Trinity and Creation

VICTORINE TEXTS IN TRANSLATION
Exegesis, Theology and Spirituality from the Abbey of St Victor

1

Grover A. Zinn
Editor in Chief

Hugh Feiss OSB
Managing Editor

Editorial Board
Boyd Taylor Coolman, Dale M. Coulter,
Christopher P. Evans, Franklin T. Harkins,
Frans van Liere

In the twelfth century the Augustinian canons of the Abbey of St Victor in Paris occupied a critical position between traditional, meditative theology and emerging scholasticism. In a series of thematic volumes, this collaborative effort will make available in new, annotated English translations many of their most important and influential works, as well as other Victorine works that deserve to be better known.

Trinity and Creation

A Selection of Works of Hugh, Richard and Adam of St Victor

Boyd Taylor Coolman
Dale M. Coulter
eds.

New City Press
Hyde Park, New York

Published in the United States by New City Press
202 Comforter Blvd., Hyde Park, NY 12538
www.newcitypress.com
©2011 Brepols Publishers, Turnhout (Belgium)

Cover design by Leandro de Leon

Library of Congress Cataloging-in-Publication Data:

Trinity and creation / Boyd Taylor Coolman, Dale M. Coulter, eds.
    p. cm. — (Victorine texts in translation : exegesis, theology and spirituality from the Abbey of St. Victor ; 1)
    Contains translations from selected members of the Abbey of St Victor.
    Includes bibliographical references and indexes.
    ISBN 978-1-56548-373-6 (pbk. : alk. paper)
 1. Trinity—History of doctrines--Middle Ages, 600-1500. 2. Creation—History of doctrines—Middle Ages,
 600-1500. I. Coolman, Boyd Taylor, 1966- II. Coulter, Dale M. (Dale Michael), 1970- III. Hugh,
 of Saint-Victor, 1096?-1141. Selections. English. IV. Adam, de Saint-Victor, d. 1192. Selections. English.
 V. Richard, of St. Victor, d. 1173. On the Trinity. English. VI. Saint-Victor (Abbey : Paris, France)
 BT109.T77 2011
 231'.04409021—dc22   2011009585

2nd printing: May 2013

Printed in the United States of America

For Michael A. Signer (d. 2009)
In memoriam

TABLE OF CONTENTS

PREFACE

The Abbey of St Victor at Paris was one of the major centers for biblical interpretation, theological reflection, spiritual guidance, and liturgical practice and innovation in the twelfth century and beyond. The Editorial Board of the series *Victorine Texts in Translation* is pleased to present this first volume in a continuing series of publications offering English translations (often for the first time) of a wide range of writings by authors resident at or formed at the Abbey.

The past several decades have seen a renaissance in the study of the Victorines, with a number of recent studies, the inception of a French translation series, a dedicated monograph series published with Brepols, the establishment of the Hugo von Sankt Viktor Institut in Frankfurt, and a Colloquium in Paris celebrating the 900th anniversary of the founding of the Abbey. The series of translated texts that this volume introduces is an American contribution to these initiatives. Our series aims to make Victorine texts more accessible to a wider English speaking audience. *Victorine Texts in Translation* uses the latest critical Latin texts being published in the *Corpus christianorum continuatio medievalis* or, where both necessary and possible, Latin texts that are improvements over the texts collected and published in the *Patrologia Latina* of Migne. Introductions to each volume and each work translated give the intellectual and historical background for understanding the work. Each text is annotated, and each volume contains a Select Bibliography.

The planning and execution of this project have been a community effort from the beginning. Our plans crystallized to a great degree at a meeting hosted by the late Michael Signer at the University of Notre Dame. His recent death was a great loss to the Editorial Board and to Victorine and Jewish-Christian studies. With memories of his personal presence and scholarship, we dedicate the first volume of *Victorine Texts in Translation* to his memory. Dale Coulter and Boyd Taylor Coolman, leaders among younger scholars of the Victorines, made some of the initial contacts with our publishers. Hugh Feiss, OSB, has exerted firm leadership developing the organization of the various elements of our volumes and managing our ongoing work. Franklin

Harkins brings the fresh perspective of one of the younger scholars in the field, as does Christopher Evans. Frans van Liere provides the knowledge of one particularly engaged in Victorine and medieval biblical interpretation generally. Our Editor at Brepols, Luc Jocqué, a distinguished scholar in the field of Victorine studies, has been a guiding light and insightful commentator on the project since the beginning. We are indebted to him for his trust in this project and his assistance in bringing it to fruition. Our goal is to have volumes available for libraries and scholars and also for students and classroom use. A joint venture between Brepols and New City Press will allow us to achieve this goal.

As Editor in Chief, it has been my pleasure to engage in this project with such a committed, creative, and cooperative group of scholars. The members of the Editorial Board have shared the decisions of what to translate, done some of the translations and reviewed together the work at each stage along the way. We have been joined by a number of other scholars engaged in Victorine studies who have offered translations or suggestions.

Planning and translation are underway for the next four volumes, so we can promise to the readers of this first volume that there will soon be more Victorine works in English translation. Each volume will be generally topical, with some works translated in their entirety, while for other works selected passages will be translated. We also intend to provide a variety of genres in each volume, from exegesis, to theological treatises, spiritual writings, and liturgical poetry.

We launch this volume, and those to come, with the conviction that the Victorine authors are important not only for understanding the intellectual and spiritual currents of the twelfth and thirteenth centuries in particular, but also for the contribution they can make to the intellectual, religious and spiritual life of the present century.

Grover A. Zinn, Editor in Chief
Oberlin College

ACKNOWLEDGMENTS

The present volume marks the beginning of an ambitious project, the origins of which reside in conversations between two doctoral students with an interest in the Victorines. As we both recall, such conversations culminated in gathering together a small group of fellow Victorine scholars who shared our enthusiasm for the production of translations that could make the depth and breadth of Victorine theology available to a broader contemporary audience. Several publishers were solicited during 2003, and a decision was made in 2004 to try to work out a joint-venture between Brepols Publishers and New City Press. With a preliminary agreement from both publishers, Michael Signer (of blessed memory) graciously sponsored a meeting at Notre Dame for the editorial board in 2005. The board hammered out the initial list of volumes, but it would take another five years to bring those plans to fruition. After much labor and under the guidance of managing editor, Hugh Feiss, OSB, we are delighted to present the first fruits of that initial conversation.

There are numerous people who helped bring this volume to completion. Hugh Feiss, Christopher P. Evans, and Juliet Mousseau were always responsive to our questions about their translations and citations. Christopher Evans provided much additional support by tracking down citations and vetting translations. The remaining members of the editorial board—Frans van Liere, Grover Zinn, and Franklin T. Harkins—also vetted translations. But the driving force behind the project as a whole, and this volume, remained Hugh Feiss, OSB. His gentle, patient prodding and readiness to help in any way possible were indispensable. We also wish to thank Dale's graduate assistants, Rachel Santiago and Sophronia Vachon who helped to edit the endnotes for the volume.

Finally, we have dedicated this volume to the memory of Michael A. Signer. His scholarship and generosity of spirit are deeply missed, but our hope is that this and subsequent volumes will birth a new generation of devotees to "all things Victorine."

ABBREVIATIONS*

ACW   *Ancient Christian Writers* (New York: Newman Press, 1946–)

CCL   *Corpus Christianorum. Series Latina* (Turnhout: Brepols, 1953–)

CCCM   *Corpus Christianorum, Continuatio Mediaeualis* (Turnhout: Brepols, 1953–)

CF   *Cistercian Fathers* (Kalamazoo, MI: Cistercian Publications, 1970–)

CSEL   *Corpus Scriptorum Ecclesiasticorum Latinorum* (Vienna: Tempsky, 1865–)

Denz.   *Kompendium der Glaubensbekenntnisse und kirchlichen Lehrentscheidungen. Lateinisch-Deutsch: Enchiridion symbolorum definitionum et declarationum de rebus fidei et morum,* ed. Heinrich Denzinger and Peter Hünermann (Freiburg: Herder, 2005)

FC   *The Fathers of the Church,* ed. R. J. Deferrari (Washington, D.C: Catholic University of America Press, 1947–)

Oeuvre 1   *L'oeuvre de Hugues de Saint-Victor* 1, Latin text by H. B. Feiss and P. Sicard, trans. (French) D. Poirel, H. Rochais, and P. Sicard, intro., notes, and appendices D. Poirel. Sous la règle de Saint Augustin (Turnhout: Brepols, 1997)

Oeuvre 2   *L'oeuvre de Hugues de Saint-Victor* 2, Intro., trans., and notes by B. Jollès. Sous la règle de Saint Augustin (Turnhout: Brepols, 2000)

PL   *Patrologiae cursus completus sive bibliotheca universalis, integra, uniformis, commodae oeconomica omnium ss. Patrum, doctorum scriptorumque ecclesiasticorum qui ab aevo apostolico ad Innocentii III tempora floruerunt . . . series* [*Latina*]. Ed. J.-P. Migne. Paris, 1844–64. 221 vols

---

*   The asterisk before the abbreviated title denotes disputed works.

SB	*Spicilegium Bonaventurianum* (Grottaferrata: Editiones Collegii S. Bonaventurae, 1963–)
SBOp	*Sancti Bernardi Opera*, 9 vols., ed. J. Leclercq, C. H. Talbot, H. M. Rochais (Rome: Editiones Cistercienses, 1957–1998)
SC	*Sources Chrétiennes* (Paris: Cerf, 1942–)
Schmitt	*Anselmi Opera Omnia*, ed. F. S. Schmitt (Edinburgh: Thomas Nelson, 1938–68)
TPMA	*Textes Philosophiques du Moyen Age* (Paris: J. Vrin, 1958–)

Hugh of St Victor

Adnot. in Pent.	*Adnotationes elucidatoriae in Pentateuchum* (PL 175.29–114)
Archa Noe	*De archa Noe* (*De arca Noe morali*) (ed. Sicard, CCCM 176)
Arrha	*De arrha animae* (*Oeuvre*, 1.227–83)
Assumpt.	*Pro Assumptione Virginis* (*Oeuvre*, 2.112–161)
BM Virg.	*De beatae Mariae virginitate* (*Oeuvre*, 2.182–253)
Cant. BM.	*Super Canticum Mariae* (*Oeuvre*, 2.24–91)
Chronicon	*Chronicon vel de tribus maximis circumstantiis gestorum* (Partial ed. W. M. Green, "Hugo of St Victor *De tribus maximis circumstantiis gestorum.*" *Speculum* 18 (1943): 484–93; ed. G. Waitz, "Chronica quae dicitur Hugonis de Sancto Victore," Monumenta Germaniae Historica, Scriptores.24:88–97)
Decalogum	*Institutiones in Decalogum* (PL 176.9–15)
Didasc.	*Didascalicon*, ed. C. H. Buttimer (Washington: The Catholic University Press, 1939); *The Didascalicon of Hugh of St Victor*, trans. and intro. J. Taylor (New York: Columbia University Press, 1991)
Diligens scrutator	Ralf Stammberger, "*Diligens scrutator sacri eloquii*: An Introduction to Scriptural Exegesis by Hugh of St Victor Preserved at Admont Library (MS 671)," *Manuscripts and Medieval Culture: Reform and Renewal in Twelfth-Century Germany*, ed. Alison I. Beach, Medieval Church Studies 13 (Turnhout: Brepols 2007). 272–83.
Egredietur	*Super "Egredietur uirga"* (*Oeuvre*, 2.270–86)

Epitome	*Epitome Dindimi* (ed. Baron, *Opera propaedeutica*, 156–223)
Eulogium	*Eulogium sponsi et sponsae* (*De amore sponsi ad sponsum*); (PL 176.987–94)
Grammatica	*De grammatica* (ed. Baron, *Opera propaedeutica*, 75–156)
In hier. cael.	*Commentariorium in hierarchiam caelestem* (PL 175.923–1154)
In Eccl.	*In Salomonis Ecclesiasten homiliae* (PL 175.113–256)
Inst. nov.	*De institutione novitiorum* (*Oeuvre*, 1.18–99)
Lament.	*Super Lamentationes* (PL 175.255–322)
Laude car.	*De laude caritatis* (*Oeuvre*, 1.182–201)
Libellus	*Libellus de formatione arche* (*De arca Noe mystica*) (ed. Sicard, CCCM 176)
Meditatione	*De meditatione* (ed. Baron, SC 155.44–59)
Misc.	*Miscellanea I: De eo Quod Spiritualis Dijudicat Omnia, et de Judicio Veri Et Boni* (PL 177.469–590)
Orat. dom.	*De oratione dominica* (PL 175.774–89)
Potestate	*De potestate et uoluntate Dei* (PL 176.839–42)
Quat. volunt.	*De quatuor voluntatibus* (PL 176.841–46)
Quid vere	*Quid vere diligendum sit* (ed. Baron, SC 155.94–99)
Quinque sept.	*De quinque septenis* (ed. Baron, SC 155.100–188)
Practica	*Practica geometriae* (ed. Baron, *Opera propaedeutica*, 15–64)
Sacr.	*De sacramentis christianae fidei* (PL 176.173–618; *On the Sacraments of the Christian Faith (De Sacramentis) of Hugh of Saint Victor*, trans. R. Deferrari [Cambridge: The Mediaeval Academy of America, 1951])
Sac. dial.	*De sacramentis dialogus* (PL 176.17–42)
Sapientia	*De sapentia Christi* (PL 176.845–56)
Script.	*De scripturis et scriptoribus sacris* (PL 175.9–28)
Sent. div.	*Sententiae de divinitate* (ed. Piazzoni, "Ugo di San Vittore 'auctor' delle 'Sententiae de divinitate,'" *Studi Medievali*, 3rd series, 23 [1982]: 861–955)
Septem donis	*De septem donis Spiritus sancti* (ed. Baron, SC 155.120–32)
Subst. dilect.	*De substantia dilectionis* (ed. Baron, SC 155.82–92)
Tribus diebus	*De tribus diebus* (ed. Poirel, CCCM 177)

Tribus rerum	De tribus rerum subsistentiis (ed. C. H. Buttimer [Washington: The Catholic University Press, 1939], 134–35)
Unione	De unione spiritus et corporis (ed. Piazonni, "Il De unione spiritus et corporis di Ugo di San Vittore," Studi Medievali 21 [1980]: 861–888)
Vanitate	De vanitate mundi (PL 176.703–39)
Verbo	De Verbo Dei (ed. Baron, SC 155.60–81)
Virtute orandi	De virtute orandi (Oeuvre, 1.126–61)

RICHARD OF ST VICTOR

XII patr.	De duodecim patriarchis (Benjamin Minor) (ed. Châtillon, SC 419)
*Abdiam	In Abdiam (PL 175.371–406)
Adnot. Psalm.	Mysticae adnotationes in Psalmos (PL 196.265–402; critical edition in preparation by Chris Evans)
Apoc.	In Apocalypsim (PL 196.683–888)
Ad me clamat.	Ad me clamat ex Seir (ed. Ribaillier, TPMA 15.256–80)
Apprehendet	Apprehendet messis vindemiam (ed. B. Haureau, Notices et extraits de quelques manuscripts latins de la Bibliothèque Nationale, 5 vols. [Paris: C. Klincksieck, 1890–1893] 1.116–17)
Arca Moys.	De arca Moysi (De arca mystica; Benjamin major; ed. Aris)
*Cant.	In Cantica Canticorum explanatio (PL 196.405A-534A)
Carb.	Carbonum et cinerum (ed. Châtillon, Trois opusc.)
Causam	Causam quam nesciebam (ed. Châtillon, Trois opusc.)
Decl. nonn. diff.	Declarationes nonnullarum difficultatum Scripturae (ed. Ribaillier, TPMA 15.201–14)
Comp. Christi.	De Comparatione Christi ad florem et Mariae ad virgam (PL 196.1031–32)
Concord.	De concordantia temporum (PL 196.241–56)
Diff. pecc.	De differentia peccati mortalis et venialis (ed. Ribaillier, TPMA 15.291–93)
Diff. sac.	De differentia sacrificii Abrahae a sacrificio Beatae Mariae Virginis (PL 196.1043–60)
Egyptus est	Egyptus est uita secularis (ed. Hareau, 1.243)

Emman.	*De Emmanuele* (PL 196.601–66)
Erud.	*De eruditione hominis interioris* (PL 196.1229–366)
Exterm.	*De exterminatione mali et promotione boni* (PL 196.1073–116)
Gem pasch.	*Sermo in die pasche* (PL 196.1059–74)
Illa die	*In illa die* (ed. Châtillon, *Trois opusc.*)
In medio	*In medio annorum* (PL 196.401–4; critical edition in preparation by Chris Evans and Hugh Feiss).
*Joel	*In Joel* (ed. Wilmart, BLE 23 (1922) 27–278 + PL 175.321–72)
Jud. pot.	*De iudiciaria potestate in finali et universali iudicio* (ed. Ribaillier, TPMA 15.142–54)
LE	*Liber exceptionum* (ed. Châtillon, TPMA 5)
Mater mentis	*Tolle puerum et matrem eius . . . Mater mentis puritas* (ed. Haureau, 1.116)
Med. plagis.	*De meditandis plagis quae circa finem mundi evenient* (PL 196.201–12)
*Misc.	*Miscellanea* 4: 43–47 (PL 177.721–25); *Miscellanea* 4: 52 (PL 177.726–27); *Miscellanea* 5: 4 (PL 177.753–54); *Miscellanea* 6: 14 (PL 177.817–19); *Miscellanea* 6: 27 (PL 177.826–27); *Miscellanea* 6: 28 (PL 177.827–30); *Miscellanea* 6:33 (PL 177.831–36); Jean Châtillon, "Autour des *Miscellanea* attribué à Hugues de Saint-Victor. Note sur la redaction brève de quelques ouvrages ou opuscules spirituels de prieur Richard," *Revue d'ascétique et de mystique* 25 (1949) 299–305
Misit Her.	*Misit Herodes rex manus* (PL 141.277–306)
Missione	*De missione Spiritus sancti sermo* (PL 196.1017–32)
*Nahum	*In Nahum* (PL 96.705–58 + Wilmart, BLE, 23 (1922) 262–65).
Nonn. alleg.	*Nonnullae allegoriae tabernaculi foedoris* (PL 196.191–202)
*Pascha	*Sermo in die Pascha* (PL 196.1067–74).
Post sex annos	*Post sex annos* (ed. Haureau, 1.112–14; critical edition in preparation by Chris Evans and Hugh Feiss)
Proles	*Tolle puerum et matrem eius . . . Proles de uirgine matre* (ed. Haureau, 1.116)
Pot. lig.	*De potestate ligandi et solvendi* (ed. Ribaillier, TPMA 15.77–110)
Quat. grad.	*De quatuor gradibus violentae caritatis* (ed. Dumeige, TPMA 3.124–77)

Quest.	*De quaestionibus Regulae sancti Augustini solutis* (ed. Coler, *Traditio* 18 (1962) 201–23).
Quid eis	*Quid eis dabis, Domine?* (ed. Haureau, 1.118–19)
Quomodo Christus	*Quomodo Christus ponitur in signum populorum* (PL 196.523–28)
Quomodo Spiritus	*Quomodo Spiritus Sanctus est amor Patris et Filii* (ed. Ribaillier, TPMA 15.164–66)
Ramis	*Sermo in ramis palmarum* (PL 196.1059–67)
Sanctific. hodie	*Sanctificamini hodie* (ed. Hareau, 1.243)
Sac. David	*De sacrificio David prophetae et quid distet inter ipsum et sacrificium Abrahae patriarchae* (PL 196.1031–42)
Serm. cent.	*Sermones centum* (PL 177.899–1210)
*Serm. Greg.	*Sermo in honorem Gregorii Magni*, partially edited by Jean Châtillon in "Contemplation, action et predication d'après un sermon inédit de Richard de Saint-Victor en l'honneur de saint Grégoire-le-Grand," *L'homme devant dieu*, Mélanges offerts au Père de Lubac, Theologie 5–58 (Paris: Aubier, 1963–1964) 2: 89–98.
Sex sunt dies	*Sex sunt dies* (ed. Hareau, 1.243)
Sp. blasph.	*De spiritu blasphemiae* (ed. Ribaillier, TPMA 15.121–29)
Statu.	*De statu interioris hominis post lapsum* (ed. Ribaillier, AHDLMA 42 (1967): 61–128)
Super exiit	*Super exiit edictum* or *De tribus processionibus* (ed. Châtillon and Tulloch, *Richard de Saint-Victor, Sermons et opuscules spirituels inédits*, 1951)
Tab. foed.	*Expositio difficultatum suborientium in expositione tabernaculi foederis* (PL 196.211–56)
Templo	*De templo Salominis* (PL 196.223–42)
Trin.	*De Trinitate* (ed. Ribaillier, TPMA 6)
Tribus per.	*De tribus personis appropriatis in Trinitate* (ed. Ribaillier, TPMA 15.182–87)
Verbo Eccl.	*Eleemonsina Patris non erit in obliuionem* (ed. Ribaillier, TPMA 15.295–96)
Verbis ap.	*De verbis apostoli* (ed. Ribaillier, TPMA 15.314–17)
Verbis Is.	*In die illa nutriet* (ed. Châtillon, *Trois opuscules spirituels de Richard de Saint-Victor*, Paris, 1986, 55–152)
Vis. Ezek.	*In visionem Ezechielis* (PL 196.527–606; ed. Schröder)

ACHARD OF ST VICTOR

Serm.	*Sermons inédits* (ed. Châtillon, TPMA 17)
Unitate	*De unitate Dei et pluralitate creaturarum* (ed. Martineau, Saint-Lambert des Bois: Franc-Dire 1987)

OTTO (ODO) OF LUCCA

Summa Sent.	*Summa Sententiarum* (PL 176.41–174)

OTHER VICTORINE WRITINGS

Sent. divinit.	*Sententiae divinitatis* (B. Geyer, *Die Sententiae divinitatis. Ein Sentenzenbuch der gilbertschen Schule, aus den Handschriften zum ersten Male herausgegeben und historisch untersucht*, Beiträge zur Geschichte der Philosophie des Mittelalters, VII, 2–3, 61–62)

AUGUSTINE

Cat. rud.	*De catechizandis rudibus* (CCL 46)
Civ. Dei	*De civitate Dei* (CCL 47–48)
Conf.	*Confessiones* (CCL 27)
Conl. Max.	*Conlatio cum Maximino Arianorum episcopo* (PL 42)
C. Faust.	*Contra Faustum Manicheum* (CSEL 25.1)
Doc. Chr.	*De doctrina Christiana* (CCL 32; CSEL 80)
En. Ps.	*Enarrationes in Psalmos* (CCL 38–40)
Ench.	*Enchiridion ad Laurentium de fide spe et caritate* (CCL 46)
Ep.	*Epistolae* (PL 33; CSEL 34, 44, 57, 58, 88)
C. ep. Parm.	*Contra epistolam Parmeniani* (CSEL 51)
F. et symb.	*De fide et symbolo* (CSEL 41)
Gn. litt.	*De Genesi ad litteram* (CSEL 28.1; ACW 41–42 [1982])
Jo. ev. tr.	*In Johannis evangelium tractatus* (CCL 36)
C. Jul. imp.	*Contra Julianum opus imperfectum* (PL 45)

Lib. arb.	*De libero arbitrio* (CCL 29)
C. s. Ar.	*Contra sermonem Arianorum* (PL 42)
Mor.	*De moribus ecclesiae catholicae et de moribus Manichaeorum* (PL 32)
S.	*Sermones* (PL 38–39; PLS 2; CCL 41)
Spir. et litt.	*De spiritu et littera* (CSEL 60)
Trin.	*De Trinitate* (CCL 50/50A)
Vera rel.	*De vera religione* (CCL 32)

Boethius

CEut.	*Contra Eutychen et Nestorium* (trans. Stewart, Rand, and Tester, Loeb 74)
Trin.	*De Trinitate* (trans. Stewart, Rand, and Tester, Loeb 74)
Con. phil.	*Philosophiae Consolatio* (trans. Stewart, Rand, and Tester, Loeb 74; CCL 94)
In cat.	*In Categorias Aristotelis Libri Quator* (PL 64.159–294)
Interp.	*Commentarii in librum Aristotelis Periermeneias* (ed. C. Meiser, 2 vols. [Leipzig, 1877, 1880])
In Isag.	*In Isagogen Porphyrii Commenta* (ed. G. Schepps and S. Brandt, CSEL 48 [Vienna-Leipzig, 1906])

Gregory the Great

Hom. ev.	*Homiliae in Evangelia* (CCL 76)
Hom. Ez.	*Homiliae in Ezechielem* (CCL 142)
Mor.	*Moralia in Iob* (CCL 143; CSEL; PL)

Isidore of Seville

Etym.	*Etymologiarum sive Originum Libri XX*, 2 vols., ed. W. M. Lindsay (Oxford: Clarendon Press, 1911); available online at LacusCurtius: Into the Roman World (http://penelope.uchicago.edu/Thayer/E/Roman/home.html)

Anselm of Canterbury

De Inc. Verbi	*Epistola de Incarnatione Verbi* (ed. Schmitt)
De proc.	*De processione Spiritus Sancti* (ed. Schmitt)
Mon.	*Monologion* (ed. Schmitt)
Prosl.	*Proslogion* (ed. Schmitt)

Bernard of Clairvaux

Csi	*De consideratione libri V* (SBOp 3)
Dil.	*Liber de diligendo Deo* (SBOp 3)
SCC	*Sermones super Cantica Canticorum* (SBOp 1–2)

Peter Abelard

SN	*Sic et Non* (ed. Boyer and McKeon)
TChr	*Theologia Christiana* (ed. Buytaert, CCCM 12)
TSch	*Theologia "Scholarium"* (ed. Buytaert and Mews, CCCM 13)
Tsum	*Theologia "Summi boni"* (ed. Buytaert and Mews, CCCM 13)

Gilbert of Poitiers

Trin.	*Expositio in Boetii librum primum De Trinitate* (ed. N. M. Häring [Toronto: PIMS 1966])
CEut	*Expositio in Boetii librum contra Euticen et Nestorium* (ed. N. M. Häring [Toronto: PIMS, 1966])
Sent.	*Die Sententie Magistri Gisleberti Pictavensis Episcopi* (ed. N. M. Häring, AHDLMA 45 [1978])

Peter Lombard

Sent.	*Sententiae in IV Libris Distinctae* (ed. Brady, SB 4–5)

ROBERT OF MELUN

Sent.   *Sententie* (ed. R. Martin, *Oeuvres de Robert de Melun,*
                 Tome III, vol. 1 [Louvain: Spicilegium Sacrum Lova-
                 niense], 1947; *Oeuvres de Robert de Melun,* Tome III, vol. 2
                 [Louvain: Spicilegium Sacrum Lovaniense], 1952)

GENERAL INTRODUCTION

Boyd Taylor COOLMAN

INTRODUCTION

Trinity and creation—fundamental *loci* in Christian theology. Both are timeless in their fascination and timely in an age of religious plurality and environmental anxiety. For its part, the doctrine of the Trinity constitutes the heart of all Christian teaching.[1] When Christians confess their creedal faith, it is the Trinity that they proclaim.[2] Yet, the fourth-century determination of Trinitarian orthodoxy did not conclude the challenge of conceiving of an adequate account of divine unity and multiplicity. Indeed, it invited on-going attempts at a formulation that could both serve apologetic purposes and satisfy the desire for an ever greater *intellectus fidei*. At the same time, the creedal statement of Trinitarian faith begins with an unambiguous claim that the Trinitarian God is the Creator—"maker of heaven and earth"—thus radically distinguishing God from all that is not God, and so positing the framework that makes all subsequent affirmations regarding the relationship between the two, including that entailed in the Incarnation, both possible and intelligible.

These two topics thus encompass all subsequent theological inquiry. As Hugh of St Victor himself says, in knowledge of the Creator and the creature "consists the whole knowledge of truth."[3] Implicated here are

---

[1] Richard of St Victor, *Trin.* 4.5: ". . . the supreme article of our faith, the very sacred and secret mystery of the Trinity . . ."

[2] Gilles Emery, O.P., *Trinity in Aquinas*, trans., Matthew Levering, Heather Buttery, Robert Williams, and Teresa Bede, with a preface by Jean-Pierre Torrell, O.P. (Ypsilanti, Mich.: Sapientia Press of Ave Maria College, 2003), xxvii.

[3] *Sacr.* 1.3.31 (PL 176.232C; Deferrari 59). See Hugh of Saint Victor, *On the Sacraments of the Christian Faith (De sacramentis)*, trans. R. J. Deferrari, Medieval Academy of America LVIII (Cambridge, MA: Medieval Academy of America, 1951). (Hereafter as *De sacramentis*; abbreviated as *Sacr.*, followed by Book Part, and Section numbers, and cited with PL reference followed by page number in Deferrari's translation).

some of the most venerable human questions: the relationship between
eternity and temporality, providence and freedom; the origin and nature of evil; and the ultimate *telos* of created reality. Questions of "theological method" emerge here too: How do humans arrive at knowledge
of this triune God? How most appropriately to conceive of God as
Trinity and to narrate the relationship between Creator and creation?
What role does creation play in mediating such knowledge? What
sources (scriptural, philosophical, empirical) should contribute to
knowledge of the world and its origins? Can such sources be harmonized and integrated? If so, how?

All these issues, of course, typically lie within the purview of what
is termed "systematic" or "dogmatic" theology. But they have been engaged by Christian thinkers less systematically from the beginning,
often with profound insight. Some of these past figures are well-known
today, and continue to make important contributions to contemporary
discussions; others, however, are less well-known or not at all—often
unjustifiably so, to the diminishment, even impoverishment of the present. The conviction of the editors of this series is that theological reflection on Trinity and creation emanating from the Abbey of St Victor in
Paris[4] during the twelfth-century has remained too long in the latter
category. Eschewing any rigid distinction between "systematic" and
"historical" theology, twelfth-century Victorine texts are here offered in
English translation, not as curious relics of the past, but as contributions
to the on-going pursuit of an *intellectus fidei* within the church.

FOUR GENERATIONS OF THEOLOGICAL DEVELOPMENT
AT SAINT-VICTOR

The texts included in this volume span a range of roughly sixty years
at the Abbey of St Victor, from ca.1115 to ca.1173, within which significant development occurred in theological reflection on both creation

---

[4]   For studies on the Abbey of St Victor, see F. Bonnard, *Histoire de l'abbaye royale et de l'ordre
des channoines réguliers de Saint-Victor de Paris* (Paris, 1904–1907); J. Châtillon, *Théologie,
spiritualité et métaphysique dans l'oeuvre oratoire d'Achard de Saint-Victor*, Études de philosophie médiévale, 58 (Paris, 1969), 53–85; *Sermons et opuscules spirituals inédits* (Paris: Desclée de Brouwer, 1951), I.xxxvi-xl; J. C. Dickinson, *The Origins of the Austin Canons and their
Introduction into England* (London: S.P.C.K., 1950); J. Longère, *L'abbaye parisienne de Saint-
Victor au Moyen Age*, Bibliotheca Victorina 1 (Turnhout: Brepols, 1991). For details concerning the religious life of St.-Victor, see the *Liber Ordinis Sancti Victoris Parisiensis* (CCLM 61);
and also F. Bonnard, *Histoire de l'abbaye*, 71–83.

and, especially, on Trinity. In fact, four different generations of theologians can be identified within this period, which are all in some way implicated in this volume. For his part, Hugh of St Victor came to St Victor in Paris from northern Germany sometime around 1115–1118. Over the next quarter century until his death in 1141, Hugh was the leading teacher and writer at Saint-Victor, authoring an impressive number of works, some of them very influential. Including Hugh's more famous contemporaries, Bernard of Clairvaux (d. 1153) and Peter Abelard (d. 1142), as well as Otto (Odo) of Lucca (d. 1145/46), this generation is perhaps the most well-known in the "long twelfth century," and it set out the main lines of subsequent reflection in the period under consideration. But its work built upon the foundation of a prior generation, including Anselm of Canterbury (d. 1109), Anselm of Laon (d. 1117), Roscelin of Compiègne (d. 1125), and William of Champeaux (d. 1122), whom Hugh succeeded at Saint-Victor, likely after William's departure for Châlons-sur-Marne in 1113 to become bishop. Following Hugh and Adam of St Victor (d. ca. 1146) at Saint-Victor, a third generation, including Andrew of St Victor (d. 1175), Lawrence of Westminster (d. ca. 1172), Peter Lombard (d. 1160), Robert of Melun (d. 1167), Achard of St Victor (d. 1172), clarified, synthesized, and transmitted the Victorine tradition to a fourth generation, including Peter Comestor (d. 1178), Clarembald of Arras (d. 1187), and especially Richard of St Victor (d. 1173), who assumed the mantle of *magister* ("teacher") at Saint-Victor in the third quarter of the twelfth century.

TWELFTH-CENTURY REFLECTION ON TRINITY AND CREATION AT SAINT-VICTOR

"The Trinitarian question constitutes the great theme of twelfth-century theology."[5] Spurred on by the controversy over the *Filioque*,[6] the Trinitarian theology of Anselm of Canterbury (d. 1109) signaled "a new period of the development in trinitarian thinking in medieval western Europe,"[7] spanning the twelfth and thirteenth centuries. If this

---

[5]   Emery, *Trinity in Aquinas*, 2.
[6]   Peter Gemeinhardt, "Logic, Tradition, and Ecumenics: Developments of Latin Trinitarian Theology between ca. 1075 and ca. 1160," in eds. Kärkkäinen, Pekka, *Trinitarian Theology in the Medieval West* (Helsinki: Luther-Agricola-Society, 2007), 11.
[7]   Gemeinhardt, "Logic, Tradition, and Ecumenics," 10.

is the "golden age of Trinitarian reflection in the West,"[8] which "still awaits a comprehensive study,"[9] the Victorine contribution to that development, especially that of Hugh and Richard, should figure centrally in accounts yet to be written. To be sure, the concurrent contributions, not only of Anselm, but also of Roscelin of Compiègne, William of Champeaux, Peter Abelard, the Chartrians (Thierry of Chartres, William of Conches, etc.), Bernard of Clairvaux, William of St Thierry, Gilbert of Poitiers, and Peter Lombard, deserve careful attention as well. The Victorine tradition is just one current (itself not monolithic) in a vigorous, twelfth-century debate swirling around Paris and elsewhere. Yet, its contribution was both distinctive in its time and influential on subsequent reflection.

In varying degrees, all thinkers in this period depend heavily and self-consciously on the thought of Augustine of Hippo and, to a lesser extent, on that of Boethius. In this, the Victorines were not exceptional. The former often provided the overarching framework and substance of Trinitarian thought; the latter offered a warrant for the application of the philosophical tools of logic and dialectic to matters theological, as well as specific formulations of neoplatonic metaphysics, e.g., the distinction between that which is (*quod est*) and that by which it is (*quo est*). Yet, Victorine reflection on the Trinity was also innovative.[10] In subtle but often significant ways, each in their own fashion, Hugh and Richard rang important changes on this patristic inheritance.[11] Perceiving these shifts in emphasis or re-configurations of the issues is often the key to appreciating the importance of their contributions. At the same time, both thinkers appear to offer wholly original insights or startling new approaches to the mystery of the Trinity. The contents of this volume assemble in one place some of the most important Trinitarian thought emanating from the school of St Victor during this period.

Hugh's Trinitarian theology does not reach to the speculative heights of Richard's, perhaps due to his own theological predilections or per-

---

8   Emery, *Trinity in Aquinas*, xxviii.
9   Gemeinhardt, "Logic, Tradition, and Ecumenics," 13.
10 Richard, for example, will find wanting Boethius' famous definition of a person—"an individual substance of a rational nature"—for matters Trinitarian.
11 Gemeinhardt ("Logic, Tradition, and Ecumenics," 12) notes that in the early twelfth century, "[w]hat appeared to be needed was a new approach to understand the mystery of the Trinity by human reason, including a hermeneutics of the doctrine of the Fathers which had to be capable of taking into account the ecumenical challenge of the Greek theology and tradition."

haps because it lacks the benefit of the developments and refinements in Trinitarian theology that occurred between their respective careers—or both. Hugh provides, nonetheless, a crucial impetus to Richard's work and at the same time offers a unique approach in his own right, one which (in contrast to Richard's almost exclusive focus on the question of the intra-Trinitarian relation between the persons) grapples with the relationship between Creator and creation, thus putting the focus on the Trinity's acts in the economy of salvation, both as Trinitarian Creator and Redeemer.[12] One might say that, whereas Richard's gift for profound speculation is on full display in his *On the Trinity*, Hugh's unique ability to put theological, especially Trinitarian, speculation to practical, even pastoral use is especially evident in his *On the Three Days* (and to a lesser extent in his *Sentences on Divinity*).

The first half of the twelfth-century also witnessed an explosion of interest in the topic of creation.[13] In the vibrant milieu of early twelfth-century theological reflection on creation, the focal point for most thinkers was the hexaemeral account of creation found in the first two chapters of the Book of Genesis. This account raised a host of exegetical, scientific, philosophical, and theological questions, many of which had been taken up in various ways by patristic thinkers, but remained to one degree or another unresolved, at least not satisfactorily so. At the same time, the twelfth-century reception of these patristic traditions was complicated by a relatively novel approach to the topic that emanated from a series of thinkers associated with the city of Chartres during the first half of the century. The members of this "school of Chartres" (including Bernard and Thierry of Chartres, Bernard Silvestris, William of Conches, Clarembald of Arras) attempted a coherent account of creation from a predominately Platonic or Neoplatonic philosophical perspective,[14] with only a secondary concern to square it with scriptural or theological accounts. This Chartrian approach provoked various reactions and exercised diverse degrees of influence on contemporary and subsequent thinkers. Beginning with Hugh, Victorine thinkers took both serious account of, and also, in various degrees, serious exception to the Chartrian claims.

---

[12] See Richard's comment below in *Trin*.1.10.
[13] See the helpful summary of these issues from a mid-twelfth-century vantage point by Marcia Colish, *Peter Lombard*, vol. 1 (Leiden: Brill, 1994), 303ff.
[14] See Edouard Jeauneau, *Rethinking the School of Chartres*, trans., Claude Paul Desmarais (Toronto: University of Toronto: 2009).

Generally speaking, the Victorine approach to creation, exemplified especially in Hugh's *On the Three Days*, is at once scientific, aesthetic, and theological. The visible creation is simultaneously both ordered, coherent, rational (the scientific) and well-formed, harmonious, beautiful (aesthetic); and, since it is both of these as direct result of the creative activity of divine Wisdom (both rational and beautiful) the creation is theologically significant; that is, it bears within it the imprint of its Creator and can, when read rightly, mediate divine self-revelation. Right reading, however, is possible only in light of God's self-revelation in salvation history, and thus Hugh's discussion of the divine work of creation, the "works of foundation" (*opera conditionis*), is always paired with, and indeed ordered toward, the divine work of salvation, the "works of restoration" (*opera restaurationis*). For Hugh, this is the Scriptural pattern, which begins with a brief account of the "works of foundation," treated "briefly and truthfully" at the beginning of its narrative, so that the correspondence between six days of creation and six ages of salvation might reveal the identity of Creator and Redeemer.[15] Ultimately, neither the "scientific" nor the "aesthetic" approach to creation are sufficient, legitimate and necessary though they are. Hugh pushes on to the theological significance of the created world, seeking out what he terms "sacramentals"—symbolic patterns that advertise and anticipate the work of salvation.[16] "The lower wisdom, rightly ordered, leads to the higher."[17]

HUGH OF ST VICTOR: POWER, WISDOM, GOODNESS IN TRINITY AND CREATION

An important theme in Victorine theology generally, which also serviceably unites the various works included in this volume, is the use of the triad power (*potentia*), wisdom (*sapientia*), and goodness (*bonitas*) to describe God, creation, and their inter-relation. As Fr. Feiss explains more fully below, drawing on the work of Dominique Poirel, this particular triad seems to have appeared for the first time in discussions of the Trinity emanating from Paris at the turn of the twelfth

---

15   *Sacr.* 1.Prol.3 (PL 176.184A-B; Deferrari 4).
16   *Sacr.* 1.Prol. 5–6 (PL 176.999A; Deferrari 5).
17   *Sacr.* 1.Prol.6 (PL 176.185C; Deferrari 5).

century.[18] The triad was an especially important feature of Hugh's theology throughout his career. Perhaps due to Hugh's influence, it found its way into Peter Lombard's *Sentences* (I.34–3–4), and thus became popular in later scholastic theology. It figures centrally in the works included in this volume; it also occupies center stage in Hugh's magisterial *De sacramentis*, which is not included here.[19] In his hands, the triad unites the doctrines of Trinity and creation, and does so in a distinctive way. Since Hugh's use of it in *De sacramentis* provides important insight into his understanding of the triad generally, that discussion is here summarized in order to facilitate a fuller appreciation of this distinctive feature of Victorine theology in the twelfth century.

In the plan of the *On the Sacraments*, governed by the scriptural order of history or the "narrative particularities of the economy,"[20] Hugh begins with a discussion of the Genesis account of creation (Part One), and then turns to what is causally prior to the work of the six days, namely, the God who creates. Thus, rather than starting with God in himself and then treating the "economic" issues of creation, etc., Hugh situates his account of Trinity explicitly within the context of God's activity in creation and history.[21] This choice to follow the "order of knowing" rather than the "order of being" has far-reaching implications for his entire theological vision.

Seeking the uncreated Source of all created things, Hugh argues that such a Cause must have three aspects. First, there must be a will or intent to create. Such a will is a function of goodness (*bonitas*). For Hugh, God is drawn (*trahebatur*), "freely without necessity" to create by the very goodness that God himself is.[22] But a good will alone can only intend. Power (*potentia*) must also be present to bring about what is intended. For "that which [is] willed through antecedent goodness [is] fulfilled through subsequent power."[23] Yet, intent and ability require knowledge or wisdom (*sapientia*) in order to dispose well, even beautifully, what is

[18]   In what are often referred to as Trinitarian "appropriations," *potentia* is associated with the Father, *sapientia* with the Son, and *bonitas* with the Holy Spirit. See Feiss' Introduction to *Tribus diebus* below.
[19]   The relevant material from the *De sacramentis* is not included here, since it is available already in English translation. See note 3 above.
[20]   The felicitous phrase is Khaled Anatolios' *Retrieving Nicaea: The Systematic Scope of Trinitarian Doctrine* (Grand Rapids MI: Baker Academic, forthcoming 2011).
[21]   See Franklin Harkins, *Reading and the Work of Restoration: History and Scripture in the Theology of Hugh of St Victor* (Toronto: Pontifical Institute of Mediaeval Studies, 2009).
[22]   *Sacr.* 1.2.4 (PL 176.208A; Deferrari 31).
[23]   *Sacr.* 1.2.5 (PL 176.208A-B; Deferrari 31).

willed and possible. Thus, "these three things [goodness-power-wisdom] were eternal and were the cause of all things; through these all were made, [but] they themselves were not made."[24] For Hugh, then, the triad is first a comprehensive way of describing the divine nature. "Whatever is truly said of God, or can be reverently believed to be in God, is contained in these three—power, wisdom, and goodness."[25] Hugh is careful here not to go where Abelard is reputed to have gone, namely, to an identification of these three aspects, respectively, with the divine persons. He allows that in God, these three are rationally distinguishable: "being able is not the same as knowing, nor is knowing the same as willing." Yet, they are not actually distinct, for in God "being able, knowing, and willing are one." So, "reason distinguishes these," but "nature does not divide them; the Trinity, which contains all, comes to us undivided."[26] Hugh insists that power-wisdom-goodness applies to the divine nature as a whole and to the persons in common. He is nonetheless willing, with due caution and proper caveat, to appropriate them, respectively, to the Father, Son, and Holy Spirit: "The Catholic faith accepted the Trinity . . . it assigned power to the Father, wisdom to the Son, goodness to the Holy Spirit."[27] But Hugh treads lightly here. To say, for example, that the Son is powerful, "not as of himself, because power belonged to the Father" (as Abelard seemed to do), would be scandalous to Catholic truth, dividing the unity, and undermining the perfection of each person. Accordingly, Hugh affirms that the triad is predicated of the Trinity "substantially" (*substantialiter*); that is, it is proper to the divine nature as such and thus each of the divine persons shares divine power, wisdom, and goodness equally and fully.[28] As Adam of St Victor hymns it: "The power of one is not less than the power of two or three persons."[29] Hugh does not define the persons on the basis of these appropriations.[30] The individual mem-

---

24 *Sacr.* 1.2.13 (PL 176.211B-C; Deferrari 35). Again: "There were three, and these three were one; these three were eternal; nothing could be perfect without these three, and with these nothing was diminished. For it was clear that if these three were present, nothing perfect would be wanting; and if one of these three were wanting, nothing could be complete. And these three were *power, wisdom, will*" (*Sacr.* 1.2.6 [PL 176.208B; Deferrari 31]).
25 *Sacr.* 1.2.6 (PL 176.208C; Deferrari 31).
26 *Sacr.* 1.2.6 (PL 176.208C; Deferrari 31).
27 *Sacr.* 1.2.6 (PL 176.208D; Deferrari 32); see also *Sacr.* 1.3.26 (PL 176.227D; Deferrari 53).
28 *Sacr.* 1.2.7 (PL 176.209A; Deferrari 32).
29 See below: "Profitentes unitatem," 7.
30 Rather, he defines the persons, more or less, in terms of mode of origin, rather than relation: the Father is from no one; the Son is from the Father, the Spirit is from both. There is "one who is from no one," and there is "one who is from Him," and "one who is from both" (*Sacr.* 1.3.22 [PL 176.226A; Deferrari 51]).

bers of the triad do *not* signify a truly "proper characteristic" (*proprietatem*) of the persons to which they are appropriated. "The Trinity was predicated *from* these, not signified *in* these."[31]

> These three in God were one, and for God they were one, but were found distinct here [i.e., in creation], where they were not one, and therefore they became an image of the Trinity. Consideration followed the peculiarity found there [i.e., in creation] even to the ineffable Trinity, and distinguished as peculiar there [i.e., in the Trinity] what was peculiar here only [i.e., in creation] . . .: there [i.e., in the Trinity], indeed, in one was all, and one was all.[32]

In short, while in created things, power, wisdom, and goodness are separable—something, for example, can be good but not powerful, or powerful but not wise—in the uncreated Trinity, they are inseparably common to all the persons of the one divine nature. What, then, is the justification for such appropriations? Teacher that he himself was,[33] Hugh was especially perceptive of the pedagogical strategies employed by the self-revealing God in Scripture. "There was reason for distinguishing in the persons what in substance was the same."[34] That reason was divine pedagogy: each member of the triad is assigned to a particular divine person in order to forestall misunderstanding. Somewhat surprising, given Abelard's purported use of the same triad, is Hugh's rationale for attributing power to the Father. Reputedly, Abelard had ascribed full omnipotence to the Father, but hesitated to ascribe the same power to the Son and even less to the Spirit. Hugh, for his part, compensates in the other direction. Given their own experience with aging human fathers, human beings might be tempted to imagine the Father as increasingly "enfeebled by the weight of years."[35] To safeguard against such a temptation, power, which is common to the divine nature, is attributed to the person of the Father.[36]

---

[31] *Sacr.* 1.2.13 (PL 176.211C; Deferrari 35). In relation to the triad, "when we wish to distinguish the persons in the Trinity, we should not attribute to one what is common to another, nor when we wish to prove the oneness of substance should we assign to another what is proper to one" (*Sacr.* 1.3.27 [PL 176.230B; Deferrari 56]).

[32] *Sacr.* 1.3.29 (PL 176.231B-C; Deferrari 57).

[33] See Paul Rorem, *Hugh of St Victor* (Oxford: Oxford University Press, 2009).

[34] *Sacr.* 1.2.7 (PL 176.209A; Deferrari 32).

[35] *Sacr.* 1.3.26 (PL 176.228C; Deferrari 54).

[36] So also, "the Son is called wise, not because He was alone so, but because of Him alone could there be greater doubt, as it were, of one posterior and still immature in age and not fully developed in mind." Similarly, "the Holy Spirit [is called] good or kind, lest God should be judged cruel; human consciousness might have been in terror before Him, if God were said

It is perhaps for this reason—to avoid the appearance of positing the triad as a genuine set of personal properties—that Hugh varies the sequence or ordering of the members of the triad in his several discussions of it. In the *On the Three Days*, the sequence is power, wisdom, goodness; in the *Sentences*: wisdom, power, will; in *On the Sacraments*: will, wisdom, power. The effect of this variation is to preclude any hasty correspondence between the persons and the members of the triad. Regarding the persons, one must always begin with the Father, and then move to the Son and the Spirit. As common to the whole Trinity, by contrast, the members of the triad are susceptible to diverse orderings.

While the triad characterizes God's nature *in se*, what interests Hugh is how it is the "face" of God's self-presentation to all that is not God. Hugh certainly affirms that God *in se* lacks nothing, enjoys the fullness of blessedness, is "alone but not lonely,"[37] and so creates freely, without any exigency stemming from some intrinsic need. But his depiction of the divine nature is already "leaning forward" toward creation and history. Whereas Richard will focus almost exclusively on the intra-divine being, Hugh's interests move rapidly to God's "economic" self-manifestation. Similarly, Hugh is less concerned than some of his contemporaries and successors (including Richard) with technical issues surrounding the definition of "person" or the applicability of human language and logic to matters Trinitiarian.[38] Rather, his concern is to characterize the divine nature as a whole in its relationship to creating as a whole.

In this light, it does not surprise that the triad functions as a "pivot" for Hugh from his consideration of the nature of the God who creates to an appreciation of the Creator-creation relation and of the creation itself. Because God *in se* is good, wise, and powerful, these characterize God's activity supremely: "these three concur to produce every effect, and nothing is accomplished unless these be present. The will moves, knowledge disposes, power operates."[39] The product of divine creation,

---

to have Spirit, and there had not been added "holy" or "kind," since Spirit of itself seems to signify a kind of harshness to mean "cruel" (*Sacr.* 1.3.26 [PL 176.228D; Deferrari 54]).

[37] *De tribus diebus*, 22.4: "sola non tamen solitaria."

[38] Gemeinhardt, "Logic, Tradition, and Ecumenics," 48–49: "Hugh renounced any contribution to the ongoing debate concerning the notion of 'person'" (49). Yet, "his tendency to leave the more technical questions of the day unresolved did not limit his influence on the forthcoming generations" (48).

[39] *Sacr.* 1.2.6 (PL 176.208B; Deferrari 31). See also, *Sacr.* 1.2.10 (PL 176.210C; Deferrari 34): "God willed by goodness, He disposed by wisdom, He made by power." *Sacr.* 1.2.11 (PL 176.210D-

moreover, profoundly reflects power, wisdom, and goodness since "perfect things followed Him who was perfect, and all things that He had made imitated their author."[40] So, as Hugh explains at length in *On the Three Days*, "the immensity of things received the form of power; beauty, that of wisdom; and utility, that of goodness. These were seen externally."[41] This derivative triad—immensity (*immensitas*), beauty (*pulchritudo*), utility (*utilitas*)—describes the created effects of the primary triad, namely, uncreated power (*potentia*), wisdom (*sapientia*), and goodness (*bonitas*).[42]

It is important to underscore at this point what has emerged here in Hugh's conception of these two triads. On the one hand, this derivative triad characterizes all created things. Nothing that God has made lacks immensity, beauty, or utility. These, then, function as what later scholastics will call "transcendentals"—concomitant perfections of all that exists.[43] On the other hand, Hugh appears to offer the original notion of what might be called "transcendentals of the divine economy." For him power (*potentia*), wisdom (*sapientia*), and goodness (*bonitas*) are themselves concomitant characterizations of all divine activity *ad extra*. Reminiscent of an axiom of patristic Trinitarian theology, namely that *opera trinitatis ad extra indivisibilia sunt*, Hugh, focusing on the divine nature as such rather than the distinction of persons, affirms that God's economic activity always and simultaneously entails divine power, wisdom, and goodness. The Trinity creates, sustains, and restores powerfully, wisely, and well.[44] For him "divine agency can only be exercised by the divine nature," the single triune divinity, and thus he is led from a meditation on divine activity to an affirmation that the triad is the common possession of the Father, Son, and Holy Spirit.

211A; Deferrari 34): "Goodness, wisdom, and power were always together, nor could these, which were the same substance, be divided or separated from one another by time."

[40] *Sacr.* 1.2.8 (PL 176.210A; Deferrari 33).

[41] *Sacr.* 1.2.12 (PL 176.211A; Deferrari 34).

[42] *Sacr.* 1.2.22 (PL 176.216C; Deferrari 41): "These [power-wisdom-goodness] are the eternal foundations of all causes and the first principle, which are ineffable and incomprehensible to every creature."

[43] Phillip the Chancellor is typically credited with articulating this doctrine in the form in which it came to be understood by later scholastics (with minor variations). Hugh's triad is different, but nonetheless functions in an analogous way to later versions. See Henri Pouillon, "Le Premier traité des propriétés transcendentals, La 'Summa de bono' du Chancellier Phillipe," *Revue néoscolastique de philosophie* 42 (1939), 40–77.

[44] See *Sacr.* 1.3.28 (PL 176.230D; Deferrari 57).

Finally, because divine activity and its non-divine result are so characterized, both provide an epistemic means by which the rational creature can arrive at a deeper understanding of its triune Creator. The immensity, beauty, and utility of created things are a "first admonition and recollection that God is threefold."[45] And, as the *Sentences* puts it, when God "brought things from non-being into being," He did so "that He might reveal the divine power." When He then "brought them from being into a beautiful being," God did so that "He might make his wisdom known." Accordingly, while treated last here in the order of causality, immensity-beauty-utility is in a certain sense first in the order of reflection. On the basis of its manifestation in created things, this triad provides a "trace" (*vestigium*)[46] or intimation of divine power, wisdom, and goodness.[47] The ineffable Trinity is found in these three, which indeed are one in divine simplicity, but "offer themselves separately to cognition" in created things.[48] Because of the triad, for Hugh, there is an analogy of being between the Creator and creation, which grounds the sacramentality of the whole creation.

Hugh's use of the triad, linking Creator and creation thus, produces a dynamic alternation between Trinity and creation in his theology. His appreciation of the immensity, beauty, and utility of creation, distinguishable as these are in created things, sends him immediately "back" behind these to the mysteriously diversified unity of divine power, wisdom, and goodness, both in God's activity and within the Godhead Itself. But meditation on these within the Trinity pushes Hugh to return again to enthusiastic pursuit of ever new manifestations of such in creation and in history. Indeed, if the conclusion of the *On the Three Days* is any indication, the entire spiritual life is an ever-increasing participation in the created dynamic and interpenetration within the human soul of the uncreated divine life of power, wisdom, and goodness. Hugh delights in the interplay between power, wisdom, and goodness. All creation reflects these three, as does salvation history, as does the spiritual life of individuals. In this way, he can give a triadic description to God's economic activity without sacrificing the affirmation of singular agency in God—the three persons act as one—

---

[45] *Sacr.* 1.2.13 (PL 176.211B; Deferrari 35).
[46] *Sacr.* 1.3.21 (PL 176.225C; Deferrari 51).
[47] See *Tribus diebus* 24.4: "Noli dubitare de potentia ejus, vide opera illius quanta sint. Noli dubitare de sapientia, vide opera ejus quam pulchra sint. Noli dubitare de benevolentia, vide opera ejus quomodo ad utilitatem tibi serviant."
[48] *Sacr.* 1.2.12 (PL 176.211A; Deferrari 34).

and without also effectively "de-trinitizing" the Trinity in the economy. That is, *ad extra* there is a clear triadic texture to God's activity without verging into effective tri-theism.

THE BENIGNITY OF THE TRIUNE GOD

In the end, a profound intuition animates Hugh's entire theology, a conviction that out of loving-kindness God is *Deus ad mundum*. Perhaps this is best captured in his use of the term *benignitas*, which he uses to describe God's deepest orientation toward all that is not God. "God in his eternal goodness wished that there be made sharers in His blessedness, which he saw could both be communicated and not at all be diminished."[49] He alternates back and forth between *bonitas* and *benignitas*, the latter glossing the former, clarifying his conception of divine goodness.[50] In his hands, *benignitas* emphasizes an active, initiating goodness, a generosity, a kindness, an eager solicitude, even zeal, for creation and for creaturely well-being: "That God created the world and all the things of the world, that He ordered the things created, that He kept and conserved in good condition what He ordered—all this He does not because it was owed, but solely from His *benignitas*."[51] In God, there is no stingy unwillingness to share: "In the highest there can be no envy, for, as Plato said: 'Envy is far removed from the best.'"[52] With pre-modern Christian thinkers before and after him, Hugh's fundamental conception of divine goodness overlaps with, while at significant points diverging from Greek philosophical traditions. For him, God is certainly the *summum bonum*, both self-communicating (*bonum sui diffusivum est*) source of creation and its desired goal, toward which all creation tends. But his God is neither a sublimely indifferent neoplatonic *summum bonum*, automatically and necessarily emanating "out of" itself (as suggested by the standard metaphors of overflowing, bubbling over, etc),[53] nor an equally indifferent passive Good in the

---

[49] *Sacr.* 1.2.4 (PL 176.208A; Deferrari 31).
[50] For divine *benignitas* in Scripture, see Rom 2:4; Titus 3:4. Hugh uses this term in several places: *Libellus* 4 (Sicard, 143.111–14; PL 176.693D); *Sent. Div.* "Appendix" (Piazzoni, 953–954.1–32, 63–68); *Sacr.* 1.2.7 (PL 176.209B–210A); *Misc.* 1.63 (PL 177.505A).
[51] *Sent. div.* (Piazzoni, 999.1–00).
[52] *Sent. div.* (Piazzoni, 999.1–00).
[53] For a description of such in Plotinus, see J. M. Rist, *Plotinus: The Road to Reality* (Cambridge: Cambridge University Press, 1967), 68.

manner of an Aristotelian "final cause," drawing all toward itself as that which everything desires. Rather, for Hugh, divine *benignitas* is goodness inflected with an initiating, solicitous modality, eager to exercise power and wisdom on behalf of all that is not God, operating always *pro hominibus*, beneficially, as befitting creaturely well-being.[54] "That good, therefore, which He Himself was and by which He Himself was blessed, was drawn by goodness alone, not by necessity, to communicate itself, since it was characteristic of *the best to wish to benefit and of the most powerful, not to be able to suffer harm*" (emphasis added).[55] It is this freedom from necessity that grounds supreme generosity in God. Hugh's conception of divine *benignitas* emphasizes the free will to benefit, to intend and communicate good for another.[56] In relation to the triad, moreover, divine power and wisdom are thus conceived as intrinsically related to divine goodness. Power is not first and foremost a *potentia absoluta*, unconstrained by anything other than itself; rather, it is the ability to communicate goodness fully without diminishment. Through wisdom, similarly, divine goodness achieves its ends aptly, fittingly, in measure, order, number. For Hugh, the consummate act of divine *benignitas* was the Incarnation, in which Christ overcame hostile powers in an act, not of brute power, but of gentle *benignitas*.[57] In his *Commentary on the Celestial Hierarchy* of Pseudo-Dionysius,[58] he observes that "the Father is moved solely by kindness [*benignitate*] and by tender pity [*pietate*] to pour out his light [i.e., Christ] upon us."[59] In short, divine "*philanthropia*," God's love for humanity, is fully expressed in the *benignitas Christi*.[60]

---

54 *Sacr.*, 1.2.1 (PL 176.205B-206C; Deferrari 28–9).

55 *Sacr.* 1.2.4 (PL 176.208A; Deferrari 31): "Illud itaque bonum quod ipse erat et quo ipse beatus erat, bonitate sola non necessitate trahebatur ad communicandum."

56 See Pseudo-Dionysius, *The Ecclesiastical Hierarchy*, 1.3 (373C-D; Luibheid 198): "The source of this hierarchy is the font of life, the being of goodness, the one cause of everything, namely, the Trinity, which in goodness bestows being and well-being on everything." *Divine Names* 1.1 (588A; Luibheid 49): ". . . the divine goodness is such that, out of concern for our salvation, it deals out the immeasurably and infinite in limited measures."

57 *Expositio moralis in Abdiam* (PL 175.375B-C): "Babylonii siquidem expugnaverunt Assyrios, Medi Babylonios, [375C] Macedones, Medos, Romani Macedones, Christus Romanos; sed ultima victoria non ex crudelitate acta est, sed ex benignitate et clementia."

58 *In hierarchiam caelestem S. Dionysii* (PL 175.937C): "Motus Patris, affectus est paternae benignitatis; sola enim benignitate et pietate sola Pater movetur, ut lumina sua effundat super nos."

59 *In hierarchiam* (PL 175.937C).

60 *In hierarchiam* (PL 175.1058C).

Richard's *On the Trinity*

At first glance, Hugh's triad of power, wisdom, and goodness does not seem to figure centrally in Richard's *On the Trinity*. In broad lines, Richard agrees with Hugh that "the power of God is identical to his wisdom, and his goodness is nothing other than his wisdom or power" and that these are "nothing other than the divine substance."[61] But, treated explicitly as such, Hugh's triad makes only brief appearances, in particular toward the end of the last book,[62] and seems wide of Richard's chief concern. Closer inspection, however, reveals that the themes of divine power, wisdom, and especially goodness recur throughout and suggests a closer connection to Hugh's thought.

Books 1 and 2 constitute a deduction of the properties of the single, unified, divine nature. In Book 1, Richard focuses on divine power and wisdom, arguing that they are identical with themselves and with the divine substance—in short, he affirms divine simplicity.[63] These affirmations of supreme power and wisdom lead, by the end of Book 2 (chs. 16ff), to an affirmation that the divine nature is also supreme goodness (*summum bonum*). Transitioning from discussions of divine unity and simplicity in Books 1–2 to divine plurality in Book 3, Richard, in effect, has the triad in view, utilizing his preferred term for divine goodness, namely, benevolence (*benevolentia*): "Just as there is then one wisdom and one power in both persons, so rightly it will be necessary that there be one supreme benevolence in both."[64]

As he proceeds in Book 3, it is apparent that divine goodness anchors and drives the argument: The divine being is supreme goodness; supreme goodness entails charity; charity is love directed toward another. Thus, "charity absolutely cannot exist where a plurality of persons is lacking."[65] The existence of multiple divine persons is a function of divine goodness. Precisely because of the presence of benevolence in God, not just power and wisdom, a Trinity of persons must be present. Supreme power and wisdom could be present in a single person, but such is *not* so once supreme goodness is also affirmed.[66]

---

[61] *Trin.* 4.3
[62] *Trin.* 6.15.
[63] As Adam of St Victor puts it: "Simple in being, simple in power, simple in willing, simple in knowing, all these are simple" (*Profitentes unitatem*, 5; see below 187).
[64] *Trin.* 3.15.
[65] *Trin.* 3.2.
[66] *Trin.* 3.16. See *Trin.* 3.20: "it is argued from the mutual fellowship (*consodalitate*) of a third

Divine Benevolence

Arguably, in fact, it is the "pressure" of divine *benevolentia*—his conviction regarding what is logically entailed in the very idea of goodness—that pushes Richard in Book 3 to complicate his strict insistence on the absolute incommunicability of the divine nature so emphatically affirmed in Book 2.[67] "But what is more glorious and what is truly more magnificent than to possess nothing that one refuses to communicate?"[68] For Richard, the will for absolute self-sharing constitutes divine *benevolentia*, from which emerges the necessity of a "sharing of community" (*consortio societatis*).[69] In a succinct summary (which includes a rare use of the term "benignity" as an equivalent for benevolence), Richard concludes: "For that reason then it is clearly concluded that the supreme degree of benignity (*benignitas*) would not have a place in divinity, if a third person were lacking in the plurality of persons."[70] And so, the highest form of love entails *benevolentia* in a crucial way: "What else is intimate and supreme mutual love for a third (*condilectio*) except the mutual concurrence of intimate benevolence...?"[71] While continuing in the remaining Books (4–6) to wrestle with technical issues regarding the notion of substance and "person" provoked by his claims in Book 3, Richard returns at key points to the theme of divine benevolence and its implications for his conception of the divine nature, especially for the relation of the persons. Arguably, *benevolentia* is his overriding concern and fundamental intuition throughout this work. In fact, it may not overstate the case to claim that in the course of this work, Richard develops a "metaphysics of benevolence." For him, the deepest, most fundamental reality is constituted by an incessant act of supreme intending of good. "Just as there is one being, so

person in the Trinity that concordant charity and consocial love (*consocialis amor*) are never found anywhere in an individual."

[67] *Trin.* 3.8: "In that discussion [in Book II] we found that the divinity cannot be common to a plurality of substances, but in this present discussion it seems clear that it is common to a plurality of persons... What then?... without a doubt each of them will be God in such a way that the two together are only one God. *And who is capable of this?* (2 Cor 2:16)... both together are one and the same substance."

[68] *Trin.* 3.4; *Trin.* 3.6.

[69] *Trin.* 3.14.

[70] *Trin.* 3.18.

[71] *Trin.* 3.19.

there is also one will. And so, one will, one love, and one indistinguish-able goodness belong to every person in the Trinity."[72]

More precisely within the divine being there is a two-fold act of willing, of intending good, or two distinct "willings" of a single, undi-vided good will. First, there is the more principal act of the Father's gratuitous self-bestowal of his entire being in the generation of the Son. The Father wills complete and utter self-communication and this act constitutes the Son—"someone to whom He would communicate the richness of His magnitude."[73] This first willing is a direct, singularly focused, even exclusive act of willing a single object of his benevolence. The Son is "someone to whom [the Father] can communicate the infi-nite abundance of his own fullness."[74] It is the opposite of envy, the desire to hoard or keep a good for oneself. Not to so share would be a grave "defect in benevolence," that is, if the Father "were enviously preferring to retain for Himself alone the abundance of His fullness, which He could, if He wanted, communicate to another."[75] The meta-physically primordial and principal act of benevolence is one of sheer generosity, what Richard calls wholly "gratuitous love."[76] It is of the very essence of the divinity to intend the good of another, but *in Deo* the good intended for the other cannot be other than the divinity itself. The Father has no other good to will for the Son than Himself, while apart from the Son He "lacks" another whose good He can intend. So *in Deo* the act of benevolence is the act of self-bestowing generosity and that good which is generously intended is the whole of the Father himself. Primordial divine benevolence eternally constitutes a duality *in Deo*: "What is the will to have a second person equal in dignity, un-less the will to have someone whom the Unbegotten loves intimately and rightly must love with a love worthy of coequality?"[77] Or "for the Unbegotten, willing to have from himself a being conformed and equal

---

[72] *Trin.* 5.23.

[73] *Trin.* 6.6.

[74] *Trin.* 3.4.

[75] *Trin.* 3.4.

[76] *Trin.* 5.17: "He, who bestows all of the fullness that he has and reserves nothing for himself alone, reveals that he has the fullness of gratuitous love. If he were to possess all plenitude, and if he were unwilling to bestow it, although he could, then he would not have the fullness of gratuitous love. Therefore, it is proven that he, who is not lacking either the power or desire to execute all his benevolence, has the fullness of gratuitous love." Note again, that power [and wisdom] are in the service of goodness.

[77] *Trin.* 6.7

in dignity to himself is identical to begetting a Son."[78] But crucially
there is a (logically, not temporally) subsequent act of willing that,
while proceeding from the same divine will, is rationally distinguishable from the first act of willing.

> But what is the will to have a third person whom they loved together
> (*condilectum*), unless to will to have someone who is loved equally both
> by the Unbegotten and his own lover and who delights with the Un-
> begotten in the pleasures of the love that was presented to the Unbegot-
> ten [by the Son]?[79]

For Richard, these two acts of willing are quite distinct: "There is a
huge difference in every respect between willing to have a person equal
in dignity and willing to have another person whom they love together
(*condilectum*)."[80] The first produces the Son, establishing a divine "duality" in a "communion of dignity;" the second produces the Holy Spirit,
establishing the divine trinity in a "communion of love."[81] Here, the
Father and the Son jointly will to share their mutual love *with* another,
a *condilectum*, one "co-loved." They give their love *to* the Holy Spirit.
And while the image of something given by or going out from two to
a third captures Richard's idea accurately, the direction of the movement can also be reversed and Richard can speak of the Spirit being
invited, welcomed *into* the mutual love of the Father and the Son.

Accordingly, while the first act of benevolent willing might be best
captured in the notion of supreme *generosity*, the second act has the
characteristic of supreme *hospitality*. Where the first has the distinguishing characteristic of exclusivity—the Father gives himself in this
way *only* to the Son and to no other, the second act has the distinguishing characteristic of inclusivity—the Spirit is invited into the communion of the Father and the Son. Where the first has the "accusative"
character of an enclosed I-Thou, the second is refracted obliquely and
opened by a "dative" modality. Or again, the first benevolence is in a
sense "interested" love; it not only wills the good of the beloved, but
also wills the beloved for itself; it seeks to love and be loved, and seeks
to enjoy the delights of such mutual, reciprocated, and requited love.
Here is divine *eros*. By contrast, the second benevolence is "disinter-

---

[78]   *Trin.* 6.17
[79]   *Trin.* 6.7; see also *Trin.* 6.17: "for the Begotten and the Unbegotten, willing to have a third
       person mutually loved by them (*condilectum*) is identical to producing the Holy Spirit."
[80]   *Trin.* 6.7.
[81]   *Trin.* 6.17.

ested"; here is divine *agape*.[82] The sharing of mutual love between two with a third does not increase the happiness of the first two, but rather allows another to enjoy it too—"but he desired to have a third person, whom they loved together (*condilectum*), so that he would have someone to whom he would communicate the pleasures of charity."[83] The supreme degree of goodness is reached when a person bestows supreme love on someone and gains nothing from it toward the fullness of his own happiness.[84] In the end, for Richard, two distinguishable acts of supreme benevolence account for the triad of persons: By an act of absolute and total self-communication—"a sharing of dignity"—the Father generates the Son. By an act of absolute and total sharing of communion—"a sharing of love"—the Father and the Son produce the Spirit.[85]

Together these two acts—divine generosity and hospitality—not only establish the divine Trinity of persons in Richard's view, but they also establish and encompass the nature and scope of divine benevolence. For Richard, the Father is most fundamentally a generous, hospitable intending of good, from which comes the Son and the Spirit: "The communion of majesty was, so to speak, the original cause of one person; and the communion of love seems, as it were, to be a certain original cause of another person. And so, even though the production of both persons proceeds, as we have said, *from the paternal will*, there are still distinct reasons and different causes for this double production or procession."[86] In short, Richard espies the fullness of benevolence within and among the trinity of persons, the perfect expression of intending good: "Certainly if the same will belongs to every person in every respect, then each person loves the other as himself and as much as himself. If each person loves the other as himself, then he desires all that is communicable in the divinity for any other as for himself. If each

---

[82] In this, arguably, Richard anticipates (influences?) thirteenth-century discussions of the nature of love, which distinguish between the "love of concupiscence," the desire to enjoy or delight in an object (thus "interested love") and the "love of friendship," which intends another's good quite apart from the lover's own enjoyment (thus "disinterested love"). See Thomas M. Osborne, Jr., *Love of Self and Love of God in Thirteenth-Century Ethics* (Notre Dame: University of Notre Dame, 2005), 32–56 (discussing William of Auxerre, Philip the Chancellor, and Alexander of Hales). Both kinds of love seem present in the two forms of Richard's intra-divine benevolence.
[83] *Trin.* 6.6.
[84] See *Trin.* 3.18
[85] *Trin.* 6.17.
[86] *Trin.* 6.6.

person loves the other as much as himself, then he does not want whatever is communicable in the divinity more enthusiastically for himself than for another, and he does not want it more unenthusiastically for another than for himself."[87]

In Deo, the dynamics of benevolence are natural and necessary. Namely, given that the divine nature is *in se* supremely benevolent— something the Richard takes as a theological first principle—a divine Trinity of persons necessarily follows. So, while Richard can characterize the love shared by the Father with the Son, and by them both with the Spirit, as "gratuitous," he does not mean by it the free contingency that marks the meaning of grace applied to the Creator-creature relationship. But it is precisely this natural and necessary character of God's Trinitarian being that establishes the possibility for the latter meaning of grace. That is, because God's benevolence is fully "discharged" (communicated or expressed) and consummated *in se*, God is free to create and communicate that goodness *extra se* without the necessity born of intrinsic need. God cannot be *this* God without a trinity of persons; but *this* triune God can be God without and apart from creation, and so can relate to it freely and graciously.[88]

The Influence of Richard of St Victor's *On the Trinity*

A common and influential, though increasingly criticized, narrative of the development of western Trinitarian theology, often traced to the work of Theodore de Régnon (1831–1893), has pitted a "western" view, which prioritizes the singular, unified divine essence over the plurality of the divine persons, against an "eastern" view, which starts with the clear affirmation of the persons, and then works to affirm their common essence or nature.[89] This narrative finds the origins of the first in Augustine and of the second in the Cappadocian fathers. The first takes as its model for the Trinitarian life the distinguishable powers/faculties

---

[87]   *Trin.* 5.23: See also *Trin.* 5.24
[88]   See David Bentley Hart, *The Beauty of the Infinite: The Aesthetics Of Christian Truth* (Grand Rapids, MI: W. B. Eerdmans, 2004), 104.
[89]   Michel Barnes, "De Régnon Reconsidered," *Augustinian Studies* 26 (1995): 55 argues that Frederick Crowe, *Doctrine of the Holy Trinity* (1966), James Mackey, *The Christian Experience of God as Trinity* (1983), John O'Donnell, *Trinity and Temporality* (1985), David Brown, *The Divine Trinity* (1985), and Catherine LaCugna, *God For Us* (1991) all inadvertently rely on Régnon's work.

or acts of the single human mind (memory-understanding-will or remembering-knowing-loving), and is thus a "psychological" model. The second sees a community of related persons as the paradigm, hence a communal or "social" model.[90] From this vantage point, Richard's *On the Trinity* has been hailed as a counter-balance or even antidote to the priority that the West places on the unity of the divine essence and the resulting tendency toward Trinitarian modalism, which allegedly stems from Augustine's own *On the Trinity*.[91] Many have seen the apparent priority Richard gives to the divine persons, who derive their essential personhood from the love relationships between them, as overcoming the deficiencies of this typical western approach and as having greater affinity with eastern models.[92] As the problematic nature of this narrative becomes increasingly apparent, the need to re-evaluate and appreciate afresh Richard's thought also becomes patent.[93] This will entail

[90] See, for example, Jürgen Moltmann, *The Trinity and the Kingdom*, trans., Margaret Kohl, (Minneapolis: Fortress Press, 1993) 199: "[t]wo different categories of analogy have always been used for the eternal life of the Trinity: the category of the individual person, and the category of community. Ever since Augustine's development of the psychological doctrine of the Trinity, the first has taken precedence in the West; whereas the Cappadocian Fathers and the Orthodox theologians, down to the present day, employ the second category. They incline towards an emphatically social doctrine of the Trinity and criticize the modalistic tendencies in the 'personal' trinitarian doctrine of the Western church."

[91] The claim is made famously by Adolph von Harnack, who argued that "Augustine only gets beyond modalism by the mere assertion that he does not wish to be a modalist" (*The History of Dogma* [New York: Dover Publications, 1960], IV.131, fn. 1. More recently see Colin Gunton, "Augustine, The Trinity and the Theological Crisis of the West," *Scottish Journal of Theology* 43 (1990): 33–58 and Cornelius Plantinga Jr., "The Threeness/Oneness Problem of the Trinity," *Calvin Theological Journal* 23 (1988), 37–53. For a penetrating rebuttal of this interpretation of Augustine, see John Cavadini, "The Quest for Truth in Augustine's *De Trinitate*," *Theological Studies* 58 (1997): 429–40 and Basil Studer, *Augustins De Trinitate* (Paderborn: Schoeningh, 2005).

[92] C. C. Pecknold argues that John Zizioulas also accepted the De Régnon thesis, and further that "King's College, London, during the 1980s and 1990s promoted an anti-Western (anti-Augustinian) formulation of the Trinity that called for sweeping retrieval of the Cappadocian contribution," which was coupled with the "social trinity" of Richard of St Victor (C. C. Pecknold, "How Augustine Used the Trinity: Functionalism and the Development of Doctrine," *Anglican Theological Review* 81:1 (2003): 127, f. 1).

[93] Contemporary Trinitarian thought among western theologians is currently in a state of flux, and arguably has been since the time of Schleiermacher. Schleiermacher inaugurated an influential trend in modern Trinitarian theology that, in the wake of the Kantian revolution, called into question any claims to know something about the nature of God *in se*, preferring to see traditional Christian claims about the Trinity strictly as claims about human experience of God. This approach was very influential on much subsequent Trinitarian theology. Reacting to this dominant approach in the mid-twentieth century, Karl Rahner most famously attempted an influential challenge to this essentially agnostic [view] . . . with the celebrated (though perhaps too easily simplified) axiom regarding the identity of the economic and

not only revisiting *On the Trinity* unencumbered by distorting narratives but also a deeper probing of the whole of this work, not just Book 3, which has been available in English translation for several decades.[94] While a summary of the whole of this work is impossible here, at least it should be emphasized that even in Book 3, after arguing for the necessity of a plurality of divine persons, Richard immediately clarifies that this plurality is unlike any kind of created plurality, such as might be found among multiple human beings.[95] However the "consocial love" (*consocialis amor*) of divine persons might best be conceived, it must be sharply distinguished from that of a community of created individuals.

At the same time, it is undeniable that Richard's approach to matters Trinitarian was bold and innovative, both in method and content. In method, the pursuit of "necessary reasons" (*rationes*), reminiscent of Anselm, would provoke negative reactions in some quarters. In content, his achievement regarding the issue of how to understand the nature of and distinction between the divine persons—"the most difficult question situated at the heart of Trinitarian speculation"[96]—was

immanent Trinity: "The 'economic' Trinity is the 'immanent' Trinity and the 'immanent' Trinity is the 'economic' Trinity". Essentially reversing the Schliermachian disjunction between God's inner being and God's relation to the world, Rahner's axiom appeared to assert a complete and exact correspondence between God's activity in salvation history and God's eternal being (Anatolios, *Retrieving Nicaea*).

[94] See Grover A. Zinn, ed., *Richard of St Victor: The Twelve Patriarchs, the Mystical Ark Book, Three of the Trinity* (New York: Paulist Press, 1979).

[95] See *Trin.* 3.23ff. Also in *Trin.* 2.12 Richard applies to God the conception of "individual substantiality," namely, "what belongs to one individual alone and cannot be common at all to several substances," (e.g., Danielness/*danielitas*), in contrast both to "specific substantiality," something common to all individuals within a species, (e.g., humanness) and to "general substantiality," something common to many different kinds of individuals (e.g., corporality). Divinity is "incommunicable" to another substance; it cannot be shared. In effect, whatever it might mean to posit three "persons" within this divinity, it must necessarily be sharply distinguished from the notion of three human individuals sharing a common humanness. This seems to mitigate against the possibility of a "social trinity" in the manner of a community of three individual human beings. Moreover, "where there is supreme simplicity, there is true and supreme unity. Therefore, whatever is in the supreme good is truly and supremely one, and *there cannot be distinct realities in it*, but it is identical to all that it is (2.17). The burden of Book 2, in fact, is to affirm the supreme simplicity and absolute unity of the divine nature. Richard insists that in the divine simplicity, God's unity far outstrips even the most unified of created things (2.20): It is not at all like the unity "which consists of a collection of many properties in one form," or "which consists of conformity of many substances in one nature," or "which occurs in a union of differently formed substances in one person," or even that "which occurs in a composition of a subsistent and subsistence in one essence." It exceeds "in an incomparable and incomprehensible way all those unities."

[96] Michael Schmaus, *Der "Liber propugnatorius" des Thomas Anglicus und die Lehrunterschiede*

far-reaching. Perhaps most crucial was his critique of the venerable Boethian definition of "person,"[97] offering a new one in its place,[98] the merits of which continue to be debated. Richard effects a "remarkable progress" in Trinitarian definitions in the twelfth century, by drawing "a lucid distinction between properties and appropriations while keeping the balance of both."[99]

Richard's achievement was of central importance to the later-medieval Trinitarian discussion.[100] A useful heuristic for analyzing different strands of late medieval Trinitarian theologies, especially those trajectories emerging in the late thirteenth and early fourteenth centuries,[101] distinguishes between those that account for the distinction of persons by an appeal to intra-Trinitarian *relations* or to intra-Trinitarian *emanations* as the distinguishing feature.[102] For the former, the persons are distinguished in terms of their relations with one another: for example, only in so far as the first person is Father to the second, the Son, are they distinct. Here, *paternitas* is the distinguishing characteristic that identifies the Father as such, and *filiation* for the Son. On the emanation account, what distinguishes the persons are their diverse modes of origin. Here, the Father is neither Son nor Spirit only because he takes his origin from no one, while the Son is generated naturally (by way of nature) and the Spirit is generated voluntarily (by

---

zwischen Thomas von Aquin und Duns Scotus, II Teil Die Trinitarischen Lehrdifferenzen, 2 vols., BGPTM 29.1–2 (1930), 385, cited in Russell Friedman, *"In Principium Erat Verbum,"* Ph.D. Dissertation, University of Iowa, 1997, 2.

[97] See Boethius, *Contra Eutychen* 3 (ed. Moreschini 214.71–72): *"naturae rationabilis individua substantia"* ["an individual substance of a rational nature"].

[98] Already in the late eleventh and early twelfth centuries, reacting to the famous Boethian definition, the proper definition of "person" in Trinitarian debate was a point of intense debate between Anselm of Canterbury and Roscelin of Compiègne, and later with Abelard and Gilbert of Poitiers (Gemeinhardt, "Logic, Tradition, and Ecumenics," 13, 17, 37–43).

[99] Gemeinhardt, "Logic, Tradition, and Ecumenics," 50–51. On the relationship between this distinction and the triad, *potentia, sapientia, benignitas*, see John T. Slotemaker, "Richard of St Victor on the Divine Appropriations and Personal Properties: A Historical Sketch of *potentia, sapientia, benignitas*," delivered at the Thirty-Third Patristic, Medieval and Renaissance Conference, Villanova University, Philadelphia, Pennsylvania, October 11, 2007.

[100] Russell L. Friedman, *Medieval Trinitarian Thought from Aquinas to Ockham* (Cambridge University, 2010) 15.

[101] An especially important period in medieval Trinitarian thought. See M. Schmaus, *Der Liber Propugnatorius* cited in Russell L. Friedman, "Divergent Traditions in Later-Medieval Trinitarian Theology: Relations, Emanations, and the Use of Philosophical Psychology, 1250–1325," *Studia Theologica* 53 (1999): 13–25, 24.

[102] Friedman, "Divergent Traditions," 24; see also Friedman's forthcoming *Intellectual Traditions at the Medieval University: The Use of Philosophical Psychology in Trinitarian Theology among the Franciscans and Dominicans, 1250–1350* (Leiden: Brill, 2010).

way of will). Thus, *innascibilitas* not *paternitas* is the personal property of the Father.[103] These are to some extent mutually compatible, and were certainly not always consciously and explicitly recognized as distinct. Indeed, they seem to stand side by side, for example, in Anselm of Canterbury's most mature statement of Trinitarian theology, *De processione Spiritus sancti*.[104] But any given account tends to privilege one over the other. While these two distinct traditions only emerged clearly after 1250, the adherents of the emanation account often looked to Richard's *On the Trinity* as the precursor to their view. Richard's definition of divine persons as "incommunicable existences of the divine nature,"[105] coupled with his insistence that modes of existence are derived from modes of origin, codified an approach to Trinitarian persons that privileged emanation over relation in conceiving the differentiation of persons.[106] Later medieval thinkers, including Bonaventure (d. 1274), John Pecham (d. 1292), Henry of Ghent (d. 1293), Matthew of Aquasparta (d. 1302), John Duns Scotus (d. 1308), and Peter Auriol (d. 1322), adopted Richard's approach.[107]

It is hoped that the availability of Richard's *On the Trinity* in its entirety here will enable and encourage greater understanding of his teaching on the matter in its own right, as well as a deeper appreciation of its subsequent contribution and influence, both medieval and modern.

CONCLUSION: DIVINE GOODNESS AT ST VICTOR

Thus it appears that the apparently distinctive Victorine accent in its fundamental view of God and creation lies in its concept of divine goodness (*benignitas/benevolentia*). That God is good is, of course, a fundamental affirmation of both Old and New Testaments, from the

---

103   Friedman, "Divergent Traditions," 14–16.
104   Gemeinhardt, "Logic, Tradition, and Ecumenics," 21–24. See also Giles E. M. Gaspar, *Anselm of Canterbury and his Theological Inheritance* (Burlington, VT: Ashgate, 2004) 140–41 and John T. Slotemaker, "The Development of Anselm's Trinitarian Theology: The Textual and Theological Origins of a Late Medieval Debate," in *Saint Anselm and His Legacy*, eds. Giles Gaspar and Ian Logan (Toronto: Pontifical Institute of Mediaeval Studies, forthcoming, 2010).
105   *Trin.* 4.22.
106   Friedman, *Medieval Trinitarian Thought*, 15f.
107   Friedman, "Divergent Traditions," 17–24.

psalmist's "taste and see that the Lord is good" (Ps 33:9, Vulgate) to Jesus' own "no one is good but God alone" (Luke 18:19). That supreme Reality is *the* good (*summum bonum*) is the well-known fundamental assumption of the philosophical traditions (especially those of Platonic pedigree) appropriated in various ways by Christian thinkers throughout the pre-modern period. That goodness is self-communicating and "self-attracting," bringing all that is not divine out from Itself and back to Itself, is a consistent refrain from Plato to Proclus, and a host of Christian neoplatonists, such as Augustine and Dionysius. For their part, Hugh and Richard synthesize these traditions in the notion of divine *benignitas* and *benevolentia*, terms that capture the specific texture of divine goodness in the Victorine vision.

It is not difficult to see here a conceptual link between the fundamental Hugonian intuition regarding extra-Trinitarian *benignitas* and the outworking of its intra-Trinitarian logic in Richard's *Ur-begriff* of divine *benevolentia* in *On the Trinity*. For Richard, as noted, God *in se* is benevolent. "How great an act of kindness, sweetness, and benevolence was it that the Father reserved nothing for himself alone from the riches of his magnitude and desired to possess nothing that he did not communicate to him!"[108] For him, it is this divine *benevolentia* that constitutes the Trinitarian nature; for Hugh, it is divine *benignitas* that characterizes the whole Creator-creation and Savior-salvation relationship as well. Richard's priority on *benevolentia ad intra*, within and among the divine persons, is an extension—more precisely, a *reductio in Deum*—of the logic of Hugh's priority on divine *benignitas ad extra*, between God and creation. It is tempting to see Richard providing an immanent Trinitarian grounding for Hugh's vision of the Trinity's economic activity. Richard's affirmation of divine *benevolentia, ad intra*, among the divine persons, provides a profound warrant for Hugh's vision of divine *benignitas, ad extra*, in relation to creation. In both cases, the Victorine insight regarding the goodness of divine being might best be epitomized in Richard's insistence that the divine *benevolentia* does not merely allow, but "seeks with longing" to share the mutual delights of love with another, namely, the "co-beloved" (*condilectum*).[109] It is precisely this longing to self-communicate that Hugh espies in God's creating and redeeming activity. All this amounts to the simple, but profound intuition that at the heart of all reality is

[108] *Trin.* 3.4; 5.10, 17.
[109] *Trin.* 3.11.

an intentional generosity and hospitality that wills the well-being and
flourishing of Itself and all else, and in the service of which the other
divine attributes—especially power and wisdom—function.[110] For the
Victorines, such divine goodness "explains" both the nature of divine
being itself, specifically its tri-unity,[111] as well as the existence and nature of all non-divine being, and, finally, the relationship between the
two.[112] So, in Victorine thought, manifest in various ways in the works
contained below, Trinity and creation are linked according to this overriding intuition regarding divine goodness.

---

[110] Similarly, Aquinas, *ST* III.1.1, ad 3: "Every mode of being wherein any creature whatsoever
differs from the Creator has been established by God's wisdom, and is ordained to God's
goodness. For God, Who is uncreated, immutable, and incorporeal, produced mutable and
corporeal creatures for His own goodness."

[111] Similarly, Bonaventure, *Itinerarium in Deum* 6.1: "the good itself is the principal foundation
for contemplating the [Trinitarian] emanations."

[112] So David Bentley Hart (*Beauty of the Infinite*, 185): "God graciously makes a place for others
in the divine interval of love's superabundance."

HUGH OF ST VICTOR

ON THE THREE DAYS

INTRODUCTION AND TRANSLATION
BY HUGH FEISS OSB

INTRODUCTION

WORK

Hugh came to St Victor in Paris from northern Germany sometime around 1115–1118, after the departure of the monastery's founder, William of Champeaux to be bishop of Chalons-sur-Marne in 1113. Hugh died in 1141. His career as a teacher and writer at St Victor spanned less than twenty-five years, during which he wrote an impressive number of works, some of them very influential.

Among these works of Hugh of St Victor is the *On the Three Days* (*De tribus diebus*), of which its editor, Dominique Poirel identified 132 manuscripts.[1] *On the Three Days* exists in two slightly different versions, the second one containing Hugh's touching up of the first.[2] It seems likely that the plan of the work also evolved between the time Hugh began the work and when he finished the first version. It is at once a sermon, a collection of wonders, a theological-philosophical treatise on creation, the existence of God and the mystery of the Trinity, allegorical exegesis, and an account of the mind's journey to God, written in a captivating Latin style.[3] More exactly, the work—especially the first of its three parts—is a meditation on the divine works, so that "through the things which God has made, a man will learn to seek out and understand him who has made them all."[4]

---

[1] On the influence of *On the Three Days*, see Dominique Poirel, *Livre de la nature et débat trinitaire au XIIᵉ siècle, Le* De tribus diebus *de Hugues de Saint-Victor*, Bibliotheca Victorina XIV (Turnhout: Brepols, 2002), 169–98. As the notes will make clear, this introduction is for the most part merely a summary of this magisterial study by the editor of the *On the Three Days*.

[2] Poirel, *Livre*, 213–33.

[3] Poirel, *Livre*, 6, 236–40. On Hugh's style, which itself suggests the variety (immensity), beauty and utility of God's creation, see Poirel, *Livre*, 199–213.

[4] *Didasc.* 3.10 (Taylor, 93; Buttimer, 59–60). I owe this reference to Jan W. M. van Zwieten, "Scientific and Spiritual Culture in Hugh of St Victor," in *Centres of Learning: Learning and Location In Pre-Modern Europe and the Near East*, ed. Jan Willem Drijvers and Alasdair A. MacDonald (New York: Brill, 1995) 183.

DATE

Poirel has confirmed and refined the opinion that *On the Three Days* is among Hugh's earliest works. In Hugh's *Booklet on the Formation of the Ark*, there is a list of popes which ends with Innocent II, who died February 13, 1130. In the *Booklet*, Hugh refers the reader to a treatise he had written entitled *On the Three Days*.[5] The *Booklet* is appended to the *On the Ark of Noah* (1125/1126); it is likely that Hugh finished the *On the Three Days* before the *On the Ark of Noah*. Abelard discusses the triad, power, wisdom and kindness in his *Theology "Of the Supreme Good,"* which its editors assign to 1120/1121.[6] As we shall see, Poirel thinks Abelard derived the triad from the *On the Three Days*, which suggests that Hugh wrote it before 1120/1121.[7] Hugh probably made corrections and issued the second version before 1130.[8] The second, corrected version was included in the official collection of Hugh's works made at St Victor by Abbot Gilduin (d. 1155).

ARGUMENT

The work is divided into three distinct sections, which are marked in the translation by bracketed roman numerals. The first section is a lyrical and well organized praise of the wonders of the things that God has made. In it Hugh, the enthusiastic twelfth-century scholar, marvels in a systematic way at the immensity, beauty and utility of the natural world. His wonder at the various dimensions of creation reminds one of the carefully constructed blessings of God and the spheres of creation in the *Benedicite*, the prayer of the three young men included in the Latin Vulgate version of the book of Daniel, a text incorporated

---

[5]   *Libellus*, IV (Sicard, 143.115–16; PL 176.693D).

[6]   Poirel, *Livre*, 284, refers to E. M. Buytaert and C. J. Mews, *Petri Abaelardi opera theologia, III: Theologia "Summi boni"; Theologia "Scholarium,"* CCCM 13 (Turnhout: Brepols, 1987) 20–21; C. J. Mews, "On Dating the Works of Peter Abelard," *Archives d'histoire doctrinale et littéraire du Moyen Age*, t. 52 (1985) 73–92, 131.

[7]   Poirel, *Livre*, 131–54, 458–60, and *De tribus diebus*, 218*-20* offer further evidence. Hugh's treatise *On the Virginity of the Blessed Mary* exists in two recensions, the second containing and appendix answering objections to the first. The manuscripts, which contain the earlier version of the Marian work, also contain the first recension of *On the Three Days*, and the later versions of both works appear in a different body of manuscripts. In addition, because of many parallels in the two works, Poirel thinks it likely that the first two books of Hugh *Explanation of Ecclesiastes* were written at the same time as *On the Three Days*.

[8]   Poirel, *Livre*, 118–21.

into the liturgy. Hugh's knowledge of the physical world draws on the encyclopedic tradition (e.g., Pliny's *Natural History* and Isidore of Seville's *Etymologies*), but his wonder seems to have been elicited by direct experience, not just descriptions in books. In the *Didascalicon*, in a rare autobiographical reference, he tells about going out at night to gaze at the stars.[9] He is particularly impressed by how creatures of very different sizes and shapes mesh together in ordered harmony, an ecosystem, and how each biological need is fulfilled (4.8; 18.2, 4–5; 20.6). The world he describes is the world of ordinary experience. He lived long before microscopes and telescopes brought knowledge of dazzling worlds beyond the reach of the senses and before the data of the senses were doubted by Enlightenment philosophers.[10]

Hugh divides the wonders of the physical world into three, because he sees in the immensity, beauty and utility of the world a reflection of the power, wisdom and kindness of God (1.3). In the first part of his treatise, he presents these as essential attributes of God, identical with the divine substance and evident in creation (1.2). His leitmotiv is Rom 1:20: "From the creation of the world the invisible realities of God are beheld through what is understood of the things which are made." He lays down a careful outline, which supplies the subdivisions of the first part of the treatise, but makes no reference to the second and third parts. Surprisingly, even in the first section, Hugh does not follow his outline exactly.

In the second part of the treatise, Hugh turns to the invisible things that have been made known through the wonders of the visible. Whereas the first part was based on experience, and the third part will be based on the authority of Scripture, this second part is based on reason.[11] Here, Hugh focuses on the link between visible beauty and invisible Wisdom. The warrant for this choice, on the one hand, is that

---

9   *Didasc.* 6.3 (Taylor, 136–37; Buttimer, 114.19–115.1).

10   Wanda Cizewski, "Beauty and the Beasts," 297–98, notes Hugh's "great delight in cataloguing the variety of qualities and species to be found on earth . . . Hugh concentrates on animal beauty . . . The category of animal beauty includes not only shapeliness or grace, but also the curious, the exotic, and the grotesque." Hugh's dictum, "Learn everything, and you will see that nothing is superfluous" (*Didasc.* 6.3 [Taylor, 137; Buttimer, 115]) is vindicated in the *On the Three Days*. In *Didascalicon* 6.3, Hugh describes how as a school boy he delighted in observing the natural world; Hugh's theory and practice directed all learning toward the *lectio divina* of the Bible. On Hugh's use of all knowledge for reading the Bible and his keen sense of observation, see Dominique Poirel, "Voir l'invisible: la spiritualité visionnaire de Hugues de Saint-Victor," in *Spiritualität im Europa des Mittelalters: L'Europe spirituelle au Moyen Age: 900 Jahre Hildegard von Bingen, 900 ans l'abbaye de Cîteaux*, ed. Jean Ferrari and Stephan Grätzel, Philosophie im Kontext 4 (St. Augustin: Gardez! Verlag, 1998) 29–30, 33.

11   Poirel, *Livre*, 249.

beauty has definite form (which power does not), and it is a habitual quality (which utility is not). On the other hand, as the image of the Father, Wisdom (or the Word) is manifested in both creation and in redemption (16.1–3; 24.3). Then, from the discussion of beauty in part one, Hugh privileges the movement proper to rational creatures, which is the highest representation of uncreated Wisdom. Because the rational creature spans the visible and invisible, it is a both a door or first access and a path to contemplation of God.

The spiritual essence of a human being had a beginning and so did not give existence to itself. For anything at all to exist, there must be an eternal Creator. The order in nature shows that this eternal Creator exerts an all-encompassing Providence (18.2–5). The Creator is "completely one and simple" (19.3), and so is unchanging (19.5) in his omnipresence (19.8), his being (20.1–4) and knowledge (20.5–10). Hugh mentions that divine knowledge is called vision, wisdom, foreknowledge and providence (he does not mention predestination at all), but says that he does not want to deal with them in this compendium (20.10; cf. 8.5)

Having discovered in the rational mind a path to the one, eternal, immutable Creator, Hugh turns to the Trinity. The rational mind generates understanding and sometimes loves and delights in what it understands. In God the generation of Wisdom is eternal, as is the Love between them (21). The Father loves his Wisdom in itself and loves Wisdom's works because of the likeness of Wisdom that he sees in them (22; 24.2).

At this point Hugh turns from meditative and devout analysis to exhortation. One might say that the first part of his treatise read the literal meaning of the book of nature (4.3), the second part to this point explored its allegorical and anagogic meaning, and from this point Hugh will urge its tropological meaning. Using as his springboard the gospel account of the Transfiguration of Christ, Hugh has the Father address the reader: "Listen to Him," and keep or return to his likeness within you (24.2–3). Then Hugh adds his own exhortation, urging his readers to turn to their Redeemer, through whom they and the beautiful world were created good (1.1) and who wishes to redeem them. If they do not wish to have him as their Redeemer, they will have him as their Judge.

The first two parts describe the way of cognition, which leads from knowledge of creation to knowledge of Wisdom, the second person of the Trinity. In contemplation of the Triune God, the rational creature is turned (converted) toward the Wisdom of God, as befits its nature. However, contemplation can last only for a little while. We (Hugh changes to the first person plural) now must reverse our path and return to the world following the way of creation, from Wisdom, to rational creation, to corporeal creation (25). However, we should bring back with us the Light that we saw there, the divine Power, Wisdom, and Kindness to which we should respond with the light of fear, the light of truth, and the light of love (26.1). These are three interior "days," which logically follow each other, without the later ones eliminating the earlier ones (26.2–3, 6).

Then Hugh relates the three days to the history of salvation. In the ark treatises, he will distinguish three eras: before the law, under the law, under grace. Here, looking at the three days from the standpoint of Christ, rather than of humanity, he distinguishes the first day, when humanity was under sin, and, under the prompting of the law, feared God the Judge;[12] the second day, when Christ brought the truth which takes away evil; the third day, when good is restored until finally charity will be perfect and fear of punishment will pass over into reverent fear (27.1–2).

What occurred in Christ was not just a remedy, but also an example and sacrament; what was external in his days we are to seek internally:

> First day: death, fear, Power, the Father
> Second day: burial, truth, Wisdom, The Son
> Third day: resurrection, charity, Kindness, the Holy Spirit.

These three days are one in the brightness and in the operation of God, but in this way "the distinction of persons can be understood in the distribution of works" (27.3). The omnipotence of God arouses our hearts to wonder and we die through fear; that is the day of the Father. The Wisdom of God enlightens our hearts to the recognition of truth and we are buried away from the clamor of this world by the contemplation of truth; that is the day of the Son. On the day of the Holy Spirit's kindness, we rise through love and desire for eternal goods (27.4).

Trinity: Power, Wisdom, Kindness

The triad power-wisdom-kindness is a connecting thread in Hugh's treatise. He saw them as divine attributes reflected in the immensity, beauty, and utility of nature. His most original contribution was to appropriate these three attributes respectively to the three persons of the Trinity.[13]

---

[12] Here Hugh adds "fear" to the dyad truth-love (*veritas-dilectio*), which he usually favored. See Poirel, *Livre*, 254–55.

[13] Poirel, *Livre*, 345–68.

Strikingly, already in 1121, Abelard was condemned at Soissons for doing something similar in his *Theology "Of the Supreme Good"* (1119–1121). Abelard aimed to describe the Trinity in terms that were more accessible to non-believers and less anthropomorphic than the Scriptural terms "Father," "Son," and "Spirit." Because it was established teaching that the divine persons are distinguished by their relations of origin, Abelard tried to show that wisdom derives from power, and goodness from the love of them both, for without power and wisdom, goodness would be without effect. This risked implying subordination in the Trinity. Reversing the traditional order, which saw attributes like power, wisdom and goodness as properly pertaining to the divine substance, but appropriated to one of the divine persons by reason of some fittingness, Abelard saw power, wisdom, and goodness as proper respectively to Father, Son and Spirit, but able, under certain conditions, to be assigned to the divine Substance. Thus, the "Father is powerful in-himself," but it can be said, with a meaning determined by the context, that "God is powerful" or "The Son is powerful." This was rejected by the church council at Soissons and again at Sens in 1141.[14] It seems very unlikely Hugh would have taken over a suspect idea from Abelard or that they would have come up with the same idea independently, so Abelard probably derived the idea from Hugh.[15]

The triad appears five times in *On the Three Days* (1.1–3; 15.2–16.1; 24.4; 26.1; 27:3–4). Only in the fourth and fifth of these passages does Hugh speak of appropriations of power, wisdom and kindness to the Trinity, and the fourth is only a brief mention. In the fifth reference, at the very end of *On the Three Days*, Hugh writes that the three days are ultimately one in God and in the divine action, but they are distinct in the works which God creates and in the stages of the spiritual life. Hugh does not identify the three attributes with the individual persons, but

[14]   Poirel, *Livre*, 283–314.
[15]   Poirel, *Livre*, 368–82. The precise chronology and source of the introduction of this triad in twelfth-century theology is still debated: Poirel (*Livre*, 372–379) opts for Hugh of St Victor, basing his argument of a dating of *On the Three Days* earlier than Abelard's *Theology "of the Supreme Good,"* whereas Matthias Perkams ("The Origins of the Trinitarian Attributes: *potentia, sapientia, benignitas*," *Archa Verbi*, 2004: 25–41) argues in favor of an "Abelardian" origin. Constant Mews (*Abelard and Heloise* [New York, NY: Oxford University Press, 2005], 38–41; 103–4; 115f), underlines the importance of oral discussions in the school of William of Champeaux in Paris; because of this, both Abelard and Hugh started using the ternary nearly at the same time (as is acknowledged by Perkams, *ibid.* 37). What is both certain and important is that Abelard's use proved immensely controversial. This particular triad would continue to draw the attention of theologians after Hugh and Abelard. Gilbert of Poitiers alludes to it (Gemeinhardt, "Logic, Tradition, and Ecumenics," 42) as does Richard (see below).

says only that they pertain to the different persons. Even then, the Trinitarian appropriations are not the primary focus of the discussion of power, wisdom and kindness in *On the Three Days*. Hugh's finesse in this regard is evident in a homily of Hugh's preserved as *Misc.* 1.99.[16] There, commenting on Mic 6: 5–8, Hugh writes that you should make an offering of discernment, piety and care, but in such a way that "you do not divide the one Trinity in distinguishing the gifts, nor confuse the Trinity of the unity in participating in the gifts, but present to each what is his and present all together to the one."[17]

The triad was discussed by theologians between 1140 and 1160. During that time, in part because of the influence of Hugh's *On the Sacraments of the Christian Faith*, the third member of the triad became fixed as "goodness" (*bonitas*).[18] Between 1160 and 1200, theologians considered the way in which essential attributes like these could be more specifically attributed to one divine person. Richard of St Victor was an important contributor; he or the anonymous author of the *Sentences on Divinity* seems to have been the first to use the term "appropriation" in this regard.[19] In *On the Spirit of Blasphemy*, he discusses the sin against the Holy Spirit, which he says is sheer malice against goodness, which is especially attributed to the Holy Spirit. "Certain [names] common to all the persons are appropriated to specific persons, not without a great mystery."[20] In *On the Trinity* 6.10,[21] he explains why the word "spirit" is applied or appropriated to the Holy Spirit as a proper name, even though it pertains to all three. In *On the Trinity* 6.15, Richard says he is going to repeat what he wrote earlier about why by a special manner of speaking, power is attributed to the Unbegotten, wisdom to the Begotten, and goodness to the Holy Spirit. The work he is referring to is a letter to an unknown Bernard, responding to his question why Augustine attributed unity to the Father, equality to the Son, and their mutual harmony to the Holy Spirit, and why the Scriptures attribute power specifically to the Father, wisdom to the Son, and charity or goodness to the Holy Spirit.[22] Richard's answer to Bernard's second question is included verbatim in *On the Trinity* 6.15. The gist of his

---

[16] PL 177.529A–532B.
[17] See Poirel, *Livre*, 334–43.
[18] *Sacr.* 1.3.26 (PL 176.227CD; Deferrari, 53–54). See Poirel, *Livre*, 383–89.
[19] *Sent. divinit.* (Geyer, 61–62).
[20] PL 196.1192BC.
[21] Ribaillier, TPMA 6.238–39, translated below.
[22] *De tribus personis appropriatis in Trinitate*, Ribaillier TPMA 15.167–87 (= PL 196.991–94).

argument is that the mystery of the Trinity exceeds the capacity of the human mind, but what we do know from daily experience—power, wisdom, charity—teaches us something about them, in a "provisory, indirect, and so to speak, mirror-like way."[23] There is no goodness without wisdom and power, no wisdom without power. In this created trinity, only power is not from the others; goodness is from both the others. In this trinity are expressed the properties of that highest and eternal Trinity. Richard does not say, as Abelard was accused of doing, that the power of the Son and Spirit is any less than that of the Father. For example, when wisdom is appropriated to the Son, an attribute common to the three persons is signified, but attention is directed toward the particular way in which this attribute is realized in that person. Or as St Thomas Aquinas put it, appropriation is "the manifestation of the persons through essential attributes,"[24] because there is some resemblance between that attribute and the unique property of that person, e.g., the relationship between unbegottenness and power.

The triad entered into the common patrimony of Western theology. Thomas Aquinas and the other thirteenth-century theologians incorporated it into their theologies of the Trinity. Among countless examples, here is one. In 1639, the Superior General of the canons regular of the Order of the Holy Cross (Crosiers) had ordered published a manuscript on the spiritual life written in the fourteenth century by his predecessor, Peter Pincharius (d. 1382). In his discussion of contemplative prayer, Pincharius lists seven reasons why such prayer is accompanied by spiritual joy. The seventh is that the contemplative is stunned by the magnitude of the divine power, and the profundity of the divine wisdom, and is in awe at the gentleness of the divine kindness.[25] The words—and the sentiments—are Hugh's.

Sources

Hugh's primary source is the Bible. He explicitly cites the Scriptures thirty-three times, most often the Psalms and the Gospel of Matthew. Beyond that, he alludes to the thought and language of the Bible constantly. Platonic thought, transmitted to the early Middle Ages through

[23] Poirel, *Livre*, 397. What follows draws upon his commentary (397–420) and Ribaillier's introduction in *Opuscules théologiques*.
[24] *ST* 1.39, aa. 7–8.
[25] Petrus Pincharius, *Vestis nuptialis* (Cologne: Henricus Krafft, 1639) 392.

Calcidius' *Commentary on the Timaeus*, Macrobius' *Dream of Cicero*, the writings of the fathers of the Church and of Boethius, is evident; e.g., the contrast between the intelligible and the physical world, the different kinds of movement, the triad reason, anger, and desire, and the pre-eminence of the sense of sight. Hugh is directly influenced by book 2 of Cicero's *On the Nature of the Gods*, which seeks to establish the existence, nature, and providence of the gods. The Carolingian theologian Paschasius Radbertus' *On Faith, Hope and Charity* anticipated and probably influenced Hugh's central ideas: the invisible creator is known from the visible things he has made, and in the creator, power, wisdom and will are co-extensive. The opening sentence of *On the Three Days* Hugh seems to have derived from a commentary on the Pauline Epistles composed by Florus of Lyons from extracts of Augustine's writings. This statement may have reached Hugh and Abelard, who also cites it, through William of Champeaux.[26]

Message

What can *On the Three Days* convey at the beginning of the twenty-first century? It provides anyone interested in the medieval world with a door into the way in which one educated, devout, and enthusiastic twelfth-century scholar, a native of Germany who chose exile in Paris, looked upon the natural world and loved it ardently (4.2). "Green, the most beautiful of all—how it enraptures the minds of those who see it" (12.2). He saw visible creation as an intricate, interconnected whole, an ecosystem, immense and beautiful. Nature was made to supply humanity's necessities, but in no sense does Hugh suggest it is humankind's plaything or possession (5). For Hugh science and theology complement each other.

For the theologian, Hugh is a charming colleague, optimistic about both the range of reason and the truth of faith. He respects the ultimate mystery of God, but reasons boldly about what faith teaches. He explores the paradox of attributes of the divine substance shared by three persons, yet somehow proper to each, which remains puzzling still to anyone who takes seriously the evidence of the Christian Scriptures. Hugh loves the beauty of the world, but knows that he must leave it behind to reach eternal beauty. He insists that the Incarnate Wisdom

---

[26] Poirel, *Livre*, 155–68.

is also the creative Wisdom, and that may be the secret of his wonder at the world. Hugh's is a sacramental world (27.3), in which nature manifests, and to spiritual person signifies, Truth itself. (4.3). The hedgehog, the human mind, and the Trinity are interconnected, and ultimately as in the Hugh's treatise *On the Ark of Noah*, Christ is the center around which all else revolves.

On the Three Days leads from visible creation to invisible creation, to contemplation of God—the order of cognition; then it leads from God to the rational creature who lives amid created realities—the order of creation. The pattern could be repeated endlessly, and deepened each time. Perhaps, that was what Hugh intended *On the Three Days* to be: an object of meditation, tracing a path that readers retrace each time they take up the book.[27]

A Note on Editions

There are translations of *On the Three Days* into modern languages, of which I have been able to consult the first:

Ugo di S. Vittore, I tre giorni dell'invisibile luce; L'unione del corpo e dello spirito. Ed. Vicenzo Liccaro. Florence: Sansoni, 1974.

Hugo van St Victor, *De drie dagen van het onzichtbare licht*. Ed. Jan Van Zwieten. Kampen: KoK, 1996.

In Poirel's critical edition, the numbers are lined, but there are no numbered divisions.[28] However, in the margins of his text he puts the section numbers into which the text is divided in Migne's *Patrologia Latina*. These section numbers are added in this translation, in order to provide a convenient way to refer to sections of the text both here and in the Latin versions. Moreover, I have divided each section into numbered paragraphs. So the third paragraph of section IX in the *Patrologia* (and Poirel) here becomes 9.3.

---

[27]   Poirel, *Livre*, 258.
[28]   Hugonis de Sancto Victore, *De tribus diebus*, ed. Dominique Poirel, Corpus Christianorum Continuatio Medievalis 177 (Turnhout: Brepols, 2002), 3–70.

Here begins *On the Three Days.*

[I]

1.1   The good Word and wise Life that made the world is perceived when the world is contemplated. The Word itself cannot be seen, but the Word both made what can be seen and is seen through what He made.[1]

1.2   "From the creation of the world the invisible realities of God are beheld through what is understood of the things which are made."[2] The invisible things of God are three: power, wisdom and kindness (*benignitas*).[3] From these three proceed all things. In these three all things subsist. By these three all things are governed. Power creates; wisdom governs; and kindness conserves.[4] Just as these three are ineffably one in God, so also they cannot be separated in any way in their operation.[5] Power creates wisely through kindness; wisdom governs kindly through power; and kindness conserves mightily through wisdom.[6]

1.3   The immensity of creatures manifests power; their beauty manifests wisdom;[7] their utility manifests kindness. The immensity of creatures lies in their number (*multitudo*) and size (*magnitudo*).[8] Number is found in the similar, the diverse, and the mixed. Size is found in bulk and extension. Bulk is found in mass and weight; extension, in length and breadth, depth and height. The beauty of creatures is found in their structure and movement, in their appearance and their quality. Structure is found in composition and order. Order lies in place, time and property. Motion is fourfold: local, natural, biological,[9] and rational. Local motion is back and forth, right and left, up and down, and around. Natural motion consists in increase and decrease; biological motion in the senses and appetites; rational motion in actions and decisions. Appearance is the visible form that the eye discerns, such as the colors and shapes of physical things. Quality is the internal property that is perceived by the other senses, such as tone when a sound is heard by the ears, sweetness in what the mouth tastes, fragrance smelled through the nose, and softness of material objects under the hand's touch. The usefulness of things consists in what makes them attractive, apt, beneficial, and necessary. The attractive is that which pleases; the apt is what is suitable; the beneficial is that which is advantageous; and what is necessary is that without which something cannot be.[10]

1.4   Now let us go through these proposed distinctions again from the beginning. For each kind in the division let us examine how from the immensity of creatures the power of the Creator is manifest, His wisdom from their beauty, and His kindness from their usefulness. Because immensity was the first division, it needs to come first in the development.

2.1   IMMENSITY

Diligently hear and consider the things that I am going to say. What kind of power (*potentia*) was it that made something to be when there was nothing? What understanding (*sensus*) could comprehend what power (*virtus*) is involved in making something from nothing, even to make anything, even to make one thing, however tiny?

2.2   MULTIPLICITY

If, then, it involves incomprehensible power to make one thing, however small, out of nothing, how can one gauge the power that makes so many things? And how many! How numerous they are! Count the stars of the heaven, the sands of the sea, the dust of the earth, the drops of rain, the feathers of birds, the scales of fish, the hair of animals, the blades of grass in the field, the leaves and fruits of trees, and countless numbers of innumerable other things.

2.3   Countless in similar things, innumerable both in diverse things and in mixed things. What are similar things? They are things in the same genus, like one man and another, one lion and another, one eagle and another, one flatfish and another.[11] Each of these and others like them are similar in their genera. What are diverse things? Those that are informed by dissimilar differences like man and lion, lion and eagle, eagle and flatfish. These are different from each other. What are mixed things? All considered together.

2.4   So, in what way are there infinite similar things? In what way are there infinite diverse things? In what way are there infinite mixed things? Listen. "Man" is one genus, but one man is not. Who can count them? "Lion" is a genus, but one lion is not. Who can count them? "Eagle" is a genus, but one eagle is not. Who can count them? Whale is a genus, but one whale is not. Who can count them? And so on in countless genera of countless things, infinite genera of things. And in each genus infinite similar things. Thus at the same time, all the infinite, innumerable things.

3.   MAGNITUDE

However, perhaps he who made so many things made small things, but could not make many and great things at the same time. On the contrary, what great things there are! Measure the masses of the mountains, the channels of the rivers, the expanses of the fields, the height of the heaven, the depth of the abyss. You are amazed for you fall short, but your amazement is better because you fall short. For those meditating on the immensity of creatures we have, as it were, laid out a seed plot. Now we move on to contemplate the beauty of these things.

4.1   BEAUTY

In extremely many and varied ways,[12] the beauty (*pulchritudo*) of creatures is perfect, but there are four in which all their beauty (*decor*) principally consists; that is, in structure, motion, appearance (*species*), and quality. If anyone were up to investigating these, he would discover the wondrous light of God's wisdom in them.

4.2   Would that I could examine these as subtly, and tell of their beauty as ably as I am able to love them ardently! I find it delightful that it is so very pleasant (*dulce*)[13] and agreeable to treat frequently of these matters where simultaneously sensation is instructed by reason and the mind (*animus*) delighted with sweetness, and feeling aroused to affection so that stunned and admiring we shout with the psalmist: "*How magnificent are your works, O Lord! You have made everything in wisdom. You have delighted me, Lord, in what you have made. I will exult over the works of your hands. How magnificent are your works, O Lord! Your thoughts have become too deep for me! A fool will not comprehend these things, a stupid man will not understand them.*"[14]

4.3   For this whole sensible world[15] is a kind of book[16] written by the finger of God,[17] that is, created by divine power (*virtus*), and each creature is a kind of figure, not invented by human determination, but established by the divine will to manifest and in some way signify the invisible wisdom of God.[18] However, just as when an unlettered person sees an open book and notices the shapes but does not recognize the letters, so stupid and carnal people, who are not aware of the things of God, see on the outside the beauty in these visible creatures, but they do not understand its meaning. On the other hand, a spiritual person can discern all things.[19] When he considers externally the beauty of the work, he understands internally how wondrous is the wisdom of the Creator. Therefore, there is no one who does not find God's works wonderful, but the foolish person admires only their appearance,[20] whereas the wise person, through what he sees externally, explores the deeper intent of the divine wisdom, just as in one and the same writing, one person notices the color or shape of the figures, whereas another praises their meaning and signification.

4.4   Therefore, it is good carefully to contemplate and wonder at the divine works, but this applies to the one who knows how to turn the beauty of physical things to spiritual use. For this reason, Scripture very strongly urges us to ponder God's wonders, so that through the things we see externally, we may come to recognize the truth within. Hence, the psalmist recalls, as though it were something important, that he had done this already, and promises that he is going to do it still: "*I was mindful of earlier days. I meditated on all your works, and I will occupy myself with all your inventions.*"[21] Hence, also, what Isaiah says about certain people who know not the Creator and give to idols the worship due to God: "*Who has measured the waters in his fist or weighed the heavens with his palm? Who grasped the bulk of the earth with three fingers, and measured out on scales the weight of the mountains and hills? The one who sits above the circular course of the earth, and to whom all its inhabitants are like locusts. The one who extends the heavens as though they were nothing and expands them like a tent.*"[22] And again in a certain place, where the psalmist was denouncing idol worshippers, he said: "*All the gods of the nations are demons, but the Lord made the heavens.*"[23] Why do you suppose that in his assertion of the true divinity, the works of God are brought to the center in this way, and he says: "*The Lord made the Heavens,*" if not because when what is created is rightly considered it shows to a human being its Creator?

4.5   So let us also consider how great are the wonderful things of God. Let us seek through the beauty of created things that beauty that is the most beautiful of all that is beautiful. It is so wonderful and ineffable that there can be no comparison between it and all transitory beauty even though the latter is a way to it.[24] We said above that all the beauty of visible things consists of four things. So, now let us run through them in order one by one and see how from them the invisible wisdom of God shines forth. Of course, I know that whatever we say will be lacking, but still it is not fitting that we be completely silent especially there where, if it were possible, we ought especially to speak in a suitable sway. We said four: structure, motion, appearance and quality. So, let us begin by discussing the first of these.

4.6   STRUCTURE

Structure consists in composition and order, that is, in composition and disposition. Composition involves two things: aptness and solidity, that is, that the things to be composed go together aptly and properly and are connected to each other solidly. Such composition is praiseworthy. Aptness is to be sought in quantity and quality; in quantity, lest the very weak and thin be with the thick and hefty; in quality, lest the very wet be connected with the dry, the very hot with the cold, the very light with the heavy. If there are such, they are conjoined in a disorderly way.

4.7   See if any of these are lacking in the beauty of the divine works. If you see nothing is lacking, then in this regard you already have something to arouse your wonder. First of all, if you gaze at the structure of this universe, you will find that the composition of all things is perfect because of wonderful thought and wisdom. How apt, fitting, seemly, how complete in all its parts! In it not only do similar things protect concord, but also diverse and incompatible things, which have come into existence by the Creator's power at the command of wisdom, come together in some way in one friendship and federation. What could be more incompatible than water and fire? Yet, the foresight of God has so mixed them in the natural world that not only do they not dissolve the common bond of association between them, but they are also able to provide vital nourishment to all growing things so that they can subsist.[25] What shall I say of the joining of the human body where the junctures of all the members preserve such a great concord with each other that we cannot find a single member whose function does not seem to provide support to another. Thus does all nature love itself and in the same wondrous way a concord of many dissimilar things joined together in unity fashions one harmonious whole in all of them.[26]

4.8   Therefore, the composition of all things is apt and suitable. But how is it firm? Who does not see it? Who is not amazed? Behold the heavens, which include all things in their ambit, how solid they are. They seem to be molded out of air and spread out above in every direction. The earth held down by its weight remains ever immobile in the middle, so that the solidity of the heavens on the one side and the stability of the earth on the other force and constrain into one the other

fluctuating things in between, lest these, spreading out beyond legitimate limits disrupt the concord of the universe. Notice how within the
bowels of the earth channels of water spread out.[27] These lead outward
through hollow places into diverse locations, and within they compact
together what is weakening so that it does not dissolve, while on the
outside they water the ground lest it crumble.

4.9   Notice how in the structure of the human body the connecting
sinews bind the joints of the bones. By means of the marrow dispersed
within the hollow places of the leg bones, channels conduct the vital
blood of the veins throughout the whole body. Then the covering of
skin wraps around the tender flesh so that the stiffness of the bones
supports the body interiorly, while the protection of the skin guards it
by defending it on the outside. Who can spell out the hardness of rocks,
the solidity of metals, the knotting of wood, the tenacity of glues? Who
can enumerate the innumerable other things? From this it is clear how
firm are the bonds of things, since each created thing defends its nature
and being with such effort, yet at the same time all things cannot be
completely loosed from the concord of their association.

5.   THE DISPOSITION OF PLACES

After considering composition, let us consider what is the disposition
of things. There will be no small amazement if one diligently examines
how divine providence distributes its causes for each and every place,
time and thing. The result is that in absolutely nothing is the order of
things disturbed. See how the heavens are above and the earth below.
She[28] situates the stars and the luminaries in heaven, so that they illu-
mine everything below. She makes a path in the air for the winds and
clouds, so that dispersed by their movements they pour down rain
from above. In the womb of the earth, She orders reservoirs of water
to form so that through their streams they run here and there where
the nod of their commander carries them. She suspends birds in the
air and immerses fish in the waters. She fills the earth with beasts and
serpents and various kinds of other reptiles and worms. She endows
some regions with rich produce, some with lush vines, others with
fertile olive trees, others with productive livestock, others with powerful herbs, others with precious gems, others with monstrous animals
and beasts, others with various colors, others with the study of different
arts,[29] others with various kinds of metals or incenses. As a result there
is absolutely no region that does not possess something new and special

by comparison to other regions. There is also no region that cannot receive something new and special from other regions. The providence of the Creator positions the things that are necessary for human uses in the midst of the common concourse of people.[30] Why is it then that She hides in the hidden hollows of the earth those things which nature does not seek out of necessity, but which cupidity craves[31] for their appearance? It is so that a person whom love of virtue does not restrain from immoderate craving will at least come to rest when overcome by weariness from his labor.

6.1   THE DISPOSITION OF TIMES

We have said these things about the disposition of places. What shall we say about the disposition of times? Who can admire sufficiently the wondrous rationale by which divine providence distinguishes the courses of time? Notice that after night comes day so that the movement of working may arouse the drowsy. After day comes night, so that rest may rescue the exhausted to revivify them. It is not always day, nor is it always night. Day and night are not always equal, lest excessive labor break those who are worn down or continual rest spoil nature, or perpetual sameness give rise to mental fatigue.[32]

6.2   Likewise, just as the alternation of days and nights renews living things, so the four seasons of the year, which succeed one another in order, change the face (*speciem*)[33] of the whole world. First, through the gentle warming of spring the earth is reborn with a kind of renewal. Then, through the heat of summer it receives youthful strength. After this, when autumn follows, it reaches maturity. Then, when winter follows, it turns toward decline.[34] However, it always declines so that it can always be renewed after its decline, for unless old things first deteriorated from their condition (as if they were occupying a certain space), new things could not arise.

6.3   One can also discern in this disposition something else which is quite wonderful. The seasons themselves, by the immutable law of their changeableness, keep their places so that they never fail to fulfill their service nor by coinciding mix up the order given at their original founding.

7.1   THE DISPOSITION OF PARTS

Let the things that have been said about the disposition of times suffice as examples. Now let us investigate that order that can be considered in each thing regarding the fitting disposition of its parts. Here there is an intrinsic order; the others, those according to place and time, are extrinsic. Here also the effectiveness of divine wisdom is no less wonderful. She[35] distributed each thing in a suitable way within the whole, so that never, never would the joining of the parts give rise to a conflict of qualities.

7.2   Here, by way of example, we can adduce a few things from among many. What great wisdom of the Creator shines forth in the composition of the human body! In its upper part, the human body is single, but below it is divided into two, because the principal aspect of the mind (*mentis*), reason (*ratio*),[36] which regards invisible things, is uniform, while the aspect of the soul (*animae*)[37] which turns down toward earthly things is dual, anger and desire. The structure of the human body extends to the side through the arms and is fixed beneath by the legs. This is because the intention to act extends the mind (*animum*) and the affect of desires focuses it. The outreach of the human body is completed in a fivefold way, outward and sideways by the fingers, and downward by the toes, for whether the mind (*animus*) moves outward by the intention of doing something or is focused downward through affect's desire, it goes out through the five senses. A division into three parts characterizes the fingers and toes. They stick out from the palm of the hand and from the sole of the foot, because from the one sensorium the five senses go out. In them, too, one finds a threefold articulation: first, the sense; then, the sensing; finally, the sensible. Next, at the outer end of each digit one finds tips with nails on them like helmets. So, wherever an extended hand or forward-moving foot finds an obstacle, it can remain unharmed, shielded by the protection they provide. In like manner those earthly things, which like nails are attached to the external senses, guard us as if in necessity; but insofar as they do not pertain to necessity, they can be cut off without that being felt for they are external to the flesh.[38]

7.3   Notice in the human face how the organs of sensation are located with such reasonable differences. Vision occupies the highest place in the eyes, then hearing in the ears, then after that smell in the nose, and after that taste in the mouth. However, we know that all the senses come from outside to within; only sight goes to the outside from within.[39] Set in the highest place, with wondrous agility sight perceives before the others do. Therefore, it is well that like a sentinel it occupies a higher place than all the rest, and before danger arises can detect what things are coming toward the other senses. Hearing is second to sight in location and mobility, then smell. However taste, which can sense only what it touches, rightly resides after the other senses at the bottom. Touch has no special location. It is universal insofar as it cooperates with all the other senses. So also among the fingers, when the others are held together to form a single fist, the thumb, which signifies touch, alone responds to all, for without touch none of the senses can exist.[40]

7.4　See also how in the human body the bones are connected internally, so that their strength supports the body. Next the flesh clothes the bones, so that their brittleness softly receives touch. Finally, the skin covers the flesh so that by its adhering it guards the body from unsuitable things coming at it from the outside. Note also how what is soft and weak is placed in the middle in a safer place, lest lacking an intrinsic support it be destroyed, or not having any external protection it deteriorate.

7.5　What is seen in this one example can be found in all kinds of things. Thus, bark protects trees; their feathers and beaks, birds; and scales, fish. The providence of the Creator has arranged defenses for every single thing according to what suits its nature. Thus far we have spoken of structure. Now let us turn to movement.

8.1　MOVEMENT

Movement is fourfold: local, natural, biological and rational. Since we cannot say many things about these, let us briefly touch lightly on each of them.

8.2　See how the wisdom of the Creator is apparent in local motion. Think about from what cause a never-failing watercourse is always served by down-flowing waters; from what cause the motion of the wind is sustained; who regulates the unfailing course of the stars; who commands the sun to descend through the winter constellations and then makes it ascend again through those of summer; who leads it from the east to the west and again conveys it back from the west to the east. All these are wonders, and only for God are they possible!

8.3　Moreover, what shall I say about natural motion? Who do you suppose grants growth to all growing things, and as from some hidden bosom of nature brings germinating things into the open, and when those same things are withering makes them return again to the place from which they came? These things will seem amazing (*mirabilia*) enough to whoever looks at them carefully.

8.4 Next comes biological movement, which occurs in the senses and the appetites. Think what He must be like who makes the senses of all living beings, creates their appetites, and for each and every animal ordains what and how much it should desire.

8.5 Next, rational movement, which occurs in deeds and deliberations, will cause you wonder enough, if you wish to examine how indescribable is the wisdom which so educes all the deeds of human beings, all their volitions, and all the thoughts of their hearts according to the judgment of Her will and so tempers and moderates them, that nothing can happen in the universe which wisdom does not wish to happen either by commanding or permitting it for the adornment of Her works.

9.1 APPEARANCE (*DE SPECIE*)

For the sake of brevity, those things just said will suffice regarding motion. There follows appearance. Appearance is the visible form that contains two things: shapes and colors. The shapes of things appear marvelous in many ways: sometimes because of their great size, sometimes because of their smallness, sometimes because they are rare, sometimes because they are beautiful, sometimes because, so to speak, they are in some fashion suitably inept, sometimes because there is one in many, sometimes because there are diverse things in one. Let us pursue these one by one in order.

9.2 Shape draws attention to its large size when something exceeds in quantity the usual measure of its kind. Thus we are astonished by a giant among human beings, the whale among fish, the griffin among birds, the elephant among quadrupeds, the dragon among serpents.

9.3 One gives thought to smallness in shape when something cannot equal in quantity other individuals of its kind. Such are a louse and a moth, a termite and a stinging insect, and other such things that live among other living things but are different from all the rest because of their small bodies. Notice, therefore, which you should admire more: the teeth of a wild boar or of a moth, the wings of a griffin or of a stinging insect, the head of a horse or of a locust, the legs of the elephant or of a gnat, the snout of a pig or of a tick; the eagle or the ant, the lion or the flea, the tiger or the tortoise.[41] In one instance you are amazed at their great size, in the other at their smallness, a small body created with great wisdom, great wisdom which no negligence negates. She gave eyes to those that the eye can scarcely grasp. In every instance, in bodies so tiny She distributed the features befitting their natures, so that you see that, in the least of them all, there is lacking nothing that nature formed in the largest.

10   It remains to speak about the things that are rare, and from this more wonderful things are seen. Among created things there are certain ones which are more wonderful because they rarely come to human notice either because few individuals of that kind of thing have been created, or because they are concealed in remote places or hidden in nature's hollows. The providence of the Creator wished to set these apart so that human society may not be damaged by intermingling with those which are harmful, human greed may be tested by the appearance of those that are precious, and human dullness of heart may learn to wonder when aroused by their rare novelty.[42] Finally, providence aimed that these, both good and bad, when placed at a distance, would speak to humanity in such a way that its members would attend to what great zeal they should show in fleeing eternal evils and seeking eternal goods, if they undergo such great labors to acquire these temporal goods and to avoid these temporal evils.

11.1   Next, about those things which are wonderful because of their beauty (*pulchritudinem*). We wonder at the shape of certain things, because they are seemly in a certain special way and suitably fit together so that the very disposition of the work seems somehow to suggest the special diligence that its Creator devoted to them.[43]

11.2   Again we are amazed at other things because they are in some way monstrous or ridiculous. The more their shape is alien to human reason, the more readily it can compel the human mind to amazement. Why does the crocodile not move its lower jaw when it is eating? And how does the salamander stay unharmed in a fire? Who gave the hedgehog spines and instructed it to wrap itself with fruits scattered by a storm with the result that freighted with them it goes along sounding like a wagon? And the ant that knows winter is approaching and so fills her granary with grains? The spider, too, fashioning its webs from its own innards to capture prey? These are witnesses to the wisdom of God.

11.3   There is still another true and clear proof of divine wisdom, namely that every kind of thing procreates offspring like itself, so that in so many the one propagated likeness does not alter the form of the first beginning. A sheep does not give birth to a calf, or a cow to a lamb, or a doe to a rabbit, or a lion to a fox. Rather, every existing thing extends its line in progeny like itself.

11.4   Even nature devoid of sensation keeps to this. The linden is one kind of tree, the beech another, and the oak another. Every one has its own appearance, and every one keeps the likeness of its kind. Look at a leaf, how around the edge it is differentiated by serrated teeth, how the ribs produced inside it are woven in this direction and that. Count one, count another, you will find that all of one kind have the same likeness: as many teeth in one as in another; as many ribs in one as in another; the same form in one as in the other; the same color in one as in another. Notice how the blackberry, how the strawberry are divided into grains pressed together all around. Such is one, such is another, and all nature, as though it has received the command of one ruling from within, never presumes to exceed its limits.

11.5   This, too, is wonderful, that in a single body are formed so many members, so many forms of members, so many locations, so many tasks. Look at how many members are in one human body! The ear is one thing, the eye another, the tongue another, the nose another, the foot another, the hand another, each with its own form, location, tasks. Although each of them is so different from the rest, all still cooperate with each other.

12.1   After shape comes color. There is no need to discourse at length about the color of things, for sight itself declares how much beauty is added to nature when it adorns different things with such varied colors. What is more beautiful than light, which, although it does not have color in itself, in some ways gives colors to all the things that it illumines?[44] What is more delightful to behold than a clear sky; resplendent like a sapphire, it draws one's gaze by the extremely pleasing mildness of its glow and softens the view? The sun shines like gold; the moon is pale like electrum. Certain stars radiate a flaming appearance; others sparkle with a rosy light; others alternately display a rosy glow, then green, then white.

12.2   What can I say about gems and precious stones, which not only have practical uses but also a wonderful appearance. Behold the earth wreathed with flowers! What a pleasing show it puts on, how it delights the eyes; how it arouses feeling! We see blushing roses, white lilies, purple violets. Not only do they look wonderful, but their origin is also wonderful—how God's wisdom produces such beauty from the dust of the earth. Finally, there is green, the most beautiful of all.[45] How it enraptures the minds of those who see it, when in a truly new way shoots come forth with new life and standing up in their stalks, which seemed to have been trodden down by death, bud forth together into the light in a symbol of the future resurrection. But what can we say about the works of God, when we admire even their imitations produced by human industry that so deceive the eyes with their artificial (*adulterina*) beauty.[46]

13.1 QUALITY

After appearance we need to discuss the quality of things. The Creator's providence endowed things with such diverse qualities that every human sense may find its delights. Sight perceives one thing, hearing another, smell another, taste another, touch another. The beauty of colors nurtures sight; the sweetness of song soothes hearing; the fragrance of scent, smell; the sweetness of savor, taste; bodily feel, touch. Who could list all the delights of the senses? Those delights are so manifold in each, that if anyone looks for himself at any one thing, he will think to himself how singularly endowed that thing is.

13.2   We find as many delights for the ear in the variety of sounds, as we have shown there are delights for the eyes in the variety of colors. First among these are the sweet exchanges of speech[47] by which people communicate their wishes to each other, tell of past events, point to present-day things, announce future things, disclose secrets. So true is this that if human life lacked these things, it would seem comparable to that of brute animals. But what shall I call to mind of the melody of birds, the pleasant sound of the human voice, or the sweet modes of all sounds. There are so many kinds of harmony, that thought cannot traverse them all nor can speech easily display them. Yet all of them are at the service of hearing and have been created for its pleasure.

13.3   It is thus with smell. Incenses have their odors, ointments their aromas, roses their scent. Thickets have their smell, and meadows have theirs. Wastelands have their odors; wood, flower and fruits have theirs. All things that emit a sweet fragrance and breathe out sweet smells serve the olfactory sense and were created for its pleasure. In the same way taste and touch have various delights that can be adequately pondered on the basis of the foregoing.

14.1 UTILITY

We have spoken of the immensity of created things and of their beauty insofar as we could, though not as we should have done. It remains for us to consider the usefulness of these same things. The utility of things includes four elements: the necessary, the beneficial, the fitting, and the pleasing.[48] What is necessary to each thing is that without which it could not exist;[49] for example, for human nourishment, bread and water; in clothing, wool or skins or some kind of clothes. The beneficial is that which, although sometimes it gives more delight, is not required for life; for example, for nourishment a glass of wine or the eating of meat, in clothes, cotton and silk, or some other softer cloth. The apt or fitting is what, although it does not benefit the users, nonetheless is fittingly used. Such are colored dyes, precious stones, and other things of this kind. The pleasing is what is not suitable for use, but is still delightful to look at. Such are certain kinds of plants, animals, birds and fish, and the like.

14.2   It is worthwhile to inquire why God wished to create these things that He foresaw would not be necessary for the use of humankind, for whom He created all things. But this will be quickly understood if one examines the cause and manner of the creation of humankind. God made humankind for Himself; God created all other things for human beings. He made humankind for Himself, not because He needed humankind, but so that humankind could enjoy Him,[50] for He could give nothing better. The rest of creation was so made that it would both be subject to humankind from its creation and would serve the use of humankind. Therefore, humankind, as though situated in a kind of middle place, has God above itself and the world below. By the body humankind is connected to the world below, and by the spirit it is lifted up toward God above. It was necessary that the creation of visible things be so arranged that human beings would recognize in them exteriorly what the invisible good they were to seek within was like; that is, that human beings would see beneath them what they were to desire above them.[51]

14.3   Hence, it was not fitting that in any aspect the array of visible things suffer a defect,[52] because it was instituted above all to announce the inconceivable profuseness of eternal goods. This is what we have said about why God also wished to create those things that He foresaw would not be necessary for human uses. If He created only what was necessary that would be goodness but not richness. So when God also joined the beneficial to the necessary He showed the riches of His goodness. When, however, the beneficial are augmented by the fitting, that manifests the abundance of the riches of His goodness. Then, when to the fitting the pleasing are also added, what does that tell other than how superabundant are the riches of his goodness.

15.1   Let these things briefly recounted about the usefulness of created things suffice. But it is pleasant to pay a bit more attention to the totality of divine praise—how wondrously God has kept these three together in His work. We probably understand this more easily—what great wonder it deserves—if first we have reflected on how these things cannot exist simultaneously in a human work. Certainly, when a human being wants to make many things, he cannot make great things, because he can accomplish less, in regard to each, the more numerous are the things toward which the focus of his attention is divided. Again, when he strives for size, he is kept back from multiplicity. This is because he is not able to devote his strength to many things when he expends it particularly on a single result. In the same way, when the mind is occupied with achieving multiplicity alone or size, less diligence is given to the beauty of a work. We see that a scribe forms more quickly those shapes that are thin; he labors more when forming large shapes. The faster he pushes the pen, the more deformed are the letters it executes. It is the same in making clothes: those who like great beauty often lose utility; those who want to maintain utility cannot have beauty. However, in God's work multiplicity does not diminish size, nor does size limit multiplicity. Nor, at the same time, is multiplicity or size detrimental to beauty, nor does beauty take away utility. All things are done as though each were done singly, so that when you look at the whole of them, you are in awe of each.[53]

15.2   Perhaps to someone it will seem that we have spoken much about visible things, in view of the constraints of our treatment.[54] However, he should realize that such difficult material cannot be explained easily with a few words. Since the Apostle says that through visible things in the world the invisible things in God are manifested, it is necessary that whoever desires to attain knowledge of invisible things through visible ones must first be familiar with those visible things. For this reason when I proposed to investigate these things as far as I was able, after the three invisible things had been listed in the beginning, and the three visible things had been arranged over against them, I decided this was the most suitable order for the discussion. First, I would bring to the fore some knowledge of those visible things and then, after an entry for contemplation had been opened, I would proceed through an investigation of invisible things. Therefore, now that we have finished with the things that needed to be said about visible things, we must consider how and by what order we ascend through these to invisible things.

[II]

16.1 We said that there are three invisible things: power, wisdom and kindness. One needs to ask which of these first occurs to those who are contemplating. I believe that the first invisible thing to be grasped in contemplation is what is more explicitly and obviously shown in its visible representation (*simulacrum*). Visible things are said to be representations of the invisible; namely, the immensity of creatures is the representation of invisible power; the beauty of created things is the representation of invisible wisdom; and the usefulness of creatures is the representation of invisible kindness. However, every creature more closely declares its Creator the more closely it approaches its Creator's likeness. Hence, that visible representation that contains expressed more perfectly within itself the image of the divine likeness (*similitudinis*) ought to be the first to show its invisible exemplar.

16.2 The immensity of creatures pertains more to the essence, the beauty of creatures more to the form. The essence considered without the form is formlessness. What lacks form is like God in as much it exists, but in as much as it lacks form, it is unlike God.[55] What has form is more like God than what does not have form. Hence the beauty of creatures, which pertains to form, is a more evident representation than the immensity of creatures, which concerns only the essence.

16.3 Likewise the beauty of creatures deriving from their natural form pertains to something habitual, whereas utility pertains to act because creatures are useful inasmuch as they are subjected to humankind and render service and obedience. But what pertains to habit is more proper and more certain than what pertains to act, because nature is connected to habit, but resolve is connected to act. The representation of beauty precedes both immensity and utility in cognition. It is first in cognition because it is more evident in its manifestation. Therefore in this representation we must situate the first step of contemplation, so that when we have properly undertaken the first step of inquiry, with it as the guide we seek, we may with sure step advance to the rest. In the search for wisdom, the representation of wisdom makes a beautiful starting point, because through His wisdom the Father is manifested not only when He sent His wisdom into the flesh, but also when He created the world through His wisdom.[56]

16.4 The beauty of created things, which we have said is the representation of God's wisdom, includes four things: structure, movement, appearance and quality. There is no doubt that, among these four, movement has pride of place. For things that can move are more akin to life than things that cannot move. Movement is fourfold: local, natural, biological, rational. Natural motion is more excellent than local motion, because in natural movement not only is the image of life expressed, but also life itself is in some way begun. Likewise, biological movement ranks above natural movement insofar as what has sensation ranks above that which is incapable of sensation. Finally, rational movement is situated above all the rest, because in it not only does sensation move to animate life, but reason also moves to understanding. No representation in creatures can be more evident than this one, because that which knows (*sapit*)[57] shows forth invisible wisdom (*sapientia*) more clearly than does anything else.

17.1   Therefore, the first and principal representation of uncreated wisdom is created wisdom, that is, the rational creature, which because in one aspect it is visible and in another invisible, becomes a door and path of contemplation.[58] It is a door insofar as it is visible; it is a path insofar as it is invisible. It is a door because for the one entering into contemplation it offers a first access. It is a path because it leads the mind that is hastening along in contemplation to its goal. It is a door because in some fashion it shows invisible things visibly. It is a path because it leads those going from the visible through the invisible to see the one who is Creator equally of the visible and the invisible.

17.2   One can recognize this in oneself. No one is wise at all who does not see that he exists. Nevertheless, if one begins to pay attention to what one truly is, one will understand that he is none of all the things that are or can be in him. For truly that in us that is capable of reason, although it is, so to speak, infused into and mixed with the flesh, can distinguish itself by its own reason from the substance of the flesh and understand that the latter is foreign to it. Why then does anyone have any doubt at all about the existence of invisible things, when he sees that what is truly human, whose existence no one can doubt, is itself invisible? Therefore, the door to contemplation opens for one who, under the guidance of his reason, enters to know himself.

17.3   It remains for the one who has entered to run the path to the end, so that whoever it is may arrive at knowledge of the Creator from a consideration of himself. For that in us that does not have the essence of the flesh cannot have matter from the flesh. But just as it is different from the flesh so it is aware of itself as alien from the flesh's origin. However, it recognizes that it really did have a beginning. The reason is this: it understands that it is, but it does not remember that it always was. But non-knowing understanding cannot be. If, then, understanding cannot be unless it is actively understanding, the conclusion is that one whom we know has not always been understanding did not always exist, and for this reason we believe that at some time he began to be.

17.4   However, as was already said, what has a spiritual essence cannot have a bodily origin, because whatever is drawn out of pre-existing matter proves to be corporeal. If, therefore, our invisible side had a beginning, it follows that it was made not from pre-existing matter, but from nothing. However, what is not cannot give existence to itself, and for that reason there is no doubt that whatever had a beginning received its being from another. Now, what is not from itself cannot give existence to others. Therefore, whoever he is who gives being to things did not receive being from another. From this it is also clearly proven that if we believe that *whatever is* is a creature, we will find no end in things.

17.5   Therefore our nature tells us that we have an eternal Creator. It is proper to Him to subsist, because if He had received being from another, He could not truly be said to be the first origin of things. If there was a time when He was not, He did not have His beginning from Himself. Neither could He be said to be first if He received being from another. Therefore if there is a Creator, He always was.[59]

17.6   Likewise, what is from itself cannot *not* be. In whatever is from itself, *to be* and *what it is* are identical. It is also clear that no thing can be divided or separated from itself. Therefore, if *whoever there is for whom to be* and *what it is* are the same; then it necessarily always is, because nothing can be separated from itself. Therefore, if in whatever is from itself to be and what it is are the same, for it did not receive being from another, it follows necessarily that it always is, and that what was not given by another cannot be taken away by another.

17.7   It is therefore necessary that we confess that the one whom we believe to be Creator can have neither beginning nor end. What always was can have no beginning; what never ceases can have no end. Therefore, no one is eternal except the Creator alone, and He cannot be the Creator unless He is eternal.[60]

18.1   We have found in rational movement this knowledge, namely, that we have an eternal Creator who lacks a beginning because He always was, and who will meet with no end because He always will be. However, the other kinds of motion, biological, natural and local, also attest to this form of knowledge.

18.2   Now, in *biological movement* there are sensation and appetite. However, all natural appetite in things finds what satisfies it. Nor is there any ordered affective impulse (*affectus*) that cannot achieve its goal (*effectus*). For example, animals are hungry; they find what they may eat. They are thirsty; they find what they may drink. They are cold; they find what will warm them. It is clear, therefore, that providence has preceded. By its counsel, providence then provided that the support required for those in need of things is not now lacking. The one who establishes desires provides the objects of those desires. If outcomes were fortuitous, there is no way that it could come about that, among all things, objects corresponded to all their effects.[61]

18.3   *Natural motion* proves the same thing. Just as it is impossible that something comes to be from nothing on its own, so it is utterly impossible that on its own something receives increase; that is, something which cannot give itself its beginning cannot give itself its increase. Whatever increase occurs in a growing thing proves to be different from what it was in itself, because previously on its own it was without the increase. If, therefore, nothing can increase unless there is added to it what it previously did not have, it is clear that no growing thing achieves increase through itself. Therefore, the one who gives increase to growing things is He who gave a beginning to existing things.

18.4   *Local motion* proves the same thing. We notice that some things are stirred by perpetual motion. We see that some things move from time to time, some things in one way, others in another. Although things thus move in dissimilar ways, the order of things is never upset. Hence, there is no doubt whether there is an internal arrangement by a provident being who moderates all things with a certain law.[62]

18.5   By what argument can we deny providence, if all natural appetite finds the sustenance that it seeks naturally prepared for it, and never does it happen that what nature seeks in one thing nature does not have in another? Similarly, since movement and growth running externally in various and dissimilar ways still never cause disorder, how can we deny that there is some intrinsic ordering? Therefore, one cannot doubt that there presides from within some ruler who precedes the outcomes of all things by His providence and arranges them with His wisdom.

19.1   I say "one." For nature herself teaches this also, namely, that there is one maker of all things and one ruler.[63] For if the counsels of those presiding differed internally, the courses of things externally would sometimes be at odds with each other. Now, however, when all things hasten harmoniously toward one goal, they surely show that there is one fount and origin from which they proceed.

19.2   But because "one" can be taken in different ways, it is necessary to consider in what way the Creator of things is said to be one.[64] For there is oneness in a collection, and oneness in composition, and oneness in likeness, and oneness in essence, and oneness in identity. Oneness in a collection resembles somewhat the way in which we say a flock of many animals is one. There is oneness in composition, as for instance when we say that a body in which there are many members is one. There is oneness in likeness when, for example, we say one word that is uttered by many.

19.3   But none of all these is truly one. They are said to be one in some respect, because they approach unity in some way. It is not right that we think that the Creator of things is one either by a collection of different things, or a composition of parts, or a likeness among many. What is rational in us can discover nothing at all of these in itself. Our reason itself establishes that what in us is observed to be composed of a multitude of parts is not the rational, but rather that which is joined with the rational. If therefore the rational in us is truly one, how much more ought we to believe that its Creator is truly one? That is truly one which is essentially one, which as a whole has one existence and which is a simple being. Whatever, therefore, is truly one is simple and cannot in any way be separated into other parts. Therefore, it admits no cutting up into parts, because it admits no composition of parts. Therefore, in the Creator of things what He is truly, is to be, because the being which he is is completely one and simple.

19.4   But we still need to consider that certain things are found which truly are one, and nevertheless are not supremely one. Thus souls are essentially one, but they are not one without any variation. What is truly and supremely one is one essentially and invariably. It remains for us, therefore, if we believe that God is truly one, to inquire whether God can be said also to be supremely one. We will truly show this if and when we prove Him to be completely invariable. But we cannot know how God is invariable unless we first recognize in how many ways something can vary. First, then, we need to describe all the modes of mutability, and then show how each is removed from God.

19.5   All mutability occurs in three ways: in place, form, and time.[65] Something changes with reference to place when it passes from one place to another, that is, when it ceases to be where it was and begins to be where it was not. This change is extrinsic, and nothing varies regarding the essence of the thing. This is because if it ceases to be where it was, it does not cease to be what it was. If it begins to be where it was not, it does not begin to be what it was not.

19.6   Something changes formally when it stays in the same place in regard to its essence, but either receives through increase something which it did not previously have or loses through decrease something that it previously had, or, by alteration, begins to have in a different way something that it previously had.

19.7   Change in regard to time arises from the two previous modes of change, because nothing can change temporally which is not changed either formally or in location. From this it can be concluded convincingly that something is wholly immutable if it can change neither in form nor in place. If, therefore, it is established that God can change neither in form nor in place, there will be no doubt that God is wholly immutable.

19.8   We can easily eliminate change in place from Him if we show that He is everywhere.[66] For what is everywhere is in every place. What is in every place cannot change from place to place. Now there are multiple proofs that God is everywhere. First, there is our soul itself, which reason does not doubt is a single essence, and sensation proves to be diffused throughout the entire body that it vivifies. No matter what part of the ensouled body is injured, there is one awareness (*unus*) to which every sensation of pain returns. This would not occur at all unless one (*unus*) and the same awareness were diffused throughout.[67] If therefore the rational spirit of a human being, although it is simple, is spread throughout the whole body in which it presides, it is not right to believe that the Creator Spirit who rules and possesses all things is confined in some one place rather than filling all things. For the very movements of things, which everywhere run with such certain and so rational governance, show that there is a moving life within.

19.9   Not that one is to believe in any way that as the human spirit is personally joined with the body to which it gives sensation, so the Creator Spirit is also joined personally with the body of this sensible world. For God fills the world in one way, and the soul fills the body in another. The soul fills the body and is contained because it is circumscribable. God fills the world but is not enclosed by the world, because being present everywhere He can nowhere be enclosed.

19.10   Besides, since we see that the effects of the divine power are nowhere lacking, why do we doubt that the same power of God is in all things? Now if the power of God is everywhere, since God's power is not other than God, it follows that God is not absent from any place. For God does not need an outside power in order to act, as a human being does, because a human being often finishes by means of another's assistance what he is not able to do by his own strength. According to a usual way of speaking, a human being is sometimes said to be working in a place where he himself is absent. For example, it is said that a king residing in his city attacks, conquers or overcomes his enemies at a distance, because his soldiers, at his will and command, attack, conquer or overcome. Such is the case when someone extends a pole toward something set on a high place or throws a rock at it and is said to touch whatever the rock or pole touched. There are many such instances, but in none of these is the action properly attributed, because what one does is attributed to another. However, it is necessary that God, who does all things Himself by His own power, is present by His Godhead everywhere where He is present by His working.

19.11   But if someone asks how the divine essence, which is simple, can be everywhere, he should know that a spirit is said to be simple in one way, a body in another. A body is said to be simple because of its insignificance, but when a spirit is called simple that signifies not its insignificance but its unity. Therefore, the Creator is simple because He is one, and He is everywhere because He is God. Existing in every place, He is nowhere enclosed because, filling all things, He contains but is not contained. Therefore, because He is in every place, He cannot change locally, and because He is enclosed by no place, He is not in a place.

20.1   Neither can mutability in form occur in Him. Whatever changes in regard to form changes either through increase or decrease or alteration. But the divine nature admits none of these, which can easily be seen in regard to each of them.

20.2   The divine nature is not augmented. Whatever increases by augmentation receives something more to itself. Whatever accepts something other than what it has in itself necessarily receives from another, because no thing can give itself what it does not have. But from what will the Creator of things receive something that it does not have, since everything that exists proceeds from it? Therefore, He who can receive nothing more into Himself cannot increase.

20.3   Nor can the divine nature be diminished. For whatever can become less than itself is not really one, because what divides itself by separation was not identical in its conjoining. Therefore God, for whom

ON THE THREE DAYS II

to be what He *is* is completely one, can in no way become less than Himself. Therefore, neither can His perfection be augmented, nor can His unity be diminished, nor can His immensity be enclosed, nor can He who is present everywhere change location.

20.4   Now all that remains for us is to show why alteration does not befit the divine nature. The alteration of bodies is one thing and that of spirits is another. It is clear from what was said above that God is not a body but a spirit. Since, then, we are talking about God, it is not necessary to say many things about change in bodies. However, let us touch upon it briefly, so that we may arrive more suitably at alteration in spiritual beings.

20.5   Change in bodies occurs through rearrangement of parts and alteration of qualities. Change in spirits occurs through knowledge and affect. Spirits change according to affect as at one time they are sad and at another joyful. They change according to knowledge when they know now less, now more.

20.6   There are two things that are usually the principal causes of change in the affect of an agent; that is, either because something causes him to repent what he did in the past, or because he proposes something disordered for the future. But the unvarying course of all things, which by a perpetual law never forsakes the measure of its original arrangement, shows with sufficient clarity that God does not, in fact, repent. That He never proposes anything disordered is proven by the reasonable outcome, which nowhere in the whole body of nature is at odds with itself. Therefore, God's will is always unchanging, because He never changes His decision regarding the past nor His plan for the future.[68]

20.7   Likewise, He ought to be believed to be immutable in knowledge. Human cognition is subject to change in three ways: through increase, through decrease, through alteration. Through increase, when we learn what we do not know; through decrease, when we forget what we know. Alteration is fourfold: in essence, form, place, and time. Human cognition suffers alteration in essence when we think now of this, and then of that, because we cannot comprehend everything in our consciousness at one time. In form, when we pay attention now to one sort of thing and then to another, because we cannot focus on both at once. In place, when we turn our thought now here, now there, because we are not capable of turning our thought everywhere at once. Human cognition alters in time when now we consider things past, now present things, and now future things, because we cannot be aware of all at the same time. Cognition also varies in time when we interrupt what we are thinking, and then resume what we have interrupted, because we are not able to keep at it without interruption.

20.8   Divine knowledge (*cognitio*) admits none of these changes. It does not increase, because it is full. Nor can the one who creates, governs, penetrates, and supports all things be ignorant of any of them. The one who is present to all things by His divinity cannot be absent from them in His seeing. He cannot decrease who is not anything that He is from another; rather His very self, whatever it is, is from itself, from one and wholly one in what it is. What shall I say of alteration? How can the Wisdom (*sapientia*), which in one glance of vision comprehends everything simultaneously and once-and-for-all (*simul et semel*)[69], undergo alteration? Simultaneously, because She embraces every essence, form, place, and time; once-and-for all, because She admits no interrupted vision, nor does She interrupt a vision once begun, because what She is all at once She is always, and what She always is She is totally. She sees all things, she sees all things about all things, She sees always and She sees everywhere. Nothing is new to Her. Nothing alien happens to Her. Nothing of Hers recedes. When it is future, She foresees it; when it is present She sees it; when it is past She retains it. Nothing in Her is other. She foresees; She sees; She retains. What happens in time was in Her vision and what went before in time remains in Her sight.

20.9   For example, if your whole body were an eye, then your being would not be one thing and your seeing another. In whatever direction a thing turned it could not *not* be present to you. While remaining immobile you would, with one glance of your sight, comprehend whatever thing you had in your sight in any direction. In fact, you would see whatever was around you as though it were in front of you. A thing might pass by, but your vision would remain stationary. In whichever direction its movement took it, it would still be present to you because you remained stationary. Now, however, because you see in part, you see changeably. When a thing passes by someone who is looking at it, it either ceases to be seen or draws the onlooker's sight after it and so brings about change. But if you were wholly eye, you would not see thus in a changeable way.[70] Therefore, whatever is partial is mutable, and whatever is not partial is immutable. For God, to *be*, to *live*, and to *understand* are identical. Since He is not in His essence partially, neither could *He* be partial in *His* wisdom. Just as He is immutable in His essence, so also is He immutable in His wisdom.

20.10 Let what has been said about divine knowledge suffice. But it should be known that this is called knowledge and vision, and wisdom, foreknowledge and providence. Vision, because it sees; wisdom, because it understands; foreknowledge, because it anticipates; providence, because it arranges. Regarding these,[71] many difficult and puzzling questions arise, which we are afraid to put into this compendium. So let us pass on to the remaining topics.

21.1 From where we first advanced with the eye of contemplation from visible things to invisible things we have traversed the path of inquiry to the point that now we have no doubt that the Creator of things is one, without a beginning, without an end, and without change. We found this not outside ourselves, but within ourselves. We might therefore consider whether that same nature of ours may still teach us something further about our Creator. Perhaps it may show us that He is not only one, but three.

21.2 Certainly, the rational mind is one and generates from its one self one understanding. Sometimes when it sees how fine, true, suitable and pleasant something is, it immediately loves it and takes pleasure in it. Simultaneously it sees and is awestruck and is amazed that it could have found something like that. It would be very glad to gaze upon that thing always, to have it always, to enjoy it always, to delight in it always. That something pleases the mind through, and because of, itself. There is nothing beyond that something that the mind seeks, because in it the whole is loved. In it, contemplation of truth is delightful to see, pleasant to have, sweet to enjoy. With it, the mind is at peace with itself and never affected with tedium regarding its secret, as it rejoices in its only, but not solitary, companion.

21.3 Consider these three: the mind, understanding, love. From the mind is born understanding; from the mind and understanding together, love arises. Understanding arises from the mind alone, because the mind generates understanding from itself. But love arises neither from the mind alone nor from understanding alone, for it proceeds from both. First there is mind, then mind and understanding, and afterwards mind, understanding and love.[72]

21.4 This is the way it is in us. Reason truthfully suggests that it is far different in the Creator. Because we believe that He always was, we must confess that He always had wisdom also. For if He is said to have been at some time without wisdom, there is no way someone could be found who would later make Him wise or from whom He would receive wisdom. It would be totally absurd and foreign to all reason to believe that He who is the fount and origin of all wisdom existed at some time without wisdom. Therefore, wisdom was always in Him, always from Him, and always with Him. Wisdom was always in him, because He who always was wise always had wisdom. Wisdom was always from Him, because He gave birth to the Wisdom that He had.[73] Wisdom was always with Him, because once born He did not separate Himself from the one who bore Him. He is always born and is always being born, neither beginning to be when He is born, nor ceasing to be born after He has been born. He is always being born because He is eternal; He is always born because He is perfect. Hence, there is one who gives birth and one who is born. The one who gives birth is the Father; the one who is born is the Son. Because the one who has given birth has always given birth, He is the eternal Father. Because the one who has been born has always been born, He is the coeternal Son of the Father. The one who always has had Wisdom, always has loved Wisdom. He who always has loved has always had Love. Therefore, Love is coeternal with the eternal Father and Son. Moreover, the Father is from no one, the Son is from the Father alone, but Love is simultaneously from the Father and from the Son.

21.5   However, because we asserted above that it is necessary that the Creator of all things is supremely and truly one, let us confess that these three[74] in God are substantially one. For just as the one who has been born cannot be He from whom He has been born, likewise neither can the one, who proceeds from the one giving birth and from the one born, be the one who gives birth or the one born. So we are forced by unassailable, true reasoning to acknowledge in the Godhead both a trinity of persons and a unity of substance. Therefore, for the three in the Godhead there is one common and equal eternity and eternal equality, because what the one Godhead does in common for all cannot be dissimilar in each. Therefore, the three are one (*unum*), because in the three persons is one substance, but the three are not one (*unus*), for just as the distinction of persons does not divide the unity of the Godhead, so also the unity of the Godhead does not confuse the distinction of persons.[75]

22.1   But it is desirable to consider a little more closely how it may be said that the Father loves His wisdom. It is often customary for people to love a science for the work to which it leads, not the work for the science. Such are the sciences of agriculture, weaving and milling,[76] and others like them, where to be sure expertise is judged useless unless it results in some work that yields a useful product.[77] But if one is speaking of the Wisdom of God, then doubtless the work yields precedence to the worker. Moreover, one must say that Wisdom is always more precious than Her work, and Wisdom is always to be loved on Her own account. If sometimes Wisdom's work is preferred to Wisdom, this results not from a true judgment, but from human error. For Wisdom is life, and the love of Wisdom is life's happiness. For this reason, when it is said that the Father of Wisdom takes delight in that Wisdom (*illa*), let it be far from our minds to believe that God loves His Wisdom on account of the works which He did through Her, when, on the contrary, He loves all His works only on account of Wisdom.

22.2   Therefore, He said: "This is my beloved Son in whom I am pleased."[78] He did not say He was pleased with the earth or the heaven, or with the sun and moon and stars, or even with the angels and what things are the most excellent in creatures, because even these things, though in their way are pleasing, nevertheless cannot please except in Him and through Him. They are the more worthy of my love, the more closely they approach His likeness. Therefore, God does not love Wisdom on account of Her works, but Her works on account of Wisdom. In Wisdom is all beauty and truth. She is totally desire, invisible light and immortal life. Her appearance is so desirable that She can delight the eyes of God. She is simple and perfect, full but not excessive, alone but not solitary,[79] one and containing all.

23.1   But because we believe in three persons in the Godhead, it remains to inquire whether what is said of each of these can also be said of the others. It has been said that the Father loves the Son. It remains for us to consider if it can be said equally that the Love-of-Father-and-Son loves the Son, and that the Son loves Himself. Likewise, that the Father loves Himself, that the Son loves the Father, that the Love-of-Father-and-Son loves the Father; likewise, that the Love-of-the-Father-and-Son loves Himself, that the Father loves the Love-of-the-Son-and-Himself, that the Son loves the Love-of-the-Father-and-Himself. Finally, whether it is one and the same Love by which each loves Himself and each of them reciprocally loves the other. But we will easily find out these things, if we recall to memory the things that have already been said.

23.2   In the above line of reasoning we asserted that God is the first cause and origin of all good things. No good can surpass Him who is the fount and beginning of all. Therefore, God is the supreme good. Blessedness (*beatitudo*) is nowhere more rightly situated than in the supreme good. Therefore, God alone is properly and principally blessed (*beatus*).[80] How could someone be blessed who is not pleased with what he is? Therefore, it is necessary that whoever is blessed loves himself. But how could anyone who hates what he is love himself? Therefore, whoever is blessed both loves Himself and loves what he is. If, therefore, the Father and Son and the Love-of-the-Father-and-the-Son are one and are one God, then, since in God alone is true beatitude, it is necessary both that each loves himself and each loves the others reciprocally. For it cannot truly be said to be beatitude; indeed, on the contrary, it would be supreme unhappiness if they were divided by an opposing will, yet on account of the same nature could not be separated from each other.

23.3   Therefore, as Father and Son and the-Love-of-Father-and-Son are one in nature, so also they cannot *not* be one in will and love. They love themselves with one love because they are one. What each loves in the other is not different from what each loves in Himself, for what each *is* is not different from what the other is. What the Father loves in the Son is identical with what the Son loves in Himself, and what the Love-of-the-Father-and-the-Son loves in the Son is what the Son loves in Himself. Similarly, what the Son loves in the Father, that the Father loves in Himself, and what the Love-of-the-Father-and-Son loves in the Father, that the Father loves in Himself. Likewise, what the Father and Son love in their Love is what the Love-of-the-Father-and-Son loves in Himself. Likewise, what the Father loves in Himself is what He loves in the Son and in their Love, and what the Son loves in Himself is what He loves in the Father and in their Love, and what the Love-of-the-Father-and-the-Son loves in Himself is what He loves in the Son and in the Father.

24.1   Listen whether the voice of the Father is in harmony with what we are saying: "*This*," He says, "*is my beloved Son in whom I am pleased.*"[81] He did not say separately, "I am well pleased," nor did He say separately, "He pleased me." Nor, indeed, did He say conjointly: "I am well pleased," and "He pleased me"; but He said: "I am well pleased in Him," that is, "what pleases me regarding myself is in Him, not outside of Him, because what I am He is. For because I am not other than He, I cannot be pleased outside of Him. '*This is my beloved Son in whom I am pleased.*'"[82]

24.2 "Whatever pleases me does so in Him and through Him. For He is the Wisdom through whom I made all things. In Him I have eternally arranged whatever I have made in time. And the more perfectly I see each work of mine to be in harmony with that first arrangement, the more fully I love it. Do not think that He is only the mediator in the reconciliation of humankind, for through Him also the creation of all creatures becomes praiseworthy and pleasing in my sight. In Him I consider all the works I do, and I cannot *not* love what I see is similar to Him whom I love. The only one that offends me is the one who departs from His likeness.

24.3 "Therefore, if you wish to please me, be like Him, 'Listen to Him.'[83] And if by chance you have departed from His likeness by acting badly, return by imitating Him. In Him are given the command and the counsel; the command so that you may remain steadfast, the counsel so that you may return. Would that you had kept the commandment! But because you have transgressed the command, at least listen to the admonition, 'Listen to Him.' An angel of great counsel[84] is sent to you, and the one who was given to created things for their glory is the same one who comes to the lost for their healing. 'Listen to Him.' He is the creator and He is also the redeemer. As God, He created you with me; He alone came to you as a human being with you. 'Listen to Him.' For He is the form; He is the medicine; He is the example; He is the remedy. 'Listen to Him.' It would have been a happier situation to have always maintained His likeness, but now it will be no less glorious to return to imitation of Him. 'Listen to Him.'"

24.4 O humanity! What is the cause of your ignorance? Look, your own nature reproves you; it convicts you. You know what you are like, whence you come, whom you have as your Maker;[85] what Mediator you need; and you still clamor insolently against God by defending yourself! You know that you are wicked and that you have not been made evil by a good Maker. You quit; you do not call to Him who made you to come and restore you, or to the one who created you to redeem you. Have no doubts about His power; see how great are His works. Do not doubt His Wisdom; see how beautiful are His works. Do not doubt His good will; see how His works serve you by their usefulness. Thus, He shows you in His works what a great thing your redemption can be. He shows you also how you can await the fearful Judge, if you do not wish to have a Redeemer. No one can resist Him, because He is almighty. No one can deceive Him, because He is most wise. No one can corrupt Him, because He is most good. No one can turn away from Him, because he is everywhere. No one can sustain[86] Him, because He is eternal. No one can bend Him, because He is immutable. Therefore, if we do not wish to have experience of the Judge, let us seek the Redeemer.

[III]

25.1   When we long since began to proceed from visible things to the investigation of invisible ones, we passed first from the corporeal creation to the incorporeal, that is, to the rational creation, and then from the rational creation we arrived at the Wisdom of God. Now, on our return, we will proceed first from the Wisdom of God to rational creation, then from consideration of the rational creation to corporeal creation.

25.2   The former is the order of knowledge; the latter, the order of creation (*conditionis*). For corporeal creation, which is visible, first comes into our awareness; then knowledge passes from corporeal creation to incorporeal creation. Finally, the open road of inquiry reaches the Creator of both. In the creation, at the top level,[87] rational creation was made in the image of God, then there is the corporeal creation, so that the rational creature would recognize in what was outside what it had received from the Creator interiorly. In the Wisdom of God is truth; in the rational creation, the image of truth; in the corporeal creature, the shadow of the image. Rational creation has been made for the Wisdom of God; corporeal creation has been made for the rational creature. For this reason, every movement and turning[88] of the corporeal creation is toward the rational creation, and every movement and turning of the rational creature ought to be toward the Wisdom of God. Then, when each thing clings to it superior through conversion, it does not disturb the order of the first creation or the likeness of that first exemplar within itself.

25.3   Therefore, whoever travels by the way of inquiry from visible things to invisible ones must first lead the gaze of his mind from the corporeal creation to the rational creation and then from the rational creation to consideration of his Creator. However, when he returns[89] from the invisible to the visible, he descends first from the Creator to the rational creation, then from the rational creature to the corporeal creation. In the human mind the order of cognition always precedes the order of creation, because it is we who are outside cannot return from the things within, unless we first have penetrated the interior things with the eye of the mind.[90] However, the order of creation always comes again after the order of cognition because, although human weakness is sometimes given tenuous admittance to contemplate interior realities, the ebb and flow of its mutability does not allow it to stay there long.[91]

26.1   Therefore, after we have, to the extent that God deigned to grant us, arrived at knowledge of invisible things from visible things, let our mind now return to itself and pay attention to what use can come to it from this knowledge. For what good is it to us if we know in God the height of his majesty, but glean from it nothing useful to us? But notice, when we come back from that interior, secret place of divine contemplation, what will we be able to bring with us? Coming from the region of light, what else except light? For it is fitting and necessary that if we come from the region of light, we carry with us light to put to flight our darkness. And who will be able to know what we were there, if we do not return enlightened? Therefore let what we were there appear; let what we saw there appear. If there we saw power, let us bring back the light of the fear of God. If we saw wisdom there, let us bring back the light of truth. If we saw kindness there, let us bring the light of love. Power rouses the sluggish to fear; wisdom illumines those who were blind from the darkness of ignorance; kindness enflames the cold with the warmth of charity.

26.2   Look, please! What is light if not the day, and what is darkness if not the night? And just as the eye of the body has its day and its night, so also does the eye of the heart[92] have its day and its night. Therefore, there are three days[93] of invisible light by which the course of the spiritual life within is divided. The first day is fear; the second day is truth; the third day is love.[94] The first day has power as its sun. The second day has wisdom as its sun. The third day has kindness as its sun. Power pertains to the Father, wisdom to the Son, kindness to the Holy Spirit.

26.3   Our days that we have exteriorly are one thing; those that we have interiorly are another. Our exterior days pass by, even if we do not want them to. Our interior days can, if we want them to, remain for eternity, for it is said of the fear of the Lord that it *"remains forever and ever."*[95] There is no doubt that truth remains forever. Even if truth begins in this life, it will be full and perfect in us then, when He who is truth will appear clearly after the end of this life. It is also said of charity that *"charity never fails."*[96]

26.4   Good are the days that never fail! For those days are bad which
not only do not last forever, but which cannot stand even for a little
while. The prophet says of these days: "*Man, his days are like straw.*"[97]
The latter are the days that our guilt deserves; the former are the days
that grace gives. The prophet spoke about these days: "*In my days I will
call out.*"[98] For if he spoke of those other days, why would he not call
out also at night, for elsewhere he said: "*I rose in the middle of the night
to praise you*"?[99] But he calls these days his own, because he does not
love those other days, as Jeremiah says: "*Lord you know that I have not
desired the day of man.*"[100] Job was full of this sort of days. Of him it
was written: "*He died an old man full of days.*"[101] He could not have
been full of that other kind of days, which he had not yet passed
through. The only days that the wicked have known are those external
days. But the good, who have already deserved to see interior days, not
only do not love those that are outside, but they also curse them. Blessed
Job says: "*Let the day on which I was born perish, and the night in which
it was said, 'A human being has been conceived.' Let this day be turned
into darkness, and let God not look at it from above, and let it not be
illumined by the light.*"[102] Instead, we should love those days that are
within, where darkness does not follow light, where the interior eyes
of the clean of heart are illumined by the splendor of the eternal sun.
26.5   Of these days the psalmist sang: "*Announce from one day to the
next His salvation.*"[103] What is "His salvation" if not His Jesus? For that
is how "Jesus" is translated, that is, "salvation." He is spoken of as salvation because through Him humanity is reformed for salvation. John
spoke of Him, saying: "*The law was given through Moses; grace and truth
have come to be through Jesus Christ.*"[104] Likewise, the Apostle Paul calls
Christ Jesus "*the power of God and the wisdom of God.*"[105] Therefore, if
the wisdom of God is Jesus Christ, and truth came to be through Jesus
Christ, it follows that truth came to be through the wisdom of God.
The day of wisdom is the truth. Concerning this His day, Wisdom
himself speaks to the Jews, saying: "*Abraham, your father, rejoiced that
he saw my day; he saw and was glad.*"[106] The truth of God is the redemption of the human race. He had first promised it; when later He showed
it, surely what else did He show than His own truthful self? Rightly this
truth was fulfilled through Wisdom, from whom all truth is. The one
who was sent to fulfill the truth was nothing else than He in whom all
the fullness of truth resides. Rightly, then, does Abraham exult at the
day of truth, because he wanted the truth to be fulfilled. How surely
then did he, through the Spirit, see the day, when he recognized the

Son of God coming in the flesh for the redemption of the human race.

26.6   Therefore let it be said: "*Tell from one day unto the next his salvation.*"[107] The second day, from the first day unto the third day; the day of truth, from the day of fear unto the day of charity. First, there was one day, the day of fear. A second day came, the day of truth. It arrived, but did not replace, because the first day did not cease. Behold, two days! There was movement toward the third day, the day of charity. But when it came, it did not expel the former days. Blessed are those days! Human beings can be fulfilled by these days, when future things supervene but the present things do not pass away, when their number will increase and their brightness will multiply.

27.1   First, human beings, placed under sin, were rebuked by the law and began to fear God, the Judge, because they knew their wickedness. Now, to fear Him was already to recognize Him, because surely they could not fear Him at all, if they had no inkling of Him. Already this recognition was some measure of light. It was already day, but not yet bright, because it was still shadowed by the darkness of sin. Therefore, there came the day of truth, the day of salvation, which destroyed sin and illumined the brightness of the previous day. It did not take away fear, but turned it into something better. But there was not yet full brightness, until charity was added to truth. For Truth himself says: "*I have many things to say to you, but you cannot bear them now. However, when that Spirit of truth comes, he will teach you all truth;*"[108] "all truth," in order both to take away evils and to reform good things. Notice, there are three days: the day of fear, which makes evil manifest; the day of truth, which takes away evil; the day of charity, which restores good. The day of truth brings light to the day of fear; the day of charity brings light to the day of fear and to the day of truth, until charity is perfect and all truth completely manifest, and fear of punishment will pass over into reverent fear. "*So announce from day unto day his salvation.*"[109]

27.2   Hosea the prophet spoke of these days, when he said: "*He will bring us to life after two days, and on the third day he will raise us up.*"[110] For we have heard and rejoiced about how our Lord Jesus Christ rising from the dead on the third day enlivened us in Himself and raised us up. But it was very fitting that we reimburse Him for his favor, and, just as we have risen in Him as He rose on the third day, so, too, let us, rising on the third day for Him and through Him, make Him rise in us. We should not believe that He wishes to be paid by us what He first wished to grant us. As He wished to have three days in order to work out our salvation in Himself and through Himself, so he gave three days to us in order that we might work out our salvation in ourselves through Him. But because what was done in Him was not only a remedy, but also an example and a sacrament, it was necessary that it happen visibly and outwardly, so that it might signify what needed to happen in us invisibly.[111] Therefore, His days are external; our days are to be sought internally.

27.3   We have three days internally by which our soul is illumined. To the first day pertains death; to the second, burial; to the third, resurrection. The first day is fear; the second is truth; the third is charity. The day of fear is the day of power, the day of the Father. The day of truth is the day of wisdom, the day of the Son. The day of charity is the day of kindness, the day of the Holy Spirit. In fact, the day of the Father and the day of the Son and the day of the Holy Spirit are one day in the brightness of the Godhead, but in the enlightening of our minds it is as if the Father had one day, the Son another, and the Holy Spirit another. Not that it is to be believed in any way that the Trinity, which is inseparable in its nature, can be separated in its operation, but so that the distinction of persons can be understood in the distribution of works.

27.4   When, therefore, the omnipotence of God is considered and arouses our heart to wonder, it is the day of the Father; when the wisdom of God is examined and enlightens our heart with recognition of the truth, it is the day of the Son; when the kindness of God is observed and enflames our hearts to love, it is the day of the Holy Spirit. Power arouses fear; wisdom enlightens; kindness brings joy. On the day of power, we die through fear. On the day of wisdom, we are buried away from the clamor of this world by contemplation of the truth. On the day of kindness, we rise through love and desire of eternal goods.[112] Therefore, Christ died on the sixth day, lay buried in the tomb on the seventh, and rose on the eighth day, so that in a similar way through fear the power of God on its day may first cut us away from carnal desires outside, and then wisdom on his day may bury us within in the hidden place of contemplation; and finally, kindness on its day may cause us to rise revivified through desire of divine love.[113] For the sixth day is for work; the seventh, for rest; the eighth, for resurrection.

Here ends *On the Three Days*.

NOTES

1.   See John 1:1–4; Sir 1:5; Heb 4:12.

2.   Rom 1:20. The Latin text of the Vulgate is not transparent: "*invisibilia enim ipsius a creatura mundi per ea quae facta sunt intellecta conspiciuntur.*" The Douai-Rheims (ca. 1750) translation reads "For the invisible things of him, from the creation of the world are clearly seen, being understood by the things that are made." Ronald Knox (1945) translated: "From the foundation of the world men have caught sight of his invisible nature [as] known through his creatures." Achard of St Victor, "On the Unity of God and the Plurality of Creatures," 1.37, 2.4 (tr. Hugh Feiss in *Achard of St Victor, Works*, Cistercian Studies Series 165 [Kalamazoo: Cistercian, 2001], 407, 441), refers to Rom 1:20, when he states that he does not develop his theology of the Trinity on the basis of what God has made. In *On the Trinity* Richard of St Victor cites Rom 1:20 more than any other biblical passage: *Trin.* 1.8; 1.10; 5.6; 6.1; 6.15; 6.17.

3.   Throughout *On the Three Days*, Hugh designates *benignitas* as the third of the three divine attributes he discusses. The Latin term means having a kind or affable bearing towards others, kindness, benevolence, mercy. For the *benignitas* of God see Rom 2:4; Titus 3:4. Hugh uses the same triad with *benignitas* in a number of places: *Libellus* 4 (Sicard, 143.111–14; PL 176.693D); *Sent. div.* "Appendix" (Piazzoni, 953–54.1–32, 63–68; *Sacr.* 1.2.7 (PL 176.209B-10A; Deferrari 32); *Misc.* 1.63 (PL 177.505A).
Elsewhere, in discussing this triad, Hugh substitutes other similar words for *benignitas*: for example,
bonitas: *Misc.* 1.83 (PL 177.518BC);
bonitas and *benignitas*: *Sacr.* 1.3.26–28 (PL 176.227C-231A; Deferrari, 53–57);
gratia: *Didasc.* 3.11 (Taylor, 93; Buttimer, 60.6–8);
voluntas: *Sent. div.* 2 (Piazzoni, 938.74–91); *Sent. div.* 3 (Piazzoni, 948.3–5);
libertas: *Sacr.* 1.5.12 (PL 176.251D; Deferrari, 80);
amor: *Sent. div.* 3 (Piazzoni, 953.177–86); *Sacr.* 1.2.6–13 (PL 176.208B-13C; Deferrari, 31–35);
caritas: *Eulogium* (PL 176.988C-989A); *Misc.* 1.99 (PL 177.531A-532A).
On *Misc.* 1.83, see Poirel, *Livre*, 140–44, 338–39; he concludes that it is probably earlier than the *On the Three Days*. It does not mention the Trinity. On the other texts in which Hugh mentions the triad, see Poirel, *Livre*, 327–43.

4.   See *In Eccl.* 10 (PL 175.180A).

5.   *Sacr.* 2.1.3 (PL 176.373A, 373D; Deferrari, 207); 2.1.4 (PL 176.376C-D; Deferarri, 211).

6.   Hugh does not follow exactly the division of the first part (of three) that he sketches in 1.3. On this initial outline, see Poirel, *Livre*, 240–60, who suggests that in 1.3 Hugh is not so much giving the plan of his treatise as he is inculcating a (di-)vision of the world.

7.   Richard of St Victor, *Exterm.* 3.16 (PL 196.1112BC): "Happy are those for whom the beauty of temporal things is an incitement toward eternity." Achard of St Victor, *Serm.* 9.4 (tr. Feiss, 67–68), writes that each created thing mirrors the Trinity by its existence, beauty and useful goodness. Regarding his preoccupation with beauty see Feiss's comments in *Sermons*, 58. However, in "On the Unity of God," where he deals with the Trinity apart from creation, Achard focuses on unity, duality and equality as the relational attributes of the divine persons.

8.   Hugh uses these same two terms in a discussion of the quadrivium in *Didasc.* 2.6 (Taylor, 67; Buttimer, 30.1–5). There he says that quantity is the visible form in its measured dimensions as impressed on the mind's imagination; it has two parts, one continuous, such as a tree or stone which is called magnitude, the other discrete, like a flock or a people, which is called multitude.

9.   "*animalis*" from *anima* (soul). Literally the adjective means "soul-bearing," "ensouled," or "animate," and at times, "animalistic." Generally when it is used in a neutral sense I have translated it as "biological." When it is used pejoratively, I have translated it as "carnal."

10.   *gratus, aptus, commodus, necessarius*. Later, Hugh will substitute *congruus* for *aptus*. The four qualities form a continuum from what is pleasant to what is necessary. In the translation I try to be consistent: *gratus*: attractive or pleasing; *aptus*: apt, for which sometimes Hugh

substitutes *congruus* = fitting; *commodus*: beneficial, for which Hugh sometimes substitutes *conveniens* = suitable; *necessarius*: necessary.

[11]   *honoruscopa*: see Pliny, *Historia Naturalis* (Thayer, 32.24.69), available online at http://penelope.uchicago.edu/Thayer/L/Roman/Texts/Pliny_the_Elder; Isidore of Seville, *Etym.* (Thayer, 12.6.35), available online at http://penelope.uchicago.edu/Thayer/E/Roman/Texts/ Isidore. The name is a corruption of "uranocscopus" ("sky-gazer"). The fish was so named because its eyes are both on the top of its head. The *Oxford English Dictionary* has a helpful entry for "uranocscopus."

[12]   Cf. Heb 1:1.

[13]   *Dulcedo* (*dulce*) and *suavitas* (*suave*) seem to be synonyms. They refer to sweetness in taste, something much rarer in the Middle Ages than now, when the prime sweetener was honey rather than sugar. Most often the terms mean charm, delightfulness, agreeableness.

[14]   Ps 91:5-7 (Vulg.). Cf. *In Eccl.* 2 (PL 175.138C).

[15]   On *mundus sensilis*, see *Sacr.* 1.1.29 (PL 176.204C; Deferrari, 27): "The works of creation, that is, this world perceptible to the senses (*sensilis*) with all its elements, were made in matter before any day together in time and with time . . ?").

[16]   On the *book* of nature, see *Archa Noe.* 2.10 (Sicard, 48.1-6; PL 176.643D-644A): There are three books: one made by human beings from something, the second created by God from nothing, the third to whom God gives birth, God from very God. The second book is the work of God, which will never cease to be; in this visible work the invisible wisdom of the Creator is visibly written. See Wanda Cizewski, "Reading the World as Scripture: Hugh of St Victor's *De tribus diebus*," *Florilegium* 9 (1987): 65-88; Alan of Lille, *Rhytmus* (PL 210.579AB); *Anticlaudianus* (PL 210.491).

[17]   On nature as revelatory, see *Didasc.* 6.5 (Taylor, 145; Buttimer, 123.4-6): "all nature bespeaks God; all nature teaches humanity; all nature produces knowledge, and nothing in the universe is sterile"; *In Eccl.* 2 (PL 175.142B). Dominique Poirel, "Voir l'invisible: la spiritualité visionnaire de Hugues de Saint-Victor," in *Spiritualität im Europa des Mittelalters: L'Europe spirituelle au Moyen Age: 900 Jahre Hildegard von Bingen, 900 ans l'abbaye de Cîteaux*, eds. Jean Ferrari and Stephan Grätzel, Philosophie im Kontext 4 (St. Augustin: Gardez! Verlag, 1998), 34-36, points out how Hugh's theology and spirituality "can be interpreted as an effort to get beyond the contradiction between the visible and the invisible." God must be known and loved by way of his visible creation, which is a pledge of His love.

[18]   On God's invisible Wisdom and Word made visible, see *Sacr.* 1.3.20 (PL 176.225B; Deferrari, 50) and *Sacr.* 1.6.5 (PL 176.266D-267A; Deferrari, 97-98): Divine Wisdom is the intrinsic, invisible Word of God; this invisible Word is made known through a visible, extrinsic word, which is God's work. Cf. Augustine, *En. Ps.* 26.2.12 (Dekkers and Fraipont, 161.10-21).

[19]   On "*spiritalis . . . omnia diiudicare potest*" (1 Cor 2:15), see *Didasc.* 6.4 (Taylor, 144; Buttimer, 122.4-5); *Sacr.* 1.1.13 (PL 176.198A; Deferrari, 20); *Sacr.* 2.2.4 (PL 176.418C; Deferrari 256). *Misc.* 1.1 (PL 177.469B-477C) is an extended commentary on this verse of St Paul, summarizing some central themes of Hugh's theology: (1) The Holy Spirit makes people spiritual. The Spirit's anointing instructs them about everything, because it contains all. There is one Wisdom, in which are all things. Thus the universe is one, and greatness (*magnitudo*) and simplicity coalesce. God is the Light by which we see and the Beauty (*species*) which we see. God is the one delight of all the spiritual senses. (2) The eye of the flesh sees the world and what is in the world; the eye of reason sees the rational soul (*animus*) and all that is in it; the eye of contemplation sees God and all else in God. (3) Hence, spiritual persons judge all things. They judge truth through wisdom and goodness through experience. (4) Like corporeal light, spiritual light both illumines to knowledge of the truth and warms to love of goodness. (5) True judgment is made according to a right rule; the supreme rule is the supreme truth and goodness, that is, God. (6) God is the supreme spiritual good; human beings are the supreme good among bodily beings, and for them all other bodily beings were made for their use and instruction. Spiritual goods are from God; bodily goods are for humankind. Hugh reiterates this conviction that God created physical things for human beings at: *Misc.* 1.35 (PL 177.494D); *Archa Noe.* 4, 5 (Sicard, 100.51-52; PL 176.671D); *Sac. dial.* (PL 176.21D); *Sent. div.* 3 (Piazzoni, 928.23-24); *Sacr.* 1.Prol.3 (PL 176.184B; Deferrari, 4); *Sacr.* 1.1.3 (PL 176.188C-189B; Deferrari,

8–9), where Hugh says that if someone does not like this explanation, they should find a better one; *Sacr.* 1.1.29 (PL 176.204D; Deferrari, 27), *Sacr.* 1.2.1 (PL 176.205B-206C; Deferrari, 28–29). He believed there was a hierarchy in creation, in which each level is subject to the one above: God, spirit, body, and world. This does not imply that human beings had unlimited scope to exploit nature; they are subject to God, and were to use God's creation to meet their needs and learn from it about its maker. Some things were made solely for the latter purpose. Moreover, Hugh had a very strong sense of the interconnectedness of the whole material universe; everything is interconnected (*Sacr.* 1.2.1 [PL 176.206 D; Deferrari 29]). See 14.2 below. (7) That is good which participates in and leads to the Supreme Good. (8) All the forms, figures, colors and beauties of things are said to be good insofar as they delight the human senses. (9) Properly speaking, evil is what people do, not what happens to them. By God's grace, the bad things that happen to people can be turned to good.

20   On this contrast between the wise and foolish person, see *In Eccl.* 10 (PL 175.182A), 17 (PL 175.241B); *Archa Noe* 3.5 (Sicard 59.12–19; PL 176.649BC).

21   Ps 142:5.

22   Isa 40:12, 22.

23   Ps 95:5.

24   *In hier. cael.* 2 (PL 175.949BC); *Assumpt.*(*Oeuvre* 2, 118.89–94; PL 177.1211D; 148.501-150.507; PL 177.1220AB); *Laude car.* 6 (*Oeuvre* 1, 188.97–99; (PL 176.972D); *Arrha* (*Oeuvre* 1, 232.101-5; PL 176.954B).

25   Van Zwieten, "Scientific and Spiritual Culture," 184, traces this idea back to Macrobius, *In somnium Scipionis* 2.10.10–22 (Eyssenhardt [Leipzig, 1893] 618–19; available at http://la.wikisource.org/wiki/Commentariorum_in_Somnium_Scipionis), where the discussion of fire and water occurs in section VI.

26   *Inst. nov.* 12 (*Oeuvre* 1, 72.926–27; PL 176.943A).

27   *Adnot. in Pent.* (PL 175.35B); *In Eccl.* 2 (PL 175.137D-138A); *Sent. div.* 1 (Piazzoni, 932.157–61; *Sac. dial.* (PL 176.20A); *Sacr.* 1.1.6 (PL 176.190C; Deferrari, 11); *Sacr.* 1.1.22 (PL 176.201D-202A; Deferrari, 24). Hugh will return to this idea of the harmonious interconnection of disparate parts a number of times in *On the Three Days*. Achard of St Victor also emphasizes this congruence: "On the Unity of God," 1.5–9, 1.48 (tr. Feiss, 381–84, 425–26).

28   The subject of the verbs in this paragraph is divine providence ("*divina providentia . . . creatoris providentia*"). One could refer to "divine providence" as "he," (referring to God in the masculine and recognizing that divine providence is only a personification of one aspect of the simple fullness of God), "she," ("*providentia*" is feminine in Latin) or "it" ("*providentia*" as a neuter power of foresight). When in Latin the pronoun was the subject of a verb, Hugh did not have to make this choice, since the pronouns are not expressed in Latin. I have chosen to use the feminine pronoun, both because the grammatical subject is the feminine word "providentia" and as a counterweight to my use of "he" for God elsewhere in the translation. Hugh will use feminine pronouns when referring to divine Wisdom and Knowledge (both feminine words in Latin), except in a few instances where he is speaking directly of Christ; in those instances he uses masculine pronouns. I will follow his usage.

29   The inclusion of the study of the arts in a list of natural resources is striking. Perhaps Hugh thought that the special contribution to human society of places like Paris or St Victor was scholarship rather than some sort of material resource.

30   The idea that Providence arrange that one region supplies what is lacking in another occurs in Walahfrid Strabo, *Hortulus*, ed. and tr. Raef Payne, comm. Wilfrid Blunt (Pittsburgh, PA: Hunt Botanical Library, 1966) 52–53: ". . . Oh, how wise, / How good is God! Let us praise Him as we ought. / From no land He withholds His bounty; what is rare / Beneath this sky, under another lies / In such abundance as the cheapest trash / We have among us here: some things we scorn / Rich kingdoms pay great prices for. And so / One land helps another; so the whole world, / Through all its parts, makes one family." (". . . O magni laudanda Tonantis / Virtus et ratio, nullis quae munera terris / Larga suae non pandit opis: quae rara sub isto / Axe videre soles, aliis in partibus horum / Copia tanta jacet, quantam vilissima tecum / Efficiunt; rursus quaedam quae spreta videntur / Forte tibi, magno mercantur ditia regna, / Altera ut alterius potiatur foenore tellus / Orbis et in toto per partes una domus sit.")

[31] Cf. *Misc.* 1.174 (PL 177.573C), which says that it is not a fault (*vitium*) to drink the waters of the lower cistern (Is 22:9), but it is a fault to hoard them, because although we may use temporal goods for our needs, we may not love them to the point of superfluity.

[32] Cf. *Didasc.* 2.12 (Taylor, 69; Buttimer, 32.14–17); *Inst. nov.* 4 (*Oeuvre* 1, 24.107–12; PL 176.927D-28A).

[33] "*Species*" is difficult to translate. It means a seeing or sight, shape, beauty, appearance, apparition, reputation, quality.

[34] Cf. *Archa Noe* 2.3 (Sicard, 37.6–8; PL 176.638A).

[35] Like "*providentia,*" "*sapientia*" is a feminine noun personifying a divine attribute.

[36] The notion that the soul has a higher part (Hugh here speaks of the *ratio* of the *mens*) directed toward the world of the invisible above humans and a lower part, directed toward knowledge of physical things, is part of the diffuse Platonism of medieval thought. The distinction between *sapientia* and *scientia*, stemming from Augustine, corresponds to this division. Here, however, when Hugh speaks of this latter dimension of human existence, he does not think of reason knowing physical things, but of instincts and feelings. Following again the Platonic tradition, he divides these into the irascible and the concupiscible, that is, we might say, adrenalin and desire. On these, cf. *Didasc.* 2.4 (Taylor, 65; Buttimer, 27.30–28.10; PL 176.754AB); *Didasc.* 2.12 (Taylor, 69; Buttimer, 33.6); and for desire, see *In Eccl.* 12 (PL 176.192B).

[37] *Anima*, soul, is the basis for the adjective *animalis*. The word means "ensouled," "soul-bearing," "animate," or even "animalistic." It is misleading to translate it the same way in each context. Generally, when it is used neutrally, I have translated it as "biological" or "animal," and when it is used pejoratively, I have translated it "carnal."

[38] Prompted by his mention of the nails on fingers and toes, Hugh draws a moral regarding earthly things. Some are almost necessary for us to live; others are not and can be trimmed painlessly. The first are needs (*necessitates*), the second superfluous wants. Cf. *Eulogium* (PL 176.990D); *Unione* (Piazzoni, 887.130–32; PL 177.288BC).

[39] Rather as we understand radar, medieval thinkers thought that seeing occurred when the eyes sent out a ray which was then reflected back to the eye. Cf. *Unione* (PL 177.287B).

[40] *In Eccl.* 2 (PL 175.141A); *Sacr.* 2.16.3 (PL 176.585B; Deferrari, 438–39); *Misc.* 2.11 (PL 177.595A).

[41] The Latin names of some of the creatures Hugh lists here are not easy to identify. In her translation of this passage, Wanda Zemler-Cizewski ("Beauty and Beasts," 298) opts for alternate translations for the following animals: moth = bookworm, stinging insect = gnat, gnat = fly, tick = mosquito. Professor Zemler-Cizewski elsewhere ("Animal and Plant Lore in Hugh of St Victor's *De tribus diebus*," unpublished paper delivered at the 43rd International Congress on Medieval Studies, Western Michigan University, May 9, 2008) made the interesting suggestion that one of Hugh's pedagogical goals may have been to increase his readers' (or students') Latin vocabulary.

[42] *In Eccl.* 2 (PL 175.140B); *Sacr.* 1.6.8 (PL 176.268D-269A; Deferrari, 100).

[43] The inclusion of "beauty" here does not perfectly fit the logic of his outline. Since par. 4, Hugh has been writing about beauty as a manifestation of divine wisdom. He subdivided it into four categories: structure, motion, appearance, and quality. In 9.1, he divided appearance into shape and color. He then listed a number of ways in which shapes can be marvelous: great size, smaller, rarity, beauty, oddity, one in many, many in one. In this paragraph he mentions that the appearance of some things is strikingly beautiful, and in the next he mentions things that are particularly odd-looking.

[44] *In hier. cael.* 7 (175.1063D); *Misc.* 1.122 (PL 177.546D).

[45] Hugh's high estimate of the color green recurs in *Assumpt.* (*Oeuvre* 2, 148.501–2; PL 177.1220A); *Libellus* 1 (Sicard, 122.38; PL 176.682A; 122.44; PL 176.682B), *Misc.* 1.183 (PL 175.567C; PL 175.568D). This love of the color green seems to reflect his own sensibility, but it may also have derived from Sir 40:22: "*gratiam et speciem desiderabit oculus tuus et super hoc viride sationis*" ("Thy eye desireth favour and beauty, but more than these green sown fields" [Douai-Rheims]; "Grace and beauty charm the eye; best of all, the green wheat" [Knox]); cf. Sir 40:16. One thinks of Hildegard of Bingen's notion of *viriditas* ("greenness"), the God-given life force of the biological and spiritual worlds.

46 In *Didasc.* 1.9 (Taylor, 56; Buttimer, 16.17), *Didasc.* 2.1 (Taylor, 62; Buttimer, 24.24), and *Didasc.* 2.20 (Taylor, 75; Buttimer, 39.16–17), Hugh speaks of mechanical arts which imitate nature. These are "artificial" (*adulterinae*) because they are the work of an artisan in which the form is not from nature. The Latin word "*adulterina*" was usually pejorative, and Hugh may have chosen it for its negative connotations. However, his treatment of these "mechanical" arts (such as cloth-making and navigation), which aim to meet human needs, is positive and original.

47 "*dulcia sermonum commercia.*" In *Inst. nov.* 13–17 (*Oeuvre* 1, 82–90.965–1113; PL 176.943D–949A), Hugh treats in detail of what, to whom, where, when, and how to speak.

48 The four categories are *necessarius, commodus, congruus,* and *gratus.* They are on a continuum from necessary to unnecessary. It is not easy to capture the nuances of the middle two, which I have translated as beneficial and suitable, the latter being less necessary than the former. In *Sacr.* 1.9.7 (PL 176.327AB; Deferrari, 164), Hugh divides "sacraments" into three kinds: Those which are necessary to salvation (Baptism, Eucharist); those helpful toward salvation (ashes, holy water); and those preparatory to the other sacraments (e.g., relating to Holy Orders).

49 In his edition, Poirel has corrected the reading in the manuscripts from "*Necessarium unicuique rei est quominus ipsa subsistere commode non potest*" to "*Necessarium unicuique rei est, quo minus ipsa subsistere omnimodo non potest.*" See Poirel, *De tribus diebus,* *243–*245.

50 Cf. 1 Tim 6:17.

51 See note 15 above.

52 "*Non igitur decebat, ut rerum visibilium copia aliqua in parte defectum sentiret.*" The subject of *sentiret* could also be understood to be "*homo*": "it was not fitting that humanity perceive a defect in some aspect with respect to the array of visible things . . ."

53 Cf. Richard of St Victor, *Serm. cent.* 69 (PL 177.1114BC).

54 *compendium tractandi:* As Poirel notes (*Livre* 235–40), here and in 20.10 Hugh refers to *On the Three Days* as a *compendium.* This is not one of the genres he lists in *Didasc.* 3.6. Hugh refers to many of his works as *compendia* or *compendiosa.* In doing so, he seems to indicate a pedagogical concern for brevity. *Tractactus* is also a flexible term, but implies a monograph treating of a unified theme.

55 In *Sacr.* 1.1.3–6 (PL 176.188C–192D; Deferrari, 8–13), Hugh draws a parallel between the formation of material creation and humankind. God first created unformed matter, and then gave it form, and so showed that it first received from God existence, which was the prerequisite for receiving ordering and form. Newly created matter was not totally without form, but it lacked the beautiful and apt disposition and form that it now has. So human beings are first created, then turn in thanks and love to their Creator to be formed. They first receive being (existence), then beautiful being (sanctification), then blessed being (eternal consummation). Newly created matter was not totally without form, but it lacked the beautiful and apt disposition and form that it now has.

56 *Misc.* 1.184 (PL 177.580D–581A) says that the Wisdom of God, without departing from where it was (in the Trinity), came out to us in three ways: in the creation of things, when it appeared to us clothed in the beauty of created things; when it assumed the vesture of the flesh and appeared to us visibly; when, clothed under the sacred veil of words, it presented itself to our understanding. Cf. *Decalogum* 1 (PL 176.11BC); *Sacr.* 1.12.6 (PL 176.354AB; Deferrari, 194).

57 *Sapere,* from which the noun *sapientia* is derived, means to taste, have good taste, be discreet or wise. This connection was often noted by medieval authors; see, for example, the citations in Henri de Lubac, *Medieval Exegesis,* vol. 2: *The Four Senses of Scripture,* tr. E. M. Macierowski (Grand Rapids: Eerdmans, 2000), 397–98.

58 In *Sacr.* 1.2.12–13 (PL 176.211AB; Deferrari, 34–35), having just said that the immensity of created things bears the form of power, their beauty the form of wisdom, and their utility the form of goodness, Hugh adds that the rational creature has a more perfect likeness of these three in its knowing, choosing and power. The primary and principle mirror of the invisible God is his image and likeness, which is near and kin to God (*Sacr.* 1.3.6 [PL 176.219A; Deferrari, 43)]). Humans, therefore recognize their invisible God, when they understand that they are made in his image (*Sacr.* 1.3.21 [PL 176.225BC; Deferrari, 50–51]).

59 In 17.4–5, Hugh may be drawing on the argument of St Anselm's *Monologion* 4–6, ed. Schmidt, *Obras completas de San Anelmo* (Madrid: Biblioteca de Autores Cristianos, 1952) 1:201–9.

60   Cf. *Didasc.* 1.6 (Taylor, 52–54; Buttimer, 12.4–13.4).
61   Hugh often plays on the words *affectus* and *effectus*; e.g., *Adnot. in Pent.* 7 (PL 175.47B) *Orat. dom.* 10 (PL 175.782B), *Arrha* (*Oeuvre* 1, 248.350; PL 176.959C), *Potestate*, where he adds *respectus* (PL 176.789C), *Sacr.* 1.3.11 (PL 176.291D-292A; Deferrari, 45), where he distinguishes in human beings *appetitus justi* and *appetitus commodi* and their respective *effectus* that, unlike those in the natural world, are not always attained, because their attainment depends on human choice. *Misc.* 1.64 (PL 177.504D-505A) tersely distinguishes *affectus*, *defectus* and *effectus*. These three would not exist apart from the providence of God. Hugh immediately goes on to say that another triad —magnitude, beauty and utility— in creation testify to the power, wisdom and kindness of God.
62   Boethius, *Con. phil.* 3, prosa 12 (Loeb 74.286.15–288.24).
63   On the oneness of God, see *Adnot. in Pent.* 4 (PL 175.33B); *Sacr.* 1.1.1 (PL 176.187AB; Deferrari 7–8); *Sacr.* 1.3.9 (PL 176.220A; Deferrari, 44); *Sacr.* 1.10.4 (PL 176.333B; Deferrari, 171); *Misc.* 1.185 (PL 177.581BC).
64   For the kinds of unity discussed in this and the next paragraph, see *In Eccl.* 16 (PL 175.233B); *In hier. cael.* 7 (PL 175.1070C); *Sent. div.* 1 (Piazzoni, 930.81–88); *Sent. div.* (Piazzoni 951.119–952.140); *Sacr.* 1.3.12 (PL 176.220BD; Deferrari, 45); *Sacr.* 1.6.37 (PL 176.285D-286B; Deferrari, 119); *Sacr.* 2.1.3 (PL 176.375AB; Deferrari, 209); *Sacr.* 2.1.11 (PL 176.408C-409A; Deferrari, 245–46); Achard of St Victor, "On the Unity of God," 1.1–4 (ed. Martineau, 71–72; tr. Feiss, 379–81).
65   Cf. *Sacr.* 1.3.15 (PL 176.221C; Deferrari, 46).
66   *Sacr.* 1.3.17 (PL 176.223D-224A; Deferrari, 49); *Sacr.* 2.1.13 (PL 176.413A-416A; Deferrari, 250–53): Christ's risen humanity is in heaven; by his divinity he is everywhere; *Misc.* 1.118 (PL 177.543D-544C).
67   *unus*: As Poirel points out, *De tribus diebus*, 247–48, the antecedent of these two occurrences of the masculine "one" is not clear. He notes that Licarro, translates "one (same) reality" and Van Zwieten has "one (same) faculty." Poirel himself suggests that one supply *animus* or *spiritus* or interpet *unus* as "*one person*," the spiritual dimension of a human being.
68   Cf. Ps 32:11.
69   Hugh uses this expression in a number of contexts: *Sacr.* 1.1.2 (PL 176.187C; Deferrari, 8): regarding the creation of the matter of physical things; *Sacr.* 1.6.12 (PL 176.270D; Deferrari, 102): regarding the knowledge infused into Adam at his creation; *Sacr.* 2.1.6 (PL 176.384A; Deferrari, 219): regarding the divine knowledge the soul of Christ received at the Incarnation; *Didasc.* 2.1 (Buttimer, 23.12): thus divine knowledge embraces past, present, and future.
70   Elsewhere, Hugh discusses the limitations of the bodily eye, contrasting it with the spiritual eye. See *Vanitate* 1 (PL 176.704BC).
71   See *Potestate* (PL 176.840CD); *Sent. div.* (Piazzoni, 938.94–7); *Sacr.* 1.1.9 (PL 176.210B; Deferrari, 33); Achard of St Victor, "On the Unity of God," 2.3 (tr. Feiss, 440).
72   *Sent. div.* 3 (Piazzoni, 952.151–62): *mens, intelligentia, gaudium* (mind, understanding and joy).
73   Here for the first time Hugh appropriates an essential attribute, wisdom, to one person of the Trinity, the Son.
74   Here Hugh uses *tria* (neuter plural); it would have been more consistent with his own practice and argument to have used *tres* (masculine plural).
75   *unum* is neuter; *unus* is masculine.
76   *pinsendi*: This rather unusual verb means to beat, pound, crush. As Poirel points out, *De tribus diebus*, *248-*249, earlier editors, including Licarro, have corrected it to *pingendi* ("of painting"), a reading found in some manuscripts. *Didasc.*1.9 (see reference in next note) encourages this when it lists "texendi, sculpendi, fundendi" among the arts which imitate nature. However, in *Didasc.* 3.2 (Taylor, 85; Buttimer, 51.6) Hugh uses "*molendi et pinsendi*" in relation to the culinary activities connected with hunting, and so Poirel chose to retain this reading.
77   On these useful skills (*artes mechanicae*), see *Didasc.* 1.9 (Taylor, 56; Buttimer, 17.16–17), *Didasc.* 2.20–27 (Taylor, 74–79; Buttimer, 39–44), and note 34 above.
78   Matt 3:17 = 2 Pet 1:17; cf. Mark 1:11; Luke 9:35; Matt 17:5.

79   *sola non tamen solitaria*: The same two adjectives are paired in *Sacr.* 1.3.31 (PL 176.232B; Deferrari, 59); cf. *Sacr.* 2.1.4 (PL 176.381B; Deferrari, 216); *Arrha* (Feiss and Sicard, 248.337–38; PL 176.959B).

80   "*Beatitudo*" means the condition of being happy, felicity. The word seems to have been coined by Cicero from the adjective "*beatus*," which means happy, fortunate, or blissful. In Christian Latin the terms came to have connotations of final bliss (e.g., "the blessed in heaven"). The adjective "*benedictus*," from *benedico*, to bless, is also rendered into English by "blessed."

81   Matt 3:17; cf. 2 Pet 1:17; Mark 1:11; Luke 9:35; Matt 17:5. This text is cited with reference to the Trinity in *Sacr.* 2.1.4 (PL 176.376C; Deferrari, 211).

82   Matt 3:17.

83   Matt 17:6.

84   Isa 9:5.

85   A very similar passage occurs in *Epitome* 1 (Baron, 190.92–98), where it is called the triple way of self-knowledge that the search for wisdom follows.

86   *Tolerare* means to sustain, bear or endure. I think that here it probably means to "outlast."

87   "*primo gradu*": This could be translated "at the first step," but that could suggest temporal succession, or, "the bottom rung of a ladder", which would not fit with the argument.

88   "*conversio*": Conversion or turning is an important idea of Neoplatonic thought. In Christian Platonism, beings go out from God through creation and return by conversion, that is, by contemplation. Here, then, the turning or conversion is intellectual contemplation, not moral change.

89   Most manuscripts have the plural "*revertentes*" which Poirel corrects to the singular "*revertens*."

90   *Verbo* 4, 4 (Baron, 72.180–82; PL 177.292C). Hugh's argument is that we have to reach God by traveling the way of cognition, from external things to rational creation, then to the Creator. But inevitably we will then follow the order of creation back to created realities, because we cannot remain long in the contemplation of God.

91   Human mutability and the limits it puts on contemplation are frequent themes in Hugh's writings; e.g. *Didasc.* 5.9 (Taylor, 133; Buttimer, 110.19–23); *In Eccl.* 12 (PL 175.104C); *Archa Noe* 2.11 (CCCM, 35.3–5; PL 176.636C); *Misc.* 1.8 (PL 177.483A); *Misc.* 1.81 (PL 177.517A); *Misc.* 2.19 (PL 177.599A).

92   The image of "eyes" is prominent in Hugh's writings: *Didasc.* 6.14 (Taylor, 154; Buttimer, 131–32.32); *Meditatione* (Baron, 56.158–59; PL 176.996); *In Eccl.* 7 (PL 175.163C); 10 (PL 175.173A, 182C); *Archa Noe* 2.14 (CCCM, 52.22–23; PL 176.545C); *Archa Noe* 4.9 (CCCM, 116.159–60); *Vanitate* 1 (PL 176.703C, 704 BC); *Sent. div.* 3 (Piazzoni, 949.38–39, 950.67–68); *Verbo* 4, 2 (Baron, 72.177–80; PL 176.292CD). Sometimes, as in *Misc.* 1.1 (PL 177.471BC; see note 19 above) and *Sacr.* 1.10.2 (PL 176.329C; Deferrari, 167), Hugh distinguishes the eye of the flesh, the eye of reason, and the eye of contemplation. The eye of reason was blurred by sin, and the eye of contemplation was blinded. *Doctrina* (teaching) and grace are means to restore their sight. In other passages Hugh distinguishes two eyes, usually the eye of the flesh and the eye of the heart (*cordis*) or mind (*mentis*). The eye of the heart is cleansed by training in virtue (*disciplina*) and instructed by teaching (*doctrina*). Stupid people walk in the dark and their eyes do not see what the eyes of the wise see.

93   This is the first mention of "the three days" which gave this work its title. Christ's humanity corresponds to the eye of the body, whereas his divinity refreshes the eye of the heart (*Misc.* 1.87 [PL 177.519D–520A]).

94   See 1 John 4:18. In *Septem donis* (Baron, 124.63–66), Hugh speaks of God coming first to arouse fear and finally to make one loving. In this passage, Hugh also refers to the divine Light. See *Libellus* 4 (CCCM, 140.53–143.98; PL 176 692C–693B); *Misc.* 1.75 (PL 177.510CD).

95   Ps 18:10.

96   1 Cor 13:8.

97   Ps 102:15.

98   Ps 114:2.

99   Ps 118:62; cf. Ps 53:8.

100 Jer 17:16.

[101] Job 42:16.
[102] Job 3:3–4.
[103] Ps 95:2.
[104] John 1:17.
[105] 1 Cor 1:24.
[106] John 8:56.
[107] Ps 95:2.
[108] John 16:12–13.
[109] Ps 95:2. A schema in the Ark treatise (*Libellus* 3 [CCCM, 132.20–133.22]; PL 176.689A, 136.103–10; PL 176.690B) distinguishes three states/eras of humanity: under the natural law, under the written law, and under grace.
[110] Hos 6:3.
[111] *Sacr.* 2.3.6–7 (PL 176.466BC; Deferrari, 308–9) explains that Christ's death was a real event and an example, that is, visible appearance (*species*), truly Christ's body (*veritas corporis*), and a power of spiritual grace. *In hier. cael.* 2 (PL 175.951D-952A) explains that Christ's death and resurrection are pattern or appearance (*figuram*), image, likeness, sacrament, and example, just as the Sacrament of the altar is both appearance and truth. Cf. *Misc.* 1.81 (PL 177.546C).
[112] *Eulogium* (PL 176.988C): "First, the Spouse (Christ) kills the concupiscence of the flesh through abstinence, then through purity of heart he wipes away the ignorance of the mind, finally, as though on the third day, coming to converse, he fires the soul with desire for him."
[113] The second volume of this series, devoted to Victorine discussions of love, will show how Richard of St Victor, *On the Four Degrees of Violent Love*, and Achard of St Victor, *Sermon* 15, speak of the same ascent to contemplation and return. However, where Hugh says only that one comes from contemplation "revivified through the desire of divine love," Richard and Achard say that one leaves contemplation filled with loving compassion for others, and so follows the path traveled by the Son of God who became incarnate out of compassion for fallen humanity.

HUGH OF ST VICTOR

SENTENCES ON DIVINITY

INTRODUCTION BY DALE M. COULTER
TRANSLATION BY CHRISTOPHER P. EVANS*

* Fr. Hugh Feiss, OSB, produced the notes and English translations for Lawrence's opening letter and the second part on the primordial causes. Christopher P. Evans produced the rest of the notes and translations. This work was profited by initial drafts produced by Dale Coulter and Boyd Taylor Coolman and editorial help from Frans Van Liere.

INTRODUCTION

The *reportatio* Lawrence of Durham sent to Maurice of Rievaulx when the latter was abbot of Rievaulx gives insight into the teaching of Hugh during the latter half of the 1120s. The title of the work stems from Lawrence's opening letter to Maurice in which he relates that he was asked to record Hugh's "opinions on divinity" (*sententiae de divinitate*). In the letter Lawrence describes how his fellow students took him to Hugh with their request that he record Hugh's lectures. Evidently, Hugh was so enthusiastic about the request that he pledged his own support by way of checking the notes to ensure that Lawrence had recorded everything correctly. With such support at hand, Lawrence took on the task of being the "crafter" (*artifex*) of Hugh's thoughts, setting them down in a rather straightforward manner rather than with polished Latin prose.

While it would take Hugh at least another decade to put his theological "opinions" into the final form of his magnum opus, *On the Sacraments of the Christian Faith*, the structure of this program is already visible in the *Sentences*. The *reportatio* follows closely the first three books of the first part of *On the Sacraments*, breaking off with a brief sketch of Hugh's thoughts on the triune nature. In addition, Hugh outlines his larger program in the prologue and provides valuable information that serves as a preliminary guide to the more expansive *On the Sacraments*. For these reasons, the *Sentences* stands as an important witness to Hugh's vision, even though through the hand of another.

The beginning of the prologue establishes the primary purpose of Hugh's project as aiding the rational soul to know what is genuinely good through knowledge of God and knowledge of self. As Hugh states, "whoever achieves these two, namely to know oneself and his God, that person is perfect."[1] System building serves the journey toward the supreme good by helping rational beings, who naturally desire to know the true good, orient themselves to what is truly good. Hugh's early lectures function as a guide to aid persons in their quest to satisfy their desire for knowledge of God.

---

[1]   *Sent. div.*, Prologue.

These concerns about how humans come to know themselves and God are also apparent in the opening chapter of the *Didascalicon*'s first book in which Hugh describes the purpose of the liberal arts in terms of the acquisition of divine Wisdom in the service of self knowledge and restoration.[2] Whereas the *Didascalicon* sets forth a program of reading and meditation necessary to return to Wisdom and thereby restore "our nature's integrity," the *Sentences* extends this program through a grand historical narrative that supplies a framework for knowing God and the self. When one considers that *On the Three Days* involves reading the "book of nature" correctly so that knowledge of the creation leads to knowledge of God, then the full breadth of Hugh's emphasis on the knowing process begins to emerge. Taken together, these works suggest that in the 1120s concerns about how one acquires genuine knowledge of God and the self were important features of Hugh's agenda.

Behind Hugh's pedagogical strategies resides a basic paradigm. Hugh sketches this paradigm at the beginning of the section on the Trinity where he considers "how humans have finally come to know [God]."[3] He suggests that rational beings gain knowledge of God in four ways, which he subdivides in terms of the sources, foci, and modes of knowledge. For convenience, these may be placed in a chart:

	Internal (focus)	External (focus)
Nature (source)	Reason (eye of the mind) (mode)	Creation (mode)
Grace (source)	Inspiration (mode)	Teaching (mode)

Within prelapsarian humanity, all four modes of knowledge worked together to form a coherent picture of the world and of God. The operation of divine grace accentuated the modes of nature to allow the individual to form a coherent vision of life, what Hugh would later call the "eye of contemplation."[4] In the post-lapsarian context, however, sin's debilitating effects on nature created a need for the remedial interven-

---

[2]   *Didasc.* 1.1 (Buttimer, 4–6; Taylor, 46–47).
[3]   *Sent. div.*, Part Three.
[4]   See Hugh of St Victor, *Misc.* 1.1 (PL 177.469C-77B) and *Sacr.* 1.10.2 (PL 176.329C-330A; Deferrari, 167 in which Hugh discusses the three "eyes." See also Patrice Sicard, *Diagrammes médiévaux et exégèse visuelle: Le Libellus de formatione arche de Hugues de Saint-Victor*, Bibliotheca Victorina IV (Paris-Turnhout: Brepols, 1993) 187–92.

tion of grace through the incarnation. One of the most basic dimensions of restoration is a recovered harmony among the four modes, and Hugh envisions this restoration as occurring in and through the hermeneutical process itself as grace enables humans slowly to learn afresh the art of interpretation.

Hugh's basic paradigm informs the multiple divisions at various points in the work. For example, he divides salvation history into two periods of time: (1) the beginning of the world until Christ; (2) Christ until the end of the world. These two periods of time also correspond to three states (*status*) of human existence that Hugh identifies as the natural law, the written law, and grace. The first two states fall under the initial period of salvation history in which God allowed humans first to use their reason to bring about restoration (natural law) and then began to teach them externally (the written law). The divisions into different states reflect Hugh's basic paradigm for the acquisition of knowledge of self and God. As he states, "This period is called the time of the natural law, because at that time man was aided neither through the internal inspiration of grace nor through the external teaching of the law, but all men were left only with the natural reason."[5] Hugh envisions history unfolding according to a divine pedagogy in which God sought to work within given structures of human existence.

Not only do Hugh's concerns about knowledge of God and self inform the divisions and subdivisions of salvation history, they also dictate that his starting point is the visible creation rather than the invisible Creator.[6] This creates a striking contrast to his contemporaries and successors, most of whom begin with God after prolegomena.[7] At the end of the prologue, Hugh anticipates an objection to his approach, noting that since God is higher in dignity than creation, it would seem that God should be the opening topic in the structural order of the treatise. Hugh responds,

---

5   *Sent. div.*, Prologue.
6   Numerous scholars have pointed this out with respect to Hugh's method in *On the Sacraments of the Christian Faith*. See Marcia Colish, *Peter Lombard*, vol. 1 (Leiden: Brill, 1994) 57 and also fn 51, in which Colish confirms the judgment of older scholarship that Hugh's structure corresponds to how humans come to knowledge of God, as well as the citations she provides.
7   This would include the sentence collections of Peter Abelard from the 1130s, Otto of Lucca's *Summa Sententiarum*, and Peter Lombard's *Sentences*.

the Creator is indeed prior to the creatures in dignity but not in knowledge. After all a rational creature first forms its mind in the knowledge of visible and sensible things, from which afterwards it raises itself to a knowledge of higher things, that is, invisible things. About this the Apostle says: "For the invisible things of him, from the creation of the world, are clearly seen, being understood by the things that are made" (Rom 1:20). Therefore, because the knowledge of created things provides a path to the knowledge of the Creator, it seems proper for us to start with the creation of the world, so that the following discussion on the Creator may thus be established in an easier and more intelligible way.[8]

Hugh's structure reflects the emphasis on the processes of human knowing, and, in particular, on the modes by which humans come to know God. In an important sense, Hugh seems to intend the *Sentences* to be a form of external teaching that itself is a manifestation of grace for his students. The treatise is *doctrina*, teaching as an external aid on the journey to read the book of creation and the book of scripture correctly.[9]

The contents of the *Sentences* unfold in connection to Hugh's agenda. Beyond Hugh's treatment of prolegomena to his larger project, what the reader receives in the remainder of the *reportatio* is an analysis of the work of creation and how this analysis can lead to knowledge of God and the self. In the strict sense, an analysis of creation concerns "the world and all its elements."[10] However, Hugh indicates that there are several subsidiary issues that must be addressed within the doctrine of creation as he understands it. These are the primordial causes of creation and the Triune God as the origin of all causality. While Hugh ultimately planned to include discussions of providence as well as the creation of angels and humans in his analysis of creation, the *reportatio* concludes with the Trinity. These topics would later appear in *On the Sacraments* as parts 4–6 of the first book.

An outline of the contents of the *Sentences* reveals how the structure follows this outline:

> Prologue: prolegomena related to knowledge of God and self
> Creation of the World: issues in initial creation and the six days

---

8   *Sent. div.*, Prologue.
9   *Doctrina* ("teaching") is the second mode of knowledge that stems from grace according to Hugh.
10   *Sent. div.*, Prologue.

Primordial Causes: divine ideas and their origin in wisdom, power, and will
Holy Trinity: how knowledge of the Trinity comes through the four modes

The *Sentences on Divinity* provide an important witness in the early stages of Hugh's thought. As Hugh's attempt at *doctrina*, the *reportatio* reveals his aim to aid his students in the tasking of reading the books of creation and scripture correctly. The prologue offers a way of reading scripture through a method guided by a theological account of history. Hugh's analysis of creation argues that God created the world through a developmental process as part of a divine pedagogical strategy to aid humans in their quest to know the truth. These first two parts lead naturally into the third and fourth parts in which Hugh deals with the ideas in God and the triune nature. What emerges from the *Sentences* is a correspondence between the importance Hugh himself had placed on developing pedagogical strategies for his own students through texts like the *Didascalicon* and what he perceived as a divine pedagogy within creation itself. In this sense, Lawrence offered an apt description of his task. He was the "crafter" (*artifex*) of Hugh's vision, which was itself a reflection of the divine artist.

To his lord[1] and most dear friend, the monk Maurice, his Lawrence[2] sends unwavering good wishes in the Lord.

You asked me countless times, as I remember, to spend my time with Master Hugh of St Victor among others and even more than others and to follow most diligently his teaching on the divine word (*eloquio*).[3] Although you do not know him, you love him, and although he is away from you, you venerate him. Not unmindful of this very sound advice of a prudent man, as quickly as I was able I chose him as my principal and special teacher. With the greatest zeal I embraced his teaching, even as the uprightness of his life adorns his knowledge, and the holiness of this teacher illumines the teaching founded on the grace of his way of life. When he began to articulate his opinions on divinity (*sententias de divinitate*), I was asked by many of my associates to do a task that they assigned to me, which, if they had not been impeded by other activities, they might have performed much more easily. They asked to commit to writing and memory his opinions for the common benefit, theirs and mine. When they had reminded me of their request two or three times, and I did not agree, they finally took me (since I knew him better than they did) with them to Master Hugh with the same request. He enjoined this task of writing (*onus scribendi*) on us and pledged to faithfully check it (*fiduciam perficiendi*) in a timely manner. So I submitted, not because I trusted in my own strength or relied on the security of my own knowledge or the force of my eloquence, but rather because I was anxious to respond worthily to the requests of such great men to whom I should refuse nothing. Their just demand added strength to my feeble knowledge and their continued entreaty completely repulsed my fearful diffidence. So that there would be no occasion for accusations from those who rightly found fault or from those who were sharply critical out of envy, once a week I took my tablets to Master Hugh. Then, if in his judgment there was anything superfluous, it was cut out; if anything was left out, it was added; if anything was incorrectly stated, it was changed; if sometimes by chance something was well stated, it received the approval of the great man's authority. So let harmful criticism from those who oppose every good thing be silent—I beg, let it be silent—and if too much faint-heartedness blocks understanding or perverse subtlety prompts distorted understanding, let them ascribe this to their own fault (*vitio*) rather than make it the basis for accusations regarding the ignorance of the teacher or the negligence of the scribe. I do not pronounce myself the author of this work, but only in some way its fashioner (*artificem*).[4] It is as if another sowed some opinions as seeds, and we by our efforts brought together into a single body of discourse what another sowed. If there is anyone whom the dryness of our discourse displeases, I ask him to notice that we have preferred to work at a humble and simple exposition of deep and subtle theology than to be concerned about rhetorical niceties that give little understanding and refresh the ears rather than the mind.

Therefore, I have decided to direct this little work to you, the dearest friend to whom I owe all things. Although it is based on the authority of a man of such eminence as Hugh, nevertheless it will appear to have attained the highest peak of its authority when it has been confirmed by your scrutiny, which it awaits as a singular and supreme favor.

PROLOGUE

The desire to know the true good belongs to the soul and is naturally implanted into every soul. But although every rational soul naturally desires this, yet it is often deceived in discerning how it ought to desire the truth.[5] Indeed, to desire the truth incorrectly is to desire it with curiosity or cupidity or iniquity.[6]

The truth of curiosity is like someone wandering around the entire day through the streets and plazas and inquiring about the condition of the kingdom and the itinerary of the king and similar things, even though this information probably does not concern him at all nor does it give him any benefit. But he only does this because he is enslaved to his curiosity. The truth of cupidity is like a merchant seeking the truth about the sale of merchandise or of other things for sale. And he does this on account of his covetousness, so that he may export his merchandise to that place where it is sold at a higher price. But some benefit of whatever kind does result here because the man does make some profit here, although there is no profit at all in the truth of curiosity. The truth of iniquity occurs when someone seeks the truth about someone's route in order to ambush him, namely in order to rob or kill him and thus complete his iniquity. But if there are any other truths of this kind, then perhaps one will be able to apply them to these three or assess them based on these three.

The truth that is good is either the supreme good or not the supreme good. The truth that is good and not the supreme good is like the truth that is contained in philosophy or the liberal arts. This truth is indeed good and must be desired but not for its own sake but rather for the sake of the supreme good, which we approach more easily through that truth. To know oneself is also a path of truth, on which one arrives at the knowledge of the supreme good. Moreover, the truth that is the supreme good is of such a kind that everyone knows how to know his Creator. And this is that good that one must desire only for its own sake, and every man should strive after it, so that he may know this good and, once it is known, love it. Moreover, to know oneself is to know what sort of person one is so that one may correct oneself and what sort of person one ought to be so that one may desire this.[7] To know the Creator is to believe that God exists, that he is supreme, to attribute every good to him, and to subject oneself utterly to his command. And whoever achieves these two, namely to know oneself and his God, that person is perfect. And these two are taught in every divine scripture, both in the Old Testament and in the New Testament. Let us consider each of these, namely what is the divine scripture, why is it called a "testament," and why is one called "old" and the other "new".

This word "testament" is derived from human usage.[8] For this custom had grown among men that when someone who owned a certain estate wanted to appoint for himself an heir who would succeed him after his death, and after he had summoned several particular friends, that is, several men of authority, he wrote certain documents that specified who gave the estate and to whom he was giving it, and the witnesses who were present also signed it. And these documents were called a "testament," both because the person who had written it testified in it about what person he wished to have his estate, and because the witnesses were present there as subscribers[9] who sanctioned the same testament with their authority. Moreover, this testament was always unknown and hidden until the death of the testator,[10] and it did not have any validity while he was alive,[11] because as long as he was alive he could have changed it at will. But it became valid at his death and could not be made void afterwards.[12]

For a similar reason the old law is called a testament. For God wanted to appoint for himself someone as heir of his estates. And so, he chose a man not as a successor after his death but as a collaborator with the one who endures forever. And because the eternal beatitude cannot be perceived by sight and is very much removed from the thought of men, God did not offer it immediately as his first word, but he chose a certain nation as the possessor, namely the Jewish people, and promised that they would possess by an inherited right a certain part of his estate, that is, the promised land. He did this so that he might arouse desire in them and propose, as it were, a certain example through which they would both learn how to seek greater things and not despair of the greater promises when they saw that this was fulfilled just as it had been promised. And so, that this promise might remain unbroken, God wrote for them documents as witnesses of this pact, that is, he gave them the law through his servant Moses. These documents specified who was giving it, what was given, and to whom it was given. The pact was also ratified between the giver and those to whom it was given, namely this: *You shall not kill; you shall not commit adultery*, and other such things.[13] And the witnesses also signed it, namely Moses, Aaron, Abiu and the other fathers who were present when the law was given. And for this reason and according to this similitude those documents are called a testament. And because a testament is made valid through the death of the testator and yet it was impossible for this testator, that is, God, to die,[14] God commanded that the paschal lamb would be sacrificed in his place and that the testament, that is, the book of the law, would be sprinkled with the lamb's blood so that the promise might be found permanent and immutable.

For a similar reason the New Testament is also called a testament, in which God certainly provided heirs for himself, that is, the sons of the holy Church, and promised them his estate, that is, eternal beatitude. God made a testament, namely, the gospel, and the witnesses, that is, the apostles and holy fathers, signed it.[15] All the things of the new law are prefigured in the old law. For the promised land and the earthly Jerusalem, which were promised to the sons of Israel, prefigured the eternal fatherland and the heavenly Jerusalem, which was to be promised to the sons of the Church. Even the fathers of the Old Testament, namely Moses and the others, prefigured the fathers of the new law, that is, the apostles and the others. And just as that testament was made valid at the death of a lamb, so this testament was made valid through the death of the true paschal Lamb, that is, Jesus Christ. At his death the previously hidden testament was revealed because the seven seals, which John discussed in Revelation,[16] which were previously hidden and obscure, and from which the whole gospel is woven, were revealed and made clear through the death of Christ

And so, we know why each is called a testament, but we do not know why one is called old and the other new. The one is called old, either because the old was to be annulled by another succeeding it, or because it concerned earthly things that are transitory and perishable. Conversely, the other is called new, both because it was to be annulled by no other ‹testament› succeeding it and because it concerns eternal things that are always new and permanent.

One must note that each testament is divided into three groups. The Old Testament into Law, prophets, and Hagiographers. The New is divided into gospels, apostles, and fathers.[17]

The Law contains the five books of Moses, namely Genesis, Exodus, Leviticus, the Book of Numbers, and Deuteronomy. The books of the prophets contain eight volumes, namely the Book of Joshua, the Book of Judges, the Book of Samuel, the Book of Kings, Isaiah, Jeremiah, Ezekiel, and the book of the twelve prophets.

But one must note that this is based on a Hebrew reckoning. For the Latins call both the Book of Samuel and the Book of Kings "the Book of the Kings," which contains four volumes. The Hebrews call the first two volumes "the Book of Samuel," and they call the latter two volumes "the Book of the Kings," in which the times and deeds of the kings and their successors are especially described.

The books of the Hagiographers contain nine books, namely Job, the Psalms, the Parable of Solomon, Ecclesiastes, the Canticle of Canticles, the Book of Daniel, Paralipomenon, the Book of Esdras, and Esther.

At this point the question arises: Why are some of the prophets counted among the Hagiographers like Job, David, and Daniel; and why are some of the historical writings, which only referred to historical deeds without predicting the future, like the Book of Joshua, Judges, and the Kings, counted among the prophets? In order to answer this question one must consider that someone is called a prophet for three reasons: office, grace, or mission.[18]

They are called prophets according to office because they were chosen for this purpose, that when the people wanted something to be destroyed or when they ought to have begun a different activity, they might consult a divine response regarding whether this ought to be done or not. They were called prophets not because they predicted the future but because they reveal secret things; and they were called "prophets" by the common voice of the people. But others are prophets according to grace because they foresaw the future through divine inspiration even though they did not have the obligation of office to reveal it to the people. About this Isaiah says: *My secret to myself, my secret to myself.*[19] It is as if he says that if I understand something by divine grace, then I am keeping it to myself because I do not have an obligation of office to reveal it to you. But others were prophets according to mission because they were not prophets according to office nor did they previously have the grace of prophecy; but when God chose them for the sake of sending them to someone in order to announce some command, they received the spirit of prophecy. And one must know that some who were prophets according to office were prophets according to grace and others were not. Likewise, some who were prophets according to grace were prophets according to office and others were not. But all who were prophets according to mission were prophets according to grace.

And so, because "prophecy" is used in three ways, not only were the prophecies of those who were prophets according to grace reckoned among the prophetic books, but so also were the prophecies of those who were prophets according to office or mission, that is, those who were called prophets by the common voice of the people. The prophecies of others were reckoned among the Hagiographers. And it is known that hagiographers are called "sacred writers" or "writers of sacred things" based on the etymology of the word.

From this a question arises: Why are those authors called hagiographers rather than the others, given that based on the ‹above› interpretation this word ‹"hagiographer"› is applicable to all these ‹sacred› authors? In response to this one must say that some authors had a certain special character on account of which they utilized this word specifically for themselves. Moreover, because they did not have a precise word, they chose a word that is common to all ‹sacred› authors as though it were a proper name. For example, let us say that there were three men, one of them was a deacon, the second a subdeacon, and the third a layperson. If someone had asked them, "Who are you?" the first would reply, "I am a deacon," the second would reply, "I am a subdeacon," and the third would reply, "I am a man" or "I am a Christian." Hence, the third person assumed for himself a name that was common to the others as though it were a proper name.

It remains to enumerate the books of the New Testament that are divided into gospels, apostles, and fathers. The gospels contain the books of the four evangelists: the Books of Matthew, Mark, Luke, and John. The books of the apostles also contain four: the Epistles of Paul, the Canonical Epistles, Revelation, and the Acts of the Apostles. Moreover, the books of the fathers are not reckoned with a number. The fathers are those who do not add new things to the previous writings but explain obscure things, as do blessed Augustine, Gregory, Jerome, Bede and other sacred fathers.[20] And it is known that these three groups of the New Testament correspond to those three groups of the Old Testament: the gospels correspond to the Law, the apostles to the prophets, and the fathers to the Hagiographers.

And one must know that some books are apocryphal and others are not.[21] Apocryphal means the same as doubtful, and an apocryphal book is one whose author is dubious. Moreover, they are called apocryphal in two ways, either according to the first authority by which they were dictated or according to the second authority by which they are approved. For example, Job is apocryphal according to the first authority because it is not known who wrote it. Some say that Job wrote it, others say Samuel, and others say Moses. Yet other writings are apocryphal because the church fathers did not approve of them. Either it is not known who wrote them or it is, like the Book concerning the Infancy of the Savior, the Itinerary of Peter, and other such writings.[22] There are also other books that are enumerated in these six orders and are not written in the canon, like the Book of Maccabees, the Book of Judith, the Book of Tobias, and other such books.[23] However, all these books that are written in the canon have been discussed.

At this point the question arises why this writing is called "sacred" or "divine writing" more than some other writings, given that certain other writings, like the books of the philosophers, discuss divine and invisible things, virtues, and other celestial things[24] while those writings that we call "divine" often do not contain a discussion of divine things but of earthly things, likes wars, kings, and generations. But these books are called "divine," because they lead man to a perfect knowledge of divinity, namely so that he may know how to know himself and his Creator.[25] In these two the consummation of all knowledge consists.

One must note that divine scripture has three meanings: the historical, moral, which is also called tropological, and the allegorical, which is sometimes called anagogical.[26] Now history is the first meaning of a word with respect to things (res).[27] The word "history" is derived from the Greek, which is ἱστορέω, that is, "I see," because the things that happened and are visible are recorded specifically in history, although in the divine page some things are sometimes recorded as if they happened, even though they did not happen, so that one may examine the tropological or allegorical meaning in them. But there is this difference between tropological and allegorical meaning: In allegory one deed is understood through another deed, but in tropology what must be done, that is, what we ought to do, is understood through the deed. And tropology is called, as it were, "a word turned around ‹to us›,"[28] so that we may establish in ourselves what we hear in others. But allegory is twofold:[29] simple allegory and that allegory that is called anagogy. A simple allegory occurs when visible things signify other visible things, as when the bronze serpent that was lifted up in the desert signifies Christ being lifted up on the gibbet of the cross.[30] But when visible things signify invisible things, this allegory is what is called anagogy; for example, if the conversion of the good angels to their Creator is understood to have been signified through the creation of light, and the illumination is understood through conversion, or if the washing of all sin (vicia) in the water of baptism is understood through the submersion of the Egyptians in the Red Sea.[31] And this is called anagogy, as it were, "a leading up" (ana means "up," and gogo means "I lead"). Hence, "pedagogy" means "a leader of a child," and "isagoge" means "introductions." In this sense the anagogical meaning occurs when the intelligence leads us from these visible things to the things that are not seen.

Moreover one must note that in other books, that is, in the books of pagans, there are only these three: things, thoughts, and words. In those books the words signify the things through the mediation of thoughts. This is very different in the divine utterance. For in it not only do words signify thoughts and things, but the things themselves also signify other things.[32] For that reason it is clear that the knowledge of the liberal arts is very useful for understanding the divine scriptures. In fact, grammar concerns the utterance of words, dialectics concerns the meaning of words, but rhetoric concerns a combination of each. The quadrivium provides knowledge of things. And thus both the trivium and quadrivium serve divine utterance, where the understanding of both words and things is necessary, because there the meaning of each is treated.[33] And although these two are there, namely the meaning of words and the meaning of things, yet the meaning of things is far more subtle than the meaning of words. For words derive their meaning from human imposition, but things derive their meaning from the institution of God. And just as man indicates what he wants to man through words, so God reveals his will to man[34] through things. Likewise, words are either unequivocal or equivocal. If they are unequivocal, then they have one meaning; if equivocal, then they only have a few meanings, that is, two, three, or four meanings, in accordance to what is imposed by man. But this is very different with respect to things. For there will undoubtedly be as many different meanings for things as there are forms, figures, properties, and natures.

But although there are so many various multiplicities in things, yet one can easily discern them with this rule: the meaning of all things is determined either by external form or by internal nature.[35] It is said according to external form: *You will wash me, and I will be made whiter than snow.*[36] For according to its external form, that is, whiteness, snow means the soul. Indeed, whiteness designates two things: it admits no contagion and it retains in itself the appearance of luminosity. In this sense any rational soul ought to be clean from every contagion of sins and shine with the radiance of virtues.[37] Moreover, according to its internal nature, it is said in the Canticle: *Your hair is like a flock of goats.*[38] There is no similitude between hairs and goats according to the external form, but there is much similitude according to internal nature. For a goat feeds on high with an erected head, and it has very bright eyes according to physiologists.[39] Indeed, the head is the reason of the soul[40] and the hairs are rational thoughts, which raise themselves on high so that they may be refreshed there through desire, and gaze into the depths of divinity by the intellect. And so, although the meaning of things is extensive and manifold, yet one discerns it with these two rules that we have indicated. For that reason it is clear that the knowledge of the arts, namely mathematics and physics, is very efficacious for these rules. After all, mathematics deals with external forms, and physics deals with internal natures.[41]

We have first discussed these things for a better understanding of the divine scriptures; now let us consider what the subject matter is that is common to all these writings. There would be an easier access to the literal understanding through the aforementioned knowledge of things.

In this regard we must first mention this division: everything that exists either exists from the work of creation or from the work of restoration.[42] The work of creation is to make what did not exist or to form what was formless. The work of restoration is to reform what had been ruined. Likewise the work of creation is to create something new, the work of restoration is to renew what was created. Likewise, the work of creation is less worthy; the work of restoration is more worthy. For the work of creation is for service, because all things were created for the purpose of serving man who was standing upright. The work of restoration is for salvation, because it happened to erect man who was fallen down. Likewise, the work of creation was accomplished in six days, the work of restoration was accomplished in six ages,[43] so that the same number in both respects might indicate the perfection of both works. For six is a perfect number, because it is the first that consists of its own parts. For instance, half of it is three, a third part of it is two, and a sixth part of it is one, which make a total of six.[44] But although there is no difference in number, yet there is much diversity in the quantity of time. For, the former, that is, the work of creation, was completed in six days, but the latter, that is, the work of restoration, will be completed in six ages. For that reason it is clear that it was much more difficult to renew man when he sinned than to create man when he did not exist, just as Augustine says: "It is more difficult to justify one sinner than to create from nothing heaven, earth, and everything in the world."[45] And why is this so? He himself supplies the reason.[46] For when God created something that did not exist or formed something that was formless, the matter did not cooperate with him but only submitted and yielded to the will of its maker. But when God restores man who had been ruined, it is necessary for the will of man to cooperate with the grace of God in such a way that if man does not obey God then this work can not be brought to effect. For that reason it is clear that the work of restoration is far more worthy than the work of creation.

And, in order to briefly describe these two works, we say that the work of creation is the world with all its elements, but the work of restoration is the incarnation of the Word of God with all its sacraments,[47] both all the sacraments preceding that incarnation for its prefiguration and signification and all the sacraments following it for its confirmation and attestation.

All of these and others up to the coming of Christ were the sacraments that preceded the incarnation of the Word of God for its prefiguration—Adam was created; Eve was formed out of Adam's side; Abel offered a lamb ‹to the Lord›; Cain killed Abel; Noah built the ark, in which eight souls were saved while everyone else died in the flood; the land was made where mankind was separated; Abraham was led out of his land, that is, Ur of the Chaldees, into the land that God promised him; the sons of Israel descended into Egypt from where the Lord afterwards led them through Moses; later God gave the law to them in the desert, where they stayed for forty-two years; after all their enemies were submerged in the Red Sea, God led them to the promised land and went before them in a pillar of cloud during the day and in a pillar of fire at night. These are all the sacraments that followed the incarnation of Jesus Christ for its confirmation—After the resurrection and ascension of Christ the apostles were sent throughout the whole earth to preach the Word of God; the sacrament of baptism, the sacrament of the Body and Blood of the Lord, and the other sacraments were instituted, all of which are still observed in the Church. And we have first discussed the work of creation and the work of restoration so that the common subject matter of the divine scriptures may become manifest more easily. Because there are two works, as we have said, the work of creation is the subject matter of pagan books and the work of restoration is the subject matter of the divine scriptures; and all of the divine scriptures have this common subject matter.

But it is questioned: Is it not the case that at the beginning of Genesis Moses discussed the creation of the heaven and earth and other things that pertain to the work of creation? Yes indeed. But this was not the subject matter of his work, because he primarily intended to discuss the work of restoration, that is, the renewal of man. So that he might demonstrate more appropriately the renewal of man, he first attested to the fall; and to make the fall more apparent, he first demonstrated his condition. And so, Moses first discussed the work of creation, so that he might penetrate more appropriately into the work of restoration, which he intended to discuss.

We have already discussed the subject matter and distinguished it in three ways: sacraments of the incarnation, the sacraments preceding the incarnation since the beginning of the world, and the sacraments following the incarnation up to the end of the world. From now on we must consider these sacraments in order to explain completely the whole subject of the divine scriptures. And the first sacrament to be considered is the incarnation of Christ, which is the primary, greatest, and highest sacrament. I say "primary" not with respect to time but dignity, because it is, as it were, the sacrament of sacraments,[48] and all other sacraments, either before or after the incarnation, were instituted on account of it.

Let us now consider why this sacrament was instituted and why it was instituted at such a time and in such a way. Then we will discuss the remaining sacraments in order. If we accomplish all these things as we ought, then we will have completely finished our intention to explain the subject matter of the divine scriptures.

We say that the sacrament of the incarnation was necessary for the renewal of man. But, so that we may better understand the reason for the renewal, let us first consider the fall. Among the other creatures God created man, for the sake of whom God had created all things insofar as he was the more worthy and more excellent creature, namely because all other creatures were subjected to man, whereas man was subjected to God. Moreover, God created man out of two pure and clean substances: one was corporeal and the other incorporeal, that is, from a body clean from any corruption and a soul pure from any iniquity. Thus with regard to each part God constituted him clean from any vice and immune from any occasion of sin. He also gave him a free will, that is, a voluntary desire, so that whichever he willed, either the good or evil, he could desire and by his own will incline his mind to either one.

But, in spite of this, man abused his freedom by stooping to evil, withdrew himself from the service of God, and sold himself into the bond of sin after despising the command of his God.[49] In this incident a twofold offense is indicated: the first is that man brought upon God the loss of his service[50] because he withdrew his service from God; the second is that he despised the command of his Creator.[51] Wherefore one must seek a twofold remedy against the twofold illness. For man could not be reconciled to God otherwise, unless he restored his lost servant to God and then compensated his despised command with a worthy satisfaction. But he could not do this by himself. For what servant would he give back ‹to God› in place of the lost servant? Not himself! For he forsook ‹his position as› a servant who was just and immune from any vice, and he became polluted with the blemish of many sins. There was no other servant because he found no one except a sinner. Nor can some loss be worthily restored without a similar and greater compensation.[52] But how would he, who did not find a similar servant, give back ‹to God› a better servant? Likewise, he could not satisfy the contempt because it is first necessary to repay the debt and then satisfy the contempt. And so, because man could not manage on his own either to restore the loss or satisfy the contempt, the divine aid was necessary to discover some counsel for healing his infirmity.

And so, God had mercy on man and decided to assist human nature, which was weak on its own, by conferring his grace on it, and to accept a sacrifice from it and on its behalf.[53] In other words, just as man had seduced himself by sinning, so a man would restore man to his previous dignity with a worthy satisfaction. Thus, God by his mercy desired to give to man what man could repay to God by his justice. And so, God assumed our substance in order to be our sacrifice, but he refused our work in order to be a clean sacrifice. God was thus made man. Indeed, it was not sufficient for him to be only a man. If he were a pure man, however just and however holy and immune from any vice, then he would be able to restore the loss by giving back ‹to God› a similar servant, but he could not worthily recompense the long period of lost servitude. Therefore, it was necessary for him to be greater than man so that the dignity of the restored servant may be a worthy compensation for the service that was lost for such long time. But he could not be greater than man unless he was God in man. Therefore, the Son of God became incarnate and the God-Man was given to man. Therefore, that Christ was given to man was the mercy of God; but that Christ was given by man and for man was the justice of man.

But after this happened it still remained ‹for man› to satisfy the contempt, so that just as he appeased the wrath ‹of God› ‹by› restoring[54] the loss, so he would avoid punishment by making satisfaction for the contempt.[55] However, man the sinner could not make this satisfaction because however much punishment he accepted, he did it because his faults required it. And so it was necessary for a man, who owed no punishment, to assume such a punishment ‹for man the sinner›. However, no such person could be found except Christ because he had no preceding guilt nor owed any subsequent punishment.[56] Yet Christ still wanted to suffer for the sake of man so that when he assumed an unmerited punishment man would be liberated from a merited punishment, and when the God-Man paid ‹the debt› that he did not owe (about which it is written in the Psalm: *I paid that which I did not ravage*)[57] he made a worthy satisfaction to God because man refused to pay the debt that he owed.

Therefore, God was made man and appeased the wrath of God by restoring in himself the loss of service. In other words, ‹Christ› suffered an unmerited death thereby making satisfaction for contempt, and he liberated man from a merited punishment. In this way man was completely reconciled to God. Indeed, guilty man could not be liberated otherwise, unless the God-Man suffered for man.

But perhaps someone asks why that restoration did not occur through an angel, namely that an angel would become incarnate. He would thus be both man and angel, that is, man and greater than man. He would restore the loss of service to God through his righteousness, make satisfaction for the length of the lost service through his dignity, and satisfy the contempt through his own unmerited suffering. But we say that this could not duly happen in that way. For if God were the Creator and another were restorer, then indeed the love of man would be divided between the Creator and the restorer because, as it was said above, it is a greater benefit to renew than to create, and perhaps man would love the angel the restorer more than God the Creator because the angel had conferred more benefits on him. But God wants the whole heart of man and desires his whole love, just as it is written: *Love ‹the Lord your› God with all your heart,* etc.[58] Therefore, unity preceded in God who was both renewing and creating, so that there may be unity in the man who is loving and the whole love of man may be directed toward one object, that is, God. This is even perceived from the unity of the number, namely six, which was found both in the work of creation and in the work of restoration, as we also taught above. Therefore, the restoration of man could not have rightly occurred through anyone other than God, through whom the first creation of the same man had occurred.

We have now explained how the incarnation of Christ pertained to the restoration of man; now let us consider why it pleased the Son of God to become incarnate at such a time. Indeed, someone could question why God delayed his advent for so long and respond that if Christ were to come immediately at the first moment after the fall of man, then the unpunished who are afterwards damned would have been saved in the faith of Christ. Likewise, neither would the pagans have been divided into so many sects, as they are now, and very many other advantages would have proceeded from this, which are too long to enumerate at this time.

In response we say that the Son of God wanted to delay his advent for this reason, that it was proper that just as man transgressed by his own will, so he would return by his own will; and he who had withdrawn from God through fear would draw near to God again through humility. Hence, God willed that man would first test in himself whether he who had fallen by himself could return by himself. Therefore, God left man completely to himself. But after man was forsaken by God and left without a leader and guide, he began to go astray, to wander off to any kind of idol, and to sink down into anything more degenerate. And the more he ought to have corrected himself, the more prone he was to start plunging down into any kind of evil. This period is called the time of the natural law, because at that time man was aided neither through the internal inspiration of grace nor through the external teaching of the law, but all men were left only with the natural reason.[59]

It is known that "nature" is found in the divine utterance with three meanings.[60] Sometimes it is used for the first state of any thing, according to which it is said: "All things are good by nature."[61] Likewise, it is used for the remnants of truth and virtue that were corrupted in our first parent, although they were not totally destroyed.[62] Indeed, these two goods were given to the rational soul at first creation, namely knowledge of truth and love of goodness. And these were true goods of the soul against which two vices are opposed, namely ignorance and concupiscence. And so the knowledge of truth was corrupted at the sin of the first man and ignorance came upon ⟨him⟩; likewise, the love of goodness was corrupted and concupiscence pressed upon ⟨him⟩.[63] And yet this ⟨knowledge and love⟩ were not totally destroyed, because the soul always and naturally retains some memory of them in itself. And with regard to this meaning ⟨of nature⟩ the Apostle said: *For when the Gentiles, who do not have the law, naturally do those things that are of the law,* etc.[64] He said *naturally,* that is, from the remnants of truth and virtue that were corrupted in them through the opposing vices. In a third meaning, "nature" is used for a vice, namely for concupiscence or ignorance, according to which the Apostle says: *We are by nature sons of wrath.*[65]

Therefore, as we have said, this period is called the time of the natural law, namely when all men were left completely to themselves. But when man by himself could not conquer ignorance nor subdue concupiscence, ‹it was› as if God visited man and said the following: "You have sinned and promised satisfaction. Behold I have granted you a truce for so much time, and what have you accomplished?" But when man could not excuse his weakness, that is, when he understood that he could not rise again by himself, he asked for help and heedlessly promised that whatever the divine counsel would impose on him, he would accomplish it, saying: "There is no lack of someone to fulfill, but there is lacking someone to instruct."[66] And so the law was given to man as an aid, which would teach the knowledge of the truth and thereby expel the blindness of ignorance from men, saying: *Hear, O Israel: ‹the Lord› your God is one* etc.[67] But man could not be completely renewed in this way. Although man now had the knowledge of truth through the law, and although he fully learned in the law what he must do and what he must not do, yet the concupiscence that removed the love of truth in him was pressing upon him and dragged him to all kinds of evil. For when the law said: *You shall not kill; you shall not commit adultery,*[68] concupiscence said the reverse: "See the gold, kill! See the brides,[69] fornicate!" Indeed the more the law prohibits something, the more it habitually causes man to do it because of concupiscence. According to ‹the poet›:[70] "We strive after the forbidden,[71] and we always desire what we are denied."[72] And so the law did not extinguish the malice of man but increased it; and it does not restrain sin but makes the one who sins a transgressor.

Because neither the natural reason nor the written law could be sufficient for the restoration of man, a third period followed, that is, the time of grace, when God sent his Son so that man, who could not be saved by nature or by the law, might hasten back to him alone like a sick person to the doctor. He would both heal the injury of ignorance through the external instruction of preaching and totally expel the vice of concupiscence through the internal inspiration of grace.[73] And so the God-Man was given for man and guilty man was restored completely. This is why God wanted to delay the advent of his Son for such a long time.

Note there are three periods which we have distinguished, that is, men of natural law, men of written law, and men of grace.[74] The first men are called openly evil, the second fictitiously good, and the third truly good. This diversity of men is found not only in these three periods but also in each one of them. For there are always certain people who are prone to any kind of evil both with respect to their will and work; and these are openly evil. There are others who withhold only their hand and not their mind from perverse work; and these are fictitiously good. And there are others who do no wrong in either; and these are truly good.

We have now made clear what the subject matter of the divine scriptures is. Next we clearly demonstrated how the sacrament of the incarnation pertained to the restoration of man. And afterwards we plainly showed why the Son of God delayed his advent for such a long time. Now it remains to discuss that subject in succession. In order to make this evident, let us divide this subject of the whole world into two: that which occurred from the beginning until Christ and that which occurs from Christ until the end of the world.

Now that time that came before Christ is called the old age, and whoever lived right up to Christ was the old man.[75] I say "old" here on account of either part, that is, the soul and body, because ‹the old man› was subject to iniquity in his soul and to mortality in his body. But that time, that is, from Christ until the end of the world, is called the new age, and anyone living during this time is called the new man because at that time the soul both took off the old age of iniquity and put on the new age of righteousness, and later the liberated body will be renewed from mortality to immortality. And so, both the internal and external man are thus renewed after the old age of either man was put off.

But it is known that all of these advance in succession. For just as the soul in the old age of sin was first subjected to iniquity through guilt, afterward the body was subjected to mortality through punishment, so the whole man was corrupted both internally and externally. In the same order in the new age of grace the soul is first liberated from guilt when it puts on sanctity, and thus the internal man is made clean, which occurs in this life. And afterward the body will be liberated from the punishment of mortality when it will put on immortality, and thus the external man will made clean. This will happen fully in the future life when man will receive a double stole because at that time the whole man will be blessed both in the soul and in the body.

And because we have thus divided the whole world into two parts, let us first discuss in order the sacraments of the first part and then the remaining sacraments. But because we intend to discuss the restoration of man, we must first say something about the fall ‹because› it is not fully understood without first knowing something of the fall. Likewise, because we do not know the fall very well without first knowing man's status—that is, how man was created—that was fashioned with certain precepts, and by transgressing these precepts man fell, for that reason, I say, we must first consider the creation of man. Likewise, because the world and everything in the world was created for the sake of man, let us begin our discussion in the proper order with the creation of the world.

Therefore, the first chapter of our discussion will contain the creation of the world. But because there is no beginning of anything that reason and a legitimate cause do not precede, we must therefore discuss the primordial causes in the second part. In the third part we will discuss the Holy Trinity, namely God himself who is the font and origin of all causes. In the fourth part we will discuss the will of God, where we will discuss whether or not all things, both good and evil, happen by his will. And if evil happens by his will, then how is he who wills the existence of evil called the supreme good? However, if evil does not happen by his will, how then is he, against whose will something happens, called omnipotent? In the fifth part we will discuss the creation of angels. In the sixth part we will discuss the creation of man and his instruction through the ‹divine› commands. In the seventh part we will discuss the fall of man. In the eighth part we will discuss the restoration of man, namely with what counsel God decreed the restoration of man. In the ninth part we will discuss the institution of the sacraments. In the tenth part we will discuss faith, because there are three things necessary for salvation: faith, works, and the sacraments. None of these can be sufficient without the others or any two without the third because we can possess all of them together. In the eleventh part we will discuss the sacraments of the natural law. In the twelfth part we will discuss the sacraments of the written law up to Christ

Let us discuss each of these aforementioned parts in the same order beginning with the creation of the world. But perhaps someone questions why we begin our discuss with the creation of the world and not rather with the Creator himself, that is, God, so that just as God holds the first place in dignity of station, so he may also be the the first topic in the order of our discussion. In response to this we say that the Creator is indeed prior to the creatures in dignity but not in knowledge. After all a rational creature first forms its mind in the knowledge of visible and sensible things, from which afterwards it raises itself to a knowledge of higher things, that is, invisible things. About this the Apostle says: *For the invisible things of him, from the creation of the world, are clearly seen, being understood by the things that are made.*[76] Therefore, because the knowledge of created things provides a path to the knowledge of the Creator, it seems proper for us to start with the creation of the world, so that the following discussion on the Creator may thus be established in an easier and more intelligible way.

Part One

On the Creation of the World

Different people have offered different opinions about the creation of the world. Some say that God created the whole world from nothing and at once, ‹that is›, at the same time and moment, both complete in all its parts and perfect in forms exactly in the same state as it is now. But others say that God created it successively over the course of six days; to the things that were at first formless, God afterwards gave forms.

Those who hold the first opinion support it with these arguments and authorities. They say that those who ascribe succession to the works of God diminish the divine power, as if "God could not create all things at once,"[77] but only over a period of time as it happens in human works.[78] Likewise, they support the same with the authority of Genesis, where it says: *These are the generations of the heaven and earth on the day that God created the heaven and the earth and every plant of the field.*[79] From this it seems that all these things were created in one day, which is false according to others. Likewise, in the book of Wisdom it says: *He who lives forever created all things at once.*[80] And they thus strive to prove that all things were created at once. But the author could not describe at once what was created at once. And so, in order to entice a human mind more easily into believing, he recorded that these things were accomplished in the order that they would have had to be accomplished, if they had needed to be accomplished in that order. Thus, according to them this distinction of days does not express the accommodation of God's work but the necessity of the narration.[81]

But we can respond to their arguments and authorities in this way.[82] The statement that this ‹succession› diminishes the divine power is not true. For even though God is said to have created in this way, yet this does not deny that he could have created in another way. But the author was not considering what God could have done but what was more expedient for man, for the sake of whom everything else was created.[83] And so, God did not want to create the world at once but successively. He did not want to create it at once with form, but he first brought it from non-being into being and afterwards into a beautiful being.[84] He created it successively that man might put faith more easily in the divine operation. Because man understood that things were made thus, he saw how it was possible for it to happen according to reason.

Likewise, God created it successively that he might reveal the divine power when he brought things from non-being into being and that he might make his wisdom known when he brought them from being into beautiful being. And so, men might thus learn to fear God, whom they understood to be supremely powerful, whom nothing could resist, and supremely wise, from whom nothing could be hidden. And so, God built his construction in such a way that he might strike fear into all men.

Just as he first fashioned all things in a good state but not the highest state, namely by creating formless things from nothing, and afterward he brought formlessness of things into the highest state by bringing them into form and order, so God did not immediately place the rational creature, that is, men and angels, in the highest state but in a good state, so that there might be a place for virtues, free choice, and meriting, because in this state a rational creature could advance through virtues and by advancing reach the highest state, in which it would merit to be made secure and endure forever. And so, led by this plan, God first created the world formless and afterward he formed it so that a rational creature, instructed by this ‹plan›, might not believe that his state was immediately perfected, but might learn to advance from that state to the highest. Likewise, because God saw that man was going to sin and fall through sin, and lest man would believe that this was his only state and despair of the possibility of advancing to the better advanced state, he put before them the construction of the world as an exemplar, so that just as the divine arrangement brought them from their first formlessness to the highest beauty, so with the cooperation of divine grace man could be brought back from the formlessness of vices to the conformity of virtues. For these reasons, God did not create the world either at once or immediately with form. And in this there will not be any diminishing of the divine power but the greatest commendation of both his power and wisdom.

Moreover, ‹in response to› the statement that it is not fitting for God to create something imperfect, we say that what lacks nothing of what it properly has in such a state is not imperfect.[85] We therefore do not conclude that something is imperfect if it is lacking nothing of what is fitting for it to have in a particular state. Likewise, we respond to the authorities from which they draw support in this way: What does not remain in that state, but soon arrives at the perfect state should not be called "imperfect." In this sense the world was not imperfect at first because it did not remain in that formlessness but immediately the work of the Creator came to highest perfection.

Authors explain in diverse ways this verse, *He who lives forever created all things at once.*[86] "At once," that is, without intermission, namely that God did not rest from his work until he had completed everything: Either "at once" in its matter, or "at once," that is, all kinds of things, namely both visible and invisible.

Moreover, when Moses says: *on the day that God created the heaven and the earth,* etc.,[87] this stands for "day" as time, or if "day" should be interpreted in its proper meaning, then "to create" is understood here in matter alone not in a temporal ordering.

Therefore, it is clear that the world was perfected successively in six days, namely, it was first formless and afterward formed. But as to why God completed his work within a span of six days, this was already discussed above, namely, on account of the perfection of that number.

Likewise, because it is clear that that matter in the first creation was formless, the question arises whether it was entirely without any form or whether it is called "formless" with respect to that beauty that it was going to have afterwards.[88]

Some say that there was no form in it at all at that time. I do not see how this can be, because ‹even› they admit that that matter was a corporeal substance at that time, unless they prefer to say that at first God created some simple substance,[89] that is, something indivisible (*attomum*)[90] from which the whole construction of the world, increased and multiplied by God's working, grew up.[91] Perhaps we can explain this more easily through the following distinction.

Whatever is, as it was said, is therefore good because it is one in number.[92] Moreover, sometimes one is one in union, and sometimes is it is one in unity. One in union is what consists of diverse parts joined together to bring about one single thing. One in unity is what does not draw its essence from some joining of parts, like the simple atom. But one of this kind, which does not consists of parts, either pours itself out into many, such as the atom from which the construction of the world grew,[93] or does not pour itself out into other things, such as the spirit in the body of the substance that neither exists from other things nor pours itself into other things.

But yet between these, that is, spirits, there is some difference. For the created spirit is changed with diverse accidents, like anger, joy, fear, and other such things. But the Spirit-Creator remains unchangeable, and this is perhaps why it is said that the matter of the world was formless in the sense that no form preceded in it. The simple atom formed the matter of the world,[94] as we have said, and this seems to be what Augustine intended when he said: "The world is not greater in essence than a millet seed, nor is the whole seed larger than its half,"[95] as if the matter and essence of all these things were in the same, namely, the simple atom, just as Augustine himself also seems to hold to the first opinion, namely that all things are created at once.[96] But one must say that Augustine frequently offers the opinion of others rather than his own, just as he himself testifies.[97] Therefore, it is better to say that matter is called "formless" not because it lacked all form, but in comparison to that beauty that things now have.

But now let us see of what nature that formlessness was that preceded in the matter of the world, and in what manner, for what reason, and in what order the divine operation brought it from that formlessness to this beauty.

One must know that God first created from nothing four elements of so great a quantity and of so great a capacity as they are now,[98] although they were not arranged in this order, but were confused. The earth occupied its proper place that it now has, that is, the middle and lowest place, and already had certain channels in it, that is, future reservoirs of water. But the other three elements—that is, water, air, fire—were confused and mixed together, and they did not have their proper place or proper form. They were upon the face of the earth on every side,[99] so that that confusion extended from the earth up to the extremity of corporeal substance. And this was the formlessness of earthly matter in the first creation that afterwards was formed in the following way.

On the first day God separated the fourth element, that is, fire, from that confusion and put it in the place where the sun is now located.[100] At that time the sun was a fire of minimal glow and minimal luminosity, as if it were suppressed by the darkness of the surrounding confusion like sparks in ashes; as long as they are buried under a pile of ashes, they cannot shine. But after the ashes are spread out and dispersed, the fire fully reveals its luminosity. Thus the light of fire was first suppressed by the surrounding confusion. After the light was cleansed and purified in the following operation, the solar body was made from it in such a way that the whole element, that is, fire, transformed into the substance of the sun.[101] If someone should ask why, we say that this was not remarkable, just as the seat of fire, that is, heat, in man is located in the heart, although the heart is not in the highest part of the body but in the middle, from which it diffuses itself throughout all the parts of the body. And so, as we have said, this was the work on the first day, namely the creation of light in the middle of that globe. Two elements, that is, water and air, were still confused. Their confusion extended from the earth up to the extremity of that corporeal substance.

On the second day God created the firmament and placed the above fire in the middle of that confusion in such a way that it intersected and divided that confusion, and it enclosed one part of it within itself but drew the other part above itself.[102] And for that reason the authors said that the firmament was placed between waters and waters.[103] And they called that confusion of air and water "water" because it was somewhat moist and slippery. Moreover, it also derived its name from the more powerful element because the species of water was more apparent there than the species of air.

The question arises here: from what matter was the firmament made?[104] We say that from the watery substance there; after it was so solidified by the removal of heat and reduced to the strongest hardness, it became the most firm and solid body.

There are various opinions about this firmament.[105] Some say that the firmament is moved and driven with such a great force that within twenty-four hours it is moved around from point to point, that is, from the east to the west and back again into the east. They say that all the stars are fixed in this firmament except the seven ‹planets›,[106] and one is moved with the firmament. Moreover, they say that those seven planets are moved by the force of the firmament, some more quickly and some more slowly according to the nature of their position, that is, in proportion to how far they are from the force of the firmament. And some say that these planets advance along a straight path with the firmament but are overtaken by the velocity of the firmament. But others say that the planets are moved in the opposite direction, which is discussed very clearly in the prophecy.[107] But it seems to us that the firmament is immobile, while the whole company (*chorus*)[108] of stars is moved.[109] Some of these stars have an equal orbit, some have an unequal orbit. Those that have an equal orbit are, as it were, fixed. They are not fixed in the firmament as some think. But because they have a uniform and invariable orbit, they are called "fixed" in comparison to the lower stars, that is, the seven planets, which have an irregular and variable motion, as they change locations and points daily. Thus on the second day God created the firmament, which he placed between waters and waters, as we have said.

But on the third day God gathered together the waters under the firmament into one place,[110] so that the surface of the earth would become visible and was made bare.[111] The question arises here: what is that place into which the waters were gathered together? We say that it was a certain place in the middle of the earth, which is called the great abyss which is the font and origin of all waters. From it the other waters go out and run through their conduits,[112] that is, either through the higher hollows or through the channels, that is, the lower passages.[113] The question arises here: How can the water, which first filled all the space above the earth, be contained within one place in the earth? We say that at that time in that confusion those waters were tenuous, dispersed, and rarified.[114] Afterwards, condensed and compressed, they could be collected properly into one place. Similarly, when water under pressure from heat rises into the air as vapor and becomes a cloud, what occupied a small place in the cavity proper to it, later, diffused in the air and rarified, grows to a larger matter.[115] And so the work of the third day was the receding of all the waters into one place. Thus, when the waters had been received into their cavities, the space under the firmament which these two, water and air, had previously occupied, remained just for the air.

Thus in these three preceding days the four elements—that is, the matter of the world—were created formless and then they were distinguished from one another.[116] But in the remaining three days the adorned world was completed.[117]

On the first of these three days, that is, the fourth of six days, the bodies of stars, that is, the ornaments of fire, were constructed from the matter of water and air, as we have said.[118] They did not have from themselves heat or luster, but they are well purified and luminous bodies like glass or crystals which, when they reflect the rays of the sun, shine forth and appear clear to us and pour out on us a luster without heat. Similarly, when water in a cup meets a ray of the sun, it projects a certain luster without heat on the adjacent wall. This is the reason why there is luster and heat from the sun but only luster from the moon and other ‹stars›.

On the second of these three days, that is, the fifth of six days,[119] God adorned two elements, that is, air and water, with their animals, that is, air with the birds and water with the fish,[120] both of which were created out of the matter of water.[121] About this the question arises: Why were the animals of the air not created out of the matter of air, just as the animals of the water were made out of the matter of water? The reason is that the place of air and water was the same at first. And for that reason it is not surprising if, on account of this affinity between water and earth, the animals of each kind should be made out of the substance of another. Or, to put it differently, water is a more solid element than air, and for that reason it was more adapted for forming solid bodies.[122] Or what is better, because of the mystical sense different animals are said to proceed from the same matter ‹but are not allotted the same habitation›. Part of them remains at the bottom and part is raised on high. The waters signify people, hence many waters signify many people. Some of these people remain at the bottom through their desires for earthly things, and some are raised on high through the contemplation of celestial things. Part of them is of the elect, but part is of the reprobate.[123]

On the third of these three days, that is, the sixth of all the days, God created on the earth four-footed creatures and creeping things that are the only ornament on the earth that was lacking thus far.[124] Among these creatures man was also created, for the sake of whom all the other preceding works were done.

And in this way and in this order, as we have said, God completed his work in six days, at first by creating it from nothing, and then by disposing it in form.

Moreover, if the reason for this order should be sought, namely why God first created light, then the firmament, and then the other subsequent things, as we have said, the reason is clear. For it was fitting for God to work first on that element, that is, the first and highest. God first created light out of fire, but afterwards, because he wanted to render an orderly arrangement, not that whole confusion that still remained but some part of it, he immediately separated the lower part, which he intended to order and adorn, from the higher part, which he left in its confusion, by placing the firmament between them. After making that division, it was fitting for God to work on that part which he separated from the other part in order to form it. In this way he gathered the waters together in one place so that their former place would remain for the air. With these places divided in this way, it remained to adorn each ‹habitation› with its living things. In this way God first decorated the heaven with stars, then he decorated the air with birds and the waters with fish, and finally he decorated the earth with four-footed creatures and creeping things.

Likewise, with respect to the mystical sense, this order seems probable because it is in the invisible world, that is, in the soul, in the same way.[125] For it is fitting that the soul should first have a light in itself, namely so that it may know itself and learn how to discern between good and evil, so that it may desire the former and avoid the latter. Afterwards the firmament follows, namely so that it may strengthen itself in the good after it has rejected evil entirely. After this happens, it remains to gather the waters together into one place, that is, to enclose the carnal desires within measure, that is, under necessity lest in something they may exceed beyond what is necessary. Immediately following that the earth produces herbs and fruit-bearing trees because at that time the soul begins to bear fruit in the virtues of good works. After this it follows that as the heaven is adorned with stars, so the soul is decorated with the Holy Spirit's gifts, which are signified by the stars. After this happens, the air is clothed with birds and the water with fish. Through these two, that is, birds and fish, spiritual thoughts are understood, one part of which is raised to the contemplation of celestial things and another part is directed toward the right service of temporal goods. After all of this, it follows that the earth receives its animals, that is, the four-footed creatures and creeping things, by which the robust works of love are signified. These works ought to proceed in the right order from the aforementioned things. And in this way and through this mystery the aforementioned order in creation is proven. And God completed all these works in six days, as it was said previously, because the number six is perfect. Note, as Augustine says, that six is thus the perfect number and God thus chooses it in his work.[126] Indeed, the number six consists entirely of its parts.[127] For it is not superfluous so as to make the union of assembled parts excessive, nor is it diminished so as to make the connected parts less. Indeed every reprehensible work is shown to be reprehensible for these reasons, either because something is done there that should have not been done, which is signified by a superfluous number, and this is called "sin" in the old law, or because something is not done there that should have been done, which is known as a diminished number, and this is called a transgression because something is neglected there that should be done. And for that reason it is commanded in the law to offer a sacrifice for a transgression and a sacrifice for sin.[128]

Now *God rested on the seventh day from all his work that he had accomplished.*[129] *On the seventh day*, that is, the sabbath, which is interpreted as rest. One must know that many mysteries (*sacramentum multiplex*) of the sabbath are found in the sacred scriptures.[130] The first sabbath is that on which the Lord rested from his work. The second sabbath is that on which man rests from every servile work. The third sabbath is that on which man rests from every work of sin.[131] The fourth sabbath occurs when Christ rests entirely in the eternal beatitude with all his members. The first of these occurs in the beginning when it is said: *And God rested on the seventh day*.[132] Regarding the second the Law says: *Observe the sabbath*.[133] Regarding the third the prophet says: *Month after month, and sabbath after sabbath*.[134] Regarding the fourth it is said in the Psalm: *To these men I swore in my anger: if they will enter into my rest*.[135] And so because there are four sabbaths, the first and the last pertain to God, the two in the middle pertain to men. And two mysteries pertain to the two outer sabbaths: The second is a sacrament of the first and the third is a sacrament of the fourth. That man ceases on the seventh day from all his works,[136] at which he had toiled for six days, signifies that Christ ceased on the seventh day from all his works which he had completed in the preceding six days.[137] Moreover, that man in this life rests from perverse thoughts in the tranquility of a good mind signifies the rest that Christ the head will entirely have in eternal life together with his members. And about this it is said: *Sabbath after sabbath*,[138] that is, because Christ refused to consent to evil ‹in this life›, they will not feel evils in the future. And it is said *Month after month*:[139] the moon completes its course in a month, so man obtains the perfection of retribution in the future life because of the perfection of his work in this life. But the second of the four sabbaths is ‹also› a sign of the third. For as man keeps the sabbath on the seventh day, that is, on the Sabbath, he abstains from servile work that is both vile and laborious, so in the sabbath of this life, all of which extends within the number seven, man ought to abstain from the work of sins, in which there are both labor because it weighs on the conscience, and vileness because it pollutes nature.

And note that it does not say that God rested 'in' his work, but *God rested 'from' his work*.[140] When a man builds a house or bed, he does not only rest from his work after it is done, but he also rests in it, that is, in the house or on the bed, because man needed that work and the building itself adds something to the good of man. But after God has completed his work, he rests from it but not in it because the beatitude of God is not augmented at all by his works because he had absolutely no need for them when they did not exist

A question arises when it is said in this verse: *God rested from all his work*.[141] Why is it that the Truth says in the Gospel: *My Father is working until now, and I am working*?[142] But one must see that there are four works of God:[143] the work of creation, the work of disposition, the work of enlargement, and the work of administration. The work of creation is what was done in the beginning, so that what did not exist came into existence; and about this it is said: *In the beginning God created the heaven and the earth.*[144] The work of disposition is what was done in the six days, so that what existed came into a better existence; and about this it is said: *God rested on the seventh day from all his work that he had accomplished.*[145] The work of enlargement is completed in the six ages,[146] so that what was less becomes more; and about this it is said: *My Father is working until now* and so on.[147] The work of administration occurs when God maintains the enlarged existences in the good lest they fail. Unless the things of the world are guided by God's help, ⟨they will fail⟩. Just as they first came forth from nothing, so by being dissolute and continually being carried[148] into a lower state they would eventually return to nothing. And thus God rested on the seventh day from the work of disposition, but he continues daily his work of enlargement.

One must note that the Jews honor the seventh day, but we honor the eighth day. Thus their feast and joy are within the number seven because only temporal goods are promised to them and they only hope for the good of this present life, all of which extends within the number seven. But God does not promise us temporal goods but eternal goods, not the goods of this life but of the future. And thus it is demanded of us to observe not the seventh day but the eighth day, which follows right after the number seven. And notice that the eighth day is the same as the first because we were created in the beginning for the same beatitude that we will perceive at the end.

Let these discussions on the creation of the world suffice for now.

Part Two

On the Primordial Causes

It was logical to treat immediately the creation of humanity, for humanity was also made within those six days, and on account of them all other things were made. It was as though a home had been prepared for them with all the furnishings, and finally they would be brought in. However, let us see first the reason why humans were made; and to make this clearer, let us also precede that with a treatment of the primordial causes of the creation of the world. To understand better what a primordial cause is, let us first say what a cause is pure and simple.

A cause is that from which something proceeds, and an effect is what proceeds from a cause. According to this, one can say that whatever exists is either a cause or effect. But of these, some are only causes, others are effects and causes but in relation to different things, that is, causes of what follows, effects of what precedes.[149]

Those things that generate but are not generated are only causes. Those things that are generated but do not generate are only effects. Those things are causes and effects that both are generated and generate. The scriptures[150] also call those things that are only causes the "prime" (*prima*) and "supreme causes" (*causalissima*); those which are only effects are called "last." Those that are both are called "intermediate" (*media*). The more the intermediate ones approach the prime causes the more they can be called "greater causes" (*causaliora*), that is, causes of more effects. And thus those that hold the first place after the prime causes are the prime effects; those that hold the last place before the last effect are the last causes. Notice that in the universe which is so great and in the great multiplicity of things, all things cohere with each other by the firmest bond, so that there is no lack of connection there and absolutely no discord because whatever is in the universe is either the cause of another or the effect of the same.

Having posited these things about causes and effects together, from this point let us treat separately of causes. We will say that some causes are prime, others not; of those that are prime, some are prime within their kind (*genus*), others are universal prime causes. The prime cause in its kind is the one that no cause preceded in that genus. Thus, Adam was the prime cause of the human race, because no cause preceded him in that kind. However, he was not a universal prime cause, because he had preceding him another cause of his creation (*conditionis*).[151] Therefore, I call "universal prime causes" those from which all other things had their origin. They are from nothing else,[152] and I call these universal prime causes "primordial causes of all things." About them we need to see what they are, of what sort they are, and where they are. So, let us follow this proposal and first see what they are.

Note that all things have one existence in act and another in reason. Something is in act when it is complete in work and temporal arrangement. Something exists in reason when some artificer, in order not to approach his work heedlessly, before moving his hands to work, thinks ahead in his mind what it is he is going to do, what sort of thing, how great, and generally what kind of thing it is he is going to make. Then he goes to work in order to complete in his work what he had laid out in his mind. So being in reason precedes what is in the work, which is clear enough. Thus, suppose someone intends to fabricate a chest or a house. Before he sets to work, he draws in his mind the whole form of the thing that he is going to make.

It happens the same way in divine actions. Before God began to work in time, he acted like a skilled artisan. He conceived in eternity in his wisdom, which is coeternal with him, the forms of all creatures. These forms are coeternal with that wisdom and are called the "reasons" (*rationes*) of things in the divine mind, or "ideas," or "notions".[153] And these primordial forms of all things are what can be described as primordial causes, reasons of things established from eternity in the divine mind. These are called "causes" because from them other things proceed, and "primordial" because they are prime and universally prime, that is, they are causes in such a way that they had no causes because they are eternal.

Let us see how some say[154] that the primordial causes are causes below God and above every creature. Whence it seems that they are neither God nor any creatures, and so, since the primordial causes are something, there will be something that will be neither the Creator nor creatures, which cannot be. To this we reply that because the primordial causes are above every creature, they are not any created thing; and this is completely true because they are in the wisdom of God from eternity and are identical with it. This wisdom is the primordial cause of all things; that is, God Himself. But regarding how they are below God, let us consider that the primordial cause of all things is, as we said, the very wisdom of God, which foresees and arranges all things. When this wisdom humbles itself and stoops from the eminence of divinity to arrange and govern lesser things, that is, earthly things, it seems as if it is inferior to and beneath the divine nature. And so, although those forms in the mind of God that are called primordial causes are nothing else than God himself, they are still said to subsist below God.

We now know what the primordial causes are. It remains to say what kind of reality they are. They are such that they generate without handing on any thing (*sine traductione*),[155] and they produce results without motion, which does not happen in other causes. For example, when we say that the father is the cause of his son, we say that he generated him by handing something on (*per traductionem*). Likewise, when we call a man the cause of a house, we do this because he brought it about through some motion. It works the same way in other ‹causes› which are not prime causes. Let this suffice regarding what kind of reality they are. Now where they are must be addressed.[156]

We said above that the primordial causes are in the mind of God. However, that we may teach this more plainly and clearly, we posit three foundations, as it were, on which they subsist; that is, the will of God, his wisdom, and his power. The will of God is the prime cause of all things. All things originate in the will, are directed by wisdom, and are developed in power in working. And these same three are also found in any[157] human being, who first applies his mind so that he wills to do something; then[158] he plans out how he may do what he has already willed; finally through power he completes the work that he has already willed and planned. However, these are different in a human being and in God. In a human being, these three proceed successively, so that the will is first, then wisdom, and finally power. For a human being first wills to do something, then arranges it, and finally completes it. In God, however, these three are simultaneous; there is no before or after in God (*ibi*),[159] because as soon as God wills, he arranges, and at that very moment he is also able. And these three are not different in God, but the wisdom of God, which is God himself, is called by different names for different reasons. And because we have posited three foundations, as it were, of the primordial causes, let us consider each of them more thoroughly, beginning with wisdom, then power, and finally will.

Although it is one and simple, the wisdom of God is assigned different names for different reasons. It is called knowledge (*scientia*), foreknowledge, providence, arrangement (*dispositio*), and predestination. It has these five names for different reasons. For it is called knowledge of present things, foreknowledge of future things, providence of the things subject to it, arrangement of things to be done, predestination of those to be saved.[160]

But why is the wisdom of God called "knowledge" only when applied to present things, and how could it be from eternity since things were not from eternity? Therefore, before the things had existed it ought to have been called foreknowledge, that is, foresight of future things, rather than knowledge, that is, thought about present things. But one should remember what we said above, that all things have one being in act and another in reason. According to their being in reason, all things were from eternity in the mind of God, and in this regard present to God from eternity. Thus, according to one state of being the wisdom of God is really called knowledge of present things that were still future things according to the other state of being. So in reality, in regard to one state it is called knowledge of present things, which in regard to another state were still future. Therefore, other things are said to be both present and future with reference to different states. The same mental comprehension is called both knowledge and foreknowledge. Insofar as things are present, knowledge is said to be in God; insofar as things are future, foreknowledge is said to have been in him.

But in regard to foreknowledge one can ask: since God will have seen from eternity what was going to happen and how it would happen, will it be possible or impossible that the foreknowledge of God be made void, or that something happen other or otherwise than what God foresaw? The foreknowledge of God would be voided in two ways: either what God foresaw was going to happen did not happen, or its opposite happened. However, this is impossible. Therefore, all things happen by necessity. That is impossible. To this we say that those who argue thus are deceived in (*in*) the foreknowledge of God.[161] For foreknowledge is not the cause of things so that things foreseen happen out of necessity, nor are future things the cause of foreknowledge so that things that have changed induce mutability into foreknowledge. For if other things had had to happen or if things had had to happen otherwise, God would have foreseen from eternity that these things were going to happen otherwise. Therefore, foreknowledge cannot be changed or voided, for it so anticipates things from eternity that it foresees that they are going to occur in a certain way. They need to happen in that way even though that foreknowledge does not impose necessity on things.

This is what we say about providence. Providence is God's care through which he supplies to subjects what they ought to have. All things are subject to God, both good things and bad.[162] Nature is subject to him through creation, justice through will, wickedness through necessity. Thus God provides nature with governance, justice with glorification, wickedness with damnation, because eternal damnation is the wages of wickedness. As the Apostle said: "The wages of sin is death," then adding, "but the grace of God is eternal life."[163] But notice that he did not says that the wages of "justice" is eternal life, but rather he says, "the grace of God" is eternal life. For when sin receives the retribution of death, human work (that is, fault [*culpa*]) is rewarded. However, when glorification is rendered for justice, the gift of God (that is, justice) is rewarded. No human being's merit could suffice for this. Therefore, no one is just if God should choose to deal strictly with him; rather, he could justly damn him.[164]

The arrangement (*dispositio*) of God is twofold: God arranges for both his own and for those who are alien to him, that is, for the good and the wicked. His arrangement for his own is also twofold, that is, that they are and that they are as they are. He makes only a single arrangement for those who are alien to him, that is, not that they are, but that they are thus.[165] So, he arranges both the merit and the reward of the good, but for the wicked he arranges reward but not also merit.[166]

Predestination, however, is only concerning the elect. Nevertheless, authors sometimes use the word with a wider meaning so that it becomes the equivalent of "arrangement." Thus Ambrose said: "God predestined the hell of the impious," rather than the "fault" (*culpam*) of the impious.[167] God predestined what he was going to do. He did not predestine what he was not going to do, but only foresaw it.[168]

Now that we have spoken of wisdom, let us treat of power.[169] Here some will be found to have erred because they pronounced opinions in order to show off their brilliance rather than being solicitous to consider the truth or to imitate the authoritative teachings of the holy fathers. They assert that God's power is equal to his will[170] so that neither exceeds the other. Thus they say that whatever God can do, that he wishes to do. From that they conclude that whatever he wishes to do, that he does, and so they necessarily conclude that God can do nothing except what God does. We strongly reject this because it runs contrary to all reason to impose a limit or boundary on divine power, which is infinite. But that is what will happen if divine power is made commensurate with things that necessarily have a fixed limit.

Those who hold the above opinion, or rather error, try to prove that God cannot do anything other than what he does and cannot do otherwise or better than he does. They say that they prove through fore-knowledge that he cannot do something other, and through reason that he cannot do otherwise, and through goodness that he cannot do better.

Through foreknowledge they argue thus: if God did something other than what he does, he would do something other than what he foreknew. If he did something other than what he foreknew, he would do it contrary to his foreknowledge, which cannot happen. Therefore, he cannot do anything other than what he does. The objection was adequately answered above in the treatment of wisdom when we spoke of God's foreknowledge. Let us deal with the others.

Through reason they assert that God cannot do otherwise then he does. They say[171] that if there is a reason why he acts in this way, there is no reason why he should not act in this way. For reason does not relate equally to two opposites; both of them cannot occur according to reason. So if there is a reason for one of them to occur, there is also a reason why the other does not occur; contraries fit with contraries. However, if there is not a reason why God does not do something in this way, he is able not to act in this way; therefore, he cannot do otherwise.[172]

However, those who argue thus do not understand that one sort of reason is compelling (*cogens*) and another is permissive (*patiens*).[173] A compelling reason is one that is so related to two opposites that if one of them happens then according to reason something else (*aliud*) nec-essarily happens. However, if the other of the two happens, in no way is it in accord with reason. For example, to love one's neighbor or not: reason enjoins one of these two necessarily, but it necessarily rules out the other. This is called compelling reason. Permissive reason is so related to two alternatives that either of the two possibilities can occur according to the choice of the one acting. If one of them happens, it happens in accord with reason. If, however, the other of the two occurs, it does not happen against reason; for example, for me to sit or not to sit. If I sit, that happens well; if I do not sit, this too happens well be-cause there is no reason compelling one of the two to happen and the other not to happen. In this case, the whole reason is in the will of the doer. Similarly, for me to give you my cloak or not to give it—either can occur reasonably. And many others things happen in this manner. Therefore, a compelling reason is one by which something happens in accord with reason, which if it happened otherwise would be against reason. A permissive reason is one by which something happens with reason, though it would not be without reason for it to happen otherwise.

Since therefore compelling reason is one thing, permissive reason another, in God there is no compelling reason with respect to creation, but only a permissive reason. Indeed, whatever God does,[174] however he does it, he does it with reason. If he does not do it thus or so, that too happens with reason. Because all reason is located in his judgment, no reason can compel him to do this or not do this or to do it thus or otherwise, because whatever he does, in whatever way he does it, he acts in accord with reason. Whatever he does not do, in whatever way he does not do it, this also happens well and in accord with reason. Therefore what they say is false, namely that when God does something reason is the cause that he does it thus and if he did it otherwise it would be contrary to reason. Therefore, they are mistaken who say that God can do nothing otherwise than he does it.

Let us now see about how they try to prove through the goodness of God that God can do nothing better than what he does. For they say that if he can do something better than he does it and he does not will to do so, this would seem to be envy. However, in the highest there can be no envy, for as Plato said: "Envy is far removed from the best."[175] Since, then, God is supremely good, he does all good things in such a way that he could do nothing better than he does it. Likewise, if God is supremely good, then he loves the greater good more than the less good because the more something is good the more it is in harmony with the divine nature, which is all good. If God loves the greater good more than the less good, it is therefore irrational to abandon the greater good in order that he may do the lesser good. It is not in accord with reason, then, for God to make some creature less good when he could make it better, because the greater good is to make the thing better. If this is so, then God can make nothing better than he does, because he can do nothing against reason.

To them we answer that it is not envy if he could confer on the creature greater good but does not confer it. Nor does he act against reason if he could make it better and does not do so. For when God confers some good on a creature, all of what is conferred is totally from the grace of the one conferring and not as a result of the merit of the one on whom it is conferred. That God created the world and all the things of the world, that he ordered the things created, that he kept and conserved in good condition what he ordered—all this he does not because it was owed but solely from his kindness. Whatever God gives he gives from grace alone, and what he does not give he does not give from justice alone. That he gives is deserving of highest praise and that he does not give is not to be criticized, since the former he does only through mercy and not because it is deserved, and the latter he does not do, but out of justice and not out of envy. For example, if now I had twenty solidi and gave ten of them to a man to whom I owed nothing, I would not be seen as unjust although I did not give all. Indeed, thanks would be given me for what I did, since no merit preceded it. No injury was inflicted by what I did not do because there could not be any wrongdoing there.

From the things that have been said it is evident that they did not prove what they intended: through foreknowledge that God could not do something else; through reason that he could not do otherwise; through goodness that he could not do better. Therefore we say that divine power, which is indeed infinite and eternal, could do something other or otherwise or better than what it does. Augustine is a witness to this when he says: "Although God did all things in weight and measure and number, nevertheless his power is not bound by number."[176] But it would be bound if he could not do more things than he has done.

Those referred to above say that the universe (*universitas*) could be made better than it has been made because its nature is not incompatible with becoming better, but for the reasons set out earlier God could not make it better than he made it or is going to make it. It is like a voice that is audible although there is not anyone who can hear it, and like a field that can be cultivated even if there is no one who can cultivate it. Even if no animated thing exists the field can be cultivated and the voice can be heard.

For my part I would think that the contrary opinion should be chosen if I thought one of them should be embraced, that is, that God could have made the universe better although it could not have been made better. Perhaps the nature of the universe is not capable of more goodness than has been granted, but God, if he wanted, could have given it twice the capacity and thus doubled its goodness and made it doubly better, and doubled this again, and so on endlessly (*infiniter*). However, just as if time, if it were extended twice beyond where it began, and was doubled again, and so on endlessly, it could never equal eternity that is infinite (*infinita*), so there could be no end to divine power, which is infinite, in creating things or in conferring good things on them, however many times it was doubled. So while saying that the universe could not have been made better, one should strongly declare that God can make it better.

However, they cite a statement of Augustine as an objection: "God is said to be omnipotent not because he is capable of all things, but because he is capable of all things he wishes."[177] We interpret this as follows. When Augustine says, "not because he is capable of all things," he includes under "all" both good and bad things. However, God is capable only of good things. And he adds: "but because he is capable of all the things he wishes," by which he means that nothing can resist his will. Again Jerome says: "Although God is capable of all things, still he cannot make the incorrupt (*incorrupta*) from the corrupt (*de corrupta*)."[178] This has to be understood in a reasonable way. Whether we say this regarding corruption of the flesh or corruption of the mind, it seems to be false because God could restore corruption of the flesh to pristine virginity and return corruption of the mind to prior integrity. So, "God cannot make the incorrupt from the corrupt" is to be understood thus: he cannot make what has been corrupted incorrupt because what has happened cannot not happen. Jerome spoke to arouse fear. Because he was speaking to virgins to urge virginity very strongly, he also aimed to deter them from the opposite. For the same Jerome said in *On Hosea*: "The work of God and the work of a human being are different because a human being can make something corrupt (*corruptam*) from what is incorrupt, but God can make a virgin from a corrupt woman (*de corrupta*)."[179]

After we have spoken of the wisdom and power of God, it remains for us to treat his will also.[180] Concerning this too, many uncertainties have arisen.

The question arises: Since God is best and supremely good, how can some parts in what belongs to him (*in eius re*) be evil?[181] If evil things are there, either this occurs with God willing or with God unwilling. If willing, then the question is this: How is he said to be supremely good if his will is that evil things occur? However, if unwilling, what reason is there for calling him omnipotent if something happens against his will? Likewise, Scripture says: "Who can resist his will?"[182] Still, it seems that many resist his will. By allowing this he orders it to happen, but he also completely forbids those doing it from doing it. Likewise God does all that he wishes and he wishes all people to be saved,[183] but that does not really happen. Because of these things and others of this sort, what according to the authoritative scriptures is to be decided and held regarding the will of God?

According to the sacred authors, the will of God consists of two things: the good pleasure of God and the sign of his good pleasure. Sometimes God's will refers to his good pleasure; at other times his will refers to a sign of his good will. We call "signs" exterior things through which we recognize interior movements of the mind. Thus we say that noticeable pallor on someone's face is a sign of fear and blushing is a sign of embarrassment, because through these externals we say that the soul within is afraid or embarrassed. In the same way, when God gives us temporal prosperity, bodily health, affluence, peaceful times, and so forth, we say that all these are signs of God's benevolence toward us. However, when we see their contraries happen, we say these are signs of God's anger. But although both the good pleasure and the sign of the good pleasure of God are called the will of God, his good pleasure is properly called his will, and the sign of good pleasure is called his will improperly and figuratively, just as we are accustomed[184] through human usage to call signs of piety, "piety" and a sign of wrath, "wrath."

The will of God (*voluntas*), which refers to his good pleasure (*beneplacitum*), is one and simple because whatever he wills once he wills always; and what he does not will once he does not will ever, because his willing (*velle*) never becomes not-willing and vice versa.[185] However, the will, which refers to a sign of his good pleasure, is multiple and varied because there are many signs through which the good pleasure of God is pondered, whereby all of them are called willings (*voluntates*) of God, though figuratively. For example, there is the Psalm: "The works of God are excellent in all his willings."[186] However, although the signs of God's good pleasure are multiplied so much, nevertheless we distinguish their multiplicity with the following four-part division. The sign of God's good pleasure may be operation, permission, precept or prohibition. All the signs of God's good pleasure fall into these four. For when God does something, that is a sign that he wills it, for unless he willed it he would not do it. Likewise, when he permits something, it is a sign that he wills it, for if he did not will it he would not permit it. The same is true of precept and prohibition. He would command or prohibit nothing unless he wanted it to happen or not happen. Therefore, although we speak figuratively of these five wills of God, we nevertheless posit that they bespeak the good pleasure of God. There are four divisions of the sign of good pleasure, that is, operation, permission, precept and prohibition.

The good pleasure of God is the prime cause of all things in such a way that whatever happens in accord with it happens justly. It happens according to it, and whatever happens thus is just and so it is just because what is just happens according to the good pleasure of God.[187] If one asks why the good pleasure of God is just, it is not possible to give a cause because it is the first cause of all things and it has no prior causes. This good pleasure of God is such that whatever is in it comes to effect and whatever comes to effect is in it. He can in no way waver or change because neither can what pleases him not come to be, nor can anything that displeases him come to be.

Hence, since evil displeases him, how did it happen? To solve this, we posit four things: namely, good and evil, to be good and to be evil. Of these four, three are good but the fourth is not good. For good is good, and to be good is good, and to be evil is good, but evil is not good. Those three that are good, God assumes to himself;[188] the fourth, which is not good, he utterly repudiated. God wishes good and wishes good to be and wishes evil to be. But God does not in any way wish evil. So that this may be more easily understood, let us posit the following division: the good pleasure of God is sometimes directed to the thing and sometimes to the act of the thing.

Good pleasure is directed to a thing when a thing is such that it does not have in itself a way to please God; the good pleasure of God is directed to the act of a thing when some thing has in it what does not please God, but from it comes some good effect that does please God. Insofar as God's good pleasure is directed to the thing, we say that God wishes good and does not wish evil. Insofar as his good pleasure is directed to the act of the thing, we say that God wishes a certain evil to be and a certain good not to be because there is a particular evil from which, if it exists, although it itself is not good, nevertheless some good act can[189] come forth, and there is some good which, although it is good in itself, nevertheless, if it exists, no good act will come forth from it.

That is why in what concerns the act God wishes the former to be but not the latter. But let us look at the meaning of these statements, namely this: "God wishes good and does not wish evil," and whether this is different from "God wishes good to be and evil not to be." God wishes all good; all good pleases God because God is of such a nature that all good is in harmony with his will, which is supremely good. This is because similar things rejoice in similar things,[190] and just as all good is in harmony with the nature of God, so all evil is discordant to his nature because dissimilarity is hateful and contrary. Therefore, we say there is no difference between "God wishes the good and does not wish the evil" and "God loves the former, but not the latter." The former pleases him, but the latter does not. And as "I want fire" is different from "I wish fire to be" because "I want fire" is the same as "I love fire" and "I want to be warmed." But "I wish fire to be" is the same as "I wish that fire be" in the house so the heat may reach others although I do not care about the fire. Just as these are different, so "God wishes good" is different from "God wishes good to be," and "God does not wish evil" is different from "God does not wish evil to be."

Therefore we say that God wishes all good and he wishes no evil. Evil is nothing else than a lack[191] of good. In God the lack of good could not be fitting[192] since he is all-good and the supremely good. If in creatures the lack of some good is fitting, through this the universe appears more beautiful because in some part of some good a defect appears. Just as superior goods are judged more beautiful compared to inferior ones, so the least goods are set off more favorably when compared to evil. Just as the good of the whole is more beautiful because the good of a part is less, so it should be more beautiful because some part suffers a defect of good. For example, if all (*totus*) of some wall[193] is painted with a certain color that is best suited to it, it will seem less beautiful than if less good colors are sometimes mixed with the best colors. And so the whole painting (*pictura*) gleams more beautifully because by the artistry of the painter there is a lack of good color in some part of the painting. Although in the Creator the lack of no good is beautiful, nevertheless in creatures the lack of some good is beautiful. Therefore we have said that although God wishes good and does not wish evil, yet he sometimes wishes a particular evil to be and a particular good not to be. Therefore, when I say "God wishes good; he does not wish evil," I am referring to the Creator only in whom no good can be lacking. When I say "God wishes evil to be and good not to be," I am referring to creatures in which, as we said, sometimes it is good for there to be a lack of good. "God wishes this to be" and "God wishes this to be in creatures" are the same thing. Therefore, we say that God wishes good because good pleases him and is in harmony with his nature. He does not wish what[194] does not please him and is out of harmony with his nature. He wishes an evil to exist because its occurrence is useful to the universe; he wishes a good not to exist because its occurrence is not useful to the universe.

So that this may be easier to understand, let us use this division: good is one thing in itself, another thing in relation to something else. According to this, let us say that everything that is either is good in itself and for another, or it is good in itself and not for another, or it is good for another and not in itself, or it is not good in itself and not good for another. What is good in itself and for another is good and it is good for it to exist. What is good in itself and not for another is good, but it is not good that it exists. What is good for another and not in itself is not good, but it is good that it exists. What is not good in itself nor good for another is not good and it is not good that it exists.

Now let us look at these statements that state him to be—which are true and which are false.[195] They are these: "God wishes all good to be," "God wishes a particular good not to be," "God wishes good not to be," "God wishes this good not to be," and again, "God wishes all evil not to be," "God wishes a particular evil to be," "God wishes evil to be," "God wishes this evil to be." These affirmative statements are true without doubt: God wishes "a particular good to be," and "good to be," and "this good to be." Likewise, these negative statements are true: God wishes "a particular evil not to be," and "evil not to be," and "this evil not to be."

But it is necessary to look at universal statements of the following kind: "God wishes all good to be, or no evil to be." From these, there are statements—particular (*particulares*), indefinite, and even singular—that can easily be identified as contradictory to them: "God wishes all good to be." This seems to be false.[196] For if you say "God wishes all good to be," namely in creatures, that is, he wishes as much good to be in creatures as in the Creator, this is plainly false. Likewise, if you say, "God wishes all good to be," that is, he wishes no lack of any good in anything, this likewise is false. It was said above that from a defect in a part the whole appears more beautiful. If, however, you understand "God wishes all good to be," that is, a lack of any good is not good for that in which it is, this will be true, and in this sense the following will be false: "God wishes a particular good not to be," or "a particular evil to be," or "this good not to be," or "this evil to be." However, according to the earlier meanings, all these were true. Likewise this is false: "God wishes no evil to be, that is, he wishes no lack of good to be in anything." But "no evil is good for that in which it is" will be true in this sense. Particular, indefinite, and singular statements are easily judged according to these examples.

We have dealt with the good pleasure of God, and we have said that this good pleasure so harmonizes with the effects in things that whatever is in it comes to effect and vice versa, and that what does not come to effect is not in it and vice versa, because whatever is always in it is sometimes in act, and whatever is sometimes in act is always in it. Now it remains to speak about the signs of God's good pleasure, which we said above are four: operation, permission, precept, and prohibition.

Operation and permission of the prime effect are the prime signs of God's good pleasure. Whatever happens is either in his working or in his permitting. But these two signs work in different ways. For when God does (*operatur*) something, that operation is a sign that God wills it and that he wills it to be thus. When God permits something, this is a sign that God wills it to be—even if he does not will it (*illam*)—and because he wills it (*illud*) to be he permits it.[197] But because if he does not will it, he himself does not do it. Therefore we say that the good of operation is both good in itself and good for another. The good of permission is good for something that is good, although in itself it not good. And so we distinguish the good of operation and the good of permission. The operation of God is twofold: God does one thing by operating, and another by cooperating. He does by operating what he does by himself; he does by cooperating what he does with another. By acting he made, orders, and arranges the world and all things of the world, because he made them by himself. By cooperating he makes the merits of human beings and the virtues in them because he does these things with another. In this work human free choice is necessary with God cooperating.

Likewise, precept and prohibition are signs of God's good pleasure. However, they are different signs than the prior ones and function differently because the prior signs are general, but these are singular. Those pertain to all things, these only to the rational creature. Whatever is in the universe occurs either by the operation of God or his permission, but precept and prohibition pertain only to human beings. The universe is not capable of any precept or prohibition because it is not a rational creature. Likewise precept and prohibition are signs of God's good pleasure in ways that differ from the two previous signs, that is, operation and permission. Operation and permission are signs that God wishes or does not wish something to be, whether he wishes these things or not. Whatever God commands, that he wishes because God commands nothing that is not good and he wishes every good. He does not wish what he prohibits because he prohibits nothing except evil, and God wishes no evil. However, he does command something which, although he may wish it to be, he nevertheless does not wish it, yet he wishes it to be because its effect is beneficial (*commodus*) to creatures.[198]

Here a question arises: When God does not wish something to be, why does he command it? Likewise, when he wishes something to be, why does he forbid it? Regarding this one should know that God is the Creator of every single thing in such a way that he is also the originator (*auctor*) of the whole universe. It is therefore fitting that he so provides for the good of each without impeding the good of all. To those of whose creation he is the originator, he is bound to be the provider of good to the extent that he instructs without deceit those whom he created without vice (*vitio*),[199] and those he did not lead into vice in creating he does not lead into vice in instructing. It is clear, moreover, that the good of one individual among several is sometimes not the good of the universe. For often what involves detriment to the individual (*singularitas*) increases the good of the universe, because as we said above, sometimes[200] a defect in a part makes the beauty of the whole greater. God must so provide for the utility of each in such a way that it does not threaten the benefit of the whole.[201] It is clear that the good of the part sometimes is not the good of the whole. Therefore, God commands certain things that he nevertheless does not wish to be and he prohibits certain things that he wishes to be. He commands what is good for someone for whose utility he must provide, but nevertheless he does not wish it to exist because it is bad for the universe. Likewise he prohibits something because it is bad for some individual (*alicui singualaritati*), yet he wishes that it be because it is a good of the whole universe, the utility of which he should (*debet*) not impede.[202]

Let this suffice for the present regarding the will of God.

PART THREE

ON THE HOLY TRINITY, NAMELY ON GOD HIMSELF
WHO IS THE FONT AND ORIGIN OF ALL CAUSES

I have already specified what those three ‹divine attributes› are in which the primordial causes of all things subsist, that is, God's wisdom, power, and will; and I have discussed each ‹attribute› separately.

Now we must consider the fact that just as all things consist in these three, so these three have their being in one origin,[203] which is the supreme and first origin of all things. Moreover this origin is God in whom and from whom all things receive their being,[204] but he is from no one. With God's help I will say something about him. First let us consider why God has so tempered knowledge ‹of himself› on the part of humankind ‹that› he was neither completely hidden nor completely manifest.[205] Next let us consider how humans have finally come to know him.

And so in the beginning God desired to conceal ‹himself› in such a way that nevertheless he was not completely hidden, and he desired to reveal ‹himself› in such a way that nevertheless he was not completely manifest.[206] He did not want to be completely hidden so that both faith might be aided and unbelief might not be excused.[207] He did not want to be completely manifest so that both faith might have merit and un-belief might have a place. Indeed, if God had been completely manifest, then faith could not have been exercised because faith pertains to things not seen[208] "and it does not have merit when human reason provides experience to it."[209] Moreover, if there were no faith, then there would be no merit; and if there were no merit, then there would be no reward, and there would thus be no beatitude. And so merit must pre-cede so that there may be a reward. Consequently, faith will be neces-sary. Likewise, ‹if God were completely manifest› then unbelief would not have a place. If there were no place for unbelief, then there would be no place for free choice because then no one could not believe and thus all would believe by necessity. Therefore, free choice would be lost. Likewise, if God were completely hidden, then neither faith nor hope would have any place. In fact how would someone believe what he did not know at all? Likewise, ‹if God were completely hidden› then unbe-lief could be rightly excused. Of this the Apostle accuses men: *Because, although they had known God, they did not glorify him as God.*[210] From this it is clear that if they had not known God at all and could not know him, then by all means they would be excusable. And so God desired neither to be completely known nor completely unknown, but to be partly hidden and partly manifest, as we have said.

Therefore, let us consider how the knowledge of God could be discovered by men.[211] There are four ways through which a creature could know the Creator. Two are according to nature and two are according to grace; two are internal and two external. Reason and creation are according to nature; reason is internal and creation external. Inspiration (*aspiratio*) and teaching are according to grace; inspiration is internal and teaching external.[212] Indeed, reason, like a kind of mental eye, internally contemplated the truth that was revealed externally through the creation.[213] But because reason itself was constricted by sin, inspiration was joined inwardly to it for illumination, just as the scripture was joined externally to creation for demonstration. But ignorance came upon ‹the soul› and snatched away the knowledge of truth; concupiscence weighed upon ‹the soul› and snatched away the love for goodness.[214] And so whenever nature failed, grace drew near and nature was aided by grace. Therefore, inspiration and teaching were given to man; inspiration was joined inwardly to reason and teaching was joined externally to creation. By these two, upon their arrival, the eye of nature was both illuminated for knowledge and kindled for love. Indeed, these three, as if three witnesses, draw near to examine the judgment of reason—creation, teaching, and inspiration. Inspiration is the last witness because afterwards no one doubts.

The Apostle sufficiently explained with concise words these four ways together with the previous dispensation, namely because God wanted to be partly known and partly unknown. For when he said: *What is known of God,*[215] that is, what is knowable about God, he had sufficiently suggested that something is knowable about God and something is not knowable. And then he added: *is manifest in them.*[216] He did not say "is manifest to them" but *in them* because reason is natural in them, to which what is knowable about God is revealed naturally.[217] Afterwards he added: *For God has manifested it to them,*[218] namely either through interior inspiration or through exterior teaching. But when he added: *For the invisible things of him, from the creation of the world, are clearly seen, being understood by the things that are made,*[219] he explained the fourth way, which is according to creation.

And so because there are four ways, as we have said, through which the Creator could be revealed in creation, we must consider how and how much each one of these ‹ways› by itself comprehended about God, and how much all of them cooperating together ‹comprehended about God›. In other words, how much could reason by itself advance in the knowledge of God or how much could it advance with the aid of inspiration? Similarly how efficacious is creation by itself for demonstrating God or how efficacious is it for demonstrating with the aid of teaching?

Let us begin with reason, which is, as it were, the first eye with which the mind of man contemplates God.[220] We say that reason, through the light ‹of truth› naturally implanted in it, could first know that God exists, next that God is one, and afterwards that God is triune. Reason certainly could know these three things about God: God exists, God is one, and God is triune. Reason comprehended eternity and immeasurability in unity, immutability in eternity, simplicity in immeasurability, that is, eternity without time, immeasurability without quantity.[221] But in trinity it discovered the communion of unity, coevity of eternity, and the equality of immeasurability, and indeed the communion of unity without division, coevity of eternity without succession, and equality of immeasurability without diminution. In each there is whole in unity, full in immeasurability, and perfect in eternity.

Now let us consider how, whence, and what reason discovered about these things, namely, how it knew that God exists, how God is one, and how God is triune. There are two natures in man, one corporeal and the other incorporeal, that is, the body without and the rational mind within. As soon as the rational mind began to understand, it immediately began to discern what it was and what is was not because it could not be ignorant that it was something.[222] And so when it was looking at all these external ‹bodily parts›, it discerned that it was none of them, that is, it was neither the hand, nor foot, nor another bodily part in man, nor something outside of man, because none of these has the power of knowing, which is characteristic of the rational soul. Therefore, when the rational mind perceived that it is not anything corporeal, it understood that it is something incorporeal and invisible, namely something more excellent than any corporeal creation. Indeed, it is more like God than all other creatures[223] and it approaches closer to the knowledge of God. Moreover, just as a rational soul understood what it was, just as it also knew that it did not always exist because it did not always understand, and just as it began to understand, so also it began to exist.[224] Moreover, if it began to exist, then it received this from some source. Now it could not possess ‹being› from itself, because how would it confer being on itself when it did not exist? Therefore, ‹it received being› from another. Likewise, this other being had being either from another or not. If it were from another being, and this same being were from another, and it were also from another, then in this way the sequence would continue forever. Therefore, it is necessary for something to preexist that does not receive being from another. Yet this being will necessarily be eternal because if it began to exist, then it is necessary for it to receive its being from another and thus an inappropriate proposition would follow. And so it will be eternal. Moreover, they have given the proper name "God" to this eternal being. All things have being from God, but he is from no one. And in this way the rational mind, through the light ‹of truth› naturally implanted in it, perceived the existence of God.

But when the rational mind understands the existence of God it will conjecture whether there is one God or several, that is, whether all things are from one God, or each creature has its own creator.[225] But it is impossible for several gods to exist because then either the plurality will be superfluous or the individual will be imperfect, that is, either some one of all the gods will be superfluous or each one of the individual gods will be imperfect. But either one of these premises is inappropriate. For if one of them were perfect, namely because he was lacking nothing, then all the others would be superfluous. But if on the contrary none of them were superfluous then anyone of them would be imperfect. Yet the rational mind could in no way assent to this, so that it believed that some imperfection has a place in that supreme good from which all things have being. Hence, reason devoted itself naturally to this, so as to believe that there are not several gods but only one God who is absolutely perfect and supremely happy, the one origin of all things, from whom anything that exists receives being. And the rational mind thus avoided an inappropriate proposition both of superfluity and imperfection. And it thus discovered by itself that God exists and is one, but it did not comprehend this as completely as it did afterwards with the assistance of inspiration.

But because the word "one" is used in different ways, let us consider which of these usages is appropriate for God.[226] "One" is used with respect to a collection, like a herd in which there are several animals. Or "one" is used with respect to a composition like the body in which there are several members. Or "one" is used with respect to a similarity, like the voice of one and the voice of another because they are distinctly similar. Or "one" is used with respect to essence like the soul that lacks parts. Or "one" is used with respect to the deity, namely what is not changed by forms. And so even though "one" is used in these five ways, something is improperly called "one" in the first three ways, because none of them is one as a unity but only as a union. And for that reason they should be called "unity" rather than "one." Hence God is not called "one" according to any of these three ways, that is, neither with respect to a collection, nor a composition, nor a similarity, but God is one with respect to essence. And thus God is one in essence because he is one in deity as well. For just as God lacks every multiplication of a part, so he does not receive some variation of forms. This cannot be said about the soul. For although the soul does not admit to being composed of parts, yet it does admit mutability[227] of forms. For the soul is changed by different accidents like anger, joy, sadness, fear and other such things, all of which do not affect the divine essence.[228] God is thus one both in essence and in deity. Moreover, what is one in essence is truly one; and what is one in deity is supremely one. And so the Lord is both truly one and supremely one. And therefore the rational mind confesses that its God is one because he is perfect, and that God is truly one because he is so substantially, and that God is supremely one because he is so invariably.

Because we have explained how the rational soul knew by itself that God exists and how God is one, we must consider how it discovered that God is triune as well. In order to show this, Augustine demonstrated in his book *On the Trinity* that a certain trinity is found even in any of the most trifling things, so that he thus ascended to explain more easily the trinity of the Creator through the trinities of created things. But because it takes far too long, namely to discover the trinity in every ‹created› thing, let us return to the same likeness that we established earlier, that is, to the rational mind which is, as it were, the image and likeness of God, so that just as we knew through it that God exists and is one, so we may know through it that the same God is triune.[229]

First the rational soul considers itself and discovers a certain trinity in itself. For the soul discovers in itself a natural power that is called the "mind," that is, the power of understanding, which is naturally implanted in the soul. Intelligence, that is, knowledge itself, is born from this power of understanding. This intelligence is, as it were, a continuous action of natural power and it is called "the offspring of the mind"[230] because it is produced by the mind that precedes it. Thus a soul perceives that these two are in it, namely the mind and intelligence. And because the desire to know the truth is naturally implanted in the soul, therefore the soul of man is always involved in a question and is always driven by some doubts to seek knowledge of the truth. And when it obtains through its intelligence the knowledge of previously unknown truth, it proceeds for a time in joy because the mind in its intelligence is very pleased with itself that it attained the truth which it desired.

And thus the soul discovers these three things in itself: mind, intelligence, and joy, which are in it in such a way that they are not different from it. For intelligence is born from the mind. From each of the two, that is, from the mind and from the intelligence, joy proceeds. These three are certainly the same in essence, but they are distinguished by different properties.

Thus at first the inspection of the rational mind was directed toward itself, in which the first vestige of the trinity was found, and eventually, based on what was in itself, the rational mind began to investigate even what was above itself when it discovered the same trinity also in the Creator.[231] For it discovered that power, wisdom and joy were in God. If the soul of man has the natural power of understanding or discerning, then that divine essence, which is supremely wise, will have much more of the natural power of foreseeing and discerning anything. Moreover, if God is wise, then he is wise by wisdom.[232] And so, wisdom is in God. Moreover, if the soul has joy from its own wisdom however slight, then God rejoices much more within himself over his wisdom that is supreme and coeternal with him.

And thus these three are found in one, that is, power, wisdom, and love.[233] There is power, and wisdom from power, and love from power and wisdom. And a certain trinity draws near and unity does not withdraw. But, although these three are both in God and in the soul, yet they are in God and in the soul in different ways. For they are in the soul in such a way that the mind precedes in time, afterwards understanding arises from it, and finally joy proceeds from each of the two. But these are in God at once and from eternity, that is, power, wisdom born from power, and joy proceeding from each of the two. For just as God is from eternity, so he had wisdom from eternity and loved his own wisdom from eternity. And in this way his love is coeternal with his eternal one and with his coeternal wisdom. And it is not surprising if reason could discover this trinity by itself, because even the pagan philosophers, who have been led only by natural reason, perceived this same thing, as Plato did who said that there is a "νοεμα ταγον", and a soul of the world.

NOTES

LETTER OF LAWRENCE (pp. 111-112)

[1] *"Dominus,"* "lord" or "master," became a title for monks, which is still used in France (e.g., Dom Leclercq). This seems to be Lawrence's intent in using the word here.

[2] On the probable identity of Lawrence and Maurice (abbot of Rievaulx), see F. E. Croydon, "Abbot Laurence of Westminster and Hugh of St Victor," *Medieval and Renaissance Studies* 2 (1950): 169–71. This letter was edited earlier by Bernhard Bischoff, "Aus der Schule Hugos von St. Viktor," in *Aus der Geisteswelt des Mittelalters: Beiträge zur Geschichte der Philosophie und Theologie des Mittelalters*, Supplementband 3.1 (Münster: Aschendorff, 1935), 250.

[3] There are several ambiguities in this sentence. The "others" could be other teachers or other students or both. This letter is written in the elevated rhetorical style popular in monastic letters of the time, e.g., in the letters of Anselm of Canterbury.

[4] *Artifex* might mean *scriptor* (scribe). This interpretation finds support in the phrase *onus scribendi* employed above. If so, this would be interesting because the distinction between *auctor* and *scriptor* with respect to God as the author of the Bible and man as the writer does not seem to appear until the thirteenth century.

PROLOGUE (pp. 113-129)

[5] Cf. Hugh of St Victor, *Sacr.* 2.13.7 (PL 176.532D-533A).

[6] Cf. *Speculum de mysteriis ecclesiae* 8 (PL 177.374A-B).

[7] Cf. Richard of St Victor, *XII patr.* 70 (SC 419.294), 83 (SC 419.332).

[8] Cf. Richard of St Victor, *LE* 1.2.10 (TPMA 5.120-21).

[9] *Testes subscripti* is a common phrase at the end of medieval charters that follows a list of names from various ranks (e.g., archbishops, abbots, etc.).

[10] Cf. Heb 9:16.

[11] Cf. Heb 9:17.

[12] Cf. Heb 9:17.

[13] Exod 20:13-14; cf. Deut 5:17-18.

[14] On the necessity of the testator's death, see Heb 9:17.

[15] Cf. Hugh of St Victor, *Script.* 12 (PL 175.19A-C); Richard of St Victor, *LE* 1.2.10 (TPMA 5.120–21), where the *testes* are the apostles and martyrs; Ambrose, *Ep.* 75 (PL 16.1258B); Isidore of Seville, *De ecclesiasticus officiis* 1.11 (PL 83.745C); Rabanus Maurus, *De clericorum institutione* 53 (PL 107.365D-365A); Aimon of Auxerre, *Expositio in divi Pauli epistolis* 3 (PL 117.688B); Bruno Carthusianorum, *In Psalmum* 83 (PL 152.1015A). Isidore, Rabanus, and Aimon all regard the *testes* to be the apostles.

[16] Cf. Rev 5:1, 5.

[17] Cf. Hugh of St Victor, *Didasc.* 4.2 (Buttimer, 71–72), *Script.* 6 (PL 175.16A-B), *Chronica* (Douai, Bibliothèque 364.123ra; Vatican City, Reg. lat. 88.15v-16r), *Sacr.* Prol. 7 (PL 176.185D-186D); Richard of St Victor, *LE* 1.2.9 (TPMA 5.119–20). See also *Speculum de mysteriis ecclesiae* 8 (PL 177.374B-D); Adam Scot, *Liber de quadripertito exercitio cellae* 18 (PL 153.832A-B); William Durant, *Rationale divinorum officiorum* 7.44.3 (CCCM 140B.116). Much of the discussion here is based on Jerome, *In libros Samuel et Malachim* (PL 28.552ff), and Isidore of Seville, *Etym.* 6.1-2 (Lindsay, 1.216-24).

For studies on this enumeration, see G. Paré, A. Brunet, and P. Tremblay, *La renaissance du XIIᵉ siècle: Les écoles et l'enseignement*, Publications de l'institut d'études médiévales d'Ottawa 3 (Ottawa: Institut d'études médiévales, 1933), 220; C. Spicq, *Esquisse d'une histoire de l'exégèse latine au moyen âge* (Paris: J. Vrin, 1944), 107–8; Ludwig Ott, "Hugo von St. Viktor und die Kirchenväter," *Divus Thomas* 27 (1949): 181–84; Roger Baron, *Science et sagesse chez Hugues de Saint-Victor* (Paris: P. Lethielleux, 1957), 102–5; George Tavard, *Holy Writ or Holy Church:*

The Crisis of the Protestant Reformation (New York: Harper and Brothers, 1959), 16–17; J. Châtillon, "La Bible dans les écoles du XIIᵉ siècle," in *Le Moyen Age et la Bible*, ed. P. Riché and
G. Lobrichon, Bible de tous les temps 4 (Paris: Beauchesne, 1984), 179–80; Rainer Berndt,
"Gehören die Kirchväter zur Heiligen Schrift? Zur Kanontheorie des Hugo von St. Viktor,"
in *Zum Problem des biblischen Kanons*, Jahrbuch für Biblische Theologie, vol. 3 (Neukirchen-
Vluyn: Neukirchener Verlag, 1988), 191–99; Grover Zinn, "Hugh's of St Victor *De scripturis
et scriptoribus sacris* as an accessus treatise for the study of the Bible," *Traditio* 52 (1997):
123–24; Dominique Poirel, *Hugues de Saint-Victor*, Initiations au Moyen Âge (Paris: Cerf,
1998), 65–69.

18 Cf. Hugh of St Victor, *Sacr.* Prol.7 (PL 176.186B), *Script.* 12 (PL 175.19C-20A).

19 Isa 24:16.

20 As Hugh previously discussed, the "fathers" along with the apostles are authoritative witnesses to the new "testament," so it is only natural that he includes them in the list of divine
writings (*diuine scripture*) along with the gospels and apostles. For that reason, modern
scholarship sometimes attributes to Hugh an innovative theory of the canon with his category
"fathers." However, it seems more probable that Hugh was simply affirming a traditional list
of sanctioned books or divine writings that includes both canonical and non-canonical writings without confusion. There are several reasons for this.
First, enumerations like "evangelists—apostles—fathers" are found throughout the Latin West
from the third to twelfth centuries. Whether the evangelists and apostles are coupled with
the fathers, doctors, councils, or the Church, these enumerations routinely contain canonical
and non-canonical ecclesiastical writings of popes, bishops, saints, or councils (see e.g., Au-
gustine, *En. Ps.* 49.3 [CCL 38.576-77]; Pope Felix III, *Ep.* 4 [PL 58.913A, 915C]; Gregory the
Great, *Hom. Ez.* 2.9.7 [CCL 142.362]; Pope Agatho, *Ep.* 3 [PL 87.1223D]; Emmo Senonensis,
Praeceptum [PL 88.1168B]; Pope Zacharias, *Ep.* 11 [PL 89.944B]; Bernold of Constance, *Ep.*
[PL 148.1084C]; Hincmar of Reims, *Ep.* [PL 126.504A]; Berengar of Tours, *Ep. ad Ascelinum
Carnotensem* [CCCM 171.149]; Ascelinus of Chartres, *Ep. ad Berengarium* [CCCM 171.152];
Aelred Rievaulx, *De speculo caritatis* 2.17.43 [CCCM 1.87]; Adelmann of Liège, *Ep. ad Beren-
garium* [CCCM 171.199]; Baldwin of Ford, *De commendatione fidei* 77 [CCCM 99.422]; Pas-
chasius Radbertus, *Expositio in Psalmum* 1 [CCCM 94.3]; Pope Pachal II, *Concilium
Lateranense* [Mansi, 21.50-51]; Hugh of St Victor, *Misc.* 1.81 [PL 177.517B]; Richard of St Victor, *Joel* [PL 175.352D]; *Apoc.* 2.2 [PL 196.752A]; *Apoc.* 2.9 [PL 196.774B]; *Apoc.* 7.10 [PL
196.885B-886C]; *LE* 2.8.12 [TPMA 5.350]; *Trin.* 4.5 [TPMA 6.167]; and so on).
Second, Hugh's enumeration corresponds to the list of canonical and ecclesiastical writings
that are sanctioned for liturgical readings. For example, in *De questionibus regule sancti
Augustini* Richard argues that, in accordance with the decrees of the fathers, nothing should
be read or chanted in the Church except canonical writings or authentic books sanctioned
by a council (*Quest* 10 [Colker, *Traditio* 18 (1962): 211-12]). The most notable sanction is the
Gelasian Decree, which lists the canonical writings along with four Ecumenical councils and
all the holy fathers who must be "received into the Catholic Church," a list that Hugh reproduces in his *Didascalicon* (*Decretum Gelasianum* 4.2 [Dobschütz, *Das Decretum Gelasianum*
(Leipzig: J. C. Hinrichs, 1912)], 8; *Didasc.* 4.14 [Buttimer, 88–89]). Moreover, the table readings
of the Abbey of St Victor include every category of these sanctioned books (see *Liber ordinis
s. Victoris Parisiensis* 48 [CCCM 61.212-15]; cf. also *Speculum* 4 [PL 177.347B-348A]; *Liber
Quare* Appendix II, additio 20 and 50 [CCCM 60.146-48, 193–94]. See also Benedict, *Regula* 9
[SC 182.512]).
Third, Hugh lists the fathers along with the gospels and apostles, simply because he regards
them all as "divine writings" (*diuine scripture*) that have been divinely inspired for the di-
vinization of readers (e.g., *Script.* 1 [PL 175.10d-11a]; *Didasc.* 4.1 [Buttimer, 70]). Whenever
Hugh juxtaposes the "divine writings" with other kinds of writings, he does so with respect
to non-ecclesiastical writings, like the philosophical or poetical writings (*Didasc.* 4.1
[Buttimer, 70-71]; *Script.* 1 [PL 175.9A-10A]; *In hier. cael.* 1.1 [PL 175.927A]). Such writings do

contain some divine wisdom by the very fact that they were written *per Spiritum*; nevertheless, they do not pass the criterion of inspiration and ecclesiastical sanction. With regard to the inspiration of councils, decrees, or creeds, Hugh notes that the four principal councils were sanctioned by the holy fathers, "who were filled with the Spirit" (*Didasc.* 4.12 [Buttimer, 87]; see also Isidore of Seville, *Etym.* 6.16.10 [Lindsay, 1.235]; Richard of St Victor, *Trin.* 3.10 [TPMA 6.145]). In *On the Trinity* 4.5 (TPMA 6.167), Richard will regard the Athanasian Creed, universally cited by the Latin Church, as divinely inspired; and in *Serm. cent.* 99 (PL 177.1205B-C), he regards Augustine as divinely inspired: "We have no doubt that this verse [Ps 44:2] is truly applicable to blessed Augustine, whose feast day we celebrate today . . . His tongue is the pen of the scribe writing swiftly, because he most elegantly discharges the Word of God through the instruction and guidance of the Holy Spirit [*Spiritu sancto docente et ducente*] . . . The Holy Spirit is the scribe, the tongue of the doctor is the pen, grace is the ink, Christ is the ink-horn, our heart is the parchment, and truth is the writing . . ."

[21]   Cf. Hugh of St Victor, *Didasc.* 4.7 (Buttimer, 77); Isidore of Seville, *Etym.* 6.2 (Lindsay, 1.218–24).

[22]   Cf. Hugh of St Victor, *Didasc.* 4.15 (Buttimer, 90–91). This list of apocryphal writings comes from the *Gelasian Decree* 4.2–11.263–353 (Dobschütz, 49–60).

[23]   Following Jerome, neither Hugh nor Richard will regard the Deuterocanonical writings as canonical, but, like the fathers, they are still among the divine writings that must be read. Cf. Hugh of St Victor, *Didasc.* 4.2 (Buttimer, 71–72); *Script.* 6 (PL 175.16A-B); *Sacr.* Prol. 7 (PL 176.185D-186D); Richard of St Victor, *LE* 1.2.9 (TPMA 5.119–20).

[24]   See note 20.

[25]   Cf. *Speculum de mysteriis ecclesiae* 8 (PL 177.374B).

[26]   Cf. *Glossa ordinaria* (PL 113.601C); Hugh of St Victor, *Didasc.* 5.2 (Buttimer, 95); *Script.* 4 (PL 175.12D-13A); *Libellus* 4 (CCCM 176.142); Richard of St Victor, *LE* 1.2.8 (TPMA 5.119).

[27]   According to basic medieval theories of biblical interpretation, the exegetical process begins at the level of 'signs' (*signa*) and 'things' (*res*), a distinction that goes back to Augustine's *De doctrina christiana* (1.2 [CCL 32.7]). Words (*verbi* or *voces*) are signs that point to a thing signified (*res*), as the word 'ram' makes us think about an actual ram (e.g., according to the historical or literal meaning). But in the Bible that actual ram is capable of further signification according to the allegorical and troplogical meaning. For example, the 'ram', which Abraham sacrificed in place of Isaac (Gen 22:13), signifies an actual ram according to the historical meaning, but it signifies Christ according to the allegorical meaning. Hence, as Hugh explains later, the Bible, unlike other non-ecclesiastical writings, is able to signify an allegorical and tropological 'thing' beyond the literal 'thing' of the word.

[28]   Cf. Hilary of Poitiers, *Tractatus super psalmos* 120.6 (CSEL 22.562): *ad eum . . . sermo conversus est*; Hrabanus Mauros, *Expositio in Matthaeum* 8 (CCCM 174A.706). Hugh's definition (*tropologia quasi conuersus sermo*) is also found in the anon. *Speculum* 8 (PL 177.375A): *tropologia dicitur conversiva locutio;* Robert of Melun, *Sent.* 1.1.6 (Martin, 173); Alan of Lille, *Liber in distinctionibus dictionum theologicalium* (PL 210.981A); Peter Comestor, *Historia scholastica* (PL 198.1055): *tropologia est sermo conversivus.* See also Henri de Lubac, *Medieval Exegesis*, vol. 2, trans. E. M. Macierowski (Grand Rapids: Eerdmans, 2000), 129.

[29]   Cf. Hugh of St Victor, *Script.* 3 (PL 175.12B); anon. *Speculum* 8 (PL 177.375A). These allegories are also called "sacraments," which Hugh will discuss below. Augustine, for example, offers the following generic definition in *De civitate Dei* (CCL 47.277; see also *Contra adversarium legis* 1.9.34 [PL 42.658]): "Therefore, the visible sacrifice is a sacrament, that is, a sacred sign, of the invisible sacrifice" (*Sacrificium ergo uisibile inuisibilis sacrificii sacramentum, id est sacrum signum est*), which becomes the basis for the generic medieval definition of a sacrament: "a sacrament is a sign of a sacred thing" (see *Summa sent.* 4.1 [PL 176.117A]; Peter Lombard, *Sent.* 4.1.2 [SB 5.232]) or "the visible sacrament is a sacrament, that is sacred sign, of an invisible thing" (Alger of Liège, *De sacramentis corp. et sang. Domini* 1.4 [PL 180.751C]; cf. Magister Herman, *Epitome theologiae christianae* 28 [PL 178.1738C]; Peter Abelard, *TSch.* 1

[CCCM 13.321]). Because of the popularity of these generic Augustinian definitions, any visible thing that signified something sacred was considered a sacrament, whether a crucifix on the wall, the tonsure, a crosier, or any sacred liturgical object and ritual. Sometime after the 1120s or 1130s we find theologians struggling for a narrower definition of NT sacraments by offering certain modifications of the Augustinian formulas. While Hugh of St Victor was one of the first to narrow the definition of a NT sacrament in his *On the Sacraments* (Sacr. 1.9.2 [PL 176.317D]), he makes no such attempt here.

On the definition of a sacrament, see P. Pourrat, *Theology of the Sacraments* (St. Louis: Herder, 1914), 37–44; A. Michel, "Sacraments. Notion, Le Moyen Age," in *Dictionnaire de Théologie Catholique* 14.1 (Paris: Librairie Letouzey et Ané, 1939), 527–32; J. de Ghellinck, "Un chapitre dans l'histoire de la définition des sacrametns au xii⁰ siècle," in *Mélanges Mandonnet. Études d'histoire littéraire et doctrinale du Moyen Age.* Bibliothèque thomiste, vol. 14 (Paris: J. Vrin, 1930), 79–96; N. M. Häring, "Berengar's Definitions of *Sacramentum* and Their Influence on mediaeval Sacramentology," in *Mediaeval Studies* 10 (1948): 109–46; D. van den Eynde, "The Terms «*Ius positiuum*» and «*signum positiuim*» in twelfth-century Scholasticism," *Franciscan Studies* 9 (1949): 41–49; ibid., *Les Définitions des Sacrements pendant la première période de la théologie scolastique (1050–1240)* (Rome: Antonianum, 1950).

30   Cf. Num 21:9; John 3:14.

31   Cf. Exod 14:26–28.

32   In his *Didascalicon* Hugh will specify the order of signification in the divine scriptures as *vox-intellectum-res-[divina] ratio-Veritas* ("through the word [or spoken sound] to thought [or intellect], through the intellect to the thing, through the thing to the ‹divine› meaning [or idea], through the ‹divine› meaning to the Truth" (5.3 [Buttimer, 96]); see note 27). Because the triad *vox-intellectus-res*, which is common to both pagan and divine writings, is the basis for the historical or literal interpretation, Hugh insists on the necessity of the liberal arts for interpreting the Bible. See also *Sacr.* Prol. 5 (PL 176.185A-B); *Script.* 14 (PL 175.20D-21D). For the triad *res-intellectus-vox*, see Boethius, *Interp.* 1.1 (Meiser, 1.37); see also discussion in J. Magee, *Boethius on Signification and Mind*, Philosophica Antiqua 52 (New York: Brill, 1989), 69–71, 114.

33   Cf. Hugh of St Victor, *Script.* 13 (PL 175.20C).

34   Cf. Hugh of St Victor, *Didasc.* 5.3 (Buttimer, 96).

35   Cf. Hugh of St Victor, *Sacr.* Prol. 5 (PL 176.185B); *Script.* 14 (PL 175.24B); Robert of Melun, *Sent.* 1.6 (Martin, 171–72); Richard of St Victor, *LE* 1.2.5 (TPMA 5.116–17); 2.10.8 (TPMA 5.391).

36   Ps 50:9.

37   If Hugh is interpreting Ps 50:9 (and Song 4:1) according to the tropological meaning of the things signified based on some similitude with the external form (i.e., not according to the historical meaning of 'words'), then he would not be regarding the simile as part of the literal meaning of the biblical passage, which is a common ambiguity among some Patristic and Medieval exegetes. For instance, the biblical passage in question already uses a simile to express the 'literal meaning' of spiritual purity; hence, one does not need to utilize allegory to arrive at that meaning (see also Hugh's treatment of 'lion' in *Didasc.* 5.3 [Buttimer, 97]). Elsewhere, however, Hugh does seem to suggest that figurative language is not part of the allegorical or tropological but the literal meaning, see *Script.* 5 (PL 175.14B-C).

38   Song 4:1; 6:4.

39   Cf. Hugh of St Victor, *Didasc.* 2.16 (Buttimer, 35–35).

40   Cf. Augustine, *Lib. arb.* 2.13 (CSEL 74.51); *En. Ps.* 3.3 (CCL 38.8).

41   Cf. Hugh of St Victor, *Sacr.* Prol. 5 (PL 176.185B-C); *Script.* 13 (PL 175.20C-D); anon. *Speculum* 8 (PL 177.375C-376A).

42   For the contents of this paragraph, see Hugh of St Victor, *Sacr.* 1 Prol. 2 (PL 176.183A-184A).

43 Cf. Hugh of St Victor, *Chronica* (Douai, Bibliothèque 364, f. 110ra): *Sex diebus perfecta est rerum conditio, et sex etatibus perficitur hominum reparatio.* After the first six days of creation, the first age of restoration is the time from Adam to Noah's son Sem (*prima etas continens annos ĩdclvi*); the second age is from Sem to Thar the father of Abraham (*secunda etas continens annos ccxcii*); the third age is from Abraham to Saul (*tertia etas continens annos dc-cccxlii a Dauid*); the fourth age is from David to Sedechias (*quarta etas continens annos cccclxxii*); the fifth age is from Jesus the priest to King Herod and the birth of Jesus Christ, the Son of God, in Bethlehem that ushers in the sixth age (*quinta etas finitur continens annos dlxxxvi*) (Douai, Bibliothèque 364, ff. 110v-112r and 117r-v; Vatican City, Reg. lat. 88, f. 7r-8v). For an alternative delineation of the six ages, see Hugh of St Victor, *Sacr.* 2.6.8 (PL 176.454D-455D), where Adam is not considered, and Noah and the flood are located in the second age and Abraham is in the third age. All the other ages correspond to the *Chronica*.
44 Cf. Augustine, *Civ. Dei* 11.30 (CCL 48.350).
45 Cf. Augustine, *Jo. ev. tr.* 74.3 (CCL 36.509).
46 Cf. Augustine, *Jo. ev. tr.* 74.3 (CCL 36.509).
47 As discussed in note 29, the word "sacraments" (*sacramentum*) is used very broadly here to refer to any signs, whether words or deeds, of sacred things. We find no attempts here to narrow the use of *sacramenta* in order to distinguish the NT sacraments from other sacred signs. As such, I have retained the ambiguity of the word *sacramenta* by simply translating it as "sacraments" without attempting to distinguish its generic meaning as mysteries or sacred signs from "sacraments" in the strict sense.
48 This designation will later be given to the sacrament of the Body and Blood of Christ, see *Summa Sent.* 2 (PL 176.139B) and *Speculum de mysteriis ecclesiae* 7 (PL 177.366D).
49 Cf. Num 15:31. For the contents of this paragraph, see Hugh of St Victor, *Sacr.* 1.8.4 (PL 176.307D-308C).
50 The word "service" (*seruitium*) here indicates the worship that is owed to God alone, which, according to Augustine, is what the Greeks call *latreia*; see Augustine, *Civ. Dei* 10.3 (CCL 47.275); *Contra sermonem Arrianorum* 29 (PL 42.703). See also Hugh of St Victor, *Sacr.* 1.10 6 (PL 176.353C).
51 Cf. Hugh of St Victor, *Sac. dial.* (PL 176.29B); *Misc.* 2.8 (PL 177.591A-B); Peter Lombard, *In ep. ad Romanos.* 5 (PL 191.1386A).
52 On this notion of satisfaction, see Anselm of Canterbury, *Meditatio* 3 (Schmitt, 3.86).
53 For the contents of this paragraph, see Hugh of St Victor, *Sacr.* 1.8.4 (PL 176.308C-309A).
54 The Latin here reads *restituendum*, but I have emended it to *restituendo* to make better sense of the sentence. The emended reading is supported by the parallel reading in the next clause (*satisfaciendo* "by making satisfaction") and by the same reading in *Sacr.* 1.8.4 (PL 176.309A).
55 For the contents of this paragraph, see Hugh of St Victor, *Sacr.* 1.8.4 (PL 176.309A-B).
56 Cf. Gregory the Great, *Mor.* 25.9 (CCL 143B.25–28): . . . *ut et praecedens culpa sit causa subsequentis, et rursum culpa subsequens sit poena praecedentis.*
57 Ps 68:5.
58 Deut 6:5; Matt 22:37; Mark 12:30; Luke 10:27.
59 Cf. Hugh of St Victor, *Sacr.* 1.8.11 (PL 176.312D-313A).
60 Cf. Hugh of St Victor, *Libellus* 3 (CCCM 176.133); *Misc.* 1.169 (PL 177.561A-B); and the anon. *Quaestiones in Ep. ad Eph.* 11 (PL 175.570D).
61 Cf. Augustine, *Contra Jul.* 6.20 (PL 44, col. 834): *in rerum natura bona sunt omnia*; Ambrosiaster, *Quaestiones Vet. et Novi Test* 9.2 (CSEL 50.33): *Itaque omnia in sua natura bona sunt, quia utilia.* Cf. also Gen 1:31; I Tim 4:4.
62 Cf. Hugh of St Victor, *Libellus* 3 (CCCM 176.133); Richard of St Victor, *Serm. cent.* 70 (PL 177.1120B-1121B); *LE* 2.12.5 (TPMA 5.464); *Adnot. Psalm.* 118 (PL 196.352C).
63 See Hugh of St Victor, *Sacr.* 1.7.26, 27, 28, 31 (PL 176.298B, 298D, 299A, 301B-C), where he argues that the ignorance of the mind and the lust of the flesh are a result of original sin;

Archa Noe. 4.5 (CCCM 176.99). See Augustine, *Ench.* 24 (CCL 46.63); *C. Jul. imp.* 6.50 (PL 45.851).

64   Rom 2:14.

65   Eph 2:3.

66   Augustine, *Jo. ev. tr.* 3.11 (CCL 36.25): "God wanted to subdue their pride and gave the law, as if saying: 'Behold, fulfill ‹it› and do not think that there is one lacking to command. There is no lack of One to command, but there is lacking one to fulfill" (*Superbiam illorum uolens domare Deus, dedit legem, tamquam dicens: ecce implete, ne putetis deesse iubentem non deest qui iubeat, sed deest qui impleat*). This version is found in Peter Lombard, *In Psalmos Davidicos Commentarii* 57 (PL 191.606C); and the anon. *Quaestiones et decisione in Ep. ad Gal.* 19 (PL 175.560A). Hugh alters this reading not to reflect the divine discourse after the law was given but the discourse of man before it was given. See also Peter Lombard, *Ad Romanos* 5 (PL 191.1398C); *Ad Galatas* 3 (PL 192.122B and 127C); Peter of Poitiers, *Sententiae* 4.3 (PL 211.1146B).

67   Deut 6:4.

68   Exod 20:13–14; cf. Deut 5:17–18.

69   The Latin edition reads *sponses* but should read *sponsas*.

70   The Latin edition reads here *iusta illud*, which makes no sense in the context. The problem is probably due to a faulty transcription. The Latin should read *iuxta illud ‹poeticum›* as reflected in the translation.

71   The Latin edition reads *nitimur inuetitum* ("we strive after the unforbidden"), which does not make sense in the context. The proper reading is *nitimur in uetitum*. Medieval manuscripts frequently lack a space between the preposition and the noun.

72   Ovid, *Amores* 3.4.17 (R. Ehwald, 1.51).

73   This notion of inspiration is commonly employed to indicate the salvific operation of the Spirit in the affective faculty of the soul that usually entails the infusion and arousal of love or the desire for good. This operation can either precede the determination of the will or cooperate with it, the results of which is union with Christ, an ordered or good will, good works, and understanding. As such, volitional inspiration is simply an extension of operative and cooperating grace, as Hugh succinctly states: "The Holy Spirit first operates a good will in these virtues, which arise through the restorative grace; then He cooperates with the good will that is moving itself and working. The Holy Spirit first inspires a good will so that it may exist (i.e. operative-volitional inspiration), and he then inspires so that it may move and work lest it be idle (i.e. cooperative-volitional inspiration). The Holy Spirit first works it, then he works through it" (*Sacr.* 1.6.17 [PL 176.274B]). Richard argues similarly: "God requires voluntary consent in the work of our justification . . . It is clear then that this work, in which God cooperates with his creatures, is accomplished by two. In this work there is a need for one's own effort and divine grace . . . Our justification is accomplished by our own deliberation and divine inspiration" (*Arca Moys.* 3.16 [Aris, 74]). See Hugh of St Victor, *Sacr.* 1.5.27 (PL 176.258C); *Sacr.* 1.8.11 (PL 176.313A); *Sac. dial.* (PL 176.32B); *Misc.* 2.36 (PL 177.607A); *Septem donis* 2.3 (SC 155.124, 126); *Eulogium* (PL 176.986D); *Archa Noe* Prol. (CCCM 176.3–4); *Archa Noe.* 3.3 (CCCM 176.57); *Archa Noe* 3.6 (CCCM 176.67); *Libellus* 5 (CCCM 176.134–5); *Misc.* 2.5 (PL 177.590C); *Misc.* 2.51 (PL 177.618B); *Misc.* 2.77 (PL 177.631A); *Meditatione* 3.3 (SC 155.52); Richard of St Victor, *LE* 2.7.24 (Châtillon, 332); *LE* 2.12.2 (Châtillon, 461–2); *Trin.* 6.14 (TPMA 6.245–6); *Sp. blasph.* (TPMA 15.123); *Erud.* 1.27 (PL 196.1276B-C); *Erud.* 1.34 (PL 196.1289B); *Erud.* 2.9 (PL 196.1309A); *XII patr.* 3, 4 (SC 419.96, 98, 100); *XII patr.* 29 (SC 419.170); *Arca Moys.* 2.21 (Aris, 48); *Arca Moys.* 3.17 (Aris, 75); *Arca Moys.* 3.24 (Aris, 83–4); *Tab. foed.* (PL 196.197D); *Diff. sac.* (PL 196.1058B); *Adnot. Psalm.* 121 (PL 196.364D). *Adnot. Psalm.* 134 (PL 196.368D); *Adnot. Psalm.* 28 (PL 196.301B); *Adnot. Psalm.* 104 (PL 196.336B); *Statu.* 7 (AH-DLMA 42.69–70); *Serm. sent.* 38 (PL 177.998A); *Misc.* 4.107 (PL 177.742C); Achard of St Victor, *Serm.* 5.4 (Châtillon, 72). See also *Questiones in ep. Pauli.: ad Cor. II* 27–28 (PL 175.535C); *Summa sent.* 3.7 (PL 176.99D); *Summa Sent.* 3.17 (PL 176.114D); *Misc.* 5.58 (PL 177.758A).

74   Cf. Hugh of St Victor, *Sacr.* 1.8.11 (PL 176.312D-313A); *Sac. dial.* (PL 176.32B); *Libellus* 5 (CCCM 176.134-5); *Misc.* 1.18 (PL 177.487D); cf. also *Misc.* 3.50 (PL 177.669A-B).

75   Cf. Hugh of St Victor, *Chronica* (Douai, Bibliothèque 364, f. 105vb): *De duobus statibus et iii temporibus. Presens seculum distinguitur in duos status siue in tria tempora. Primus status qui dicitur uetus est ab Adam usque ad Christum. Secundus qui nouus appellatur ab aduentu Christi usque ad finem seculi. Primum tempus est naturalis legis ab Adam usque ad Moysen. Secundum scripte legis a Moyse usque ad Christum. Tercium tempus gracie ab aduentu Chrisi usque ad finem seculi.*

76   Rom 1:20.

Part One (pp. 130-139)

77   Cf. Augustine, *Civ. Dei* 11.30 (CSEL 40.557): *quasi qui non potuerit creare omnia simul.* Cf. also Augustine, *Gn. litt* 4.3 (CSEL 28.1.98): *Nec quisquam ita demens est, ut audeat dicere non potuisse Deum facere uno die cuncta, si uellet . . .*; Ambrosiaster, *Quaestiones ueteris et noui testamenti* 106.18 (CSEL 50.244): *Nam potuit utique simul facere cunta sed ratio multiformis prohibuit.* This text of Ambrosiaster is usually cited in discussions on God's omnipotence, e.g., Peter Abelard, *SN* 35.7 (Boyer and McKeon, 185); *TChr* 5.39 (CCCM 12.364).

78   Cf. Ambrosiaster, *Quaestiones ueteris et noui testamenti* 106.18 (CSEL 50.244): *. . . quare non omnia simul fecisse dicatur? Nam hic hominum mos est, ut per partes fecisse credatur. Ad potentiam ergo Dei magis facere videtur, si uno die omnia ab eo facta dicantur.* Cf. *Sententiae Atrebatenses* 2 (ed. O. Lottin, "Les Sententiae Atrebatenses" *Recherches de théologie ancienne et médiévale* 10 [1938]: 208): *Fecit autem Deus in sapientia sua, id est in Filio, omnia simul, non distincte quedam prius, quedam posterius per seccessiones temporum creando; quod Augustinus super Genesim affirmat dicens quod que a Deo facta sunt simul ab homine similiter non potuerint dici. Fecit ergo Deus omnia simul . . .*

79   Gen 2:4-5.

80   Sir 18:1.

81   Cf. Augustine, *Gn. litt.*, 1.15 (CSEL 28.1.21-22); the anonymous (vi-viii sec.) *Dies dominica* (CCL 108B, 183-84): *Quod diuisit sermone, quod potuit Deus facere momento, diuisit scriptura per tempora.*

82   Hugh of St Victor developed the content of this paragraph in *Sacr.* 1.1.3 (PL 176.188B-189B). See also Hugh of St Victor, *Adnot. in Pent.* 4 (PL 175.33A-34A).

83   Cf. 1 Cor 8:6.

84   Cf. Jerome, *Hebraicae quest. in libro Gen* 1.1 (CCL 72.3); Gregory the Great, *Mor.* 32.12.16 (PL 76.644D-645C); Bede, *In principium Genesis* 1 (CCL 118A.3, 32, 39-40); Ps.-Bede, *De sex dierum creatione* (PL 93.220D-221A); and Isidore of Seville, *De differentiis rerum* 2.11.27-31 (PL 83.74B-75A), where he makes a distinction between the "creation of the world" (*creationem mundi*) and the "formation of it" (*formationem ejus*). Everything was created at once according to matter, which was confused and without form, but the confused and unformed matter was formed over the period of six days according to the distinction of species. See also *Summa sent.* 3.1 (PL 176.90B); *Sent. divinit.* 1.1.3 (Geyer, 9-12); Peter Lombard, *Sent.* 12.2 (SB 4.384-85).

85   Cf. Hugh of St Victor, *Sacr.* 1.1.2 (PL 176.188A); 1.5.15 (PL 176.252D).

86   Sir 18:1. Hugh of St Victor developed the content of this paragraph in *Sacr.* 1.1.2 (PL 176.187C-188B); 1.1.5 (PL 176.189C-190A).

87   Gen 2:4.

88   Cf. Hugh of St Victor, *Sacr.* 1.1.4 (PL 176.189C-D).

89   Cf. Hugh of St Victor, *Sacr.* 1.6.37 (PL 176.286B-C). See also Isidore of Seville, *Etym.* 8.6.15-16 (Lindsay, 1.318). According to Epicurean philosophy, the origin of all things is attributed to indivisible and corporeal atoms. The universe was made from these atoms after they accidently collided together. Hence, based on this philosophy, God did nothing. See also

Boethius, *Commentaris in Porphyrium* 2 (CSEL 48.139), which Hugh of St Victor cites in *Didasc.* 1.11 (Buttimer, 19-20).

90   An atom is something corporeal that is indivisible and simple, or as Hugh calls it later "simple bodies" (*corpora simplicia*) that are not matter but become matter, see *Sacr.* 1.6.37 (PL 176.286B). See also Bede, *De temporum ratione* 1.3 (PL 90.304A); *Sent. divinit.* I (Geyer, 18). See esp. Isidore of Seville, *Etym.* 13.2.1, where he discusses a corporeal atom with the analogy of a stone. A stone is broken in sand, and sand into fine dust, and the fine dust can be broken down further into its most minute form (i.e., an atom) that cannot be seen or divided again.

91   This paragraph in the Latin edition reads: *id est attomum, ex quo augmentata et diuina operatione multiplicata, tota mundi machina excreauerit* (Piazzoni, 930). There are two difficulties here. First, *atomus* is a feminine noun, hence the *ex quo* should read *ex qua*, as the next paragraph correctly reads: *ut attomus qua.* Second, the verb *excreavert* from *excreare*, attested elsewhere in this text, is extremely rare and not even found in Latin dictionaries with the exception of Blaise, where it is defined as "to create from oneself" ("créer de soi", A. Blaise, *Dictionnaire Latin-Français des auteurs chréteins* [Turnhout: Brepols, 1954], 325). Because *excreauerit* does not make sense in this context, I have emended it to reading the perfect form of *excrescrere* (i.e., *excreuerit*), hence "... from which the whole construction of the world ... grew up." These grammatical peculiarities are a reminder that the *Sententiae de divinitate* are a student's notes.

92   Cf. Hugh of St Victor, *Sacr.* 1.6.37 (PL 176.285D-286C).

93   Again, *excreauit* is amended to *excreuit*, see note 91.

94   The Latin reads *simplicem attomum constituentes materiam mundi. Constituentes* should read *constituentem.*

95   Cf. Augustine, *Vera rel.* 80 (CCL 32.240).

96   Cf. Augustine, *Gn. litt* 1.15 (CSEL 28.1.21-22).

97   Augustine says in his *Retractationes* that many questions in his *De Genesi ad litteram* were resolved with tentative conclusions, see 2.24.1 (CCL 57.109). In the Prologue of *Sic et Non* Peter Abelard offers hermeneutical keys for reading the fathers, one of which is to determine whether or not the fathers are citing the opinion of another (Boyer-Mckeon, 92–93); see also Peter Abelard, *Commentariorum ad Romanos* 2 (CCCM 11.174).

98   Cf. Hugh of St Victor, *Sacr.* 1.1.6 (PL 176.190B-191B).

99   Reading *circumquaque* for *circum aque.*

100 Cf. Hugh of St Victor, *Sacr.* 1.1.9 (PL 176.193D-194D); *Adnot. In Pent.* 6 (PL 175.34C-35A); cf. also *Sent. divinit.* I (Geyer, 13).

101 Hugh is less certain of this in *Sacr.* 1.1.15 (PL 176.199A).

102 Cf. Hugh of St Victor, *Sacr.* 1.1.6 (PL 176.191D); 1.1.17 (PL 176.200A-B).

103 Cf. Gen 1:6-8.

104 Cf. Hugh of St Victor, *Sacr.* 1.1.18 (PL 176.200B-C), in which Hugh argues that one can know nothing of this question.

105 Cf. Augustine, *Gn. litt* 2.10.23 (CSEL 28.1.47-48); *Sent. divinit.* I (Geyer, 15); Peter Lombard, *Sent.* 2.14.5.2 (SB 4.397). For a list of the different views, see Ps-Bede, *De mundi coelestis terrestrisque constitutione* (PL 90.895A-B).

106 Cf. Haymo of Auxerre, *Expositio in Epistolam II ad Corinthios* 12 (PL 117.661A): *Julianus Pomerius* (v sec.), *vir sanae prudentiae, primum coelum dicit isto in loco appellatum esse aerium, a quo aves coeli vocantur: secundum sidereum, ubi continentur duodecim signa caeteraque astra, praeter septem planetas, quod et firmamentum appellatur . . .*

107 I cannot identify the prophecy here.

108 *Chorus* is a difficult word to translate. It means a dance, a troop of dancers (or singers), the movement of heavenly bodies, a crowd or company.

109 Cf. *Sent. divinit.* I (Geyer, 15): *Magister Hugo dicit quod [firmamentum] est immobile, quia significat ipsum creatorem, stellae sanctos, iuxta illud: Stella a stella differt in claritate* (I Cor 15:41),

ideoque ut melius videamus id, quod immutabilem repraesentat, est immobile, sed quod mutabile ut stellae mobiles sunt, et secundum hoc non sunt infixae, sed parili motu moventur illa talis chorea stellarum. At the time, Geyer was unaware of the *Sententiae de divinitate*, hence he rightly noted: "Hunc locum in operibus Hugonis a S. Victore non inveni" (15, n. 3). It seems, therefore, that the author of the *Sent. divinit.* was familiar with Hugh's oral and written teachings.

110 Cf. Gen 1:9.

111 Cf. Hugh of St Victor, *Sacr.* 1.1.21 (PL 176.201C-D).

112 The Latin here is faulty: *Et in omnes cetere exeunt et per recepta sua discurrunt. Et in* has been emended to *in quo* and *recepta* to *receptacula.*

113 Cf. Hugh of St Victor, *Sacr.* 1.1.6 (PL 176.190C); 1.1.22 (PL 176.202A); Hugh of St Victor, *Adnot. In Pent.* 6 (PL 175.35B). See also the *Sent. divinit.* I (Geyer, 15–16). See also Bede, *Libri quatuor in principium Genesis usque ad nativitatem Isaac et eiectionem Ismahelis adnotationum* 1.1 (CCL 118A.12–13), which is cited by Peter Lombard, *Sent.* 2.14.8.1 (SB 4.398).

114 Cf. Hugh of St Victor, *Sacr.* 1.1.21 (PL 176.201C-D); cf. *Sent. divinit.* I (Geyer, 16).

115 I am reading *excreuit* for *excreauit* here. Cf. Augustine, *Gn. litt* 1.12 (CSEL 28.1.18–19); Beda, *Libri quatuor in principium Genesis usque ad nativitatem Isaac et eiectionem Ismahelis adnotationum* 1.1 (CCL 118A.12–13), which is cited by Peter Lombard, *Sent.* 2.14.8.2 (SB 4.398); *Sent. divinit.* I (Geyer, 16).

116 Cf. Hugh of St Victor, *Sacr.* 1.1.24 (PL 176.202D).

117 Cf. Hugh of St Victor, *Adnot. in Pent.* 6 (PL 175.35C-D); *Sacr.* 1.1.29 (PL 176.204C); cf. also *Sent. divinit.* I (Geyer, 13); Peter Lombard, *Sent.* 2.14.9.2 (SB 4.398–99).

118 Cf. Gen 1:16.

119 Cf. Gen 1:20.

120 Cf. *Sententiae Atrebatenses* 2 (O. Lottin, 208).

121 Cf. Hugh of St Victor, *Sacr.* 1.1.26 (PL 176.203B); *De sacramentis legis naturalis* (PL 176.20C). See also the *Sent. divinit.* I (Geyer, 17); Peter Lombard, *Sent.* 2.15.1 (SB 4, 400).

122 Cf. Hugh of St Victor, *Sacr.* 1.1.26 (PL 176.203C).

123 Cf. Hugh of St Victor, *Sacr.* 1.1.27 (PL 176.203C-D). See also the *Sent. divinit.* I (Geyer, 17); Richard of St Victor, *LE* 2.1.6 (TPMA 5.225–26).

124 Cf. Gen 1:23–25.

125 Cf. Hugh of St Victor, *Sacr.* 1.1.12 (PL 176.195C-197B); Richard of St Victor, *LE* 2.1.26 (TPMA 5.223–26).

126 Cf. Augustine, *Gn. litt* 4.7 (CSEL 28.1.103); *Trin.* 4.7 (CCL 50.169).

127 Cf. Augustine, *Quaestiones* 2.107 (CCL 33, 122); Isidore of Seville, *Etym.* 3.14 (Lindsay, 1.127–29); Bede, *Explanatio Apocalypsis* 1.5 (CCL 121A.283).

128 Cf. Lev 7:7.

129 Gen 2:2.

130 Cf. Hugh of St Victor, *Sacr.* 1.12.6 (PL 176.354C-355A).

131 Augustine argued that when God is said to rest from all his works, we should interpret this as God making us rest after we do good works. The main idea is this: "God is rightly said to do whatever we do by ‹his› work in us" (. . . *recte dicitur Deus facere, quidquid ipso in nobis operante fecerimus*), see *Gn. litt* 4.9 (CSEL 28.1.104).

132 Gen 2:2.

133 Deut 5:12.

134 Isa 66:23.

135 Ps 94:11 (Vulg.); Heb 3:11.

136 Hugh uses the verb *cessat* ("he ceases") not *requescit* ("he rests"). According to Bede "to rest means to cease" (*requiescere enim cessare dicitur*), see *Libri quatuor in principium Genesis usque ad nativitatem Isaac et eiectionem Ismahelis adnotationum* 2.2 (CCL 118A.33–34), cited by Peter Lombard, *Sent.* 2.15.7 (SB 4.403–4).

137 Augustine mentions another interesting allusion here: "And the Lord Jesus Christ, who suffered only at the precise time he willed, also underlined the mystery of this rest by his burial.

It was of course on the day of the sabbath that he rested in the tomb, and he had the whole day as a kind of holy vocation, after he had finished all his works on the sixth day, that is, Preparation Day, which they call the sixth of the sabbath, when what had been written about him was fulfilled on the very gibbet of the cross" (*Gn. litt* 4.11 [CSEL 28.1.107]; trans. E. Hill, Works of St Augustine 1.13.253).

138   Isa 66:23.

139   Isa 66:23.

140   Gen 2:2. Cf. Odo of Tournai, *De operibus sex dierum* (PL 171.1219A): *Nempe Deus mundum sola bonitate creavit, indiguit mundi non tamen ille bonis. Et nec in his, sed ab his requievit, nullius horum indigus; et tribuens, non requiem accipiens.*

141   Gen 2:2.

142   John 5:17.

143   Cf. Hugh of St Victor, *Sacr.* 1.6.37 (PL 176.285A-288A; Deferarri 118–20); Richard of St Victor, *LE* 1.2.8 (TPMA 5.119). See also Bede *De natura rerum* 1 (CCL 123A.7); Alcuin, *Interrogationes et responsione in genesin* 19 (PL 100.519A), which is cited by Peter Lombard, *Sent.* 12.6 (SB 4.388–89). See also the *Sent. divinit.* 1.1.3 (Geyer, 10).

144   Gen 1:1.

145   Gen 2:2.

146   On the six ages, see note 43.

147   John 5:17.

148   I emended the reading *congenerando* to *congerendo*.

PART TWO (pp. 140-154)

149   For this and the next paragraph see Hugh of St Victor, *Sacr.* 1.2.2 (PL 176.206C-207C; Deferrari, 29–30).

150   The "scriptures" here are the writings of Pseudo-Dionysius and Eruigena.

151   Hugh uses *conditio* as a synonym for *creatio*.

152   Richard of Victor, *Trin.* 2.13, mentions "*substantiis quasi divinis*," which Salet (*La Trinité.* SC 63. Texte latin, introduction, traduction et notes de G. Salet [Paris: Cerf, 1959], 473–74) refers to these platonic primordial causes that are from nothing. Eriugena connected the *causae primordiales* of Pseudo-Dionysius with the *rationes aeternae* of St Augustine, as Hugh does as well.

153   See Augustine, *Eighty-Three Different Questions*, 46.1–2, (Vernon Bourke, *The Essential Augustine* [New York: Mentor, 1964]: 62–63).

154   Hugh may be referring to Eriugena, *Periphyseon* 3 (CCCM 163.4): *Ab intellectuali siquidem creatura, quae in angelis est constituta.*

155   The term "*traductio*" was associated with the theory ("traducianism") that the soul of newly conceived child was handed to it from its parents, although the term had other applications as well. Augustine considered the theory of the *traductio* of the soul, but never fully adopted it. See Augustine, *Gn. litt* 10.6–26, (CSEL 28.302–32). For other references and bibliography see Allan D. Fitzgerald, "Traducianism," in *Augustine through the Ages: An Encyclopedia* (Grand Rapids: Eerdmans, 1999): 843. However, Hugh seems to be using the term in a more general sense.

156   Hugh of St Victor, *Sacr.* 1.2.3 (PL 176.207CD; Deferrari, 30). Hugh states, "Now these effect without movement and produce without handing on, since eternity did not fail in its state by ordaining time, nor did it minister substance from its own store by creating corruptible things, but remaining what it was it made what was not, containing in itself the power of making, not taking from itself the matter of what was made." Hugh also deals with primordial causes in *Didascalicon* 1.6 (Buttimer, 12–14; Taylor, 52–54). See also Robert of Melun, *Sent.* 2.1 (3.1.263–4). Robert discusses the different causes in the same way that Hugh does. He even employs Hugh's language at times: "Now there is a great difference between these primary

causes and other causes. All other causes bring about by moving and generate by handing on (*traducendo*), but these 'effect without motion and generate without handing on' (quoting from Hugh). In God no variation occurs and because of this there is no motion for 'remaining immobile [God] moves everything else' (Boethius, *Con. phil.* [CCL 94.3, poem 9]). He brings none into being by handing on who is simple and from whom nothing can be taken away in the same way that nothing can be added to him. For he can be neither greater nor lesser . . . Now he has not created anything by handing on parts of himself, which is why the creation of things cannot occur by the handing on of parts."

157 Reading *quolibet* for *quodlibet*.
158 Reading *deinde* for *dum*.
159 Cf. Pseudo-Athanasian Creed, *Quicumque vult*, (Denz., 51): "*in hac Trinitate nihil prius aut posterius.*"
160 See *Sacr.* 1.2.9 (PL 176.210B; tr. Deferrari, 33). See also Richard of St Victor, *Arca Moys.* 2.20 (Aris, 46–47, tr. Zinn, 206), who employs a fourfold scheme, which leaves out providence.
161 Uncharacteristically, Hugh seems to be making a pun here. One could paraphrase it thus: Those who argue for fatalism because God's foreknowledge cannot fail, are failures in God's foreknowledge.
162 For providence, see *Sacr.* 1.2.19 (PL 176.213B-D; Deferrari, 37).
163 Rom 6:23.
164 This emphasis on human sinfulness and the sovereignty of grace is a clear indication of Hugh's dependence on the harsh anti-Pelagian theology of Augustine's later works.
165 See *Sacr.* 1.2.20 (PL 176.213D; Deferrari, 38: [altered]). Hugh states, "Divine regulation (*dispositio*) is considered in two ways. To be sure good things receive their regulation from above, both that they might be because they are good and that they might be in a particular way because they are ordered (*ordinata*). Evil things, however, do not possess what they are from heavenly arrangement (*dispositio*) because they are evil, and yet they possess what they are in a particular way because they are ordered. For God does not make evil, but when it occurs he does not allow it to be unordered (*inordinatum*) since he is not the author of evil things, but their orderer (*ordinator*)."
166 The last two statements are somewhat confusing. Hugh's points seem to be that God arranges that the good have merit and so a reward, whereas for the wicked he arranges only that they are punished (because they have no merit). Both groups receive their just deserts, but only for the good does God arrange the basis for those deserts.
167 Cf. Ambrose, *De fide* 5.6.82 (PL 16:693).
168 See *Sacr.* 1.2.21 (PL 176.213D-214A; Deferrari, 38).
169 See *Sacr.* 1.2.22 (PL 176.214A-216C; Deferrari, 38–41).
170 Werner II of Küssenberg, Abbot of St Blaisen (d. 1126), *Liber deflorationum* (PL 157.828D-829A) argues *amplius facere non potest quam facit*; see also Hildebert of Lavardin (?), *Tractatus theologicus* 11 (PL 171.1095A-C); *Summa sent.* 1.14 (PL 176.69A-B). In making this assertion, these writers draw on Augustine, *Conf.* 7.6 (CCL 27.95; trans. Boulding, 162): *nec cogeris inuitus ad aliquid, quia uoluntas tua non est maior quam potentia* ("Nor are you forced unwillingly into anything, because your will is not greater than your power"). Abelard makes a similar assertion in *Christian Theology* 3.73 when he is discussing the Trinity. Abelard concluded on the basis of divine goodness and divine reason that God could not do more than he does, or do anything better than he does it. He based his view partly on Plato's idea that God could not make a better world than the present one because this would imply a lack of goodness in God. Abelard would not entertain the idea that there could be more than one course of action for God. This claim, he believes, diminishes the goodness of God. See Abelard *TChr* (CCCM 12.361), *TSch* 3.27–28 (Mews, 511–2). See also John Marenbon, *The Philosophy of Peter Abelard* (Cambridge: Cambridge University Press, 1997), 217–21. Whether Hugh included Abelard among those who held this opinion depends on the relative dating

of Abelard's *Christian Theology* (ca. 1125) and the lectures of which the *Sentences on Divinity* are a *reportatio*.

171   Cf. Ambrosiaster, *Com. in Pauli ep. ad Romanos* (recensio gamma) 8.7 (CCL 184.263): *o prudentes mundi, qui putant Deum non debere aliter facere quam facit condita ab eo creatura, ut ipse similis creaturis putetur!* This text of Ambrosiaster is usually cited in discussions on God's omnipotence, e.g., Peter Abelard, *TChr* 5.39 (CCCM 12.364); *SN* 35.7 (Boyer-McKeon, 185).

172   By "through reason" (*per rationem*), Hugh seems to have Abelard's appeal to rational cause in mind. Abelard borrows the idea that there must be a rational cause for everything from Plato's *Timaeus* (28a). He concludes that God must have a reason or cause for everything he does. "If, therefore, there is a reason for God either doing or leaving off, then the activity must be carried out or the cessation must come into effect" (translation taken from J. R. McCallum, *Abelard's 'Christian Theology'* [Oxford: Blackwell, 1948], 94).

173   See *Sacr.* 1.8.9 (PL 176.311BD; Deferrari, 147–48) where Hugh discusses "permissible justice and compelling justice" (*patiens et cogens iustitia*). Hugh states, "Permissive justice is that in which if some action occurred, it is just, and it is not unjust if it did not occur. Compelling justice is that in which something happened in such a way that it would be unjust for it not to happen. For this reason, permissive justice deals with governance and compelling justice deals with necessity." Hugh goes on to use this distinction in order to argue that salvation and damnation are both within God's right because they pertain to permissive justice. It would not be unjust if God saved or condemned the same person based on his/her merits. Hugh's reason for this position is that the exercise of divine power ultimately resides in the divine will. He states "Those who are justly damned according to their merits, could have been justly saved by God's grace if God had willed it. On the other hand, God could have damned according to their merits those who are justly saved by God's grace, if he had not willed to save them. Consequently, what God willed for each group was just so that even if God had willed something else it would not have been unjust. It is because power resides in God's will that whatever he so willed is permissible for him to do without it being unjust."

174   The verb "*facere*" is prominent in what follows. It means "do" or "make." Most often this translation opts for the more general "do."

175   *Timaeus* 29e. The reading here is identical to the following Latin translation attributed to Chalcidius: *Plato secundum translationem quam fecit Chalcidius* (after 400 AD), *Timaeus* 1 (J. H. Waszink, *Plato latinus* 4.22). It is most likely that Hugh takes this quotation from Abelard's *Christian Theology*, which Abelard had composed in the early 1123–1125 (Buytaert dates the first redaction to 1123–1125 [CCCM 12.49–50]). The specific passage is part of a larger quotation from the *Timaeus* that Abelard inserts into his discussion about whether God could do more than he does or better than he does. See also L. Moonan, "Abelard's Use of the *Timaeus*," *Archives d'histoire doctrinale et littéraire du moyen âge* (1989): 7–90.

176   Wis 11:21. Piazzoni includes a reference to Augustine, *Civ. Dei*, 11.30. Augustine does cite Wis 11:20 in *CD* 11.30, but the quotation Hugh offers from St Augustine does not occur there. Hugh may be paraphrasing Augustine, *Gn. litt.* 4.3 (CSEL 28.1.99): "*Magnum est paucisque concessum, excedere omnia quae metiri possunt, ut videatur mensura sine mensura; excedere omnia quae numerari possunt, ut videatur numerus sine numero; excedere omnia quae appendi possunt, ut videatur pondus sine pondere.*" ("It is a great thing, granted to few, to go beyond all things that can be measured, so that one sees the measure without measure; to go beyond all things that can be numbered, so that one sees the number without number; to go beyond what can be weighed, to see weight with without"). In 4.4. (CSEL 28.1.100), Augustine continues: "*numerus sine numero est, quo formantur omnia, nec formatur ipse; pondus sine pondere est, quo referuntur, ut quiescant, quorum quies purum gaudium est, nec illud iam refertur ad aliud.*" ("Number without number is that by which all things are formed; it is itself not formed; weight without weight, is that by which they are brought back so that they rest; their rest is pure joy, which is not referred back to anything else.")

The *Sententiae divinitatis*, (Geyer, 17), which follow Hugh rather closely (even at times the *Sententiae de divinitate*), says: "*Item quod dicit Augustinus: Omnia fecit Deus in pondere et mensura et numero, non praetermittendum esse videtur, quoniam ad ea, quae diximus alludere iudicatur. Creavit omnia in pondere etc., id est: In se ipso, qui est numerus sine numero, mensura sine mensura, pondus sine pondere.*" ("Likewise what Augustine says should, it seems, not be passed over—'God made all things in weight, measure and number'—for it is judged to pertain to the thing we have said. 'He created all things in weight, etc.,' that is, in himself, who is number without number, measure without measure, weight without weight.")

177 Augustine, *Civ. Dei*, 5.10 (CCL 47.140): "*Dicitur enim [Deus] omnipotens, faciendo quod vult, non patiendo quod non vult.*" (God "is said to be omnipotent, because he does what he wishes, not because he suffers [= cannot do] what he does not wish.")

178 Jerome, *Epistula* 22.5.2 (CSEL 54.150): "*Audenter loquor: cum omnia Deus possit, suscitare virginem non potest post ruinam.*" ("I speak boldly, although God is capable of all things, he can not restore a virgin after her downfall.") In Hugh's paraphrase, "corrupt" is a singular feminine adjective, whereas "incorrupt" seems to be a neuter plural adjective; perhaps one should read *incorruptam* for *incorrupta. Corrumpere*, the Latin verb from which these adjectives are derived, means to destroy, seduce, bribe, or corrupt.

179 Jerome, *In Osee prophetam* 1.2 (CCL 76.8).

180 Cf. *Sacr.* 1.4.1–26 (PL 176.233D–246C; Deferrari 61–74).

181 I have emended "mala" to "mal[a]e" so that it agrees with "alique partes."

182 Rom 9: 19.

183 1 Tim 2.4.

184 I have amended "*consecuimus*" to "*consuevimus.*" *Consecuimus* is the first-person, plural, perfect form of *consecare*, a rare verb meaning to cut to pieces or prune.

185 See *Sacr.* 1.4.8 (PL 176.237AC; Deferrari, 63–64).

186 Ps 110.2 (Vulg.).

187 This seems to be a convoluted way of saying that whatever happens according to God's will is right, and all things happen according to his will, therefore all things are right. The Latin text may be corrupt.

188 Hugh is referring to the incarnation by which the Son of God assumed a human nature (= *homo assumptus*).

189 In order to make sense of this sentence it seemed necessary to amend the text by changing "cannot" to "can."

190 See *Didasc.* 1.1 (Buttimer, 5; Taylor, 46). There Hugh utilizes the idea that "similars are comprehended by similars" to reinforce his claim that the human soul can ascend from the visible to the invisible.

191 *defectus*: want, lack, absence, defect. Most of the ideas in the discussion of evil which follows can be found in the writings of St Augustine; e.g., *Ench.* 10–11, J. Rivière, *Exposés généraux de la foi*, Oeuvres de Saint Augustin, Série 1: Opuscules, 9 (Paris: Desclée de Brouwer, 1947) 118–19.

192 Emending "deesse" to "decere," the verb used in the next sentence.

193 *paries*: may mean mural or wall-painting here. The possibility of painting the whole surface with one color suggests that this not the case, but the word *pictura* does suggest a mural. It is not clear whether the "all" goes with the first clause or the second. One can't help thinking about the (real or imagined) drawing of the ark of Noah described in Hugh's *Libellus*.

194 Emending "*quia*" to "*quod.*"

195 In the discussion that follows it appears that Hugh is borrowing from contemporary dialectics. He may be drawing on Boethius' commentary *On Cicero's Topics* (cf. *In Ciceronis Topica* 4.11.47–49; Stump, 117–21) or *De divisione liber* (Magee, 22–27). Hugh could also be borrowing from William of Champeux. Notes of William's teaching on dialectic written by William himself from *ca.* 1113 state, "The nature of contradictories is such that they always divide into true and false. From which they take this inference: if one is true, the other is false, and the

converse. For example, if it is true that 'every man is an animal,' it is false that 'this man is not an animal' [*quidam homo non est animal*]. This is proven in this way: If it is true that 'every man is an animal,' it is also true that 'everything not an animal is not a man' (an inference from the part); and if it is true that 'everything not an animal is not a man,' it is false that 'something that is not an animal is not a non-man' [*quiddam non animal ‹non› est non homo*] (an inference from contradictories). If this is the case, then it is false that 'this man is not an animal.'" (*Introductiones dialecticae secundum Wilgelmum* 3.3; Iwakuma, 61). A *reportatio* of William's early teaching (*ca.* 1080s), has him state, "I said earlier that one type of categorical proposition is affirmative, another is negative, another is universal, another is particular, another is indefinite, and another is singular. On the basis of these divisions, one can have a division by complex part in this way: one is a universal affirmative while another is a universal negative. For example, 'every man is an animal' and 'no man is an animal.' Another complex part is a particular affirmative and a particular negative. For example, 'a certain man is an animal' and 'a certain man is not an animal.' Another complex part is an indefinite affirmative and an indefinite negative. For example, 'man is an animal' and 'man is not an animal.' There is also an individual affirmative and an individual negative as, for example, 'Socrates is an animal' and 'Socrates is not an animal.'"

196 Based on William's examples, this statement appears to be a universal affirmative: *Deus vult omne bonum esse* is akin to *omnis homo est animal*.

197 The meaning of this sentence hinges on the distinction between willing something (in itself) and willing something to be (for the sake of something else). The shift from neuter pronouns (*id, illud, quod*) to a feminine one (*illam*) is puzzling. In *Sacr.* 1.5.27 (PL 176.258D; Deferrari, 88) Hugh asks: *quare permittit ut faciant quod non vult, cum fieri non possit nisi eo permittente, nec permitti nisi eo volente?* Even God's passive will is not really passive. Maybe the following captures the sense of the passage: "this is also a sign that God wills *it to be*, even though he does not will *it*, but he permits *it* because he wills *it to be*." Hence, the only difference between the active and passive will is the *illud uelit* (= active will), but they both entail the *illud esse uelit*. In the same passage in *Sacr.* (PL 176.258C; Deferrari, 88), Hugh will argue that God is the regulator (*ordinator*) of an evil will but not its creator, that is, he permits a creature's evil activity, but he did not inspire an evil will in him. God grants evil people the freedom or ability to carry out evil (*potestatem*), not an evil will (*voluntatem*). This makes sense if evil is a privation; hence, all this is very Augustinian.

198 The Latin reads: *Sed tamen aliquid precipit quod cum velit esse tamen non vult, esse tamen vult quia eius effectus commodus est creaturis.* Piazonni put the comma after *esse*, which seems to make no sense. As translated, the sentence seems to mean that God sometimes commands something that although he may wish it, he wishes it *to be* only because its effect is beneficial to creatures. Alternatively, one could emend the verb to *prohibet*. Three considerations can be advanced in support this emendation: First, the "*sed tamen*" points to the previous sentence in which the verb is *prohibet*. Second, this corresponds to his previous definition of a prohibition as *illud non uult* (hence, this sentence is adding the unexpected proposition of a prohibition of what God wills to be even though he does not will it). Third, this makes sense of the following question, which results from this sentence, namely, "Why does God prohibit what he wills to be?"

199 In Hugh of St Victor's Latin usage, *vitium* has a wider range of meaning than does the English word "vice." It can mean any bad habit or an impulse or thought that needs to be restrained or properly directed.

200 The Latin has *non umquam* (not ever), but the logic of Hugh's argument requires *non numquam* (not never = sometimes).

201 *quem igitiur Deus ita singulorum providere debet utilitati ut . . .* The antecedent of the *quem* is not clear and I have not translated it.

202 The subject ("he") of *debet* could be the individual of the previous sentence, God, or an indefinite "one."

PART THREE (pp. 155-160)

203 Cf. Col 1:17.

204 Cf. Augustine, *Soliloquia* 1.3 (CSEL 89.5).

205 Cf. Hugh of St Victor, *Sacr.* 1.3.1 (PL 176.216D; Deferrari, 41); 1.3.31 (PL 176.234B).

206 Cf. Hugh of St Victor, *Sacr.* 1.3.2 (PL 176.217B; Deferrari, 41–42).

207 Cf. Hugh of St Victor, *Archa Noe* 4.3 (CCCM 176.94); cf. Otto of Lucca, *Summa sent.* 1.3 (PL 176.45C-D); *Summa sent.* 2 (PL 171.1071A-B). See also Augustine, *Jo. ev. tr.* 40.9 (CCL 36.355); Peter Lombard, *Sent.* 3.23.2.1 (SB 4.141); 3.23.7 (SB 4.145–46).

208 Cf. Heb 11:1.

209 Gregory the Great, *Hom. ev.* 2.26.1 (CCL 141.218). Peter Lombard uses this citation to explain why the body and blood of Christ in the Eucharist is hidden under two species, see *In ep. I ad Corinthios* 11.23 (PL 191.1641D-1642A); *Sent.* 4.11.3 (SB 4.299).

210 Rom 1:21.

211 Cf. Hugh of St Victor, *Sacr.* 1.3.3 (PL 176.217B-218B; Deferrari, 42).

212 This epistemological function of divine inspiration, which is common in the twelfth century, may not be apparent to the modern reader who usually views inspiration as a special chrism of the canonical authors. Cognitive inspiration, which will be clarified further by Richard of St Victor, occurs whenever Christ is present to the rational soul in such a way that it acquires knowledge of truth in a way not otherwise possible. The content of knowledge acquired through cognitive inspiration varies. First, cognitive inspiration sometimes entails what Richard calls "intellectible" truths, that is, invisible things that reason cannot understand without grace, as opposed to sensible truths (i.e., visible and perceptible by the corporeal senses) or intelligible truths (i.e., invisible things that reason can understand). After such truths are inspired, reason can then affirm and "the authority of divine scripture" sanctions the intellectible truth infused into the soul (cf. Richard of St Victor, *Arca Moys.* 1.7 [Aris, 14]; see also *XII patr.* 82 [SC 419.326, 328]). Consequently, the content of knowledge acquired through external and internal grace can be the same; their difference lies in the mode in which that knowledge is infused into the heart. The source of revealed or inspired knowledge is the Triune God: the internal, inner-Trinitarian communication becomes the exterior speaking that can be infused internally into the heart by means of divine inspiration or externally by means of the external graces (e.g., Richard of St Victor, *Trin.* 6.12 [TPMA 6.243]). Second, cognitive inspiration can also convey knowledge of future contingencies or the secret intentions and deeds of other people, both of which are beyond human nature to know without the grace of inspiration (e.g., Richard of St Victor, *Erud.* 1.6 [PL 196.1241a]; Andrew of St Victor, *In Genesim.* 27.42 [CCCM 53.76]). It was reported, for example, that once while Hugh was too ill to retain food, the brothers brought him an unconsecrated host; Hugh, however, was "divinely inspired" (*divinitus inspiratus*) and knew of their deception (*Catalogi duo veteres operum Hugonis a S. Victore* [PL 175.146A]). Third, cognitive inspiration sometimes conveys universal moral truths. Hugh argues, for example, that the good that one ought to accomplish and the evil that one ought to avoid are contained in two kinds of commands: "the precept of nature" and the "precept of discipline." The discipline is an external precept, while the precept of nature is the natural moral law that is "inspired" into the soul at original creation. These moral laws are natural moral instincts—what Hugh calls "natural discernment" (*discretionem naturalem*)—that are infused into the soul, so that it can naturally pursue the good and avoid the evil (see Hugh of St Victor, *Sacr.* 1.6.7 [PL 176.268C; Deferrari, 99–100]; *Sacr.* 1.6.28 [PL 176.281B; Deferrari, 113–14]; *Sac. dial.* [PL 176.23D]; cf. also *Sacr.* 1.4.25 [PL 176.245C; Deferrari, 72–73]). See *Summa sent.* 3.4 [PL 176.95D]). In addition to natural discernment, Richard makes a further distinction between what is profitable and more profitable (what he calls "deliberation"). Concerning deliberation, see *Arca Moys.* 3.23 [Aris, 82–83]; *Adnot. Psalm.* 143 [PL 196.381D]; *Erud.* 1.12 [PL 196.1248C]; *Super exiit* [Châtillon, 104]. Concerning discretion, see Richard of St Victor, *XII patr.* 67–69 (SC 419.282–92);

Arca Moys. 3.7, 23 [Aris, 65, 82]; *Adnot. Psalm.* 118 [PL 196.359b-363b]; *Erud.* 1.12 [PL 196.1248c]; *Erud.* 2.3 [PL 196.1301c]; *Super exiit* [Châtillon, 74]. On the difference between the two, see *Decl. nonn. diff.* [TPMA 15.208]. See also Peter Abelard, *Dialog. inter phil.* [PL 178.1652a]; Bernard of Clairvaux, *SCC* 49.5 [SBOp 2.76]) Because of the fall, Richard argues that humanity has sustained a moral blindness toward the deliberation of actions that are more expedient for their well being. And yet, because of divine inspiration, some people can decide the most profitable actions for themselves and others (See Richard of St Victor, *Statu.* 28, 30, 31 [*AHDLMA* 42.95-96, 97-98]). In *De statu interioris hominis* Richard makes a distinction between deliberation of counsel, which determines how good something is, and discernment of judgment, which determines how expedient something is (*Statu.* 28, 29 [*AHDLMA* 42.95, 96]). Both are a gift of God and require divine inspiration, see *Statu.* 31 (*AHDLMA* 42.97-98).

The overarching framework for the theology of cognitive inspiration may be identified as the anatomy of divine revelation. Here in the *Sentences on Divinity* Hugh summarizes this anatomy under the rubrics of internal or external nature and internal or external grace. This anatomy of divine revelation is found throughout the writings of Hugh and Richard (see references below). The advantage of this construct is that it clearly singles out divine inspiration as a distinct operation from other modes of divine revelation. The object of natural revelation is the visible world (external-natural revelation) or the soul (internal-natural revelation). Despite the importance of these modes of revelation as a source for Victorine theology, they are insufficient in themselves unless external or internal grace was added as an aid to nature (see Hugh of St Victor, *Sacr.* 1.3.3 [PL 176.214C-218B; Deferrari, 42–43]; see also *Summa sent.* 1.3 [PL 176.46A]). Divine revelation as an internal grace is the illumination of human ignorance by means of the divine operation of inspiration, while divine revelation as an external grace is the instruction of divine truth through external means like the ecclesiastical writings (canonical and non-canonical), teachings of the Church, miracles, and even the sacred liturgy (see Hugh of St Victor, *In hier. cael.* 2.1 [PL 175.944D]; *Archa Noe* 4.7 [CCCM 176.103]; Richard of St Victor, *Arca Moys.* 5.13 [Aris, 139–40]). All these "revelations" entail a single *vox Dei* working throughout the ages and in different aspects of human existence. The presence of the Spirit ensures the reliability, consistency, harmony, and unity of truth diffused in all its parts, so that knowledge acquired by divine inspiration is corroborated and sanctioned by the authority of the external graces, and vice versa. Even internal-natural revelation can confirm what is discovered through inspiration (Richard of St Victor, *Arca Moys.* 1.7 [PL 196.72A-C; Aris, 14]). But, although these are all valid sources for acquiring knowledge of divine things, they are not of the same value. Truth acquired from creation is the lowest kind of knowledge, while inspired truth is usually the sweetest kind of knowledge. External revelation is mediate, visible, varied, and time consuming, while inspiration is immediate, internal, invisible, simple, and instantaneous (Hugh of St Victor, *In hier. cael.* 2.1 [PL 175.954C]; *In hier. cael.* 7 [PL 175.1054C]). The very fact that the Scripture must present information externally means that it is a limited vehicle for dispensing knowledge. Inspiration infuses information without external restrictions; hence, it is a loftier vehicle for imparting information. "The light of knowledge," Hugh argues, "which is infused inwardly through invisible inspiration (*per invisibilem aspirationem*), is loftier and more worthy than the light that is possessed externally through the instruction of doctrine" (Hugh of St Victor, *In hier. cael.* 7 [PL 175.1054C]; see also Richard of St Victor, *Adnot. Psalm.* 118 [PL 196.351b-352A]; *Missione* [PL 196.1023D]). Cf. Hugh of St Victor, *Sacr.* 1.3.3 (PL 176.214C-218B; Deferrari, 00); 1.3.30 (PL 176.232B); 1.6.12 (PL 176.270D); 1.6.14 (PL 176.271C-D); *In hier. cael.* 2.1 (PL 175.944D); *Misc.* 1.63 (PL 177.504C-505A); *Verbo* 5 (SC 155.74); Richard of St Victor, *Arca Moys.* 3.16 (Aris, 74); 5.1 (Aris, 123); *Erud.* 1.32 (PL 196.1268D); *Adnot. Psalm.* 28 (PL 196.308A and 310A); *Adnot. Psalm.* 80 (PL 196.325D); *Adnot. Psalm.* 118 (PL 196.351C-D); *Apoc.* 1.1 (PL 196.686B-D); *Apoc.* 2.1 (PL 196.744D); *Missione* (196.1023D); *Serm. Greg.* 8 (Châtillon, 391); *Serm. cent.* 41 (PL 177.1006D); *Serm. cent.* 61 (PL 177.1087D); *Serm. cent.* 90 (PL 177.1182A);

LE 2.7.23 (Châtillon, 330–31); cf. also *Quaestiones in ep. Pauli: ad Rom.* 34 (PL 175.439D-440A); *Quaestiones in ep. Pauli: ad Cor. I* 116 (PL 175.535C); *Speculum* 9 (PL 177.377A); *Summa sent.* 1.3 (PL 176.46A. Regarding this juxtaposition between external revelation and internal inspiration, see also William of St Thierry, *Super Cantica Cant.* 34 (CCCM 87.145); Ambrosius Autpertus, *Sermo in purificatione* 14 (CCCM 27B.999); Peter Lombard, *In Psalmos Davidicos Commentarii.* 32 (PL 191.329C); Gerhoh of Reichersberg, *Expositiones in Psalmos* 9.84.9 (PL 194.519D); Gottfried of Admont, *Homiliae dominicales* 10 (PL 174.67); *Homiliae festivales* 60 (PL 174.942); Radulphus Ardens, *Homilia* 1.71 (PL 155.1934A); *Homilia* 2.21 (PL 155.2019A); *Homilia* 2.39 (PL 155.2084D); *Homiliae de tempore* 9 (PL 155.1332D); *Homiliae de sanctis* 4 (PL 155.1503C).

[213] Cf. Rom 1:19–21.

[214] See references in Prologue, note 63.

[215] Rom 1:19.

[216] Rom 1:20.

[217] Cf. Gilbert of Poitiers, *Expositio ad Romanos* 1.19 (Lisbon, Biblioteca Nacional *Fundo Alcobaça* XCVII/178, f. 3rb): Manifestum est *non dico illis sed* in illis, *quia nobiles philosophi per naturalem racionem quesierunt et omnium rerum specie‹m› tanqum uoce sibi respondente, ex arte artificem cognouerunt. Nec defuit diuinum auxilium sine quo ratio nichil cognesceret: Deus enim manifestauit uel reuelauit illis*; William of St Thierry, *Expositio ad Romanos* 1 (CCCM 86.440).

[218] Rom 1:19.

[219] Rom 1:21.

[220] Cf. Hugh of St Victor, *Sacr.* 1.3.4 (PL 176.218B-C; Deferrari, 43).

[221] Cf. *Speculum de mysteriis ecclesiae* 9 (PL 177.378B).

[222] Cf. Hugh of St Victor, *Sacr.* 1.3.7 (PL 176.219A-B; Deferrari, 44).

[223] Cf. Hugh of St Victor, *Sacr.* 1.3.6 (PL 176.219A; Deferrari, 43).

[224] Cf. Hugh of St Victor, *Sacr.* 1.3.8 (PL 176.219B-C; Deferrari, 44).

[225] Cf. Hugh of St Victor, *Sacr.* 1.3.12 (PL 176.220B-C; Deferrari, 45).

[226] See *supra* Pars Prima and Hugh of St Victor, *Sacr.* 2.1.12 (PL 176.408D-409B; Deferrari, 34).

[227] The Latin reads *immutabilitatem*, but *mutabilitatem* makes better sense.

[228] Cf. Hugh of St Victor, *Sacr.* 1.3.25 (PL 176.227B; Deferrari, 52–53).

[229] Hugh of St Victor, *Sacr.* 1.3.6 (PL 176.219A; Deferrari, 43).

[230] Cf. Guibert of Nogent, *Moralia in Genesin* 6.23 (PL 156.174C).

[231] Cf. Hugh of St Victor, *Sacr.* 1.3.21 (PL 176.225B-D; Deferrari, 50–51).

[232] Cf. Augustine, *Trin.* 6.2 (CCL 50.229); Hugh of St Victor, *De sapientia animae Christi* (PL 176.848B).

[233] Cf. Richard of St Victor, *Trin.* 5.15 (TPMA 6.247; n. 72).

ADAM OF ST VICTOR

SEQUENCES

INTRODUCTION AND TRANSLATION
BY JULIET MOUSSEAU

INTRODUCTION

Adam of Saint Victor was the leading liturgical theologian of the Abbey of Saint Victor. His sequences provide a window onto the life and liturgy at Saint Victor and explore Victorine theology in poetic form.

The story of Adam's life remains largely unknown, and there is some controversy over his identity and works.[1] He lived at the Abbey during the same time period as Hugh, dying there in the late 1140s. Adam's literary corpus consists of approximately forty-seven sequences.[2] A sequence is a poem composed to be sung during the mass, between the Alleluia and the gospel reading.[3] It bridges the Old Testament or

[1]   The clearest recent source of information about Adam's life is Margot Fassler's "Who Was Adam of Saint Victor? The Evidence of the Sequence Manuscripts." *Journal of the American Musicological Society* 37 (1984): 233–69. In this article, Fassler reviews the primary source material for Adam's biography and makes conclusions, often contradicting earlier scholarship, that will be assumed here. Using the Victorine liturgical manuscripts as her major source, Fassler wades through the legends of Adam of Saint Victor, as well as the confusion of Adam with different authors and Victorines. While the sequences from all Parisian sources are related to each other, Fassler asserts a process of redaction at the Abbey (not present at the Cathedral) that allows for a consistent expression of the Victorine theology throughout the sequence repertoire.

[2]   The number of Adam's authentic works is difficult to establish, and throughout the centuries numerous other works have been attributed to him that are not authentic. The most recent text to examine this problem is that of Jean Grosfillier, *Les séquences d'Adam de Saint-Victor: Étude littéraire (poétique et rhétorique) textes et traductions, commentaires* (Turnhout: Brepols, 2008). However, I have used the list by Josef Szövérffy in *Die Annalen der lateinischen Hymnendichtung: Ein Handbuch* (Berlin: Erich Schmidt Verlag, 1965), 107–8, which assigns forty-eight sequences to Adam. My amendation of Szövérffy's list is simply to exclude from that list the sequence written at Saint Victor for St Thomas of Canterbury, who died several years after Adam.

[3]   The sequence developed from the ninth century forward. Connected at first to the Alleluia, which is proclaimed before the gospel during mass, the sequence became a separate poem that was sung between the Alleluia and the gospel reading. See Peter Dronke, "The Beginnings of the Sequence," *Beiträge zur Geschichte der deutschen Sprache und Literatur* 87 (1965): 43–73; and John F. Benton, "Nicolas of Clairvaux and the Twelfth-Century Sequence with Special Reference to Adam of St Victor," *Traditio* 18 (1962): 149–79. For later development of the Parisian sequence, see Michel Huglo, "Origine et diffusion de la séquence parisienne (ou séquence de second époque)," in *Musicologie médiévale: notations et séquences*, edited by Michel Huglo, 209–12, (Paris: H. Champion, 1987); Nancy Van Deusen, "Polymelodic Sequences and a 'Second Epoch' of Sequence Composition," in *Musicologie Médiévale*, 213–25, and "The Use and Significance of the Sequence," *Musica Disciplina* 40 (1986): 5–47.

Epistle readings and the gospel, both literarily and musically. During Adam's lifetime, the sequence was at its poetic and musical height, retaining a determined form and regular rhyme scheme. Scholars refer to this particular stage of development as the late or second-epoch sequence, and Adam is the recognized master of this poetic form.[4]

The sequences *Mundi renovatio, Profitentes unitatem,* and *Qui procedis ab utroque* illustrate the Victorine theology of Trinity and creation. *Mundi renovatio,* an Easter sequence, presents the theme of the renewal of all creation through the resurrection of Christ. *Profitentes unitatem,* for the feast of the Trinity, and *Qui procedis ab utroque,* for the Pentecost octave, focus on the theology of the Trinity and the relationship of the Trinitarian God to humanity.

Mundi renovatio celebrates the resurrection of the Lord by expressing the beauty of the natural world as the work of the Creator God, which is then wonderfully re-created and renewed by the work of Christ, for "as the Lord resurrects, all things rise together."[5] Adam describes creation as beautified and calmed by the work of God in Jesus Christ. As Genesis illustrates creation as the movement from chaos to order, so also Adam understands the redemption of the fallen world. Verses three through five clearly state that the elements of earth, sky, sea, wind, ground, and water become calm and spring-like. The weather changes from the cold of winter into the verdant warmth of spring. The re-creation begins with the elements of the earth, but its center is the salvation of humanity, and the end of certain death: "The frost of death is brought to an end, the prince of the world fails and his empire is destroyed in us . . . Life overcomes death, for man recuperates what he first lost, the joy of paradise."[6] Quite clearly, the ordered world is one of continued regeneration and growth through the work of the Trinitarian God.

Mundi renovatio ends with praise for the Trinity, by declaring that the glory for victory over death and the renewal of God's creation be-

---

[4]   Most late sequences consist of a number of strophes, each divided into two sections of identical rhyme and meter. The strophes are arranged to music that consists of repeated lines, with each half-strophe assigned to one repetition of the line while the next strophe receives new music. The length of the strophes and of the sequences as a whole varies widely. The highly developed and repetitive rhythm of the poem is masked by the musical shape given to the text. Fassler analyzes the musical and textual characteristics of the sequences in *Gothic Song: Victorine Sequences and Augustinian Reform in Twelfth-Century Paris* (Cambridge: Cambridge University Press, 1993), 72–78.

[5]   *Mundi renovatio* 2.

[6]   *Mundi renovatio* 7–8.

longs to the Trinity, that is, "to the Father and the Son, with the Holy Spirit."⁷ This theme continues in *Profitentes unitatem*. Adam vocalizes nearly every technical term used in reference to the Trinity. He uses philosophical language of the Aristotelian categories of causality to explain the function of God in creation. Then, using credal terminology, Adam asserts the equality of the three persons of the Trinity: they are one substance, essence, *ousia*, being, power, willing, and knowing. They function as unity, yet Adam also affirms their distinction by relationship, a distinction that cannot be removed or overwhelmed by their divine unity. The Western theology of the *filioque* is found here: "The connection of the Spirit proceeds from both the Father and equally from the Son."⁸

Even amid the technical language, Adam asserts that belief in the Trinity is a matter of faith rather than understanding, for "to speak of the persons worthily transcends the power of reason, exceeds all ingenuity."⁹ Perhaps for this reason, the sequence is scattered with paradoxes, such as "simple Trinity."¹⁰ It is impossible for the human mind to comprehend fully the sublimity of the Godhead. This fundamental faith is a source of pride for Adam of Saint Victor and his companions.

Drawing further upon the role of God in the life of the human person, *Qui procedis ab utroque* paints a more intimate portrait of that relationship. This sequence directly calls upon the Holy Spirit by employing the second person "you." The prayer speaks of the gifts of the Holy Spirit, which establish the presence of the Trinity in the human heart. The relationship demands gratitude and love for God, not only for the initial creation and re-creation, but also for the continued work of God in daily human life. Thus, the sequence connects the actions of the Trinity to human history, to the lives of the apostles and to each person alive today. An air of humility pervades the sequence: through the Holy Spirit, the human person can learn, be cleansed of sinfulness, and follow Christ's path of peace.

Thus, in Adam's poetry, a theology of a three-fold creation emerges. The Father God creates, Christ renews his creation, and the Holy Spirit sustains that restored life. The three sequences, *Mundi renovatio, Profi-*

---

⁷   Mundi renovatio 9.
⁸   Profitentes unitatem 10.
⁹   Profitentes unitatem 15.
¹⁰ Profitentes unitatem 20.

tentes unitatem, and *Qui procedis ab utroque,* draw together the theology of creation with the Trinity, thereby illustrating the same theology promoted throughout Victorine writings.

The present translation of the sequences will utilize the critical text of Clemens Blume and Guido Dreves published in *Analecta hymnica: Thesauri hymnologici prosarium* in 1915 and 1922.[11] A translation of the complete corpus of Adam's sequences is forthcoming.[12]

[11]   Vols. 54 and 55 of *Analecta hymnica medii aevi* (Leipzig: O. R. Reisland, 1915 and 1922).
[12]   My translation of Adam's corpus will be published with the Blume/Dreves Latin text, introduction, and notes as a volume in the Dallas Medieval Texts and Translations Series, general editor Philipp Rosemann (Leuven: Peeters, 2010).

MUNDI RENOVATIO

EASTER SEQUENCE

1.
The renovation of the world
produces new joy:

2.
As the Lord resurrects,
all things rise together.

3.
The elements serve
and sense how great
is the power of their Author.

4.
The sky becomes more serene
and the sea more tranquil,
the breeze moves more gently,
our valley flourishes,

5.
Darting fire flies,
as does shifting air.
Falling water flows,
earth remains stable.
Light things reach for the heights,
heavy things hold the center.
All are restored.[1]

6.
Dry things grow green again,
cold things become warm again,
after spring has begun.

7.
The frost of death is brought to an end,
the prince of the world fails
and his empire
is destroyed in us.
While he willed to hold

that in which he had no right,
he lost what was his right.

8.
Life overcomes death,
for man recuperates
what he first lost,
the joy of paradise.
The cherubim hold out the easy way,
removing the turning sword.

9.
Christ opens the heavens
and frees the captives,
whom guilt bound
under the ruin of death.
For such a victory
may glory be to the Father and the Son,
with the Holy Spirit.

PROFITENTES UNITATEM

Sequence for the Feast of the Trinity

1.
Professing the unity,
let us worship the Trinity
in equal reverence,

2.
upholding three persons,
distinct from each other
by a personal characteristic.

3.
They are distinguished relatively
although they are of one substance,
not three principles.

4.
Although you may say three or of three,
they are of a single *ousia*,
not a triple essence.

5.
Simple in being, simple in power,
simple in willing, simple in knowing,
all these are simple:

6.
Father, Offspring, Holy Flame.
One God, yet they each
have certain properties of their own.

7.
The power of one
is not less than the power
of two or three persons.

8.
One virtue, one divinity,
one splendor, one light,
in one as in the others.

9.
The Son is equal to the Father,
but this does not remove
the distinction of each person.

10.
The connection of the Spirit
proceeds from both
the Father and equally from the Son.

11.
Neither these persons
nor their distinctions
can be grasped by reason.

12.
There is no temporal order here,
no place, or local
limitation of things.

13.
Nothing is in God except God,
no cause except he who
creates causable things.

14.
Effective cause and also formal cause,
and final cause—God—
but at no time is he the material cause.

15.
To speak of the persons worthily
transcends the power of reason,
exceeds all ingenuity.

16.
What is it to be begotten? What to proceed?
I profess to be ignorant myself,
but in faith there is no doubt.

17.
Let the one who thus believes not act rashly,
and not turn aside insolently
from the royal way.

18.
Let that one keep the faith, form morals,
and not consider the errors
that the Church condemns.[2]

19.
Let us glory in faith.
Let us sing in one
constant faith.

20.
Praise be to the threefold Unity,
and coeternal glory
to the simple Trinity.

QUI PROCEDIS AB UTROQUE

SEQUENCE FOR THE OCTAVE OF PENTECOST

1.
You who proceed from both
begetter and begotten,
equally, Paraclete,

2.
give us eloquent tongues,
make our minds burn in you,
and enrich them by your flame.

3.
The love of the Father and of the Son,
equal of both, and
equal and entirely similar to each,

4.
You replenish everything, you foster all,
you rule the stars, you move heaven,
remaining unmoved.

5.
Dear light, clear light,
you put to flight the darkness
of the internal shadows.

6.
Through you the pure are cleansed.
You destroy sin and
every trace of sin.

7.
You make truth new
and show the path of peace
and the way of justice.

8.
You shun the hearts of the wicked
and enrich the hearts of the good
with your gift of knowledge.

9.
You teach and nothing is obscure,
you are present and nothing is impure.
Under your presence

10.
the joyful soul glories,
the conscience—happy through you,
pure through you—rejoices.

11.
You change the elements.
Through you the sacraments
have their efficacy.

12.
You drive away the hurtful power.
You overthrow and refute
the wickedness of the enemy.

13.
When you come
you ease the heart.
When you draw near,
the darkness of the black cloud
takes flight.

14.
Sacred fire,
heart of fire,
you do not burn,
but when you visit,
you clear away cares.

15.
You educate and awaken
minds formerly unskilled,
asleep and forgetful.

16.
You warm our tongues. You form the words.
Your charity given inclines
the heart toward good.

17.
O aid of the oppressed,
o comfort of the miserable,
refuge of the poor,

18.
give contempt of earthly things,
lead desire
to love of celestial things.

19.
Consoler and founder,
dweller and lover
of humble hearts,

20.
Drive out evil. Wipe away filth.
Make what is discordant harmonious.
Bring us protection.

21.
You who once visited,
taught, and comforted
the frightened disciples,

22.
may you consider us worthy to visit,
and if it pleases, may you console us,
your believing people.

23.
The majesty of the persons is equal,
their power and
common divinity are equal.

24.
You, proceeding from two
are equal to both,
in no way dissimilar.

25.
For you are as great and
of the same kind as the Father.
May the humility of your servants

26.
return the praises
due to God the Father and the Son
Redeemer also to you.

NOTES

1   Verse 5 is found only in the footnotes of Dreves and Blumes' edition.

2   Verses 17–18 represent one of two alternative verses present in the footnotes of the critical edition.

RICHARD OF ST VICTOR

ON THE TRINITY

INTRODUCTION AND TRANSLATION
BY CHRISTOPHER P. EVANS

INTRODUCTION

Richard of St Victor was active as a theologian at Paris in the third quarter of the twelfth century.[1] His predecessors, who were pioneering the nascent scholastic theology within various schools of thought, were assembling the teachings from the treasuries of the Scriptures and church fathers as the starting points for their own theological investigations. These sacred sources, however, also presented theological problems at times (e.g., problems with meaning of words and concepts, and problems with harmonization), and the need was recognized for greater systemization and solutions based on dialectical methods developed from the liberal arts. The rapid development of early scholastic theology was largely the work of the urban schools, and one such school of importance was the Abbey of St Victor, where Richard achieved some success as a teacher and writer.[2]

---

[1] For studies on the life of Richard of St Victor, see John of Toulouse, *Vita* (PL 196.9–14); F. Hugonin, *Notice sur Richard de Saint-Victor* (PL 196.12–32); G. Buonamici, *Riccardo di S. Vittore. Saggio di studi sulla filosofia mistica del secolo XII* (Alatri, 1898); G. Fritz, "Richard de Saint-Victor," DTC (Paris, 1899–1950), 13.2.2676; C. Ottaviano, *Riccardo di S. Vittore: La vita, le opera, il pensiero*, Memorie della R. Accademia Nazionale dei Lincei. Classe di scienze morali, storiche e filologiche, serie VI, vol. IV, fasc. V (Rome: Dott. Giovanni Bardi, tipografo della R. Accademia nazionale dei Lincei, 1933), 411–22; J. Châtillon, "Richard de Saint-Victor." DS (Paris, 1937), 13.593–654; E. Cousins, "The Notion of Person in the *De Trinitate* of Richard of Saint Victor" (Ph.D. diss., Fordam University, 1966), 52–76; M. Purwatma, "The Explanation of the Mystery of the Trinity Based on the Attributes of God as Supreme Love: A Study on the '*De Trinitate*' of Richard of St Victor" (Ph.D diss., Pontificia Universitas Urbaniana, 1990), 21–29. See also the introduction in *Selected Writings on Contemplation*, trans. and introduction by Clare Kirchberger (London: Faber and Faber, 1957), 15–31; *The Twelve Patriarchs, The Mystical Ark, and Book Three on the Trinity*, The Classics of Western Spirituality, trans. and introduction by G. A. Zinn (New York: Paulist Press, 1979), 1–10; J. Châtillon, *Les douze patriarches*, SC 419, 7–12.

[2] Indeed most of his smaller treatises (or letters) were written at the request of others seeking out his opinion on certain matters. This admiration is also attested in several letters written to Richard that are preserved in Vatican City, Reg. lat. 179 (Abbey of St Victor, sec. xii/xiii), some of which are still unedited. In one letter of this collection, William, prior of the Cistercian Abbey of Ourscamp, writes Richard, prior of St Victor, to request a copy of two works that he does not yet have: *De sompno Nabuchodonosor* [= PL *Eruditione hominis interioris*] *uel Illumina faciem tuam super seruum tuum* [= PL *Adnot. Psalm.* 118b] (f. 266a; cf. John of Toulouse, *Vita* [PL 196.9]; *Ep.* 3 [PL 196.1226C–1227A]). The second work is interesting, because William is requesting it as if it was an independent work. Migne's insertion of it among the *Adnot. Psalm.* is based on a 13th century conflation (see fn. 18). The earliest existent witness

Richard's life is relatively unknown. John of Toulouse, who wrote a short *vita* in the 17th century, said that Richard, of Scottish origin, was received into the community by Abbot Gilduin (1114–1155) and that he was a student (*discipulus*) under Hugh of St Victor.[3] This would mean that he entered the community before Hugh's death in 1141. This traditional view has been challenged by others, such as Ottaviano in 1933, who claims that Richard had no direct contact with Hugh's teachings.[4] Consequently, such views must situate Richard's entrance into the community sometime between the deaths of Hugh and Gilduin. Nevertheless, whether or not he was a *discipulus* of Hugh, the manuscripts of his early writings gives him the title *magister* ("teacher").[5] Châtillon is no doubt correct in arguing that Richard was charged with teaching responsibilities, but whether or not he was the Novice Master, as he

---

of it, however, is found in a collection called *Sermones et sententie magistri Richardi* (e.g., Troyes, Bibliothèque municipale 259). Presumably then these independent writings were later collected into the single corpus, *Sermones et Sententie*. Moreover, the incipit of this work in that corpus is generally preceded by the introduction: *sanguine cognato . . . stilum conuerto,* which is the opening to Migne's *De superexcellenti baptismo Christi* (PL 196.1011D-1013A); cf. Châtillon, *Un sermon theologique,* 24–25. Another letter attributing upmost reverence for Richard comes from John, subprior of Clairvaux, who requests a short prayer to the Holy Spirit (f. 248v; for an abbreviated version, see John of Toulouse, *Vita* [PL 196.10]): *Domino et patri suo R‹ichardo› priori de sancto Victore, Johannes dictus su‹b›prior Claraeuallis modicum id quod est. Rogo uos, domine mi, in Spiritu sancto pro Spiritu sancto scribite michi orationem deuotam de Spiritu sancto. Scribite, domine mi, iuxta sensum et scientiam, quam dedit uobis Spiritus sanctus, iuxta deuotionem, quam amministrabit uobis Spiritus sanctus. Scribite, pater mi, et mittite michi. Nolite super hoc contradicere michi. Scribite, domine mi, non sub nimia, non sub nimia breuitate nec sub nimia prolixior, sed sic ut eam memoriter ualeam retinere, et Spiritui sancto siue in die siue in nocte saltem semel offerre. Karissime pater ut nos exaudiat Spiritus sanctus, ut consoletur nos indefinenter Spiritus sanctus. Nolite negligere clamorem mendici uestri. Nolite uilipendere petitionem amici uestri, sed et in orationibus uestris memento Iohannis seruuli uestri. Valete.*

3 *Vita* (PL 196.9). On the Victorine program of learning, see Hugh of St Victor, *Didasc.*; Richard of St Victor, *LE*; cf. also introduction in *The Didascalicon of Hugh of St Victor,* Records of Western Civilization Series, trans. and intro. Jerome Taylor (New York: Columbia University Press, 1991), 3–45; Nico den Bok, *Communicating the Most High: A Systematic Study of Persons and Trinity in the Theology of Richard of St Victor (d. 1173),* Bibliotheca Victorina VII (Turnhout: Brepols, 1996), 95–149; Beryl Smalley, *The Study of the Bible in the Middle Ages* (Oxford: Blackwell Publishers, 1983), 83–111; F. Copleston, *A History of Philosophy II: Augustine to Scotus* (Westminster, Maryland: The Newman Press, 1952), 175–82.

4 See Ottaviano, *Riccardo di S. Vittore,* 414–15. Châtillon finds Ottaviano unconvincing here and regards it plausible that Richard entered the community before 1141 as Hugh's student; see, "Richard de Saint-Victor," *DS* 13.594 and *Les douze patriarches,* 8.

5 For example, the title of his first published work reads as follows: *Liber exceptionum magistri Ricardi canonici sancti Victoris parisiensis (ca.* 1153–1160). See J. Châtillon, *Liber Exceptionum,* Textes philosophiques du moyen âge 5 (Paris: J. Vrin, 1958), 77–78.

hypothesizes, is still uncertain.[6] Nevertheless, all scholarship agrees that *magister* Richard was promoted to subprior in 1159 and to prior in 1162, a position he held until his death on March 10, 1173.[7]

The paucity of historical facts leaves scholars without the possibility of an absolute chronology of Richard's writings.[8] Scholars can at best offer tentative theories of a relative chronology, but even this is difficult, because Richard makes few allusions to his previous writings, and his epistolary correspondence is incomplete.[9] Nevertheless, based on internal (e.g., development of ideas) and external evidence (e.g., the manuscript tradition), scholars usually situate his writings within the three aforementioned periods of his life. The first period dates before 1159, while he was a teacher. Here most scholars will place the *Book of Class Notes*.[10] The second period dates between 1159 and 1162, while he was a subprior, during which time Richard may have written his two mystical works *On the Twelve Patriarchs* and *On the Ark of Moses*. The

---

[6]   See Châtillon, "Richard de Saint-Victor," *DS* 13.596. He arrives at this hypothesis based on Richard's *Tractatus super ps.* 28 (or *Super Afferte Domino*) (= PL *Mysticae Adnotationes in Ps.* 28), in which he addresses novices (*Vobis dicitur, nouitii*). In fact, some of the earliest Parisian manuscripts even provide marginal titles: *Ad nouitios* (Paris, Bibliothèque Mazarine 770; Paris, Bibliothèque Nationale 2588) and *De nouiciis* (Paris, Bibliothèque Mazarine 769). However, Châtillon leaves open the possibility that Richard addressed the novices here as part of his responsibilities as sub-prior (after 1159) or prior (after 1162). While most scholars tend to situate the *Tractatus super quosdam psalmos* (= PL *Mysticae Adnotationes in Psalmos*) during his years has subprior (1159–1162), nevertheless the external evidence suggests a date prior to 1159 while Richard was a *magister*. After all, there are 119 manuscripts that contain all or parts of the *Tractatus*, and *magister Richardus* is the only attribution made among the mss that designates a title. While such evidence is not conclusive, it does provide some support to Châtillon's hypothesis.

[7]   See John of Toulouse, *Vita* (PL 196.9–11).

[8]   See Ottaviano, *Riccardo di S. Vittore*, 422–46; Châtillon, *Richard de Saint-Victor* (DS 13.598–627); Kirchberger, *Selected Writings*, 20–25. For a complete list of Richard's writings, editions, and alternative dates see P. Cacciapuoti, *Deus existentia amoris: Carità e Trinità nell'itinerario teologico di Riccardo di San Vittore (d. 1173)*, Bibliotheca Victorina IX (Turnhout: Brepols, 1998), 49–96; R. Goy, *Die handschriftliche Überlieferung der Werke Richards von St. Viktor im Mittelalter*, Bibliotheca Victorina 18 (Turnhout: Brepols Publishers, 2005), see esp. 20–23.

[9]   In *In Apocalypsim* Prol. (PL 196.683B) Richard refers to a previous work (*sicut alibi diximus*) that most likely refers to the *Liber Exceptionum*. In *Trin.* 6.15 (TPMA 6.247) he says: "It is appropriate for me to repeat at this time what I remember writing elsewhere," after which he reproduces the second part of his *De tribus peronis appropriatis*. With regard to his epistolary correspondence, see fn. 2 where there is a reference to *Eruditione hominis interioris* and *Illumina faciem tuam*.

[10] Richard of St Victor, *LE* (Châtillon, TPMA 5). In this text Richard offers his friend a synopsis of learning needed for the study of Scripture.

third period dates after 1162 and before his death in 1173, while he was prior. Here belongs *On the Trinity*.

The external evidence is not conclusive for dating *On the Trinity*, because all but three manuscripts refer to Richard as a *magister* not *prior*. The earliest and most reliable witness, Paris, Maz. 769 (Abbey of St Victor, sec. xii), which Ribaillier believes to be the archetype, simply resists giving Richard any title. And, as preserved in the memory of the Victorines in the 15th century, "the whole book was written by the most elevated contemplative *magister* Richard, formerly the prior of the Monastery [sic] of St Victor near Paris."[11] While acknowledging Richard as the former prior, this Victorine witness never says that Richard wrote as the prior but *magister*. Perhaps this confusion of attribution suggests that this treatise, which was started earlier in his teaching career, was not finished until shortly before his death[12] and hence published post-humously when he was no longer the prior.[13]

The internal evidence better indicates the theological milieu of the treatise. First, the earliest possible *terminus post quem* would be 1148, because in *On the Trinity* 1.13–14, 2:20, and 4.1 Richard is familiar with the condemnation of Gilbert of Poitiers' Trinitarian teachings at the Council of Rheims. Second, the controversy in *On the Trinity* 6.22 (see notes 572 and 575) bring us closer to the theological milieu of the 1160s. Here Richard engages in a heated polemic against "many" who deny "substance begets substance or wisdom begets wisdom" (*substantia gignat substantiam uel sapientia sapientiam*). Richard may have one and/or two theologians in his crosshairs here: Peter Abelard and Peter Lombard. While the language *substantia gignat substantiam* corresponds better to Abelard (*TChr.* 3.109 [CCCM 12, 235]), nevertheless it was Lombard who denied "wisdom begot wisdom, and essence begot essence" (*Sent.* 1.5.1.7 [SB 4, 82]: *sapientia sapientiam et essentiam es-*

---

11   Paris, Arsenal 239, f. 121 (Abbey of St Victor, sec. 15; cited in Ribaillier, TPMA 6.35): *totus liber editus ab eleuatissimo contemplatiuo magistro Richardo quondam priore monasterii Sancti Victoris prope Parisius.*

12   See *Trin.* (TPMA 6.12–13); Cacciapuoti, *Deus existentia amoris*, 89–90. Ribaillier suggests that Richard's responsibilities as subprior and/or prior left him with little time for writing. For example, in the prologue of his *De status interioris hominis* Richard expresses the following apology: "I was late in sending what I promised according to your petition. But, most beloved man, it was out of necessity not intention that I did not finish earlier what I first intended. With many occasions interfering and hindering my plan, I was not able to complete your command" (TPMA 6.61).

13   On Ribaillier's theory of a posthumous publication, see *Trin.* 5.25, note 112.

sentiam genuerit),[14] thereby situating more precisely the *terminus post quem* (at least of book 6) to after the early to middle 1150s. Third, in *On the Trinity* 6.15 Richard reproduces the second part of his *On the Attributions of the Three Persons*, in which he discusses the method of appropriation whereby the essential attributes of power, wisdom, and goodness are attributed respectively to the person of the Father, Son, and Holy Spirit. The method, which was adopted by Peter Abelard, was highly controversial and led to his condemnation at the Council of Sens (1140), thanks in part to Bernard of Clairvaux. L. Ott, followed by Ribaillier, argues that *On the Attributions of the Three Persons* must have been written sometime after Bernard's death, when the method was no longer controversial.[15] The title *magister* is given to Richard in many manuscripts,[16] which, if correct, *On the Attributions* must be dated around 1159. However, in one twelfth-century manuscript (Munich, CLM 23434), Richard is designated 'prior'. If correct, as Ribaillier believes it is, then *On the Attributions* must be dated after 1162.[17] Regardless, either designation would place *On the Trinity* within the theological milieu of the 1160s.

The success of Richard's *On the Trinity* is evident from the numerous existent manuscripts that is only exceeded by *Tractate on Psalm* 28 (86 mss), *On the Ark of Moses* (98 mss), *On the State of the Interior Man* (106 mss); *On Allegory* (139 mss), and *The Twelve Patriarchs* (224 mss).[18] This treatise is found today in 74 manuscripts (not including

14 This is the consensus, see Th. de Régnon, *Études de théologie positive sur la Sainte Trinité* (Victor Retaux et Fils, 1892), 2.252–62; Ottaviano, *Riccardo di S. Vittore*, 522; Éthier, *Le «De Trinitate» de Richard de Saint-Victor*, 28; Ribaillier, TPMA 6.11; M. Schniertshauer, *Consummatio caritatis*, 211–14.
15 See L. Ott, *Untersuchungen zur theologischen briefliteratur der frühscholastik* (Munich: Aschendorff, 1937), 592–93; Ribaillier, *Opuscules Théologiques*, 174.
16 Paris, B.N. 12325 (sec. xii); Troyes, Bibl. mun. 198 (sec. xii); Valenciennes, Bibl. mun. 198 (sec. xii); Vatican City, Bibl. fondo Chigi B.VII.106 (541) (sec. xiv); and Venice, Bibl. Nazionale Marciana Lat. Z.86 (1928) (sec. xiv).
17 Ribaillier, *Opuscules Théologiques*, 174.
18 R. Goy's *Die handschriftliche Überlieferung der Werke Richards* (2005) is the first comprehensive catalogue of the manuscript tradition of all the writings of Richard (see my review in *Manuscripta* 50.2 [2006]: 317–22). Based on the number of existent mss, Goy divides the popularity of Richard's writings into five categories (389–91). First, Richard's least popular writings are those with fewer than 20 mss (e.g., *De questionibus regule, In expositione tabernaculi, De uerbis Apostoli*). These writings, however, were written as letters at the request of others, and so they were rarely copied for that reason. Second, about two-thirds of his other exegetical and theological writings received moderate attention with fewer than forty mss (e.g., *In Apocalypsim, In uisione Ezechielis, De spiritu blasphemie, De Emanuele*, and so on). Third, three works in particular have a more extensive dissemination with forty to seventy mss (*Tractatus super Psalmos, Afferte domino*, and *De potestate ligandi*). Fourth, other writings

the many fragments).[19] The majority are found in 13th and 14th century manuscripts and mostly in monastic libraries (Benedictine and Cistercian) and some university libraries (esp. Sorbonne), which is typical of all of Richard's writings.[20]

In this treatise, Richard draws together all of his psychological, rational and theological insights in order to produce one of the most profound and original treatments of the Trinity since Augustine.[21] In it he intends to prove through reason the Church's profession of the

received widespread distribution with more than 70 mss but fewer than 100 mss, and it is here that we find *On the Trinity* (as well as, *De statu interioris hominis, De exterminatione, De arca Moysi, De mystico somnio, De oratione domica,* and *De qutuor gradibus*). Fifth, his best sellers with over 100 mss are *De statu interioris hominis* (106 mss), *De Allegorie* (139 mss), and the most popular of all is *De duodecim patriarchis* (224 mss) not including the many vernacular versions). Goy's third category with the *Tractatus super Psalmos* and *Afferte domino* is incorrect for three reasons. First he considers the first two writings as independent, but all the earliest Parisian mss contain *Afferte domino* (Ps. 28) as part of the *Tractatus super Psalmos.* Only the Germanic mss witness the *Tractatus* without *Afferte domino* (most notably Admont, Stiftsbibliothek 82), which receives an extensive and independent dissemination (and either anonymous or attributed to Bernard of Clairvaux). Second, Goy presumes that Migne's edition of the *Mysticae Adnotationes in Psalmos* is not a composite work. But in fact Migne's edition is actually based on an early 13th conflation of two independent works *Tractatus super Psalmos* and the *Sermones et Sententie* (the conflation is found in two 13th century manuscripts: Paris, Bibliothèque Mazarine 769 and Mâcon, Bibliothèque municipale 84). Hence, many sermons in Migne's *Adnot.* like Ps. 90, 4, 118:135, 118:136, 143, 71, 136 are actually part of the *Sermones et Sententie.* Consequently, there are not 44 mss of the *Tractatus super Psalmos,* as Goy lists, but only 32 mss (not including the 87 mss with only selected sermons). Third, Goy indentified 48 mss that contains *Afferte domino* independently of the *Tractatus,* but there are actually 61 mss. And when included with the 24 other mss containing the complete *Tractatus,* there is a total of 86 mss, which makes it the fourth most copied work.

19   See R. Goy, *Die handschriftliche Überlieferung,* 174–87. I know of seven other mss not found in Goy's impressive catalogue. Moreover, in preparing his critical Latin edition Ribaillier consulted fifty-five of these ninety mss; however, the mss unknown to Ribaillier are all outside Paris dating from the thirteenth to fifteenth century.

20   See R. Goy, *Die handschriftliche Überlieferung,* 391–96. Goy notes that when taken as a whole, the dissemination of Richard's writings was most extensive in the thirteenth century; however, individual writings enjoyed more or less popularity in each century. For example, while Richard's theological writings like *On the Trinity* were copied less in the fifteenth century, his mystical writings like *On the Twelve Patriarchs* were copied the most during that time. Moreover, his writings spread mostly in French, Austrian, Germanic, and Gallic regions. Finally, as Goy notes, the vast majority of manuscripts (about 85%) are found in monastic libraries (esp. Benedictine), and most of the others are found at the Abbey of St Victor and university libraries (esp. Sorbonne).

21   E.g., Th. de Régnon, *Études de théologie positive sur la Sainte Trinité* (Paris: Victor Retaux et Fils, 1892), 2.20; see also, J. Châtillon, "Richard de Saint-Victor" in *Dictionnaire de spiritualité* (Paris: Letouzey et Ané, 1937–), 13.609; Paul Vignaux, *Philosophy in the Middles Ages: An Introduction,* trans. E. C. Hall (New York: Meridian Books, 1959), 64–65. For studies and summaries on *Trin.,* see bibliography.

triune God as depicted in the so-called Athanasian Creed or *Qui-cumque*, which would have been recited during Prime at the Abbey of St Victor.[22] Although he never doubts the validity and certitude of this confession of faith, nevertheless he will seek the rationale for it by utilizing all the visible and invisible evidences before him, as opposed to citing other authorities, such as canonical Scripture or ecclesiastical writings.[23] Richard himself perceives this task as a "bold undertaking,"[24]

[22] According to the *Liber ordinis Sancti Victoris Parisiensis*, the *Quicumque Vult* was recited during Prime (54 [CCLM 61.533]); see also the ordinal for the Abbey of St Victor in Paris, BN lat. 14506, ff. 267v, 292r. Richard quotes from this creed throughout his study, see *Trin.* 1.5 (TPMA 6.90–91); 3.8 (TPMA 6.143); 3.20 (TPMA 6.155); 3.25 (TPMA 6.159); 4.25 (TPMA 6.192); 5.5 (TPMA 6.200); 6.11 (TPMA 6.240); 6.13 (TPMA 6.244); 6.20 (TPMA 6.256); 6.22 (TPMA 6.260). A typical medieval manuscript of the Psalter ends with various biblical canticles followed by the *Quicumque*, usually along with the Apostles' Creed and Nicene Creed (see V. Leroquais, *Les psautiers: Manuscrits latins des bibliothèques publiques de France* 1 [Mâcon, 1904–1941], lv; J. Mearns, *The Canticles of the Christian Church Eastern and Western in Early and Medieval Times* [Cambridge: Cambridge University Press, 1914], 21, 23, 53, 55, 66, 70, 78, and 81; P. Salmon, *Les manuscrits liturgiques latins de la bibliothèque vaticane*, Studi e testi 251 [Vatican City: Biblioteca apostolica vaticana, 1968], 3–45; A. Hughes, *Medieval Manuscripts for Mass and Office: A Guide to Their Organization and Terminology* [Toronto: University of Toronto Press, 1995], 76). Given that it was deeply embedded in the liturgical and theological milieu of the twelfth-century, it is not surprising to find commentaries on it in the manuscript tradition (see, N. Häring, "Commentaries on the Pseudo-Athanasian Creed," *Mediaeval Studies* 34 [1972]: 225–46). Some of these come from illustrious, twelfth-century theologians like Peter Abelard, Gilbert of Poitiers (ed. Häring), and Hildegard of Bingen (C. Evans, CCCM 226). It comes as no surprise then to find suggestions that even Richard's *On the Trinity* is an extended commentary on this liturgical text (e.g., O. González, 'Sobre las fuentes de Ricardo de San Víctor y su influjo en San Buenaentura', *La Ciudad de Dios* 176 [1963]: 570–74).

[23] E.g., *Trin.* 1.3 (TPMA 6.88); *Trin.* 1.4 (TPMA 6.89). This approach explains why there is a paucity of biblical and patristic citations in the treatise. The greatest number of biblical citations appears in the Prol.-1.4, where he justifies with the Bible his speculative theology as dictated by faith and love, and in Book 6, where he discusses the divine names. And, as Ribaillier notes (*Trin.*, 18), Richard's choice of biblical passages is not unique; they are found in the writings of Augustine and Peter Lombard's *Sent.* (esp. in Book 6). Moreover, Richard's cites from the fathers rarely, in fact only four times and all in Book 4 (see *Trin.*, [TPMA 6.18]; although Ribaillier misses the dependency on Peter Lombard here). The first occurs in 4.3 (see note 283), where he cites Pelagius, attributed to Jerome (*Sermo.* 236.3 [PL 39.2182]), which he derived from Peter Lombard, *Sent.* 1.33.1.2 (SB 4.241). The second occurs in 4.4 (see note 284), where he mentions Jerome's suspicion of the word hypostasis (*Ep.* 15.4 [CSEL 54.66]), again which Richard derived from Peter Lombard, *Sent.* 1.26.1 (SB 4.197). Third, in 4.20 (see note 329) the Latin confession of one substance and the Greek confession of three substances strongly echo Augustine, *Trin.* 7.7 (CCL 50.255), which was cited by Peter Lombard, *Sent.* 1.23.2 (SB 4.182–83); cf. also Peter Abelard, TChr 4.27–28 (CCCM 12.277–78). Finally, in 4.21 (see note 337) Richard cites Boethius' definition of a person. Besides these explicit references, Richard also makes numerous allusions. Richard's notion of love was inspired by Gregory the Great and Augustine in 3.2 (see notes 193 and 194), and his notion of perfection in 2.16 (see note 150) was probably inspired by Boethius and/or Hugh of St Victor.

[24] *Trin.* 3.1 (TPMA 6.135). In fact, Richard even thinks of himself as undertaking something

especially since the content of this creed concerns eternal truths that are seemingly beyond the proofs from experience and reason, although they are known with certainty through faith.[25] Due to the delicacy of the subject matter, Richard must first demonstrate the soteriological rationale for his own rational investigation (Prol.), before he clarifies his subject matter (1.1–10). He by no means divorces his undertaking from spirituality. The ascent toward eternal truths is both intellectual and spiritual. And so, experienced souls, which are steadfast in the certitudes of faith and inflamed with the love of God, should want to seek the divine mysteries in other ways of knowing, such as experience or reason.[26] Such an approach not only moves toward and increases understanding in illumined minds, but it also intensifies and is supported by the ardor of love in inspired souls.

Richard begins his investigation with the uniqueness, unity, and attributes of the divine substance (1:11–2:1–25), before he discusses the rationale for the plural persons (3:1–6:25). Like the entire western tradition before him, Richard's point of departure is the divine substance, to which the name "God" refers. Such a departure allows him to establish two fundamental assertions, which he will weave throughout the remainder of his investigation: the principle of simplicity and aseity ("being from itself"). He first discusses in some detail the necessary existence of a single divine substance which derives all that it has— existence, being, essence, power, wisdom, goodness, happiness, and so on—from itself. He will later adapt this principle to the level of person in order to demonstrate the uniqueness of the Father from whom the Son and Spirit proceed (e.g., 5:2–5). At the substantial level such a principle ensures not only that the divine substance is supreme, but also that it is the source of all existence, being, power, wisdom, and so on. These substantial qualities then can be predicated of God or creatures, but not in the same way. Unlike created substances, the divine substance possesses these qualities to a superlative or infinite degree and is identical to them, that is, God is a supremely simple being.[27] For all these reasons, Richard concludes that there can only be one true

---

new in this book and that perhaps some of his contemporaries may not approve, see *Trin.* 1.5 (TPMA 6.91); 3.1 (TPMA 6.135).

[25]   E.g., *Trin.* Prol. (TPMA 6.84); 1.1 (TPMA 6.87); 1.4 (TPMA 6.90).

[26]   See *Trin.*1.1 (TPMA 6.87); 1.4 (TPMA 6.89–90); *Arca Moys.* 2.24 (Aris, 50–52); 4.5 (Aris, 90–91). For an analysis of Richard's use of experience and reason, as well as the distinction between necessary and probable reason, see notes 41, 42, and 56 in Book 1.

[27]   For example, God, strictly speaking, does not *have* supreme power but *is* supreme power.

God, who alone is uncreated, immeasurable, incomprehensible, and eternal (that is, as he defines eternity, an immutable being without beginning or end).

Richard investigates the plural divine persons through an analysis of the nature of love, in order to demonstrate the existence of *at least* three coequal persons (3:1–25),[28] and through a definition of person and personal properties, in order to demonstrate the necessary existence of only three persons, distinguished by three incommunicable properties, without compromising the unity of substance (4:1–6:25). Book three proceeds methodically. Richard first considers the existence of two divine persons (3.2–5), their perfect and incomprehensible equality (3.6–10), after which he considers the existence of a third divine person (3.11–20) as well as the perfect, incomprehensible equality of the three (3.21–25). Supreme charity ensures the existences of at least three persons of equal dignity. Such charity, by Richard's definition, must be mutual, and, lest this mutual love be disordered, it requires a second person of equal dignity with the first (*condignum*). But, in order for supreme charity to be perfectly consummated, two mutual lovers require a third to be loved equally by them (*condilectum*). In this sense, the mutual fellowship of three coequal persons in the divinity is a perfect community where love is entirely unified and complete.

In book 4 Richard develops a logic of personhood and existence in order to account for the otherness of persons without otherness of substance. Richard reduces the whole matter into two considerations: the mode of being (*modum essendi*) and the mode of obtaining being (*modum obtinendi*). Etymologically speaking, this makes perfect sense to him. The Latin verb *existere*, which is a compound of *sistere* ("to be") and the preposition *ex* ("from"), refers to the notion of substance (*sistere*) and the origin of being (*ex*), either from itself or from another source. According to Richard then existence denotes a substance in connection with a personal property indicating origin, for which he uses a two-part formula: existence is "to have or be a substantial being" and "from some origin." The three in the divinity are three persons or existences possessing an identical, uncreated, supersubstantial being from three different origins. Consequently, Richard must seek the rationale for the otherness of divine persons not in substantial qualities (*sistere*) but in an incommunicable personal property or origin of being (*ex*), which is the topic of book five.

[28]   In Book 5 Richard will argue for the existence of *only* three coequal persons.

Books 5 and 6 are various applications of Richard's logic of person-hood, developed in book 4. According to book 5, an incommunicable personal property is what differentiates one divine person from another based on the mode of their origin, that is, whether a person has his being from himself (personal aseity) or from another person. Aseity, as a personal property, belongs to the unbegotten Father alone, and, for that reason, this property is incommunicable to the other persons. However, 'being from another person' is the personal property of the Son and Spirit; consequently, it is not incommunicable. Richard must find another property that distinguishes them. For this he turns to the *Filioque* doctrine, which is absolutely essential for his logic. The Spirit's procession from the Father 'and Son' (*filioque*) is the incommunicable personal property, which alone distinguishes the persons of the Son and Spirit. This seems obvious to Richard, because, according to his logic, divine personal properties can be reduced to two possible considerations: giving or receiving. The Father, who has his being from himself, can only give the divine substance (or love, or any other substantial property); the Son both receives it immediately from the Father and gives it to the Spirit; while the Spirit has an immediate-mediate relationship with the Father in that he receives the fullness of divinity from the Father and the Son at the same time.[29] Richard also utilizes this logic of personhood to exclude the possibility of more than three divine persons. A fourth person, for example, would not only confound the symmetrical differences among the three persons,[30] but there would also be no possible property for him to possess, since there can only be one incommunicable property per person.[31]

In book 6 he further utilizes this logic of personhood to distinguish between the processions of the Son and Spirit and to give the rationale for the various divine names found in the Scriptures. According to Richard, the Father does not have the same kind of relationship with the Son as with the Spirit on account of their different modes of origin

[29]   Obviously Richard is not thinking in terms of temporal succession, nor does he think that divine substance is something divisible, cf. *Trin.* 5.7 (TPMA 6.203).

[30]   According to Richard's principle of proportionality, between two opposite natures there is a mediating nature that possesses a likeness to both natures in the pattern aa-ab-bb. For example, the Father, who gives alone, is the exact opposite to the personal property of the Spirit, who receive alone. The Son, who both gives and receives, creates symmetry between these opposite natures by possessing a likeness to both. According to Richard, then, a fourth person would disrupt this symmetry. See *Trin.* 5.14 (TPMA 6.213).

[31]   In fact, one could probably even say that there wouldn't really be two different persons at all, if they had identical incommunicable personal properties.

and the different intentions of the paternal will. The Father desires to have an immediate relationship with the Son, because he wants a fellowship with a person of equal dignity (*condignum*), and he desires to have an immediate-mediate relationship with the Spirit, because he wants to delight in a third who is mutually loved by him and the Son (*condilectum*). For that reason, the names "Father" and "Son" are appropriate for describing the relationship between them, just as a father and child is the most immediate kind of human relationship. And, even though no familial term captures the reality of their relationship with the third person, the use of "Spirit" is appropriate to indicate the same relationship of the Holy Spirit with the Father and Son, in the same way that the word "spirit" (*spiritus*) can indicate the like-mindedness or same desires and purposes of plural persons (cf., Acts 4:32). All such names, therefore, indicate something about the inner-Trinitarian relationships in light of the incommunicable personal properties.

The influences that enriched Richard's Trinitarian theology have already been the object of careful research.[32] Even though Richard rarely supports his assertions with direct citations from the authorities, his arguments are nevertheless thoroughly entrenched in the theological traditions of the Latin West and the theological milieu of his day. The most predominate influence is Augustine, who dominated the attention of all the medieval theologians. The very numerous allusions and common ideas to Augustine's writings in the endnotes of the translation bear witness to this. Even the hallmark of Richard's Trinitarian theology based on the love of friendship was inspired by Augustine and Gregory the Great (notes 193, 194, 195, and 200), though they never develop it to the extent that Richard does. Another significant influence on Richard, especially his dialectical method, is Boethius. The division of substance in 2.12 as "general, specific, or individual" comes from Boethius' *In Categorias Aristotelis* (see note 137), and Richard's invention of the word "Danielness" echoes Boethius' "Platoness" in *In librum Aristotelis Peri hermeneias* (see note 139). With regard to the influences within Richard's own theological milieu, his expression "necessary reasons" no doubt goes back to the writings of Anselm of Canterbury that found its way into the writings of John of Salisbury, Gilbert of Poitiers, Robert Melun, and Achard of St Victor (see note 56 in book one). Moreover, Richard's optimism in natural reason, with which even the pagan philosophers conceived in part the Triune God, was shared by

---

[32] See Ribaillier (TPMA 6.20–33).

others like Peter Abelard and Hugh of St Victor.[33] Another important influence, discovered more recently, is his former Abbot, Achard of St Victor, whose work *On the Unity of God and the Plurality of Creatures* may have inspired Richard to write his own treatise.[34] Achard's treatise, found in only one manuscript, is unpolished and incomplete, yet the similarities between the two treatises are striking. Ribaillier has shown that the two treatises share the same order of argumentation that corresponds to Anselm's *Monologion*, many similar ideas, and even common formulas and vocabulary.[35]

This translation follows the Latin critical edition: ed. J. Ribaillier, *De Trinitate* (Paris, 1958). Richard's treatise is also found in the following translations that I have consulted:

La Trinité. Latin text, introduction, translation, and notes by G. Salet. Sources Chrétiennes 63. Paris, 1959.

The Twelve Patriarchs, The Mystical Ark, and Book Three on the Trinity. Translated by G. A. Zinn. New York, 1979.

Die Dreieinigkeit. Christliche Meister 4. Translated by Hans Urs von Balthasar. Einsiedlen, 1980.

Salet's French translation is based on a Latin text adapted from the 1650 edition of John of Toulouse, which was reprinted in Migne's *Patrologia Latina* in 1855 and 1880.[36] Both von Balthasar's German translation and Zinn's English translation of book three are based on Ribaillier's critical edition. As such, the present work represents the first published English translation of the entire treatise.

The majority of the references in the footnotes are taken from Ribaillier's edition. The purpose of the footnotes is to put Richard in the context of the theological discussion in the twelfth century, but these references should not necessarily be regarded as direct sources for Richard.

The chapter titles in *On the Trinity* are original to Richard's text, but the book and section titles have been inserted for clarity.

---

[33] See note 16 in Prologue and Hugh of St Victor, *Sent. div.* Part 3 (Piazzoni, 950, 953), although note that while Hugh, like Richard, is optimistic about natural reason, nevertheless they are not referring to naked reason here but to an illumined natural reason.

[34] *De unitate Dei et pluralitate creaturarum*, ed. by E. Martineau (Saint-Lambert des Bois: Authentica, 1987); trans. H. Feiss, *Works*, CS 165 (Kalamazoo: Cistercian Publications, 2001).

[35] Ribaillier (TPMA 6.27–33).

[36] PL 196.887C–992B.

My just one lives by faith.[1] This is both an apostolic and prophetic opinion. The Apostle declares what the Prophet proclaimed: *the just lives by faith.* If this is so, or rather because this is so, then we ought to consider carefully and review frequently the mysteries (*sacramenta*) of our faith.[2] For *it is impossible to please God without faith.*[3] Hope cannot exist where there is no faith. *It is indeed necessary that those who draw near to God believe that he exists and that he is a rewarder to those who seek after him.*[4] Otherwise, what sort of hope will be possible? Charity cannot exist where there is no hope. Indeed, who loves something from which he hopes for nothing good? Therefore, we are moved toward hope through faith, and through hope we advance to charity.[5]

Moreover, *if I do not have love, then* whatever I have *profits me nothing.*[6] You hear from the mouth of Truth what the fruit of love is: *If someone loves me, then he will be loved by my Father, and I will love him and manifest myself to him.*[7] And so, manifestation derives from love, contemplation from manifestation, and knowledge (*cognitio*) from contemplation.[8] Moreover, *when Christ, our life, appears, then we will also appear with him in glory,*[9] and *we will be like him* at that time, *because we will see him just as he is.*[10] You see our starting point, our destination, and the steps of our ascent: by means of hope and love ‹we ascend› from faith toward divine knowledge, and through divine knowledge ‹we ascend› toward eternal life. *Eternal life,* he said, *is to know you, the true God, and Jesus Christ whom you have sent.*[11] And so, life derives from faith, and life derives from knowledge. Internal life derives from faith, and eternal life from knowledge.[12] Internal life, in which we live well in the meantime, is from faith; and eternal life, in which we will live blessedly in the future, is from knowledge.[13] Therefore, faith is the beginning and the foundation of all good.[14]

How appropriate it is that we be ardent in faith, from which all good receives both foundation and support! But just as the beginning of all good is in faith, so the consummation and perfection of all good is in knowledge. And so, let us press on toward perfection; and, by what steps of progress we can ‹make›, let us hasten from faith toward knowledge; let us strive, insofar as we are able, to understand what we believe.[15] And let us consider how ardent the philosophers of this world have been, or how far they have advanced, in this kind of knowledge.[16] It should cause us shame to be found inferior to them in this regard: *For that which was known of God was manifested to them.*[17] Indeed the

Apostle testifies: *Because, although they knew God, they did not glorify him as God*.[18] Therefore, they did know God. What then are we to do—we who received the tradition of true faith since the cradle? The love of truth ought to be something more in us than the love of vanity could be in them, and it will be necessary that we can be something more in these things where faith guides, hope draws, and love compels.[19] Therefore, it should not be enough for us to believe what is right and true about God, but, as it has been said, let us strive to understand what we believe.[20] Inasmuch as it is right and possible, let us always strive to comprehend with reason what we hold by faith.[21]

What wonder is it if our mind is blind to the divine mysteries, when, at almost every moment, it becomes dirty with the dust of earthly knowledge?[22] *Shake off the dust, O virgin daughter of Zion*.[23] If we are sons of Zion, let us erect that sublime ladder of contemplation,[24] and let us put on *wings as eagles*,[25] with which we can hover above earthly realities and rise to heavenly realities. Let us taste *not the things that are on the earth*[26] but heavenly realities, *where Christ is seated at the right hand of God*.[27] Let us follow the lead of Paul, who flew up to the secrets of the third heaven, where *he heard secrets which he was not able to speak to men*.[28]

Let us ascend after our head.[29] For this purpose Christ ascended to heaven, that he might provoke our desire and draw it after him.[30] Christ ascended, and the Spirit of Christ descended. For this purpose Christ sent his Spirit to us, that he might raise our spirit toward him. Christ ascended bodily, let us ascend mentally. And so, his ascension was corporeal, but ours is spiritual. Why did he present the Spirit as the teacher and leader of our ascension, unless because he wanted our ascension to be spiritual in the meantime? For the purpose of that corporal ascension which is in our future, Christ will come corporeally in the same flesh that he assumed for us, as it is written: *He will come in the same way that you see him going into heaven*.[31] Therefore, let us ascend spiritually, and let us ascend intellectually (*intellectualiter*) to that place where we may not yet ascend corporeally.[32]

Now, it should not be enough for us to ascend in the contemplation of the mind to the secrets of the first heaven. Let us ascend from the first heaven to the second and from the second heaven to the third. For those who are ascending in contemplation from the visible to the invisible and from the corporeal to the spiritual, a consideration of immortality occurs in the first heaven, a consideration of incorruptibility occurs in the second heaven, and a consideration of eternity occurs in the third heaven.[33] Behold the three regions: immortality, incorruptibility, and eternity. The first is the region of the human spirit, the second is the region of the angelic spirit, and the third is the region of the divine spirit.[34] Indeed the human spirit possesses immortality as some inheritance of its own right, which at no time and at no duration can it ever lose permanently. For it must always live either in glory or endure in punishment. And so, whenever this spirit actually inclines toward earthly and transitory things, it forsakes itself, so to speak, and falls below itself. Therefore, the ascension to the first heaven is nothing other than for it to return to itself and to ponder and perform things that are worthy of itself and pertain to immortality.[35] Moreover, far above the first region is incorruptibility, which the human spirit cannot possess at the present time, but it can obtain through the merit of virtues what it does not have at the present time. And so, the human spirit's ascension to the second heaven is to secure the glory of incorruptibility through merits. Certainly, as by right of inheritance, the angelic spirit already possesses this incorruptibility, which it maintained in the same condition through the merit of its perseverance, so that from now on it cannot ever part with it. Moreover, the third heaven pertains to divinity alone, because it is written that God alone *dwells in eternity*.[36] But all other beings, which began to exist in time, are unable to possess eternity for the reason that they did not exist from eternity. But it is a unique gift and superior to everything else to fly up to this heaven on the wings of contemplation and to fix the eyes of the mind on his radiance.[37]

One ascends, therefore, in actuality (*actualiter*) to the first heaven, one ascends in virtue (*virtualiter*) to the second heaven, and one ascends in intellect (*intellectualiter*) to the third heaven. Toward this highest heaven the Spirit of Christ certainly raises spiritual people, whom with the prerogative of revealing grace he illumines more loftily and fully than other people. We are moved toward the understanding of eternity by the grace of contemplation as often as we are lifted up by the Spirit who raises us to this heaven. And so, it should not be enough for us to believe what is true of the eternal realities unless it is also granted to us to demonstrate the object of our faith with the testimony of reason. Nor should we be satisfied with the knowledge (*notitia*) of eternal truths which is through faith alone, if we do not also apprehend that knowledge which is through rational comprehension (*intelligentiam*), and if we are not capable of that knowledge which is through experience.[38]

We have introduced these reflections in the prologue of our work, so that we can make our minds more attentive and more ardent for this kind of a study. We think it is very meritorious to be extremely zealous in this kind of exercise, even if what we intend to accomplish is not granted to the extent we wanted.[39]

BOOK ONE

THE DIVINE SUBSTANCE

METHOD OF STUDY

CHAPTER ONE. We acquire knowledge (*notitiam*) of things in three ways: experience, reason, and belief.

If we desire to ascend toward the knowledge (*scientiam*) of lofty truths through insights of the mind, it is first worthwhile to know that we usually acquire knowledge (*notitiam*) of things in certain ways. Unless I am mistaken, then, we acquire knowledge of things in three ways:[40] we demonstrate some things by experience;[41] we conclude other things by reasoning;[42] and we are certain of other things by believing.[43] We acquire knowledge of temporal things through experience itself, but we rise to knowledge of eternal things sometimes by reasoning and sometimes by believing. Indeed some of those truths which we are ordered to believe seem to be not only above reason but also contrary to human reason,[44] unless they are scrutinized with a profound and very subtle investigation, or rather unless they are revealed by divine revelation. And so, in the knowledge (*cognitione*) or assertion of those truths we usually rely more on faith than on reasoning and on authority rather than argumentation,[45] just as the Prophet said: *Unless you believe, you will not understand.*[46] But it also seems that we must pay careful attention to the meaning in this verse. When it is said: *Unless you believe, you will not understand*, this authority is certainly proposing that we must deny an understanding of those things, not in general but conditionally.

Therefore, those who have trained senses should not despair of acquiring an understanding of such matters,[47] provided they feel steadfast in their faith and in all respects are of proven constancy in the assertion of their faith.[48]

CHAPTER TWO. Nothing is held more firmly than what is apprehended with a steadfast faith.

But the truth in these words is wonderful beyond measure: all of us who truly are believers hold nothing more certainly and nothing more steadfastly than what we apprehend by faith.[49] These truths have been revealed from heaven to the fathers and divinely confirmed with signs or wonders so numerous, so great, and so wonderful that it seems like great madness to have even a little doubt in these matters.[50] And so, the innumerable miracles and other such wonders, which can only happen by divine influence, produce faith in people like us, and they cannot be doubted. Thus, we utilize signs for arguments and wonders for proofs in the attestation or even confirmation of these truths. If only the Jews would have paid attention to them; if only the pagans would have observed them! With such a great security of conscience in this regard we will be able to approach the divine judgment. Will we not be able to say to God with all confidence: "Lord, if this is wrong, then we have been deceived by you; for these truths have been confirmed to us with such great signs and miracles and with other such wonders that can only be done by you. Certainly they were passed down to us by men of the highest sanctity, and they were proven with a supreme and authentic witness, that is, you yourself *worked and confirmed the word with the signs that followed it*"?[51] This is certainly the reason why believers are entirely more prepared to die for the faith than to deny it. Without a doubt, nothing is held more firmly than what is apprehended with a steady faith.[52]

CHAPTER THREE. This book discusses eternal truths that we are prescribed to believe.

It is therefore necessary for us to enter by faith into the knowledge (*notitiam*) of truths concerning which it is correctly said to us: *If you do not believe, you will not understand.*[53] Nevertheless, we must not stop immediately at the entrance, but we must always hasten toward a deeper and more profound understanding and pursue it with every effort and with supreme diligence, so that we may be able to advance daily toward an understanding of what we hold by faith.[54] Eternal life is obtained in full knowledge and perfect understanding of these truths. There is certainly supreme usefulness in acquiring them; there is supreme pleasantness in contemplating them. These truths are the highest riches; they are the everlasting pleasures. There is very intimate sweetness in tasting them and infinite delight in enjoying them.[55]

Therefore, in this work we intend to discuss not just any kind of truth but those eternal truths that we are ordered to believe by the rule of the Catholic faith. We do not intend to discuss anything in this work about the mysteries (*sacramentis*) of our redemption accomplished in time, which we are prescribed to believe and do believe. For the method of examination is different for these two topics.

CHAPTER FOUR. The method of examination in this work is to pursue logical reasoning rather than to cite authorities.

Our intention in this work will be to introduce, insofar as the Lord allows, not only probable but also necessary reasons (*necessarias rationes*) for what we believe and to season the teachings of our faith with an exposition and explanation of truth.[56] I believe without a doubt that, with regard to the explanation of any being that necessarily exists, not only are probable arguments not lacking, but neither are necessary arguments; although, at the moment, they happen to escape our undertaking.

For everything which begins to exist in time according to the good pleasure of the Creator, it is possible to exist and possible not to exist.[57] The source and cause of their being is demonstrated by experience rather than concluded by reasoning. But those beings that are eternal absolutely cannot not exist; just as they have never not existed, so certainly they will never not exist, or rather they are always what they are; they cannot be different or otherwise. Moreover, it seems absolutely impossible for any necessary being to lack necessary reason. But it does not belong to any soul to elicit such reasons from the profound and hidden bosom of nature, and to draw them out into the open as if uprooting them from some inmost secret sanctuary of wisdom.[58] Many are not worthy enough for this task; many are not qualified enough for this task; many are not diligent enough for this task. And what we should always have before our eyes, if that could happen, we scarcely or rarely consider. With what kind of eagerness, I ask, and with how much longing should we have applied ourselves to that matter and gazed longingly at that sight upon which the supreme happiness of everyone to be saved depends? I believe that I have produced something, if I am allowed to assist even modestly studious minds in this sort of study and to provoke lukewarm minds to great zeal with my effort.[59]

SUBJECT MATTER OF THIS STUDY

CHAPTER FIVE. A brief preview to what is discussed in the following chapters.

I have often read that there is only one God; that he is eternal, uncreated, immeasurable; that he is omnipotent and the Lord of all; that everything that exists is from him; that he is everywhere, he is every-

where whole and not divided into parts. I have read that my God is one
and three—one in substance but three in persons. I have read all this,
but I do not remember having read how all these assertions are proven.
I have read that there is only one substance in true divinity; that in the
unity of substance there is a plurality of persons, each of whom is distinguished from each of the others by a ‹distinct› property; that in the
unity of substance there is a person who is from himself but not from
any other, that in the unity of substance there is a person who is from
only one person but not from himself, and that in the unity of substance there is a person who is from two persons but not from one
person alone. Daily I hear that the three are not three eternals but one
eternal; that the three are not three uncreated nor three immeasurable,
but one uncreated and one immeasurable. I hear that the three are not
three omnipotents but one omnipotent; I hear, nevertheless, that the
three are not three Gods but one God, nor are there three Lords, but
the Lord is one. I find that the Father is neither made nor begotten, that
the Son is not made but begotten, that the Holy Spirit is not made nor
begotten but proceeds.[60]

I frequently hear or read all these assertions, but I do not recall
having read how all these assertions are proven. Authorities abound in
all these issues, but argumentations are not equally abundant; proofs
(*experimenta*) are lacking in all these assertions and argumentations
are rare. Therefore, as I have already said above, I think that I have accomplished something if I am able to assist even to a modest degree
studious minds in a study of this kind, even if it is not granted that I
can satisfy them.[61]

CHAPTER SIX. Every mode of being can be generally comprehended
under a threefold classification.

So that the order of our reasoning may stand upon a solid ground
of plain and clear truth as on an unshakable foundation, let us begin
with an assertion that no one can doubt or presume to repudiate. Everything that is or can be either has its being from eternity or begins
to exist in time. Likewise, everything that is or can be either has its
being from itself or from some source other than itself.

Therefore, every being is generally differentiated in three modes
according to reason.[62] The being of anything existing will either be
from eternity and from itself, or, conversely, neither from eternity nor
from itself, or, mediately between these two, from eternity but not from

itself. Nature itself in no way allows there to be a fourth mode of being, which seems to correspond as an opposite to the third group. Indeed absolutely nothing can be from itself that is not from eternity. There was certainly a time when whatever begins to exist in time was nothing; but as long as it was nothing, it had absolutely nothing, nor could it do anything at all; therefore, it gave being neither to itself nor to another, so that it would exist or could do something. Otherwise, it gave what it did not have, and it made what it could not make. Therefore, conclude from this how impossible it is for some being which is not from eternity to be absolutely from itself. Behold, therefore, we conclude with clear reason our previous assertion: all being is distinguished in three modes according to reason.

CHAPTER SEVEN. On that mode of being which is not from eternity and for that reason not from itself.

We ought to begin from the kind of realities, about which we can in no way doubt; and through those truths, which we know through experience, we ought to conclude by reasoning what is necessary for us to think concerning those truths that are above experience.[63] Clearly, through daily and multiple experiences we are made certain about that mode of being that is, according to the aforementioned reason, not from eternity and for that reason not from itself. We constantly see some things seceding, other things succeeding, and things coming into actuality that did not previously exist. We constantly see this in humans and in animals. Through daily experience we can demonstrate the same thing in trees and herbs. We see in our diligent operations the same as what we see in natural operations. Therefore, daily experience does not allow us to hide that fact that there are innumerable beings that were not from eternity.

A previous argument discovered that whatever was not from eternity could not be from itself;[64] otherwise, it is clearly proven that some being gave to itself the beginning of existence in that instant when it had nothing and when it could do absolutely nothing. How utterly impossible this is can never escape the notice of a person with a healthy mind. It is certain that everything which began to exist in time has that being in common which is not from eternity and for that reason not from itself, as was said above.[65] Behold, we have already discussed that mode of being about which we cannot doubt, namely that mode of being which we demonstrate from everyday experience.

CHAPTER EIGHT. On that mode of being which is from itself and for that reason from eternity.

But that being that is from itself and for that reason also from eternity is deduced by reasoning from that being that is neither from eternity nor from itself. If nothing had existed from itself then there would be no possible source for the existence of those beings which do not have nor can have their own being from themselves. It is demonstrated then that some being is from itself and for that reason also from eternity, as was said already;[66] otherwise, there was a time when there was nothing. And then no one will have ever existed, because there was absolutely no one around to give or able to give the beginning of existence to himself and others.[67] What is obvious shows how false this is, and the experience of existing realities also demonstrates how false this is. Hence, through reasoning we infer the beings that we do not see from what we see, eternal things from transitory things, things beyond the world from things of the world, and divine things from human things. *For since the creation of the world the invisible things of God are seen, having been understood through those things which are made.*[68]

CHAPTER NINE. On that mode of being which is from eternity but not from itself.

It should not seem impossible to anyone that there was some being from eternity which is not from itself, as if it is necessary for a cause always to precede its effect and for every being that is from another always to follow its origin. Certainly, a ray of the sun proceeds from the sun and draws its origin from the sun, and yet the ray is coeval with the sun. From the time it existed the sun produced its ray from itself, and at no time was it without the ray. Therefore, if corporeal light possesses a ray coeval with itself, why should the spiritual and inaccessible light not have a light beam coeternal with itself?[69]

We read in created nature what we ought to think or estimate about uncreated nature.[70] We see daily how existence produces existence by a natural operation, and how existence proceeds from existence. What then? Will it be necessary that that superexcellent nature does not have and cannot have any operation of nature? Will that nature which gave the fruit of fertility to our nature remain absolutely sterile in itself? And will that nature which bestowed reproduction to others be sterile and without reproduction?[71] From this, therefore, it seems probable that in that superessential immutability there is some being which is not from itself and was from eternity. But we will discuss this subject with a greater and more effective reason in another chapter.[72]

CHAPTER TEN. The whole purpose of this work is only concerned with the two modes of being that are from eternity.

We intend to discuss in this work the two modes of being which we said are from eternity and those matters that seem to pertain to such a consideration. We will discuss on occasion temporal realities—that is, those realities which pertain to the third mode of being—only to the extent that we regard their consideration necessary or useful to the investigation of eternal realities, as we learned from the Apostle and quoted earlier: *The invisible things of God are clearly seen, having been understood through those things which are made.*[73]

Therefore, as often as we climb up to the contemplation of invisible realities through the speculation of visible realities,[74] what else are we doing other than erecting some ladder, as it were, by which we ascend mentally to those realities that are above us? This is why the whole process of our reasoning in this work takes its point of departure from those truths that we know through experience. Therefore, what is said in this work about eternal things is the deliberate focus, but what is said about temporal things is occasional; for the whole purpose in this work concerns the two modes of being that are from eternity.

The One Supreme Substance and its attributes

CHAPTER ELEVEN. On the supreme substance which is from itself and for that reason from eternity and without any beginning.[75]

We must now discuss in more detail that being which is from itself and, consequently, is clearly from eternity, as we have already said.[76] It is most certain and thus, as I believe, no one can doubt that some supreme being necessarily exists amid the great multitude of existing realities and so many different grades of beings. We call the highest of all beings that-than-which-nothing-is-greater and that-than-which-nothing-is-better.[77] Now, without a doubt rational nature is better than irrational nature. Thus, it is necessary for some rational substance to be the highest of all beings. Moreover, it is certain that this substance, which holds the highest place in the universe of realities, cannot receive the very thing that it is from a source inferior to it. Thus, it is necessary that some substance exist that possesses both, namely, to hold the highest place and to exist from itself. Indeed, just as we have said and proven earlier,[78] if nothing were from itself then nothing would be from eternity and in that case there would be no origin and succession of things.

Therefore, the evidence of experienced realities clearly demonstrates that some substance must be from itself.[79] If no substance were from itself then absolutely no beings would exist that draw their origin from another and cannot exist from themselves. The substance that is only from itself pertains—it pertains, I say—to that being which is from eternity and without any beginning.

CHAPTER TWELVE. Likewise, one substance alone is from itself, all other substances exist from it, and this one substance has all that it has from itself alone.

We can further demonstrate our previous assertion about the supreme substance with a greater reason.[80] Now it is most certain that in the whole universe of realities nothing can exist unless it either possessed the possibility of being from itself or received it from another source. What cannot exist absolutely does not exist. Therefore, in order for something to exist it is necessary for it to receive the ability to exist from the power of being. And so, everything which subsists in the universe of realities receives its being from the power of being. But if all things are from the power of being, then the power of being certainly exists only from itself and it has nothing except from itself.[81] If all things are from the power of being, then every essence, all power, and all wisdom come from it. If every essence is from the power of being, then the power of being is the supreme essence. If all power is from the power of being then it is supremely powerful. If all wisdom is from the power of being, then it is supremely wise. Indeed, it is impossible to give something greater than one has. Wisdom can certainly be bestowed by one who possesses all wisdom, and at the same time wisdom can be withheld by one who bestows all wisdom. But you absolutely cannot impart greater wisdom than what you have. Therefore, it was necessary for the wisdom from which all wisdom draws its origin to exist supremely.

But where there is no rational substance there absolutely cannot be wisdom. Indeed, wisdom can only belong to a rational substance. Therefore, the highest substance of all, in which there is supreme wisdom, is also a rational substance. The highest substance of all, I say, is the source of every essence and certainly every nature, both rational and irrational. And so, the power of being is nothing other than the supreme substance. Therefore, just as the power of being only exists from itself, so the supreme substance, which is nothing other than the power of being, can only exist from itself.

It is certain then that everything that exists comes from the supreme substance. But if everything comes from the supreme substance, then nothing exists from itself except the supreme substance alone. And if every being, every power, and every possession is from the supreme substance, then without a doubt the supreme substance has all that it has from itself. Rightly therefore this substance, from which everything that exists obtains its beginning and origin, is called primordial.

CHAPTER THIRTEEN. The supreme substance is identical to its power and wisdom; and for that reason any of these properties is identical to the others.

At this time let us consider our previous assertion: the supreme substance is supremely powerful. It is most certain that whatever is powerful is so by power itself; whatever is wise is so by wisdom itself. Now we have already demonstrated that the supreme substance has all that it has only from itself. Therefore, in order for it to have only from itself what it has from power and from wisdom, it is necessary that wisdom and power be entirely identical to it; otherwise, the supreme substance, which cannot be powerful and wise without power and wisdom, would have what it has from them from another source rather than from itself. Moreover, it follows that if each of these properties is identical to the supreme substance, then any of them is identical to each other.[82]

CHAPTER FOURTEEN. The supreme substance cannot have an equal, just as it cannot have a superior.

Now at this point we must carefully notice that if this substance is the very thing that supreme power is, then the Self-same (*idipsum*) cannot be a different substance; otherwise, different substances would be one and one substance would be different, and this is absolutely impossible.

But perhaps you respond to this: "What if some diverse substance can *have* the supreme power even if it cannot *be* the supreme power?

RICHARD OF ST VICTOR

Will both these substances not be equally powerful if they have the highest power?"[83]

I affirm without doubt or hesitation that if one of these substances can *have* the supreme power and cannot *be* the supreme power, then it does not have power equal to the substance that can have and be the supreme power. After all what is entirely possible for one substance is partly possible and partly not possible for the other: this is to delight in the participation of that power not in the fullness of it. However, it is much greater and far more excellent to have the fullness of some great attribute than to obtain the participation of it. From this therefore it is clearly concluded that the primordial substance cannot have an equal,[84] just as it is clear from the above discussions that the primordial substance cannot have a superior.

CHAPTER FIFTEEN. It is impossible for the supreme substance to have a partaker of its own nature.

And so, it seems that the inability to have an equal or superior and the supervision over everything naturally belongs to the primordial substance. Without a doubt what belongs substantially to it also belongs naturally to it. That the primordial substance is supremely powerful and cannot have a superior or equal in its power naturally belongs to it from the fact that it is entirely identical to supreme power. Therefore, let us see if perhaps the primordial substance can have an inferior partner of its own nature. But how, I ask, will any substance possibly be inferior to the primordial essence, if it naturally shares the following property with the primordial essence: the inability of having an equal or superior? According to this any one substance will be greater and lesser than the other, or rather every substance will be superior and inferior to itself. Therefore, it is impossible for the primordial substance to have a partaker of its own nature.[85]

CHAPTER SIXTEEN. The supreme substance is identical to the divinity, and God is only one in substance.

According to the previous argument,[86] we now maintain as certain that everything that exists comes from the supreme substance alone, and that this substance has all that it has from itself. But if everything is from the supreme substance, then the divinity itself is also from it. But if the supreme substance gave that divinity to another and did not retain it for itself, then the supreme substance, which cannot have a superior according to our previous conclusion,[87] has a superior. It is certain then that the supreme substance possesses and at the same time has retained the divinity for itself. Moreover, God is the one who has deity and has the very thing that is God from deity. But if the supreme substance, which has nothing unless from itself, has the very thing that is God from divinity, then the deity itself is really nothing other than the supreme substance.[88] Therefore, the supreme substance could not give the divinity to any other substance (I am not saying that the supreme substance possessed the deity, but it was the deity itself);[89] otherwise, he would have an equal, which is impossible. For that reason, therefore, it is concluded that true divinity is in a unity of substance, and a true unity of substance is in the divinity. And so, God is only one in substance.

CHAPTER SEVENTEEN. Likewise, there is only one God; all that exists comes from God; he has all that he has only from himself; and he is identical to his power and wisdom.

Now hear how easily we are able to demonstrate that God is only one. From the fact that God has nothing except from himself it is certain that divinity itself is nothing other than God, so that no one should conclude that God has what he has from divinity from a source other than himself. And so, the divinity itself will either be incommunicable or common to other substances. But if the divinity is incommunicable, then it follows that God is only one. However, if the divinity is common to other substances, then the substance which is nothing other than the divinity itself will also be common. But the one substance cannot be common to multiple substances; otherwise, one and the same substance would be multiple, and multiple substances would be one; reason does not allow how false this is to be hidden. But if it is said that the divinity is common to multiple persons, then based on our previous statement, that substance which is nothing other than the divinity itself will certainly also be common to multiple persons.[90] According to this, there will certainly be multiple persons, but only one substance, in the one divinity. Whether, therefore, it is said that there is only one person or multiple persons in the one divinity, God will still be only one in substance. And so, the one and only God is from himself and for that reason from eternity. And, according to our previous demonstration on the supreme substance that is nothing other than God,[91] all that exists comes from God; he has all that he has from himself; and he is identical to his power and wisdom.

CHAPTER EIGHTEEN. It is absolutely impossible that even God himself can determine what is better than God.

If God's wisdom and power are one and the same in every respect, then no perfection and no consummation is contained by one property that is not contained by the other under the same measure of integrity.[92] And so, there is nothing greater and nothing better in his knowledge than in his power and, for this reason, in his being, because his power is identical to his being. Therefore, whatever is apprehended or determined by God's wisdom as best or excellent, all this is comprehended by his power according to the same fullness of integrity, and all this is comprised by his essence.[93] Indeed, with regard to this pinnacle of perfection, if God were reaching something through his intelligence that he could not apprehend through his efficacy, then he would undoubtedly extend himself more magnificently through wisdom than through power, and one and the same substance would be both greater and lesser than itself.[94] For if the substance of God would extend itself further through wisdom than through power (even though it is nothing other than its power or wisdom), if it had been able to extend itself further through the one than through the other, then one and the same substance would certainly be greater than itself through wisdom in comparison to its power, and one and the same substance would be lesser than itself through power in comparison to its wisdom. Therefore, God himself cannot either define or attain by understanding something better than God.

CHAPTER NINETEEN. If God himself cannot attain through his intellect to something that is better than him, then how much less can human thought.

If divine knowledge (*scientia*) cannot comprehend through intellect anything that is more perfect than God, then how much less can human knowledge devise something greater than God and something better than God! For what human thought comprehended through intellect could not be hidden from divine intelligence. It is a kind of insanity to believe that a human being, who cannot attain the very thing that God is through any investigation, can ascend in thought above that which God is.[95] And so, the more human thinking attains to what is best and perfect, the closer it ascends to that which is God, even though it does not attain him.[96]

CHAPTER TWENTY. For those who are investigating and discussing God, he is usually like a highest principle and a common conception of the mind.

It seems to happen by some endowment of nature, as it were, that almost every erudite person and every unlearned person usually accepts this as something familiar and holds it like a rule, namely, they conclude without hesitation that whatever is the best is attributed to God. And what reason does not teach some people through reasoning about this clear rule, devotion persuades them without the uncertainty of doubt. This is the reason why even those people who do not know how the Self-same (*idipsum*) can be proven indubitably affirm that God himself is immeasurable, eternal, immutable, supremely wise, and omnipotent. And so, attributing to God all that human estimation attains of the loftier truths is like a highest principle for erudite people and like a common conception of the mind for everyone in general.[97] From this solid principle of certitude, as on the foundation of the most profound truth, even the highest teachers everywhere assume the beginning of their disputation when they intend to discuss the divine properties very closely and deeply.

CHAPTER TWENTY-ONE. God is supremely powerful inasmuch as he is omnipotent.

That God exists as the supreme power is sufficiently clear from the above discussions.[98] But it still can be asked whether God is called supremely powerful because no one is higher than God in power or because he is supremely powerful in the sense that he can do all things and is really omnipotent. But if we reject his omnipotence, then we are found guilty of thinking that there is something greater than God. For it is greater to have omnipotence than to have any kind of power that is lacking some of the fullness of omnipotence. And indeed what is very easy for humans to understand cannot escape divine wisdom. And so, if God understands something of the fullness of power that he cannot have, then there will be something greater in his knowledge than in his power, both of which are identical to his being. Therefore, according to the above argumentation[99] one and the same being will be both greater and lesser than itself, and nothing is more impossible than this. Therefore, from this one can conclude without doubt that God is capable of all things of which 'to be capable' involves real power (*omnia potest [Deus] quecumque posse potentia est*).[100]

We are said to be able to do many things, which would be much better not to have been able to do than to be able to do. The power to decrease, the power to fail, the power to be destroyed, and the power to be reduced to nothing—in such cases non-power is greater than power. Indeed these powers are indications of weakness more than signs of majesty. Therefore, God is capable of all those things and only those things which, as we have already said, 'to be capable of' involves real power. And we say that God is omnipotent all the more correctly and rightly when we remove all evidence of weakness from his power.[101]

CHAPTER TWENTY-TWO. God's wisdom is supreme just as it is wholly perfect.

We can investigate divine wisdom with a similar reason applied to divine power in our previous discussion. Can it be that God's wisdom is called supreme because nothing can ever be greater than it? Or is it truly supreme in the sense that it is wholly perfect? But it is most certain that the fullness of wisdom cannot be lacking where there is omnipotence. For if God were lacking any perfection from the fullness of his wisdom that he could not have, then without any ambiguity God would not be omnipotent. And so, it is certain that God's wisdom absolutely is not lacking at all any sort of perfection of knowledge and prudence—an addition of which could make him greater or better. One must note how the fullness of his power is discovered from a consideration of divine wisdom, and conversely the fullness of wisdom is manifested and clearly demonstrated from a consideration of omnipotence.

CHAPTER TWENTY-THREE. Another reason further corroborates our assertion about the wisdom of God.

We can demonstrate our previous assertion about the fullness of divine wisdom with another reason. It is indeed certain that any wise person is wise either through the fullness of wisdom itself or through participation of wisdom.[102] But we already know from previous discussions that the divine substance is identical to wisdom itself.[103] Who else except an insane person would say that the substance of God, which is his very self, partly has and partly does not have wisdom and that God is not able to have the fullness of himself? Therefore, as it is impossible that the substance of God cannot have its whole self, so God cannot be lacking in fullness of wisdom.

CHAPTER TWENTY-FOUR. The same reason corroborates our previous assertion about the fullness of divine power.

A similar reason corroborates our previous assertion about omnipotence.[104] Indeed, just as every wise person is wise either through the fullness of wisdom or through the participation of it, so clearly every powerful person is powerful either through the fullness of power or through the participation of it. Moreover, it is impossible for something to participate in itself. Therefore, God cannot be omnipotent through the participation of power, because the fullness of power is nothing other than God. Thus, it is certain that God is powerful from the fullness of power. Moreover, no power can be lacking where fullness of power exists. It follows therefore that God, in whom all power resides, has omnipotence and truly is omnipotent.

CHAPTER TWENTY-FIVE. There can only be one omnipotent being, and it follows that there can only be one God.

Now it is impossible for several omnipotent beings to exist. Indeed he who truly is omnipotent can easily be able to render any other power powerless;[105] otherwise, he certainly will not be omnipotent. Behold such omnipotent ones who can become powerless with ease! Behold how easily it is proven that the very nature of realities does not allow but only one omnipotent being! We have concluded with clear reason that God is omnipotent, and from now on we cannot doubt it. And so, just as there can only be one who is omnipotent, so there can only be one God. Hence, our faith and previous assertions are clear: true divinity remains in unity of substance, and unity of substance remains in true divinity.[106] Behold, we have already said so much about the unity of divinity. Now it remains that we say something about the singularity of that nature.

BOOK TWO

THE ATTRIBUTES OF GOD

THE ETERNITY AND IMMEASURABILITY OF GOD

CHAPTER ONE. The divine properties are discussed in this book. The first topic to be discussed is that God is uncreated.

After we have discussed above what we thought needed to be said about the unity of divinity,[107] it remains for us to say something about the properties of the divine nature and especially about those things that we celebrate daily in the divine office.[108] In the divine office some of these attributes are such that the mind easily gives assent to them and willingly accepts them, even though it does not know how they are proven with reason. But certainly the mind would not at all, or less firmly, adhere to other attributes, if the faith, handed down in the Catholic Church, were not guiding it in this matter. For the human mind easily receives and freely accepts the fact that God is uncreated, eternal, and immeasurable; however, it would not easily believe that there cannot be several eternal beings and several immeasurable beings unless the rule of faith were to persuade it, especially since three are believed to exist whose eternity and infinity every mouth should confess.

Now, the fact that God is uncreated is sufficiently clear from the above discussions and a new exposition is not needed.[109] Indeed, if God were created, then he would have a creator. But he who is only from himself cannot have a creator. After all what do we mean by 'created' except 'made from nothing'? But God, who was never nothing and has being both from himself and from eternity, could never be made from nothing.[110]

CHAPTER TWO. God is everlasting.

Behold, it is now certain that God, who is from eternity and lacks any beginning, is uncreated. Now we must investigate whether God also lacks a beginning just as he lacks an end, and whether he has an everlasting being. For this is an everlasting being: To lack a beginning and an end.[111] Now, therefore, from the fact that this is most certain, let us clearly demonstrate something that someone could doubt.

It is most certain that no falsehood can be in the wisdom that is God; otherwise, he, who either desired to deceive or had been able to be deceived, would not be supremely wise. It is certain then that God is truthful and that very attribute belongs to him from truth. And so, truth is nothing other than God, because it can truly be demonstrated that he has only from himself what he has from truth. Moreover, just as truth always existed, so it will always exist. The fact that this universe could exist was true from eternity and will be true in eternity. For if this universe were not able to exist, then it would absolutely not exist. And so, there was truth from eternity, on account of which whatever was true from eternity was true; and there will be truth in eternity, on account of which whatever will be true in eternity will be true. Therefore, if God had true being, which was always true and will always be true, from the truth that is God, then surely God the Truth will also lack a beginning just as he also lacks an end. And so, God is everlasting and has an everlasting being. In other words, he lacks a beginning and an end.

CHAPTER THREE. God is incorruptible and absolutely immutable.

Because it is now certain that God has an everlasting being, it follows that we investigate whether he also has an immutable being. And so, one must know that every change is either from one position to a better position, from one position to a worse position, or from one position to a position equal to the first. However, there is true immutability where none of these changes are possible. Therefore, let us carefully examine each of these premises.

But how can God, who is omnipotent, be made worse? Indeed what is it to be made worse except to be corrupted? But no corruption can have dominion over him who is truly omnipotent, rather who is omnipotence itself. It is now certain that God cannot decrease, but let us now see if he can at least increase. But everything that increases receives some kind of increase of the good, on account of which it can be made better. However, from what source would he, who has and must have nothing except from himself, have this increase of good? For if he had the good before, then how did he attain to it by increasing? And if he did not have the good before, then surely he could not give to himself or to another what he absolutely did not have? From these arguments, therefore, one can conclude that God cannot increase or be diminished.[112]

But now we must see if perhaps God can be changed from one position to an equal position. But in order for something to pass from one position to another equal position, it is necessary for it to withdraw somehow from some position, which it had before, and to add to itself another, which it did not have before, in compensation for the same loss. And then God will be subjected to the two aforesaid changes in one and the same alteration, both of which the above reason rejected. And so, he, who cannot be made worse, is incorruptible; he, who cannot be made better or be changed in any way whatsoever, is absolutely immutable. Without any ambiguity, then, God certainly has an immutable being.[113]

CHAPTER FOUR. How we can conclude that God is eternal.

But if we combine those three aforementioned properties into one, then we demonstrate that God is not only everlasting but also eternal. There seems to be a distinction between everlasting and eternal.[114] Everlasting seems to indicate what lacks a beginning and end, and eternal seems to indicate what lacks a beginning, end, and any mutability. And, although perhaps neither is discovered without the other, it is still correct to distinguish between the meanings of these words. And so, what else is eternity other than duration of time without a beginning and end, and the absence of all mutability? But he who is uncreated and everlasting lacks a beginning and end; and he whose condition is invariable remains without any mutability. With regard to these three attributes, therefore, it is proven that God is eternal; for without ambiguity these three attributes grant that God has eternity and is eternal.

CHAPTER FIVE. God is infinite and for that reason immeasurable.

It is undoubtedly certain that what lacks a beginning and end is infinite. And so, one can ask whether God, who is infinite on account of his eternity, is also infinite on account of his magnitude.[115] We have demonstrated above that the divine substance is identical to its power and wisdom.[116] Indeed, we can prove with the same reason that the eternity, from which it is eternal, and the magnitude, from which it is great, are nothing other than that substance itself, which has nothing except from itself. If then we demonstrate that the eternity of God is infinite, then without a doubt we cannot deny that his magnitude is infinite; otherwise, we are proven wrong by clear reason in confessing that one and the same substance is both larger and smaller than itself.[117] If his eternity is infinite, but his magnitude is finite, then, according to its eternity, one and the same substance will be greater than its magnitude (that is, than itself), and, according to its magnitude, it will be less than its eternity (that is, than itself). It is clearly concluded then that if his eternity is infinite, then his magnitude will also be infinite. And so, God has an infinite magnitude, and, for that reason, God is immeasurable. Indeed what is infinite cannot be contained by any measurement. Therefore, God is rightly called immeasurable, whose magnitude is not contained by any measure.

Only God Alone is an Immeasurable, Eternal, and Uncreated Being

CHAPTER SIX. There is, or rather can be, only one immeasurable God alone.

It is suitable now to consider also whether several immeasurable beings are possible.[118] Surely what is not contained by measure is rightly called immeasurable. And what is found equal or comparable to no measure is called immeasurable. If therefore we assert that there are several immeasurable beings, then they will each be incomprehensible and immeasurable to each other. And so, the measure of any one of these beings is not contained by the measure of any other, and, consequently, they each surpass the other. Therefore, each one will be greater than each other, and each one will be less than each other.[119] But if this is impossible—or rather because this is impossible—then it will also be impossible for several immeasurable beings to exist. But if no being is greater or lesser than any other, then just as each one of them is comprehensible and measurable to themselves, so each will be comprehensible and measurable to each other. From these assertions we can conclude as certain that several immeasurable beings absolutely cannot exist, but there can be only one immeasurable being.

CHAPTER SEVEN. How it is proven that there is only one eternal God from the fact that there is only one immeasurable God.

We now know that it is impossible for several immeasurable beings to exist; now let us see whether several eternal beings are possible. We already recognize from the previous discussions and ascertain with certainty that the divine substance is nothing other than its immeasurability and eternity;[120] hence, it is also certain that both its immeasurability and eternity are identical to each other. And so, it is certain that

God who has eternity certainly must have immeasurability. But if God who is eternal cannot lack immeasurability, then without a doubt he will be eternal and immeasurable at the same time. Therefore, just as several immeasurable beings cannot exist, so several eternal beings cannot exist.

At this time there is a fact that must be especially noted and deserves careful consideration. In our rational conclusions, we elicit some truths from an analysis of the property in question of one divine attribute, and we prove other truths from a consideration of the property of another attribute and the mutual relationship between the two attributes. For instance, we conclude from the property of immeasurability that there can only be one immeasurable God, but we concluded the impossibility of several eternal beings both from the same property of immeasurability and from the mutual relationship between immeasurability and eternity.

CHAPTER EIGHT. God alone is uncreated; he alone is from eternity, and everything else is created *ex nihilo*.

We are certain that the divine substance alone is from itself and that everything else is from it. But whatever is or even can be from the divine substance either exists according to the operation of nature or according to the communication of grace. But, as it is certain that the divine nature cannot be diminished or that the omnipotence cannot be degraded, so it will necessarily be certain that a being, which was not God, could not be from the divine substance through an operation of nature. But we have sufficiently demonstrated above that God can only be one in substance.[121] Thus, there cannot be a second God from God himself—from that unique and singular substance of God—, but neither can any other being that is not God come from God. It is certain then that whatever is other than God is from him according to the operation of grace. But whatever comes from God through an operation of grace rather than necessity of nature could be created by him or could also not be created by him according to the decision of his good-pleasure. And so, those beings created by God cannot have as matter that divine substance, which is incorruptible and immutable. It is certain then that, except for the divine substance alone, all creatures are either created *ex nihilo* or they have something mutable for their matter.

But, I ask, what was the origin of primordial matter, which absolutely cannot exist from itself or have the divine substance for its matter? If one says that primordial matter has matter, then he must affirm that it is primordial and not primordial at the same time.[122] Therefore, it is clearly concluded from this that absolutely everything—primordial matter, all material things ⟨formed⟩ by means of that matter, and anything immaterial—was created *ex nihilo*.[123] The content of our faith then is certain: God alone is uncreated.[124] Just as God alone is from himself, so also God alone is undoubtedly from eternity.

CHAPTER NINE. Another way of proving that God is eternal and that there is only one eternal God.

Now, there was undoubtedly a time when whatever receives being from creation was absolutely nothing; otherwise, it could not be created *ex nihilo*. Thus, everything created begins to exist in time; however, what is uncreated preceded all time. But what existed when there was no time undoubtedly could not be mutable; otherwise, it was subject to time, when there was not yet any time, which could not happen at all. Indeed what is subject to mutability is, for that reason, subject to time. After all, time is always in motion, and it absolutely cannot remain still even for a moment.[125] And if there were no change, then without a doubt there absolutely would not be time. It is certain then, as I have already said above, that what is subject to mutability is also subject to time. However, something could not be subject to mutability when there was no time.

Therefore, what is uncreated could not be mutable, because it existed before any time. Moreover, just as what is immutable cannot be changed from being to non-being, so it cannot be changed from being to a different being. In fact, what cannot be changed from being to non-being endures without end. What cannot be changed from being to a different being remains without any change.[126] And so, what is uncreated not only lacks a beginning, but it also remains without an end and any mutability. Moreover, to lack a beginning, an end, and any mutability means to be eternal. It is demonstrated then that what is uncreated is also eternal. Conversely, moreover, it is certain that whatever is eternal is also uncreated. For what is eternal was from eternity, and, for that reason, it could not be created. Therefore, it is concluded from these arguments that if there is only one uncreated, then there is only one eternal; and conversely if there is only one eternal, then there is one uncreated.

CHAPTER TEN. Another way of demonstrating that God is immeasurable and that there is only one immeasurable God.

We can also conclude God's immeasurability, which we discussed above, with another reason by considering the property of immeasurability.[127] Whatever is contained within a measure would be greater if its size were doubled, it would be much greater if it grew tenfold, and even more if it grew a hundredfold. What if it grew a thousand times, or rather a million times more? For that reason, therefore, you are able, I believe, to notice that to have measurable magnitude, that is, to participate in it, is not to be magnitude.[128] However, as the previous reason demonstrated,[129] God is magnitude itself, and absolutely nothing can participate in itself, nor can it partially be and partially not be the very thing that it is. Thus, God, who is magnitude itself, cannot have measurable magnitude. And so, what is contained or even regarded as comprehensible with no measure is understood to be beyond every measure and, for that reason, immeasurable. Therefore, the content of our faith and our daily confession remains unshaken: God is immeasurable.[130]

This confession can be proven from a consideration of omnipotence. But, because this is very easily considered, it is not necessary to linger on this point. We have ascertained from the previous discussions that God's omnipotence is identical to his immeasurability and eternity.[131] It follows then that God, who is immeasurable and has eternity, also has omnipotence at the same time. Thus, just as there can only be one omnipotent, so there can only be one immeasurable and one eternal.

INCOMMUNICABILITY OF THE DIVINE PROPERTIES

CHAPTER ELEVEN. God's immeasurability and eternity are incommunicable, and these attributes cannot be common to several substances.

We have established far above that the divinity is absolutely incommunicable and cannot be common to several substances.[132] We can discuss God's immeasurability as well as his eternity with a similar reason that was applied to our previous discussion on the divinity. Indeed, as any one substance cannot be communicable to several substances,[133] so immeasurability and eternity cannot be communicable to several substances, because both immeasurability and eternity is nothing other than the divine substance.

But at this point a great question arises that can trouble simple listeners unless it is resolved with a clear explanation.[134] It was proven above that the divine substance is identical to its power and wisdom,[135] but who can actually say that power is incommunicable and wisdom is not common to several substances? If the reason why we say that God's immeasurability and eternity are incommunicable is because they are demonstrated to be identical to the divine substance, then why do we not also say that his power and wisdom are also incommunicable and cannot be common to several substances for the same reason? Why is a different conclusion drawn when the same reason is premised? But, in order for us to untie this knot of perplexity more easily, let us further discuss with deeper scrutiny our previous argument about the singularity of the divinity.[136]

CHAPTER TWELVE. A clearer and fuller explanation of our previous argument about the incommunicability of the divinity.

One must know that every substance possesses being from its own substantiality. After all, a substance, in which there is no substantiality, cannot rightly be called a substance. Substantiality is what we call that property of the substance that enables it to be called and to be a substance. The substantiality of human substance is humanness itself, because a substance that does not contain humanness cannot accurately be called man. Moreover, what we say about this substance can be considered equally in other substances. Substantiality is general, specific, or individual.[137] General substantiality is what is common to every species, such as corporality, which belongs to everything physical both animate and inanimate. Specific substantiality is what belongs to all the individuals of only one species, such as humanness, which is common to every human. And individual substantiality is what belongs to one individual alone and cannot be common at all to several substances.

We do not have a term in use for specifying individual substantiality, but, in order to establish greater clarity of what needs to be discussed, we can make up a term from a proper name.[138] And so, let us say "Danielness" from Daniel, just as we say humanness for a human.[139] And so, Danielness is understood as that substantiality, or, if it seems better, that substance from which Daniel is able to have that substance which is Daniel and in which no other substance can participate. Humanness then, like corporality, is common to many substances, but Danielness is absolutely incommunicable. We say incommunicable because Danielness belongs to Daniel in such a way that it cannot belong to another. After all, someone, who has this substantiality, will certainly be Daniel; but someone, who did not have it, will not be able to be the same Daniel. Different substantiality makes a different substance, but a singular and individual substantiality can only make one substance. Danielness then is incommunicable, as we have said, because this substance belongs to one substance in such way that it cannot belong to another. Thus, if Danielness is called an incommunicable being, because it cannot belong to a different substance, then how much more incommunicable would it be if the substance of Daniel were identical in every respect to its own substantiality? Now the divinity is identical in every respect to the divine substance; identical, I say, to a single substance, which alone is also from itself and from which alone every other being exists.[140] Thus, just as divinity cannot be communicable, so diverse substances cannot be one substance, and one substance cannot be diverse substances.

Behold how we have shown that the divinity itself is incommunicable with such clarity that a reader, who still had doubts, seems to be more blind than stupid. According to the aforementioned reasoning, immeasurability and eternity belong to one substance in such a way that they cannot belong to another substance; and, for that reason, we consider those attributes incommunicable. Let us also add that they are identical to the divine substance, and, for that reason it is also certain that they are incommunicable.

CHAPTER THIRTEEN. According to the various ways of speaking, wisdom or power can sometimes be called communicable and sometimes incommunicable.

But let us return to the question that prompted this discussion: If God's power and wisdom are truly proven to be identical to the divine substance, then why not say that they are incommunicable for the same reason? But one must realize that we misuse the words "power" and "wisdom", when we apply them interchangeably to God and humans, so that we seem to have made an unequivocal predication rather than an equivocal one.[141] We say that God is wisdom, and we do not say that a man is wisdom, but that wisdom is in a man. In the first assertion, the word "wisdom" designates something that is the substance and more than a substance. In the second assertion, the word "wisdom" designates something that is not a substance. In both assertions one word is used but with different meanings. If equivocation occurs when one word with diverse meanings designates diverse substances, then how much more equivocal is it when one word is used separately in order to designate both what we do not call a substance and what we call a substance. We say that a human being has wisdom; yet, we also say that God has wisdom. It seems that the expression is equivocal, but it is used incorrectly only with respect to God. It seems to be no less an incorrect expression than if someone said that Abraham *is* not a human being, but he *has* a human being.[142] This incorrect use of language or this equivocation of words confuses the meaning and does not allow power and wisdom to be called incommunicable.

In short, let us utilize such a word that can only be appropriate for the divine power or for the divine wisdom, and we will see that both are incommunicable. For the word "omnipotence," which can only be appropriated to the divine power, is understood to be absolutely incommunicable, because, just as we have already demonstrated, only the one God can be omnipotent.[143] But in order to express divine wisdom, we do not have a word similar to omnipotence, but we often designate it with adjuncts; for example, when we say "supreme wisdom," "wisdom itself," or "the fullness of wisdom." But whenever the divine and uncreated power or wisdom is expressed in such way that they absolutely cannot be realized in any other substance, then both properties will undoubtedly be incommunicable and will not be able to be common to several substances (I am referring not just to angelic and human substance, but I am also referring to certain quasi-divine substances).[144]

CHAPTER FOURTEEN. There are multiple ways of demonstrating that there is only one God. ·

Leaving aside what we already said above about the singularity of the divinity,[145] behold how many ways we can prove that there is only one God. One uncreated, one eternal, and one immeasurable—each property proves and clearly demonstrates that there is only one God. If you pay careful attention, you will be able to prove the same truth from a consideration of ‹unity›.[146] If someone claims that there are several gods, then the following consideration will be able to prove that person wrong: if any one of these gods comes from any of the other gods, then the property to exist from themselves alone belongs to each of them. But, because we know that this can be weighed and examined from our previous discussions,[147] we deliberately omit this issue and leave it to the sagacity of the reader to work out.

CHAPTER FIFTEEN. There can only be one Lord, just as there can only be one God.

Now let us ask whether, according to our daily confession, there can be only one Lord alone.[148] Indeed, one is truly called the Lord, whose freedom is not checked by any power and whose power or dominion is not hindered by any impossibility. But one truly could not be called the Lord who unwillingly yields or is subjected to the will of another.[149] And so, it seems impossible for several lords to exist. If it is asserted that there are several lords, then see what kind of inconsistent conclusion follows from it. If, for example, any one of these lords should desire to enslave some other lord, and if the lord being attacked cannot repel the violence of the attacker, then how will he not be a slave more than a lord? But if the perpetrator of the assault surrenders after being violently repelled and conquered, then how will he be a true lord who is subjected to the will of his conqueror indeed not by his own will, yet by surrendering? It thus happens that if we assert that there are several lords and several equal powers, then we undoubtedly prove that none of them is truly the Lord.

But what was proven from a consideration of the property of lordship is confirmed by a consideration of omnipotence. Indeed, just as it will only be possible for one God to exist who is omnipotent, so it will only be possible for one Lord to exist. Who will be able to resist the force of him, who is clearly and truly all-powerful? Therefore, one must regard as certain that there is only or can only be the one Lord just as there is the one and only God alone.

THE SUPREMELY PERFECT GOOD AND HAPPINESS

CHAPTER SIXTEEN. God himself is his own good and the supreme good, and that the supreme good is entirely perfect.

But he who is truly omnipotent cannot lack anything to be desired. No fullness and no perfection can be lacking where there is omnipotence; otherwise, if God's supreme power were lacking even a little perfection that he could not have, then he absolutely would not be omnipotent. However, he is entirely perfect who lacks or can lack no perfection in any way.[150] Nothing can be better and nothing can be greater than that which is full and perfect in every respect. And so, it is certain that the Almighty himself is the supreme good and, consequently, is his own good to himself. Indeed, just as he who holds the highest place cannot have a superior, so the supreme being of all cannot be made good or blessed by a being inferior to it. How could he, who has all that he has from himself, be made good or blessed by another? Thus, he is good from himself and is blessed from himself. Therefore, he is himself his own goodness, he is the supreme goodness; he is himself his own happiness, he is the supreme happiness. It is certain then, as it was said, that God is the supreme good, and the supreme good is entirely perfect. After all, what is blessedness other than the fullness and perfection of all good things?[151] It is certain then that the supreme good and absolute perfection lacks absolutely nothing, the addition of which could make it better.

CHAPTER SEVENTEEN. There is true unity and supreme simplicity in the supreme and absolutely perfect good.

But if the fullness of all the good is in the true, supreme, and absolutely perfect good, then surely that entirely perfect good is not a composite of many good things? But what is a composite of several parts is naturally divisible, and what is naturally divisible is naturally mutable, and eternity cannot exist where there is mutability, and thus neither can there be true happiness.[152] But neither eternity nor true happiness can be lacking in the universally perfect good. For, leaving aside the other attributes, it is proven from a consideration of omnipotence alone that no perfection and, consequently, none of those other attributes can be lacking in the good. Thus, it is certain that there is true immutability and, consequently, true and supreme simplicity in that eternal happiness and truly happy eternity. Moreover, where there is supreme simplicity, there is true and supreme unity. Therefore, whatever is in the supreme good is truly and supremely one, and there cannot be distinct realities in it, but it is identical to all that it is.[153]

CHAPTER EIGHTEEN. How another reason can corroborate our assertions about the simplicity or unity of the supreme good.

What we are asserting here about the simplicity or unity of the true good can be demonstrated further with another argument and likewise be inferred from those attributes that we have already established above. In the previous arguments reason discovered that the divine substance is identical to its power and wisdom, and from that it is proven that any of its attributes is identical to its other attributes.[154] It was previously asserted, or rather it was proven by a similar reason, that the same substance is true immeasurability and is identical to its eternity.[155] Note then that all these attributes are one and the very same and can even be mutually predicated of one another. From what we say about those attributes, we can draw a similar conclusion about God's goodness and blessedness. Those attributes, like previous ones, receive a mutual predication about themselves and about the aforementioned attributes; and absolutely everything, which is said to be in the divine substance or from which the divine substance is said to possess something, runs into the same conclusion. And so, because whatever is in the supreme substance, or rather whatever the supreme substance is, is truly and supremely one, its being is the same as its living, its living is the same as its understanding, and its power and wisdom will be the same as its being, living, and understanding; and even its being good and blessed is not different from one another nor from those other attributes. One can conclude from such reason and consideration that whatever is in the supreme good and true divinity is truly, substantially, and supremely one.[156]

CHAPTER NINETEEN. The universally perfect good is supremely one and uniquely supreme.

It is necessary for the supreme good to be supremely one, and not only supremely one but also uniquely supreme. Indeed, there cannot be two supreme goods, just as there cannot be two universally perfect beings. If we grant that there are two equally perfect beings, then it is necessary for us also to grant consequently that all the fullness and perfection in one will also be in the other according to the same manner and measure. And so, in each being there will be one and the same fullness and one perfection without distinction. But absolutely no one can rightly speak of or discover plurality where there is no difference. And so, just as several entirely perfect beings absolutely do not exist, so several entirely perfect beings absolutely cannot exist. And indeed, just as those before us have argued, if one entirely perfect being exists, then it is sufficient in every way;[157] otherwise, it will never be perfect. And if one perfect being is entirely sufficient, then a second will be superfluous; and if a second is entirely superfluous, then how is it useful? And if it is useless, then how is it good?[158] And so, as it was said, the entirely perfect good will be not only supremely one but also uniquely supreme.[159]

Behold, as you see, our assertion about the supreme good comes to the same conclusion as our previous rational argument for the unity of the divine substance.[160] For if God is truly the supreme good, then as there can only be one supreme good, so what we believe is truly certain: there can only be one God.[161] Therefore, there is, I say, supreme and substantial unity in that true and supreme happiness, in the truly and supremely happy divinity, and in the true unity and supreme simplicity, where it is identical to all that it is, as it was previously demonstrated.[162]

The Incomprehensibility of the Divine Substance

CHAPTER TWENTY. The simplicity of true and supreme unity is incomprehensible.

But if there is true and supreme simplicity in that unity, then nothing in the supreme simplicity pertains to that unity which consists of a composition of parts in one substance. If it is identical to all that it is, then nothing in it pertains to that unity which consists of conformity of many substances in one nature. If it is truly and supremely simple, then what is in it that pertains to that unity which occurs in a union of differently formed substances in one person? If a simple identity is in it, then what is in it that pertains to that unity which occurs in a composition of a subsistent and subsistence in one essence? Nevertheless, this is also far above and beyond that unity which consists of a collection of many properties in one form.[163] Moreover, it is certain that the supreme simplicity, which has a supremely simple and immutable being in the identity of infinity, will transcend in an incomparable and incomprehensible way all those unities.[164]

And so, there is true unity in that supreme and universally perfect good, there is supreme simplicity in it, and there is a true and supremely simple identity in it. This is more wonderful still: in that good there is true unity with the totality of plenitude, supreme simplicity with the immeasurability of perfection, and a supremely simple identity with the infinity of total consummation. Therefore, note how incomprehensible and absolutely inestimable the simplicity of true and supreme unity is.

CHAPTER TWENTY-ONE. How someone can conclude in one's own knowledge by means of comparison what one ought to think concerning the unsurpassable incomprehensibility.

So that some of the more simple readers may not suppose that I am building conflicting and contradictory arguments one on top of the other, as if those assertions could not stand together, I am showing such readers how they can look, as it were, into a mirror and conclude in themselves by means of comparison what they ought to think concerning the unsurpassable incomprehensibility.[165] If someone were holding a kernel in his hand, would he not really think and readily affirm that none of the other kernels were the same as his one kernel? If then we were to question him about each individual kernel of corn or herb one at a time, would he not constantly reply that one kernel is different from each and every kernel? He would think the same about every hair and affirm the same about every strand of hair. What about some drop of sea? What about a leaf of some tree? If the whole earth were dissolved into dust, and if we were able to question him about each of the minute particles of dust, then he would constantly and truly reply the same in each interrogation. If the size of the earth were growing infinitely, then he would hold the same opinion about the minutest parts of it. I have sought to express this carefully, so that anyone, however simple in his knowledge, may read and understand how infinite truths are comprehended under one simple truth. Therefore, what wonder is it if in that wisdom, which is God and in which everything is true—otherwise, it would not be perfect if some truth were eluding his wisdom— I say, what wonder is it if there is supreme simplicity according to one perspective, and there is infinite multiplicity according to another perspective? What wonder is it, I say, if there is harmony and convergence of identity with the infinity of multiplicity, of simplicity with the immeasurability of magnitude, and of true unity with the entirety of complete fullness? Behold everyone knows how they can conclude in their own knowledge what they ought to think concerning the unsurpassable incomprehensibility.[166]

CHAPTER TWENTY-TWO. What is said more correctly about the substance of God. And God is great without quantity and good without quality.

We know from the previous discussions that there is true unity and supreme simplicity in that nature which is God, there is no composition or coalescence in it, and the divine nature is inherent in nothing, and nothing is inherent in it just as in a subject.[167] The divine nature is called and is the highest power; it is called and is the supreme wisdom;

and it is called a substance, lest it is regarded as being in a subject. But because, contrary to the nature of substances, nothing is discovered to inhere in it just as in a subject, it is shown to be not so much a substance as a supersubstantial essence.[168]

The above reason discovered, unless it was forgotten, that God's goodness is identical to his immeasurability.[169] What then? If his immeasurability is identical to his goodness, then surely God will not be good on account of his immeasurability? If his goodness is identical to his immeasurability, then surely God will not be great on account of his goodness? But his goodness seems to pertain to quality, and his immeasurability to quantity. What then? Will God be great according to quality and good according to quantity? *And who is capable of these questions?*[170] Because God's immeasurability or his goodness is not different from his substance, surely God will not be good without quality and great without a quantity?[171] *And who is capable of these questions?*[172] From these considerations, I think that it is very easy to understand how ineffable and indeed incomprehensible it is what a rational argument compels us to think about our God.

CHAPTER TWENTY-THREE. God is incomprehensibly in every place and is invariably in every time; and how God is uniform and multiform.

We maintain from our previous assertions that God is omnipotent and that he can undoubtedly do anything. If then he is truly omnipotent, it follows that he can be omnipresent.[173] If he can be omnipresent, then he is omnipresent in power. If he is omnipresent in power, then he is omnipresent in essence. Indeed, his power is not different from his essence. Moreover, if he is omnipresent in essence, then he is both where there is place and where there is not place. And so, he will be within every place, and he will also be outside every place. He will be above all, and he will be below all; he will be within all, and he will be outside of all. But because God has a simple nature, he will not be divided into parts in different places, but he will be everywhere whole. He will then be whole in a however small part of the whole; he will be whole in the whole; and he will be whole outside the whole. And so, if he is whole outside every place, then he is contained in no place. If he is whole in every place, then he is excluded from no place; therefore, he is locally nowhere, who can be contained by no place and excluded from no place. And just as he is presently in every place and locally in no place, so he is eternally in every time and temporally in no time.

Just as he who is supremely simple and not compounded is not extended through spaces, so he who is eternal and immutable is not altered through time. And so, as none of those things, which do not yet exist, are future for him, so none of those things, which no longer exist, are past time for him, and none of those things that presently exist are transitory for him. He is therefore incomprehensibly in every place and invariably in every time.[174]

And in a wonderful way God, who is always uniform with regard to himself, is found multiform in a variety of beings. If you seek the position of him who lacks a position, then, with regard to himself, he uniformly contains himself everywhere according to the simplicity of his nature. And yet, according to the participation of grace, he presents himself multiform in a variety of beings. He is in some beings according to the participation of power, and yet not according to the participation of life; he is in other beings according the participation of life, and yet not according to the participation of wisdom. He is in some beings according to the participation of goodness, and yet not according to the participation of blessedness. Indeed, it is clear that he is in other beings according to the participation of goodness and blessedness. And he, who is uniform in himself and unable to change, shortens the hand of his bounty in some beings; he extends generously the hand of his bounty in other beings; and he extends more generously the hand of his bounty in other beings.[175]

CHAPTER TWENTY-FOUR. God's activity is his will that something be done by him; God's permission is not to refuse that something be done ⟨by another⟩; and God equally possesses both what actually is and what actually is not.

And because God is truly omnipotent, whatever exists subsists either through God's activity or his permission. If whatever happens were not taking place according to his will, then he would undoubtedly not be omnipotent. And so, God's activity is his will that something be done by him, but his permission is not to refuse that something be done by another. And just as all of his passivity is without any passion, and all of his compassion is without propassion,[176] so all of his activity is without self-agitation, and his unfailing activity is without fatigue.[177]

But if God's activity is identical to his will that something be done by him, then can it be that, when he does something that was not previously done, can it be, I ask, that he wills something that he previously did not will? But he who is truly immutable cannot will himself to change. Therefore, he always willed what he willed once. Can it be then that he accomplished from eternity what he accomplished by his will, given that he willed that they be done from eternity? And if he accomplishes those things that are in the future, then can it be that he is still doing and will do those things that are already in the past and will no longer be in the future? Surely he does not preserve something by his activity in the same way as his will? And, when some being ceases to exist, surely he does not cease to possess what he had before; and, when some being begins to exist, surely he does not begin to possess what he did not have before? For what ceases to exist or what does not yet begin to exist is nothing; and what is nothing cannot be possessed. But the Almighty Owner can neither grow rich nor wane in his wealth.

What then? But consider whether perhaps the very thing that exists in actuality is more excellent where it does not exist in actuality than where it does exist in actuality. For it is transitory in the latter place and eternal in the former.[178] And *that which was made was life* in God,[179] even at a time when it did not exist yet in actuality. Therefore, he who can lose or acquire nothing possesses equally what is in actuality and what is not in actuality.

CHAPTER TWENTY-FIVE. All of our assertions about the divine properties until now seem to pertain to that being which is from eternity and from itself.

At this time we want to refrain from a discussion of those divine properties expressed in terms of relationship; for their meaning extends further than what can be understood in a brief summary. Indeed, in my opinion, the meaning of relative properties extends to every category.[180] In addition to the relation that they denote, their connotation pertains at times to one category and at other times to another. For we say in terms of substance: "one is consubstantial with another;" in terms of quantity, "equal or unequal;" in terms of quality, "similar or dissimilar." Place connotes "above or below;" time connotes "before or after;" situation connotes "one sitting near or a sitting together;" condition connotes "possessor and possession." "Begetter and begotten, lover and beloved" pertain to activity and passivity. And so, it is better at the moment to refrain from this discussion than to attempt to study what we cannot furnish in a concise manner.

Now one should note here that all of our assertions until now about the divine properties seem to pertain to that being which is from eternity and from itself. For whatever was said about such a being until now would stand no less, even if there were no being from eternity that drew its origin from a source other than itself.[181]

BOOK THREE

THE PLURALITY

Questions to Be Studied

CHAPTER ONE. The unity of the divine substance has been analyzed thus far; now it is necessary to investigate what we must think concerning the plurality of divine persons.

We have completed thus far our discussion on the unity and property of the divine substance, as it seemed to us. Henceforth, we intend to investigate what we ought to think concerning the plurality and properties of the divine persons. And so, it first seems necessary to investigate whether there is true plurality in the true and simple divinity, and if the number of persons comes to three, as we believe?[182] Second, how the unity of substance can be consistent with the plurality of persons.[183] Third, it will be necessary to investigate whether, according to the teachings of our faith,[184] there is among the three one person alone who is from himself, and whether each of the other two persons proceeds from another, and if there are other questions to be investigated concerning the same consideration.[185] If it is granted that we prove these issues from reason, then it will still be necessary in the end to investigate whether there are diverse modes of procession in those two persons who proceed from a source other than themselves, what sort of mode is proper to each, and what we can learn about their names according to the property of each person.[186]

Now it is necessary for us to pursue more ardently and devote greater care to these issues that remain to be investigated, inasmuch as we find less in the writings of the fathers from which we can demonstrate those issues from the testimony of reason (not, I say, from the testimonies of the Scriptures). But he who wishes let him laugh at the intention of my investigation, and he who desires let him ridicule; this is indeed an appropriate response. For, to tell the truth, it is not so much knowledge that prompts me but rather the ardor of a burning mind stimulates me to this bold undertaking.[187] What if it is not granted that I attain the goal for which I strive? What if I fail in the race? Nevertheless, I will rejoice that I have always run, labored, and exerted all my strength to seek the face of my Lord.[188] And if it should turn out that I fail on account of the excessive length, difficulty, and steepness of the course, I have still accomplished something;[189] if it should turn out that

I can truly say: "I did what I could; *I have sought him and I have not found him; I have called him and he did not responded to me.*"[190] And, behold Balaam's ass, which hindered its rider on his journey;[191] somehow that ass urges and persuades me to run down the road that I have begun. I hear this ass still speaking and saying to me: "He, who was able to give me the ability to speak, will undoubtedly also be able to give you this ability." But let us now apply ourselves with all diligence to our proposed discussion.

THE FULLNESS OF GOODNESS, HAPPINESS,
AND GLORY REQUIRES A PLURALITY OF PERSONS

CHAPTER TWO. How the fullness of goodness demonstrates from the property of charity that a plurality of persons cannot be lacking in true divinity.

We have learned from the previous discussions that the fullness and perfection of all goodness lies in the supreme and universally perfect good.[192] Moreover, where the fullness of all goodness is, true and supreme charity cannot be lacking. Indeed, nothing is better than charity, and nothing is more perfect than charity. However, no one is properly said to have love on account of a private and exclusive love of oneself. And so, it is necessary that *love be directed toward another, so that it can be charity.*[193] Therefore, charity absolutely cannot exist where a plurality of persons is lacking.[194]

But perhaps you say: "Even if there were one person alone in the true divinity, nevertheless he would still be able to have, or he would have, charity toward his creation." But surely God would not be able to have supreme charity toward a created person. After all, his charity would be disordered, if he were loving supremely someone who should not be loved supremely.[195] However, it is impossible that charity be disordered in the supremely wise goodness. And so, a divine person could not have supreme charity toward a person who would not be worthy of supreme love. Moreover, in order for charity to be supreme and supremely perfect, it is necessary that it be so great that no greater love can exist, and that it be so excellent that no better love can exist.[196] As long as someone loves no one else as much as himself, that private love, which he has toward himself, proves that he has not yet apprehended the highest degree of love. But a divine person would surely not have someone whom he could love as worthily as himself, if he absolutely were not having a person of equal dignity. However, a person who was not God would not be of equal dignity to a divine person. Therefore, so that the fullness of charity can occur in true divinity, it is necessary for a divine person not to lack the fellowship with a person of equal dignity and, for that reason, a divine person.

See therefore how easily reason proves that a plurality of persons cannot be lacking in true divinity. Surely, only God is supremely good. Only God therefore ought to be supremely loved. And a divine person could not show supreme love to a person who lacked divinity. But the fullness of divinity cannot be without the fullness of goodness; the fullness of goodness cannot be without the fullness of charity; and the fullness of charity cannot be without the plurality of divine persons.[197]

CHAPTER THREE. The fullness of divine happiness confirms the same as what the fullness of goodness says about the plurality of divine persons.

The fullness of happiness confirms with a similar reason what the fullness of goodness demonstrates and proves about the plurality of persons. One property confirms what another property says, and, in one and the same confirmation of truth, one property acclaims what another property proclaims.

Let each person examine his own conscience, and without a doubt or without contradiction he will discover that just as nothing is better than charity, so nothing is more pleasant than charity.[198] Nature herself teaches us this, and so do many experiences. And so, just as that—than-which-nothing-is-better cannot be lacking in the fullness of true goodness, so that—than-which-nothing-is-more-pleasant cannot be lacking in the fullness of supreme happiness. It is necessary then for charity not to be lacking in supreme happiness. Moreover, in order for charity to be in the supreme good, it is impossible that there can be lacking either someone who communicates charity or someone to whom charity is communicated. Moreover, your longing to be loved greatly by one whom you love greatly is a property of love, without which it absolutely cannot be love. Therefore, love cannot be pleasant if it is not also mutual. And so, just as a pleasant love cannot be lacking in that true and supreme happiness, so a mutual love also cannot be lacking. Moreover, it is absolutely necessary that in mutual love there be one who bestows love and one who requites loves. And so, one will be the bestower of love and the other will be the requiter of love. Moreover, a true plurality is discovered where two persons are demonstrated to exist. And so, a plurality of persons cannot be lacking in the fullness of true happiness. It is certain, moreover, that the supreme happiness is identical to divinity. Therefore, the communication of a gratuitous love and the return of an owed love demonstrate without a doubt that a plurality of persons cannot be lacking in true divinity.[199]

CHAPTER FOUR. What was established about the plurality of persons in the two aforementioned witnesses is confirmed by considering the fullness of divine glory.

Certainly, if we maintain that there is just one person in true divinity, just as there is just one substance alone, then consequently this person will definitely not have someone to whom he can communicate the infinite abundance of his own fullness. But, I ask, why is that the case? Is it because he is not able to have someone to share with, although he wants it? Or is it because he does not want to have someone with whom to share, although he is able? But he who is undoubtedly omnipotent cannot be excused by the impossible. But, because it is certain that this is not from a defect of power, surely it will not be from a mere defect of benevolence? But if he absolutely were not willing to have someone with whom to share, although he really could have someone if he wanted, then bear in mind, I say, what the nature or gravity of that defect of benevolence would be in the divine person![200] Certainly, as we have said, nothing is sweeter than charity, and nothing is more pleasing than charity.[201] A rational life experiences nothing sweeter than the pleasures of charity, and it never enjoys anything more delightful than the delight of charity. A divine person will lack these pleasures in eternity, if he lacks a fellowship and remains isolated on the throne of majesty. And so, from these reasons we can consider what the nature and gravity of that defect of benevolence would be, if he were greedily preferring to retain for himself alone the abundance of his fullness, which he could, if he wanted, communicate to another with such great overflow of joys and with such a great increase of pleasures. If this were the case, then he would rightly shun the sight of angels and everyone. He would rightly be ashamed to be seen or to be recognized by them, if there were such a grave defect of benevolence in him. But far be it! Far be it that there is something in his supreme majesty, in which he cannot glory and for which he ought not to be glorified. Otherwise, where will the fullness of glory be? After all, as we previously demonstrated, no fullness can be lacking in the divinity.[202] But what is more glorious and what is truly more magnificent than to possess nothing that one refuses to communicate? It is certain then that in that unfailing good and supremely wise counsel there can be neither a greedy withholding nor a disordered profusion. Behold, you clearly understand, as you can see, that the fullness of glory requires a partaker of glory from not being absent in the highest and supreme exaltation.

CHAPTER FIVE. The aforementioned assertion about the divine plurality is confirmed by a threefold testimony.

Behold we have taught concerning the plurality of the divine persons with such clear reason that anyone who desires to oppose such evident attestation would appear to suffer from the affliction of insanity. Indeed who else, except a person suffering from insanity, would assert that that than-which-nothing-is-more-perfect and that than-which-nothing-is-better lacks the supreme goodness? Who else, I ask, except a person destitute of mind, would deny that that than-which-nothing-is-more-pleasant and that than-which-nothing-is-sweeter are in the supreme happiness? Who else, I say, except a person devoid of reason, would think that that than-which-nothing-is-more-glorious and that than-which-nothing-is-more-magnificent can possibly be lacking in the fullness of glory. There is certainly nothing better, nothing more pleasant, and absolutely nothing more magnificent than true, genuine, and supreme charity, which is absolutely not known to exist without a plurality of persons.

Therefore, a threefold witness confirms the assertion about the divine plurality. For the fullness of glory acclaims with confirmation and confirms with acclamation what supreme goodness and supreme happiness harmoniously proclaim about this matter. Behold, we have a threefold witness concerning this article of our faith: the supernal concerning supreme matters, the divine concerning the divine matters, the most high concerning profound matters, and the most open concerning the secret matters. And we know that *in the mouth of two or three witnesses every word is established*.[203] Behold *the triple cord*, *which is broken with difficulty*,[204] and, for that reason, it firmly binds by the gift of God's wisdom any madman who opposes our faith.

PERFECT EQUALITY AND UNITY
IN THE PLURALITY OF DIVINE PERSONS

CHAPTER SIX. It is absolutely necessary for the divine persons to be coeternal.

As we can conclude clearly from the previous discussions, see how the perfection of one person requires a fellowship with another person.[205] We found that there is nothing more glorious and more magnificent than the desire to have nothing that you refused to communicate. And so, a person, who was supremely good, would refuse to be without a partaker of his majesty. Moreover, it was undoubtedly necessary that what he, whose will is omnipotent, desired to exist did exist, and that he, whose will was immutable, always desired what he desired once.[206] Therefore, it was necessary for an eternal person to have a coeternal person: one could neither precede the other, nor could one succeed the other. For nothing old, as it were, can pass away in the eternal and immutable divinity, and nothing new can be added. And so, it is absolutely impossible for the divine persons not to be coeternal. For supreme goodness and complete happiness are found where the true divinity is. But, as it was said, supreme goodness cannot exist without perfect charity, nor can perfect charity exist without a plurality of persons.[207] Complete happiness certainly cannot exist without true immutability, nor can true immutability exist without eternity.[208] True charity requires a plurality of persons, and true immutability requires coeternity of persons.

CHAPTER SEVEN. It is necessary for both supreme equality and supreme similitude to exist in that plurality of persons.

One surely ought to note that just as true charity requires a plurality of persons, so supreme charity requires an equality of persons.[209] Supreme charity is not yet proven to exist where the beloved is not truly loved supremely. And love does not show discretion, when someone is supremely loved who must not be supremely loved.[210] But the flame of love in the supremely wise goodness does flare up neither differently nor more intensely than the supreme wisdom mandates. And so, it is undoubtedly necessary that he, who ought to love supremely according to the supreme abundance of charity, ought to be love supremely according to the supreme rule of discretion. But the very property of love itself proves that it is not sufficient for the one loving supremely if the one supremely loved does not requite the supreme love.[211] In a mutual love then the fullness of charity requires that each of the two persons be supremely loved by the other, and, consequently, according to the aforementioned norm of discretion, each ought to be loved supremely. Moreover, where each of the two persons ought to be loved equally by the other, it is necessary that each be equally perfect. And so, each ought to be equally powerful, equally wise, equally good, and equally blessed. Thus, the supreme fullness of love requires the supreme equality of perfection in those mutually loved. And so, just as the property of charity requires a plurality of persons in true divinity, so the integrity of the same charity requires the supreme equality of persons in true plurality. Moreover, in order that they may be equal in every respect, it is necessary that they be similar in every respect. After all similitude can be possessed without equality, but equality can never be possessed without mutual similitude.[212] How can those, who do not have any likeness in wisdom, desire to be equal in wisdom? But what I say about wisdom, I say the same about power; indeed, you will find the same in every other property, if you run through them individually.[213]

CHAPTER EIGHT. How through a wonderful reason there is a substantial unity in that plurality and a personal plurality in the true unity of substance.

We have sought and found that, in order that supreme love should exist worthily in the ‹two› aforementioned persons who are mutually love and ought to be loved mutually, there must be in each supreme perfection and the fullness of total perfection.[214] And so, the fullness of power, the fullness of wisdom, the fullness of goodness, and the fullness of divinity will be in each person. Behold much earlier in this work we made mention of something without specifying it.[215] In that discussion we found that the divinity cannot be common to a plurality of substances,[216] but in this present discussion it seems clear that it is common to a plurality of persons. But, as we have said, if every perfection is common to two persons mutually loved,[217] then it is certainly clear that if one is omnipotent, then the other will also be omnipotent; if one is immeasurable, then the other will also be immeasurable; if one is God, then the other will be God.

But, as our previous discussions have shown with sufficient evidence, there can only be one omnipotent being, only one immeasurable being, and only one God.[218] What then? Certainly each person will undoubtedly be omnipotent in such a way that the two together are only one omnipotent being; each will be immeasurable in such a way that the two together are only one immeasurable being; and without a doubt each of them will be God in such a way that the two together are only one God. *And who is capable of this?*[219] But, as we have said, if the divinity is surely common to both, then the divine substance will certainly also be common to both, since, as we have demonstrated above, the divine substance is identical to the divinity.[220] And so, it is proven that each person has one and the same substance, or, if this sounds better, both together are one and the same substance.[221] Hence, what wonder is it if both together are only one omnipotent being, one eternal being, one immeasurable being, and only one God and Lord, when both together are only one in substance? Therefore, consider how through a wonderful reason there is a substantial unity in that plurality of persons, and there is a personal plurality in a true unity of substance, in such a way that there is also *property in the persons, unity in substance, and equality in majesty.*[222]

CHAPTER NINE. In the divine nature there is a plurality of persons in the unity of substance, and in human nature there is a plurality of substances in a unity of person.

Perhaps you, who hear or read this, wonder—you wonder, I say—how there can be more than one person, when there is only one substance alone. But what wonder is it—what wonder, I say—is it that if he, who is wonderful in so many of his works, is wonderful in himself above all? You wonder how there is more than one person in the divine nature, when there is not more than one substance; and yet you do not equally wonder how there is more than one substance in human nature, even when there is not more than one person. After all man consists of a body and soul, and these two together are only one person. And so, human beings have in themselves the means to read and learn what they ought to think about God through contrasts.

If it is acceptable, let us compare in one place what reason discovers in the divine nature by reasoning and what experience discovers in human nature. There is unity and plurality in both cases: there is a unity of substance in divine nature, but a unity of persons in human nature; there is a plurality of persons in divine nature, but a plurality of substances in human nature. In divine nature indeed there is a plurality of persons in a unity of substance, but in human nature there is a plurality of substances in a unity of person. Behold how human nature and divine nature seem to gaze mutually at one another and as if from an opposite direction, and either nature responds to the other as if through contrasts.[223] Hence, created nature and uncreated nature, time and eternity, corruptible and incorruptible, mutable and immutable, tiny and immense, ephemeral and infinite—they have each other in sight, and they ought to respond mutually.

CHAPTER TEN. How humans are instructed from the plurality and unity found in themselves what they should think through contrasts, as it were, concerning the things that are proposed to them to be believed about their God.

Let us add that there is full similitude and supreme equality in the plurality of divine persons, but there are many dissimilitudes and great inequalities in the plurality of human substances. In the plurality of divine persons one is incorruptible and the other is incorruptible; one is immutable and the other is also immutable; one is boundless and the other is also boundless; the one and the other are equally powerful; the one and the other are equally wise, equally good, and equally blessed. But in the plurality of substances, of which the human person consists, one is corporeal and the other is incorporeal; one is visible and the other is invisible; one is mortal and the other is immortal; one is perishable and the other imperishable; one is destructible and the other is indestructible. Nevertheless, these plural substances have been so joined into one by virtue of a personal property that they cannot be distinguished—I do not say to be separated—in experiencing or being delighted.

You have now seen how great the dissimilitude or diversity of substances is in human nature; and you have likewise heard how great the similitude or equality of persons is in divine nature. Explain to me, I ask, how there is personal unity in such great dissimilitude and diversity of substances, and I will tell you how there is substantial unity in such great similitude and equality of persons. "I do not understand," you say, "I do not comprehend it; but experience itself still convinces me of what my understanding does not grasp."[224] Well said indeed and rightly spoken! But if experience teaches you that something in human nature is beyond understanding, then, for that reason, ought it not to have taught you that something in divine nature is beyond understanding?[225] And so, humans can learn from themselves what they should

think through contrasts, as it were, concerning the things that are proposed to them to be believed about their God. These things have been
said for the sake of those who strive to define and determine the profundity of divine secrets according to the measure of their own capacity
and not according to the tradition of the holy fathers, who have clearly
learned from and been taught by the Holy Spirit.[226]

FROM DUALITY TO TRINITY:
HOW THE FULLNESS OF DIVINE CHARITY, GOODNESS, HAPPINESS,
AND GLORY AFFIRMS THE TRINITY

CHAPTER ELEVEN. How it is demonstrated from the integrity of charity
that true Trinity is in true unity and true unity is in true Trinity.

But let us now pursue the method of our reasoning in the order in
which we began. It is already certain that there is a plurality of divine
persons, but it is not yet certain that there is a Trinity. After all, plurality
can even occur where there is no trinity; for example, duality itself is
plurality. And so, concerning the affirmation of the Trinity let us interrogate the same witnesses, whom we summoned above to bear witness
for the plurality.[227]

If it is agreeable, let us first ask supreme charity what it testifies
about this matter. Now it is necessary for supreme charity to be entirely
perfect. But, in order for it to be supremely perfect, it is necessary for
it to be so great that no greater love can exist, in the same way that it
must also be so excellent that no better love can exist.[228] For, just as
what is the greatest cannot be lacking in supreme charity, so it is certain
that what is excellent will not possibly be lacking in it. The desire for
another to be loved as oneself certainly seems excellent in true charity.
In fact in a mutual and very ardent love nothing is rarer and more
excellent than your desire for the person, whom you supremely love
and who supremely loves you, to love equally another person. And so,
the proof of perfected charity is the votive communion of the love that
was bestowed to oneself. The excellent joy for someone, who loves
supremely and desires to be loved supremely, usually lies in the fulfill-
ment of his desire, that is, the acquisition of a desired love. And so, the
fact that someone is not yet able to be satisfied in the sharing of his
excellent joy proves that he is not perfect in charity. The inability then
to permit a partaker of love is an indication of great weakness, but the
ability to permit a partaker of love is a sign of great perfection. If the
ability to permit is great, then it will be greater to undertake it with joy;

however it will be the greatest to seek it with longing. The first is very good, the second is better, and the third is the best. Therefore, let us give to the supreme what is excellent, and let us give to the best what is best.[229] And so, in order for perfection to be completed in the two mutually loved persons, whom our previous discussion treated,[230] it needs, for the same reason, a partaker of the love which was shown to them. Indeed if he does not desire what perfect goodness requires, then where will the fullness of goodness be? But if he desires what cannot be done, then where will the fullness of power be?[231]

Therefore we concluded from clear reason that there cannot be an excellent degree of charity—and, for that reason, the fullness of goodness—where a defect of will or ability excludes a partaker of love and a communion of excellent joy. Therefore, each of the two persons, who is supremely loved and ought to be loved supremely, must seek with equal desire a third person mutually loved (*condilectum*) and must possess him freely with equal concord.[232] Therefore, you see how the perfection of charity requires a Trinity of persons, without which charity absolutely cannot subsist in the integrity of its own fullness. Therefore, just as complete charity cannot be lacking, so neither can the true Trinity be lacking where all that is is entirely perfect. And so, there is not only plurality but also a true Trinity in true unity, and true unity in true Trinity.

CHAPTER TWELVE. How the supreme good and the supreme happiness shout harmoniously the proclamation of the Trinity and confirm it with a mutual attestation.

If someone contends that there are only those two mutually loved persons in the true divinity, which the above reason discovered,[233] then what reason, I ask, will he possibly give for his assertion? Can it be, I ask, that each of these persons will lack a partaker of their excellent joy? Maybe this is because neither wanted to have a partaker, or maybe because one wanted it but the other did not?[234] But if the one person did not want what the other wanted, then where will that property be which usually always belongs and must always belong to true and perfect friends?[235] Where, I ask, will that special prerogative of intimate love be, namely, the unanimity and intimate concord of minds? And certainly, if someone asserts that one desires a partaker but the other does not, then he will concede that whoever cannot prevail in his volition will be denied the supreme power. But if someone asserts that neither can be satisfied with the communion of the love which was shown to them, then how, I ask, will he be able to excuse them from the defect of love which was previously specified? But we know that nothing can be hidden from those who are supremely wise. And so, if they truly and supremely love one another, then how will any one of them be able to see the defect of the other and not grieve? After all if one of them sees the defect of the other and does not grieve, then where will the fullness of love be? If one does see it and grieves, then where will the fullness of happiness be? But it is certain that the fullness of happiness will not be able to exist where a cause for grieving is never absent.

For that reason, therefore, it is concluded and apprehended with unquestionable reason that the fullness of happiness removes every defect of charity, whose perfection, as we have said,[236] requires the Trinity of persons and also shows that a Trinity of persons cannot be lacking. Behold how the supreme goodness and supreme happiness shout harmoniously the proclamation of the Trinity and confirm it with mutual attestation.

CHAPTER THIRTEEN. The fullness of divine glory seems to shout approval for the testimony of highest goodness and highest happiness.

The inability to experience a fellowship of love is undoubtedly a great defect of charity. Who does not know this or who can conceal this fact? If then that frequently mentioned defect were present in the two mutual lovers,[237] then each would have not only what causes grief in the other but at the same time what also causes shame in himself. For just as a true and intimate friend cannot see the defect of one, whom he loves intimately, and not grieve, so surely he cannot avoid being ashamed of his own defect in the presence of his friend. But if something that rightly ought to cause shame is present in that plurality of persons, then where, I ask, will the fullness of glory be that cannot possibly be lacking in true divinity? But just as a cause for grieving cannot belong to supreme happiness, so also a matter of shame cannot belong to the fullness of supreme glory. For who does not see how utterly insane it would be to suppose even slightly that anything could belong to the supremely happy majesty that can obscure however moderately the splendor of such great glory?

Behold how the fullness of divine goodness, happiness and glory coincide with one another in one attestation of truth, and how they clearly show what ought to be understood about the fullness of divine love in the plurality of persons. Together they condemn the suspicion of any defect in the supreme charity, and they proclaim in one accord the fullness of total perfection. Charity requires a plurality of persons in order that it may be true; but it requires a Trinity of persons in order that it may be perfected.

CHAPTER FOURTEEN. The communication of love absolutely cannot exist in less than three persons.

If we acknowledge that we cannot doubt an issue after so many reasons have been set before us; if, I say, we acknowledge that any one person in the true divinity is of a benevolence so great that he desires to have none of those riches or delights that he refuses to share, of a power so great that nothing is impossible for him, and of a happiness so great that nothing is difficult for him, then, consequently, it is necessary to confess that there cannot be lacking a Trinity of divine persons. But, so that this may become clearer, let us gather our diffused discussions into one place.[238]

Certainly if there were only one person in the divinity, then he would not have someone to whom he could communicate the riches of his magnitude; but, conversely, the abundance of pleasures and sweetness, which could have grown in him on account of the acquisition of an intimate love, would be lacking in eternity. But the fullness of goodness does not allow the supremely good one to hoard greedily the riches of his magnitude, nor does the fullness of blessedness allow the supremely blessed one not to obtain the abundance of pleasures and sweetness. And, with regard to the magnificence of his honor, he takes as much delight in the bounty of his riches as he glories in the enjoyment of his abundance. You notice from these arguments how impossible it is that any one person in the divinity lacks the fellowship of a fraternity (*consortio societatis*).[239] But if he were possessing only one companion, then certainly he would not lack someone, with whom he would communicate the riches of his magnitude, but he absolutely would not have someone with whom he could share the pleasures of charity. Nothing is found to be more pleasant than the sweetness of love; there is nothing in which the mind is more delighted. He alone possesses the pleasures of such sweetness, who does [not] have a companion and lover who is loved mutually (*condilectum*) in the love that was presented to him.[240]

And so, there absolutely cannot be a communion of love in less than three persons. But, as we have said,[241] there is nothing more glorious and more magnificent than to share in common whatever you have that is useful and pleasant. But this cannot be hidden from supreme wisdom, nor can this be unsatisfying to supreme benevolence. And as the happiness of the one supremely powerful or the power of the one supremely happy cannot be lacking in his pleasure, so a third person must be united to two persons in the divinity.

CHAPTER FIFTEEN. Two persons in the divinity must seek a third person with equal desire and for a very similar reason.

One must surely note that with regard to the divine persons the perfection of one requires the union of a second, and, consequently, with regard to two persons, the perfection of each requires the union of a third person. For, with regard to two persons, just as I have already said elsewhere,[242] in order for each person to be loved worthily and supremely by the other, it is necessary that both be supremely perfect. Just as then there is one wisdom and one power in both persons, so rightly it will be necessary that there be one supreme benevolence in both. Moreover, it is a property of supreme and altogether perfect benevolence to share in common all the abundance of its fullness. But where equal benevolence exists in both persons, it is necessary for each of them to seek with the same desire and for a very similar reason a partaker of their excellent joy. After all, when two mutually loving persons embrace one another with supreme longing and are delighted in each other with supreme love, then the supreme joy of the one is in the intimate love of the second, and, conversely, the excellent joy of the second is in the love of the first. As long as the first person alone is loved by the second, then he alone seems to possess the pleasures of his excellent sweetness; similarly, as long as the second does not have a third mutually loved person (condilectum), then he lacks a communion of excellent joy. But so that the two persons can communicate such pleasures, they must have a third mutually loved person (condilectum).

And so, as we have said, when two mutually loving persons have benevolence so great that they desire every perfection to be shared in common, then, as we have said, it is necessary for them both to seek with the same desire and for the same reason a third person mutually loved (condilectum), and to possess that person freely according to the fullness of their power.[243]

CHAPTER SIXTEEN. The fullness of power and wisdom seems to be able to consist in a single person.

There is usually a significant difference between the pleasures of charity and wisdom. The pleasures of wisdom are able to be drawn and are usually drawn from one's own heart; but the intimate pleasures of charity are drawn from the heart of another. After all he, who loves intimately and longs to be loved intimately, is not delighted but anxious if he does not draw from the heart of his beloved the sweetness of love for which he thirsts. But the pleasures of wisdom delight more when they are drawn from one's own heart. Therefore, nothing is defined in a manner contrary to nature, if it is asserted that the fullness of wisdom can subsist in a single person. For it seems that, even if there were only one person in the divinity, he could still have the fullness of wisdom. However, the fullness of wisdom cannot exist without fullness of power, just as the fullness of power cannot exist without the fullness of wisdom.[244] For he, who would not know how he could obtain what he lacked in omnipotence, would undoubtedly not have the fullness of wisdom; conversely, however, he, who could unwillingly sustain a defect of wisdom, would undoubtedly lack the fullness of power. And so, the fullness of one cannot be possessed without the fullness of the other. It follows then that we understand the same about power as we have asserted about wisdom. After all, if omnipotence cannot be lacking where there is the fullness of wisdom, then certainly it seems that the fullness of both power and wisdom can be possessed by a single person.

CHAPTER SEVENTEEN. The completion of happiness does not seem to be able to subsist without two persons.

Now the completion of true and supreme happiness in no way seems to be able to subsist without two persons. This is now known more clearly than day from our previous discussion.[245] For if there were only one person in true divinity, he would certainly not have someone on whom he could bestow supreme love, nor someone who could requite supreme love to him. Therefore, from what source would those supremely sweet pleasures, which, as we have said,[246] are usually drawn not from his own heart but from the heart of another, abound in him? Indeed, as we have already said,[247] there is nothing sweeter than these pleasures, nothing more delightful, nothing more wholesome, nothing more excellent and more pleasant than this sweetness. Therefore, how had the divine happiness obtained the abundance of total fullness without always having supreme sweetness and pleasantness? And so, as we have said, happiness requires two persons, so that it can subsist in the integrity of all fullness.[248]

CHAPTER EIGHTEEN. The perfection of true and supreme goodness does not seem capable of subsisting without the completion of the Trinity.

Let no one be disturbed and let no one be angered, if we should speak in a human way in order to understand more clearly the truth about the divine and supernatural. The more frequently we find this mode of speaking in the Holy Scriptures, the more confidently we utilize it in service of our poverty.[249]

The supreme degree of goodness seems to occur when a person bestows supreme love to someone and gains nothing from it toward the fullness of his own happiness. But, as it is most evident from our previous discussion,[250] this degree of supreme perfection cannot be found between only two mutually loved persons. For, in that situation, each of the two who are loved bestows love, from which each undoubtedly draws the mellifluous delights of love; and they absolutely would not have that love, from which each could draw, if each was alone and lived in solitude. And so, a great accumulation of joy and pleasantness grows in each on account of a fellowship of love having been bestowed and received.[251] For that reason then it is clearly concluded that the supreme degree of benignity would not have a place in divinity, if a third person were lacking in the plurality of persons; and in only two persons there certainly would not be anyone with whom either of the two persons could communicate the excellent pleasures of his joy. For this reason, it is given to be understood that the consummation of true and supreme goodness cannot subsist without completion of the Trinity.

CHAPTER NINETEEN. How a vestige of the Trinity can be apprehended simply by observing the property of the mutual love for a third person (*condilectionis*).

What has been demonstrated with multiple attestation of reason about the assertion of Trinity can be confirmed by a sufficiently brief and very lucid consideration.[252] And so, let us examine with careful consideration the virtue and property of the mutual love for a third person (*condilectionis*), and we will find more quickly what we are seeking.

When one person bestows love to a second, and he alone only loves the other, then this is indeed love but not the mutual love for a third person (*condilectio*). When two people mutually love one another and bestow to one another the affection of supreme love, and when the affection of the first person extends to the second, and the affection of the second extends to the first, extending, as it were, in different directions, then there is indeed love in both, but there is not the mutual love for a third person (*condilectio*). But, this kind of love is described correctly when a third person is loved harmoniously and communally by two people, and when the affection of two is melted together into a single affection for the third by the flames of love.²⁵³ From this description then it is clear that the mutual love for a third person (*condilectio*) would not have a place in divinity itself, if there were only two people, and they were lacking a third. Indeed we are not discussing here any kind of mutual love whatsoever but the supreme mutual love. A creature never merits such a love from the Creator, nor is it ever found worthy of it.

Who, I ask, can correctly convey how great the virtue of supreme and altogether perfect benevolence is? Who, I ask, is qualified to accurately assess what or how great the dignity of intimate and supreme unity is? If then such great dignity is inherent in each of those two virtues when each virtue is considered in itself, then what kind of virtue, I ask, what kind of dignity will be in them when each is produced from the other, when each is magnified by the other, when each is perfected by the other? Moreover, what else is intimate and supreme mutual love for a third (*condilectio*) except the mutual concurrence of intimate benevolence and supreme concord?²⁵⁴ And so, just as the virtue of so great a dignity and unsurpassable excellence cannot be lacking in supreme and universally perfect good, so it cannot subsist without a Trinity of persons.

CHAPTER TWENTY. How it is argued from the mutual fellowship (*consodalitate*) of a third person in the Trinity that charity is always concordant and love consocial (*consocialis amor*), never individual.

Pay attention now to how the bond of a third person unites concordant affection everywhere and binds together a consocial love through all and in all. If you pay attention to any one of the three persons, you will see that the other two concordantly love the third. If you look at the second person, you will likewise find there that the rest are united in love of him with equal desire. If you bring the third person into consideration, then you will undoubtedly see the affection of the other two flowing together in him with equal concord. If the creation is considered,[255] then the cord of love is tripled there, so that certitude is strengthened by greater solidarity where a suspicion about a defect of love could arise more easily.[256] Behold how it is argued from the mutual fellowship (*consodalitate*) of a third person in the Trinity that charity is always concordant and love consocial (*consocialis amor*), never individual.[257] Behold in the assertion of the Trinity the attestation of truth is everywhere so great and so certain that the person who finds such great assurances inadequate seems to be mad.

Perfect equality in the Trinity of Persons

CHAPTER TWENTY-ONE. There is supreme equality in the Trinity, where every person must be equally perfect.

What was previously demonstrated about the two persons can also be concluded with the same reason about the three persons, namely, each one ought to be loved supremely and is supremely loved by each other, because they are supremely perfect.[258] The fullness of supreme happiness requires fullness of supreme pleasantness. The fullness of supreme pleasantness requires the fullness of supreme charity. The fullness of supreme charity requires the fullness of supreme perfection. And so, where every person must be equally perfect, it is necessary that every person coincide in supreme equality. Hence, equal wisdom, equal power, indistinguishable glory, uniform goodness, eternal happiness will be in all three persons, so that what the daily profession of Christian instruction teaches is truly correct: the three persons together are *one divinity, equal glory, and coeternal majesty*.[259] No one person in the divinity is greater than the other, no one is lesser than the other, no one comes before another, and no one comes after. And so, it is certain that every person in the Trinity is at once coequal and coeternal. After all if they were not coeternal, then, for that reason, they would not be coequal.

CHAPTER TWENTY-TWO. There is supreme simplicity in each person, there is true and supreme unity in all together, and in both cases there is wonderful identity.

And so, in the supreme and altogether perfect equality of persons, the supreme and supremely simple being is common to all. Therefore, for every person being is the same as living, living is the same as understanding, and understanding is the same as being able.[260] And so, wisdom is not different from power, and power is not different from essence, and, according to this method, a similar idea is found in similar statements.[261] Thus you see that every thing in each person is identical. But if supreme perfection is in the equality, and supreme equality is in the perfection, then the supreme fullness of wisdom and the supreme fullness of power will be in each person and in all the persons at the same time. But what is supreme and full power except omnipotence?[262] However, we know that it is called omnipotence because it can do all things. But if it is true that omnipotence truly means all-powerful, then it will easily be able to render every other power powerless.[263] For that reason, then, it is obvious that there can only be one omnipotence. But it was previously demonstrated that omnipotence is identical to the divine essence.[264] If then to have omnipotence, rather to be omnipotent, is common to all the persons together, then to be one and the same essence will also be common to all the persons, since for them being is identical to possessing. After all the divine essence, just like omnipotence, can only be one. And so, all that each person is is not only identical, but also each one is identical to what each of the others is. And so, there is supreme simplicity in each person; there is true and supreme unity in all together; and, if you paid attention well, there is wonderful identity in both cases.

CHAPTER TWENTY-THREE. How the aforementioned equality ought to be understood in these persons where there is such great unity and such excellent identity.

We can understand our discussion of the equality of persons both correctly and incorrectly. It seems that there is more identity than equality in such great simplicity and unity of persons. We can and usually say that three golden statues are equal, if they are of the same purity, weight, and similitude in every respect. But that kind of equality is very foreign to the equality which is in the Trinity of divine persons.[265] For in the equality of statues, the mass of gold in one statue is one thing, and the mass of gold in another statue is another thing; and, based on that distinction, the statues are different from each other. However, we should not think about that true and supreme Trinity, as if there are distinct things in it, but one thing is equal to the other thing. For, just as we have already demonstrated, whatever is in any one person exactly the same is entirely in any other person. We do not say unworthily that three rational spirits are equal, if they are of the same power, the same wisdom, the same purity and goodness. But just as there are three persons in this trinity of spirits, so there are obviously three substances in it. The supreme Trinity, however, exists in a unity of substance. And so, distinct things, although equal, are found in the former trinity, but such equality is far from the divine Trinity. But we say that there are equal persons in the supreme Trinity, because that supreme and supremely simple being, which belongs to one person in fullness and perfection, also belongs to each of the other persons in the same fullness and perfection.[266]

CHAPTER TWENTY-FOUR. How every aspect (*omniformitas*) of supreme coequality is incomprehensible.

Certainly one and the same substance is not something greater or lesser, better or worse than itself. And so, any person in the Trinity will not be something greater or better than any other person, since each person is truly one and the same substance. Moreover, the very same substance is in each person and in all at once; hence, any two persons will not be something greater or better than any one person, nor will all three persons taken as a whole be something greater or better than any two persons or any one person by himself.[267] However, in that trinity of ‹human› persons where there are several substances, then one person alone is something less than two persons, and all three persons taken as a whole are something greater than any two persons. Therefore observe now how incomprehensible the multifaceted and manifold coequality of magnitude is in the supreme Trinity, where unity does not negate plurality, nor does plurality remove unity![268]

CHAPTER TWENTY-FIVE. A person in the Trinity is never dissimilar to himself, nor is he unequal to any other person in any way.

But, so that you may have greater admiration for equality of divine persons, observe the following situation in every ‹human› person: In one and the same person there is neither singularity without plurality, nor unity without inequality. I pass over in silence that he can grow or be reduced, and that he can become unequal in himself. I pass over in silence that his power is one thing, his wisdom is another, and his justice is yet another, and that he can be greater in relation to one thing and lesser in relation to another, and better in relation to one thing and worse in relation to another. His power alone is certainly dissimilar to itself, and his wisdom alone is unequal to itself. The same result occurs in other properties. Consider his power, and you will discover that one thing is easy for him, another is difficult, and a third thing is impossible; and it is thus discovered that his power is also dissimilar and unequal to itself. In the same way, one thing is comprehensible for his wisdom, but another thing is incomprehensible. How will human or angelic understanding ever be able to comprehend the very immensity of divinity, not to mention other attributes? And so, while one and the same nature is effective in one thing and ineffective in other things, it is discovered to be lesser in part and greater in part; and both dissimilar and unequal to itself. From this therefore it can be concluded that true equality cannot exist where there is no true simplicity.[269] But nowhere in the Trinity is someone dissimilar to himself, nor is he unequal to any other person in any way. There surely can be no earlier and later where there is true eternity, just as there can be no greater or lesser where there is immutable immeasurability.

Hence, the vicissitude or alteration of inequality can in no way belong to those who have the same principle for eternity and infinity, because there is *no change or shadow of change* in them.[270] *There is nothing earlier, nothing later, and nothing greater or lesser, but all three persons are coeternal and coequal to themselves.*[271] Behold we have now proven with clear and multiple reason how what we are commanded to believe is true, namely, that we *venerate one God in Trinity and Trinity in unity.*[272]

BOOK FOUR

THE PERSONS OF THE TRINITY

THE CHALLENGES TO THIS INVESTIGATION AND LIMITING THE TERMS FOR DISCUSSION

CHAPTER ONE. How it seems incomprehensible to human understanding that there is a plurality of persons in a unity of substance.

At the beginning of this work,[273] we have proven what we believe about the unity of the divine substance with such obvious explanation and with such clear reasons that those, who paid careful attention, must have no more doubts that should cause them to hesitate even a little. Similarly, in a separate place,[274] what our faith teaches about the plurality of persons was proven with such certain reason and confirmed with so many reasons that one would appear to be destitute of mind, who cannot be satisfied by such great attestation of truth. Indeed, nothing seems more credible and nothing seems more correct than when each of these considerations and assertions is considered separately and independently. However, if we ever discuss the unity together with the plurality and consider how they can stand together harmoniously, then whatever was proven by the various rational arguments runs straight into ambiguity, unless the steadfastness of faith stands in the way. Indeed, human understanding does not easily comprehend that there can be more than one person where there is not more than one substance. This is why countless errors of unbelievers and multiple heresies of the schismatics arise. That is why some tear apart the unity of the divine substance, and others confound the plurality of persons.[275] This is why the Arians and Sabellians are mutually divided through opposite heresies. This is also why some today understand the word "person" under so many meanings; they have shrouded into greater ambiguity the understanding of truth so profound, which they should have made clear. For if anyone should desire to understand the word "person" under the common and normal meaning, then no one would think that several persons, understood with that meaning, can subsist in a unity of substance.[276]

CHAPTER TWO. How there are many things that human understanding does not comprehend, yet personal experience does not allow them to be hidden from human understanding.

But, I ask, can it be that this designated unity of Trinity and Trinity of unity cannot exist, because it cannot be comprehended? Who thinks this except a person who lost his mind? Who presumes to say this? How many things are there that human understanding does not comprehend, and yet multiple experiences do not allow their veracity to be hidden from the human mind?[277] Explain to me, I ask, if you can, this fact that you absolutely cannot doubt: why is it that the physical eye does not perceive by seeing the place where it is, and it does perceive by seeing the place where it absolutely is not. In the sky, where the eye certainly is not, it sees the arranged stars; yet, after it is covered with the eyelid, it does not see the eyelid under which it is covered. The other senses of the body perceive and discern only what they touch; only the sense of the eyes are inactive to what they touch and active to what is distant and very far away. Can it be that you contest this truth, because you do not understand how it happens? Explain to me, if you can, this fact that you dare not deny: how the body and soul in you, natures so different indeed, are one and the same person; and then you may ask me how the Trinity of persons is one and the same substance in a supremely simple and common nature. But if 'how something is' is incomprehensible, and yet the human mind knows it through experience, then how much more incomprehensible is that which is beyond any human experience!

CHAPTER THREE. How there are many incomprehensible things for which experience is insufficient, yet clear reason does not allow them to be hidden.

If you say that you can in no way doubt those things you have experienced, even if they seem to transcend the limit of human capacity, then I say in addition that you do not doubt that some things, which are incomprehensible, do exist, yet you do not demonstrate them through experience. In fact, clear reason does not allow many things to be hidden, and yet the human mind is insufficient in comprehending them.[278] Surely you do not comprehend the eternity of God, and yet you do not distrust his eternity? Surely you do not doubt the immeasurability of God, although you are not able to comprehend it? Surely the omnipotence of God is not comprehended by everyone who preaches and believes it? If you interrogate every theologian,[279] you will receive this response from all of them: the power of God is identical to his wisdom, and his goodness is nothing other than his wisdom or power.[280] If you ask them what these three properties are, then you will discover that they are nothing other than the divine substance. Clear reason proves all these truths and does not allow them to be hidden. Every theologian truly consents to this, and they all together defend this. Which of these statements, I ask, is more comprehensible and better understood: one substance is the three aforementioned properties, or three persons are one substance? Both statements are incomprehensible, yet neither is unbelievable.

Nevertheless it seems to me that it is because of this incomprehensibility that, according to some, the meaning of "person" changes based on its many usages. There are those who say that the word "person" sometimes means substance, sometimes subsistence, and sometimes the properties of persons.[281] Moreover, according to their preference, the word "person" means substance whenever it is used in the singular, but never in the plural, lest those, who confess three persons, actually seem to confess three substances.[282] Moreover, in order to prove that persons are the properties of persons, they cite the authority of Jerome, who says in this passage: "In order to avoid the Sabellian heresy, we distinguish three distinct persons by property. For we confess not only the names, but also the properties of the names, that is, persons, or, as the Greeks express it, *hypostases*, that is, subsistences."[283] But it seems to me that in this passage Jerome did not say that persons are "the property of persons" but "the properties of their names," that is, what the names of persons properly mean.

CHAPTER FOUR. For a clear understanding of doctrine, it is necessary to determine the meaning of person and to specify the unity of the Trinity according to that definition.

Let us pass over the word *hypostasis*, in which there is a suspicion of poison according to Jerome;[284] let us, who are not Greek,[285] pass over that Greek word. But we should not pass over in silence the word "subsistence."[286] Some propose that persons are subsistences, and they say, more than they demonstrate, that there are three subsistences and one substance in the one divinity; indeed, they pass through this statement without explanation, as if it is well-known to all readers that there could be three subsistences, even where it is well-known that there is only one substance. I do not denounce their opinion; I do not criticize it; I do not assert that it is false. But I am compelled to confess what is true: this doctrine of theirs does not satisfy my simplicity. If you want to satisfy people like me, then you must first determine carefully the meaning of both substance and subsistence, and to specify, based on your definition, how there can be more than one subsistence where there is only one substance. Otherwise, I ask, what does it profit me to be shown the unknown through the more unknown? The word "person" is constantly on the lips of everyone, even the illiterate; but the word "subsistence" is not understood by anyone, not even the literate. Therefore, I ask, how will any of the more simpleminded people be able to conclude from the property of a word, which they do not understand, that there can be three subsistences and, therefore, three persons in a unity of substance? How, I ask, will that doctrine, which resolves disputed matter with a disputed matter, be able to satisfy?

Therefore, because my intention in this work is to serve diligently more simpleminded people[287] and not, so to speak, teach Minerva,[288] I will strive, to the extent that the Lord will have granted, to determine not the meaning of subsistence but the meaning of person and, according to the specification of the proposed definition, to demonstrate how a plurality of persons can be consistent with the unity of substance.

CHAPTER FIVE. By what necessity did those before us seek to call the three in the Trinity "persons," and it remains to be sought by what truth the three are called "persons."

I must say—I must certainly say—what I think and what I firmly and indubitably believe: the word "person" was by no means ascribed to the very sublime and supereminent mystery of the Trinity without the divine inspiration and magisterium of the Holy Spirit.[289] Let us consider how the same Spirit prophesied through the lips of the prophets, formulated through the lips of the evangelists, and expounded through the lips of the doctors so many mysteries of our faith, redemption, sanctification, and glorification. He who considers this will in no way be able to believe that the Holy Spirit has subjected to human estimation rather than ordained through his inspiration the supreme article of our faith, the very sacred and secret mystery of the Trinity, and the very word that he wanted every heart to believe and every tongue to confess.

Now let us acknowledge that there were those who first transferred the word "person" to the divine reality,[290] and let us also acknowledge that they did this out of necessity, so that they might have some kind of response to those who asked: "The three in the Trinity are three what?" because they could not reply: "Three Gods."[291] They did this out of necessity, but the Holy Spirit, who directed their hearts, knows the reason and truth for which he wanted this to be done. But if we really believe this, then let us investigate with all diligence not the meaning of the word "person" that was first established by humans, nor the necessity out of which it was later transferred to the divine reality, but the truth in which it was both inspired by the Spirit of truth through those who translated it ‹to the divine reality› and recited frequently and universally by the Latin Church. Moreover, no opinion is rendered more certain than what is formed from a common conception of the mind.[292] Therefore, I will strive to form a method for our assertions based on the simple and common concept of the mind, which everyone conceives with regard to the word "person."

AN ANALYSIS OF THE WORD "PERSON"

CHAPTER SIX. The meaning of person and substance are very different.

Let us first repeat what others have said: the word "person" is spoken in reference to substance, and it seems to indicate a substance.[293] Yet, the meaning of the two words is very different. But let us explain this same point more clearly in order for our argument to become more apparent.

Who denies and doubts that an animal indicates a substance? Yet the meaning of these two words is very different. Indeed, the word "animal" indicates an animate, sensible substance. And so, animal does indicate a substance, but it also consignifies another meaning. Indeed, substance is indicated by the word "animal," but the word "animal" adds a specific difference to the idea of substance. Likewise, the word "human" also seems to indicate an animal, and, for that reason, a substance. Indeed, what else is a human except a mortal, rational animal? Therefore, the word "human" consignifies a meaning in addition to what it principally indicates. And so, animal indicates a substance, and not just any substance, but a sensible substance; however, a human is not any kind of sensible substance, but a rational substance. Moreover, the word "person" is never used unless it refers to a rational substance. And whenever we use the word "person", we always comprehend a single substance alone and some individual.

And so, a property common to every animal is implied in the word "animal" as it relates to the conception of substance; a property common to every human is implied in the word "human;" similarly, in the word "person" a certain property is implied that is applicable to only one ‹individual›, yet not determinately as in a proper name. Therefore, a general property is sometimes implied, and at other times a specific property is implied; however, an individual, singular, and incommunicable property is implied in the word "person." From these arguments, I think you will easily be able to notice the many differences between the meaning of person and substance.

CHAPTER SEVEN. Something rather than someone is indicated by the word "substance;" someone rather than something is indicated by the word "person."

If you deliberated well and paid careful attention, then ‹you would notice that› a 'what' rather than a 'who' is indicated by the word "substance," but, conversely, a 'who' rather than a 'what' is designated by the word "person."²⁹⁴ When something is so far away from us that we cannot discern it, we ask: "What is that?" And we usually receive this in response: "That is an animal, man, or horse," and so on. But when it comes close enough for us to see that it is man, then we no longer ask: "What is that?" but "Who is it?" And we receive this response: "Matthew, Bartholomew, a father or his son." You see that the response to a 'what' question is a general or specific term, a definition, or other such responses, but the usual response to a "who" question is a proper name or something equivalent. And so, a common property is sought through a 'what' question, and a singular property is sought through a 'who' question.

We must note, moreover, that if one person asks another in the presence of an angel's appearance: "Who is this," and the he receives this in response: "An angel of the Lord," then certainly this response does not correspond to the linguistic norms, but to the intention of the inquirer, as though he said to the inquirer in clearer terms: "This is not a human, as you think, but an angel of the Lord." For, if he were aware that it was an angel, then he would not ask such a question, nor would he receive such a response unless foolishly. And so, as we have said, a common property is sought through a 'what' question, and a singular property is sought through a 'who' question. We ask a 'what' question in order to be informed about the nature of substance, and we ask a 'who' question in order to be informed about the identity of a person.

And we must note that with regard to the question "who is that person?" or "who is it?" we usually give the same response: a proper name or something equivalent. I think that this is enough for someone to understand that something rather than someone is implied in the word "substance;" but, conversely, someone rather than something is indicated by the word "person." Moreover, only one someone alone, who is differentiated from everyone else by a singular property, is understood in the word "person."

CHAPTER EIGHT. It is not necessary to believe that there are several substances wherever there are plural persons.

When we say three persons, what else do we mean other than three 'someones'? We use the word "person" both in the singular and plural with exactly the same meaning, provided that we do not mean that a single person is plural and the plural is only one person. When we say person, a single someone, who is a rational substance, is certainly understood. When we say three persons, three someones are undoubtedly understood, each of whom is still a substance of rational nature. But regardless of whether several of them or all of them are one and the same substance, it makes no difference to the property and truth of person.

But humans make judgments based more on what experience proves than what a rational argument asserts.[295] We certainly see human persons, but we cannot see divine persons. In human nature there are as many substances as persons, and daily experience compels humans to make a similar conclusion about the divine persons. Indeed, a carnal mind is content with what it learned through experience to such an extent that it can hardly believe something that does not approximate those things, which it knew by experience, by some similitude. But at least he, who is asleep in the faith, is awake to a clear reason. We have now demonstrated with a clear reason that it is not necessary to believe that there are plural substances wherever there are plural persons.

CHAPTER NINE. We declare without contradiction that our God is both one in substance and three in persons.

Certainly, wherever there are three persons, it is absolutely necessary for there to be one someone, a second someone, and someone else who is a third after the other two; for each of them to exist separately;

and for each one to be distinguished from the other two by an individual distinction and distinct property. In the same way, wherever there are three substances, it is absolutely necessary for there to be one something, a second something, and something else that is third after the other two. For if they were not in any way different from each other, then they certainly would not be able to be plural. In fact, plurality cannot exist where there is no difference.

Now, we have previously discovered that in the supreme Trinity a supreme and supremely simple being has all things in common, and that any one person is not something different from any other person;[296] and, for that reason, we do not say that there are three substances in the Trinity. For, a diversity of substances produces something and something else to exist in a rational nature, and otherness of persons causes someone and someone else to exist.[297] But we do find that otherness ‹of persons› in the divine and supremely wise nature, yet we do not find the aforementioned diversity ‹of substances›.[298] For that reason, we believe that there are plural persons in the divine nature, and we deny that there are plural substances. Behold, in our opinion, we have now sufficiently demonstrated with a lucid and succinct reason that we are not contradicting ourselves when we say that our God is both one in substance and three in persons.

CHAPTER TEN. A plurality of substances does not dissolve the unity of a person in human nature, nor does a plurality of persons divide the unity of substance in divine nature.

We must carefully note and compare the following parallel: just as 'being something and something else in substance' certainly does not destroy the unity of a person, so certainly neither does 'being someone and someone else in person' divide the unity of substance. For, in human nature a body is one substance and the soul is another substance, although they are still only one person. But in the divine nature one someone is one person and a second someone is another person, although they are still only one and the same substance. And we certainly know and have already demonstrated above that there is supreme similitude and supreme equality in the plurality of divine persons; however, there are many dissimilitudes and great inequalities in the plurality of the substances of human nature.[299] Therefore, what wonder is it if true unity of substances remains in such great equality of persons, since a unity and identity of person is found in such diversity of contrary qualities? After all, in human nature one and the same person consists of one corporeal substance and one incorporeal substance, of one visible substance and one invisible substance, and of one mortal substance and one immortal substance;[300] nevertheless a unity of person still consists of so many diverse substances. And so, the plurality of substances does not produce a plurality of persons in human nature, and neither does a plurality of persons produce a plurality of substances in the divine nature. Moreover, let us also add the following logical consequence: a plurality of substances does not divide the unity of a human person in human nature, neither does a plurality of divine persons dissolve the unity of substance in the divine nature.

An Analysis of the Word "Existence"

CHAPTER ELEVEN. A twofold consideration is needed in order to distinguish persons: we should know what sort of thing it is and from what source it has being.

Behold we have discovered that it is not impossible for plural persons to exist in a unity of substance; however, it follows that we investigate how there can be otherness of persons without otherness of substances.[301] I think that a twofold consideration is needed in order to distinguish persons: we should know both what sort of thing it is and from what source it has being. The first consideration is engaged in distinguishing the nature of being, and the second in investigating its origin.[302] It pertains to the first consideration to seek carefully what it is in itself, with what it is common, what is general, what is specific, and finally what is the particular characteristic of the specified nature. It pertains to the second consideration to investigate carefully the source from which the very thing that it is has being: either from itself or from another source; and if it possesses being from a source other than itself, then one must investigate whether it possesses being from this or that mode of existing, or any other mode of existing. And so, the first consideration seeks the definition of the thing itself or some description and designation of its property. The second consideration seeks the order of nature, the origin of being itself, and any other distinctions of this sort. And so, the first consideration is engaged in the mode of being (*modum essendi*), but the second consideration is engaged in the mode of obtaining being (*modum obtinendi*). The first is engaged with the notion of essence; the second is engaged with, so to speak, the notion of obtaining.

Putting aside other terms, I know that this word "obtaining" is not proper for the divine reality.[303] But let this word scandalize no one if I explain what I think about God in the words in which I am able.[304] Moreover, I gladly accept and consider it a great gift if some truth, which I expressed in unsuitable and improper words, is explained by someone else with more appropriate and exact terminology.[305] I use the word "obtaining" in this sense: the mode in which someone obtains what one is substantially or what one possesses naturally. In fact, the mode of obtaining is very different in different people—whether in receiving, or in not receiving; whether in the mode of giving or in the mode of receiving.

CHAPTER TWELVE. We can imply both considerations from the word "existence:" what pertains to the notion of essence or what pertains to the notion of obtaining.

We can imply both considerations from the word "existence," namely, what pertains to the notion of essence and what pertains to the notion of obtaining—in the first, I say, the 'what sort of thing it is' of any being is sought, and in the second the 'from what source it has being' is sought. The word "existence" is derived from the verb "to exist" (*exsistere*). What pertains to the first consideration can be noted in the verb "to be" (*sistere*); similarly, what pertains to the second consideration can be noted through the added preposition "from" (*ex*). By asserting that something is (*sistere*), we first remove those existences that have a being in something (*alicui inesse*) rather than a being in themselves (*in se esse*), in other words they do not have a being (*sistere*) but a 'being in' (*insistere*), that is, they adhere in a subject. But what is said "to be" (*sistere*) seems to be related both to what is able 'to be under' (*subsistere*) in some way, and what is not able 'to be under' in any way, that is, both to what is necessarily a subject and to what is not necessarily a subject at all. The first belongs to created nature, the second to uncreated nature. For what is uncreated exists in itself in such a way that nothing is in it as in a subject. And so, what is said "to be" is related both to created and uncreated essence. But what is said "to exist" (*exsistere*) is implied not only in what has being, but also in what has being from another source, that is, possessing being from something. This is the meaning in the compounded verb joined with the preposition "from" (*ex*). For what does 'to exist' (*ex-sistere*) mean except 'to be' (*sistere*) 'from' (*ex*) something, that is, 'to be' (*esse*) from something substantially? Those considerations that pertain both to the nature of being and to the origin of a being are understood in the single verb "to exist" or under the one noun "existence."

CHAPTER THIRTEEN. The general difference of existences is distinguished in three ways.

As one can conclude from the previous arguments, existence in general can be differentiated in three ways. Existence can be differentiated either according to the nature alone of being or according to the origin alone of a being, or according to a concurrence of both. ‹First,› existence is differentiated according to nature alone when one and the same origin belongs to several persons in every respect; yet, a singular and individual substance belongs to each. After all, plural substances absolutely cannot exist without a different nature; however, such a difference of existence is based on nature alone with any difference of origin. ‹Second,› the difference of existence according to origin alone occurs when several persons are one and the same being without differentiation; yet, they appear to have a mutual difference according to origin. They are different according to origin, if one person possesses an origin and another lacks an origin, or if, among those who have an origin, the origin of one differs from the origin of another. Therefore, such existence is differentiated according to origin alone but not according to some difference in nature. ‹Third,› existence is differentiated according to both the nature of being and its origin, when individual persons have a singular and individual substance and a different origin. See what we have now discussed: a general difference of existences is distinguished in three ways according to either the quality alone of what exists, or according to the origin alone of it, or according to an alteration of each.

CHAPTER FOURTEEN. Based on what is the existence of persons differentiated in human nature, and based on what is it differentiated in angelic nature.

Certainly in human nature, which we know through experience, we see that the existence of persons is differentiated according to both the nature of persons and their origin. Every human person certainly has a singular and individual nature, through which each person differs without any doubt from any other person. In the same way, every single person also has a particular origin that is different from everyone else and distinguished by an individual property. After all, different persons have different beginnings, because different persons have different fathers. And where several people have the same father, there is still a different separating of the paternal substance from which different people are propagated. And so, as we have said, we see that the property of existences in human persons is differentiated according to both the nature of individual persons and their origin.

However, there is no propagation in angelic nature; there is only simple creation. Therefore, all individual angels have at once only one beginning without difference. Indeed they all have only one beginning, the Creator, and each and every angel exists at once according to creation alone. Moreover, in angelic nature there are as many substances as persons, and for that reason, it is necessary that they differ in nature. After all, if there were no difference in nature, then without a doubt there would not be plural substances. A difference of existences in angelic nature is differentiated according to nature alone, but, as we already discussed, the difference of existences in human nature is differentiated according to both nature and origin.

CHAPTER FIFTEEN. It is necessary to seek the difference of the divine existences in origin alone.

As we have proven, there is absolutely no dissimilitude and inequality among the divine persons.[306] Whatever one person is, so is the second person, and so is the third as well. They cannot be differentiated according to nature when they are all entirely similar and equal to one another. Indeed, as a clear reason already proved,[307] in no way can they, who have one and the same supremely simple being in every respect, be different from one another through some difference of nature. And so, since they can by no means differ from one another according to some property of nature, it remains that we believe that they do have some difference according to the mode of origin. After all, there absolutely cannot be any plurality where there is no difference. And so, a plurality of persons does prove that a distinctive property and difference of properties cannot be lacking in the Trinity. But because the identity of substance completely excludes every difference of nature, it will be necessary to seek the differentiating properties of persons in the origin alone. And so, in order to glance briefly over our very diffuse discussion, it is clear that a plurality of existences in the divine nature is differentiated according to origin alone, in the angelic nature according to nature alone, but in human nature according to both nature and origin.

See how we now have discovered what we intended to seek above: how there can be otherness of persons without any otherness of substances.[308] We discovered that although the plural persons in the divinity have one and the same being without any differentiation at all, which pertains to the identity of substance, they nevertheless can have mutual difference according to the mode of origin,[309] if one person exists from himself, if the second person draws his origin from another, and if those who have an origin ‹from another› are different in the mode of obtaining. Without a doubt, moreover, the property of the persons is made different for exactly the same reason that the property of existences is different.[310] After all, it is necessary to seek in the divine nature the difference of both persons and existences in origin alone.

CHAPTER SIXTEEN. In the divine nature there is an existence that is common to several persons, and there is an existence that is absolutely incommunicable.

As it is clear from the previous discussions, the word "existence" indicates both 'the possession of a substantial being' and 'from some property'.[311] It is the property of animals to have a substantial being from propagation alone. It is the property of humans to have a substantial being from propagation and procreation at the same time—the flesh is propagated, the soul is procreated. It is the property of angels to have a substantial being from creation alone. And it is the property of the divine nature to have a supersubstantial being without creation and beginning.

One existence is common to several persons, but another existence is absolutely incommunicable. For, passing over those beings who are not referred to as persons, possessing a rational being belongs at once to the divine, angelic, and human nature, but it is the property of both angelic and human nature to have a being not from themselves but from another source; however, it is the property of the divine nature alone to have a being not from another source but from itself. But the existence, which can only be applicable to any one person, is incommunicable. But passing over the other natures, there is without a doubt an existence in the divine nature that is common to several persons, and there is an existence that is absolutely incommunicable.

We have demonstrated above that existence denotes substance, yet not directly, but with the indication of some property that pertains to the consideration of original cause.[312] It pertains to the consideration of the original cause not only to seek and find the origin of being where there is one, but also to seek and find the non-origin of being where there is not one. And so, the possession of a substantial being belongs to the divine existence—or rather the possession of a supersubstantial being without creation and without beginning—because it is the property of every substance, whose name truly derives from its reality,[313] to be a composite being and to be subject to accidents. However, only the divine substance that transcends the nature of substance has a simple being both without composition and subject to no inherent accidents.[314] And for that reason the divine substance is rightly said to have a supersubstantial being rather than a substantial being.

One must know that existence does denote a substantial being, but one that is either from a common property or from an incommunicable property. Moreover, we call existence 'common' when possessing being from a common property is understood, and we call existence 'incommunicable' when possessing being from an incommunicable property is understood. Just as it is the property of the divine substance not to exist from some other substance, but only from itself, so it is truly the property of a person not possessing origin not to exist from any other person. In the first instance a common property is understood, but in the second instance an incommunicable property is understood. It is common to every divine person to be that substance which does not exist from any other substance but from itself. And so, the divine substance is identical to a common existence when it is said or understood to exist from itself. We know what a common existence is, now let us see what an incommunicable existence is.

CHAPTER SEVENTEEN. For what reason incommunicable existences can exist in the divinity. And there are as many incommunicable existences as persons.

What is not common nor can be common is truly incommunicable. And so, we must consider whether or how there can be an incommunicable existence in the divinity.

But in the Trinity it is undoubtedly necessary that there be as many personal properties as persons. A personal property, moreover, is certainly incommunicable. A personal property is that from which each one can be the one that he is. We call a property "personal," because through it each one is different from everyone else. Indeed, we only use the word "person" for a single someone distinct from everyone else by an individual property.[315] If then you argue that a personal property is communicable, then this is the same as saying one person can be two. But if one person is said to be two persons, and if two persons are said to be one person, then it is easily proven that neither of them is a person, because neither of them is distinguished from the other by an individual property. This is why, therefore, we clearly conclude, as we have already discussed above, that a personal property is absolutely incommunicable.[316]

In the Trinity of persons it is undoubtedly necessary that there be personal properties, that is, incommunicable properties. But, as we have proven, the difference of persons and existences is the same. If then the persons are different through incommunicable properties, then certainly existences are also different through incommunicable properties. Moreover, it is necessary for the existence, which has an incommunicable difference, to be incommunicable. And so, there are as many persons in the divinity as there are incommunicable existences.

CHAPTER EIGHTEEN. With regard to the divine nature, a person is nothing other than an incommunicable existence.

If we examine this matter more carefully, then with regard to the divine nature a person is nothing other than an incommunicable existence. As we have demonstrated above, every personal property is absolutely incommunicable,[317] and the difference of persons in the divine nature is exactly the same as the difference of existences. And so, what sort of incommunicable existence will be in the divinity, except an existence that possesses a supersubstantial being from a personal property? And what is a divine person, except a person who possesses the divine being from an incommunicable property? But what is the divine being except a supersubstantial being? Whether you say divine, supersubstantial, supremely simple, omnipotent being, or any such expressions, it seems that you are considering the same thing. And so, both a divine person and a divine existence have the divine being; both have a supersubstantial being; both are a personal property; and both are incommunicable. You see that everything that is said about one can be said also about the other. And so, just as we have said, with regard to the divine nature, a divine person is nothing other than an incommunicable existence.[318]

CHAPTER NINETEEN. There can be plural existences and consequently plural persons, where there is only a unity of substance.

Because we maintain from our previous discussions that there can be plural existences in the divinity,[319] we must now consider if there can be plural existences in the divinity without compromising the unity of substance.[320] If common usage were to allow this, then just as what we call essence (*essentia*) could derive from the word "to be" (*esse*), so what we call "sistence" (*sistentia*) could be derived from the word "to exist" (*sistere*).[321] Perhaps you, who hear or read this, are laughing, but I prefer that you laugh at what I intend to say rather than not understand it enough and carelessly deride it. If then common usage were allowing us to speak of "sistence" (*sistentia*) as essence, then it would simply signify the being of a subject. Now then it is necessary to understand something more under the word "existence" (*existentia*). Just as we can use the word "subsistence" to speak of what is under something, so we can use the word "existence" (*existentia*) to speak of what has being from something. And so, existence indicates the 'being of a thing' and 'this being from some property'.

Who does not see that an omnipotent being from one property and an omnipotent being from another property are different existences? Indeed, although both are one mode of being, yet both are not one mode of existing. Who, I ask, says that it is impossible or even incredible, if one says that two or three are equally powerful and equally wise? Or why is it impossible or even incredible, if one says that one has from one property the very thing that they are in common, and the other has from another property the very thing that they are in common? And so, it does not seem impossible or incredible for plural existences and consequently plural persons to exist in the divinity. If we assert that we prove with clear reason that they are equally powerful, then it will be necessary to for us to assert that if one possesses omnipotence, then the other will also possesses omnipotence.[322] Every theologian knows with indubitable reason that there is a supremely simple being in the true divinity. Therefore, it will be necessary that in the divinity being omnipotent is identical to having omnipotence, and that omnipotence is nothing other than the divine substance. Moreover, there can only be one omnipotence, as we have previously demonstrated;[323] therefore, there can be only one divine substance. Hence based on what is probable to everyone and necessary for theologians, we have concluded our investigation: plural existences can exist where there is only a unity of substance.

In order to say something even more subtly for the sake of more subtle ‹readers›, in natural and created things "there is a difference between being and the thing that is;"[324] however, being and the thing that is are identical in uncreated things. Thus it is certain that the divine substance is nothing other than a substantial being, or rather a supersubstantial being—a substantial being insofar as it is such a thing existing in itself, and a supersubstantial being insofar as nothing is in it as in a subject.[325] And so, those who fear *where there is no fear*[326] would rightly be afraid to confess that the word "person" refers to the substance, if it were simply to mean a substantial being without consignifying another meaning. However, it means one having a substantial being from some individual property. For that reason, therefore, we confidently confess that the persons in the divinity refer to substance and indicate substance, and that the plural persons in the divinity are not plural substances, because they are plural persons possessing one undifferentiated being from a different property. And so, there is unity in the divinity according to the mode of being, and there is plurality according to the mode of existing. There is a unity of essence, because there is one undifferentiated being; and there are plural persons, because there are plural existences. These arguments, I think, should satisfy those who are investigating piously. After all, no one ought to demand or expect that in this life one can fully exhaust such great profundity.

But one must note how person and existence are related to one another. For the uncertainties of one are demonstrated in turn by the other. For instance, based on the notion of person one proves very easily the necessity of a plurality in the divinity; but based on a consideration of existence one demonstrates very easily the possibility of a plurality in a unity of substance.[327]

CHAPTER TWENTY. How these formulas must be understood, or how they can be harmonized: three substances and one essence, three subsistences and one substance, and three persons and one substance or essence.

Perhaps someone expects to hear me discuss how one must understand these formulas, or how they can be harmonized: three substances and one essence, three subsistences and one substance, and three persons and one substance or essence.[328] The confession of one substance in divinity by the Latins and the confession of three substances by the

Greeks seem to be very different and completely contradictory.[329] But far be it that we believe something different from them, and their confession or ours errs in the faith! Therefore, among the variety of formulas one truth must be understood, although the meaning of words is different with different people. It seems to look the same whether some call persons "substances" or others call them "subsistences." It is certain that persons are called "substances" or "subsistences" with respect to the things which are usually inherent in them and under which they seem to be. We know that everywhere in the world the Church of Christ chants: "property is in the persons and unity in the essence."[330] Because of these properties which seem to inhere in the divine persons, by which they are distinguished from each other, the persons, according to some likeness to what truly are under the things which inhere in them, can be called, though less properly, substances or subsistences. Whether the three in the Trinity are called persons, substances, or subsistences, it is necessary to understand these terms in no other way than three having a substantial being under a distinct and different property. For that reason, moreover, by playing with the words, I have said "under a distinct property" and not "from a distinct property," so that you may understand from this that the three in the Trinity are called, although improperly, substance or subsistences. We even say that properties inhere in the persons, but, if you observed correctly, their inherent properties do not give them subsistence but existence. And, for that reason, it is more correct to call the persons "existences" rather than "substances" or "subsistences."

People, who consider only the divine reality, do not find a property that makes the divine essence different from some other divine essence, because there is only one essence in the divinity, just as one person in the divinity differs from another person by properties. And so, based on this consideration these people do not understand how the unity is called a "substance," and, for that reason, they call it simply and properly enough "essence." And they call, although improperly, the plurality, in which the properties are inherent, "substance." Moreover, in an uncreated essence no one finds a property through which one uncreated essence differs from another uncreated essence, since, as we have already said, there is only one essence;[331] yet, one certainly finds there a property through which the uncreated essence differs from every created essence. When taking this into account, these people call the unity not only essence but also substance; yet they transfer the word "subsistence" from its proper meaning to the designation of persons.

Now in order to distinguish briefly between substance and subsistence as they define it, take substance to mean what I previously called a "common existence,"[332] and take subsistence to mean what I previously called an "incommunicable existence."[333] And so, he, who knows from my previous explanations how there can be plural existences in the unity of substance, knows no less how there can be plural subsistences in the unity of substance. I am not unaware that this can be discussed with more subtle reason, but I think that this ought to satisfy the more simpleminded people and those to whom I am devoted.

But one must note and firmly uphold this point, so that if you ever hear the three in the Trinity being called "substance," "subsistence," or "persons," then you should understand these terms to be spoken 'according to substance'.[334] After all, as far as the truth of the matter is concerned, it is necessary to understand these terms in no other way than "three having a rational being from a different and personal property." For it is certain that a rational being cannot be possessed where rational substance does not exist. Moreover, it is agreed that every person has a rational being from an incommunicable property. I will not say anything about the Greeks who, as Augustine wrote,[335] utilize the word substance in a different way than we do; but, with the Latins, I think that no word can be found more suitable for the divine plurality than the word "person." Certainly there should be nothing more authoritative for a faithful mind than what is heard by every ear and confirmed by Catholic authority.

DEFINITION OF PERSON

CHAPTER TWENTY-ONE. A definition of person, not any person whatsoever but a created person alone.

See what we have previously suggested and developed insofar as we were able, namely, what are the different meanings of substance and person, and why several persons can exist in a unity of substance.[336] Now let us consider, if it is agreeable, whether Boethius' famous definition of person can be appropriately applied to all persons and to persons alone. If we find his definition to be generally and sufficiently applicable, then we undoubtedly seek in vain for another definition.

In order for a definition to be perfect, it is necessary for it to comprehend the entire reality and only the reality of the object being defined. For instance, in order for it to have its name from its reality, it is necessary for it to extend up to the limits of its definition without exceeding it, to be appropriately applied to all the defined objects and only the defined object, and to be an interchangeable proposition. Now, Boethius defines person as "an individual substance of a rational nature."[337] In order for this definition to be universal and perfect, it is necessary for every individual substance of a rational nature to be a person, and, conversely, for every person to be an individual substance of a rational nature. And so, seeing that there is only one divine substance alone, I ask this question; I ask, I say, whether the divine substance is individual? As we have proven above, we undoubtedly believe and clearly prove that the divine substance is a Trinity of persons.[338] And so, if we must call divine substance 'individual', then an individual substance of a rational nature will be something that is not a person. After all, the Trinity is neither a person, nor can we rightly call it a person. Accordingly, it does not seem that this definition of person can be applicable to a person alone. But if we must not call that substance 'individual', then it is certain that there is some person who is not an individual substance, because this person is divine. And so, that definition of person cannot be applicable to all persons. Therefore, whether or not we call the divine substance 'individual', Boethius' definition is not found to be related to all persons.[339]

CHAPTER TWENTY-TWO. A definition of a person, not any person whatsoever but only an uncreated person.

Without a doubt, we cannot correctly define what is infinite; nevertheless, perhaps we will be able to make some advances in our knowledge of God, if, as the Lord permits, we strive to formulate a definition of a divine person. According to the meaning of existence, which we have previously discussed,[340] we will be able to assert, perhaps not improperly, that a divine person is an incommunicable existence of divine nature. As it is clear from previous discussions,[341] the word "existence" indicates what and from what source a substantial being is, and this is certainly common to every substance. Moreover, there is a general existence that is common to all substances; there is a general existence that is common to all rational substances and to them alone; and there is a specific existence that is common only to angelic and human substances. But all these existences are excluded in the case where the meaning of existence is restricted and confined by the addition of "divine nature." Likewise, if we look carefully, then we will be able to find in the divine nature both an existence common to plural persons and an existence appropriate for one person alone and, for that reason, incommunicable. But an existence that is common to plural persons is excluded in the case where existence is called "incommunicable." Not improperly, I believe, we can thus say that a divine person is an incommunicable existence of the divine nature.

CHAPTER TWENTY-THREE. A definition of person that seems to be applicable to every person and to a person alone.

And if we define "divisible" as that which can be divided both among several persons and among several substances and be possessed jointly by several and completely by each one, and if we define "individual" as that which can only be applied to one substance alone, and if, I say, we want to define those two words, divisible and individual, in that way, then, perhaps not improperly, we will be able to assert that it is true, on the one hand, that any created person is an individual substance of a rational nature, and, on the other hand, it is true that any person is an individual existence of a rational nature.

But so that our discussion may become clearer, let us discuss the same point more carefully. We have said previously that the word "existence" indicates a substantial being.[342] According to our aforementioned definition, the word "existence" undoubtedly does not mean what the word "substance" means, but what is the principal thing in a substance and what is applicable to every substance. Moreover, the principal thing in a substance is neither what stands under being nor what has something inherent in it as in a subject, but it is such a thing that subsists in itself without inhering in something as in a subject. This is certainly common to every substance, whether human, angelic, or divine. Indeed, one correctly regards the principal thing in a created substance as more worthy and more principal to the extent that it draws closer to the divine similitude. After all, a created substance seems to fall away from the divine similitude to the extent that it is subject to accidents. And so, on account of what is principal in every substance, it can be more correct to call it essence than substance.

Moreover, as we have said, the word "existence" denotes what has being in itself and what possesses being from another source,[343] and it is certain that this is common to every substance. For instance, everything that exists either exists from itself or from another source. The other issues that pertain to the same definition of person are sufficiently clear from the previous discussions, and they do not require a new exposition, namely, why any existence whatsoever is not called person, but only an individual and incommunicable existence.

CHAPTER TWENTY-FOUR. Likewise, a definition of person that seems to be applicable to every person and to a person alone.

Perhaps it will be clearer and more expedient for our understanding, if we define person as someone existing through himself alone according to a singular mode of rational existence. How we ought to understand the word "existing" is sufficiently clear from the previous discussions.[344] Moreover, we are adding "through himself alone," because the word "person" is never used correctly unless one someone alone is differentiated from everyone else by a singular property. But 'to exist through himself alone' is common to every individual, both animate and inanimate. However, the word "person" is never used correctly unless it refers to some rational substance. For that reason, we added the phrase "according to a singular mode of rational existence," to the first phrase, "existing through himself alone." Moreover, the mode of rational existence is threefold: the first mode is common to plural natures; the second mode is common to plural substances of the same nature, the third mode is common to plural persons of the same substance. But a personal property requires a 'singular mode of rational existence', without which a person never subsists. Therefore, so that 'existing through himself alone' can be a person, it will be necessary to have 'a singular mode of rational existence.' How we ought to understand this word "singular" is sufficiently clear from the previous discussions;[345] therefore, it is not necessary for us to linger in these explanations.

As we were able according to our own limited capacity, we have considered the meaning, differences, and description of the word "person." If someone understands the words "individual," "person," or "existence" differently than we have defined them, if he continues by arguing not for our meaning but his own, and if he arrives at improper conclusions from his reasoning, then let him know that he is doing nothing against me. And if he thinks that he is doing something against me, then he deceives himself and does not know it.

CHAPTER TWENTY-FIVE. It is the property of divine nature to have a plurality of persons in the unity of substance; and, for that reason, the divine nature is different from other natures.

It is a property of the divine nature to have a plurality of persons in a unity of substance. Conversely, it is the property of human nature to have a plurality of substances in a unity of person. After all, the fact that a human person is sometimes found in the simplicity of substance is explained not by a condition of its own nature but by the corruption of its condition. This is why it is easy to assess how the human property seems to be opposite from the divine property. And so, the two properties standing, as it were, on opposite sides stare at one another and correspond to each other as through contrasts.[346] The angelic property, like an intermediate, is placed in between those two properties and is connected to both on either side with the likeness to both properties, resembling the divine property by never possessing a plurality of substances in a unity of person, and resembling the human property by never possessing a plurality of persons in a unity of substance. See how, by its interposition, the angelic property arranges the contrariety of opposites as in a kind of symmetrical proportion and composes the dissonance of alternating sounds into one consonance.[347]

Yet, having said this, I know that several people have a different opinion of angels. There are many even today who think that angels have a body. But if they were searching more vigorously, and if they were investigating more carefully, then they would quickly discover, I believe, the truth of my investigation. What sensible person will dare to deny that the more sublime and worthy the property of rational nature is, the closer it approaches the similitude of the supremely simple nature without composition? Who says that a creature, which is incorporeal and foreign to any adhesion of corporeal matter, does not come closer to and is not more intimately connected to the divine simplicity by the similitude of its property than that nature which is composed of corporeal and incorporeal substance and is united to the singleness of one person from two essences? Without a doubt the best kind of creature is what consists of a single and simple purity of spiritual nature.

Therefore, when we see in human handiwork statues of a human body without a head, this seems to be like the formation of the universe without the best kind of creature in divine handiwork. This comes near to what was previously argued concerning the angelic property. Which, in your opinion, seems to be a more appropriate order, which, I ask, seems to be more befitting for the arrangement of one who is supremely wise: if among that trinity of natures—namely, the divine, angelic, and human natures—the properties of two natures are opposed to the third through absolutely contrary natures without the intervention of an intermediate nature, or if it is said that the third nature intervenes between the two extreme natures and, having been connected alternately through the similitude of both natures, reconciles the aforementioned contrariety into one harmony?

But if, by chance, someone still finds this evidence of our argument suspect, then let him consider the testimony of the Gospel, which ought to convince him. Is it not clear from the Gospel that the Lord expelled a legion of demons from one man?[348] One legion contains 6,666 demons. If that many demons were expelled from one man, then there were that many demons in him before the expulsion. If demons have bodies, where, I ask, were they in him? In his spirit or in his body? It is certain that every body has a length, width, and height, that is, a body has spatial dimensions, and, for that reason, it is not able to subsist without a spatial capacity; the spirit absolutely does not have such a spatial capacity. Therefore, the demons were not in his spirit but in his body. But how or in which part of that man could so many demonic bodies be? But perhaps you say that angelic spirits, both good and bad, have subtle bodies. But however subtle their bodies are, two bodies, especially of the same size, cannot occupy one and the same place. Therefore, how small, I ask, do you think an angelic body can be, if you believe that the man's skin alone, even if flayed from the body, can contain so many angelic bodies?

We have now discussed this issue by means of a digression, and we have strayed far beyond our subject. I think that a pious and simple mind should be and can be satisfied with what was said about the proposed investigation, namely, how nothing is contrary to reason in our obligation to venerate "one God in the Trinity and the Trinity in a unity."[349]

BOOK FIVE

THE ETERNAL PROCESSIONS

Summary and Thesis

CHAPTER ONE. Because we are now certain about the unity of the divine substance, the plurality of persons, and also the concord and mutual relationship between unity and plurality, it remains to investigate the properties of the persons.

As we have already said elsewhere, it is appropriate for every person to have a rational being from an incommunicable property.[350] However, a divine person still requires something more than this, so that he can rightly be called divine. Now the property of a divine person requires the divine being. The divine being is identical to the supersubstantial being and to the supremely simple being. For the supremely simple being, being is identical to wisdom. Moreover, the divine substance alone has this being, and, for that reason, it is rightly called the supersubstantial essence. And because there is only one supremely simple and undifferentiated being in the divine nature, we thus confess the unity of substance in it. But the unity of substance is truly just as certain as the plurality of persons. But there can be no plurality without any otherness, and there can be no otherness without any difference.

How then can we harmonize plurality with the undifferentiated being? Where there is no diversity of being, there can be a different and distinct existence. Indeed, where several existences have an undifferentiated being from a different origin, they preserve the unity of substance in such a way that there are still several existences. Moreover, as we have previously demonstrated, a divine person is nothing other than an incommunicable existence.[351]

And so, one must note that if any divine existence is found to have some or even one incommunicable property, then from that fact alone it is discovered and clearly proven to be a person. For even if a divine existence should have several incommunicable properties, yet only one is sufficient for proving that it is a person. From this it is clear that there is a single someone who is differentiated from all others by that property.[352] We have glanced over this as a recapitulation of our previous discussions, so that the more versed we are, the more ready we are to approach those issues that still remain to be investigated.

But because we are certain about the unity of the divine substance, the plurality of persons, and the concordant and mutual relationship between unity and plurality, the occasion now requires that we investigate the properties of each person and specify the particular characteristics of each person. For instance, we already know that the three in the Trinity—whether they are called "persons," "existences," or some other name—the three, I say, are differentiated by certain properties;[353] and we already realize that we must seek those properties only in the distinction of their original cause.[354] But we have not yet discovered through reasoning those properties that are applicable to them individually. And so, let us now pursue these issues in the same manner that we have already pursued previous issues, so that it may be granted to us to apprehend with reason what we hold by faith and to support it with the testimony of demonstrative certitude.[355]

Proof of the First Individual Property from Mode of Existing: The 'Person from Himself' is Distinct from the 'Two Persons from Another Source"

CHAPTER TWO. The most pleasant relationship of persons cannot be lacking in supreme happiness, nor can the most ordered relation of properties be lacking in supreme beauty.

Let us first say what we all together know through some natural instinct and what we all prove through continuous use of our daily experiences. It is certainly clear that the more familial the plurality of persons is, the more intimate it is; and the more intimate it is, the more pleasant it is. But who has the audacity to attest or who dares to think that what is regarded as more pleasant is lacking in the fullness of supreme happiness and what is undoubtedly less pleasant exists in it?[356] And so, if one says that each person exists from himself, then such a plurality is certainly not united by any affinity among them, nor is it connected by any mutual relationship. Moreover, who can believe or who dares to affirm that that plurality of supreme unity is, on the one hand, so united and, on the other hand, so distant as if entirely estranged from itself that there is supreme indistinguishability insofar as the persons are united, and there is no union at all insofar as that plurality is separated in several persons? Which plurality, I ask, is more beautiful to you? Which plurality, I ask, seems more appropriate to you: the plurality that is differentiated by the most ordered variety of properties and unified in the most appropriate

manner of proportionality through a marvelous reason, or the plurality that is connected by no concord of differences or concordant difference between the persons and adorned by no order of otherness?
In my opinion, no one thinks that what is more beautiful can be lacking in the supreme beauty and what is less beautiful can be in it. And
so, we must believe that the most pleasant relationship of persons
cannot be lacking in the supreme happiness, nor can the most ordered variety of properties be lacking in the supreme beauty.[357] But
lest perhaps someone regards our proposed argument as probable
rather than necessary, let us investigate our argument further with a
more profound reason.

CHAPTER THREE. The nature of things requires that there be some person who exists from himself and not from any other.

What we said about the substance at the beginning of this work can
be repeated here decisively and verbatim about the person.[358] The same
reason suggests itself in both cases, and a similar conclusion derives
from similar arguments. What we have previously said about the substance, let us repeat here about the person: it is necessary for some
person to exist who is from himself and not from any other; otherwise,
an infinite number of persons would undoubtedly exist in the one divinity. For instance, if one person were from a second person, and that
second person were from another person, and if, according to this
manner of progression, any one person were from some other person,
then without a doubt the extension of this sort of sequence would
continue infinitely, and no end of this sort of extension would occur;
and it would so happen that the series and order of things, which cannot be without a beginning, would not have a beginning—a beginning,
I say, not of time, but of origin or of any originator.

The truth in these and other such assertions is so evident and the
reason is so clear that they absolutely do not need any proof. All of the
following assertions are obvious to everyone who has understanding
and to everyone who uses reason: nobody makes what is impossible to
make, and no one can give what he does not have;[359] there was a time
when whatever began to exist did not exist, and whatever exists that
did not formerly exist begins to be in time the very thing it is;[360] there
is no composition without a composer, and there is no distribution
without a distributor; and there exists a being than-which-nothing-is-
greater and than-which-nothing-is-better.[361] He who hears such asser-

tions, if he understands the meaning of the words, immediately gives assent to them and is unable to doubt them.

And so, lest we go against our conscience and extend the number of divine persons to infinity, it is undoubtedly necessary for us to concede that some person exists from himself and absolutely does not draw his origin from another person. Moreover, because it is certain that this person does not exist from any person other than himself, it is necessary consequently to investigate whether this existence is communicable or incommunicable, that is, if it belongs to one person alone to exist from himself, or if this property can be common to several persons.

CHAPTER FOUR. There can only be one person alone who exists from himself.

Because this subject demands a more careful consideration and summons us to a more sublime understanding, we must, in the manner of a builder, dig deeper into it and establish the foundation of our reasoning on the solid depth of certainty, upon which it is necessary for us to raise the structure of our work up to the higher sublimities of the more mysterious understanding. For this reason, therefore, we must begin with something that no one can doubt.

It is certainly clear that everything that exists either has a composite being or a simple being.[362] It is no less clear that everything that is possessed is possessed either according to participation or according to plenitude.[363] It is one thing to compose a single being from several diverse elements, and it is another thing to divide one being into many parts and to distribute it intentionally throughout many parts. But, as we have already said, there is no composition without a composer, and there is no distribution without a distributor.[364] Therefore, let us see if that being which is truly known to exist from itself can have a composite being.

It is clear that every composition requires a composer, and what cannot exist without the favor of a composer undoubtedly does not possess from itself the very being that is. Therefore, it is clear that a being that is from itself cannot have a composite being. It is necessary then for a being that lacks any origin or originator to have the supremely simple being. In fact, it is necessary for a person with the supremely simple being, that being be identical to power and wise being identical to powerful being.

We have answered our question about his being, now let us examine his power. Let us inquire whether he possesses his power according to plentitude or according to participation. But where there is participation, there is also distribution, because there is no participation without distribution, nor is there distribution without a distributor. And so, the one who can only have power according to participation undoubtedly requires the service of a distributor. It is clear then that if that person who exists from himself received power by participation, then he derives his own power from the favor of another. But if he derives his power from the favor of another, then surely he also derives his being from the favor of another, because, as we have already demonstrated, his being and power are identical.[365] And so, he either has both power and being from himself, or he has neither from himself.

For that reason, therefore, it is concluded that he who exists from himself cannot have power from the participation of power. He thus has according to plentitude what he cannot have according to participation. But all-power exists where there is plentitude of power. Thus, if that person, for whom being and power are identical, possesses his being from himself, then he also has his power from himself. But his power is all-power. Therefore, every power is from him. If every power is from him, then every being is from him, and every existence is from him. And so, all that is is from him: every essence, every existence, every person; I say, every human, angelic, and divine person is from him. If, therefore, all others have being from him, then it is certain that this person alone lacks a beginning; and it is no less clear that no other can exist unless from him, from whom is every power. You certainly see that such existence is absolutely incommunicable, and it cannot be common to several persons.

CHAPTER FIVE. Two persons in the divinity have their being from a source other than themselves according to that mode of existing that is from eternity yet not from itself.

We now know for certain that a person existing from himself is absolutely an incommunicable existence. Therefore, we can clearly conclude from this that a person existing from another source rather than himself is not an incommunicable existence; otherwise, there would not and could not be more than two persons in the divinity. And so, it is specifically the property of one person to exist from himself, but not existing from oneself is common to the other persons. You see therefore that an incommunicable existence produces a communicable existence, or rather a common existence; and you see how the communicable existence proceeds from the incommunicable existence and derives its origin from it.

We have deduced with a now indisputable argument that mode of existing, about which we have spoken in the beginning of this work,[366] where we utilized probable reason rather than necessary reason. Indeed, as we have already discussed there, there are three modes of existing: one mode is from eternity and from itself; a second mode is neither from eternity nor from itself; and, in between these two modes, a third mode is from eternity yet not from itself. As we have proven above, "all three persons are coequal and coeternal to each other."[367] Therefore, just as that existence that exists from itself is from eternity, so it also has from eternity a being which proceeds from the same source. And so, that mode of existing that is common to two persons has being from eternity but not from itself.

See therefore how much the properties of the first two modes of existing are different or rather completely opposite. The third mode of existing connects the contrariety of these two properties into a kind of symmetrical proportion, and by its mediation arranges the two extreme modes into a mutual harmony—having a being from eternity like the first mode of existing and having a being not from itself like the second mode of existence.[368] We now know that there is a property that specifically belongs to one person, and we know what property is common to two other persons, but we have not yet apprehended through reasoning what the properties are of each of these two persons.

PROOF OF TWO INDIVIDUAL PROPERTIES
FROM NOTION OF PROCESSION

CHAPTER SIX. The procession of one person from another person is either only immediate, only mediate, or both mediate and immediate at the same time.

We are informed from things that we know through experience what we must seek in the divine reality that is beyond experience: *For the invisible things of God are seen, having been understood through the things that have been made.*[369] Whenever we desire to ascend to lofty truths, we, who are human and unable to fly, usually use a ladder. Therefore, let us use the similitude of visible things for a ladder, so that from such a watchtower and as if through a mirror, we may merit to see the things in themselves that we cannot see by sight.[370]

In the human reality we see that a person proceeds from a person, and this procession can happen in three ways. A person proceeds from a person, sometimes only immediately, sometimes only mediately, but sometimes both mediately and immediately at the same time. Both Jacob and Isaac proceeded from the substance of Abraham, but the procession of one was only mediate and the procession of the other was only immediate. For instance, Jacob came from the loins of Abraham through the mediation of Isaac.[371] Eve, Seth, and Enoch proceeded from the substance of Adam, but the first procession was only immediate,[372] and the second procession was both mediate and immediate at the same time. For instance, Seth certainly proceeded immediately from the substance of Adam insofar as he was from Adam's seed, but he proceeded mediately insofar as he was from the seed of Eve.[373] See how the procession of a person in human nature is distinguished in three ways.

Although this seems very foreign to that unique and superexcellent nature, nevertheless there is some similitude inasmuch as human nature was made in the similitude of God.[374] And so, it is necessary for us to rise from our nature to that watchtower of contemplation,[375] and, according to the aforementioned consideration, to investigate with supreme diligence what is in the divine nature or what is not in it based on the proportion of similitude or dissimilitude. But if we say that there are three such existences in the divine nature, which we previously distinguished, in addition to the existence that is understood to exist from itself, then we undoubtedly seem to introduce four persons into that nature. For that reason, we must investigate carefully which of these properties truly belong to God, if they all cannot belong to him at the same time.

CHAPTER SEVEN. On the procession that is only immediate. It is necessary for a person to exist in the divinity who is from one person alone.

This fact is most certain and we can in no way doubt it: it is necessary for a single person to proceed immediately from the very first existence; otherwise, it will be necessary for the very first existence to remain alone. It is clear that absolutely none of the other persons can exist without proceeding from the first existence either immediately or mediately. Moreover, there cannot be a mediate procession without an immediate procession; nor can there be a procession that is equally mediate and immediate without it. But there is nothing preventing an immediate procession from sometimes occurring even where a mediate procession happens to be lacking. The immediate procession exists in a duality of persons, but a mediate procession is never without a trinity of persons. After all, two persons are necessary in an immediate procession: one person, who produces a second person, and that second person, who proceeds from the first. A mediate procession also requires a third person, in whom the mediation consists, in addition to those two persons in whom it begins and ends. Moreover, a duality is naturally prior to a trinity. For a duality can exist without a trinity, but a trinity can never exist without a duality.[376] And so, the immediate procession, which can subsist in a duality of persons, naturally comes before the mediate procession, which cannot exist without a trinity of persons.

But in the plurality of the persons and in the true eternity nothing precedes another, nothing succeeds another, and, for that reason, nothing is temporally prior, and nothing is temporally posterior. But what cannot be temporally prior can be causally prior and, for that reason, naturally prior. Indeed, as we have said far above, the perfection of one person requires a fellowship with another person.[377] And it thus happens that one person is the cause of another. In fact, where the fullness of divinity is, there is also the fullness of goodness and, consequently, the fullness of charity. Moreover, the fullness of charity requires one person to love another person as himself; otherwise, his love still contains the possibility of growth. It is also necessary for him to have an equal in dignity, so that someone may exist whom he could and rightly must love as himself.[378] If then it is certainly true that the primordial person is supremely good, then he will not be able to refuse what supreme charity requires; and if it is certainly true that he is omnipotent, then whatever he desires to exist will not be able not to exist. And so, due to the requirement of charity, he will want to have an equal in dignity; and, due to the exercise of his power, he will have the one whom he wants to have. See what we have said: the perfection of one person is the cause of another person's existence.[379] The second person receives the cause of existence from the first person who is the source of his existence.[380] Indeed, he was not able not to exist from him, who, as we have already said, is the source of all power.[381]

See how reason corroborates with reason. What is clearly proven by one reason is confirmed by another reason. Behold you know now that a person proceeds from a person, existence from existence, one person from one person alone, one capable of proceeding from one incapable of proceeding, the Begotten from the Unbegotten, and finally one immediately uniting to one person, because one person proceeds immediately from one person. We undoubtedly recognized that such an existence is in the divine nature, but we have not yet concluded with demonstrative reason whether it is communicable or incommunicable.

CHAPTER EIGHT. On the procession that is both mediate and immediate at the same time. It is necessary for a person to exist in the divinity who proceeds from two persons.

Because it is clear that the third person in the Trinity draws his origin from a source other than himself, it is necessary for him to possess his being either from any one of the aforementioned persons or from both together. And it remains for us to inquire which of these can be proven and for what reason.

We have already demonstrated above with clear reason that it will be necessary for a supremely worthy person to have a ‹second› person of equal dignity.[382] Moreover, in order for this ‹second› person to have dignity equal to ‹the first› omnipotent person, it was necessary for this person to receive his omnipotence from that omnipotent person, so that he would have equal, or rather the same, power. As we have often said, there can only be one omnipotence.[383] But if he received the same power, then certainly he received that power from him who is the source of all power, all being, all existence, and from whom, as we have said above, every essence and every existence has being.[384] If then the same power is undoubtedly common to both persons, then it follows that the third person in the Trinity both received his being and possesses existence from these two persons.

But perhaps someone will reply to this argument: "If the Begotten person receives and possesses the same power as the Unbegotten, then he receives and has the power of existing from himself, which is a specific property of the Unbegotten." Surely he who says this, as far as it seems to me, does not correctly understand what he is saying. But in order for our argument to become more apparent, let us discuss this matter more carefully.

You are saying that if the Unbegotten gave the fullness of his power to the Begotten who proceeds from him only immediately, then he also gave to the Begotten the power to exist from himself inasmuch as he is omnipotent and can do all things. I respond to this argument and confidently affirm that if the Begotten is able to exist from himself, then he does exist from himself. After all, the divine nature is absolutely invariable.[385] If then he exists from himself, then it is clear that he is what he is without the gift of another. But if the Unbegotten gave this power to him, then he had it from the gift of another. What then? Does he have from himself and, for that reason, without the gift of another what he has from the gift of another? You see now, I believe, how that assertion is contrary to itself. It is entirely contradictory that exactly the same thing is possessed from the gift of another and is possessed without the gift of another. What is more impossible than one being both existing and not existing at the same time? Therefore, just as we have said above, in order for a supremely worthy person to have a ‹second› person of equal dignity, as the fullness of goodness required, he gave to the existence which proceeds immediately from him whatever he who is omnipotent could truly give.[386] And so, that power which is the source of the being and power of everything else is common to both persons. And so, both existences are the source of every essence, every person, every existence, and, therefore, even that existence which is the third person in the Trinity.

The assertion is undoubtedly affirmed with a rational proof that we established earlier in our investigation on the Trinity. In that investigation we proved with clear reason, or rather we established with multiple demonstrations, that just as the perfection of one person is the cause of a second person, so the perfection of both persons is the cause of a third person in the Trinity.[387] Just as the perfection of one person requires a second person of equal dignity, so the perfection of both persons certainly requires a third who is mutually loved (*condilectum*). But because we have carefully discussed these issues above,[388] we do not need to consider the same issues here again, because anyone can return to that place again whenever he wants.

But we must be absolutely certain about this point, and we ought to uphold it firmly: the third person receives the cause of existence from the two persons who are the source of his existence.[389] Behold we now have a reason for affirming that the third person in the Trinity possesses his being from the other two persons. And so, we accept the fact that the third person draws his origin from the two persons, but we have not yet comprehended through reasoning whether such an existence is communicable or incommunicable.

CHAPTER NINE. The procession, which belongs to a person only mediately, cannot exist in the divine nature.

Behold now we have discovered for the most part what we have previously intended to investigate. We have discovered that it is necessary for a single existence to exist that is united only immediately to the Unbegotten. We have also discovered a third existence united to the same ‹Unbegotten› existence both through an immediate and mediate relationship.[390] We must now investigate the matter at hand: whether there is, or can be, some existence that is united to the Unbegotten only mediately.

There is one thing that I do not believe anyone in his right mind can think, namely, that there is some person in the divinity who is not permitted or does not wish to see immediately the Unbegotten, so to speak, *face to face*.[391] What else does it mean for a divine person to see unless to know by seeing and to see by knowing?[392] And what else does it mean to know the Unbegotten unless to have the fullness of wisdom? Moreover, wisdom and being are identical for a divine person. Thus, he receives wisdom and being from the same source, the Unbegotten. The same source who gives him wisdom also gives him existence.[393] And if he receives wisdom immediately from the Unbegotten, then he certainly also receives existence immediately from him. But if someone asserts that this person does not see the Unbegotten immediately, then he consequently admits that this person does not have a fully formed contemplation of the truth. And if that is true, then neither does he have complete plenitude and, consequently, true divinity.

Perhaps someone opposes these arguments and says: "Just as any person sees the one who proceeds from him, so any person proceeding sees the one producing. Why, therefore, is it not demonstrated that that person is from this person for the same reason as it is proven and demonstrated that this person is from that person?" I briefly reply to this question and say that any divine person receives full wisdom, and consequently, the divine being at the sight of another divine person, unless he possesses full wisdom and the divine being from another source. After all, it is necessary for him to possess wisdom and being from that source, if he does not have them from another source. But if he has them from another source, then it is not necessary for him to have them also from that source.

This may be better understood by an example: a truth written in a letter was sent to two people, the first who knew the truth from another source, and the second who did not know the truth at all from another source; nevertheless, both persons read the letter and understand the truth, but only the person, who did not have the truth from another source, obtained knowledge of the written truth by reading the letter. Therefore, because all of the divine persons gaze at each other mutually and immediately, they receive from or emit to each other the rays of supreme light.[394] And because they see each other immediately, they are united to each other immediately. It is therefore impossible for a person to exist in the divine nature who is united to another divine person by a mediate relationship alone.

This reasoning also confirms what we have said above about the procession of the third person.[395] Who can deny that the third person knows the other two persons by seeing them and sees them by knowing them? Moreover, these two persons are one and the same wisdom. Therefore, because it is clear that the third person has nothing from himself, it follows that he receives wisdom from seeing wisdom, and, for that reason, he also receives being, because being and wisdom are identical for them.

Behold we have sought and now found what we previously intended to investigate.[396] We have discovered that there is a procession in the divine nature that is only immediate and a procession that is both immediate and mediate, and that a procession that is only mediate absolutely does not exist, nor can it exist, in the divine nature.[397]

There is One Divine Person Per Mode of Procession

CHAPTER TEN. There cannot be more than one person in the divinity who is only from a single person, and there can only be one person alone who receives being only from two persons.

From our previous discussions we can truly and undoubtedly conclude as certain that if a fourth person had been able to exist in the divinity, then it would undoubtedly be necessary for him to draw his origin immediately from the other three persons;[398] otherwise, he would be united to some of them only through a mediate relationship, and he would see them only mediately. And if a fifth person had been able to exist in the divinity, then he would proceed immediately from the other four persons for the same reason. According to this manner of reasoning, the same conclusion will be found in subsequent persons no matter how far such a sequence is intellectually extended.

We can confirm our present discussion with our previous investigations.[399] Just as power is common to the two persons from whom the third person clearly draws his origin, so power would undoubtedly be common to the three persons from whom a fourth person would necessarily exist, if there were a place for a fourth person in the divinity. Otherwise, the two persons would greedily reserve for themselves what they could give to the third person without violating their own property. What we are saying about these three, you will undoubtedly discover the same conclusions in subsequent persons. After all, no matter how far you extend this line of explanation, you will see that the same consistency always and everywhere occurs.

One must notice how the difference of such properties consists only in the number of persons who are producing being. The first person has his being from no one else, the second person has his being from the first person alone, and the third person has his being from both. If the number of persons were to increase more, then it would be necessary for the same tenor of progression to be found throughout. See how this order of differences arises and extends according to the mode and order of numbers.

One must also notice that it is impossible for more than one person to exist according to any one difference ‹of properties›. For instance, only one person can exist from only one person. Similarly, there can only be one person alone who is only from two persons. If two persons were proceeding from only one person, then neither of them who are proceeding would be united immediately to the other person. A previous reason clearly taught how impossible this is.[400] What is said about one difference ‹of properties› it given to be understood about any other difference.

Behold in these arguments we have a solution for those two questions that we previously left unanswered.[401] It is indeed clear that if there can be only one existence alone from only one person, and if there can be only one existence alone from only two persons, then it is also clear, I say, that both existences are incommunicable. And so, just as only one person alone in the divinity can exist who is from himself, so there cannot be more than one person who is from only one person, nor can there be more than one person who has his being from only two persons.

CHAPTER ELEVEN. It is necessary for a person to exist in the divinity from whom no other person proceeds, even though this same person is still not from himself.

In the previous discussions we have found differences among the personal properties, and we have also found how the persons are mutually united to one another, or how they proceed based on the mode and succession of numbers. But if there were as many divine persons as possible differences, then there would certainly be an infinite number of divine persons. Thus it is necessary for us to examine the properties of the divine persons more carefully, so that no improper suspicion can rise concerning their number.

We have previously demonstrated that in the plurality of divine persons some person necessarily exists who cannot draw his origin from any source other than himself.[402] But just as it is necessary for a person to exist in the divinity who is not from another person, so it is necessary for another person in the divinity to exist from whom no other person proceeds. Both arguments are proven with a similar reason, and both are confirmed with the same demonstration. For instance, if some person in the true divinity were not existing from whom no other person would proceed, but every person proceeding from another would have a person proceeding from him, then the extension of this sort of deduction would continue infinitely, and the series of persons infinitely extended would find no end for its plurality. But no one accepts this opinion, nor does anyone admit it for any reason.[403] And so, it is necessary for such a person, from whom no other person draws his origin, to exist in the plurality of divine persons. It is no less necessary for this very same person to possess the origin of his existence from another person, just as it is necessary for that person, who is not from any other person, to communicate the cause of existence to another person. The reason for both affirmations is the same; both are proven with a similar argument. Indeed, because clear reason proves that only one person can exist from himself, if that person, who is not from another person, were to have no one proceeding from him, then he would remain alone forever. If, for a similar reason, that person, who does not have a person proceeding from him, were proceeding from no other person, then he would lack a divine fellowship forever. But, as we have previously shown with sufficient clarity, a multitude of reasons excludes solitude from true divinity and demonstrates a plurality of persons.[404] Therefore, it is necessary for a person in the divinity to exist who does not assume an origin of existence from another person but communicates it to another person; and it is equally necessary for a person in the divinity to exist who, conversely, receives the being that he is from another person and does not communicate it to another person.

CHAPTER TWELVE. Only one person from whom no other person proceeds can exist in the divinity.

It is certainly necessary for such a person to exist in the divinity from whom, as we have already said, no other person proceeds.[405] But one can still doubt whether this very property belongs exclusively to one person alone, or whether it can also be common to others. But if there were two persons who possessed this property in common, then without a doubt neither of them would proceed from the other. If neither were proceeding from the other, then neither one would be united immediately to the other. If neither were united immediately to the other, then they would certainly be united to one another through a mediate relationship alone. But our previous argument demonstrated with very clear reason how impossible this is.[406] And so, it is exclusively the property of only one person to have no person at all who proceeds from him. Therefore, just as only one person alone in the divinity can exist who does not proceed from another, so only one person alone can undoubtedly exist from whom no person proceeds. This first existence will be incommunicable in the same way that the second existence is also incommunicable, and neither will be able to be common to the other persons. Indeed, only one person in the plurality of persons receives and possesses being from another person, in such a way that absolutely no other person either receives or possesses being from that person. Behold, we have deduced the properties of two persons in the Trinity with a reason so clear that we can in no way doubt them even a little.

CHAPTER THIRTEEN. It is necessary for such a person in the divinity to exist who proceeds from one person and has another person proceeding from him.

From the two properties of the two aforementioned persons we can conclude without any scruples what we ought to think concerning the property of him who is in the middle of these two persons. If there can be only one person alone in the divinity who is not from any other person, then it follows that the person, about whom we are now discussing, is not from himself. Likewise, if there can be only one person alone in the divinity who does not have a person proceeding from him, then it is necessary for this person, about whom we are now discussing, to have a person proceeding from him. And so, he proceeds from another person, yet in such a way that another person still proceeds from him. Behold therefore, as we have said,[407] we have no doubts about what we must think concerning his property.

This testimony undoubtedly agrees with that assertion which the aforementioned disputation already discovered as certain. It seems, or rather it is clearly demonstrated, that the person, who proceeds only immediately from the Unbegotten, has both properties. For instance, without any diminution of his integrity, he certainly communicates to another person the being that he is in the same fullness that he receives from the Unbegotten. Indeed, the third person in the Trinity proceeds both from the Begotten and the Unbegotten at the same time.

See how reason converges with reason, and how one affirmation alludes to another affirmation. Behold, as we now know more clearly than day, we have found three distinct properties in the three persons. It is the property of the first person not to proceed from another person but to have a person proceeding from him; it is the property of the second person both to proceed from one person and to have another proceeding from him; but it is the property of the third person to proceed from another and not to have a person proceeding from him. And we already know that two of these properties are incommunicable; but we have not yet apprehended by reason what we should think about the third.

CHAPTER FOURTEEN. There can only be one person alone in the divine nature who proceeds from another person and who has a person proceeding from him.

But because we already know from the testimony of reason that two of the aforementioned properties are incommunicable, we are, consequently, urged to think the same about the third. But lest this reason seems probable rather than necessary, let us investigate this argument more thoroughly.

First, we must note and carefully consider how both properties of the two persons gaze at one another as opposites, and they correspond to one another as contraries.[408] For instance, it is the property of one person not to receive the fullness but to give it; conversely, it is the property of another person not to give the fullness but to receive it. Moreover, where there is supreme beauty and where no perfection can be lacking, then the logical consequence is clear and no healthy mind can doubt at all: the plurality of the divine persons is entirely united in the most congruous beauty and differentiated in the most ordered otherness. And so, it is necessary for the different concord and concordant difference in both properties to exist mutually with one another in divine plurality of persons, which is supremely beautiful and the most ordered of all. It thus seems to be necessary then that between the person, whose property is to give and not receive the fullness, and the person, whose property is to receive and not give it, there is one person alone in the middle whose particular property is both to give and receive it, so that this person, who was established in the middle, is united to one person on one side and connected to the other person on the other side. It will thus happen that by giving he is united with the person giving, and by receiving he is united with the person receiving. And, conversely, by giving he is different from the person not giving, and by receiving he is different from the person not receiving, so that, as we have already said, there is a different concord and concordant difference in both properties.[409]

However, if we should say that there are two intermediate persons between the two outer persons, then let us see what inconsistency follows this assertion. Certainly the first of them will derive from no person, the second will derive from one person alone, the third will derive from two persons, and the fourth will derive from the three, just as we have sufficiently and carefully explained above. And in light of this consideration this arrangement seems to have something in common with an arithmetic mean. But let us only see how in light of another consideration this arrangement of four persons confounds a kind of geometric mean, which, as it is clear above, the Trinity of persons indicates. Certainly the property of the person, who is first according to cause, will only be the giving of the fullness; the property of the two intermediate persons will be both giving and receiving it; but the property of a fourth person will only be receiving and not giving it. Behold the first of them is united with the second person in one way alone; the second is united with the third not in one way alone but in two ways; but the third person is united to the fourth person not in two ways but in only one way. You certainly see how the doubling and communication of one property confounds rather than extends the principle of proportionality, and how it decreases rather than augments the beauty of order. But what kind of person asserts that there is or could be something in the supreme beauty that reduces its beauty and confounds its order? The arithmetic mean according to one consideration, the geometric mean according to another consideration, and the harmonic mean according to the comparison of Trinity and unity converge face to face in the aforementioned arrangement of properties and allude to one another by a marvelous reason.[410] And so, it is clear that the particular property of one of the persons is to give and receive the fullness, and that this property, just like the other two, is incommunicable.

CHAPTER FIFTEEN. There cannot be four persons in the divine nature.

It is absolutely certain that possessing all plenitude is common to every divine person. Moreover, the differentiation of properties pertains to two things: it consists in giving and in receiving. As it is clear from the previous discussion, the property of one person consists in giving alone, the property of the other person consists in receiving alone, but the middle property between these two consists in both giving and receiving.

But perhaps someone will respond to this assertion: "If one property consists in giving alone, and another property consists in receiving alone, and the middle property between these consists in both giving and receiving, then why couldn't there be a fourth property consisting in having alone without giving or receiving? And if we accept this, then we are apparently acknowledging a quaternary of divine persons." But in the previous discussions we already resolved the difficulty of this question with such a clear reason that a careful reader, however ignorant he may be, can hardly be uncertain concerning this matter. As we have demonstrated above, a clear reason proves that only one person in the divinity can be from himself.[411] And so, if this person, who does not receive being and power from another source, were not bestowing what he possesses to another person, then, as we said elsewhere, he would undoubtedly remain alone forever. And so, we know that a fourth property has no place in the divinity, and, for that reason, the suggestion of a quaternary is totally excluded. It is clear then that a fourth person absolutely cannot exist in the divine nature.

THE DISTINCTION OF PERSON THROUGH A REFLECTION OF LOVE

CHAPTER SIXTEEN. On the fullness of true love, and on the distinction of properties considered with respect to this love.

We can further confirm with a more thorough and clearer reason our previous discussion on excluding the suggestion of quaternary from the divine nature.[412] If we bring into consideration the fullness of true love, and if we pay careful attention to the distinction of properties pertaining to the same consideration, then perhaps we will sooner discover what we are seeking.

The fullness of true love consists only in the supreme and entirely perfect love. But only that love can be called supreme love which is so great that there cannot be a greater love and is so excellent that there cannot be a better love.[413] From this also one may observe that the fullness of true love cannot be possessed by a person who is not God; otherwise, if someone had prevailed above God to possess the plenitude of true love, then a person who was not God would have been able to be equal to God in love and, for that reason, in goodness. But who can say or presume to think lightly about this?

Moreover, it is clear that true love can either be a gratuitous love alone, an owed love alone, or a combination of both, that is, on the one hand, an owed love, and, on the other hand, a gratuitous love.[414] Love is gratuitous when someone gladly bestows love to a person from whom he did not receive any favors. Love is owed when someone requites nothing but love to the person from whom he freely receives it. And love is a combination of both when by loving in both ways a person freely receives love and freely bestows it. But the fullness of gratuitous love, the fullness of owed love, and also the fullness of a love perfected in both loves can in no way be possessed by a person who is not God. But because this is sufficiently clear from the previous discussions, there is no need for an additional explanation.

CHAPTER SEVENTEEN. To which person in the Trinity is possessing the fullness of gratuitous love alone applicable?

It is already most certain that one person in the Trinity possesses nothing except from himself, receives absolutely nothing from any other source, and has nothing at all from a foreign gift. It does not seem at all possible for this sort of owed love, which we described to you above, to belong to a person who is discovered to have received nothing from anyone for which he would become obliged to him or become a debtor to him.[415] But when he bountifully, generously, and freely bestows the abundance of his fullness to those who proceed from him, he shows that he possesses a gratuitous love. Indeed what can those persons proceeding from him demand from him, what, I ask, can they demand from him as an obligation, seeing that they even receive as his gift this owed love which they are returning for his gratuitous love? Otherwise, they would have something that they had not received from him, and the previous discussions showed how false this is.

And so, he has a gratuitous love and only a gratuitous love. He has, I say, a gratuitous love, and, what is greater still, the fullness of gratuitous love. He, who bestows all of the fullness that he has and reserves nothing for himself alone, reveals that he has the fullness of gratuitous love.[416] If he were to possess all plenitude, and if he were unwilling to bestow it, although he could, then he would not have the fullness of gratuitous love. Therefore, it is proven that he, who is not lacking either the power or desire to execute all his benevolence, has the fullness of gratuitous love.

CHAPTER EIGHTEEN. Having the fullness of an owed love alone is applied to which person in the Trinity?

It is necessary for the fullness of an owed love to belong to the person whose property is to proceed and yet not have a person proceeding from him, because he receives all that he has from another source; otherwise, if he were not returning the supreme love to those loving supremely, then he would not deserve the supreme love.[417] He is certainly loved by them with a supreme love, and he is known to have received all plenitude from them. What kind of love, which is not owed, can he return to those from whom he clearly received freely all plenitude? And, as we have already discussed before, because it is his property not to have a person proceeding from him, a person does not exist in the divinity to whom he can bestow the fullness of a gratuitous love.[418] He can certainly have gratuitous love toward a created person, but he who cannot have a disordered love cannot have the fullness of gratuitous love toward a creature.[419] Indeed love would be disordered, if he were to love with the supreme love someone who is not worthy of the supreme love.[420] After all, he who is not supremely good absolutely does not deserve the supreme love. A person, who is not God, cannot be supremely good, because he cannot be equal to God. And so, the aforementioned ‹divine› person can have and does have the fullness of an owed love according to the aforementioned reason, but he absolutely does not have, nor can he have, the fullness of a gratuitous love. Therefore, as we have said, it is necessary for the person, who does not have a person proceeding from him, to have the fullness of an owed love alone.

CHAPTER NINETEEN. Obtaining the fullness of both a gratuitous and owed love is the property of which person in the Trinity?

The important considerations that we have just offered about the two persons sufficiently reveal what we should think about the last person.[421] Because it is the particular property of one person both to proceed from another and have a person proceeding from him, it is necessary for him to abound in both a gratuitous and owed love and to bestow completely the fullness of both loves, namely, the fullness of a gratuitous love to one person and the fullness of an owed love to another person. It is obviously an obligation that he loves with a supreme love the first person from whom he receives everything and to whom he gives nothing; but it is gratuitous that he supremely loves the other person from whom he receives nothing but bestows everything.

We now comprehend through clear reason how we ought to differentiate the properties of each person according to this consideration. It is clear that a supreme and gratuitous love alone belongs to one of the three persons; a supreme love belongs to a second person in such a way that it is an owed love alone; but a supreme love belongs to a third person in such a way that it is, on the one hand, an owed love and, on the other hand, entirely gratuitous. Behold the three distinctions of properties in supreme love, although it is still one and the same love in every person, namely, a supreme and truly eternal love. And so, from this speculation of the supreme and true love we can conclude whether there can be a place for a fourth person in the plurality of divine persons.

THE EXCLUSION OF A FOURTH PERSON
THROUGH AN ANALYSIS OF LOVE

CHAPTER TWENTY. Reason clearly demonstrates why there can be no place for a fourth person in the Trinity.

The previous discussions sufficiently prove and demonstrate that there can only be one person in the divinity who is from himself.[422] Moreover, a careful investigator of the truth can conclude with an unquestionable reason that no love can exist in that mutual charity of persons that is not either gratuitous alone, owed alone, or both owed and gratuitous at the same time. Concerning the three aforementioned persons, it is no less clear that the fullness of a gratuitous love belongs to one person alone, the fullness of an owed love belongs to a second person alone, and the fullness of both an owed and gratuitous love belongs to a third person alone.

But what are we to say to this? Surely each of the three persons and their love are not distinct things? Surely, for each of these persons, being is not distinct from loving, nor is loving distinct from being? Therefore, where is that true and supreme simplicity that we previously sought, found, and proved with many attestations from reason?[423] And so, it is necessary without a doubt that being be identical to loving in supreme simplicity. Therefore, for any of the three, their person will be identical to their love. And so, "several persons are in one divinity" will denote nothing other than "several persons have," or better, "several persons are one and the same love, namely, the supreme love, from a different property." In the divinity, then, the first person is nothing other than the supreme love distinguished by one property; the second person is nothing other than the supreme love distinguished by a second property; and the third person is nothing other than the supreme love distinguished by a third property.[424] And so, the number of persons will be consistent with the number of properties. Therefore, as we have said, because any person is identical to his love, and because the designated differentiation of each person consists only in the three aforementioned properties, just as we will in no way be able to find a fourth property in the divinity, so we will not be able to find a fourth person in it.

So as to prevent someone from not sufficiently understanding us and thereby inconsiderately criticizing us for maintaining a gratuitous or owed love, it certainly does not escape our notice that we do not always use these words with the same meaning. We say that one person owes love to another, because the latter deserves to be loved. We also say that one person owes love to another, because the latter justly rendered the former a debtor of some gift or favor. In the same way, we could also comprehend the word "gratuitous" with different meanings in different contexts. But so as to avoid an occasion for accusations, we have determined with additional explanation the meaning with which we want others to comprehend both words in this context. But let no one be surprised and let no one be angry, if we say what we think about such great profundity with the words in which we are able.[425]

We have now explained how reason clearly demonstrates according to our previous confirmation that there can be no place for a fourth person in the divinity.[426]

CHAPTER TWENTY-ONE. How we can conclude many things from our last speculation.

But if anyone, having trained perceptions in such matters,[427] desires to pursue carefully this last speculation, then perhaps from it alone he will be able to conclude without doubt and demonstrate with probable assertion many arguments that have been disputed above and proven with diverse demonstrations. If anyone thoroughly understands that there is one God and apprehends with clear reason that God is supremely good and supremely blessed but despairs about the plurality of persons,[428] then through this watchtower he will be able to lift himself up from what he already believes to what he does not yet apprehend. I think that from this single speculation one will be able to draw out and establish with probable proofs the plurality of persons, indeed the entire Trinity. As a previous argument demonstrated,[429] this speculation excludes the suggestion of four divine persons. To those who believe and truly confess the true divinity this speculation gives evidence for the plurality of persons in such a way that it also demonstrates the unity of substance. From this speculation the property of each person is made clear and goes forth into manifestation. For instance, after seeking out clear reason, it proclaims that there is a person in the divinity who does not have being from any other person, a person who is from one person alone, and a third person who draws his origin from two persons. Let him, who reads this, consider how important and useful it is to have a familiar and ready answer *for every person who requests the reason* for all these truths from a single speculation.[430] But because we have furnished a passable route for an investigation of these things from what we have already discussed, we leave them to be discussed more fully by more diligent investigators.

CHAPTER TWENTY-TWO. When we say that the fullness of gratuitous love consists in giving alone, and the fullness of owed love consists in receiving alone, it is necessary for someone to understand this not as a work of grace but as an operation of nature.

When we said that one person possesses or is the fullness of gratuitous love, but the other person possesses or is the fullness of owed love,[431] let no one interpret this to mean that any one person surpasses any other person in some way or that one person has or is something better or more perfect than another. There is no difference of degrees in God; there is no diversity of dignity. Behold, it is clear that the property of one person is to give the fullness and not to have received it, but the property of another person is to have received it and not give it. Surely it is not necessary therefore for us to believe that one person is better than another, and one person is more worthy than another? Far be it! Remove any such suspicion from your mind! Such suspicion deceived and divided many through various errors. The person, who received nothing that he has from another person, has nothing greater and absolutely nothing better than the person, who has nothing that he had not received. It is the property of one person only to give all that he has of his perfection, goodness, and beatitude; and the person, whose property is to have received everything, also possessed these qualities in the same fullness.

Moreover, when we say that the fullness of gratuitous love consists in giving alone, and the fullness of owed love consists in receiving alone, no one should take this to mean that in that equality without differentiation this is a work of grace rather than an operation of nature.[432] But the depth of such a great mystery is very profound, and it can hardly or never be explained with suitable words by any human being.[433]

Therefore, let no one be surprised, and let no one be angry if, in the example of the Virgin Mother, I bring forth the truth that I conceived and wrap it in the rags of my words, because I am not able to wrap it in the silk of eloquent speech, which I realize that I do not have. But where the truth of a thought is certain, nothing remains for the prudence of a wise reader except to employ accurate words, which I receive with all gratitude, for asserting truth.

CHAPTER TWENTY-THREE. With respect to the substance of love, the supreme and one love belongs to every person, although it is differentiated by distinction of properties in each person.

It is the property of a true and intimate love to cause the following even in those persons who have a different being: "to will the same and not to will the same."[434] How much more does an identical will belong to those persons for whom being is the same as willing. Consequently, just as there is one being, so there is also one will. And so, one will, one love, and one, indistinguishable goodness belong to every person in the Trinity.

Therefore, with respect to the substance of love, there will be one and the same love in every person. And, because the one and supreme love is in every person, in no way can it be greater in one person than in another, and in no way can it be better in one person than in another. Certainly if the same will belongs to every person in every respect, then each person loves the other as himself and as much as himself. If each person loves the other as himself, then he desires all that is communicable in the divinity for any other as for himself. If each person loves the other as much as himself, then he does not want whatever is communicable in the divinity more enthusiastically for himself than for another, and he does not want it more unenthusiastically for another than for himself. And so, such a love will be, on the one hand, so excellent that there cannot be a better love, and, on the other hand, so great that there cannot be a greater love.[435]

. And so, as we have said, with respect to the substance of love, there will be one and the same love in every person; nevertheless, in a wonderful way that love will be differentiated by the distinction of properties in each person.[436] Based on the meaning that we previously defined,[437] the first person will have gratuitous love alone toward the second person, the second person will have owed love alone toward the first,[438] and the third person will have owed love toward the first and gratuitous love toward the second. According to a human manner of speaking, we correctly call love "gratuitous" that receives nothing and bestows everything, but we call that love "owed" that bestows nothing to someone from whom everything is received. And so, one can say that the wave of divinity and the flow of supreme love in the first person is only pouring out and not poured in, in the second person it is both pouring out and poured in, and in the third person it is not pouring out but only poured in, even though love is still one and the same in every person. And there is one truth in all these statements, although there is a multiformity of expressions for it.

CHAPTER TWENTY-FOUR. With respect to the integrity of perfection, there is no difference of love or dignity in the Trinity.

Meanwhile perhaps someone, who thinks about the divine persons in a human way, grants greater dignity to that person, who possesses from himself all that he possesses, and concludes that he is more excellent than the other persons. But far be it that someone believes that there is some difference of dignities in the divinity where there is truly and undoubtedly supreme equality![439] But he, who does not yet understand this truth through rational comprehension, can restrain his own thinking about it with another consideration.

And so, as I have already said above, one must know that each person desires both for the other persons and for himself whatever is communicable among every person in the divinity,[440] and, conversely, he must also know that each person loves his own incommunicable property more for himself than for another. In fact, each person must be the same substance with the other persons, because this is common to every person; and each person must be an individual person who is distinguished from the other persons, because this is his own incommunicable property. If, therefore, any person were loving his own property more for another than for himself, and if any person were loving the property of another more for himself than for another, then what would this mean or what could this indicate other than the refusal to be the person that he is and the desire to be a person that he is not? But I do not think that anyone is so insane that he would dare think this or that he could patiently listen to it. And so, without any ambiguity the person who possesses the property that you regard a prerogative of dignity desires it more for himself than for the other persons, and without any contradiction the other persons desire it for him more than for themselves. What then? Surely we must not consider those persons, who prefer for another person rather than for themselves that property which you consider preeminent in excellence, to be of more benevolence than that person who prefers it more for himself than for any other person? But if they are rightly considered to be more benevolent, then why not consider them more worthy for the same reason?[441]

Perhaps you still say that possessing and giving the fullness is far more glorious than only possessing it and not giving it to another. Again, as it seems to you, if we are judging according to human standards, then we find in the two persons a certain prerogative of glory. But I say again that, according to the aforementioned reason, the third person in the Trinity prefers this property, which you consider a prerogative, for the others rather than for himself; nevertheless, the others prefer it for themselves rather than for the third person. Surely, therefore, one will not assert that the third person is more generous than the other two persons, and, for this reason, more glorious?

As long as we proceed according to human judgment, each divine person is found more or less benevolent and more or less worthy than the other persons. See how false this opinion is which is found contradictory to itself! And so, we ought to cast such mental images away from our hearts, and we ought to believe with an absolute firmness what we are not yet able to understand through rational comprehension. It is certain and not at all ambiguous that, with regard to the integrity of perfection, there is no difference of love or dignity in the Trinity.

CHAPTER TWENTY-FIVE. What is common to every person, or what is proper to each person; and what issues still remains to be investigated.

And so, if it is acceptable, let us now briefly summarize here what we have investigated with reasoning in this book. To possess all plenitude is common to every divine person. To give all plenitude is common only to two persons;[442] to have received all plenitude is common only to two persons;[443] and not to possess both is common only to two persons.[444] For the property of one person is in giving alone;[445] the property of a second person is in receiving alone;[446] and the property of a third person is both in receiving and giving.[447] To have a person proceeding from himself is common only to two persons;[448] to proceed from another person is common only to two persons;[449] and not to have both properties is common only to two persons.[450] After all, to have a person proceeding only from himself is the property of one person;[451] but to proceed only from another is the property of a second person;[452] and both to proceed from another and to have a person proceeding from himself is the property of a third person.[453] To proceed from no one is only the property of one person;[454] to proceed from one person alone is only the property of a second person;[455] and to proceed from both persons is the property of a third person.[456] Moreover, there is only one person from whom no person exists;[457] likewise, there is only one person from whom only one person exists;[458] and there is only one person from who two persons proceed.[459]

And so, because it is the common property of two persons not to exist from themselves but to proceed from another, there still remains to investigate with supreme diligence how the procession of one person and the procession of the other person differ from one another. Moreover, after finding the differences of their mutual relation based on the principle of similitude, it is finally necessary to determine their proper names.

I had intended to reveal publicly what I thought about these issues, but because there is intense profundity in them, it will be better to leave them to be discussed more thoroughly by those who have greater abilities.[460] It will also be better to prove from the judgment of others what sort of gratitude or ingratitude I deserve from those things that I have said up until now.

BOOK SIX

THE NAMES OF THE DIVINE PERSONS

THE APPROPRIATION OF FATHER, SON, AND HOLY SPIRIT

CHAPTER ONE. Nothing is in true divinity according to the gift of freely-given grace, but everything is according to the endowment and property of nature.

As we have said, it is clear that it is the common property of two persons alone to exist not from themselves but to proceed from another.[461] From this it appears that it remains to investigate whether both persons have an identical mode of proceeding or rather two different modes of proceeding. The matter is sufficiently limited but very profound and most worthy of a careful investigation. Nevertheless, I think that an argument shines forth brilliantly from our previous discussions that can be very effective in the explanation of this perplexing problem. But because according to the Apostle the *invisible things* of God, *are seen, having been understood by those things which are made,*[462] where something profound about the divine persons is sought, we rightly return to that nature where the image of God, painted by the work of God, appears. Everyone knows that man was made in the image and likeness of God;[463] and although the principle of dissimilitude is incomparably more copious than the principle of similitude, yet there is some or rather much similitude between human nature and divine nature.[464] And so, as I believe, we can look in this mirror of the divine image, or rather we can distinguish according to the judgment of a reasoning mind what we must approve in the mirror on the basis of the principle of similitude, or what we must reject in it on the basis of the principle of dissimilitude.

And so, in the case of human persons, we find that the production of a person from a person is not everywhere uniform.[465] If we return to the origin of our propagation, we see in the case of the first man that the production of his wife and the production of his children were very different and very diverse. The production of his wife was beyond nature; the production of his children was according to nature. The production of his wife was according to the operation of creative grace alone; the production of his children was according to the operation of nature.[466] But in the case of divine nature nothing is, or can be, from the operation of grace.[467] After all what derives only from the operation of grace can exist or not exist by virtue of the goodwill of the author.[468] But there cannot be any such thing in the deity; otherwise, there would be mutability in God, and he would not have true eternity.[469] There is nothing then in God according to the gift of freely-given grace, but everything is according to the property of a necessary nature. Indeed, just as it is natural for the Unbegotten not to proceed from another, so clearly it is natural for him to have one who proceeds from himself.

CHAPTER TWO. The relationship between a father and child seems to exist entirely between the Unbegotten and the person proceeding directly from him.

We ought to examine carefully the natural order of procession in humanity and, with all acuteness, search for what the divine reality has in likeness to it. After finding and understanding it, according to the practice of the theological discipline we ought to transfer the terms of the proprieties from the human to the divine according to the principle of similitude.[470]

And so, we see in human nature, as we have already discussed above, that the production or procession of a person from another person is either only immediate, only mediate, or both mediate and immediate at the same time.[471] Immediate procession is the production of a child from either parent without any intermediate person. Mediate procession is the production that we see only in a grandson of some person, and this only occurs through the intermediacy of his son. Moreover, there is both mediate and immediate procession in the situation when one and the same person is the son and grandson of someone.[472] In human nature mediate procession is various and manifold which absolutely cannot exist in the divine nature. But the degrees and names of the relationship are varied and multiplied in human nature according to the different order of procession and different mode of affinity. Indeed, the relationship that a man has with his son is different from the relationship that a man has with his grandson. One can also understand other relationships according to what I said about these relationships. But the relationship between the parent and child holds the primary and principal[473] place among such a great multitude of relationships. Indeed, if this relationship had not preceded the other relationships in human nature, then absolutely none of the other relationships would have existed. Even if absolutely none of the other relationships were to exist, then, without a doubt, the principal relationship would have still existed nonetheless. Moreover, where it happens that one and the same man has many children, certainly they are all called his children for one and the same reason. And if it happens that one and the same man is a grandson and son of the same person, then he is certainly called a grandson and son, yet not for the same reason but for a very different reason.

One must note, moreover, that Eve was immediately produced from the substance of Adam, yet, as we have already said above, not according to the operation of nature.[474] And this is why she is not called Adam's child, nor is Adam called her parent. But when the person of someone is produced from the substance of another person, and produced, I say, by the principal order of procession and according to the operation of nature, then without a doubt we are accustomed to call the one person a parent and the other person a child.

And so, because according to the example of divine Scripture we are accustomed to transfer the terms of human relationship to the divine reality on the basis of the principle of similitude, we can properly say that the relationship that is between the parent and child is between the Unbegotten and the person proceeding directly from him. Indeed, that procession of one person from another person is entirely immediate, and it is according to the principal order of procession and according to the operation of nature.[475] Because this is clear enough from the previous discussions, there is no need for further explanation.

CHAPTER THREE. There is a diverse mode in begetting offspring according to the diversity of nature.

I do not think that anyone can call into question the fact that there is a diverse mode in producing a child according to the diversity of nature. But if we desire to know what the singular mode of procession is in the supereminent and superexcellent nature of deity, then let us think about the goodness, wisdom, and power of the Unbegotten, and perhaps we will discover what we seek more quickly. Certainly he who possesses supremely wise goodness can desire absolutely nothing, especially with regard to the divine reality, unless on account of a reason that is, so to speak, intimate and supreme. And if it is truly clear that he is omnipotent, then whatever he desires to exist in the divinity will exist by virtue of his will. If solely by his willing he cannot obtain what he desires, then how, I ask, can he truly be called omnipotent? And so, to produce from himself a consubstantial and equal person will be for him to will it immutably on account of a necessary reason. Without a doubt to produce a son will be for him to have complete pleasure in his son.[476]

CHAPTER FOUR. Conventional language has properly maintained that one of the two persons in the Trinity is called Father, and the other is called Son.

One ought to note that there are two sexes in human nature, and, for that reason, the terms of relationship are varied according to differences in gender. We call the parent in one gender "father" and in the other gender "mother." We call the child in one gender "son" and in the other gender "daughter." However, as all of us together know, there is absolutely no gender in the divine nature. It was appropriate for the terms of relationship to be transferred from that gender that is known to be more worthy[477] to that being who is the most worthy of all. Therefore, you see how conventional language has properly maintained that one of the two persons in the Trinity is called "Father," and the other is called "Son."

But in this investigation let us not leave a question unanswered that rightly ought to disturb a feeble listener. Let us examine further with a more careful consideration our same discussion of the transference of terms. Perhaps someone will wonder why certain terms are transferred to the divine from where the principle of similitude is incompatible and not rather from where the comparison of relations is partially compatible. Indeed, human nature does not allow for a son to proceed from his father alone according to the operation of nature. Only one man in the human race proceeded from his mother alone without a father in the flesh, and this was still not without the operation of nature.[478] If therefore it is not appropriate to transfer the terms of relationship to the divine reality from where some principle of similitude alludes to it, then how fitting will it be to transfer it when no proportionate congruence suggests itself?

And so, one ought to note above all that if in the deity he who proceeds from one alone is correctly called the Son, and if he from whom alone the Son draws his origin is correctly called the Father, then we are reminded by these terms that a principal relationship undoubtedly exists in the divinity in a manner that absolutely cannot exist here in our nature. From these terms, I say, our carnal mind is compelled not to understand anything carnal about the divine generation, but to as-

cend with our heart toward a higher understanding, and not to conclude rashly anything according to human measure about the mystery
of such great profundity.[479]

CHAPTER FIVE. How we maintain with a firm and clear argument the
reason for calling the one person "Father" and the second person "Son."

But if we return to the above conclusion that we have already deduced with an indubitable reason, then we will be able to ascertain a
satisfactory solution for explaining this perplexing issue. We have
sought and found that for the Unbegotten to produce an offspring from
himself is to will this very thing in virtue of a necessary reason.[480]
Without a doubt, if Adam, the first man, possessed the natural ability
to produce at will and from himself alone an offspring who was consubstantial with him and equal in every way, then they would be united
no less by a principal relationship, and they would rightly be called by
the same terms of relationship: the first would be called "father" and
the second "son." After all, if they were entirely alike, then they would
not differ in sex. You certainly see how a clear reason appears from this
consideration and plainly shows how appropriate it is for one of the
two in the Trinity of persons to be called Father in relation to the second person, and the second person to be called Son in relation to the
one and same Father.[481]

See how in the profundity of such great mystery neither dissimilitude without similitude nor similitude without dissimilitude is apparent in the reflection of divine similitude and the consideration of our
infirmity. It is no doubt the part of dissimilitude that, with respect to
our nature, a son cannot proceed from a father alone; but it is the part
of similitude that if this production had been able to exist and if it were
to happen, then the same terms of relationship would be applicable to
each person in a similar relationship. Behold now, as I believe, we
maintain with a firm and clear argument the reason for calling the one
person Father and the second person Son: the Father is from no one
and his Son is from the Father alone.[482]

CHAPTER SIX. Because the procession from the Father is common to
the other two persons, what is the difference between their two
processions?

We now know what the relationship of the first person is to the
second person. It still remains to investigate what we ought to know

about the relationship of the first two persons to the third. Perhaps someone will think that the third person, who proceeds immediately from the first two persons, can be called the son of both. But if he is the son of the Son, then will the Unbegotten not be his father and grandfather, and will he not be a grandson and son of the Unbegotten? The more mysterious these questions which are not yet investigated and ascertained with a rational explanation, the more they should be pondered with a very careful investigation.

Now this is already very certain: the procession from the Unbegotten is common to the other two persons. And so, one must investigate above all what sort of difference there is between their two processions according to the intention of the one who produces. Indeed, even though both persons proceed from the paternal will, there can still be a different reason for the two processions.

But if we keep in mind what we have previously ascertained with reasoning, then perhaps it is not necessary for us to labor long and hard on this question. There clear reason openly discovered that the Unbegotten desired to have a person equal in dignity (*condignum*), and it was necessary for him to have this person according to his will, so that there would be someone both to whom he would bestow supreme love, and who would requite the supreme love to him.[483] And not only did he desire to have a person equal in dignity, but he also desired to have a third person who is loved equally by both (*condilectum*). It was necessary for him to have this third person according to his will, so that he would have a partaker of his love, lest perhaps he would reserve exclusively to himself what he had been able to share.[484] And so, he desired to have a person equal in dignity, so that there would be someone to whom he would communicate the richness of his magnitude; but he desired to have a third person who is loved equally by both, so that he would have someone to whom he would communicate the pleasures of charity. The communion of majesty was, so to speak, the original cause of one person; and the communion of love seems, as it were, to be a certain original cause of another person. And so, even though the production of both persons proceeds, as we have said, from the paternal will, there are still distinct reasons and different causes for this double production or procession.

CHAPTER SEVEN. The Unbegotten does not have the same relationship with one person as he does with the other person.

There is a huge difference in every respect between willing to have a person equal in dignity (*condigum*) and willing to have another person who is loved equally by both (*condilectum*). But let us see now which of these wills is first and which of these wills is second. Now we want it to be understood that first and second in this context are not according to temporal succession but according to the order of nature. What is the will to have a second person equal in dignity, unless the will to have someone whom the Unbegotten loves intimately and rightly must love with a love worthy of coequality? But what is the will to have a third person who is loved equally by both, if not to will to have one who is loved equally with oneself by one's own lover and delights with oneself in the pleasures of the love shown to oneself? The first will can consist only in a duality of persons, but the second will absolutely cannot subsist without a trinity of persons. But with respect to the order of nature duality comes before trinity. After all a duality cannot be lacking where there is a trinity; but there can be a duality even where a trinity happens to be lacking.[485] It is clear then that the Unbegotten naturally has his beloved (*dilectum*) before he has the person who is loved equally by both (*condilectum*). Therefore, with respect to the order of nature the procession that has the more principal cause of procession is the more principal procession.[486]

Moreover, we know that the order of relationship will undoubtedly correspond to the order of procession. Certainly the relationship that a man has with his son holds first place in human nature; the relationship that a man has with his grandson holds second place; and the relationship that a man has with his great-grandson holds third place; and after this we may ascertain the same conclusion in subsequent relationships. But what brings about these different grades of relationship in this nature of ours, unless a different mode of procession in different people? After all, there is no difference in a relationship without a multiformity of processions in several individuals. In fact, it happens that one and the same man has several children, but he has a single relationship with all of them on account of the same mode of procession.

And thus the nature of relationship is undoubtedly varied according to a similar or dissimilar mode of procession. But it is already known more clearly than day that each of the two persons proceeds from the Father. Yet the mode of procession in one person is different from the mode of procession in the other person. Therefore, it is necessary that the Unbegotten does not have the same relationship with one person as he does with the other person.

CHAPTER EIGHT. The person who proceeds from the Father and the Son cannot rightly be called their son.

More principal is the procession of the one in the manner of nature who is known to proceed only from the Unbegotten. There is a principal relationship where a principal procession occurs; and the relationship between father and son occupies the principal place. Therefore, as we have already discussed previously, he who is proven to proceed directly from the Unbegotten is rightly called his Son. But if, as we have already demonstrated, the Unbegotten does not have the same relationship with one person as he does with the other person,[487] and if one of these persons is correctly called his Son, then the other person cannot be called his son. Indeed, what does it mean for one person to be the Son of another other than to be united to him by a principal relationship? But, as we have demonstrated, the person, who is the third person in the Trinity, is not united to the Unbegotten by a principal relationship; hence, he cannot rightly be called his son.[488]

But, just as we have sufficiently demonstrated in the previous discussions, we know that the third person in the Trinity proceeds from the other two persons.[489] If then he is not the son of one person, then he will not be the son of the other person. For he proceeds both from the Father and the Son in absolutely one and the same mode; indeed in both persons there is absolutely one and the same reason for the procession. But because this is sufficiently clear from the previous discussions, it is not necessary to repeat the same information.

But if the third person is not the son of the Son, then the Father of the Son will not be his grandfather, nor will he be his grandson. But no intermediate relationship occurs in human nature between the relationship that a father has with his son and the relationship that he has with his grandson.

Therefore, I ask, what kind of relationship will the Father and the Son have with him who is the third person in the Trinity? Certainly every immediate procession of a person from a person is a principal procession in human nature; however, as it is most evident already, the principal procession occurs differently in the divine nature. You find in the divine nature one person who is immediate and principal, but you find another person who is immediate and yet not principal. And so, because there is absolutely no person in human nature who is immediate and not principal, a word for such a relationship cannot be transferred from human nature to the divine nature. You certainly see that the poverty of our ordinary language is entirely insufficient for describing the relationship of the Father and the Son with the person who proceeds from both.

CHAPTER NINE. Why the one who proceeds from the Father and the Son is called the Spirit of God.

And so, a word for relationship could not be adapted to the third person from our conventional usage. But the fact that he is called the "Spirit of God" or the "Holy Spirit" in the divine Scriptures was not totally contrary to the principle of similitude. The word "breath" (*spiritus*) indicates that which proceeds from human beings and without which they absolutely do not have life. If one asserts that the person, about whom we are discussing, is called the Spirit of God (*Spiritus Dei*) based on such similitude, then perhaps someone will find this word play very strange with reference to him. For it is clear that the breath, which proceeds from humans, is not consubstantial with humans themselves. But the Spirit of God is certainly consubstantial and wholly equal in every way to the one from whom he proceeds.[490] Yet, what wonder is it if he, who was called the Finger of God in the divine Scriptures, is called the Breath of the Father and the Son on account of the principle of similitude?[491] The name "Finger of God" indicates no inequality in him, but it refers to some similitude of his own property. We naturally extend our finger when we desire to direct the eyes of someone to something. And so, when God reveals to someone the internal secrets of his wisdom through the illumination of his Spirit, what is this other than that God points with his own finger to what he desires to be seen? After all, the Father and the Son—one and the same God in every respect—teach us all things through the inspiration of his Spirit.[492] Did the Teacher of Truth not teach us that the Holy Spirit is the divine breath as through a similitude, when, appearing to his disciples, he breathed on them and said: *Receive the Holy Spirit*?[493] Just as we have discussed previously, the breath (*spiritus*) proceeds from humans and without it they absolutely do not have life. And so, the eternal procession from him who is eternal is indicated in the fact that the Holy Spirit is called the Spirit of God (*Spiritus Dei*); or rather, in the fact that the eternal procession from God belongs to the Holy Spirit. In this very fact, I say, we are given to understand that he is consubstantial with God, because a being that is not God cannot proceed from God and have eternity.

We will explain more fully in the following sections how the names Breath, Breathing, or Spirit of God indicates some individual property of him.

CHAPTER TEN. Why the one who proceeds from the two is called the Holy Spirit.

As we have said, he who proceeds from two persons is called the Holy Spirit—a fact not devoid of great mystery, and one that invites us to a deeper understanding. The Father is a spirit, and the Son is a spirit, just as we have learned from the Gospel: *God is Spirit*;[494] similarly, the Father is holy, and the Son is undoubtedly holy: both expressions can truly designate both persons. Therefore, given that these terms are appropriate to both persons for the same reason, how is it that the third person alone receives these terms as his proper name?[495]

But the appropriation of such a designation absolutely does not seem to be contrary to the reason for describing any property.[496] But if the breath (*spiritus*), which proceeds from a human body and is corporeal, has some resemblance to the divine property, then wouldn't that breath (*spiritus*), which proceeds from the human spirit (*spiritu*) and is spiritual, have a much greater resemblance to the divine property? Indeed, what sort of breath is it, which blows more gently from the human heart in some people and more vehemently in others, and which burns more tepidly in some people and more ardently in other, except the intimate affection of the mind and impulse of a burning love? This is the reason why certain people are said to have one spirit (*spiritum*) and to walk in one spirit: there is one intention and the same purpose in them, and they love the same, desire the same, and long for the same thing with equal desire. But this spiritual breath (*spiritus*) is truly holy and can truly be called holy only when it is animated by piety and moved according to truth. Without this breath (*spiritu*), none of the spirits (*spirituum*) are holy, neither human nor angelic spirits. Indeed, the human spirit undoubtedly begins to be holy only when it loves what pertains to piety and hates and detests what pertains to impiety. Certainly this affection of piety, this breath (*spiritus*), when it blows from the hearts of many, causes many to be *one heart and one mind*.[497]

And so, with respect to the similitude of such a breath (*spiritus*) that proceeds and blows from the hearts of many, the one who proceeds from two in the Trinity of persons is called the Holy Spirit. Who else, except one prompted by complete insanity, can doubt that there is truly the same affection of piety and one and the same love in the Father and Son? Thus, this love that is common to both persons is called the Holy Spirit. He is the one who is inspired into the hearts of the saints by the Father and Son.[498] He is the one who sanctifies men, so they may merit sainthood. Just as the human spirit is the life of the body, so that divine Spirit is the life of spirits. The former is life endowing sensation; the latter is life which sanctifies. Rightly, therefore, he is called the Holy Spirit without whom no spirit is made holy. He possesses a name from reality; he possesses a name according to a similitude of reason.[499]

The Appropriation of other names

CHAPTER ELEVEN. Why the Son of God alone is called the Image of the Father.

The name Holy Spirit is attributed only to one person as a proper name; although, this name seems to be common to every ‹divine› person by reason of substance. We should note that there are certain terms for properties that can in no way be applied to anyone except one person alone. This is why only one person is called Father, and only one person is called Son, just as we have sufficiently demonstrated above.[500] This is also why the Son of God alone is called the Image of the Father, and he alone is called the Word. The Catholic faith confesses and many reasons affirm that "of such a nature as the Father is, so is the Son, so is the Holy Spirit."[501] Without a doubt both persons are entirely similar to the Father, and both are coequal in every respect to him. If you consider their wisdom and power, and if you reflect upon their goodness and beatitude, then you will find without any ambiguity at all that none of these qualities are greater in one person, and none of them are less in the other person.

If then the Son of God is rightly called the Image of the Father because of an explicit similitude in him, then why is the Holy Spirit not rightly called the Image of God as well, since he is similar and coequal to both? But, as I believe, we can untie the knotty point of this question more quickly, if we return to the consideration of their properties. As we have already said above, possessing all plenitude is common to every person;[502] and both possessing and giving the fullness is a property common to the Father and Son; yet, possessing and not giving it to another is the particular property of the Holy Spirit. In that common property then the Son alone possesses the explicit similitude of the

Father in himself, and he possesses the image, because just as the plenitude of divinity flows from the Father, so the bestowing of the same
plenitude flows from the Son. The Holy Spirit does not receive something less, or in a different way, from one person than from the other
person. However, absolutely no person receives the plenitude of the
divinity from the Holy Spirit, and consequently the Holy Spirit does
not express the image of the Father in himself. You know now why the
Son alone is called the Image of the Father,[503] and not also the Holy
Spirit.

But let us repeat this same discussion still more explicitly or more
crudely, so to speak, for the sake of simpler readers. According to human conventions we usually speak about the image more for the sake
of an external likeness than an internal one. We call some statue the
image of man, and we especially say this only on account of external
likeness. If you consider the interior of the statue, you will find dissimilitude rather than similitude. Thus so that we may say something
about the Trinity of persons according to a human manner of speaking,
what one person is in himself, so to speak, is intrinsic to each person,
but the relationship that each person has with another is, so to speak,
extrinsic to them. Moreover, it is known that the Son has exactly the
same relationship with the Holy Spirit that the Father has. And so,
because the Son seems to manifest the relationship of the Father in the
bestowing of his own plenitude, he alone is correctly called the Image
of the Father.[504] The Holy Spirit is not called the Image of the Father
nor of the Son, since he is not considered similar to either one in the
relationship that we are discussing. See how we are groping for the
truth by the touching on similitudes amid such a great profundity of
mysteries where we cannot see clearly.[505]

But we must not overlook the fact that perhaps he is correctly called
the Holy Spirit in order to prevent a false opinion, that is, lest it appear
that some think less worthily about his benevolence on account of his
aforementioned property.[506]

CHAPTER TWELVE. Why the Son of God alone is called the Word.

Likewise, if we seek the reason why the Son of God alone is called
the Word, then it seems that here too one ought to draw the answer out
from the consideration of properties. Let us say that a word that someone utters is usually indicative of the perception and wisdom of the one
who utters it. Rightly, therefore, the Word refers to the person through

whom the knowledge of the Father, who is *the font of wisdom*, is revealed.[507]

But perhaps you respond to this and say that the name of the Father is revealed not only through the Son but also through the Holy Spirit. After all, the Holy Spirit himself is the *Anointing* that *teaches us all things*;[508] he is the one who teaches and suggests all things to us and leads us to all truth.[509] If this is the reason why we call the Son the Word, then why do we not call the Holy Spirit the Word for the same reason?[510] Let us add then that a word originates from the heart alone, and the intention of one who speaks is manifested by a word. And so, the only Begotten of the Father alone is correctly called the Word, through whom the Father, who is the primordial wisdom, is revealed. Accordingly, then, the name Word seems to be suitable for the Son alone in virtue of the principle of similitude.

But perhaps you respond yet again that there is a difference between the word of the heart and the word of the mouth.[511] The former arises from the heart, but the latter is uttered through the mouth. The former is hidden interiorly, but knowledge of the heart is usually revealed through the latter. And neither of them possesses both of the previously mentioned properties, but one seems to possess one of the properties and the other possesses the other property. But I say that if you consider the matter more subtly, then you will find that the word that is conceived from the heart is identical to the word that is uttered with the voice. For what is a voice except the vehicle of a word, or, if it is more pleasing, a garment of a word? Surely a clothed person is not someone different than when he was not clothed? Is it not the case, I ask, that you had not been able to utter a word, which you utter with your mouth, unless you would have first possessed it in your heart through thinking? And when a spoken word has been understood by a listener, is it not the case that the same word that was first in your heart begins to exist in his heart? But if he had an ear for the speech of the heart, just like he has for the speech of the mouth, then he absolutely would not have a need for someone to speak to him externally. From these arguments, as I believe, you clearly understand that the word of the mouth is identical to the word of the heart, but a word is without a voice in the heart, and it is with a voice in the mouth. Without a doubt, one and the same truth is conceived by the heart, uttered by a word, and learned by a listener. A word possesses its origin from the heart alone, but hearing has its origin from both the word and the heart.[512] Therefore, because the word proceeds from the heart alone, and because sagacity of the heart becomes known through it, the Son of God is likewise correctly called the Word of the Father through whom the paternal glory is revealed.[513]

The conception of all truth is in the Father, the articulation of all truth is in his Word, and the hearing of all truth is in the Holy Spirit, according to what we read in the Gospel about the Holy Spirit: *For he will not speak from himself, but he will speak whatever he will hear.*[514] And so, the Father who is not from another cannot be called Word, nor can the Holy Spirit who is not from one alone, but only the Son is called the Word who is from one alone and from whom the revelation of all truth emanates. You know about this Word in the Psalm: *My heart emits a good Word.*[515] In this Word the Father speaks to the Holy Spirit, and in this Word he speaks to the created spirit, the angelic and human spirit. But according to our previous discussion speech is either internal or external. Internal speech is what the Holy Spirit alone understands, and external to it is the speech that a created spirit understands. And, just as the internal speech in us occurs without the cooperation of human breath, but the external speech never occurs without its cooperation, so the internal speech in the supereminent nature is delivered by the Father alone, the originator. Indeed, the Father alone speaks, and the Holy Spirit alone listens. But external speech is delivered by the originator and also the divine breath, that is, the Holy Spirit. This is why the same Spirit is sometimes called Breathing, sometimes Breath, and sometimes the Spirit of God, through whom the Word of God is inspired in angelic spirits and human spirits.

You now understand what we proposed above to discuss: Why only one person in the Trinity was called the Spirit of God? You know no less why only the Son was called the Word of God.[516]

CHAPTER THIRTEEN. According to which mode of glorification the Son alone glorifies his Father, for which reason also he is correctly called the Word.

Behold while we are laboring to answer one question, we have incidentally run into another question. We said that the Son of God is called the Word, because he proclaims the paternal glory and reveals the nature and magnitude of this glory through himself. But as it is certainly the case that the Son glorifies his Father,[517] it is not also the case that the Father also *glorifies his own Son* with his revelation,[518] as indicated by what the Son said to Peter: *You are blessed, Simon son of John, because flesh and blood did not reveal this to you, but my Father who is in heaven?*[519] But notice whether perhaps the Son glorifies his Father according to a certain mode of glorification, yet the Father does not glorify his Son according to this same mode. The Son is indeed from his Father, but the Father is not from his Son. The Son reveals the magnitude of the glory of the Father's property, who desired and was able to have a Son so excellent and equal to himself in every respect.[520] How great an act of kindness, sweetness, and benevolence was it that the Father reserved nothing for himself alone from the riches of his magnitude and desired to possess nothing that he did not communicate to him![521] Behold, you have here a certain unique mode of glorifying according to which the Son glorifies his Father.

But perhaps you object to this and say that the Holy Spirit also glorifies the Father through the same mode of glorifying. After all, just as the Father wanted the Son to co-exist with himself, so that he might have someone to whom he would communicate the riches of his magnitude, so also he wanted to unite the Holy Spirit to himself, so that there might be someone to whom he would communicate the delights of his charity. Both the Son and the Spirit proclaim the paternal glory, and the paternal property is revealed in both persons. But note that the Father does not share the glorification of his paternal property, which he has in the Son, with someone else, because "the Son is from the Father alone."[522] Moreover, that glorification that shines in the Holy Spirit is not a declaration of paternity, nor does it belong to the Father alone, but the Father shares it with his own Son. After all, the Holy Spirit is not from the Father alone, but he proceeds absolutely in the same way both from the Father and the Son. Therefore, the Word or Tongue of the Father rightly refers to the Son, in whom alone the glory of the paternity is revealed according to the aforementioned mode.

CHAPTER FOURTEEN. Why the Holy Spirit is called the Gift of God; and why and how the Spirit has to be sent or be given.

Why the Holy Spirit is called the Gift of God seems to be a question worthy of careful consideration.[523] Just as we have demonstrated with a clear explanation in the previous discussions, the fullness of a gratuitous love is in the Father, the fullness of an owed love is in the Holy Spirit, and the fullness of a love both owed and gratuitous is in the Son.

Moreover, I carefully and sufficiently discussed in a previous context how all these properties must be understood.[524] To be sure, in the supremely simple nature where there cannot be any composition, there is absolutely no differentiation between the Holy Spirit and his love. And so, what is the gift or infusion of the Holy Spirit, except the infusion of an owed love? Therefore, the Holy Spirit is divinely given to humans at the moment when the owed love of the deity is inspired into a human mind.[525] Indeed, when this Holy Spirit enters a rational spirit, he ignites its affection with the divine flame and transforms it into the similitude of his property, so that it may present to its Author the love which it owes.

What is the Holy Spirit except the divine fire?[526] All love is a fire, but a spiritual fire. What a corporeal fire does for iron, the fire, about which we are speaking, does the same for an impure, cold, and hardened heart.[527] In consequence of the infusion of such a fire, the human mind gradually removes all blackness, coldness, and hardness; and the whole mind changes into the similitude of him who inflames it. The whole mind becomes white-hot from the igniting of the divine fire; it flares up and, at the same time, liquefies in the love of God, according to the Apostle: *The love of God was poured into our hearts through the Holy Spirit, who was given to us.*[528]

But why, I ask, does the Apostle say *through the Holy Spirit* rather than through the Father or Son? But we know that the Father does not have an originator or giver; hence, he can only have a gratuitous love. But, as we have said previously, the Son has both a gratuitous and owed love.[529] And so, in the divine love we cannot be conformed to the property of the Son or the property of the Father, because we are not able to have both loves together, or even a gratuitous love alone, toward God.[530] For how, I ask, can a creature love gratuitously his Creator, from whom it has all that it has? And so, we are certainly conformed to the property of the Holy Spirit to the same extent that we return an owed love to our Creator. In fact, the Holy Spirit was given to humans and inspired in them for this reason: that they may be conformed to him insofar as it is possible for them. This gift is sent, or this mission is given, at the same time and in the same way both from the Father and from the Son. For the Holy Spirit has all that he has from both the Father and Son. If then he has being, power, and will from both the Father and Son, then they are rightly said to send or give him, who received from them the power and desire to come and be present in us.[531]

CHAPTER FIFTEEN. Why, through a special kind of attribution, is power attributed to the Unbegotten, wisdom to the Begotten, and goodness to the Holy Spirit?

It is appropriate for me to repeat at this time what I remember writing elsewhere:[532] why, through a special kind of attribution, power is attributed to the Unbegotten, wisdom to the Begotten, and goodness to the Holy Spirit?[533] We all in common know and affirm through daily experience what power, wisdom, love or goodness is. And so, unless I am mistaken, in these attributes, which are obvious and known to us, we are being instructed with respect to a notion of things that exceed the measure of human capacity. A certain form and image of the supreme Trinity is represented in these three attributes,[534] and it is placed before us as a kind of mirror,[535] so that the *invisible things* of God *are seen, having been understood through those things which are made.*[536]

And so those things that are in this trinity correspond to those which are in that Trinity, three by three: likenesses to likenesses, properties to properties, singularities to singularities. We see that multiple powers can exist even where no wisdom is or can be. Putting aside the elements or all inanimate objects, there is the power of hearing, of seeing, the power of walking, of eating, of drinking, and other such things in animate creatures and animals. But there is no wisdom in these powers, nor can wisdom naturally be in them. Therefore, as we have already said above, it is clear that multiple powers can exist where there can be no wisdom.

On the contrary, however, wisdom cannot be present where there is no power. After all, the power to be wise is undoubtedly a kind of power. And so, wisdom does not give power (*potentia*) the power to exist (*esse posse*), but power gives wisdom the power to exist. Likewise, it is clear that *Lucifer* himself *who rose in the morning* has great power and great wisdom, but he absolutely does not have a good will.[537] However, to will the good belongs to goodness; and what is goodness except a good will? And so, Lucifer himself, who is hardened in his perversity, is a witness to the fact that there can be multiple powers and, at the same time, multiple wisdom where no vestiges of goodness remain.

Conversely, however, no goodness will be present where wisdom or power is totally absent. After all, the power to will the good is a kind of power. Discerning between good and evil is a property of wisdom, and without such discernment the will does not know what it ought to choose. Therefore, in order to be able to have goodness, it is necessary for you to know how to choose the good and to be able to choose the good. Power gives the ability (*posse*), wisdom gives the know-how (*nosse*), and without them goodness does not come to be (*esse*). And so, true goodness draws its own being both from wisdom and power. In this trinity, then, power alone is not from any of the other attributes; wisdom, however, is from power alone, but goodness is from both power and wisdom.

Certainly you see how the properties of the supreme and eternal Trinity are expressed in that trinity: there is the person of the Unbegotten, who is not from any other person; there is the person of the Begotten, who is from the Unbegotten alone; and there is the person of the Holy Spirit, who is from both the Begotten and the Unbegotten. Therefore, because the property of the Unbegotten is represented in power, this property is rightly ascribed to him by a special mode of consideration. But because the property of the Begotten is represented in wisdom, this property is rightly ascribed to him according to the same mode of consideration. Likewise, because the property of the Holy Spirit is found in goodness, this property is rightly assigned to him more specifically. Behold how this trinity of attributes suggests a consideration that shows us by example how we can comprehend what we read about the divine properties.

APPROPRIATION OF UNBEGOTTEN AND BEGOTTEN

CHAPTER SIXTEEN. Why the Father is called Unbegotten, the Son is called Begotten, and the Holy Spirit is not called Unbegotten or Begotten.

Why the Father is called Unbegotten and the Son Begotten is very easily understood, and there is no need for a laborious explanation. Only the Father is from no other person, and, consequently, in no way can he be called begotten.[538] If he were begotten, then he would receive what he is from another. Therefore, he who originated from no other person rightly receives the name Unbegotten. And if he had not begotten the Son, then in no way should he have been called Father.[539] Moreover, that the Father had the Son from eternity was already clear from previous discussions.[540] And so, the Son whom the Father had from eternity was begotten from eternity, and, as it is necessary to say, he received his being from eternity.[541] Therefore, he is called Begotten, and not just Begotten but also Only-Begotten. There is only one Son in the Trinity, and the Holy Spirit does not have the same relationship with the Father or Son that the Father has with the Son. In human nature where a person is born from a person, one person is called father and the other son. Rightly, therefore, the Holy Spirit is not called begotten, lest it is supposed that he, who is not a son, is a son; yet neither is he called unbegotten, lest it is said that he, who is not from himself, does not possesses an origin from another source.[542]

We utilize the word "begotten" sometimes in a stricter sense and sometimes in a broader sense. Based on conventional language, we do not attribute the same word of relationship to everyone who begets or is begotten. When a human begets a human, we have become accustomed by the norms of human language to say that the former is a parent, the latter a child; the former a father, the latter a son; the former a begetter, the latter begotten. A tree is said to beget a branch, yet a tree is not called a parent, nor is the branch called its child. A branch begets a flower, yet a branch is not customarily called a father, nor is the flower customarily called a son. A worm is begotten from the fruit, yet the fruit is not called a begetter, nor is the worm called its begotten one. Behold, we call the worm begotten according to one meaning, and we do not call the worm begotten according to another meaning.

Now, generation, when taken in a broad sense, seems to be nothing other than the production of an existent from an existent according to the operation of nature. But according to this usage a production that is not according to the operation of nature cannot be called a generation. Eve was not produced from Adam according to the operation of nature, and, therefore, she is not said to have been generated. Moreover, some natural production receives the aforementioned terms of relationship, and other natural productions absolutely do not receive these terms, as we have already said.[543] And so, as we have said, the Holy Spirit is not called begotten, because his production is not of such a kind that he ought to be called a son; but neither ought he be called unbegotten, because his procession is according to the production of nature. Reasonably then, just as we have said, he is not called begotten, lest it is supposed that he, who is not a son, is a son. And no less reasonably he is not called unbegotten, lest it is denied that he has an natural origin.

CHAPTER SEVENTEEN. What does it mean that the Father begets and that the Son is born from the Father; and what does it mean to proceed from generation and to proceed without generation.

Insofar as it pertains to human nature, to produce from oneself a being consubstantial with oneself appears to be identical to the produc-

tion of a child or the generation of a son. But if one pays careful attention, he discovers that it is very different in the divine nature. Indeed,
the Father produces from himself both the Son and the Holy Spirit, and
both are consubstantial with him; yet both cannot be called his son,
because the production of both persons is not uniform. If both productions were uniform, then one production would not be more principal
than the other according to the order of nature; however, a previous
examination found that one production is more principal than the
other.[544]

Moreover, we know that a different mode of procession corresponds
to the different grades of relationship in the propagation of human
persons, as we have already discussed above.[545] A son proceeds from
his father, a grandson from his grandfather, and a great-grandson from
his great-grandfather—these are different modes of procession. Indeed
what I say about these relationships can be seen also in subsequent
relationships. Moreover, among all the modes of proceeding, it is clear
that the mode of proceeding that is of the son from the father clearly
holds first place and is more principal than the other relationships.
After all, where the principal relationship does not first exist, the other
relationships will not be able to exist at all.

Moreover, when these words "father" and "son" are transferred from
the human to the divine reality, it is certainly clear that this happens
on account of similitude, according to what the Apostle said: *invisible
things* of God *are seen, having been understood through those things
which are made.*[546] Therefore, according to the principle of the proposed similitude, when one says that God begets God, and God the
Father produces God the Son, what else does this mean; what else, I
say, does this necessarily mean other than the Father, who produces
another, produces from himself a person proceeding according to the
principal mode of procession? We believe and have concluded with the
testimony of reason that the Father begets, and, consequently, the Son
is born from the Father. We believe that the procession of the Son is
from generation and that the procession of the Holy Spirit is without
generation.[547] If you ask what it means that God begets a divine person,
then this means that God produces from himself a person conformed
and consubstantial to himself according to the principal mode of procession. If you ask what it means that the Son is born from the Father,
then this means that the Son proceeds from the Father according to
the principal mode of procession. It seems that the procession from
generation is identical to having the principal mode of procession in

the procession. It also seems that the procession without generation is identical to absolutely not having the principal mode of procession in the procession.[548]

It is above all necessary for someone to understand generation, birth, and procession in a manner both worthy of a dignity of such great excellence and proper for the supereminent nature. If therefore you ask what the mode of procession is, then it is that which we have already discussed. With respect to the producer who is himself omnipotent, producing another person from himself will be identical to willing the very same from the most ordered cause.[549] Moreover, willing it from the more principal cause will be identical to generating it. For, although both modes of proceeding pertain to the will, yet they are different on account of the otherness of cause;[550] hence, the more principal mode of procession pertains to the more principal cause.

Do you want to hear an abbreviated account of this topic, which we have already discussed more diffusely? It seems to me that for the Unbegotten willing to have from himself a being conformed and equal in dignity to himself is identical to begetting a Son; it also seems that for the Begotten and the Unbegotten willing to have a third person who is equally loved by them (*condilectum*) is identical to producing the Holy Spirit.[551] A communion of dignity is noted in the first, and a communion of love is noted in second. But when we speak of a conformed person, seek carefully, diligent reader, whether perhaps this term is able or ought to refer to a conformity in which only the Son bears the image of the Father on account of a conformity of properties.

CHAPTER EIGHTEEN. Likewise, what it means for the Father to beget the Son is proven with a different reason.

Just as we already noted above,[552] the poverty of human language compels us often to vary the meaning of words. This is the reason why, as we have already said, that we sometimes broaden the meaning of generation, and sometimes restrict it.[553] We say the same thing about the procession as we have said about the generation. For, when we say "to proceed," we are by no means accustomed to understand the meaning uniformly. As far as the general meaning is concerned, "to be begotten" appears to be identical to saying that an existing being is produced from an existing being according to a natural operation. According to this meaning, only the Father is called Unbegotten in the Trinity, and the Holy Spirit is said not to be unbegotten.

Moreover, the production of an existing being from an existing being is undoubtedly found to be different with reference to different
natures. In comparison with every other mode of production according
to the dignity of nature, the principal mode of production appears to
be a production which is moved according to a natural appetite that
cannot be present in inanimate objects. Hence, only the one who begets
is called a begetter or father and the one who is begotten is called begotten or son. Based on this consideration we can say that the natural
production of an animate being from an animate being in the conformity of substance appears to be identical to begetting a child from a
parent. However, not every production of an animate being from an
animate being according to the operation of nature can agree with this
definition. For when a worm is born from a human, who can say that
the worm is the child of the human or the human is the parent of the
worm?

Moreover, one ought to know that if humans had not sinned, and
if they had preserved the integrity of their nature, then they would have
been motivated to produce a child according to rational consent rather
than animal appetite.[554] And so, in the production of their race, humans
would have had a willed rather than an appetitive production of children in conformity to their image. If then humans had preserved the
integrity of the primordial purity, then they would have drawn closer
to the principle of divine similitude in such a production.

But in order that we may return to that question on account of
which we inserted these remarks, with respect to God ‹the Father›,
begetting a Son is identical to naturally producing at will a person from
his own person according to a singular conformity of his property.
Possessing the fullness of divinity is common to all persons in the Trinity. But possessing the fullness of divinity and not giving it is the particular property of the Holy Spirit. However, both possessing and giving
the fullness of divinity is common to the Father and the Son.

It is right indeed that one ought to be called his Son in whom the
Father intimately stamped and clearly expressed the figure of his property and the form of his image. Because of this expression of conformity, only the Son is called the image of the Father; because of this,
only the Son is rightly called the *figure of* his *substance*.[555] Therefore,
the Holy Spirit should not be called his son, since, in producing the
Holy Spirit, the Father did not stamp, so to speak, the figure of his image into him, although he did proceed naturally from the Father. Thus,
conventional language usually does not apply the word "child" to the

one person nor the word "parent" to the other person in every situation where one existing being proceeds from another existing being according to the operation of nature.

CHAPTER NINETEEN. The Holy Spirit is not the image of the Only-Begotten, but neither should he be called the son of the Unbegotten.

But just as giving the fullness of divinity is naturally common to the Father and Son, so not possessing it from themselves is common to the Son and the Holy Spirit. If then we rightly call the Son "the Image of the Father" on account of the similitude of property that the Son has with his Father,[556] then why don't we for the same reason call the Holy Spirit the 'image of the Son,' given the similitude of property that the Spirit has with the Son? It does seem to be common to the Son and Father to produce a person from their own person in the image of their similitude. In both cases, the one proceeding from another appears to be the image of the one producing. If then the one, whom the Unbegotten produces from himself in the image of his similitude, is rightly called the Son of the Unbegotten, then why not for the same reason call the Holy Spirit, whom the Begotten produces from himself under the image of his similitude, the son of the Begotten?

But an object is usually called the image of another object, not because both objects lack the same thing, but because both have something similar. How, therefore, is it said that one person is the image of the other, because each is said not to have something? For neither has being from themselves, nor do they have anything from themselves. Otherwise, a stone is rightly called the image of man, and man is rightly called the image of a stone, because neither has from themselves what they have, nor are they able to have it from themselves. Everyone understands how frivolous this is.

But perhaps you respond to this: "Just as it is common to the Father and Son to give the fullness of the divinity, so it is common to the Son and the Holy Spirit to have received the same fullness. Why therefore is the same affinity of relationship in both cases not ascribed to both on account of the conformity of their mutual similitude?" But one ought to note that the Holy Spirit receives from both the Father and Son. But on account of this receiving the Holy Spirit cannot be called the image of the Father who receives absolutely nothing from another person, because in this respect there is more dissimilitude than similitude between the one and the other. Therefore, the Holy Spirit cannot rightly be called an image of the Father or of His Son on account of the property in which He is dissimilar to the Father. But if the Holy Spirit is not the son of the Father, then neither can He be called the son of the Son, because the relationship that He has with the Father is the same relationship that He has with the Son. And because He proceeds entirely and uniformly both from the Unbegotten and from the Only-Begotten, all that He receives from one He receives from the other in the same way. In fact, because the Holy Spirit is said to have received all plenitude, He is shown not to have it from Himself. And, as we have already said, because He is said not to have it, He is not therefore rightly said to be the image of another.[557] But where the one who proceeds is not begotten in the image and similitude of the other who produces, then the one who begets is not called father, nor is the one who is begotten called son according to our conventional language. We read that Adam is begotten *in his image and similitude.*[558] In such a generation alone conventional language usually accommodates the principal terms of relationship. And so, we conclude from our discussion that the Holy Spirit is not the image of the Only-Begotten, but neither should He be called His son.

CHAPTER TWENTY. One ought to investigate the paternal image where there is no mutual agreement without some difference, nor is there difference without mutual agreement.

Perhaps someone will think that the Son is called the image of the Father, because He is similar in every respect and absolutely equal to Him in power, wisdom, and goodness. But if we call the Son the Image of his Father on account of this consideration, then why wouldn't we call the Holy Spirit the image of both the Father and the Son for the same reason? For when ‹the Athanasian Creed› says, "of such a nature as the Father is, so is the Son," it immediately adds "so is the Holy Spirit."[559] When it first says, "the Father is omnipotent, the Son is omnipotent," it also immediately adds, "the Holy Spirit is omnipotent." It says, "the Father is God, the Son is God," where also it is added, "the Holy Spirit is God." If then the Son is called the Image of the Father on account of such similitude and equality, then why should we not think something similar about the Holy Spirit for similar reasons?

But one must definitely notice and consider with supreme diligence what is said imprecisely about the divine reality on account of our limited capacity, or what is stated more precisely. Indeed, many expressions in Holy Scripture are not exact, as if on purpose, so that they may be more easily comprehended by our limitations.[560] But often the expressions, which are not exact, are usually corrected by clearer expression. This is the reason why when ‹the Athanasian Creed› first says, "the Father is eternal, the Son is eternal, the Holy Spirit is eternal," it immediately adds as if to make the truth more explicit, "and yet there are not three eternals but one eternal." In the same way, when it says, "the Father is omnipotent, the Son is omnipotent, the Holy Spirit is omnipotent," it adds subsequently as if for correcting, "and yet there are not three omnipotents but only one omnipotent." Similarly, after saying, "the Father is God, the Son is God, the Holy Spirit is God," it immediately adds, "and yet there are not three gods but one God." Therefore, where there is simple unity and supreme simplicity, what is to be done with the expressions "of such a nature as one is" and "so is the other"? It is incorrect to say "similar to oneself" and "equal to oneself."

We can appropriately speak of identity rather than equality where true unity exists. The Father is power, the Son is power, the Holy Spirit is power; and yet Father, Son, and Holy Spirit are only one and the same power. Our assertions about the divine power can be equally applied in every respect to the divine wisdom and substance. The power or wisdom of God is nothing other than his substance. In human nature the substance of a son can appropriately be called the image of his father, because the substance of the father is different from the substance of the son. But in divine nature one and the same substance belongs to the Father, Son, and Holy Spirit. What comparison can be made where there is true unity? Similitude and dissimilitude cannot pertain to supremely simple unity. One ought to seek the paternal image where there is no mutual congruity without some difference and no difference without the greatest congruence.[561]

And so, it is necessary for us, who want to know more fully this topic about which we are discussing, to return to the consideration of properties. As we have often said above, possessing the fullness of divinity is common to every person.[562] But the property of the Father is not to have received the fullness of divinity but to give it, and the property of the Son is both to receive and to give it. And so, there is harmony in giving, but difference in receiving. But, as we have previously shown, a clear argument demonstrates how the Son bears the image of the Father in this mutual harmony.[563]

CHAPTER TWENTY-ONE. Why the Only-Begotten of God is called the figure of the divine substance.

A lofty consideration is needed, if we desire to have a more certain understanding why the Son of God, who is God, is called *the figure of his substance*.[564] When a person is called the figure of another person's substance, we can understand this, unless I am mistaken, in two ways.[565] If we resort to human reality, so that we can look through a mirror,[566] then it seems that the first meaning is the figure of a human, which forms his substance, and the second meaning is the figure of an image, which represents him. Both are still a figure, and both can be called the figure of a human. And so, where there are two substances, there can be, on the one hand, a figure which is forming, and, on the other hand, there can be a figure which is representing.[567] But the Father and the Son have one and the same substance. And so, the Son cannot be called the figure of the paternal substance in that way. But if the Son cannot be called the figure in the sense of a representing figure, then surely he cannot be called a forming figure? But if the Son were forming the Father, then, consequently, he would certainly bestow his beauty to the Father, and in this case the Son would not receive beauty from the Father, but the Father would receive it from the Son. But reason does not consent to this nor does the Catholic faith accept this.

We have learned from the testimony of Truth that *God is Spirit*.[568] And so, concerning these questions that we are investigating, let us interrogate the spiritual nature. Now your soul is a spiritual nature. Indeed your soul is either beautiful or deformed by its will. A good will makes your soul beautiful, but it becomes deformed by a bad will. Its benignity makes it beautiful; its malignity makes it deformed. From these assertions we may consider what the figure of a spiritual substance is. If the Lord grants it, the same form of perfection can undoubtedly form your soul and my soul. And so, if we seek the conformity or configuration of the Father and Son according to the similitude of will, then without a doubt and without any contradiction we will find that, just as the Father desires to have a person proceeding from himself, so that he can communicate to him the delights of a love that was bestowed to him, so also the Son desires to have and does have this in exactly the same way according to his will. Therefore, just as we have already argued regarding the image, so the configuration should be concluded from the consideration of properties, where, as we have already said, we find no mutual congruity without some difference and no difference without the greatest congruence.[569]

CHAPTER TWENTY-TWO. We should believe those truths that we accept from the holy fathers in accordance with the Catholic faith regarding the Unbegotten and Begotten substance, although, for the time being we are not able to understand through rational comprehension how they are true.

But perhaps you respond to these arguments: "Where there is no plurality, there cannot be conformity. But a plurality of substances does not exist in the true divinity, although the plurality of persons truly exists in the divinity. Why don't we say then that the Son is the figure of the paternal person rather than of the paternal substance? After all, as you have said, the Son cannot be called the figure of the paternal substance as if the Son forms the Father;[570] and if both are one and the same substance, it does not seem possible to call the figure of the paternal substance a representing figure." But one must note the following: that the Apostle called the Son *the figure of the paternal substance* can mean the same as if the Apostle called Him the figure of the unbegotten substance.[571] Nevertheless, if the Son were called the figure of the Unbegotten substance, then this would be the same as if he were called the figure of the Unbegotten person. You are undoubtedly indicating the same person, whether you say the Father, Unbegotten substance, or Unbegotten person. Without a doubt, the person of the Father is nothing other than the Unbegotten substance, and the person of the Son is nothing other than the Begotten substance.

But many rise up nowadays who do not dare say this, or rather, what is even more dangerous, who, contrary to the authority of the holy fathers and so many witnesses of the tradition of the fathers, have the audacity to deny and attempt to refute on all accounts those formulas.[572] In no way do they concede that substance begets substance, or wisdom begets wisdom.[573] They stubbornly deny what every saint affirms; they cannot find an authority to support what they say. Let them cite, if they are able, an authority; not, I say, many authorities, but at least one authority, which denies that substance begets substance! For even they cite many authorities that support what we say. Like Goliath, they are going to battle, drawing their sword which cuts their own throats.[574] They say, "But what the fathers say should be understood in this way."[575] Good! The fathers say that substance begets substance; but your explanation[576] contends that we should believe that substance does not beget substance. This is a trustworthy explanation and worthy of full acceptance[577] that contends to be false what the holy fathers affirm with one voice and contends to be true what none of the saints assert![578]

But they say: "If the substance of the Son is begotten, but the substance of the Father is unbegotten, then how will both be one and the same substance?" Without a doubt the substance of the Son is begotten, the substance of the Father is unbegotten, and unbegotten substance is not begotten nor the begotten substance unbegotten. Nevertheless, it does not follow that there are two distinct substances, but it does follow that there are two distinct persons. To be sure the situation in human nature is very different from the situation in divine nature. In human nature if the substance of one is begotten, but the substance of another is unbegotten, then it will follow without any contradiction that the substance of the one is totally different from the substance of the other. But in divine nature the substance of one is undoubtedly unbegotten, and the substance of another is begotten; nevertheless, it does not follow that the substance of one is different from the substance of the second, but it does follow that the person of one is different from the person of the second.

"I do not comprehend this," you say, "I do not understand!" But what you cannot understand through rational comprehension you can believe through the devotion of faith. Otherwise this is said to you and those similar to you: *If you do not believe, then you will not understand.*[579] Why do you not believe what, as you are aware, the universal Church confesses every day regarding Christ: "God is from the substance of the Father, begotten before time"?[580] But perhaps you do not want to believe this, because you cannot prove it with an example or understand it through rational comprehension. Surely you do not understand through rational comprehension or prove with an example that a unity of substance can exist in a plurality of persons, and that a plurality of persons can exist in a unity of substance? Surely that statement, which you stubbornly deny,[581] does not exceed human intelligence more than the statement that you truly affirm with us?[582] But if you know of an explanation for the statement that you affirm, then why don't you make it known publicly? Why do you deny your brothers the explanation? And if the explanation of both assertions eludes your understanding, then why do you believe the holy fathers in one assertion and also not believe them in the other assertion?[583] If one correctly believes them, then one believes that the person of the Father is not different from the unbegotten substance, nor is the person of the Son different from the begotten substance.

But in order to briefly mention what we think concerning the proposed question, the begotten substance bears the figure of the unbegotten substance in this way: the begotten substance produces from itself the same person whom the unbegotten substance produces, and it produces him in the same way; and the begotten substance is the cause and origin, the author and beginning of the same gift.[584] Truly the same bestowing of all plenitude flows in every respect both from the one and from the other, both from the begotten substance and the unbegotten substance.

CHAPTER TWENTY-THREE. How it can be demonstrated what the Catholic faith teaches about the Unbegotten and Begotten substance.

While we aspire to the investigation and demonstration of the sublime and invisible realities, we gladly utilize the ladder of similitude, so that those who have not yet received the wings of contemplation may have the means by which they can ascend.[585] And so, in the ‹human› nature which, as we know, was made in the divine image and similitude,[586] we draw from and search for things similar to the divine, from which we can be lifted up to the knowledge of divine realities.

Let's say there are two men. The first person discovered a science of some sort or knowledge of some art by devising them by himself, and he passed on to the second person everything that he could acquire from this and taught him fully and perfectly. What then? Is it not the case that the same knowledge and the same truth are located in both the heart of the first person and in the heart of the second person? Otherwise, he did not teach him the knowledge that he discovered. Behold one of them passed on knowledge, and the other received it. You certainly see that the knowledge of one is a knowledge received by the other, while the knowledge of the first is knowledge, so to speak, absolutely not received. Yet surely the knowledge of the first is not different from the knowledge of the second? If whatever truth is in the first person is whole and identical in the second, then the knowledge of both will undoubtedly be essentially one. Yet it is clear nonetheless that knowledge received is not knowledge not received, and knowledge not received cannot be called a knowledge received, although the knowledge not received and the knowledge received is, so to speak, essentially one.

From the speculation on these matters I believe that we can consider what is necessary for us to think concerning the divine reality. And so, by standing upon this watchtower let us see if we clearly demonstrate from those truths, which they believe with us, what some of them have not yet believed about the unbegotten and begotten substance. They believe with us that the Father has from himself all that he has. They believe with us that the Son receives from the Father all that he has from eternity. And so, it is clear that the Son receives the fullness of wisdom from the Father. They concede with us that the wisdom of the Father is not different from the wisdom of the Son, and that both the Father and the Son have one and the same wisdom in every respect. Yet it is no less clear that the Son's wisdom is received, and the Father's wisdom is not received.[587] It is equally clear that wisdom not received is not wisdom received, and wisdom received is not wisdom not received, although wisdom received and wisdom not received is without a doubt essentially one. Who is so simple or obtuse that he denies to the divine knowledge what he sees possible in human knowledge?

But in order to pursue this speculation still more carefully, we all together know that the Son has his being from the Father by means of the generation of the Father. If the Son has his being by means of generation, then he also has his wisdom by means of generation, because being and wisdom are the same for the Son. And so, the Son receives essence from the same source that he receives wisdom.[588] But because he receives his being by means of generation, it is clear that he is begotten. It is clear that the Son's wisdom, or rather the Son, is wisdom begotten from the Father. The assertion that the Father gave wisdom to the Son, or that the Son received it from the Father, is no different from the assertion that the Father has begotten the Son who is wisdom. Indeed the Father gives to the Son by begetting him, and the Father begets the Son by giving to him. Rightly, therefore, it is said that the Son is the begotten wisdom, just as it is said that the Father is the unbegotten wisdom.[589] But one absolutely does not know anything that the other does not also know in the same measure. And so, both have one and the same wisdom, although the unbegotten wisdom is not the begotten wisdom, and the begotten wisdom is not the unbegotten wisdom. And if the Son is the begotten wisdom, then, consequently, he is also the begotten substance. After all, the Son's wisdom is the same as the Son's substance. And so, what is said about the begotten and unbegotten wisdom must be granted by the same logical conclusion for the begotten and unbegotten substance.[590]

And so, it is in vain that some fear to say that substance begets substance, that wisdom begets wisdom, and that the Father is unbegotten substance, and the Son is begotten substance, as if it can be proven from these assertions that the Unbegotten and Begotten are two different substances. Indeed, just as we have already discussed above, from the fact that the Father is an unbegotten substance and the Son is a begotten substance, it does not follow that there are two distinct substances, but it does follow that there are two distinct persons.[591]

CHAPTER TWENTY-FOUR. From what consideration we can conclude that two persons can be without two substances.

But so that our previous assertions about a duality of persons without duality of substances may shine forth more clearly,[592] let us pursue still more carefully the example given above. We have taught above that there can be one and the same knowledge in two persons, if the one person fully taught the second person the knowledge of some art that he first apprehended. And so, if the word "instruction" is taken in a passive or active sense, so that it is called both the instruction of him who teaches and the instruction of him who is taught, and certainly if we accept this word "instruction" in these two ways, then the instruction of the one person will undoubtedly be different from the instruction of the other person. Just as knowledge derives from 'to know', so instruction derives from 'to instruct'. The knowing is the same for both persons, but the instructing is not the same for both. One person instructs, and the other person is instructed; one person teaches, and the other person is taught. And so, instruction that instructs pertains to one person, but instruction that learns pertains to another person. Therefore, the instruction of one person is different from the instruction of the other person. In this way then you can say that that your instruction is different from my instruction, although there is one and the same knowledge in both cases, both in learning and in instructing. And if, with respect to both of us, one's own substance were the same as one's own knowledge, then one substance would be able to exist in both of us, just as one knowledge would be able to exist in both of us. And if, with respect to both of us, one's own person were the same as one's own instruction, then one person, as one instruction, would belong to one of us, and the other person, as the other instruction, would belong to the other.

If my knowledge derives its origin from your knowledge, then wouldn't one knowledge be begotten from another knowledge in its own certain way? If knowledge is begotten from knowledge in human nature, then why is it not all the more correct to say that wisdom begets wisdom in the divine nature, where it is absolutely proven that wisdom is identical to substance? Just as knowledge that instructs and knowledge that was instructed is one and the same knowledge in human nature, but nevertheless there are two distinct instructions, so also wisdom that begets and wisdom that was begotten is one and the same wisdom in the divine nature; and, consequently, there is one and the same substance, nevertheless there are two distinct persons. With respect to human nature, from the fact that knowledge of one person is knowledge received and knowledge of a second person is knowledge not received, and knowledge received is not knowledge not received, it does not follow at all that the knowledge in them is two distinct things, but it does follow that there are two distinct instructions in them. In the same way, with respect to divine nature, from the fact that the substance of one person is begotten and the substance of a second person is unbegotten, and begotten substance is not unbegotten substance, in no way does it follow that there are two distinct substances, but it does follow that there are two distinct persons.

CHAPTER TWENTY-FIVE. From what consideration and by way of example there is corroborated what the Catholic faith believes about the Trinity and unity.

We have said that the Father is unbegotten substance and that the Son is begotten substance.[593] We must also say that the Holy Spirit is neither begotten nor unbegotten substance. But how we should understand this is clear from previous discussions. Although the Father alone is called unbegotten substance, the Son alone is called begotten substance, and the Holy Spirit alone is called neither begotten nor unbegotten substance, yet the Father, Son, and Holy Spirit are still one and the same substance, just as they are one and the same wisdom. After all, as we have often said, the divine substance is nothing other than the divine wisdom.[594] The previous example, somewhat more fully explained, informs us in our present discussion.

Behold, there are three persons. One of them discovered and instructed some knowledge, the second learned it from the same discoverer and wrote what he learned, and the third read and gained understanding. The first person has knowledge from himself, the second has knowledge from the first person alone, and the third has knowledge both from the first person and the second person. The third person arrives at his knowledge, because the first person found the knowledge and the second person wrote it. And so, if the same truth of understanding is whole and complete in all three persons, then surely, with respect to the essential truth, the knowledge of one person is not different from the knowledge of the other persons? In short, if he who learned by listening had learned by reading, or if he who learned by reading had learned by listening, then surely it would not follow that the knowledge in both cases is different. If therefore one and the same knowledge can exist in the three persons, then why is it not believed all the more that one and the same wisdom exists in the three persons of the divine Trinity? And yet wisdom received from one person alone is not wisdom not received from another person; and wisdom received from two persons is not wisdom either received from no one or received from one person alone. Yet, without a doubt, there is only one and the same wisdom in all three persons, and, consequently, there is only one and the same substance. However, the Father does not receive his substance, just as he does not receive his wisdom, from another person; the Son receives his substance from the Father alone; and the Holy Spirit receives his substance both from the Father and from the Son. And our assertion about wisdom can be applied in every respect to the substance, because the wisdom and substance in God do not establish two different things.

And if knowledge (*scientia*) of one who has been taught is called "learning" (*disciplina*), because he is fully learned,[595] so that learning means the same as, so to speak, full learning (*discentia*).[596] And if we make what we call "learning" (*disciplinam*) a reference to that mode of learning (*discendi*), then, according to this meaning, the learning of one who learns by devising, the learning of one who learns by listening, and the learning of one who learns by reading will all be different. Behold, according to this meaning, as you see, learning can be threefold in human nature, where there is only one and the same knowledge. Why wonder then if in the divine nature where substance is identical to wisdom; why wonder, I say, if there are three persons in God, where there is only one substance alone? Behold, how what the Catholic faith confesses about the divine unity or the Trinity is confirmed by a clear and obvious example.

Let us also consider this: if I were to have the same and entirely equal knowledge (*scientiam*) as you and a third person, then surely my knowledge and his knowledge would not be greater than your knowledge alone, nor would my knowledge and your knowledge be greater than his knowledge alone, nor would your knowledge and his knowledge be greater than my knowledge alone? In short, surely my knowledge, your knowledge, and his knowledge will not be greater than my knowledge alone, or your knowledge alone, or his knowledge alone? Who else, except one not understanding the assertion at all, says this? Thus any of the two persons in the Trinity or all three persons taken together are not something other than the person of the Unbegotten alone, or the person of the Only-Begotten alone, or the person of Holy Spirit alone.[597]

In the end of our work, we want to repeat and commend to memory the following: as we have shown with sufficient evidence in the previous discussions, it was easily proven from the consideration of omnipotence that there is and can only be one God; it was easily proven from the fullness of goodness that God is triune in person; and it was clearly concluded from the fullness of wisdom how the unity of substance is consistent with the plurality of persons.

Here ends Richard, *On the Trinity*.

NOTES

PROLOGUE (pp. 209-212)

1   Rom 1:17; Hab 2:4; Heb 10:38.

2   See Hugh of St Victor, *Sacr. dial.* (PL 176.36B-C).

3   Heb 11:6.

4   Heb 11:6.

5   Cf. Augustine, *Trin.* 13.25–26 (CCL 50A.417–20); *Ench.* 8 (CCL 46.52); Anselm, *Prosl.* 1 (Schmitt, 1.97–100); Peter Abelard, *TSch* 1.10–12 (CCCM 13.321–24); Peter Lombard, *Sent.* 3.23.9 (SB 5.147–48).

6   1 Cor 13:3.

7   John 14:21.

8   Cf. Richard of St Victor, *Arca Moys.* 1.4 (Aris, 9); 5.5 (Aris, 129-130); *Quat. grad.* 29 (TPMA 3.157); *Exterm.* 5 (PL 196.191B).

9   Col 3:4.

10   1 John 3:2.

11   John 17:3.

12   Cf. Bernard of Clairvaux, *Csi* 5.18 (SBOp 3.482).

13   The notion of living well and living blessed (*vivimus bene . . . vivemus beate*) is a Ciceronian theme utilized by Augustine: *Ep.* 130.3 (CSEL 44.42–33); *Trin.* 14.11 (CCL 50A.437); *Spir. et litt.* 5 (CSEL 60.157); *Mor.* 1.10 (CSEL 90.13); *C. Jul. imp.* 6.26 (PL 45.1565–66).

14   Cf. Augustine, *Trin.* 2.28 (CCL 50.119); *Civ. Dei* 22.6 (CCL 48.813); Hugh of St Victor, *Sac. dial.* (PL 176.35D); *Sacr.* 2.5.1 (PL 176.439C). Peter Abelard, *TSch* 1.11 (CCCM 13.322).

15   Cf. Anselm, *De Inc. Verbi* 1 (Schmitt, 2.7).

16   For the various opinions regarding pagan philosophers and knowledge of God, see Augustine, *Conf.* 7.13 (CCL 27.101); *Jo. ev. tr.* 2.4 (CCL 36.13); *Civ. Dei* 8.6 (CCL 47.222); Peter Abelard, *SN* 25 (Boyer, 2.167–69); *TChr* 2.1 (CCCM 12.132); *TSch* 1.16–17 (CCCM 13.325–26); Hugh of St Victor, *Sacr.* 1.4.30 (PL 176.231C-D); Peter Lombard, *Sent.* 1.3.1 (SB 4.68–71); Richard of St Victor, *Arca. Moys.* 2.2, 9 (Aris, 23–24, 31).

17   Rom 1:19.

18   Rom 1:21.

19   Cf. Richard of St Victor, *Statu.* 31 (*AHDLMA* 42.97–98); *Arca. Moys.* 3.24 (Aris, 83–84); *Quat. grad.* 38 (TPMA 3.167).

20   Cf. Augustine, *Trin.* 15.2 (CCL 50A.461); *Lib. arb.* 2.5–6 (CSEL 74.40–42); Anselm, *Prosl.* 1 (Schmitt, 1.100).

21   See *infra*, 3.10; 4.1–3; 5.22, 24; 6.22; cf. also Augustine, *Trin.* 9.1 (CCL 50.292–93); 14.4 (CCL 50A.425–26).

22   That "the dust of earthly knowledge" (*terrenarum cogitationum pulverem*) hinders our sight of the divine mysteries comes from Gregory the Great, *Mor.* 32.12 (CCL 143A.1637) and 16.23 (CCL 143A.812). Cf. also Augustine, *Trin.* 1.17–18 (CCL 50.50–55); 8.6 (CCL 50A.275); Anselm, *De Inc. Verbi* 1 (Schmitt, 2.8–9); Richard of St Victor, *Arca Moys.* 3.9 (Aris, 66–67); *XII patr.* 72 (SC 419.296–98).

23   Isa 52:2.

24   Regarding the "ladder of contemplation" (*contemplationis scalam*), see *infra*, 1.10; 5.6; 6.23. See also Richard of St Victor, *Exterm.* 3.16 (PL 196.1111C-D); Hugh of St Victor, *Libellus* 4 (CCCM 176.139–48). Richard also uses three other metaphors to describe his theological method: first as a mirror (see 2.21, 5.6, 6.15, 6.21); second as a watchtower (see 5.6); and third as wings (see Prol., 6.23).

25   Isa 40:31. Cf. Gregory the Great, *Hom. Ez.* 1.3 (CCL 142.33–34); Richard of St Victor, *Quat. grad.* 34 (TPMA 3.162–63); *XII patr.* 83 (SC 419.330–32); *Arca Moys.* 5.4 (Aris, 128).

26   Col 3:2.

27   Col 3:1.
28   See 2 Cor 12:4.
29   Cf. Richard of St Victor, *Serm. cent.* 70 (PL 177.1122B-C).
30   Cf. Augustine, *Trin.* 4.24 (CCL 50.192–93).
31   Acts 1:11.
32   Cf. Bernard of Clairvaux, *SCC* 76.3.6 (SBOp 2.257–58); 84.1.1 (SBOp 2.303).
33   On this sort of ascension, cf. Augustine, *Conf.* 9.24 (CCL 27.147–48); Hugh of St Victor, *Sacr.*
     1.10.2 (PL 176.329–30); Richard of St Victor, *Arca Moys.* 2.24 (Aris, 85–86); 4.5 (Aris, 90).
34   Richard maintains these same distinctions in *XII patr.* 74 (SC 419.302–4).
35   Cf. Augustine, *Trin.* 8.3 (CCL 50.270); *Vera rel.* 72 (CCL 32.234); *En. Ps.* 41.9 (CCL 38.466);
     Conf. 3.2–3 (CCL 27.27–28); *Gregory the Great, Vita S. Benedicti Prol. 3 (PL 66.138B-C);* Peter
     the Venerable, *Epistolarum libri sex* 20 (PL 189.99C); Hugh of St Victor, *Sacr.* 1.10.2 (PL
     176.329C); Bernard of Clairvaux, *SCC* 44.5–6 (SBOp 47–48); 82.5 (SBOp 2:295); Richard of
     St Victor, *Arca Moys.* 3.5, 8 (Aris, 61–62, 65–66); *Diff. sac.* (PL 196.1057); *Exterm.* 1.5 (PL
     196.1076D).
36   Isa 57:15.
37   Concerning the "eyes of the mind" (*intellectuales oculos*), see Hugh of St Victor, *Sacr.* 1.10.2
     (PL 176.329C-330A); Richard of St Victor, *Arca Moys.* 3.9 (Aris, 66-67).
38   Cf. *infra*, 1.1, 5. Richard's prologue is integral for situating his rational investigation of the
     divine mysteries within the overall context of his spirituality and soteriology. Such a contex-
     tualization is important for him, especially because he occasionally gives the impression that
     some of his contemporaries would not approve of his 'bold' rational investigation of the
     Trinity (e.g., *Trin.* 1.4 [TPMA 6.90]; 1.5 [TPMA 6.91]; 3.1 [TPMA 6.135]). The goal of Richard's
     investigation is divine knowledge, and this is nothing more than seeking an encounter with
     Christ (see *Trin.* 3.1 [TPMA 6.135]). Such an investigation does not operate in a rational
     vacuum, but, as he explained earlier in the Prologue, encompasses a salvific process in which
     the soul ascends from faith through hope and love to manifestation, from manifestation to
     contemplation, from contemplation to divine knowledge, and from divine knowledge to
     eternal life. In the prologue then Richard tries to convince his audience that a rational inves-
     tigation of God is useful and compatible with the soul's salvific ascent toward Christ or
     eternal life. To do this, he will have to demonstrate how his rational method of inquiry is
     incorporated into the salvific process, how the cognitive aspect of the soul functions in this
     ascent, and how the affective aspect actually supports and motivates one to this cognitive
     dimension.
     In this section of the Prologue, Richard considers contemplation from which divine knowl-
     edge derives. Here Richard presents a fuller expression of his soteriology, which is depicted
     as the ladder of contemplation. Such a process is not one-dimensional in Richard's mind. He
     can present this salvific process from the vantage point of Christ who took the initiative by
     descending to humans and, after his ascension, sent his Spirit to his own—the Christological
     scheme of salvation. Richard can also present this procession from the vantage point of the
     human soul, which returns to itself through self-knowledge and ascends to Christ—an an-
     thropological scheme of salvation. Yet these two schemes must be contextualized within
     Richard's understanding of the fall. The best expression of this was already presented early
     in his writing career—the *Liber exceptionum* and *Sermones Centum* 70 (written between
     1153–1162), both of which will clarify many of his ideas and expressions in the Prologue.
     When God created human beings, he substantially inserted (*substantialiter insita*) into them
     three primordial goods: the image of God, the similitude of God, and corporeal immortality
     (*LE* 1.1.2 [TPMA 5.104]; *Serm. cent.* 70 [PL 177.1120B], the latter text only mentions the first
     two goods). The image of God is the cognitive aspect: reason (*ratio*), knowledge of truth
     (*cognitio veritatis*), and understanding (*intellectus*). The similitude of God is the affective
     aspect: love (*dilectio*), love of virtue (*amor virtutis*), and the desire (*affectus*) (see *LE* 1.1.1
     [TPMA 5.104]; *Serm. cent.* 70 [PL 177.1119C]). Hence, Richard says, "God, the Creator, made

a rational creature in his image and similitude, so that this rational creature might know God through that which was made in the image of God, might love God through that which was made in the similitude of God, might take hold of God by knowing and loving, and might be blessed by holding" (*LE* 1.1.1 [TPMA 5.104]; *Serm. cent.* 70 [PL 177.1119C-D]). In this prelapsarian state Adam and Eve lived a blessed life in their fellowship with God; they were, as Richard says, "under God in creation, above the world in dignity" (*LE* 1.1.2 [TPMA 5.104]; cf. Gregory the Great, *Hom. Ez.* 2.5.9 [PL 76.990A]). However, according to the *Liber exceptionum*, they did not desire to persevere in their obedience to the Creator, and the three original goods became corrupt by the three principal evils: ignorance, concupiscence, and weakness (*ignorantia, concupiscentia,* and *infirmitas*) (*LE* 1.1.3 [TPMA 5.105]; cf. *Serm. cent.* 70 [PL 177.1120B]). In other words, in an attempt to rise above themselves, Adam and Eve fell below themselves and dragged humankind down with them. The nature of this corruption is discussed in more detail in *Sermones centum* 70, in which Richard states: "And so, humanity was despoiled and wounded—despoiled of the good and wounded by evil— and left half-alive (*semivivus*), since even though the divine similitude, which is in love, can be totally corrupted in human nature, yet the divine image, which is in reason, cannot be totally erased. For, although humanity can be afflicted with wickedness so great that nothing of the good is loved, yet humanity cannot be blinded with ignorance so great that nothing of the truth is known . . . Therefore, it is rightly said that humanity is half-alive, since even though they were corrupted in part by the primordial evils, yet they are not totally blind . . . Therefore, the sword of the enemy did not totally kill humanity, when it could not completely erase the dignity of the natural good in them" (*Serm. cent.* 70 [PL 177.1120B-1121B]; cf. *LE* 2.12.5 [TPMA 5.464]; *Adnot. Psalm.* 118 [PL 196.352C]).

The solution to such a problem can be seen from two vantage points—the Christological or anthropological (although they are actually a single dynamic process)—depending on what Richard wants to emphasize. In his Christological scheme, humans would have continued in their sickness if the Physician had not descended to humanity through the incarnation (*Serm. cent.* 70 [PL 177.1121B]). During the time of grace, Christ became incarnate for two reasons: to make humans aware of their illness and their need for salvation outside themselves, and to dispense grace as the medicine for sin (*Serm. cent.* 70 [PL 177.1121B-1122B]). After he ascended physically to (the third) heaven, Christ sent his Spirit, descending unto humans to illuminate them for understanding and to inflame them for the love of virtue (*Serm. cent.* 70 [PL 177.1121B-1122B]). This theme is picked up here in the Prologue. This intellectual and spiritual ascent, which encompasses Richard's anthropological scheme of salvation, is depicted through the analogy of ascending to the third heaven, where Christ is physically located. For other didactic uses of the three heavens, see *Quat. grad.* [PL 196.1219D]; *XII patr.* 74 [SC 419.302-4]; *Arca Moys.* 1.10 [Aris, 19]; 3.4 [Aris, 61]; 3.8 [Aris, 65-66]; 5.19 [Aris, 148]. This journey to Christ entails three regions or heavens, each with their own manner of penetration and object of knowing:

Region	Object for Contemplating	Examples	How the soul progresses to this region
3rd Heaven	Invisible—Eternal Things	Divine spirit	A Special Gift
2nd Heaven	Invisible—Incorruptible Things	Angelic spirit	Prepare for Glory through Merits
1st Heaven	Invisible—Immortal Things	Human spirit	Self-Knowledge
Creation	Visible Transitory Things		

Richard's point of departure for his anthropological scheme is the state of humanity. Since the original fall, the actual state of humans is not what it should be. And, because of original sin, this state is unavoidable; a human is born with ignorance, concupiscence, and weakness. In short, humankind finds itself in the "region of dissimilitude" (*regione dissimilitudinis*) (*LE* 2.7.33 [TPMA 5.228]; *Adnot. Psalm.* 28 [PL 196.313B]; *Adnot. Psalm.* 84 [PL 196.328D]; *Exterm.* 1.1 [PL 196.1073D]; see also Augustine, *Conf.* 7.16 [CCL 27.103]), having lost the similitude to

God, whereby humans have the capacity to love God, and having tarnished the image, whereby humans have the capacity to know God. In theory, however, it seems that humans through their impaired reason could obtain a measure of relief, yet experience shows that humans are incapable of such a move as long as they are no longer conscious of their dignity nor of their incorruptibility (see *Trin.* Prol. [TPMA 6.83]; see also Augustine, *En. Ps.* 42.6 [CCL 38.479]; *En. Ps.* 48.1.16 [CCL 38.564]; *En. Ps.* 48.2.11 [CCL 38.574]), and their desires are inclined toward "earthly and transitory things" (i.e., a disordered love). Such a reordering of one's inclination is made possible by grace, and the important first step for this is to ascend up to the first heaven through self-knowledge, that is, a return to oneself by recognizing one's sickness and pondering one's own dignity in the immortality of the soul. Having come closer to divine similitude through love of truth, the soul desires to become more like Christ by ascending to the second heaven, where it can make preparations for "the glory of incorruptibility through the merit of virtue" (*Trin.* Prol. [TPMA 6.83]). Afterwards, through a unique and special gift, God sometimes allows the soul, persevering in love and virtue, to have "understanding of eternal things through the grace of contemplation" (*Trin.* Prol. [TPMA 6.83]). Consequently, a theological investigation of the Trinity through the testimony of reason (the cognitive function of the soul) is an integral aspect of Richard's anthropological scheme of salvation. But, at the same time, such an aspect is never actually divorced from the affective function of the soul, which supports and motivates the cognitive dimension of the ascent. It is within this context then that Richard concludes his Prologue as he does. Richard will present the peculiarities of this rational investigation in the first section of Book 1.

39   Cf. *infra*, 1.5; 3.1.

BOOK ONE (pp. 213-227)

40   On the three ways of knowing, cf. Hugh of St Victor, *Sacr.* 1.10.2 (PL 176.327C-329A); Richard of St Victor, *XII patr.* 74 (SC 419.302-3); *Arca Moys.* 1.3 (Aris, 8); *Decl. nonn. diff.* (TPMA 15.214). The following chart is a birds-eye view of Richard's method in *On the Trinity* 1.1–5, including the corresponding levels of heaven, as presented in the Prologue, and the corresponding levels of contemplation, as presented in *The Ark of Moses* 1.6 (Aris, 12–14).

A. How an Object is Proven	B. Object		C. Levels of Heaven	D. Genre of Contemplation (*Bej. major*)
Experience	Visible/ Corporeal + Created	Visible World		1—In imagination & according to imagination alone
				2—In imagination & according to reason
Reason	Invisible/ Spiritual + Created	Human Spirit	1st Heaven (Immortality)	3—In reason & according to imagination
		Angelic Spirit	2nd Heaven (Incorruptibility)	4—In reason & according to reason.
Faith	Invisible + Uncreated (Eternal)	God — Substance / Trinity	3rd Heaven (Eternity)	5—Above but not beyond reason.
				6—Above reason and seemingly beyond reason.

As such, Richard's treatise on the Trinity is actually an example of this fifth and sixth kind of contemplation. See Joseph Ebner, *Die Erkenntnislehre Richards von St. Viktor*, Beiträge zur Geschichte der Philosophie und Theologie des Mittelalters, 19.4 (Münster: Aschendorff, 1917), 92–120; Nico den Bok, *Communicating the Most High: A Systematic Study of Persons and Trinity in the Theology of Richard of St Victor (d. 1173)*, Bibliotheca Victorina VII (Turnhout: Brepols, 1996), 99–149.

41   Experience is a way of knowing whose object is the visible, created world. Such knowledge is an important first step in the process of finding the rationale for many aspects of the divine reality which are manifested through the authorities (see *Trin.* 1.10 [TPMA 6.95]). In *On the Trinity*, Richard often begins with experience before he ascends to reason, and as such his speculative theology is rather concrete (see e.g., *Trin.* Prol. [TPMA 6.84]; *Trin.* 1.9 [TPMA 6.94]; *Trin.* 3.9 [TPMA 6.144]). The advantage of working at this level is that it introduces understood truths as a point of departure for an investigation of truths that, while certain, are not understood (see *Trin.* 1.7 [TPMA 6.92–93]; 5.2 [TPMA 6.196]; 5.4 [TPMA 6.198]; 6.15 [TPMA 6.247]; *Arca Moys.* 2.14 [Aris, 36–37]; *Erud.* 2 [PL 196.1235A]). Richard knows that in studying the mystery of the Trinity his intellect is confronted with a foreign reality. His safest point of departure is the visible, created, and experienced reality, where the human facilities of knowing are quite sufficient (e.g., *Trin.* 1.7 [TPMA 6.92]); although even at this level there are many things that human experience knows to be true but cannot explain how they are so (he uses the sense of sight as an example in *Trin.* 4.2 [TPMA 6.163]). After becoming competent in knowledge from experience, Richard ascends to created, invisible realities (e.g., the human and angelic spirit) or even uncreated reality (e.g., God), to which the visible realities serve as gateways (see *Trin.* 1.8 [TPMA 6.93]; 1.9 [TPMA 6.94]; 5.6 [TPMA 6.201]). Such a process, however, is not always a linear ascent in practice; hence, Richard is not haphazardly wandering around the tangible world in search of similitudes to invisible realities (e.g., *Trin.* 1.10 [TPMA 6.95]). In Book 6 of *On the Trinity*, for example, Richard constantly descends to the visible from invisible realities in order to confirm through similitude various terms that are provided by the authorities (e.g., person, generation, procession, and the divine names: Father, Son, and Holy Spirit). Even when no correspondence between created and uncreated reality exists, knowledge of the human reality is still useful. At the end of Book 3, for example, Richard tries to balance his lengthy discussion of the divine plurality by reaffirming the complete equality among the three persons in a manner that does not negate the plurality (*Trin.* 3.21–24 [TPMA 6.155–58]). Such equality cannot be comprehended in itself because no analogy from created reality exists whereby the human intellect can grasp it. What Richard can do, however, is use an analogy of three golden statues from human experience in order to demonstrate how *not* to think about the divine equality of persons (see *Trin.* 3.23 [TPMA 6.157]). Thus, whether in terms of similitude or dissimilitude, knowledge of human reality is beneficial as a point of departure or a reference point for the divine reality.

   See discussion in C. Ottaviano, *Riccardo di S. Vittore: La vita, le opera, il pensiero*, Memorie della R. Accademia Nazionale dei Lincei. Classe di scienze morali, storiche e filologiche, serie VI, vol. IV, fasc. V (Rome: Dott. Giovanni Bardi, tipografo della R. Accademia nazionale dei Lincei, 1933), 454–62; G. Dumeige, *Richard de Saint-Victor et l'idée chrétienne de l'amour*, Bibliothèque de Philosophie Contemporaine 1 (Paris: Presses universitaires de France, 1952) 159–60; Ebner, *Die Erkenntnislehre Richards*, 15–28; E. Cousins, "The Notion of Person in the *On the Trinity* of Richard of Saint Victor," (Ph.D. diss. Fordham University, 1966), 82–100.

42   Reason is Richard's next step after experience. As the chart above indicates, reason is a specific way of knowing which is distinct from experience and faith and whose objects are invisible created realities and even invisible uncreated realities (see e.g., *Trin.* 1.8 [TPMA 6.93]). Richard assumes that reason is enlightened by the divine wisdom, which enables it to grasp the uncreated realities in an obscure but real way. After all, strictly speaking Richard perceives himself as receiving the knowledge of the triune God or being allowed to investigate such a lofty context (see e.g., *Trin.* 1.4 [TPMA 6.89]: ". . . insofar as the Lord allows . . .;" *Trin.* 4.4 [TPMA 6.166]; 4.22 [TPMA 6.187]). The activity of reasoning is investigating the rationale for the nature and properties of invisible created realities, which can be used to correspond to the nature or properties of invisible uncreated realities (i.e., the principle of similitude). But what Richard actually intends is more specific. He wants to discover necessary reasons, as opposed to probable reasons, for many aspects of the divine reality (see *infra*, 1.4).

See discussion in Maurice de Wulf, *Philosophy and Civilization in the Middle Ages* (New York: Dover Publications, 1953), 216–17; Ebner, *Die Erkenntnislehre Richards*, 29–80; Ribailler, TPMA 6.26–27); A.-M. Éthier, *Le "De Trinitate" de Richard de Saint-Victor*, Publications de l'Institut d'Études médiévales d'Ottawa, 9 (Paris: J. Vrin, 1939), 43; E. Cousins, "The Notion of Person," 113–19.

How does Richard regard the limits of reason? In general, it seems that the more incomprehensible the reasons, the more human language lacks the words to express certain invisible realities; and the more often one runs into dissimilitude between created and the divine realities, the more difficult it is to find the reasons for the properties of the divine reality. These then are the interrelated hurdles for investigating the divine reality in *On the Trinity*: incomprehensibility, poverty of human language, and dissimilitude.

Regarding the first hurdle, even when Richard has found necessary reasons for many aspects of the divine being he still regards them as incomprehensible and utterly inestimable (e.g., divine simplicity, omnipotence, eternity, and coequality; see *Trin.* 2.20 [TPMA 6.127]; 2.23 [TPMA 6.129–30]; 3.24 [TPMA 6.158]). This is why at the beginning or end of major sections Richard counters his positive assertions about the divine reality, gathered from reason, with statements about incomprehensibility (e.g., *Trin.* 2.20–25 [TPMA 6.126–32]; 3.6–10 [TPMA 6.140–45]; 3.21–25 [TPMA 6.155–59]; *Trin.* 4.1–5 [TPMA6.162–68]). Richard is confident that he can prove with reason, for example, *that* God is omnipotent, but he never claims to grasp the very thing that God's omnipotence is (e.g., *Trin.* 4.3 [TPMA 6.164]). This is the reality of any theological investigation; "for no one ought to demand or expect that, in this life, one can fully exhaust such great profundity [of the divine reality]" (*Trin.* 4.19 [TPMA 6.183]), because the eyes of human intellect are utterly insufficient for seeing the infinite and mysterious properties of God. The divine properties are so profound that Richard regards the theologian, whose vision is otherwise fine in tangible places, as groping for the semblance of truth in a dark and alien place (*Trin.* 6.11 [TPMA 6.241]). Consequently, realizing the impenetrableness of God's very essence, Richard does try to comprehend what he can to the extent that the rule of faith allows (*Trin.* 1.19 [TPMA 6.119]; *Trin.* 5.24 [TPMA 6.224]; *Trin.* 4.22 [TPMA 6.187]).

The second hurdle to theological investigation is what Richard calls "the poverty of human language" (*Trin.* 6.8 [TPMA 6.236–37]; 6.18 [TPMA 6.252]). Richard is concrete in his theological method, which is generally an etymological analysis of different words (e.g., *Trin.* 4.5 [TPMA 6.167], 4.12 [TPMA 6.174–75]). Within human reality, for example, words are not always used with the same meaning (e.g., *Trin.* 4.6 [TPMA 6.168–69]; 6.16 [TPMA 6.249–50]; 6.18 [TPMA 6.252–53]). According to Richard, the Greeks used the formula "three substances" in their Trinitarian confession, while the Latin West used "three persons"; and so it is the task of the theologian to reconcile these seemingly contradictory formulas with a single meaning and to disentangle from ambiguities the meaning of words which are used in the Church's confession (*Trin.* 5.20 [TPMA 6.218]; cf. 4.1 [TPMA 6.163]; 4.3 [TPMA 6.164–65]). This leads to the problem of using words in human and divine contexts. These two contexts are very different, so that a word in one context can have a very different meaning in another context (hence, the problem of equivocation, see *Trin.* 2.13 [TPMA 6.120]; *Trin.* 4.22 [TPMA 6.221]). This obstacle is all the more apparent whenever Richard tries to clarify divinely inspired terms such as those used in the Scripture, Creeds or the Church's confession, with non-inspired terms (see *Trin.* 4.5 [TPMA 6.167–68]). At best Richard hopes for "suitable words" (*verba ideonea*) that are more or less accurate (e.g., *Trin.* 2.4 [TPMA 6.111]; 5.23 [TPMA 6.222]; 4.11 [TPMA 6.173]). In the process of making words suitable for the divine reality and trying to avoid misunderstanding, Richard will often qualify or vary the meaning of a word (e.g., *Trin.* 5.20 [TPMA 6.218–19]; 6.18 [TPMA 6.252]), play around with different expressions (*Trin.* 4.20 [TPMA 6.184]), or even create a neologism (e.g., *condilectum* in *Trin.* 3.11 [TPMA 6.147]; 3.14 [TPMA 6.150]; 3.15 [TPMA 6.151], 3.19 [TPMA 6.154]; 5.8 [TPMA 6.204]; 6.6 [TPMA 6.234]; 6.7 [TPMA 6.235]; 6.17 [TPMA 6.252]; *Danielitas* in *Trin.* 2.12

(TPMA 6.119); and *discentia* in 6.25 [TPMA 6.265]). Sometimes he will paradoxically negate what he has affirmed (e.g., *Trin.* 2.23–24 [TPMA 6.129–32]), and other times he will concede that human language is totally unable to capture the true reality of God's existence (see *Trin.* 5.22 [TPMA 6.221]; 6.8 [TPMA 6.236–37]).

Dissimilitude indicates a third hurdle, which represents an overall difficulty in theology: humans are simply unlike the transcendent God. Conversely, many aspects of human nature and experience are very similar to God, which provides Richard with a basis for a method of reasoning through the principle of similitude. Nevertheless, Richard acknowledges that "the principle of dissimilitude is incomparably more copious than the principle of similitude" (*Trin.* 6.1 [TPMA 6.228]). While depicting God in a human way, which is appropriate and even necessary due to human weakness (see *Trin.* 3.18 [TPMA 6.153]), and while shifting among all the similitudes and dissimilitudes according to his theological method (e.g., *Trin.* 5.6 [TPMA 6.202]; 6.1 [TPMA 6.228]), Richard always guards against positively transferring any dissimilitude to the divine reality (e.g., *Trin.* Prol. [TPMA 6.82]; 5.24 [TPMA 6.224]; 6.4 [TPMA 6.232]). In such an instance one would think of God according to one's own capacity but not according to the rule of faith (see *Trin.* 3.10 [TPMA 6.145]; 6.4 [TPMA 6.232]).

See discussion in Ebner, *Die Erkenntnislehre Richards*, 84–91; Éthier, *Le "De Trinitate,"* 49–55; Dumeige, *Richard de Saint-Victor*, 69–75; Ribaillier, TPMA 6.20–22; Salet (SC 63.33–37); Walter Simonis, *Trinität und Vernunft*, 101–14; Hugh Feiss, "Learning and the Ascent to God," 115–26; E. Gössmann, *Glaube und Gotteserkenntnis im Mittelalter* (Freiburg: Herder, 1971), 36–38; M. Melone, *Lo Spirito Santo nel De trinitate di Riccardo di S. Vittore*, Studia Antoniana, 45 (Rome: Pontificium Athenaeum Antonianum, 2001), 78–82. See also E. Cousins, "The Notion of Person," 119–26, who critiques Régnon and Bligh's assumption that Richard is using natural reason without the aid of revelation (cf. Régnon, *Études de théologie positive*, 2.52–53; and J. Bligh, "Richard of St Victor's *De Trinitate*: Augustinian or Abelardian?" *Heythrop Journal* 1 [1960]: 138–39); cf. also R. Javelet, "Psychologie des auteurs spirituels du XIIᵉ siècle," *Revue des Sciences religieuses* 33 (1959): 112–20.

43 For Richard faith as a way of knowing constitutes an absolute certainty (see *Trin.* 1.2, 1.20). Such knowledge derives from the authorities (see discussion in note 45). Richard himself was nurtured and strengthened in the content of this faith by the sacred texts sung or read during the daily liturgy at the Abbey of St Victor. The concrete actualization of this faith as presented in *On the Trinity* is the so-called Athanasian Creed (see M. Melone, *Lo Spirito Santo nel De trinitate*, 97–101), which would have been recited daily during Prime. Consequently, insofar as Richard's study is seen as an exposition of this creed, this text can be thought of as a commentary on a sacred text. One must note that Richard never calls into question the validity and certainty of the truth expressed in the Athanasian Creed; otherwise, his insistence on the contingency of his rational investigation on one's maturity in their faith would not make sense (see *Trin.* 1.4 [TPMA 6.89–90]; *Arca Moys.* 2.24 [Aris, 85–86]; 4.5 [Aris, 90–91]). He will, however, build upon authority and try to find the rationale for the statements of faith by utilizing all the visible and invisible evidences that are before him (see *Trin.* 1.3 [TPMA 6.88]). In other words, Richard will try to find the rationale for various aspects of the divine reality, as defined in the Athanasian Creed, with reason rather than another authority (see *Trin.* 1.4 [TPMA 6.89]). Hence, Richard is not trying to *prove* the truths of the faith, because he already knows them with certainty, but he is simply trying to *understand* them as much as possible. See also Ebner, *Die Erkenntnislehre Richards*, 80–91.

44 Cf. Anselm, *De Inc. Verbi* 1 (Schmitt, 2.6); Richard of St Victor, *Arca Moys.* 1.6; 4.3, 17 (Aris, 14, 87–88); 4.2 (Aris, 87). See also Hugh of St Victor, *Sacr.* 1.3.30 (PL 176.231D–232A).

45 For Richard, the authorities which are the source for the knowledge of the faith are the Sacred Scriptures, the teachings of the Catholic Church, the fathers, whom he considers inspired, and the Creeds, which are tantamount to the Sacred Scriptures. For references to the norm which Scripture provides, see *XII patr.* 81 (SC 419.322–24); *Arca Moys.* 1.6 (Aris, 14); 3.15 (Aris, 72–73); 3.17 (Aris, 75); 4.3 (Aris, 87–89); 4.17 (Aris, 109–11); *Trin.* 3.1 (TPMA 6.135); 3.18

(TPMA 6.153); 6.2 (TPMA 6.230); 6.9 (TPMA 6.237); *Apoc.* 3.4 (PL 196.781B); 7.2 (PL 196.862A). See especially *Serm. cent.* 95 (PL 177.1195C-1196A). For references to Catholic teaching, see *Arca Moys.* 2.2 (Aris, 24); *Trin.* 1.3 (TPMA 6.89): *ex catholice fidei regula*; 2.1 (TPMA 6.109); 4.20 (TPMA 6.186); 6.11 (TPMA 6.240); 6.21 (TPMA 6.257); see also *Trin.* 3.1 (TPMA 6.135): "the teachings of our faith" (*fidei nostrae documenta*); *Trin.* 3.5 (TPMA 6.140): "concerning this article of our faith" (*super hunc fidei nostrae articulum*). For reference to the fathers and their inspired status, see *Trin.* 1.2 (TPMA 6.87–88); 3.10 (TPMA 6.145); 4.3 (TPMA 6.165); *Trin.* 4.5 (TPMA 6.167); 6.22 (TPMA 6.259); *Apoc.* 1.Prol. (PL 196.683B); *Verbis ap.* (TPMA 15.319). And for references to the Creeds, see *Trin.* 1.5 (TPMA 6.90–91); 2.1 (TPMA 6.108); 2.10 (TPMA 6.117); 2.15 (TPMA 6.122); 4.20 (TPMA 6.186); and *Trin.* 6.20 (TPMA 6.256), where Richard refers to the Athanasian Creed as Holy Scripture. See discussion in Hugh Feiss, "Learning and the Ascent to God in Richard of St Victor" (STD diss., The Pontifical Athenaeum of Saint Anselm, 1979), 103–8; Salet (SC 63.468–70).

46   Isa 7:9. That one cannot understand God without faith, cf. Augustine, *En. Ps.* 128.23.3 (CCL 40.1724); *Ep.* 120.3 (CSEL 34.2.706–7); *Lib. arb.* 2.6 (CSEL 74.41); *F. et symb.* 1 (CSEL 41.3–4); *Doc. Chr.* 2.17 (CCL 32.43); *Jo. ev. tr.* 27.7 (CCL 36.273); 29.6 (CCL 36.287); 45.7 (CCL 36.391); Anselm, *Prosl.* I (Schmitt, 1.100); *De Inc. Verbi* 4 (Schmitt, 1.283–84); *De Inc. Verbi* 1 (Schmitt, 2.8–9); Peter Abelard, *TChr* 3.51 (CCCM 12.215); Peter Lombard, *Sent.* 3.24.3 (SB 5.150–52); Richard of St Victor, *infra*, 1.3; 6.22; *Exterm.* 2.8 (PL 196.1094D); *Decl. nonn. diff.* (TPMA 15.214).

47   The phrase "trained senses" (*exercitatos sensus*) is found in Heb 5:14 (Vulg.) and is very common among the writings of the church fathers. The term is very difficult to translate because it has several meanings: sense, sensation, feeling, disposition, thought, idea, and sometimes even spiritual senses.

48   Cf. *infra.*, 5.21; Anselm, *De Inc. Verbi.* 1 (Schmitt, 2.6–7); cf. also Peter Abelard, *TChr* 3.50 (CCCM 12.214–15).

49   Cf. Richard of St Victor, *Decl. nonn. diff.* (TPMA 15.214); *Emman.* 1.7 (PL 196.613D). Cf. also Hugh of St Victor, *Sacr.* 1.10.2 (PL 176.330C).

50   Richard often use this kind of argument, see *supra*, 1.7, 19, 23; 2.12; 3.5, 13, 20; 4.1, 2; 5.24; 6.10.

51   Mark 16:20.

52   Cf. Bernard of Clairvaux, *SCC* 28.4.9 (SBOp 1.198).

53   Isa 7:9.

54   Cf. Augustine, *Trin.* 15.2 (CCL 50A.460–61); *Lib. arb.* 2.5–6 (CSEL 74.39–42); Hugh of St Victor, *Sacr.* 1.10.2 (PL 176.330D-331B); Richard of St Victor, *Decl. nonn. diff.* (TPMA 15.214); *Arca Moys.* 4.21 (Aris, 117–18).

55   Delight and delightful (*delectatio, delectabilis*), pleasantness and pleasant (*jucunditas, jucundus*), sweet and sweetness (*dulcis, dulcitas*), and pleasure (*delicia*)—These become standard terms for Richard's description of one's experience with God and the experience of a communal love; see *infra*, 3.4, 5, 14–18, 21; 5.2; 6.13.

56   The distinction between necessary and probable reasons corresponds to the distinction between arguments based on necessary rational principles (i.e., universal truths) and arguments based on a similitude from experience. From the six contexts in which the word "probable" is used, it is clear that Richard regards probable reasons as arguments from experience that can be demonstrated with a measure of certainty; and as such they are useful but require more penetrating reasons in order to be considered necessary (see *Trin.* 4.19 [TPMA 6.182]; 5.2 [TPMA 6.197]; 5.14 [TPMA 6.211]; 5.21 [TPMA 6.219]; and compare *Trin.* 1.9 [TPMA 6.94] with 5.5 [TPMA 6.200]). Richard makes clear his understanding of "necessary reason" when he says later in this chapter: "But those beings that are eternal absolutely cannot not exist; just as they have never not existed, so certainly they will never not exist, or rather they are always what they are; they cannot be different or otherwise. Moreover, it seems absolutely impossible for any necessary being to lack necessary reason" (*Trin.* 1.4 [TPMA 6.89]). Con-

versely, those beings that can not exist are demonstrated by experience; they lack necessary reasons. Therefore, necessary reasons have as their object only the divine being in virtue of the fact that they cannot be otherwise. Richard's notion of necessary then is closely linked with immutability, from which he arrives at the notion of eternity (see *Trin.* 2.4 [TPMA 6.111]; 6.1 [TPMA 6.228]). In this sense, necessary reasons are regarded as 'always being the case'. Necessary reasons, therefore, derive from the invariable condition of an eternal being, from which eternal or necessary principles can be derived (see Nico den Bok, *Communicating the Most High*, 186; Cousins, "The Notion of Person," 126). This condition applies to the divine substance and divine persons since both are eternal. Accordingly, whether Richard's particular argument is considered necessary or probable is contingent on the mode of being from eternity; yet not all of Richard's arguments concerning God are necessary.

What does Richard regard as necessary? There are three aspects of the eternal divine reality for which Richard explicitly claims to have discovered necessary reasons. First, Richard consistently maintains that the divine substance is necessarily without composition (i.e., a supremely simple being); hence, the divine being is immutable and identical to its essential properties (such as power, love, wisdom)—that is, Richard has established the principle of identity, which is based on divine simplicity, as a necessary reason (see e.g., *Trin.* 1.13 [TPMA 6.97–98]; 4.19 [TPMA 6.182]). Second, the eternal processions in the divinity are necessary. The divine processions are according to an operation of nature not grace, which means that the processions cannot be otherwise (see e.g., *Trin.* 2.8 [TPMA 6.115]; 6.5 [TPMA 6.232]). For such a conclusion Richard always starts with the existence of the Father, who is from himself (the principle of aseity), and then uses this principle for the other two existences (e.g., *Trin.* 6.1 [TPMA 6.228]; 6.3 [TPMA 6.231]; 6.5 [TPMA 6.232]): the Son is necessarily related to the Father through an immediate procession (*Trin.* 5.7 [TPMA 6.202]; 6.1 [TPMA 6.228]; 6.3 [TPMA 6.231]), and the Holy Spirit necessarily proceeds from the Father and Son but does not have anyone proceeding from him, according to negation of infinite regression (*Trin.* 5.11 [TPMA 6.209]). Third, in *On the Trinity* 4.8, Richard asserts: "it is not necessary to believe that plural substances exist wherever there are plural persons" (*Trin.* 4.8 [TPMA 6.171]). The reason is that "whether there are several persons or they all are one and the same substance, it makes no difference to the property and truth of person" (*Trin.* 4.8 [TPMA 6.170]). Although this runs counter to what is normally seen in human nature, where there is one substance per person, Richard maintains that it is not necessarily impossible (*Trin.* 4.9 [TPMA 6.171–72]). Yet, according to a later context, it is necessarily the case that there are individual incommunicable personal properties in the divinity; in other words, there is one person per individual personal property based on the necessity of the divine processions (*Trin.* 4.17 [TPMA 6.180]). In summary, based primarily on the eternal principles of aseity, immutability, and simplicity, Richard has shown the necessary reasons for the existence of one divine substance which is supremely simple and three divine persons who are differentiated based on personal properties. However, Richard never claims that he can discover the necessary reasons for the compatibility between the divine unity and plurality; he only states that it is not necessarily impossible. Whenever such an issue is encountered, Richard understands what he can and believes the rest.

Richard uses thirteen principles to create a complex web of necessary arguments that demonstrate several aspects of the unity and plurality of the divine reality. They function as points of departure for his reasoning and support his conclusions about the divine reality, and Richard regards them as self-evident and indubitable principles (see *Trin.* 4.3 [TPMA 6.164]; 4.5 [TPMA 6.167]; 4.19 [TPMA 6.182]; 5.2 [TPMA 6.196]; 5.3 [TPMA 6.197]). As such, he thinks that it is a kind of insanity to deny them (see 1.2 note 50). He offers four such notions in 5.3 (TPMA 6.197–98): [1] nobody makes what is impossible to make, and nobody can give what he does not have (see *Trin.* 1.6 [TPMA 6.92]; 1.7 [TPMA 6.92–93]: 1.8 [TPMA 6.93]; 1.12 [TPMA 6.97]; 2.3 [TPMA 6.111]; 2.24 [TPMA 6.131]; 5.8 [TPMA 6.204]; 6.1 [TPMA 6.228]); [2] there was a time when whatever began to exist did not exist, and whatever exists that did not formerly exist begins to be in time the very thing it is (see e.g., *Trin.* Prol. [TPMA 6.83]; 1.4 [TPMA 6.89]; 1.6 [TPMA 6.91]; 1.8 [TPMA 6.93]; 2.9 [TPMA 6.115–16]); [3] there is no composition without a composer, and there is no distribution without a distributor (see e.g., *Trin.* 5.4 [TPMA 6.198–99]); [4] and that-than-which-nothing-is-greater and that-than-which-nothing-is-better do exist (see e.g., *Trin.* 1.6 [TPMA 6.91–92]; 1.7 [TPMA 6.92]; 1.8 [TPMA 6.93]; 1.11 [TPMA 6.95–96]; 1.19 [TPMA 6.102]; 3.2 [TPMA 6.136–37]; 3.3 [TPMA 6.138]; 3.11 [TPMA 6.146]; 5.3 [TPMA 6.197]; 5.16 [TPMA 6.214]; 5.23 [TPMA 6.222]). In addition to this list, Richard mentions several other evident principles: [5] the principles consistent with hierarchy of being, which contains three principles in Richard's texts: a) "rational nature is better than irrational nature" (*Trin.* 1.11 [TPMA 6.95]); b) a higher being cannot partake from a lower being (*Trin.* 1.11 [TPMA 6.95–96]; 2.16 [TPMA 6.123]); and c) possessing the fullness is better than participation in it (*Trin.* 1.14 [TPMA 6.98–99]; 1.19 [TPMA 6.102]; 1.21 [TPMA 6.103]; 1.24 [TPMA 6.105]); [6] the exclusion of infinite progress (*Trin.* 5.3 [TPMA 6.19–98]); [7] the principle of personal properties (*Trin.* 5.10 [TPMA 6.208]); [8] the principle of intimacy (*Trin.* 5.2 [TPMA 6.196]); [9] the principle of maximum properties (e.g., "whatever is best is attributed to God," *Trin.* 1.20 [TPMA 6.102–3]; cf. 3.11 [TPMA 6.147]; 5.2 [TPMA 6.196–97]); [10] the principles based on natural consistency, which contains three principles: a) the principle of natural sequence (see *Trin.* 5.7 [TPMA 6.203]; 6.2 [TPMA 6.229–30]; 6.7 [TPMA 6.234–35]); b) a supreme being cannot be greater or lesser than itself (see *Trin.* 1.14 [TPMA 6.98]; 1.15 [TPMA 6.99]; 1.17 [TPMA 6.100]; 1.18 [TPMA 6.101–2]; 1.21 [TPMA 6.103]; 1.23 [TPMA 6.105]; 2.10 [TPMA 6.117]; 5.24 [TPMA 6.224]); c) two beings cannot possess the same supreme property (see *Trin.* 1.16 [TPMA 6.100]; 1.25 [TPMA 6.106]; 2.6 [TPMA 6.113]; 2.15 [TPMA 6.122]; 2.19 [TPMA 6.125–26]; 3.22 [TPMA 6.156]; 5.16 [TPMA 6.214]); [11] the principle of similar conclusions (*Trin.* 2.11 [TPMA 6.118]; 3.3 [TPMA 6.137–38]; 3.15 [TPMA 6.150–51]; 4.15 [TPMA 6.178]; 5.3 [TPMA 6.197]; 5.7 [TPMA 6.202]; 5.8 [TPMA 6.205]; 5.9 [TPMA 6.207]); [12] the principle of identity (*Trin.* 1.13 [TPMA 6.98]; 1.17 [TPMA 6.101]; 2.7 [TPMA 6.1, 114]; 2.18 [TPMA 6.125]; 3.3 [TPMA 6.137–38]; 3.5 [TPMA 6.140]; 3.7 [TPMA 6.142]; 3.24 [TPMA 6.158]; 4.3 [TPMA 6.164]; 4.19 [TPMA 6.182]; 5.4 [TPMA 6.199]); [13] and the principle of proportionality (see *Trin.* 3.9 [TPMA 6.144]; 4.25 [TPMA 6.190]; 5.2 [TPMA 6.197]; 5.5 [TPMA 6.200]; 5.14 [TPMA 6.213]; 6.4 [TPMA 6.232]).

Richard uses principles 2 and 5 in contexts dealing with the divine substance, and he uses principles 3 and 6–8 in contexts dealing with the divine persons. All other principles can be used at the substantial or personal level in order to prove certain aspects of the divine reality. Richard uses the principles at the personal level primarily to demonstrate the first divine person, the Unbegotten, who is from himself alone (principles 1, 3, 6); and in Richard's method the Unbegotten is the basis for the plurality of persons (principles 4, 7, 8). At the substantial level, Richard uses these principles primarily to demonstrate the aseity, eternity (and immutability), supremacy, and simplicity of the divine substance (principles 1, 2, 4, 5, 9–12). Two notable ways in which Richard implements these principles are the method of exhaustive possibilities and the method of transference.

Richard describes the method of transference as follows: "We ought to examine carefully the natural order of procession in humanity and, with all acuteness, search for what the divine reality has in likeness to it. After finding and understanding it, according to the practice of the theological discipline we ought to transfer the terms of the proprieties from the human to the divine according to the principle of similitude" (*Trin.* 6.2 [TPMA 6.229]). The theological basis for such a method is the divine image in humans and the vestige of the Trinity in created reality. Yet, Richard is also aware of the many dissimilitudes (see 1.1, note 42). And so, while sifting through the similitude and dissimilitude (see e.g., *Trin.* 5.6 [TPMA 6.202]; 6.5 [TPMA 6.233]), Richard disregards the dissimilitude and transfers the similitude to the divine reality in order to show how to think about certain properties of the divine reality (e.g., *Trin.* 2.21 [TPMA 6.103]; 6.1 [TPMA 6.228]). In contrast, however, Richard will also bring a notion down from the divine reality to the human reality in order to show how *not* to think about such a notion (e.g., *Trin.* 3.23 [TPMA 6.157]). The direction Richard proceeds depends on the type of correspondence between the created and uncreated realities. Sometimes, for example, there is direct correspondence but in an analogous sense, as with the notion of generation (see *Trin.* 1.9 [TPMA 6.94]). Richard will even demonstrate the rationale for the names "father" and "son" through an analysis of human generation (see *Trin.* 6.16–21 [TPMA 6.249–57]). Yet sometimes there are no terms of human relationship capable of capturing the reality of the relationship that the Father and Son have with the Holy Spirit (see *Trin.* 6.16 [TPMA 6.250]). In this case there is no correspondence between human and divine realities. Finally, sometimes there is correspondence but as mirror opposites; for example, the plurality of human natures in one person is a mirror image of the divine unity of substance in plural persons (see *Trin.* 3.9 [TPMA 6.144]; *Trin.* 3.10 [TPMA 6.145]; 4.14 [TPMA 6.176]). In this situation, someone disregarding the rule of faith would not perceive this correspondence as opposites and would misrepresent the true reality of God's existence (see *Trin.* 4.8 [TPMA 6.170–71]).

Richard uses the method of exhaustive possibilities in order to establish the categories that govern his investigation. In this method, Richard chooses two properties, lists all the possible connections, and disregards the impossibility. In *On the Trinity* 1.6–10, for example, Richard establishes three modes of being that he will draw upon throughout the rest of his study. Every being can be rationally differentiated based on two properties: whether the being is from eternity and/or from itself. Such an approach could be charted as follows (The references to the mode of being as created, Father, Son/Spirit do not appear in Richard's text. I have added them for clarity. Richard does not use these proper names until Book 6):

Mode of Being	Property 1: From Eternity	Property 2: From Itself	Nec./Prob. or Certain	How are Properties 1 and 2 Proven in *Trin.* 1.6–10?
Mode 1: Created	No	No	Certain	1. Experience: Natural Operation 2. Must be No if 1 is No
Mode 2: Father	Yes	Yes	Necessary	1. Evident and Inferred from 2 2. Reasoning from Mode 1
Mode 3: Son/Spirit	Yes	No	Probable	1. Experience: Sun/Sunbeam 2. Experience: Natural Operation
Mode 4	No	Yes	Certain	Logical Impossibility

Richard uses this method at any level of being or existence—whether human, angelic, or divine—that needs to be differentiated. Such a method is even applicable to differentiate among the three divine persons based on two properties: giving or receiving. It is the personal property of the Father to give and not receive the fullness of divinity; it is the property of the Son to give and receive the fullness; and it is the property of the Holy Spirit to receive and not give the fullness (see *Trin.* 5.14 [TPMA 6.211–13]). If the notion of love is considered, then Richard can use this same method to differentiate the three persons based on whether love is given and/or received. The Father, who only bestows love, has a gratuitous love alone; the Son receives and bestows love, so he has both a gratuitous and owed love; and the Spirit, who only requites love, has an owed love alone (see *Trin.* 5.16 [TPMA 6.214–15]). With these categories in place, Richard then brings in the principle of proportionality to demonstrate how "the plurality of the divine persons is entirely united in the most congruous beauty and differentiated in the most ordered otherness" (*Trin.* 5.14 [TPMA 6.212]). The Father and Spirit, who are related with opposite properties, are balanced by the Son who possesses the same properties as they (*Trin.* 5.14 [TPMA 6.212–13]). In other words the Son is the mean between the opposite properties of the Father and Spirit in the pattern aa-ab-bb. In addition to the inner Trinitarian relationship, Richard can apply this same principle to a cosmic level. In terms of the mode of being (see chart above), the mode of the Son and Spirit harmonizes the opposite properties between the mode of the Father and the mode of created beings (see *Trin.* 1.6 [TPMA 6.91–92]); and in terms of personal property the angelic nature harmonizes the opposite natures of God and humanity. The divine being is related as a mirror opposite to human beings. While the divine being has plural persons in a unity of substance, the human being has a unity of person in plural substances (body and soul); and "the angelic property," according to Richard, "arranges the contrariety of opposites as in a kind of symmetrical proportion and composes the dissonance of alternating sounds into one consonance," by a unity of substance like the divine being and by possessing a unity of person like the human being (see *Trin.* 4.25 [TPMA 6.225]). Therefore, within the hierarchy of being ranging from the Father to humans Richard perceives a relationship of different concords and concordant differences of existences (see *Trin.* 5.2 [TPMA 6.196–97]; *Trin.* 5.14 [TPMA 6.212]). See, also Nico den Bok, *Communicating the Most High*, 177–83, F. Copleston, *A History of Philosophy II: Augustine to Scotus* (Westminster, Maryland: The Newman Press, 1952), 178–82.

Regarding "necessary reasons" (*necessarias rationes*), see Anselm, *De Inc. Verbi.* 6 (Schmitt, 2.20), where he acknowledges that he wrote the *Monologion* and *Proslogion* "to demonstrate with necessary reasons and without the authority of Scripture what we hold by faith concerning the divine nature and persons besides the incarnation"; cf. also *Mon.* Prol. (Schmitt, 1.7); Hugh of St Victor, *Didasc.* 2.30 (Buttimer, 46); Robert of Melun, *Sent.* 1.2.4 (Martin, 3.1.273); Achard of St Victor, *Unitate* 1.41 (Martineau, 111); John of Salisbury, *Metalogicon* 2.13 (CCCM 98.74–76). Concerning "probable reasons" (*probabiles rationes*), see Hugh of St Victor, *Didasc.* 2.1, 30 (Buttimer, 24, 46). For further discussion on Richard's understanding of probable and necessary reasons, see Ribaillier, TPMA 6.20–21; Salet, SC 63.465–68; M. Melone, *Lo Spirito Santo nel De trinitate*, 82–90; M. Schniertshauer, *Consummatio caritatis: eine Untersuchung zu Richard von St. Victors De Trinitate*, Tübinger Studien zur Theologie und Philosophie, 10 (Mainz: M. Grünewald Verlag, 1996), 8–90. Cf. also A. M. Jacquin, "Les '*rationes necessariae*' de Saint Anselme," in *Mélanges Mandonnet: Études d'histoire littéraire et doctrinale du Moyen Age*, Bibliothèque thomiste 14.2 (Paris: J. Vrin, 1930), 67–78.

57   See *infra*, 6.1.
58   Cf. *supra*, Prol.
59   "Studious minds" (*mentes studiosas*) and "to great zeal with my effort" (*ad tale studium . . . meo studio*) have a range of meaning which includes zeal, effort, eagerness, and study. Hence, Richard not only indicates an activity here but also the result or means by which that activity is performed.
60   The source of this paragraph is the Athanasian Creed (Denz., 50–52). According to the *Liber ordinis Sancti Victoris Parisiensis*, the Athanasian Creed was recited during Prime (54 [CCCM 61.233]). Richard quotes from the creed throughout his study: see *Trin.* 1.5 (TPMA 6.90–91); *Trin.* 3.8 (TPMA 6.143); *Trin.* 3.20 (TPMA 6.155); *Trin.* 3.25 (TPMA 6.159); *Trin.* 4.25 (TPMA 6.192); *Trin.* 5.5 (TPMA 6.200); *Trin.* 6.11 (TPMA 6.240); *Trin.* 6.13 (TPMA 244); *Trin.* 6.20 (TPMA 6.256); *Trin.* 6.22 (TPMA 6.260).
61   See *supra*, Prol.; 1.4; *infra*, 3.1.
62   Cf. *infra*, 1.10; 5.5; Boethius, *In Isag.* 1.1 (CSEL 48.4–5); Achard of St Victor, *Unitate* 1.2 (Martineau, 70); cf. also Ribaillier, "Introduction," TPMA 6.30–31. As Salet notes (SC 63.260–61, fn. 1), it seems that Richard likes to develop an argument that involves three variables: three modes of existences (1.6); three arguments to demonstrate plurality in the divinity (3.2–5); three kinds of natures (4.25); three forms of love (5.16); three kinds of processions: immediate, mediate, immediate and mediate (5.6); three modes of being (5.14); three ways of possessing knowledge (6.25).
63   On this principle that one ascends from visible realties to invisible, see *supra* Prol; *infra* 1.8, 10; 5.6; 6.15, 17.
64   See *supra*, 1.6.
65   See *supra*, 1.6.

66 See *supra*, 1.6.

67 Cf. *supra*, 1.6; Augustine, *Conf.* 11.4.6 (CCL 27.197); *Trin.* 15.6 (CCL 50A.467–68); Anselm, *Mon.* 2 (Schmitt, 1.15–16); Hugh of St Victor, *Sacr.* 1.2.2 (PL 176.206D–207B); 1.3.9–11 (PL 176.219A–220A).

68 Cf. Rom 1:20. The same verse is quoted in *infra*, 1.10; 5.6; 6.1, 15, 17. Cf. also Augustine, *Vera rel.* 101 (CCL 32.252); *Civ. Dei* 8.6 (CCL 47.224); 22.29 (CCL 48.861); *Trin.* 15.3 (CCL 50A.462); *Jo. ev. tr.* 14.3 (CCL 36.142); *Ep.* 120.12 (CSEL 34.2.714–15); 194.24 (CSEL 57.195); Robert of Melun, *Sent.* 1.2.8 (Martin, 3.1.293); 1.3.2, 3, 23, 28, 30, 31 (Martin, 3.2.7–8, 23, 78–79, 88, 92, 93–94); 1.5.54 (Martin, 3.2.274); *Quest* 1.20 (Martin, 2.24–29); Peter Lombard, *Sent.* 1.3.1 (SB 4.70); Peter Abelard, *TChr* 1.54 (CCCM 12.94); 2.6 (CCCM 12.135); *TChr* 2.12–13 (CCCM 12.137–39); *Tsum* 3.67 (CCCM 13.185–86); *TSch* 1.91 (CCCM 13.356); 2.6, 110 (CCCM 13.409, 461); Hugh of St Victor, *Sacr.* 1.3.3 (PL 176.217D–218A); 1.7.23 (PL 176.302D); Bernard of Clairvaux, *SCC* 5.1 (SBOp 1.21, 23, 24); 8.3 (SBOp 1.39); *Csi* 5.1 (SBOp 3.467); Richard of St Victor, *XII patr.* 5, 62, and 72 (SC 419.102, 268, and 296); *Arca Moys.* 2.12, 16 (Aris, 34, 40).

69 Cf. Augustine, *Trin.* 4.27 (CCL 50A.196); *S.* 117.10–13 (PL 38.666–69); cf. also Peter Abelard, *TSch* 2.116–21 (CCCM 13.465–68).

70 On the similitude between created and uncreated nature, see *infra* 3.9, 10; 4.10, 12, 25; 5.6; 6.1. Cf. also Richard of St Victor, *Arca Moys.* 5.7 (Aris, 131).

71 Cf. Isa 66:9; Peter Abelard, *SN* 19 (Boyer 2.158).

72 See *infra*, 5.5.

73 Cf. Rom 1:20. See, *supra*, 1.8.

74 Concerning the word "speculation" (*speculatio*), see Richard of St Victor, *Arca Moys.* 5.14 (Aris, 143); *Adnot. Psalm.* 118 (PL 196.342A-D).

75 After limiting his discussion to the two modes of being from eternity, Richard then proceeds to prove rationally the existence of one supreme substance and its attributes. One must note that, while attempting to understand the faith of the Triune God, Richard does not begin the rational investigation itself (where no authorities are cited) with the notion of 'God', which he does not discuss until chapter 16, but with a metaphysical inquiry on one supreme substance, from which all things derive, which has all that it has from itself, and who is identical to its power and wisdom (chapters 11–15).

76 See *supra*, 1.8.

77 For "that-than-which-nothing-is-greater" or "that-than-which-nothing-is-better" (*quo nihil est majus, nihil est melius*), cf. Augustine, *Doc. Chr.* 1.7 (CCL 32.10); *Conf.* 7.6 (CCL 27.95); *Trin.* 8.4–5 (CCL 50.271–74); Boethius, *Con. phil.* 3.10 (CCL 94.53); Anselm, *Mon.* 1–4 (Schmitt, 1.13–18); *Prosl.* 2 (Schmitt, 1.101–2).

78 See *supra*, 1.6, 8.

79 For the "evidence of experienced realities" (*rerum expertarum evidentia*), cf. *supra*, 1.7, 8.

Book Two (pp. 228-246)

80 See *supra*, 1.11.

81 Cf. Anselm, *Prosl.* 5 (Schmitt, 1.18).

82 On the fact that the attributes of divinity are identical to the divine substance, see Augustine, *Trin.* 15.7–8 (CCL 50A.468–71); Anselm, *Mon.* 16 (Schmitt, 1.30–31); Robert of Melun, *Sent.* 1.2.5 (Martin, 3.1.276).
This assertion of Richard may be against Gilbert of Poitiers, who is thought to have asserted that God is called the divine substance *qua est* not *quae est*—in the ablative as opposed to the nominative (cf. *Trin.* 1.98 [Häring, 135]). In other words, Gilbert was understood as saying that the divinity by which God is is not God Himself; He may possess the divine nature, but it is not God. The Council of Rheims (1148), however, insisted that God be called the divine substance in both senses (Denz., 327). See N. M. Häring, "The Case of Gilbert de la Porrée, Bishop of Poitiers (1142–1154)," *Mediaeval Studies* 13 (1951): 1–40.

83 Richard is writing against Gilbert of Poitiers; see discussion in 1.13, note 82. Cf. also Bernard of Clairvaux, *Csi* 5.15 (SBOp 3.479); cf. also *SCC* 80.4.6 (SBOp 2.281).
84 That the supreme substance cannot have an equal, cf. Anselm, *Mon.* 4 (Schmitt, 1.16–18); Achard of St Victor, *Unitate* 1.3 (Martineau, 72).
85 Cf. 2 Pet 1:4.
86 See *supra*, 1.12.
87 See *supra*, 1.14.
88 That the divinity is the supreme substance, cf. *infra* 1.25; 2.18–20; Augustine, *En. Ps.* 68.1.5 (CCL 39.905–6); The Council of Rheims (Denz., 327); and the Athanasian Creed (Denz., 50–52).
89 Contra the teaching of Gilbert of Poitiers, see *supra*, 1.13, note 82.
90 Cf. *infra*, 2.12; 4.16–17. Richard will begin his discussion of the plurality in 3.1.
91 See *supra*, 1.12–14.
92 Cf. *infra*, 3.22; Augustine, *Trin.* 15.7 (CCL 50A.469); 15.9 (CCL 50A.471); Peter Lombard, *Sent.* 1.5.1 (SB 4.81–82); Alcuin, *De fide sanctae et individuae Trinitatis* (PL 101.33A). Cf. also the Council of Rheims (Denz., 327).
93 Cf. *infra*, 1.21; 2.5.
94 Cf. *infra*, 1.21; 2.5, 6, 24; Augustine, *Conf.* 7.6 (CCL 27.95); Boethius, *Con. phil.* 3.10 (CCL 94.55); Anselm, *Mon.* 59 (Schmitt, 1.70).
95 Cf. Anselm, *De Inc. Verbi.* 4 (Schmitt, 2.18), where he says that the intellect cannot penetrate beyond God.
96 Cf. Augustine, *Trin.* 14.11 (CCL 50A.436); *Jo. ev. tr.* 18.10 (CCL 36.186); Anselm, *Mon.* 66 (Schmitt, 1.77).
97 Cf. Boethius, *Con. phil.* 3.10 (CCL 94.53); Anselm, *Mon.* 15 (Schmitt, 1.28–29); *Prosl.* 3 (Schmitt, 1.102–3). See also the discussion in Salet (SC 63, 470–72).
98 See *supra*, 1.12–14.
99 See *supra*, 1.18.
100 This argument derives from Hugh of St Victor, *Sacr.* 1.2.22 (PL 176.241B).
101 For similar discussions on God's omnipotence, see Augustine, *Trin.* 15.23 (CCL 50A.496); *SymbCat.* 2 (CCL 46.185–86); Boethius, *Con. phil.* 4.2 (CCL 94.66–69); Anselm, *Prosl.* 7 (Schmitt, 1.105–6); Peter Abelard, *TChr* 5.35 (CCCM 12.631–62); *SN* 32 (Boyer 2.180); *TSch* 3.19 (CCCM 13.507–8); Hugh of St Victor, *Sacr.* 1.2.22 (PL 176.214B); Peter Lombard, *Sent.* 1.42.2 (SB 4.295–98).
102 On the distinction between participation and fullness, to be and to have, see Augustine, *Trin.* 5.11 (CCL 50.217–18); Anselm, *Mon.* 16 (Schmitt, 1.30–31).
103 See *supra*, 1.13, 18.
104 See *supra*, 1.21.
105 See *infra*, 3.22.
106 See *supra*, 1.16; cf. Athanasian Creed (Denz., 51–52).
107 See *supra*, 1.11–25.
108 According to the *Liber ordinis Sancti Victoris Parisiensis*, the Athanasian Creed was recited during Prime (54 [CCCM 61.533]).
109 See *supra*, 1.8, 11.
110 Cf. Anselm, *Mon.* 6 (Schmitt, 1.18–20); 18 (Schmitt, 1.32–33); Hugh of St Victor, *Sacr.* 1.3.9 (PL 176.219C).
111 Concerning divine eternity, see Augustine, *Trin.* 15.7 (CCL 50A.469); *Jo. ev. tr.* 40.6 (CCL 36.354); *Conf.* 7.16 (CCL 27.103); Boethius, *Con. phil.* 5.6 (CCL 94.100–105); Anselm, *Mon.* 18 (Schmitt, 1.30–31); *Prosl.* 13 (Schmitt, 1.110).
112 Cf. Augustine, *Trin.* 6.9 (CCL 50.238); Hugh of St Victor, *Sacr.* 1.3.13 (PL 176.221A).
113 Cf. Augustine, *Trin.* 1.2 (CCL 50.29); 4.1 (CCL 50.160); *Jo. ev. tr.* 23.9 (CCL 36.305); 38.10 (CCL 36.334–44); *S.* 7.7 (CCL 41.75–76); Bernard of Clairvaux, *SCC* 81.5 (SBOp 2.286–86); Hugh of St Victor, *Sacr.* 1.3.14–15 (PL 176.221B-C).

[114] On the distinction between "everlasting" (*sempiternitatem*) and "eternal" (*aeternitatem*), see Boethius, *Trin.* 4 (PL 64.1253A-B); cf. also Augustine, *Civ. Dei* 11.6 (CCL 48.326); 12.16 (CCL 48.370–72); Anselm, *Mon.* 24 (Schmitt, 1.42–42).

[115] On the demonstration of the divine magnitude, see Augustine *Trin.* 5.11 (CCL 50.217–18); Anselm, *Mon.* 2 (Schmitt, 1.15); *Prosl.* 13 (Schmitt, 1.110–11); Hugh of St Victor, *Sacr.* 1.3.17 (PL 176.223C-224A).

[116] Cf. *supra*, 1.13, 18, 23.

[117] Cf. *supra*, 1.18, 21.

[118] In 2.1, Richard divides the discussion between maximum propositions and propositions that the mind does not easily except, namely "that there cannot be several eternal beings and several immeasurable beings." Hence, at this point, Richard moves to the second point.

[119] Cf. *supra*, 1.18, 21; 2.5.

[120] See *supra*. 2.5.

[121] See *supra*, 1.16, 25.

[122] Regarding "primordial matter" (*primordialis materia*), cf. Augustine, *Gn. litt* 1.15.29 (CSEL 28.1.21); *Gn. Adv. Man.*1.7.11 (PL 34.178); Peter Abelard, *Hexaemeron* (PL 178.733C); Robert of Melun, *Sent.* 1.1.19 (Martin, 3.1.211).

[123] Cf. Anselm, *Mon.* 7 (Schmitt, 1.21–22). According to Peter Abelard, there were certain philosophers in the twelth century who affirm that God did not exist prior to the world (*TChr* 4.80 [CCCM 12.302]); cf. Salet (SC 63.473).

[124] See Athanasian Creed (Denz., 50–52).

[125] Cf. Augustine, *Civ. Dei* 11.6 (CCL 48.326); 12.16 (CCL 48.370–72).

[126] Cf. Augustine, *Jo. ev. tr.* 38.10 (CCL 36.343).

[127] See *supra*, 2.6, 7.

[128] On the distinction between greatness itself and greatness through participation, see Augustine, *Trin.* 5.11 (CCL 50.217–18); Anselm, *Mon.* 2 (Schmitt, 1.15).

[129] See *supra*, 2.5, 6.

[130] See Athanasian Creed (Denz., 50–52).

[131] That omnipotence is the same as the divine essence, see *supra*, 1.24; that the divine essence is the same as its immeasurability and eternity, see *supra*, 2.7.

[132] See *supra*, 1.17.

[133] For Richard's discussion of individual substances, see *infra*, 2.12.

[134] For other references to the simple listeners, see, *infra*. 2.21; 4.4, 20, 25; 6.4, 11.

[135] See *supra*, 1.13, 18, 23.

[136] See *supra*, 1.24.

[137] Concerning this division of substances, cf. Boethius, *In. cat.* 1 (PL 64.182B-C); *Interp.* 2.7 (C. Meiser, 137).

[138] For other examples of Richard's use of language (neologisms and varying the meaning of a word), see *infra*, 4.11; 6.18; *Adnot. Psalm.* 148 (PL 196.382A-B); *Decl. nonn. diff.* (TPMA 15.209).

[139] Cf. Boethius, *Interp.* 2.7 (C. Meiser, 137), who speaks of "Platoness" in this regard.

[140] Cf. *supra*, 1.14.

[141] On an unequivocal and equivocal predication, see Boethius, *In. cat.* 1 (PL 64.163D-167A; 193B-194B).

[142] Cf. *supra*, 1.14; cf. also Augustine, *En. Ps.* 68.1.5 (CCL 39.905–6).

[143] See *supra.*, 1.25.

[144] For a discussion on and sources for this platonic notion of quasi-divine substance, see Salet (SC 63.473–74).

[145] See *supra*, 1.17; 2.12.

[146] The manuscript here reads "goodness" (*bonitatis*), but in order to make sense of the context the editor has corrected it to read "unity" (*unitatis*).

[147] See *supra*, 2.8–13.

148 See Athanasian Creed (Denz., 50–52).

149 Cf. Augustine, *Gn. litt* 8.24 (CSEL 28.1.268).

150 Cf. Boethius, *Con. phil.* 3.10 (CCL 94.54–55); Hugh of St Victor, *Sacr.* 1.5.16, 19 (PL 176.253A-B).

151 See Boethius, *Con. phil.*3.2 (CCL 94.38); 3.10 (CCL 94.53–55).

152 Cf. Augustine, *Trin.* 6.8 (CCL 50.236–37); *Conl. Max.* 2.12.2 (PL 42.768).
Anselm, *Mon.* 17 (Schmitt, 1.31); *Prosl.* 22 (Schmitt, 1.116); Bernard of Clairvaux, *Csi* 5.16 (SBOp 3.480); Peter Abelard, *SN* 8 (Boyer 2.133); Peter Lombard, *Sent.* 1.8.3 (SB 4.98).

153 Cf. Anselm, *Mon.* 17 (Schmitt, 1.31).

154 See *supra*, 1.13, 18, 23; 2.5.

155 See *supra*, 2.7, 10, 11.

156 Cf. Augustine, *Trin.* 6.4 (CCL 50.232); 7.1–2 (CCL 50.244–49); 8.1 (CCL 50.268–69); 15.8 (CCL 50A.470); 15.22 (CCL 50A.495); *Jo. ev. tr.* 20.4 (CCL 36.205); Anselm, *Mon.* 17 (Schmitt, 1.31); Bernard of Clairvaux, *Csi* 5.16 (SBOp 3.480); Peter Lombard, *Sent.* 1.8.4 (SB 4.98–99).

157 In his notes for *Trin.* 6.19, Ribaillier suggests that Richard is referring to common opinion (126), e.g., Peter Abelard, *TChr* 5.11 (CCCM 12.352); Hugh of St Victor, *Sacr.* 1.5.16, 19 (PL 176.253A-B).

158 Cf. Anselm, *De Inc. Verbi* 5 (Schmitt, 2.19); Peter Abelard, *TChr* 5.11 (CCCM 12.352).

159 See *supra*, 2.17–18.

160 See *supra*, 1.16, 25.

161 See Athanasian Creed (Denz., 50–52).

162 See *supra*, 2.17.

163 Cf. Augustine, *Trin.* 6.8 (CCL 50.236–37); Hugh of St Victor, *Sacr.* 1.3.12 (PL 176.220B-C); Bernard of Clairvaux, *Csi* 5.18–19 (SBOp 3.482–83).

164 Cf. *supra*, 1.13.

165 See *supra*, 1.7. Cf. Augustine, *Trin.* 15.14 (CCL 50A.479–80).

166 Richard often returns to this kind of argumentation; see *infra.*, 3.9–10; 4.2–3.

167 See *supra*, 2.17–20.

168 Cf. Augustine, *Trin.* 5.3 (CCL 50.207–8); 7.9 (CCL 50.260); 7.10 (CCL 50.260–61); *En. Ps.* 68.1.5 (CCL 39.905–6); Boethius, *Trin.* 4 (PL 64.1252A-B); Anselm, *Mon.* 26 (Schmitt, 1.44); 27 (Schmitt, 1.45); Peter Abelard, *TChr,* 3.118–24 (CCCM 12.237–41); *TSch* 2.77–79 (CCCM 13.445–46).

169 See *supra*, 2.18.

170 2 Cor 2:16.

171 This phrase "good without quality, great without quantity" (*sine qualitate bonus, sine quantitate magnus*) probably started with Augustine (*Trin.* 5.2 [CCL 50.207]), and is frequently found after him; e.g., Hugh of St Victor, *Sacr.* 1.1.4 (PL 176.376C); Peter Abelard, *TChr* 3.120 (CCL 12.238–39); *SN* 9 (Boyer 2.138); Peter Lombard, *Sent.* 1.8.6 (SB 4.100).

172 2 Cor 2:16.

173 See *supra*, 1.21, 24–25.

174 Cf. Augustine, *Gn. litt.* 8.39–40 (CSEL 28.1.258–61); *Trin.* 5.2 (CCL 50.207); *Jo. ev. tr.* 2.10 (CCL 36.16); Boethius, *Trin.* 4 (PL 64.1252D-1253B); Gregory the Great, *Mor.* 2.20 (CCL 143.72–73); Anselm, *Mon.* 22–24 (Schmitt, 1.39–42); Peter Abelard, *SN,* 43 (Boyer 3.199–200); Hugh of St Victor, *Sacr.* 1.3.17 (PL 176.223D-224A); Richard of St Victor, *Adnot. Psalm.* 2 (PL 196.270D); *De missione* (PL 196.1019B-D).

175 Cf. Ps 103:28; 144:16; Bernard of Clairvaux, *HomBVM.* 3.4 (SBOp 4.38).

176 The word *propassio* comes from Jerome, *Commentariorum in Matheum* 1.5.28 and 4.26.37 (CCL 77.30–31, 253). According to Jerome, commenting on Matt 5:28, *propassio* is the sensual stimulus of the human soul whenever, e.g., a man looks at a women. But *propassio* itself is not a sin. *Propassio* turns into *passio* whenever someone consents to lust with the will to sin. This is the adultery of the heart. Moreover, commenting on Matt 26:37, Jerome notes that Jesus was sorrowful not because *passio* dominated his soul but because he 'began' to be sor-

rowful through *propassio*, thereby freeing Jesus of the charges of sin. Hence, *propassio* denotes the mode and extent in which Christ's human soul was affected by defects of the soul like fear and sadness—a state in which the soul experiences an unbalanced state and is subject to sin. *Propassio* is true fear and sadness (i.e., Jesus experienced a true crisis state of the soul), although not liable to sin. See discussion in Peter Lombard, *Sent.* 3.15.2.1-2 (SB 5.98-99); Salet (SC 63.156, fn. 2). Richard is unique here in speaking of *propassio* in relation to the immanent God. Obviously in upholding the impassibility of God he will deny God of *propassio* and thereby *passio*.

177   Cf. Augustine, *Trin.* 5.2 (CCL 50.207); *Gn. litt.* 8.39–40 (CSEL 28.1.258–61); Boethius, *Con. phil.* 3.9 (CCL 94.51); Gregory the Great, *Mor.* 2.20 (CCL 143.72–73); 3.4 (CCL 143.116–17); Anselm, *Prosl.* 8 (Schmitt, 1.106); Peter Abelard, *TChr* 3.120 (CCCM 12.238–39); Robert of Melun, *Sent.* 1.2.4 (Martin, 3.1.272).

178   Richard is alluding to Augustine's theory of causal principles; see *Civ. Dei* 11.29 (CCL 48.349); 22.14 (CCL 48.833–34); *Gn. litt.* 3.14 (CSEL 28.1.80); *Gn. litt.* 6.9 (CSEL 28.1.182); cf. *Gn. litt.* 4.24 (CSEL 28.1.123–24); 7.22, 24, 28 (CSEL 28.1.221, 222–23, 225). Cf. also Achard of St Victor, *Unitate* 37–38 (Martineau, 106–8); Robert of Melun, *Sent.*1.2.8 (Martin, 3.1.295).

179   John 1:4.

180   That is, to every Aristotelian category, which Richard lists in this chapter. On the ten categories of Aristotle, see Augustine, *Conf.* 4.16.28–29 (CCL 27.54); Boethius, *Trin.* 4 (PL 64.1252A-B).

181   That is, even if there were no eternal processions in God, a fact which at this point in Richard's study is probable, not necessary, see *supra*, 1.9.

Book Three (pp. 247-267)

182   This is a topic for Book 3.

183   This is a topic for Book 4.

184   For another reference to "the teachings of our faith" (*fidei nostrae documenta*), see *supra*, 1.4.

185   This is a topic for Book 5.

186   This is a topic for Book 6.

187   For this phrase "ardor of a burning mind" (*aestuantis animi ardor*), see Prudentius, *Liber Peristephanon* (PL 60.500A); cf. also Richard of St Victor, *Quat. grad.* 14 (TPMA 3.139).

188   Cf. Ps 23:6.

189   Cf. *supra*, Prol.; 1.5.

190   Song 5:6.

191   Cf. Num 22:23–31.

192   See *supra*, 2.16.

193   Cf. Gregory the Great, *Hom. ev.* 1.17.1 (CCL 141.117) "Love cannot be possessed among fewer than two people. For no one, strictly speaking, possesses a love toward oneself, but love extends to another so that it could be love." The following authors use Gregory's quote to support the Spirit's procession from the Father and Son: Peter Abelard, *TChr* 4.117–18 (CCCM 12.323–24); 5.52 (CCCM 12.370) *Tsum* 3.88 (CCCM 13.195–96); Robert of Melun, *Sent.* 1.4.3 (Martin, 3.2.121). Cf. also Richard of St Victor, *Arca Moys.* 4.15 (Aris, 105–6). Bernard of Clairvaux also speaks of a "singular" and "private" love, see *Dil.* 12.34 (SBOp 3.148–49).

194   Cf. Achard of St Victor, *Unitate*, 1.5 (Martineau, 74): "Love, like the unity just discussed, cannot exist except in several, nor can one conceive with the mind anything better or more pleasing" (CS 165.382). Cf. also where Augustine argues that the supreme love in God necessitates the unity of substance, *Jo. ev. tr.* 14.9 (CCL 36.148); 39.5 (CCL 36.347). Anselm also argues that there cannot be several supreme loves based on the unity of the divine essence (*Mon.* 53 [Schmitt, 1.66]).

195   This notion of a "disordered love" (i.e., a love not properly ordered toward God) is vibrant in the theologies of the twelfth century. According to Fernand Guimet ("Notes en marge d'un

text de Richard de Saint-Victor," *Archives d'Histoire Doctrinale et Littéraire du Moyen Âge* 16 [1943–1945], 380), this notion of "disordered love" (*inordinata caritas*) derives from Origen's treatment of Song 2:4 ("*ordinavit in me caritatem*"). In Origen's homily on this verse, which was translated by Jerome, he will also speak of a "disordered love" (*In Cantica Canticorum* 2 [PL 23.1136C]). Lombard will quote this same passage from Origen, but attribute it to Ambrose (*Sent.* 3.29.2 [SB 5.173–74]).

Regarding a second source, Guimet also mentions two important texts by Augustine: *Doc. Chr.* 1.28 (CCL 32.22) and *Civ. Dei* 15.22 (CCL 48.488). But cf. also *De musica* 6.46 (PL 32.1187); *Conf.* 13.10 (CCL 27.246); *C. Faust* 22.28 (CSEL 25.1.622); *Ep.* 6.8 (CSEL 88.38); *Ep.* 140.4 (CSEL 44.157); *Ep.* 243.12 (CSEL 57.579); *De mendacio* 41 (CSEL 41.463); *S.* 21.3 (CCL 41.279); *S.* 37.23 (CCL 41.467); *Cat. rud.* 20 (CCL 46.145).

Cf. also Gregory the Great, *Expositiones in Cantica canticorum* 2.5 (PL 79.495D-496A); William of St Thierry, *Expositio altera super Cantica canticorum* (PL 180.518–19); Bernard of Clairvaux, SCC 49.5–8 (SBOp 2.75–78); Hugh of St Victor, *Subst. dilect.* (PL 176.145A-18B); Richard of St Victor, *Super Exiit* 4 (Châtillon, 104); *Verbis ap.* (TPMA 15.325–26); *XII patr.* 7 (SC 419.108–10); *Arca Moys.* 4.23 (Aris, 82); *Statu.* 34 (*AHDLMA* 42.101–2). See also Salet (SC 63.481–83).

[196]   Cf. *infra*, 5.23.

[197]   On the fact that love in the divinity cannot be without a plurality, see Achard of St Victor, *Unitate*, 1.5 (Martineau, 74). According to Ribaillier (TPMA 6.138), this idea becomes popular after Richard especially among the Franciscans.

[198]   Cf. *infra*, 3.7; Anselm, *Mon.* 49 (Schmitt, 1.64); Achard of St Victor, *Unitate*, 1.5 (Martineau, 74).

[199]   Richard discusses the notions of a "gratuitous love" (*amor gratuitus*) and "owed love" (*amor debitus*) in 5.16ff.

[200]   This argument is similar to one that Augustine made in *Conl. Max.* 2.7 (PL 42.762). See also Peter Lombard, *Sent.* 1.20.3 (SB 4.173) and Robert of Melun, *Sent.* 1.1.19 (Martin, 3.1.216).

[201]   Cf. *supra*, 3.3.

[202]   See *supra*, 3.2.

[203]   Matt 18:16; Cf. Deut 19:15; 2 Cor 13:1.

[204]   Eccl 4:12. Cf. Richard, *Quat. grad.* 5 (TPMA 3.129).

[205]   See *supra*, 3.4.

[206]   See *supra*, 2.24.

[207]   See *supra*, 3.2.

[208]   See *supra*, 2.17.

[209]   Cf. Anselm, *Mon.* 50–52 (Schmitt, 1.65).

[210]   Concerning the notion of discretion, see *infra*, 6.15; *XII patr.* 67–69 (SC 419.226–34); *Arca Moys.*, 4.23 (Aris, 82); Bernard of Clairvaux, SCC 49.5 (SBOp 2.75–76).

[211]   Cf. *supra*, 3.3.

[212]   Cf. Boethius, *In. cat.* 2 (PL 64.228A-B).

[213]   Cf. *supra*, 1.13.

[214]   See *supra*, 3.3–4.

[215]   See *supra*, 1.17.

[216]   See *supra*, 2.11, 13.

[217]   See *supra*, 3.7.

[218]   See *supra*, 1.21, 23, 24; 2.6, 10. Cf. also *supra*, 1.17, 25.

[219]   2 Cor 2:16. Cf. *supra*, 1.17.

[220]   See *supra*, 1.16.

[221]   Cf. Augustine, *Trin.* 7.1–2 (CCL 50.244–49); *Conl. Max.* 2.10.2 (PL 42.765); Peter Abelard, *SN* 8 (Boyer 2.128–29); *TSch* 2.68–70 (CCCM 13.441–42); Peter Lombard, *Sent.* 1.19.5–7 (SB 4.163–66).

[222]   Athanasian Creed (Denz., 50–52).

[223] Richard seems to understand this contrast in terms of a mirror image, that is, the plurality of human nature and divine persons are arranged with a reversal of left to right, and the unity of human person and divine nature are arranged with a reversal of right to left, as it would appear if the two were standing face-to-face. On the principle of similitude which is between human and divine nature but as opposites, see *infra*, 3.10; 4.10, 25; 6.22. Cf. *infra*, 1.6; *supra*, 5.5.

[224] See *supra*, 2.21; *infra*, 4.2–3. Cf. Richard, *Emman.* 20 (PL 196.623A-B); Anselm, *De Inc. Verbi* 1 (Schmitt, 2.9); Bernard of Clairvaux, *SCC* 22.2 (SBOp 1.130): "In matter of this kind, understanding can follow only where experience leads" (CF 7.15).

[225] On the incomprehensibility of three persons in one substance, see Augustine, *Conl. Max.* 2.10.2 (PL 42.765); *Trin.* 5.2 (CCL 50.206–7), 15.13 (CCL 50A.477–78); Anselm, *Mon.* 64 (Schmitt, 1.74–75); Hugh of St Victor, *Sacr.* 2.1.4 (PL 176.377A-B); Peter Lombard, *Sent.* 1.19.6 (SB 4.163–64).

[226] Regarding the fact that the fathers have been inspired by the Holy Spirit, see, *infra*, 4.5. See also 1.1, note 45.

[227] See *supra*, 3.5.

[228] Cf. *supra*, 3.2.

[229] See *supra*, 1.20.

[230] See *supra*, 3.8.

[231] Cf. Robert of Melun, *Sent.* 1.1.19 (Martin, 3.1.216).

[232] *Condilectum* is a word, probably coined by Richard, that does not have an English equivalent. He uses it twelve times in *On the Trinity*: 3.11, 14, 15 (three times), 19 (where the term is defined); 5.8; and 6.6 (twice), 7 (three times), 17. He uses this term, *condilectum*, whenever he wants to refer to the third person in the Trinity who is loved mutually by the two persons (Father and Son). See also Salet (SC 63.192, fn. 2).

[233] See *supra*, 3.8, 11.

[234] Cf. *supra*, 3.4.

[235] Cf. *supra*, 3.3.

[236] See *supra*, 3.11.

[237] See *supra*, 3.11, 12.

[238] See *supra*, 3.4, 11, 12.

[239] This expression "fellowship of a fraternity" (*consortio societatis*) is used once by Augustine, *C. Ep. Parm.*, 2.14 (CSEL 51.59).

[240] This is a difficult passage. Ribaillier brackets the *non*, which indicates an editorial omission (TPMA 6.50), even though *non* is witnessed by the entire manuscript tradition. Salet argues for the *non*-reading (SC 63.201, fn. 2) based on a parallel passage in 3.15: "As long as the first person alone is loved by the second, then he alone seems to possess the pleasures of his excellent sweetness; similarly, as long as the second does not have a third mutually loved (*condilectum*), then he lacks a communion of excellent joy."

[241] See *supra*, 3.4, 6.

[242] See *supra*, 3.2, 11.

[243] See *supra*, 3.11.

[244] Cf. *infra*, 6.15.

[245] See *supra*, 3.3.

[246] See *supra*, 3.16.

[247] See *supra*, 3.5.

[248] See *supra*, 3.3.

[249] Cf. *infra*, 5.22; Augustine, *Trin.* 1.2 (CCL 50.28–29); *Civ. Dei* 15.25 (CCL 48.493). Cf. also *infra*, 6.20 where the Holy Scriptures (*Scriptura sacra*) could also refer to the Creeds and Councils.

[250] See *supra*, 3.12.

[251] Cf. *supra*, 3.14.

[252] See *supra*, 3.11–15, 18.

253   Cf. Augustine *Trin.* 6.7 (CCL 50.235); Bernard of Clairvaux, *SCC* 8.2 (SBOp 1.37).
254   If Richard views the Holy Spirit as the union between the Father and Son, then here he seems to associate the unity between the Father and Son as the unity between benevolence and unity, which is love.
255   Instead of "creation" (*creatura*), as the critical edition reads (TPMA 6.155) and the mss tradition supports, some like Salet (SC 63.212–13, fn. 1) prefer an alternate reading, namely, "concord" (*concordia*).
256   For "solidarity" (*confederatio*), cf. Augustine, *C. Faust* 23.8 (CSEL 25.1.714), where Mary was called the wife of Joseph on account of the "solidarity of souls," although without being joined sexually.
257   See Salet (SC 63.483–84).
258   Cf. *supra*, 3.7.
259   Athanasian Creed (Denz., 50–52); cf. Augustine, *Trin.* 6.3–5 (CCL 50.229–33); Hugh of St Victor, *Sacr.* 1.3.27 (PL 176.228D-230B).
260   Cf. *supra*, 2.18; *infra*, 3.23; Augustine, *Trin.* 6.11 (CCL 50.241); Robert Melun, *Sent.* 1.5.6 (Martin, 3.2.175); Richard of St Victor, *Arca Moys.* 4.22 (Aris, 110–11).
261   See *supra*, 1.18.
262   As Salet suggests (SC 63.214, fn. 2), Richard could be alluding to the Council of Sens which listed the following as an error of Peter Abelard: "That the Father was full power, the Son some power, and the Holy Spirit no power" (Denz., 324–26).
263   See *supra*, 1.25.
264   See *supra*, 1.13–18.
265   On the similitude of three golden statues, cf. Augustine, *Trin.* 7.11 (CCL 50.264–65); Peter Abelard, *TChr.* 4.13–14 (CCCM 12.272); Peter Lombard, *Sent.* 1.19.8 (SB 4.166).
266   Cf. *supra*, 1.18; 2.18; 3.22; Augustine, *Trin.* 8.2 (CCL 50.269); Peter Abelard, *TSch.* 2.68–69 (CCCM 13.441–42); Peter Lombard, *Sent.* 1.19.7 (SB 4.165–66).
267   Cf. Augustine, *Trin.* 8.2 (CCL 50.269); 6.12 (CCL 50.242–43); Hugh of St Victor, *Sacr.* 2.1.4 (PL 176.377); Peter Lombard, *Sent.* 1.19.3 (SB 4.161).
268   On the incomprehensibility of the Trinity, cf. Augustine, *Trin.* 15.2 (CCL 50.460–61).
269   Cf. Augustine, *Trin.* 6.8 (CCL 50.236–37).
270   Jas 1:17.
271   Athanasian Creed (Denz., 50–52).
272   Athanasian Creed (Denz., 50–52).

BOOK FOUR (pp. 268-291)

273   See Books 1 and 2.
274   See Book 3.
275   The "tear apart the unity of the divine substance" could be a reference to Gilbert of Poitiers (cf. Council of Rheims [Denz., 327]; see 1.13-14, notes 82 and 83), while "cofound the plurality of persons" could be a reference to Peter Abelard (cf. Council of Sens [Denz., 324–26]; see also 6.15 note 533).
276   Cf. Gilbert of Poitiers, *CEut* 2.1–31 (Häring, 264–71); 3.1–22 (271–76); Peter Lombard, *Sent.* 1.23.1 (SB 4.181–82); Anselm, *Mon.* 79 (Schmitt, 1.85–86); Robert of Melun, *Sent.* 1.3.14 (Martin, 3.2.54). See also Boethius, *De persona* 3 (PL 64.1343).
277   Cf. *supra*, 3.9, 10; Richard of St Victor, *Erud.* 18 (PL 196.1317C); *Arca Moys.* 4.2 (Aris, 87).
278   Cf. Richard of St Victor, *Arca Moys.* 3.1 (Aris, 56).
279   Cf. *infra*, 4.19, 6.2.
280   Cf. *supra*, 1.13, 16, 17; 2.12, 18.
281   Cf. also Anselm, *Mon.* 79 (Schmitt 1.85–86); Peter Abelard, *TChr* 3.165 (CCCM 12.256); *TSum* (CCCM 13); Hugh of St Victor, *Sacr.* 2.1.4 (PL 176.377D); *Summa Sent.* 1.11 (PL 176.59B); Robert of Melun, *Sent.* 1.3.13 (Martin, 3.2.54–57).

²⁸² See Salet (SC 63.484–86).

²⁸³ Ps-Jerome, *Expositione fidei catholicae ad Alypium et Augustinum episcopas*; rather, the statement was made by Pelagius, *Libellus fidei ad Innocentium Papam* (listed as Ps-Augustine, *Sermo.* 236.3 [PL 39.2182]). The text is also found in *Scripta ad historiam Pelagianorum pertinentia* (PL 48.489B-C). Richard probably derived his citation from Peter Lombard, *Sent.* 1.33.1.2 (SB 4.241), based on the textual similarities; cf. also Peter Abelard, *TChr* 3.165 (CCCM 12.256); *SN* 8 and 9 (Boyer, 2.132, 138–39); *Summa Sent.* 1.11 (PL 176.59B); Peter Lombard, *Sent.* 1.25.3 (SB 4.195–96); Robert of Melun, *Sent.* 1.5.10 (Martin, 3.2.180).

²⁸⁴ See Jerome, *Ep.* 15.4 *ad Damasum papam* (CSEL 54.66); Peter Lombard, *Sent.* 1.26.1 (SB 4.197).

²⁸⁵ On the statement "We are not Greek," see Salet (SC 63.486–87).

²⁸⁶ Concerning subsistence with relation to the meaning of person, cf. Boethius, *CEut* 3 (Loeb, 74.84); Hugh of St Victor, *Sacr.* 2.1.4 (PL 176.379C).

²⁸⁷ See *supra*, 2.11.

²⁸⁸ In Roman mythology, Minerva is the goddess of wisdom and the arts.

²⁸⁹ Cf. *supra*, 3.10.

²⁹⁰ Cf. Gilbert of Poitiers, *Sent.* 1.6 (*AHDLMA* 45.109).

²⁹¹ Cf. Augustine, *Trin.* 5.10 (CCL 50.217); 7.7, 11 (CCL 50.225, 261–62); Anselm, *Mon.* 38 and 79 (Schmitt, 1.56, 85–86); *De Inc. Verbi.* 2 (Schmitt, 2.12–13); Peter Abelard, *TChr* 3.174–82 (CCCM 12.260–63); Hugh of St Victor, *Sacr.* 2.1.4 (PL 176.378A); *Summa Sent.* 1.9 (PL 176.55D-56A); Peter Lombard, *Sent.* 1.23.2 (SB 4.182–83); Robert of Melun, *Sent.* 1.3.16 (Martin, 3.2.64).

²⁹² Cf. *supra*, 1.20.

²⁹³ Cf. Augustine, *Trin.* 7.11 (CCL 50.261–62); Hugh of St Victor, *Sacr.* 1.3.31 (PL 176.233B-234A); *Summa Sent.* 1.9 (PL 176.55C); Peter Lombard, *Sent.* 1.23.1 (SB 4.181–82); Achard of St Victor, *Unitate* (Martineau, 84–86). See also Salet, (SC 63.487–89).

²⁹⁴ Cf. Augustine, *Trin.* 7.7 (CCL 50.255–57).

²⁹⁵ Cf. Richard of St Victor, *XII patr.* 19 (SC 419.140); *Statu.* 39 (*AHDLMA* 42.110).

²⁹⁶ See *supra*, 3.23–25.

²⁹⁷ Cf. Augustine, *Trin.* 1.20 (CCL 50.57); *Jo. ev. tr.* 49.3 (CCL 36.477); Peter Lombard, *Sent.* 3.7.1 (SB 5.59–64); Achard of St Victor, *Unitate* 1.13, 28 (Martineau, 82–84, 98–100).

²⁹⁸ Cf. Boethius, *Trin.* 1 (Loeb 74.4, 6).

²⁹⁹ See *supra*, 3.21, 23.

³⁰⁰ Cf. Augustine, *Conl. Max.* 2.14.8 (PL 42.775); Peter Lombard, *Sent.* 1.20.3 (SB 4.173–74).

³⁰¹ Cf. Bernard of Clairvaux, *Csi* 5.17 (SBOp 3.481).

³⁰² Cf. Achard of St Victor, *Unitate* 1.13 (Martineau, 82–84); Robert of Melun, *Sent.* 1.5.26 (Martin, 3.2.210–14).

³⁰³ Richard said the same about "to have" (*habere*), see *supra*, 2.13; cf. Peter Abelard, *TChr* 4.41 (CCCM 12.283); Robert of Melun, *Sent.*1.6.3 (Martin, 3.2.291).

³⁰⁴ On the poverty of human language, cf. *supra*, 2.13; and *infra*, 6.8, 18.

³⁰⁵ Cf. *infra*, 5.20, 22.

³⁰⁶ See *supra*, 3.21, 23–24.

³⁰⁷ See *supra*, 3.22; cf. *supra*, 2.17.

³⁰⁸ See *supra*, 4.1.

³⁰⁹ Cf. Achard of St Victor, *Unitate* 1.16 (Martineau, 90).

³¹⁰ Cf. *infra*, 5.9; 6.23.

³¹¹ Richard is using *exsistentia* in its literal etymological sense: *sisistere* and *ex*, that is, "to be from." Cf., *supra*, 4.15.

³¹² See *supra*, 4.12–15.

³¹³ Cf. *infra*, 4.21

³¹⁴ Richard regards creation and God as the two extreme modes of existence in such a way that their properties are a mirror image of one another. Cf. *supra*, 3.9; *infra*, 4.25.

374 RICHARD OF ST VICTOR - *ON THE TRINITY*

315 That a personal property is nothing but the very person, cf. *supra,* 4.3.

316 See *supra,* 4.16.

317 See *supra,* 4.17.

318 See *supra,* 4.17.

319 See *supra,* 4.17–18.

320 This issue is also discussed by Augustine, *Trin.* 7.9 (CCL 50.259–60); Anselm, *Mon.* 78 (Schmitt, 1.78–79); Peter Abelard, *TChr* 3.69 (CCCM 12.223); *SN* 5 (Boyer 2.126); *TSch* 2.75 (CCCM 13.444–45); Robert of Melun, *Sent.* 1.6.39 (Martin, 3.2.347).

321 Cf. Augustine, *Trin.*5.3 (CCL 50.207–8); *Civ. Dei* 12.2 (CCL 48.357); Peter Lombard, *Sent.* 1.8.7 (SB 4.100–101).

322 See *supra,* 3.10, 23.

323 See *supra,* 1.25.

324 Boethius, *Quomodo substantiae in eo quod sint bonae sint cum non sint substantialia bona* (PL 64.1311B).

325 Cf. Augustine, *Trin.* 7.10 (CCL 50.260–61).

326 Ps 13:5 (Vulg.).

327 Richard is quite convinced that he can rationally demonstrate the necessity of the unity and the plurality in the divine nature. In other words, he can demonstrate the necessary reason, not just the probable reasons, for the unity and the plurality. However, Richard does not make such claims with regard to the unity in plurality or plurality in unity. While faith makes this certain, reason only shows that it is probable and not impossible. In other words, Richard can demonstrate the probable reason for the plurality in unity but falls short of demonstrating the necessary reasons for it, not because Richard lacks proper argumentation but because of the nature of the transcendent mystery.

328 Cf. Augustine, *Trin.* 5.10 (CCL 50.217); Robert of Melun, *Sent.* 1.6.39 (Martin, 3.2.346).

329 Richard is alluding to Augustine, *Trin.* 7.7 (CCL 50.255). See Anselm, *Mon.* Prol. (Schmitt, 1.8); Peter Abelard, *TChr* 4.27–28 (CCCM 12.277–78); *TSum* 3.1.23 (CCCM 13.167–68); Peter Lombard, *Sent.* 1.23.2 (SB 4.182–83). On the variety of Trinitarian formulas, see Salet (SC 63.489–90).

330 *Praefatio Trinitatis* in the Roman Missal; cf. also Gregory the Great, *Liber sacramentorum* (PL 78.116C).

331 See, *supra,* 3.22.

332 See, *supra,* 4.16.

333 See, *supra,* 4.17.

334 See, *supra,* 4.6.

335 Cf. Augustine, *Trin.* 7.7 (CCL 50.255); 7.11 (CCL 50.261); Peter Abelard, *TChr* 4.27–28 (CCCM 12.277–78); Peter Lombard, *Sent.* 1.23.2 (SB 4.182–83).

336 See *supra,* 4.4, 19.

337 Boethius, *De persona* 3 (PL 64.1343D).

338 Cf. *supra,* 3.8, 22; Athanasian Creed (Denz., 50–52).

339 Cf. Robert of Melun, *Sent.* 1.3.13 (Martin, 3.2.54–57); Peter Abelard, *TChr* 3.178–79 (CCCM 12.262).

340 See *supra,* 4.16.

341 See *supra,* 4.16.

342 See *supra,* 4.12, 16.

343 See *supra,* 4.16.

344 See *supra,* 4.12, 16.

345 See *supra,* 4.14–19.

346 Cf. *supra,* 3.9, where Richard uses the same analogy.

347 Cf. Hugh of St Victor, *In. hier. cael.* 1.3 (PL 175.929–30).

348 Cf. Mark 5:9; Luke 8:30.

349 Athanasian Creed (Denz., 50–52).

BOOK FIVE (pp. 292-318)

350 See *supra*, 4.6, 16, 17, 20.
351 See *supra*, 4.16–18, 22.
352 Cf. *supra*, 4.7.
353 Cf. *supra*, 4.20.
354 Cf. *supra*, 4.15.
355 Cf. *supra*, Prol.
356 Cf. *supra*, 3.2.
357 On the divine beauty, cf. Augustine, *Civ. Dei* 8.6 (CCL 47.233–34); Achard of St Victor, *Unitate*
     1.5 (Martineau, 72–74).
358 See *supra*, 1.11, 12.
359 Cf. *supra*, 1.12.
360 Cf. *supra*, 2.9.
361 Cf. *supra*, 1.11, 19; 3.2, 11.
362 Cf. *supra*, 4.16.
363 Cf. *supra*, 1.23.
364 See *supra*, 5.3.
365 See *supra*, 1.21.
366 See *supra*, 1.6, 9.
367 Athanasian Creed (Denz., 50–52); see also *supra*, 3.21, 25.
368 Cf. *supra*, 4.25, where Richard says the same things about the angelic nature.
369 Rom 1:20.
370 Cf. *infra*, 6.1. See discussion in Salet (SC 63.491–92).
371 In other words, Isaac was the son of Abraham (Gen 21:3), while Jacob, Abraham's grandson,
     was the son of Isaac (Gen 25:25).
372 Cf. Gen 2:21–23.
373 Cf. Gen 4:25.
374 Cf. Gen 1:26.
375 Cf. *supra*, Prol; 1.10.
376 Cf. *infra*, 6.7.
377 See *supra*, 3.3, 4, 6.
378 Cf. *supra*, 3.2.
379 Cf. *supra*, 3.6, 15.
380 See *supra*, 5.8, where Richard uses the same formula with respect to all three persons.
381 See *supra*, 1.12.
382 See *supra*, 3.2, 7.
383 See *supra*, 1.25; 2.13, 15; 3.22; 4.19.
384 See *supra*, 5.4.
385 Cf. *supra*, 2.4.
386 Cf. *supra*, 5.7.
387 See *supra*, 3.15.
388 See *supra*, 3.11–15.
389 See *supra*, 5.7, where Richard uses the same formula with respect to the first two persons.
390 See *supra*, 5.6–8.
391 Gen 32:30; Exod 33:4; Deut 5:11; and 1 Cor 13:12. Regarding the notion of divine seeing and
     generation, cf. Augustine, *Trin.* 2.3 (CCL 50.83); Peter Abelard, *SN* 18 (Boyer, 2.155).
392 Regarding the connection between seeing and understanding, cf. Richard, *Arca Moys.*1.3; 3.9
     (Aris, 8–9, 66–67).
393 Cf. *supra*, 4.15; *infra*, 6.12, 23; Anselm, *De proc.* 11, 12 (Schmitt, 2.206–11).
394 Cf. Augustine, *Trin.* 4.27 (CCL 50.196).
395 Cf. *supra*, 5.8.

396   Cf. *supra*, 5.6.
397   Richard also uses this method of reasoning in *supra*, 1.6. See discussion in 1.4, note 56.
398   See *supra*, 5.9.
399   See *supra*, 3.15; 5.8.
400   See *supra*, 5.9.
401   See *supra*, 5.5, 6.
402   See *supra*, 5.4.
403   E.g., Augustine, *Conl. Max.* 2.12.3 (PL 42.768); Peter Lombard, *Sent.* 1.7.1 (SB 4.92); Achard of St Victor, *Unitate* 1.21 (Martineau, 92–94).
404   See *supra*, 3.2–5, 18.
405   See *supra*, 5.11.
406   See *supra*, 5.9.
407   See *supra*, 5.7–8.
408   For the same analogy, see *supra*, 3.9; 4.25.
409   See *supra*, 5.2.
410   On the arithmetic, geometric, and harmonic mean, cf. Boethius, *De arithmetica*, 2.43–47 (CCCM 94.177–205).
411   See *supra*, 5.4, 14.
412   See *supra*, 5.10, 14–15.
413   Cf. *supra*, 1.22; 3.2; 3.11; and *infra*, 5.23.
414   See discussion in Richard of St Victor, *Verbis ap.* 9 (TPMA 15.337). For gratuitous love, cf. 1 John 4:10; Augustine, *S.* 331.5.4 (PL 38.1461); 334.3 (PL 38.1469); *En. Ps.* 53.10 (CCL 39.654); 79.14 (CCL 39.1119); 104.35 (CCL 40.1550); 134.11 (CCL 40.1945). For an owed love, cf. Augustine *Cat. rud.* 4.7 (CCL 46.127). For a gratuitous and owed love, cf. *supra*, 3.3.
415   Cf. *supra*, 5.16.
416   Cf. *supra*, 3.4.
417   Cf. *supra*, 3.2.
418   See *supra*, 5.11–13.
419   Cf. *supra*, 3.2.
420   Cf. *supra*, 3.2.
421   See *supra*, 5.17–18.
422   See *supra*, 5.4.
423   See *supra*, 2.17–18.
424   Cf. Augustine, *Trin.* 15.27 (CCL 50A.501–2); Robert of Melun, *Sent.* 1.6.51 (Martin, 3.2.370–72); Bernard of Clairvaux, *Dil.* 12.35 (SBOp 3.149–50).
425   Cf. *supra*, 4.11; *infra*, 5.22.
426   See *supra*, 5.14–15.
427   Cf. Heb 5:14 (Vulg.). See discussion *supra*, 1.1, note 42.
428   Cf. *supra*, 1.17, 25; 2.16; 3.3.
429   See *supra*, 5.14–15.
430   1 Pet 3:15.
431   See *supra*, 5.17–18.
432   On the work of grace and operation of nature, cf. *supra*, 1.9; 2.8. Cf. also Augustine, *C. S. Ar.* 2 (PL 42.684–85); Robert of Melun, *Sent.* 1.4.17 (Martin, 3.2.134); Achard of St Victor, *Unitate* 1.14 (Martineau, 84–86).
433   On suitable words (*verbis idoneis*), cf. *supra*, 4.11; 5.20.
434   Sallust, *Catilinae* 20.5 (Loeb, 116.34–35).
435   Cf. *supra*, 1.22; 3.2; 3.11; 5.16.
436   See *supra*, 5.16.
437   See *supra*, 5.17–19.
438   Obviously the "first person" is the Father and the "second person" the Holy Spirit. The Latin here, as supported by the manuscripts, reads *erit in isto ad illum tantum gratuitus, et in illo*

ad istum tantummodo debitus. Ribaillier has made the following editorial correction: *ad illos* for *ad illum* and *ad istos* for *ad isto* (TPMA 6.222). Contrary to the manuscritps Ribaillier changed the reading to be more specific, that is, the Father has gratiutious love toward the Son and Holy Spirit, and the Holy Spirit has an owed love alone toward the Father and the Son. This is no doubt faithful to Richard's teaching elsewhere (see, e.g., 5.25), but I have retained the reading found in the manuscripts.

439 Cf. Augustine, *Conl. Max.* 2.14.7 (PL 42.774–75).

440 See *supra,* 5.23.

441 That the supreme beatitude requires that each person in the Trinity loves what he is, cf. *Didasc.* 7.23 (PL 175.833B).

442 That is, to the Father and Son.

443 That is, to the Son and Holy Spirit.

444 That is, to the Father and Holy Spirit.

445 That is, the Father.

446 That is, the Holy Spirit.

447 That is, the Son.

448 That is, the Father and Son.

449 That is, the Son and Holy Spirit.

450 That is, the Father and Holy Spirit.

451 That is, the Father.

452 That is, the Holy Spirit.

453 That is, the Son.

454 That is, the Father.

455 That is, the Son.

456 That is, the Holy Spirit.

457 That is, the Holy Spirit.

458 That is, the Son.

459 That is, the Father.

460 The authenticity of this paragraph is unquestionable in the manuscript tradition. Nevertheless, it is very abrupt and seems to indicate not only a conclusion to his book, but also a refusal to deal with the questions of the different processions and the divine names. But these issues, which Richard announced in 3.1, are actually discussed in Book 6. Moreover, despite the apparent termination, no scholar disputes the authenticity of Book 6, which is found in all the manuscripts and corresponds to Richard's style and vocabulary. Ribaillier speculates that Richard, who was nearing death, did write Book 6 but originally left it out, because he was dissatisfied with it and did not have time to rework it. Richard would have then signaled the end of the treatise at the end of Book 5, but after his death Book 6 was inserted back into the treaties by the copyist at the Abbey of St Victor. Hence, *On the Trinity* is a posthumous publication. See Ribaillier, "Introduction," *Opuscules Théologiques,* 8–11. For an alternative theory, which Ribaillier finds unconvincing (*Opuscules Théologiques,* 22–23), see Salet (SC 63.368–69, fn. 1).

BOOK SIX (pp. 319-352)

461 See *supra,* 5.5, 10, 25.

462 Rom 1:20. See *supra,* 1.8, 10; 5.6.

463 Cf. Gen 1:26; Richard of St Victor, *Statu.* 14 (*AHDLMA* 42.78).

464 Cf. *supra,* 5.6.

465 Cf. *supra,* 5.6.

466 On the "creative grace" (*gratia creatrice*), cf. Hugh of St Victor, *Sacr.* 1.6.17 (PL 176.273C-D). On the distinction between grace and nature, cf. Richard of St Victor, *Statu.* 20 (*AHDLMA* 42.84–85).

467 Cf. *supra*, 2.8; 5.22.

468 Cf. *supra*, 1.4.

469 Cf. *supra*, 2.8; 5.22.

470 Cf. Richard, *Arca Moys.* 2.17 (Aris, 40–44); Robert of Melun, *Sent.* 1.5.43 (Martin, 3.2.263–65).

471 See *supra*, 5.6.

472 See *supra*, 5.6, where Richard uses Seth as an example of this immediate and mediate procession.

473 The Latin word here *principalis* that Richard uses throughout book six is very difficult to translate. Based on his discussions in chapters two and eight, it indicates the immediate proximity of the Son's procession from or relationship to the Unbegotten Father. For the sake of consistency I will retain the translation "principal" throughout.

474 See *supra*, 6.1.

475 Cf. Augustine, *Trin.* 15.20 (CCL 50A.486–89); *C. S. Ar.* 1 (PL 42.684–85); Robert of Melun, *Sent.* 1.4.17 (Martin, 3.2.134).

476 This is an allusion to Matt 3:17; 17:5. See also Richard of St Victor, *XII patr.* 82 (SC 419.326–28).

477 Cf. Anselm, *Mon.* 42 (Schmitt, 1.58–59).

478 Cf. Peter Lombard, *Sent.* 3.8.1 (SB 5.67).

479 On the incomprehensibility of the divine generation, cf. Peter Abelard, *SN* 18 (Boyer 2.156–57); Robert of Melun, *Sent.* 1.6.10 (Martin, 3.2.300).

480 Cf. *supra*, 6.3.

481 Cf. Robert of Melun, *Sent.* 1.4.14 (Martin, 3.2.127).

482 Cf. Augustine, *Jo. ev. tr.* 19.13 (CCL 36.472).

483 Cf. *supra*, 3.2; 5.7–8.

484 Cf. *supra*, 3.11, 14–15; 5.8.

485 Cf. *supra*, 5.7.

486 On the distinction between the more principal procession and the less principal, cf. Augustine, *Trin.* 15.29 (CCL 50A.503–4).

487 See *supra*, 6.6, 7.

488 See *supra*, 6.7. Regarding the issue why the third person in the Trinity is not called a son, cf. Augustine, *Trin.* 15.48 (CCL 50A.529–31); *Jo. ev. tr.* 94.9 (CCL 36.587); Anselm, *De Inc. Verbi* 16 (Schmitt, 2.34–35); *De proc.* 4 (Schmitt, 2.191–94); Hugh of St Victor, *Sacr.* 1.3.23 (PL 176.226B); Peter Abelard, *TChr* 3.63–64 (CCCM 12.200–221), 4.118 (CCCM 12.324); *SN* 18 (Boyer 2.157); Peter Lombard, *Sent.* 1.13.1 (SB 4.121–23); Robert of Melun, *Sent.* 1.4.10 (Martin, 3.2.113); Achard of St Victor, *Unitate* 1.36 (Martineau, 104–6).

489 See *supra*, 5.8.

490 Cf. Richard of St Victor, *Quomodo Spiritus* (TPMA 15.165–66).

491 The Spirit is called the "finger of God" in Matt 12:28 and Luke 11:20.

492 Cf. 1 John 2:27.

493 John 20:22.

494 John 4:24. Cf. *infra*, 6:21.

495 On this question, cf. Augustine, *Trin.* 5.13 (CCL 50.220); 15.12 (CCL 50A.475–77); 15.37 (CCL 50A.513–14); Gregory the Great, *Hom. ev.* 2.30 (PL 76.1220B); Peter Abelard, *TChr* (CCCM 12.152–53); *Tsum* 3.3.88–93 (CCCM 13.195–98); Peter Lombard, *Sent.* 1.10.3 (SB 4.113–14); Achard of St Victor, *Unitate* 1.36 (Martineau, 104–6).

496 Cf. Hugh of St Victor, *Sacr.* 1.3.23 (PL 176.226).

497 Acts 4:32.

498 Cf. John 20:22.

499 For the phrase "similitude of reason" (*rationis similitudo*), see *Arca Moys.* 4.20 (Aris, 115).

500 See *supra*, 6.5, 8.

501 Athanasian Creed (Denz., 50–52).

502 See *supra*, 5.25.

503 Cf. 2 Cor 4:4; Col 1:15; Heb 1:3.

504 See discussion in Salet (SC 63.402–3, fn.1).

505 Possible allusions to Isa 59:10 and Acts 17:27.

506 That is, since the Spirit receives without giving, one may suspect the lack of benevolence.

507 Sir 1:5; cf. John 1:1, 14; 1 John 1:1–3; 5:7; Rev 19:13. Cf. Augustine, *Trin.* 6.3 (CCL 50.230–31); *Conl. Max.* 2.23.7 (PL 42.801); Anselm, *Mon.* 63 (Schmitt, 1.73–74); Peter Abelard, *TChr* 1.53 (CCL 12.93–94); Peter Lombard, *Sent.* 1.27.5 (SB 4.208–9).

508 John 17:1–6; 1 John 2:20.

509 Cf. John 14:26.

510 On this question, cf. Anselm, *Mon.* 61, 63 (Schmitt, 1.71–74).

511 On the word of the mouth and heart, cf. Hugh of St Victor, *Sacr.* 1.3.20 (PL 176.225A).

512 Cf. Richard of St Victor, *Jud. pot.* 6 (TPMA 15.148–49).

513 Cf. John 17:5, 22; Augustine, *F. et symb.* 3 (CSEL 41.6–7); *Trin.* 15.17–20 (CCL 50A.483–89).

514 John 16:13.

515 Ps 44:2 (LXX); cf. Richard of St Victor, *Missione* (PL 196.1019–20).

516 See *supra*, 6.10.

517 Cf. John 17:4.

518 John 17:1.

519 Matt 16:17.

520 Cf. Augustine, *Conl. Max.* 2.16.7 (PL 42.773).

521 Cf. *supra*, 3.4; 5.10, 17.

522 Athanasian Creed (Denz., 50–52).

523 Cf. John 4:10; Acts 2:38; 8:18–20; 10:44–46; 11:15–17; Heb. 6:4; see also Eph. 3:7.

524 See *supra*, 5.17–19.

525 That the Holy Spirit is the gift of God, cf. Augustine, *Trin.* 15.34–37 (CCL 50A.509–14); *F. et symb.* 9 (CSEL 41.12–13); Peter Abelard, *TChr* 4.150 (CCL 12.340); *TSch* 2.179–82 (CCCM 13.495–97); *Tsum* 3.96–98 (CCL 13:199–200); Peter Lombard, *Sent.* 1.18.2 (SB 4.153–55); Robert of Melun, *Sent.* 1.6.30 (Martin, 3.2.329–31).

526 Cf. Gregory the Great, *Hom. Ez.* 1.8.29 (CCL 142.119).

527 For the same imagery of iron and fire, cf. Bernard of Clairvaux, *Dil.* 10.28 (SBOp 3.143); Hugh of St Victor, *In Eccl.* 1 (PL 175.117–18); see also Richard of St Victor, *Quat. grad.* 39 (TPMA 3.166); *Apoc.*7.3 (PL 196.864D).

528 Rom 5:5; cf. Augustine, *Trin.* 15.32 (CCL 50A.507–8); *S.* 128.4 (PL 38.715); Peter Lombard, *Sent.* 1.14.2 (SB 4.128).

529 See *supra*, 5.19.

530 Cf. Richard of St Victor, *Verbis ap.* (TPMA 6.336).

531 Cf. Augustine, *Trin.* 4.29 (CCL 50.199–201); 5.12 (CCL 50.218–20); 15.36 (CCL 50A.513); Peter Lombard, *Sent.* 1.18.2 (SB 4.154); Robert Melun, *Sent.* 1.6.28–30 (Martin, 3.2.327–31).

532 See Richard of St Victor, *Tribus per.* (TPMA 6.182–87), the contents of which he incorporated into this chapter. See discussion in Ribaillier (TPMA 6.169–74); Ottaviano, *Riccardo di S. Vittore*, 443 ; Feiss, this volume, 57-58.

533 The method of appropriation is attributing an essential attribute of God (power, wisdom, and goodness) to a single divine person in order to distinguish that person in a special way. Cf. Augustine, *Trin.* 7.1–3 (CCL 50.244–50); *Civ. Dei* 11.24 (CCL 48.343); Peter Abelard, *Tsum* 1.2.1–12 (CCCM 13.86–90); *TChr* 1.1–7 (CCCM 12.72–75); 4.49 (CCCM 12:287); *TSch* 1.30–34 (CCCM 13.330–32); Hugh of St Victor, *Sacr.* 1.2.8 (PL 176.209); *Summa Sent.* 1.10 (PL 176.57C); Gilbert of Poitiers, *Trin.* 1.2.16 (Häring, 61); Robert Melun, *Sent.* 1.3.17–27 (Martin, 3.2.65–87); Peter Lombard, *Sent*, 1.34, 3–4 (SB 4.251–53); Richard of St Victor, *Statu.* 40 (*AHDLMA* 42.111); *Sp. blasph.* 1 (TPMA 15.122–23); *Ad me clamat.* 5 (TPMA 15.262–63).

534 On the fact that power, wisdom, and goodness are an image of the Trinity, see *supra*, 3.25.

535 On the mirror analogy, cf. *supra*, 2.21, 5.6, 6.1.

536 Rom 1:20; see *supra*, 1.8, 1.10, 5.6, 6.1.

537 Isa 14:12.
538 Cf. Augustine, *Trin.* 5.7 (CCL 50.211–12); *Conl. Max.* 1.18 (PL 42.756); Anselm, *Mon.* 56 (Schmitt, 1.67–68); Robert of Melun, *Sent.* 1.6.35 (Martin, 3.2.338–39).
539 That "Father" is a relational term, cf. Augustine, *Trin.* 5.7 (CCL 50.211–12); Robert of Melun, *Sent.* 1.4.14 (Martin, 3.2.125).
540 See *supra*, 3.6, 21, 25.
541 Cf. John 1:14, 18; 3:16, 18; 1 John 4:9; Athanasian Creed (Denz., 50–52).
542 That the Holy Spirit is not called begotten or unbegotten, cf. Augustine, *Trin.* 15.47 (CCL 50A.527–29); Peter Abelard, *TChr* 3.62 (CCCM 12.220); *SN* 17 (Boyer 2.152–53); *Tsum* 2.30 (CCCM 13.124–25); Peter Lombard, *Sent.* 1.13.4 (SB 4.124–25); Robert of Melun, *Sent.* 1.6.35 (Martin, 3.2.339).
543 See *supra*, 6.8.
544 See *supra*, 6.2, 7, 8.
545 See *supra*, 5.6; 6.2.
546 Rom 1:20; see *supra*, 1.8, 1.10, 5.6, 6.1.
547 Cf. Athanasian Creed (Denz., 50–52); *supra*, 6.4, 5, 16.
548 Regarding the question on procession with generation and without generation, cf. Augustine, *Trin.* 5.15 (CCL 50A.222–23); Peter Abelard, *TChr* 4.148 (CCCM 12.339); *SN* 18 (Boyer 2.156–57); Robert of Melun, *Sent.* 1.4.7 (Martin, 3.2.107).
549 Cf. *supra*, 3.2, 15; 6.3.
550 That the Father wills to generate the Son, cf. Robert of Melun, *Sent.* 1.4.19–20 (Martin, 3.2.138–39).
551 Cf. Achard of St Victor, *Unitate* 1.36 (Martineau, 104–6).
552 See *supra*, 2.12; 4.11.
553 See *supra*, 6.17.
554 Cf. Richard of St Victor, *Statu.* 17 (*AHDLMA* 42.82).
555 Col 1:15; Heb 1:3.
556 Cf. *supra*, 6.11.
557 See *supra*, 6.11.
558 Gen 1:27. Obviously, Richard identifies the possessive pronoun "his" with the Only-Begotten.
559 All the direct quotes in this chapter are from the Athanasian Creed (Denz., 50–52).
560 Richard associates the Athanasian Creed with Holy Scripture.
561 Cf. *infra*, 6.21.
562 See *supra*, 3.2–3, 8, 24–25; 5.25.
563 See *supra*, 6.11, 18.
564 Heb 1:3; see *supra*, 6.18.
565 Cf. Richard of St Victor, *Erud.* 2.48 (PL 196.1345A).
566 On the mirror imagery, see *supra*, 2.21; 5.6; 6.1, 15.
567 Cf. Hugh of St Victor, *Sacr.* 1.3.31 (PL 176.232D).
568 John 4:24; see *supra*, 6.10.
569 See *supra*, 6.20.
570 Cf. *supra*, 6.21.
571 Heb 1:3.
572 Obviously Richard is highly disturbed by the "many" (*multi*) in his day that deny the truth of the formula: "substance begets substance" (*substantia gignat substantiam*). There is no doubt that Richard has Peter Lombard (and maybe Peter Abelard) in his crosshairs. Peter Abelard seems to be the first to use and reject this formula (*TChr* 3.109 [CCCM 12.235]; *Tsum* 2.62 [CCCM 13.134]: *substantia substantiam generat*). Because he accepts the formula "God begets God," if this is taken to mean God the Father begets God the Son (i.e., God the Father begets a person not substance), then the question arises whether "substance begot substance." According to Peter Abelard, not only does every argument reject this formula, but so do the "writings of the holy fathers." He cites Augustine's *On the Trinity* (CCL 50.28): "But those,

who think that God is of such power that he begets himself, are very wrong, because not only is God not so, but neither are spiritual or created spirits. There is absolutely no thing that begets itself." Based on this Peter Abelard offers the following maxim: "It is obvious that everything that is said about God must be said with reference to the persons either individually or all together." But if God begets himself (which Peter obviously equates with 'substance begets substance'), then this would lead to a confusion of persons, because if the Father begets himself, then the Father would be his own son, and if the Son or Holy Spirit begets himself, then he would be his own father (*TChr* 3.109–10 [CCCM 12.235]). Hence, Peter Abelard will reject this formula, because he thinks that it will lead to Modalism.

In two places in book one of his *Sententiae* Peter Lombard disscusses these formulas. First, Peter does allow for the formulas "God begot God" (*Deus genuit Deum*) and "One begot One" (*unus unum genuit*), if it is taken to mean: "God the Father begot God the Son" (*Deus Pater Deum Filium genuit*), that is, similar to Peter Abelard, Peter wants *Deum* and *unum* in the two formulas to refer to the person of the Word; he does not want to concede that the divine nature, as distinguished from the divine persons, can be generated (see below). Nevertheless, he will allow for this formula, because the Constantinopolitan Creed does profess after all: "Light from light, true God from true God" (Denz., 83–85). Moreover, while not cited by Peter Abelard, Augustine does say in his *Conl. Max.* (PL 42.749): "Even if we understand that ineffable generation from the womb of the Father, what this means is this: that from out of himself, that is, from his substance God begot God" (*Illa ineffabilis generatio etiam si ex utero Patris accipitur, hoc significatum est, quia de se ipso, hoc est, de substantia sua Deus Deum genuit*) (see also *S.* 118 [PL 38.1003]). But Peter denies the following conclusion that could be drawn from this formula: "therefore God begot himself as God or another God" (*ergo genuit de Deum vel alium Deum*) for obvious reasons (see, *Sent.* 1.4.1.1 [SB 4.77–78], which is following the *Summa sent.* 1.11 [PL 176.60C-D]).

Next Peter Lombard discusses the formula "essence begot essence" (*essentia genuit essentiam*), and following Peter Abelard, he will reject it, presumably because essence cannot predicate a person. Finding support in the Catholic tradition, Peter Lombard will also say: "We consent to the Catholic expounders and say that the Father did not beget the divine essence, nor did the divine essence beget the Son, nor did the divine essence beget the essence. But we interpret this word 'essence' as the divine nature, which is common to the three persons and is whole in each of them" (*Sent.* 1.5.1.1 [SB 4.81]). While Peter cannot cite any authority that explicitly denies the formula, he makes the inference from three citations from Augustine. First, according to Augustine, "what is said relatively does not indicate a substance" (*Trin.* 5.8 [CCL 50.214]). As Peter reasons, if the Father begot the essence, then the essence would be a term relative to the Father; hence, the formula is rejected based on an inference from Augustine. Second, if the Father begets the divine essence, then he would beget that which he is (i.e., the divine essence). Here Peter Lombard refers to the same passage of Augustine that Peter Abelard cited, namely that the Father cannot beget himself (*Trin.* 1.1 [(CCL 50.28], which is cited above). Peter Lombard, however, prefers the third reason. If the Father begets the divine essence, and the Father is that divine essence, then this would mean that the Father is God by the very essence that he begets. Here Peter Lombard brings in a similar argument from Augustine, who denies that the wisdom begotten by the Father is the cause of the Father's wisdom (*Trin.* 1.2 [CCL 50.249]). Because God's wisdom is identical to his being, Peter concludes as certain that the Father did not beget the divine essence (*Sent.* 1.5.1.1–4 [SB 4.80–82]).

However, unlike Peter Abelard and Peter Lombard Richard will allow "substance" to predicate person in the formula "substance begets substance," if the subject is the Unbegotten substance, which is nothing other than the person of the Father, and the object is the Begotten substance, which is nothing other than the person of the Word (and yet the substance of the Father and Son is identical). Moreover, while Peter Lombard rejects the formula "substance begets substance," because it suggests that Father is wise by the Wisdom that he begets (see *Sent.* 1.5.1.4 [SB 4.81–82]), Richard will resolve this issue in the next chapter, where he argues the Son's wisdom is a "received wisdom" (or begotten wisdom) and the Father's wisdom is a "not-received wisdom" (or unbegotten wisdom), and yet the wisdom of the Father and Son is identical. See discussion in Robert of Melun, *Sent.* 1.4.21–24 (Martin, 3.2.141–51) and Salet (SC 63.504–7).

573   Again probably a reference to Peter Lombard, *Sent.* 1.5.1.7 (SB 4.82), who denies a similar formula: "wisdom begot wisdom, and essence begot essence (*sapientia sapientiam et essentiam essentiam genuerit*); see 6.22, note 573.

574   Cf. 1 Sam 17:51.

575   Richard is probably mocking Peter Lombard (see, *supra* 6.22, note 573). In his *Sent.* 1.5.1.5 (SB 4.82), after citing two passages from Augustine *F. et symb.* 3.4 (CSEL 41.7–8), Lombard admits the following: "[Augustine] *clearly says* from these words that God the Father begot that which he is. Moreover, that which he is is nothing other than divine essence. Therefore *it seems* that he begot the divine essence" (emph. mine). Afterward, Lombard replies: "We respond to this and say that those words are to be undersood in the following way (*illa uerba sic intelligenda esse*): 'The Father begot from himself that which he is', that is, the Son who is that which the Father is." Hence, according to Lombard, the Father did not beget the divine essence but the person of the Word. Peter Lombard also cites several other passages from Augustine and Hilary that "*seem* to mean that wisdom begot wisdom, and substance begot substance" (*videtur significare quod sapientia sapientiam et essentia essentiam genuerit*) but in each instance he interprets the meaning of the passages to refer to the person of the Word not the essence or wisdom (see *Sent.* 1.5.1.7–17 [SB 4.82–87]).

576   A number of the manuscripts read "our explanation". Salet will prefer that reading (SC 63.445), while I have adopted Ribaillier's reading (TPMA 6.259).

577   1 Tim 1:15.

578   Richard is obviously being ironic here.

579   Isa 7:9 (LXX); see *supra*, 1.1.

580   Athanasian Creed (Denz., 50–52).

581   I.e., that substance begets substance.

582   I.e., that God is from the substance of the Father.

583   On the authority of the holy fathers, cf. *supra*, 1.5.

584   Cf. Augustine, *Trin.* 10.15 (CCL 50.328); Peter Lombard, *Sent.* 1.29.3 (SB 4.215–16); Robert of Melun, *Sent.* 1.4.3 (Martin, 3.2.101–3).

585   Cf. *supra*, Prol; 1.10, 5.6.

586   Cf. Gen 1:26.

587   Cf. 1 Cor 1:24; Augustine, *Trin.*6.1 (CCL 50.228); Peter Lombard, *Sent.* 1.32.2 (SB 4.234–36); Robert of Melun, *Sent.* 1.6.1 (Martin, 3.2.285–87).

588   Cf. *supra*, 4.15; 5.9.

589   Cf. Richard of St Victor, *Quomodo Spiritus* (TPMA 15.164–66).

590   Cf. *supra*, 6.22.

591   See *supra*, 6.22.

592   See *supra*, 6.23.

593   See *supra*, 6.22, 23.

594   See *supra*, 1.17, 18, 23; 2.18; 3.22; 6.23.

595   Cf. Isidore of Seville, *Etym.* 1.1 (Lindsay, 1.25): "Discipline derives its name from learning; hence, it can also be called 'knowledge'. For instance, 'to know' is named from 'to learn,' because none of us knows unless we learn. Discipline is also used in another way, because the full thing is learned" (*Disciplina a discendo nomen accepit: unde et scientia dici potest. Nam scire dictum a discere, quia nemo nostrum scit, nisi qui discit. Aliter dicta disciplina, quia discitur plena*).

596   As indicated by "so to speak" (*ut sic dicatur*), Richard may be coining the word *discentia*. It could be a word play on "from" (*de*) and "knowledge" (*scientia*).

597   Cf. Augustine, *Trin.* 8.2 (CCL 50.269–70).

SELECT BIBLIOGRAPHY

Primary Sources

Hugh of St Victor

Hugh of St Victor. *Didascalicon: De studio legendi.* The Catholic University of America, Studies in Medieval and Renaissance Latin, vol. 10. Edited by Charles Henry Buttimer. Washington: The Catholic University Press, 1939.

_____. *The Didascalicon of Hugh of St Victor.* Records of Western Civilization Series. Translated and Introduction by Jerome Taylor. New York: Columbia University Press, 1991.

_____. *Opera omnia.* PL 175–77. Edited by J. P. Migne. Paris, 1854.

_____. *On the Sacraments of the Christian Faith (De Sacramentis) of Hugh of Saint Victor.* The Mediaeval Academy of America Publications 58. Translated by Roy Deferrari. Cambridge: The Mediaeval Academy of America, 1951.

_____. *Opera Propaedeutica.* Edited by R. Baron. Notre Dame, IN: University of Notre Dame Press, 1966.

_____. *'De archa Noe, Libellus de formatione arche'.* Edited by P. Sicard. Corpus Christianorum Continuatio Mediaevalis 176. Turnhout: Brepols, 2001.

_____. *Selected Spiritual Writings.* Translated by a Religious of C.S.M.V. with an introduction by A. Squire. London: Faber and Faber, 1962.

_____. *Hugonis de Sancto Victore: De tribus diebus.* Edited by D. Poirel. Corpus Christianorum Continuatio Mediaevalis 177. Turnhout: Brepols, 2002.

L'oeuvre de Hugues de Saint-Victor 1. Latin text by H. B. Feiss and P. Sicard. Translation (French) by D. Poirel, H. Rochais, and P. Sicard. Introductions, notes, and appendices by D. Poirel. Sous La règle de Saint Augustin. Turnhout: Brepols, 1997.

L'oeuvre de Hugues de Saint-Victor 2. Introductions, notes, and appendices by B. Jollès. Sous La règle de Saint Augustin. Turnhout: Brepols, 2000.

'Ugo di San Vittore "auctor" delle *Sententiae de divinitate*'. Edited by A. Piazzoni. *Studi Medievali, 3rd series*. 23 (1982), 861–955.

Richard of St Victor

Richard of Saint-Victor. *Les douze Patriarches ou Benjamin Minor*. SC 419. Translated and edited by Jean Châtillon and M. Duchet-Suchaux. Paris: Cerf, 1997.

_____. *Die Dreieinigkeit*. Christliche Meister 4. Translated by Hans Urs von Balthasar. Einsiedlen: Johannes Verlag, 1980.

_____. *Liber exceptionum*. Edited and introduced by Jean Châtillon. Textes philosophiques du moyen âge 5. Paris: J. Vrin, 1958.

_____. *Richardi a Sancto Victore omnia opera*. PL 196. Edited by J. P. Migne. Paris, 1855.

_____. *Opuscules théologiques*. Texte critique avec introduction, notes et tables, par J. Ribaillier. Texte philosophique du moyen âge 15. Paris: J. Vrin, 1967.

_____. *De quatuor gradibus violentae caritatis*, in Ives, *Épître à Séverin sur la charité*. Texte critique avec introduction, traduction et notes par Gervais Dumeige. Texte philosophique du moyen âge 3. Paris: J. Vrin, 1955.

_____. *De questionibus regule sancti Augustini solutis*. Edited by M. L. Colker, "Richard of Saint Victor and the anonymous of Bridlington." *Traditio* 18 (1962): 181–227.

_____. *Sermones centum*. Patrologia Latina, vol. 177, col. 901–1210. Edited by J. P. Migne. Paris, 1880, attributed to Hugh of St Victor.

_____. *L'Édit d'Alexandre ou les trois processions*. Vol. 1 of *Sermons et opuscules spirituels inédits*. Texte latin, introduction et notes par Jean Châtillon and W. J. Tulloch. Traduction française J. Barthélemy. Paris: Desclée de Brouwer, 1951.

_____. *Selected Writings on Contemplation*. Translated by Clare Kirchberger. London: Faber and Faber, 1957.

_____. "*De statu interioris hominis*." Introduction et texte critique par J. Ribaillier. *Archives d'histoire doctrinale et littéraire du moyen-âge* 34 (1967): 7–128.

_____. *De Trinitate*. PL 196, col. 887–992. Edited by J. P. Migne. Paris, 1855.

_____. *De Trinitate*. Texte critique avec introduction, notes et tables par J. Ribaillier. Texte philosophique du moyen age 6. Paris: J. Vrin, 1958.

_____. *La Trinité*. SC 63. Texte latin, introduction, traduction et notes de G. Salet. Paris: Cerf, 1959.

_____. *Trois opuscules spirituels de Richard de Saint-Victor: Textes inédits accompagnés d'études critiques et notes*. Edited by Jean Châtillon. Paris: Etudes Augustiniennes, 1986.

_____. *The Twelve Patriarchs, The Mystical Ark, and Book Three on the Trinity*. The Classics of Western Spirituality. Translated and introduction by G. A. Zinn. New York: Paulist Press, 1979.

Other Authors Cited in the Footnotes

Abelard, Peter. *Sic et Non*. Edited by Blanche B. Boyer and Richard McKeon. Chicago: University of Chicago Press, 1976.

_____. *Theologia Christiana*. CCCM 12. Edited by E. M. Buytaert. Turnhout: Brepols, 1969.

_____. *Theologia 'Scholarium'*. CCCM 13. Edited by E. M. Buytaert and C. J. Mews. Turnhout: Brepols, 1987.

_____. *Theologia 'Summi Boni'*. CCCM 13. Edited by E. M. Buytaert and C. J. Mews. Turnhout: Brepols, 1987.

Achard of St Victor. *De unitate Dei et pluralitate creaturarum*. Edited and translated by Emmanuel Martineau. Saint-Lambert des Bois: Authentica, 1987.

_____. *Works*. CS 165. Translation and Introduction by Hugh Feiss. Kalamazoo: Cistercian Publications, 2001.

Anselm of Canterbury. *The Major Works*. Oxford World's Classics. Edited with an Introduction by Brian Davies and G. R. Evans. Oxford: University Press, 1998.

_____. *Opera omnia*, 6 vols. Edited by F. S. Schmitt. Edinburgh: T. Nelson, 1938–1961.

Augustine of Hippo. *Arianism and Other Heresies*. WSA 1.18. Edited by John Rotelle. Translated by Roland Teske. New York: New City Press, 1995.

_____. *Aurelii Augustini Opera*, 1.1. CCL 27. Edited by Lucas Verheijen. Turnhout: Brepols, 1981.

_____. *Aurelii Augustini Opera*, 4.1. CCL 32. Edited by Joseph Martin and K. D. Daur. Turnhout: Brepols, 1962.

_____. *Aurelii Augustini Opera*, 8. CCL 36. Edited by R. Willems. Turnhout: Brepols, 1954.

_____. *Aurelii Augustini Opera*, 10.1. CCL 38. Edited by E. Dekkers and J. Fraipont. Turnhout: Brepols, 1956.

_____. *Aurelii Augustini Opera*, 10.2. CCL 39. Edited by E. Dekkers and J. Fraipont. Turnhout: Brepols, 1956.

_____. *Aurelii Augustini Opera*, 10.3. CCL 40. Edited by E. Dekkers and J. Fraipont. Turnhout: Brepols, 1956.

_____. *Aurelii Augustini Opera*, 11.1. CCL 41. Edited by C. Lambot. Turnhout: Brepols, 1961.

_____. *Aurelii Augustini Opera*, 13.2. CCL 46. Edited by E. Evans, I. B. Bauer, R. Vander Plaetse, *et al.* Turnhout: Brepols, 1969.

_____. *Aurelii Augustini Opera*, 14.1. CCL 47. Edited by B. Dombart and A. Kalb. Turnhout: Brepols, 1955.

_____. *Augustini Opera*, 14.2. CCL 48. Edited by B. Dombart and A. Kalb. Turnhout: Brepols, 1955.

_____. *Augustini Opera*, 16.1. CCL 50. Edited by W. J. Mountain. Turnhout: Brepols, 1968.

_____. *Augustini Opera*, 16.2. CCL 50A. Edited by W. J. Mountain. Turnhout: Brepols, 1968.

_____. *Christian Instruction*. FC 4. Translated by John Gavigan. New York: CIMA Publishing, 1947.

_____. *The City of God Books 1-7*. FC 6. Translated by D. Zema and G. Walsh. New York: Fathers of the Church, Inc., 1950.

_____. *The City of God Books 8-16*. FC 7. Translated by G. Walsh and Grace Monahan. New York: Fathers of the Church, Inc., 1952.

_____. *The City of God Books 17-22*. FC 8. Translated by G. Walsh and D. Honan. New York: Fathers of the Church, Inc., 1954.

_____. *Confessions*. FC 21. Translated by Vernon Bourke. New York: Fathers of the Church, Inc., 1953.

_____. *Exposition of the Psalms 1-32*. WSA 3.15. Edited by John Rotelle. Translated by Maria Boulding. New York: New City Press, 2000.

_____. *Exposition of the Psalms 33-50*. WSA 3.16. Edited by John Rotelle. Translated by Maria Boulding. New York: New City Press, 2000.

_____. *Exposition of the Psalms 51–72.* WSA 3.17. Edited by John Rotelle. Translated by Maria Boulding. New York: New City Press, 2001.

_____. *Exposition of the Psalms 73–98.* WSA 3.18. Edited by John Rotelle. Translated by Maria Boulding. New York: New City Press, 2002.

_____. *Letters (83–130),* vol. 2. FC 18. Translated by Wilfrid Parsons. New York: Fathers of the Church, Inc., 1953.

_____. *The Literal Meaning of Genesis.* ACW, 41–42. Translated by John Taylor. New York: Newman Press, 1982.

_____. *Opera omnia,* 16 vols. PL 32–47. Edited by J. P. Migne. Paris, 1845–1849.

_____. *Sancti Aureli Augustini Opera,* 2.1-2. CSEL 34.1–2. Edited by A. L. Goldbacher. Vienna: F. Tempsky, 1895.

_____. *Sancti Aureli Augustini Opera,* 2.3. CSEL 44. Edited by A. L. Goldbacher. Vienna: F. Tempsky, 1904.

_____. *Sancti Aureli Augustini Opera,* 2.4. CSEL 57. Edited by A. L. Goldbacher. Vienna: F. Tempsky, 1911.

_____. *Sancti Aureli Augustini Opera,* 2.6. CSEL 88. Edited by J. Divjak. Vienna: F. Tempsky, 1981.

_____. *Sancti Aureli Augustini Opera,* 3.1. CSEL 28.1. Edited by J. Zycha. Vienna: F. Tempsky, 1893.

_____. *Sancti Aureli Augustini Opera,* 5.3. CSEL 41. Edited by J. Zycha. Vienna: F. Tempsky, 1900.

_____. *Sancti Augustini Opera,* 6.1. CSEL 25.1. Edited by Joseph Zycha. Vienna: F. Tempsky, 1896.

_____. *Sancti Augustini Opera,* 6.3. CSEL 74. Edited by G. M. Green. Vienna: F. Tempsky, 1956.

_____. *Sancti Augustini Opera,* 6.7. CSEL 90. Edited by J. B. Bauer. Vienna: F. Tempsky, 1992.

_____. *Sancti Augustini Opera,* 8.1. CSEL 60. Edited by C. F. Urba and J. Zycha. Vienna: F. Tempsky, 1913.

_____. *Tractates on the Gospel of John 1–10.* FC 78. Translated by John Rettig. Washington, D.C.: The Catholic University of America Press, 1988.

_____. *Tractates on the Gospel of John 11–27.* FC 79. Translated by John Rettig. Washington, D.C.: The Catholic University of America Press, 1988.

_____. *Tractates on the Gospel of John 28–54*. FC 88. Translated by John Rettig. Washington, D.C.: The Catholic University of America Press, 1993.

_____. *Tractates on the Gospel of John 55–111*. FC 90. Translated by John Rettig. Washington, D.C.: The Catholic University of America Press, 1994.

_____. *Tractates on the Gospel of John 112–124*. FC 92. Translated by John Rettig. Washington, D.C.: The Catholic University of America Press, 1995.

_____. *The Trinity*. FC 45. Translated by Stephen McKenna. Washington, D.C.: The Catholic University of America Press, 1962.

Bernard of Clairvaux. *Five Books on Consideration: Advice to a Pope*. The Works of Bernard of Clairvaux 13. CF 37. Translated by John Anderson and Elizabeth Kennan. Kalamazoo: Cistercian Publications, 1976.

_____. *Homilies in Praise of the Blessed Virgin Mary*. CF 18A. Translated by Marie-Bernard Saïd. Kalamazoo: Cistercian Publications, 1993.

_____. *On the Song of Songs I*. The Works of Bernard of Clairvaux 2. CF 4. Translated by Kilian Walsh. Kalamazoo: Cistercian Publications, 1971.

_____. *On the Song of Songs II*. The Works of Bernard of Clairvaux 3. CF 7. Translated by Kilian Walsh. Kalamazoo: Cistercian Publications, 1983.

_____. *On the Song of Songs III*. The Works of Bernard of Clairvaux 3. CF 31. Translated by Kilian Walsh and Irene Edmonds. Kalamazoo: Cistercian Publications, 1979.

_____. *On the Song of Songs IV*. The Works of Bernard of Clairvaux 4. CF 40. Translated by Irene Edmonds. Kalamazoo: Cistercian Publications, 1971.

_____. *Opera*. Edited by Jean Leclerq *et. al.*, Vol. I-VIII. Rome: Editiones Cisterciensis, 1957–1977.

Boethius. *De arithmetica*. CLL 94A. Edited by H. Oosthout and J. Schilling. Turnhout: Brepols, 1999.

_____. *The consolation of philosophy*. Translated with introduction and explanatory notes by P. G. Walsh. New York: Oxford University Press, 1999.

_____. *In Isagogen Porphyrii commenta*. CSEL 48. Edited by George Schepss and Samuel Brandt. Vienna: F. Tempsky, 1906.

—————————. *Opera omnia.* PL 63–64. Edited by J. P. Migne. Paris, 1847.

—————————. *Philosophiae consolatio.* CCL 94. Edited by L. Bieler. Turnhout: Brepols, 1957.

—————————. *The Theological Tractates.* Loeb Classical Library, 74. Translated by H. F. Stewart, E. K. Rand, and S. J. Tester. Cambridge: Harvard University Press, 1973.

Gilbert of Poitiers. *The Commentaries on Boethius.* Edited by N. K. Häring. Toronto: Pontifical Institute of Mediaeval Studies, 1966.

Gregory the Great. *XL homiliarum in Evangelia libri duo.* CCL 141. Edited by Raymond Étaix. Turnhout: Brepols, 1999.

—————————. *Homiliarum in Ezechielem Prophetam.* CCL 142. Edited by M. Adriaen. Turnhout: Brepols, 1971.

—————————. *Liber sacramentorum.* PL 78, col. 25–240A. Edited by J. P. Migne. Paris, 1849.

—————————. *Moralia in Job libri I-X.* CCL 143. Edited by Mark Adriaen. Turnhout: Brepols, 1979.

—————————. *Moralia in Job libri XI-XXII.* CCL 143A. Edited by Mark Adriaen. Turnhout: Brepols, 1979.

—————————. *Moralia in Job libri XXIII-XXXV.* CCL 143B. Edited by Mark Adriaen. Turnhout: Brepols, 1985.

—————————. *Vita S. Benedicti.* PL 66, col. 125–204. Edited by J. P. Migne. Paris, 1847.

Hildebert of Lavardin. *Tractactus theologicus.* PL 171, col. 1067–1150B. Edited by J. P. Migne. Paris, 1854.

Jerome. *Commentariorum in Matheum libri IV.* CCL 77. Edited by D. Hurst and M. Adriaen. Turnhout: Brepols, 1969.

John of Salisbury. *Metalogicon.* CCCM 98. Edited by J. B. Hall. Turnhout: Brepols, 1991.

Liber ordinis Sancti Victoris Parisiensis. CCCM 61. Edited by Lucas Jocqué and Ludovicus Milis. Turnhout: Brepols, 1984.

Lombard, Peter. *Sententiae in IV libris distinctae.* SB 4–5. Grottaferrata: Editiones Collegii S. Bonaventurae ad Claras Aquas, 1971–81.

Peter the Venerable, *Epistolarum libri sex.* PL 189, col. 61–472B. Edited by J. P. Migne. Paris, 1854.

Robert of Melun. *Questiones de divina pagina.* Vol. 1, *Oeuvres de Robert de Melun.* Spicilegium sacrum Lovaniense: Études et documents, fasc. 13. Edited by Raymond Martin. Louvain: "Spi-cilegium sacrum Lovaniense" Bureaux, 1932.

_____. *Questiones theologice de epistolis Pauli.* Vol. 2, *Oeuvres de Robert de Melun.* Spicilegium sacrum Lovaniense: Études et documents, fasc. 18. Edited by Raymond Martin. Lou-vain: "Spicilegium sacrum Lovaniense" Bureau, 1938.

_____. *Sententie.* Vol. 3.1–2, *Oeuvres de Robert de Melun.* Spicile-gium sacrum Lovaniense: Études et documents, fasc. 21, 25. Edited by Raymond Martin. Louvain: "Spicilegium sacrum Lovaniense" Administration, 1947, 1952.

Werner of St Blaise *Libri deflorationum sive excerptionum.* PL 157, col. 721–1256A. Edited by J. P. Migne. Paris, 1854.

William of St Thierry. *Expositio altera super Cantica canitcorum.* PL 180, col. 473–545. Edited by J. P. Migne. Paris, 1855.

Select Secondary Works

Allard, Henri. *Die eheliche Lebens und Liebesgemeinschaft nach Hugo von St. Viktor.* Rome: Analecta Dehoniana, 1963.

Aris, Marc Aeilko. *Contemplatio*: Philosophische Studien zum Traktat *Benja-min Maior* des Richard von St. Victor: Mit einer verbes-serten Edition des Textes. Fuldaer Studien 6. Frankfurt: J. Knecht, 1996.

Arnold, J. "*Summa germanitas*: Zur Bedeutung des Verwandtschaftsbegriffs in den Trinitätstheologien Richards von St. Victor und Wilhelms von Auxerre." *Theologie und Philosophie* 70 (1995): 92–100.

Barbosa de Sousa, Ricardo. "A Trindade: O pessoal e o social na espiritualidade Crista." *Vox Scripturae* 5 (1995): 17–28.

Barnes, M. "De Régnon Reconsidered," *Augustinian Studies* 26 (1995): 51–79.

Baron, Roger. "L'Influence de Hugues de St.-Victor." *Recherches de théologie ancienne et médiévale* 22 (1955): 56–71.

_____. "La pensée mariale de Hugues de Saint-Victor." *Revue d'ascétique et de mystique* 31 (1955): 249–71.

_____. "Notes biographiques sur Hugues de Saint-Victor." *Revue d'histoire ecclésiastique* 51 (1956): 920–34.

_____. *Science et sagesse chez Hugues de Saint-Victor.* Paris, 1957.

_____. "Le 'sacrement de foi' selon Hugues de Saint-Victor." *Revue des sciences philosophiques et théologiques* 100 (1958):50–78.

_____. "Rapports entre Saint Augustin et Hugues de Saint-Victore: trois opuscules de Hugues de Saint-Victor." *Revue des Études Augustiniennes* 5 (1959): 391–429.

_____. "Hugues de Saint-Victor: contribution à un nouvel examen de son oeuvre." *Traditio* 15 (1959): 223–97.

_____. ed. *Hugues et Richard de Saint-Victor. Témoins de la foi.* Paris: Bloud and Gay, 1961.

_____. "Note sur la succession et la date des écrites de Hugues de Saint-Victor." *Revue d'histoire ecclésiastique* 57 (1962): 88–118.

_____. *Études sur Hugues de Saint-Victor.* Paris, 1963.

_____. "L'idée de liberté chez S. Anselme et Hugues de Saint-Victor." *Recherches de théologie et philosophie médiévales* 32 (1965): 117–21.

_____. "Hugues de Saint-Victor." *Dictionnaire de spiritualité*, vol. VII, pp. 901–39. Paris, 1969.

Barthélemy, J. "Richard de Saint-Victor, Deux sortes de pain. La consolation et l'épreuve dans l'exercice des bonnes oeuvres." *Le vie spirituelle* 83 (1950): 43–7.

Bataillon, L. J. "Bulletin d'histoire des doctrines médiévales: Richard de Saint Victor." *Revue de sciences philosopiques et théologiques* 43 (1959): 698–701.

Bautier, R. H. "Les origines et les premiers développements de l'abbaye Saint-Victor de Paris." In *L'abbaye parisienne de Saint-Victor au Moyen Âge.* Bibliotheca Victorina 1. Turnhout: Brepols, 1991.

Berndt, Rainer. *André de Saint-Victor (d. 1175): Exégète et théologien.* Bibliotheca Victorina 2. Turnhout: Brepols, 1991.

_____. "The School of St Victor in Paris." In *Hebrew Bible/Old Testament* 1.2. Gottingen: Vandenhoeck and Ruprecht, 2000.

_____. ed. *Schrift, Schreiber, Schenker. Studien zur Abtei Sankt Viktor in Paris und den Viktorinen.* Corpus Victorinum. Instrumenta 1. Berlin: Akademie Verlag, 2005.

_____. "La théologie comme système du monde. Sur l'évolution des Sommes théologiques de Hugues de Saint Victor à

Saint Thomas d'Aquin." *Revue des sciences philosophiques et théologiques* 78 (1994): 555–72.

Bonnard, F. *Histoire de l'abbaye royale et de l'ordre des chanoines réguliers de Saint-Victor de Paris*, 2 vols. Paris, 1904–1907.

Bok, Nico den. *Communicating the Most High: A Systematic Study of Persons and Trinity in the Theology of Richard of St Victor (d. 1173).* Bibliotheca Victorina 7. Turnhout: Brepols, 1996.

Bynum, Carolyn Walker. *Docere verbo et exemplo: An Aspect of Twelfth-Century Spirituality.* Harvard Theological Studies XXXI. Missoula, MT: Scholars Press, 1979.

——————. "The Spirituality of Regular Canons in the Twelfth Century." In *Jesus as Mother: Studies in the Spirituality of the High Middle Ages*, 22–58. Berkeley, CA: University of California Press, 1982.

Cacciapuoti, Pierluigi. *Deus existentia amoris: Carità e Trinità nell'itinerario teologico di Riccardo di San Vittore (d. 1173).* Bibliotheca Victorina 9. Turnhout: Brepols, 1998.

Cavadini, John. "The Quest for Truth in Augustine's De *Trinitate*." *Theological Studies* 58 (1997): 429–40.

Chase, Steven. *Contemplation and Compassion: The Victorine Tradition. Traditions of Christian Spirituality.* Maryknoll: Orbis, 2003.

Châtillon, Jean. "Les quatre degrés de la charité d'apres Richard de Saint-Victor (I)." *Revue d'ascétique et de mystique* 20 (1939): 237–64.

——————. "Les trois modes de la contemplation selon Richard de Saint-Victor." *Bulletin de littérature ecclésiastique* 41 (1940): 3–26.

——————. "Le contenu, l'autheniticité et la date du *Liber exceptionum* et des *Sermones centum* de Richard de Saint-Victor." *Revue du moyen-âge latin* 4 (1948), 23–52, 343–366.

——————. "Autour des *Miscellanea* attribués à Hugues de Saint-Victor." *Revue d'ascétique et de mystique* 25 (1949): 299–305.

——————. "Une ecclésiologie médiévale: l'idée de l'Église dans la théologie de l'école de Saint-Victor au XIIᵉ siècle." *Irénikon* 22 (1949): 115–38; 395–411.

——————. "*Misit Herodes rex manus*: un opuscule de Richard de Saint-Victor, égaré parmi les oeuvres de Fulbert de Chartes." *Revue du moyen-âge latin* 6 (1950): 277–99.

——————. "Chronique de Guillaume de Champeaux à Thomas Gallus: chronique d'histoire littéraire et doctrinale de l'école de Saint-Victor." *Revue du moyen-âge latin* 8 (1952): 139–62, 247–73.

—————. "Contemplation, action et predication d'après un sermon inedit de Richard de Saint Victor en l'honneur de Saint Gregoire-le-Grand." In *L'homme devant Dieu: Mélanges offerts au Père Henri de Lubac*. Paris: Aubier, 1963–64.

—————. "La culture de l'école de Saint Victor au 12ᵉ siècle." In *Entretiens sur la renaissance du 12ᵉ siècle*, ed. Maurice de Gandillac and Édouard Jeauneau, 147–78. Paris, 1968.

—————. *Théologie, spiritualité et métaphysique dans l'oeuvre oratoire d'Achard de Saint-Victor*. Études de Philosophie médiévale, 58. Paris: J. Vrin, 1969.

—————. "Les écoles de Chartres et de Saint-Victor." *La scuola nell'occidente latino dell'alto medioevo. Settimana di Studio del Centro Italiano di studi sull'Alto Medioevo* 19.2. Spoleto: Presso La Sede del Centro, 1972.

—————. "La Bible dans les écoles du XIIᵉ siècle." In *Le moyen âge et la Bible*, pp. 163–97. Eds. Pierre Riché and Guy Lobrichon. Paris, 1984.

—————. "Richard de Saint-Victor." *Dictionnaire de spiritualité* 13. Paris, 1987, 594–654.

—————. *Le mouvement canonial au moyen age: Réforme de l'église, spiritualité et culture*. Ed. Patrice Sicard. Biblootheca Victorina 3. Turnhout: Brepols, 1992.

Chenu, M. D. *La théologie au douzième siècle. Études de philosophie médiévale*, 45. Paris: J. Vrin, 1957.

—————. "Civilisation urbaine et théologie: L'École de Saint-Victor au XIIᵉ siècle." *Annales: Économies, sociétés, civilisations* 29.2 (1974): 1253–63.

Cizewski, Wanda. "Reading the World as Scripture: Hugh of St Victor's *De tribus diebus*." *Florilegium* 9 (1987): 65–88.

Colish, Marcia. *Peter Lombard*. 2 vols. Leiden, 1994.

Croyden, F. E. "Abbot Laurence of Westminster and Hugh of St Victor." *Medieval and Renaissance Studies* 2 (1950): 169–71.

Constable, Giles. *The Reformation of the Twelfth Century*. Cambridge: Cambridge University Press, 1996.

Coolman, Boyd Taylor. "*Pulchrum Esse*: The Beauty of Scripture, the Beauty of the Soul, and the Art of Exegesis in the Theology of

Hugh of St Victor." *Traditio: Studies in Ancient and Medieval Thought, History, and Religion* 58 (2003): 175–200.

—————. "Hugh of St Victor." In *The Sermon on the Mount through the Centuries*, eds. Jeffrey P. Greenman, Timothy Larsen, and Stephen Spencer, 72–102. Grand Rapids, MI, 2007.

—————. "Hugh of St Victor on 'Jesus Wept': Compassion as Ideal *humanitas*." *Theological Studies* 69 (2008): 528–56.

—————. *The Theology of Hugh of St Victor: An Interpretation*. Cambridge University Press, 2010.

Coulter, Dale M. *Per visibilia ad invisibilia: Theological Method in Richard of St Victor (D. 1173)*. Bibliotheca Victorina 19. Turnhout: Brepols, 2006.

Courth, Franz. *Trinität in der Scholastik*. Handbuch der Dogmengeschichte II.1. Freiburg: Herder, 1985.

Cousins, Ewert H. "The Notion of Person in the De Trinitate of Richard of Saint Victor." Ph.D. diss., Fordham University, 1966.

—————. "A Theology of Interpersonal Relations." *Thought* 45 (1970): 56–82.

Delhaye, Philippe. "Les perspectives morales de Richard de Saint-Victor." In *Mélanges offerts à René Crozet a l'occasion de son soixante-dixieme anniversaire*, vol II. Poitiers: Société d'Études Médiévales, 1966.

—————. "L'organisation scolaire au XIIᵉ siècle." *Traditio* 5 (1947): 211–68.

—————. *Le Microcosmus de Godefroy de Saint-Victor. Étude théologique*. Lille: Facultés Catholiques, 1951.

Dickinson, J. C. *The Origins of the Austin Canons and Their Introduction into England*. London: S.P.C.K., 1950.

Dronke, P., ed. *A History of Twelfth Century Western Philosophy*. Cambridge: Cambridge University Press, 1988.

Dumeige, Gervais. "Effort métaphysique chez Richard de Saint-Victor." In *Die Metaphysik im Mittelalter: Ihr Ursprung und ihre Bedeutung: Vorträge des II. Internationalen Kongresses für mittelalterliche Philosophie Köln 31. August-6. September*. Edited by P. Wilpert. Miscellanea Mediaevalia, Bd. 2. Berlin: De Gruyter, 1963.

—————. *Richard de Saint-Victor et l'idée chrétienne de l'amour*. Bibliothèque de Philosophie Contemporaine 1. Paris: Presses universitaires de France, 1952.

Duggan, Anne J. "The Deposition of Abbot Ernis of Saint-Victor: A New Letter?" *Journal of Ecclesiastical History* 45 (1994): 642–60.

Ebner, Joseph. *Die Erkenntnislehre Richards von St. Viktor*. Beiträge zur Geschichte der Philosophie und Theologie des Mittelalters, 19.4. Munich: Aschendorff, 1917.

Ehlers, Joachim. "Das Augustinerchorherrenstift St. Viktor in der Pariser Schul- und Studienlandschaft des 12. Jahrhunderts." In *Aufbruch, Wandel, Erneuerung*. Stuttgart: Frommann-Holzboog, 1995.

_____. *Hugo von St. Viktor: Studien zum Geschichtsdenken und zur Geschichtsschreibung des 12. Jahrhunderts*. Frankfurter historische Abhandlungen 7. Wiesbaden: Steiner, 1973.

_____. "Hugo von St. Viktor und die Viktoriner." In *Mittelalter* 1. Stuttgart: W. Kohlhammer, 1983.

Emery, Gilles O.P. *Trinity in Aquinas*, trans., Matthew Levering, Heather Buttery, Robert Williams, and Teresa Bede, with a preface by Jean-Pierre Torrell, O.P., Ypsilanti, Mich.: Sapientia Press of Ave Maria College, 2003.

Ernst, Stephan. *Gewissheit des Glaubens: Der Glaubenstraktat Hugos von St. Viktor als Zugang zu seiner theologischen Systematik*. Beiträge zur Geschichte der Philosophie und Theologie des Mittelalters, 30. Münster: Aschendorff, 1987.

Éthier, Albert Marie. *Le "De Trinitate" de Richard de Saint-Victor*. Publications de l'Institut d'Études médiévales d'Ottawa, 9. Paris: J. Vrin, 1939.

Fassler, Margot. *Gothic Song: Victorine Sequences and Augustinian Reform in twelfth-century Paris*. Cambridge Studies in Medieval and Renaissance Music. New York: Cambridge University Press, 1993.

Feiss, Hugh. "Heaven in the theology of Hugh, Achard, and Richard of St Victor." In *Imagining Heaven in the Middle Ages*. Edited by Jan Swango Emerson and Hugh Feiss. New York: Garland Publisher, 2000.

_____. *Learning and the Ascent to God in Richard of St Victor*. STD diss., Pontifical Athenaeum of Saint Anselmo, 1979.

_____. "Circatores in the ordo of St Victor." In *Medieval Monastery*. St. Cloud, Minn.: North Star Press of St. Cloud, 1988.

Friedman, Russell L. *"In Principium Erat Verbum,"* Ph.D. Dissertation, University of Iowa, 1997.

_____. *Medieval Trinitarian Thought from Aquinas to Ockham.* Cambridge University Press, 2010.

_____. "Divergent Traditions in Later-Medieval Trinitarian Theology: Relations, Emanations, and the Use of Philosophical Psychology, 1250–1325," *Studia Theologica* 53 (1999):13–25

_____. *Intellectual Traditions at the Medieval University: The Use of Philosophical Psychology in Trinitarian Theology among the Franciscans and Dominicans, 1250–1350* (Leiden: Brill, forthcoming).

Fritz, G. "Richard de Saint-Victor." *Dictionnaire de théologie catholique* XIII.2, col. 2676–2695. Edited by Alfred Vacant, E. Mangenot, and Emile Amann. Paris: Letouzey et Ané, 1937.

Gaspar, Giles E. M. *Anselm of Canterbury and his Theological Inheritance.* Burlington VT: Ashgate, 2004.

Ghellinck, Joseph de. "La table des matières de la première édition des œuvres de Hugues de Saint-Victor." *Recherches de science religieuse* 1 (1910): 270–89, 385–96.

_____. *Le mouvement théologique du XIIe siècle.* 2nd edition. Bruges: Éditions "De Tempel," 1948.

Gemeinhardt, Peter. 2008. "Logic, Tradition, and Ecumenics: Developments of Latin Trinitarian Theology between c. 1075 and c. 1160." In *Trinitarian Theology in the Medieval West*, ed., Pekka and Kärkkäinen. Helsinki: Luther-Agricola-Society, 2007.

Gibson, Margaret T. "The *De doctrina christiana* in the School of St Victor." In *Reading and Wisdom: the De doctrina Christiana of Augustine in the Middle Ages.* Edited by Edward English. Notre Dame: University of Notre Dame Press, 1995.

Grosfillier Jean. *Les séquences d'Adam de Saint-Victor. Étude littéraire (poétique et rhétorique). Textes et traductions, commentaires.* Bibliotheca Victorina 20. Turnhout: Brepols, 2008.

Guimet, Fernard. "*Caritas ordinata* et *amor discretus* dans la théologie trinitaire de Richard de Saint-Victor." *Revue du moyen-âge latin* 4 (1948): 225–36.

_____. "Notes en marge d'un texte de Richard de Saint-Victor." *Archives d'histoire littéraire et doctrinale du moyen âge* 14 (1943–1945): 371–94.

Gunton, Colin, "Augustine, The Trinity and the Theological Crisis of the West." *Scottish Journal of Theology* 43 (1990): 33–58.

Häring, N. M. "The Case of Gilbert de la Porrée, Bishop of Poitiers (1142–1154)." *Mediaeval Studies* 13 (1951): 1–40.

Harkins, Franklin T. *Reading and the Work of Restoration. History and Scripture in the Theology of Hugh of St Victor*. Studies and Texts 167. Toronto: Pontifical Institute of Mediaeval Studies, 2009.

——————. " Homo Assumptus at St Victor: Reconsidering the Relationship between Victorine Christology and Peter Lombard's First Opinion." *The Thomist* 72 (2008): 595–624.

——————. "Secundus Augustinus: Hugh of St Victor on Liberal Arts Study and Salvation." *Augustinian Studies* 37:2 (2006): 219–46.

Harnack, Adolph, *The History of Dogma*. New York: Dover Publications, vol. IV, 1960.

Hart, David Bentley. *The Beauty of the Infinite: The Aesthetics Of Christian Truth*. Grand Rapids, MI: W. B. Eerdmans, 2004.

Haskins, C. H. *Renaissance of the Twelfth Century*. Cambridge: Harvard University Press, 1939.

Hödl, L. *Von der Wirklichkeit und Wirksamkeit des dreieinen Gottes nach der appropriativen Trinitätslehre des 12. Jarhunderts*. Mitteilungen des M. Grabmann-Institutes 12. München: M. Hueber 1965.

Hofmann, P. "Analogie und Person: Zur Trintätsspekulation Richards von St. Viktor." *Theologie und Philosophie* 59 (1984): 191–234.

Hofmeier, J. *Die Trinitätslehre des Hugo von St. Viktor, dargestellt im Zusammenhang mit den trinitarischen Stroemungen seiner Zeit*. Münchener Theologische Studien, 2. Systematische Abteilung, 25. Munich: M. Heuber, 1963.

Hugonin, F. "Notice sur Richard de Saint-Victor." *Patrologia Latina*, 196, col. xiv-xxxi. Edited by J. P. Migne. Paris, 1880.

Ilkhani, Mohammad. *La philosophie de la création chez Achard de Saint-Victor*. Brussels: Ousia, 1999.

Javelet, R. "Thomas Gallus et Richard de Saint-Victor, mystiques." *Recherches de théologie ancienne et médiévale* 29 (1962): 206–33.

——————. "Sens et réalité ultime selon Richard de Saint-Victor." *Ultimate Reality and Meaning* 6.3 (1983): 221–43.

Karfiková, Lena. *"De esse ad pulchrum esse." Die theologische Relevanz der Schönheit im Werk Hugos von Sankt Viktor*. Bibliotheca Victorina 8. Turnhout: Brepols, 1998.

Kleinz, John P. *Theory of Knowledge in Hugh of St Victor*. Catholic University of America Philosphical Studies 87. Washington, DC: The Catholic University of America Press, 1944.

Knoch, Wendelin. "Deus unus est trinus: Beobachtungen zur fruhscholast-ischen Gotteslehre." In *Im Gesprach mit dem dreieinen Gott*. Dusseldorf: Patmos Verlag, 1985.

Kühneweg, U. "Der Trinitätsaufweis Richards von St. Viktor." *Theologie und Philosophie* 62 (1987): 401–22.

Landgraf, Artur Michael. *Introduction à l'histoire de la littérature théologique de la scolastique naissante*. Publications de l'Institut d'Études Médiévales, 22. Montréal/Paris, 1973.

Longère, Jean, ed. *L'abbaye parisienne de Saint-Victor au Moyen Age*. Bibliotheca Victorina 1. Turnhout: Brepols, 1991.

Lottin, Odon. *Psychologie et morale aux XIIe et XIIIe siècles*. Vol. 4. Louvain: Abbaye du Mont César, 1954.

Lubac, Henri de. *Medieval Exegesis*. Vol. 3: *The Four Senses of Scripture*. Tr. E. M. Macierowski. Grand Rapids: Eerdmans, 2009, pp. 211–326.

Magee, J. *Boethius on Signification and Mind. Philosophia Antiqua: A Series of Studies on Ancient Philosophy*. Edited by W. J. Verdenius and J. C. M. Van Winden. Leiden: Brill, 1989.

Marenbon, J. *The Philosophy of Peter Abelard*. Cambridge: Cambridge University Press, 1997.

McGinn, Bernard. *The Growth of Mysticism: Gregory the Great through the 12th Century*. New York, 1996.

Melone, Maria Domenica. *Lo Spirito Santo nel "De trinitate" di Riccardo di S. Vittore*. Studia Antoniana, 45. Rome: Pontificium Athenaeum Antonianum, 2001.

Mews, Constant. "The World as Text." In *Scripture and Pluralism: Reading the Bible in the Religiously Plural Worlds of the Middle Ages and Renaissance*, eds. T. J. Heffernan and T. E. Burman, 95–122. Leiden, 2005.

——————. "Philosophy and Theology 1100–1150: The Search for Harmony." In *Le XIIe siècle: Mutations et renouveau en France dans la première moitié du XIIe siècle*. Ed. Françoise Gasparri. Cahiers du Léopard d'or, 3, 159–203. Paris: Le Léopard d'or, 1994.

Moltmann, Jürgen. *The Trinity and the Kingdom*, trans., Margaret Kohl. Minneapolis: Fortress Press, 1993.

Moonan, L. "Abelard's Use of the *Timaeus*." *Archives d'histoire doctrinale et littéraire du moyen âge* 56 (1989): 7–90.

Osborne, Jr., Thomas M. *Love of Self and Love of God in Thirteenth-Century Ethics*. Notre Dame: University of Notre Dame, 2005.

Ostler, H. *Die Psychologie des Hugo von St. Viktor*. Beiträge zur Geschichte der Philosophie und Theologie des Mittelalters, Band 6, Heft 2. Münster: Aschendorff, 1906.

Ott, L. *Untersuchungen zur theologischen Briefliteratur der Frühscholastik unter besonderer Berücksichtigung des Viktorinerkreises*. Beiträge zur Geschichte der Philosophie und Theologie des Mittelalters, Band 34, Heft 2. Münster: Aschendorff, 1937.

Ottaviano, Carmelo. *Riccardo di S. Vittore: La vita, le opera, il pensiero*. Memorie della R. Accademia Nazionale dei Lincei. Classe di scienze morali, storiche e filologiche, serie VI, vol. IV, fasc. V. Rome: Dott. Giovanni Bardi, tipografo della R. Accademia nazionale dei Lincei, 1933.

Ouy, Gibert. *Les manuscrits de l'abbaye de Saint-Victor: Catalogue établi sur la base du répertoire de Claude de Grandrue (1514)*. 2 vols. Bibliotheca Victorina 10. Turnhout: Brepols, 1999.

Paré, G., A. Brunet, and P. Tremblay. *La renaissance du XII* siècle, les écoles et l'enseignement*. Paris: J. Vrin, 1933.

Pecknold, C. C., "How Augustine Used the Trinity: Functionalism and the Development of Doctrine," *Anglican Theological Review* 81:1 (2003): 127–42.

Perkams, Matthias. "The Origins of the Trinitarian Attributes: potentia, sapientia, benignitas." *Archa Verbi*, 2004: 25–41.

Plantinga Jr., Cornelius. "The Threeness/Oneness Problem of the Trinity," *Calvin Theological Journal* 23 (1988) 37–53.

Piazzoni, Ambrogio M. "L'esegesi vittorina." In *Bibbia nel Medioevo*. Bologna: Dehoniane, 1996.

Pikaza, J. "La persona y el amor." *Estudios Trinitarios* 4 (1970): 3–36.

——————. "Notas sobre la Trinidad en Riccardo de San Victor." *Estudios Trinitarios* 6 (1972): 63–101.

Poirel, D. *Hugues de Saint-Victor. Initiations au moyen âge*. Paris: Cerf, 1998.

——————. ed. *L'abbe Suger, le manifeste gothique et Saint-Denis et la pensée victorine. Actes de Colloque organisé à la Fondation Singer-Polignac (Paris) le mardi 21 novembre 2000*. Recontres médiévales européennes 1. Turnhout: Brepols, 2001.

——————. "*Symbolice et anagogice*: l'école de Saint-Victor et la naissance du style gothique." In *L'abbé Suger, le manifeste gothique de Saint-Denis et la pensée victorine: colloque organisé à la Fondation Singer-Polignac le mardi 21 novembre 2000 par Rencontres médiévales européennes*, 141–70.

Rencontres médiévales européennes, vol. I. Turnhout: Brepols, 2001.

_____. *Livre de la nature et débat trinitaire au XIIe siécle: Les "De tribus diebus" de Hugues de Saint-Victor.* Bibliotheca Victorina 14. Turnhout: Brepols, 2002.

_____. "L'ange gothique." In *L'architecture gothique au service de la liturgie,* pp. 115–42. Eds. A. Bos and X. Dectot. Turnhout: Brepols, 2003.

_____. "'Alter Augustinus—Der Zweite Augustinus': Hugo von Sankt Viktor und die Väter der Kirche." In *Väter der Kirche: Ekklesiales Denken von den Anfängen bis in die Neuzeit: Festgabe für Hermann Josef Sieben SJ zum 70. Geburtstag,* 643–68. Munich, 2004.

_____. "Hugo Saxo. Les origines germaniques de la pensée d'Hugues de Saint-Victor." *Francia. Forschungen zur westeuropäischen Geschichte* 33/1 (2006):163–69.

_____. "Voir l'invisible: la spiritualité visionnaire de Hugues de Saint-Victor." In *Spiritualität im Europa des Mittelalters: L'Europe spirituelle au Moyen Age: 900 Jahre Hildegard von Bingen, 900 ans l'abbaye de Cîteaux.* eds. Jean Ferrari and Stephan Grätzel, Philosophie im Kontext 4. St. Augustin: Gardez! Verlag, 1998.

Pouillon, Henri. "Le Premier traité des propriétés transcendentals, La 'Summa de bono' du Chancellier Phillipe," *Revue néoscolastique de philosophie* 42 (1939), pp. 40–77.

Purwatma, Matheus. "The Explanation of the Mystery of the Trinity Based on the Attributes of God as Supreme Love: A Study on the 'De Trinitate' of Richard of St Victor." Ph.D. diss., Pontificia Universitas Ubaniana, 1990.

Reyero, Arias M. "'Al principio amaba el amor' La doctrina de la Trinidad en Ricardo de San Victor." *Teología y Vida* 31 (1990): 163–90.

_____. "Fé y razón: Las razones necessarias en el *De Trinitate* de Ricardo de San Victor." *Teología y Vida* 32 (1991): 295–310.

de Régnon, Th. *Études de théologie positive sur la Sainte Trinité,* vol. 2. Paris: Victor Retaux et Fils, 1892.

Rist, John. "Love, Knowing and Incarnation in Pseudo-Dionysius," *Traditions of Platonism: Essays in Honour of John Dillon,* ed. John J. Cleary. Brookfield: Ashgate Publishing Company, 2009.

Roques, René. *Structures théologiques de la gnose à Richard de Saint-Victor.* Bibliothèque de l'École des Hautes Études. Section des

Sciences religieuses, vol. 72. Paris: Presses universitaires de France, 1962.

Rorem, Paul. *Hugh of St Victor. Great Medieval Thinkers*. New York: Oxford, 2009.

Salet, Gaston. "Les chemins de Dieu d'apres Richard de Saint-Victor." In *L'homme devant Dieu: mélanges offerts au Père Henri de Lubac*. Paris: Aubier, 1963–64.

Schlette, H. R. *Die Nichtigkeit der Welt: Der philosophische Horizont des Hugo von St. Viktor*. München, 1961.

——————. "Das unterschiedliche Personverständnis im theologischen Denken Hugos und Richards von St. Viktor." In *Miscellania Martin Grabmann: Gedenkblatt zum 10. Todestag*. Mitteilungen des Grabmann-Instituts der Universität München, 3. Edited by Michael Schmaus. München: Hueber, 1959.

Schmaus, Michael. *Der "Liber propugnatorius" des Thomas Anglicus und die Lehrunterschiede zwischen Thomas von Aquin und Duns Scotus, II. Teil Die Trinitärischen Lehrdifferenzen*, 2 vols., Beiträge zur Geschichte der Philosophie und Theologie des Mittelalters 29.1–2. Münster: Aschendorff, 1930.

Schmidt, Martin Anton. "Verstehen des Unbegreiflichen in den beiden ersten Buchern *De Trinitate* des Richard von Saint-Victor." In *Abendländische Mystik im Mittelatler: Symposion Kloster Engelberg 1984*. Edited by Kurt Ruh. Stuttgart: J. B. Metziersche, 1986.

——————. "Zur Trinitätslehre der Fruhscholastik: Versuch einer problemgeschtlichen Orientierung." *Theologische Zeitschrift* 40.2 (1984): 181–92.

Schniertshauer, Martin. Consummatio caritatis: *eine Untersuchung zu Richard von St. Victors De Trinitate*. Tübinger Studien zur Theologie und Philosophie, Bd. 10. Mainz: M. Grünewald Verlag, 1996.

Schoebel, Martin. *Archiv und Besitz der Abtei St Viktor in Paris*. Pariser Historische Studien, 31. Bonn, 1991.

Sicard, P. *Hugues de Saint-Victor et son école: introduction, choix de texte, traduction et commentaires*. Témoins de notre histoire. Turnhout: Brepols, 1991.

——————. *Diagrammes médiévaux et exégèse visuelle: Le* Libellus de formatione arche *de Hugues de Saint-Victor*. Bibliotheca Victorina 4. Paris-Turnhout: Brepols, 1993.

———. "L'urbanisme de la Cité de Dieu: constructions et architectures dans la pensée théologique du XIIᵉ siècle." In *L'abbé Suger: le manifeste gothique de Saint-Denis et la pensée victorine*, 109–40. Turnhout: Brepols, 2001.

———. *Théologies victorines: études d'histoire doctrinale médiévale et contemporaine*. Paris, 2008.

Simonis, Walter. *Trinität und Vernunft; Untersuchungen zur Möglichkeit einer rationalen Trinitätslehre bei Anselm, Abaelard, den Viktorinern, A. Günther und J. Frohschammer*. Frankfurt: J. Knecht, 1972.

Slotemaker, John T. "The Development of Anselm's Trinitarian Theology: The Textual and Theological Origins of a Late Medieval Debate," in *Saint Anselm and His Legacy*, eds. Giles Gaspar and Ian Logan (Toronto: Pontifical Institute of Mediaeval Studies, forthcoming, 2010).

Smalley, Beryl. *The Study of the Bible in the Middle Ages*. Oxford: Blackwell Publishers, 1983.

Smith, Ruth. "Cistercian and Victorine Approaches to Contemplation: Understanding of Self in a Rule of Life for a Recluse and The Twelve Patriarchs." In *Medieval Mystical Tradition in England, Ireland and Wales*. Cambridge: D. S. Brewer, 1999.

Southern, R. W. "The Schools of Paris and Chartres." In *Renaissance and Renewal in the Twelfth Century*. Edited by Robert L. Benson and Giles Constable. Cambridge, MA: Harvard University Press, 1982, 113–37.

———. *Scholastic Humanism and the Unification of Europe*. Vol. I: *Foundations*. Oxford: Blackwell, 1995.

Spijker, I. van 't. "Learning by Experience: Twelfth-century monastic ideas." In *Centres of Learning: Learning and Location in Pre-Modern Europe and the Near East*. Edited by J. W. Drijvers and A. A. MacDonald. Leiden: E. J. Brill, 1995.

Studer, Basil. *Augustins 'De Trinitate.'* Paderborn: Ferdinand Schoeningh GmbH, 2005.

Van den Eynde, D. *Essai sur la succession et la date des écrits de Hugues de Saint-Victor*. Rome, 1960.

Walther, Helmut G. "St. Victor und die Schulen in Paris vor der Entstehung der Universitat." In *Schule und Schuler im Mittelalter*. Cologne: Bohlau, 1996.

Wasselynck, R. "La part des Moralia in Job de S. Grégoire-le-Grand dans les Miscellanea Victorins," *Mélanges de science religieuse* 10 (1953): 286–94.

Weisweiler, H. "Hugos von St. Viktor *Dialogus de sacramentis legis naturalis et scriptae* als frühscholastisches Quellenwerk." In *Miscellanea Giovanni Mercati II*, Studi e Testi 122. Vatican City: Biblioteca Apostolica Vaticana, 1946, 179–219.

——————. "Die Arbeitsmethode Hugos von St. Viktor: Ein Beitrag zum Entstehen seines Hauptwerkes *De sacramentis*." *Scholastik* 20–24 (1949): 59–87, 232–67.

Willesme, J. P. "Saint-Victor au temps d'Abélard." In *Abélard et son temps. Actes du colloque international organisé à l'occasion du 9ᵉ centenaire de la naissance de Pierre Abélard*. Paris, 1981.

Wipfler, Heinz. *Die Trinitätsspekulation des Petrus von Poitiers und die Trinitätsspekulation des Richards von St. Viktor: Ein Vergleich. Beiträge zur Geschichte der Philosophie und Theologie des Mittelalters*, 41.1. Münster: Aschendorff, 1965.

Ypenga, Anko. "Sacramentum. Hugo Van St. Victor († 1141) en zijn invloed op de allegorische interpretatie van de liturgie en de sacramentele theologie Vanaf 1140 tot aan Durandus van Mende († 1296)." Ph.D. thesis. Groningen: Rijksuniversiteit Groningen, 2002.

Zinn, Grover A. "History and Contemplation: The Dimensions of the Restoration of Man in Two Treatises on Noah's Ark by Hugh of St Victor." Unpublished doctoral dissertation, Duke University, NC, 1969.

——————. "Hugh of St Victor and the Ark of Noah: A New Look." *Church History* 40 (1971): 261–72.

——————. "Mandala Symbolism and Use in the Mysticism of Hugh of St Victor." *History of Religions* 12 (1972): 317–41.

——————. "Book and Word: The Victorine Background of Bonaventure's Use of Symbols." In *S. Bonaventura 1274–1974.*, Vol. 2, 143–69. Rome, 1973.

——————. "Hugh of St Victor and the Art of Memory." *Viator* 5 (1974): 211–34.

——————. "Historia fundamentum est: The Role of History in the Contemplative Life According to Hugh of St Victor." In *Contemporary Reflections on the Medieval Christian Tradition: Essays in Honor of Ray C. Petry*, 135–58. Durham, NC, 1974.

_____. "De Gradibus Ascensionum: The Stages of Contemplative Ascent in Two Treatises on Noah's Ark by Hugh of St Victor." In *Studies in Medieval Culture* 5, 61–79. Kalamazoo, MI, 1975.

_____. "Personification, Allegory and Visions of Light in Richard of St Victor's Teaching on Contemplation." *University of Toronto Quarterly* 46 (1977): 190–214.

_____. "The Regular Canons: Deacons and Priests in Medieval Monasteries." In *Christian Spirituality*. New York: Crossroad, 1985.

_____. "History and Interpretation: 'Hebrew Truth,' Judaism, and the Victorine Exegetical Tradition." In *Jews and Christians: Exploring the Past, Present, and Future*, 100–123. New York, 1990.

_____. "Hugh of St Victor, Isaiah's Vision, and *De Arca Noe*," In *The Church and the Arts: papers read at the 1990 Summer Meeting and the 1991 Winter Meeting of the Ecclesiastical History Society*, 99–116. Oxford, 1992.

_____. "Texts Within Texts: The Song of Songs in the Exegesis of Gregory the Great and Hugh of St Victor," *Studia Patristica* xxv, 209–15. Leuven, 1993.

_____. "The Influence of Augustine's *De doctrina christiana* upon the writings of Hugh of St Victor." In *Reading and Wisdom: The De doctrina christiana of Augustine in the Middle Ages*, 48–60. Notre Dame, IN, 1995.

_____. "Hugh of St Victor's *De scripturis et scriptoribus sacris* as an Accessus Treatise for the Study of the Bible." *Traditio* 52 (1997):111–34.

_____. "Exile, the Abbey of St. Victor at Paris, and Hugh of Saint Victor," *Medieval Paradigms: essays in honor of Jeremy du Quesnay Adams*, vol. II, 83–111. New York, 2005.

Zwieten, J. van. "Jewish Exegesis within Christian Bounds: Richard of St Victor's *De Emmanuele* and Victorine Hermeneutics." *Bijdragen* 48 (1987): 327–35.

INDEX OF SCRIPTURE REFERENCES*

OLD TESTAMENT

---

* References are to the page number where the note appears and the number of the note.

DEUTEROCANONICAL BOOKS

NEW TESTAMENT

INDEX OF VICTORINE AUTHORS*

HUGH OF ST VICTOR

* References are to the page number of the note itself and the number of the note.

RICHARD OF ST VICTOR

OTHER VICTORINE WRITERS

SUBJECT INDEX*

---

* References that include notes are to the page of the note itself and the number of the note.

166 (n. 73), 192, 210, 213, 252, 253, 256, 257, 260, 264, 268, 297, 311, 317, 321, 324, 328, 334, 354 (n. 38)

Despair 114, 131, 213

Devotion 225, 346

Dignity (see also 'Son, *condignum*') 39-41, 107, 108, 122, 123, 124, 128, 129, 205, 249, 263, 299, 300, 301, 314, 316, 317, 318, 339, 340, 355-56 (n. 38)

Ps. Dionysius the Areopagite 36, 47, 170 (n. 150 and 152)

Discernment 57, 61, 64, 113, 136, 157, 160, 175 (n. 212), 176, 335

Divinity (or Deity) 64, 84, 100 (n. 66), 118, 120, 141, 158, 159, 187, 192, 205, 206, 211, 216
Identical to divine substance 222-23, 236, 254
Incommunicable to other substances 223, 234, 235, 236
Is nothing other than God 223

Doctors (teachers) 111, 162 (n. 20), 225, 271

Effect (-s) (see also 'Cause') 79, 81, 140, 152

Element (-s) 74, 108, 121, 133, 134, 135, 136, 182, 185, 191, 335

Emanations 45

Envy 35, 39, 111, 146, 147

Evangelists 117, 162 (n. 20), 271

Existence
Definition of 277-78, 283
'In act' and 'in reason' 141
Modes of — 276, 278, 280; Human and angelic 278-79, 280; Divine 279-

80; Communicable (= divine substance) 280-81, 296-97; Incommunicable (= the personal properties that distinguish the divine persons) 280-81, 281-82, 292, 294, 296-97, 305, 306-7; Necessary 215, 219

Eyes 98 (n. 39), 101 (n. 92 and 93)

Faith (virtue of, content//teachings of; see also 'Theological Method') 59, 125, 128, 130, 155, 183, 188, 189, 209-10, 213-14, 228, 233, 234, 247, 251, 268, 271, 285, 293, 329, 344, 345, 346, 347, 350, 351, 356 (n. 40), 359 (n. 43 and 45)

The Fall 122-23, 125, 128, 131, 176, 354-55 (n. 38)

Father 76, 86, 87, 88, 183, 186, 187, 188, 190, 192, 193, 204, 206
Meaning of 207, 322, 323, 338, 340
Primordial 299, 331
Specially attributed with power 30, 31, 55-58, 91, 94, 201, 335-36
Unbegotten 206, 216, 300-01, 302, 307, 320, 321, 323, 324, 325, 326, 335, 336-37, 339, 340, 341, 345-47, 349, 350

Fathers (Church) 26 (n. 11), 42, 59, 115, 117, 144, 162-63 (n. 20), 168 (n. 97), 197, 213, 247, 256, 345, 346, 359-60 (n. 45), 371 (n. 226), 382 (n. 583)

Fear 55, 89, 91, 93, 94, 101 (n. 94), 111, 125, 131, 132, 148, 149, 159, 284, 369 (n. 176),

Fellowship 205, 207, 249, 250, 252, 258, 259, 262, 263-64, 299, 305, 371 (n. 239)

Filiation 45

Florus of Lyons 59

Freedom, Divine 36, 42

Communicable and incommunicable 236-37
Identical to Being 292; Divine substance 226, 230, 235, 236, 239; Power 221, 223, 224, 230, 235, 239, 240, 343
Primordial (=Father) 331
Specially attributed to the Son 55-58, 91, 94, 201, 335-36
"Wisdom begets wisdom" 200-1, 345, 348, 349, 350

World (see also 'Creation', 'Universe') 24, 28, 35, 52, 53, 54, 55, 59, 60, 61, 65, 67, 74, 75, 76, 81, 94, 95 (n. 2 and 6), 96 (n. 15 and 19), 97 (n. 30), 98 (n. 36), 100 (n. 61), 106, 107, 108, 109, 120, 121, 122, 127, 128, 129, 130, 131, 132, 133, 135, 136, 139, 140, 146, 153, 160, 167 (n. 84), 168 (n. 91), 171, 176, 182, 185, 218, 285, 356 (n. 40), 357 (n. 41)

Works, good and evil 70, 89, 128, 130, 137, 138, 166 (n. 73), 176

Worship 64, 165 (n. 50), 187

Zeal 71, 111, 212, 215, 364 (n. 59)

ABOUT THE EDITORS

This volume is edited by Boyd Taylor Coolman (PhD, University of Notre Dame; Theology Dept. Boston College), author of T*he Theology of Hugh of St. Victor: An Interpretation* (2010), and Dale M. Coulter (DPh, Oxford University; School of Divinity, Regent University), author of *Per Visibilia ad Invisibilia: Theological Method in Richard of St. Victor (d. 1173)* (2006).